PROCEDURAL LAW AND ECONOMICS

ENCYCLOPEDIA OF LAW AND ECONOMICS, SECOND EDITION

General Editor: Gerrit De Geest
School of Law, Washington University, St Louis, MO, USA

1. Tort Law and Economics
   Edited by Michael Faure

2. Labor and Employment Law and Economics
   Edited by Kenneth G. Dau-Schmidt, Seth D. Harris and Orly Lobel

3. Criminal Law and Economics
   Edited by Nuno Garoupa

4. Antitrust Law and Economics
   Edited by Keith N. Hylton

5. Property Law and Economics
   Edited by Boudewijn Bouckaert

6. Contract Law and Economics
   Edited by Gerrit De Geest

7. Production of Legal Rules
   Edited by Francesco Parisi

8. Procedural Law and Economics
   Edited by Chris William Sanchirico

Future titles will include:

Regulation and Economics
Edited by Roger Van den Bergh and Alessio M. Pacces

Methodology of Law and Economics
Edited by Thomas S. Ulen

Corporate Law and Economics
Edited by Joseph A. McCahery and Erik P.M. Vermeulen

Intellectual Property Law and Economics
Edited by Ben Depoorter and Michael Meurer

For a list of all Edward Elgar published titles visit our site on the World Wide Web at http://www.e-elgar.co.uk

Procedural Law and Economics

Edited by

Chris William Sanchirico

Samuel A. Blank Professor of Law, Business, and Public Policy, University of Pennsylvania Law School and Wharton School, USA

ENCYCLOPEDIA OF LAW AND ECONOMICS, SECOND EDITION

Edward Elgar
Cheltenham, UK • Northampton, MA, USA

© The Editor and Contributors Severally 2012

All rights reserved. No part of this publication may be reproduced, stored in a retrieval system or transmitted in any form or by any means, electronic, mechanical or photocopying, recording, or otherwise without the prior permission of the publisher.

Published by
Edward Elgar Publishing Limited
The Lypiatts
15 Lansdown Road
Cheltenham
Glos GL50 2JA
UK

Edward Elgar Publishing, Inc.
William Pratt House
9 Dewey Court
Northampton
Massachusetts 01060
USA

A catalogue record for this book is available from the British Library

Library of Congress Control Number: 2009941093

ISBN 978 1 84720 824 8

Typeset by Servis Filmsetting Ltd, Stockport, Cheshire
Printed and bound by MPG Books Group, UK

Contents

List of contributors		vii
Introduction		ix
1	Adversarial versus inquisitorial justice *Luke M. Froeb and Bruce H. Kobayashi*	1
2	Appeal and supreme courts *Lewis A. Kornhauser*	19
3	Attorney-client confidentiality *Gillian K. Hadfield and Shmuel Leshem*	52
4	Class action *Robert G. Bone*	67
5	Conflict of laws and choice of law *Erin O'Hara O'Connor and Larry E. Ribstein*	85
6	Criminal procedure: empirical analysis *Thomas J. Miles*	116
7	Detection avoidance and enforcement theory *Chris William Sanchirico*	145
8	Discovery *Robert G. Bone*	188
9	Evidence: theoretical models *Chris William Sanchirico*	203
10	Fee shifting *Avery Wiener Katz and Chris William Sanchirico*	271
11	Judicial organization and administration *Lewis A. Kornhauser*	308
12	Negative-expected-value suits *Lucian A. Bebchuk and Alon Klement*	341
13	Preclusion *Robert G. Bone*	350
14	Self-incrimination *Alex Stein*	366
15	Settlement *Andrew F. Daughety and Jennifer F. Reinganum*	386
16	The social versus private incentive to sue *Thomas J. Miceli*	472

vi *Procedural law and economics*

17 Trial selection theory and evidence 487
     Keith N. Hylton and Haizhen Lin

Index 507

Contributors

Lucian A. Bebchuk, William J. Friedman and Alicia Townsend Friedman Professor of Law, Economics, and Finance, Harvard Law School, USA

Robert G. Bone, G. Rollie White Excellence in Teaching Professor of Law, The University of Texas at Austin School of Law, USA

Andrew F. Daughety, Professor of Economics and Professor of Law (by courtesy), Department of Economics and Law School, Vanderbilt University, USA

Luke M. Froeb, William C. and Margaret M. Oehmig Associate Professor of Entrepreneurship and Free Enterprise at Owen Graduate School of Management, Vanderbilt University, USA

Gillian K. Hadfield, Richard L. and Antoinette S. Kirtland Professor of Law and Professor of Economics, University of Southern California, USA

Keith N. Hylton, Honorable Paul J. Liacos Professor of Law, Boston University, USA

Avery Wiener Katz, Vice Dean and Milton Handler Professor of Law, Columbia University, USA

Alon Klement, Professor of Law, Radzyner School of Law, Interdisciplinary Center Herzliya, Israel

Bruce H. Kobayashi, Professor of Law, George Mason University School of Law, USA

Lewis A. Kornhauser, Alfred B. Engelberg Professor of Law, New York University School of Law, USA

Shmuel Leshem, Associate Professor of Law, University of Southern California, USA

Haizhen Lin, Assistant Professor, Indiana University, Kelley School of Business, USA

Thomas J. Miceli, Professor, Department of Economics, University of Connecticut, USA

Thomas J. Miles, Professor of Law, University of Chicago Law School, USA

Erin O'Hara O'Connor, Professor of Law, Vanderbilt University Law School, USA

Jennifer F. Reinganum, E. Bronson Ingram Professor of Economics and Professor of Law (by courtesy), Department of Economics and Law School, Vanderbilt University, USA

Larry E. Ribstein, Mildred Van Voorhis Jones Professor of Law, University of Illinois College of Law, USA

Chris William Sanchirico, Samuel A. Blank Professor of Law, Business, and Public Policy, University of Pennsylvania Law School and Wharton School, USA

Alex Stein, Professor of Law, Cardozo Law School, USA

Introduction

This volume of the *Encyclopedia of Law and Economics* gathers entries on the main issues covered in the scholarly, economics-based literature on litigation, procedure, and evidence. This second edition of the volume includes several new entries. Some of these bridge gaps in the first edition; others reflect significant new trends in research. Moreover, several entries that appeared in the first edition have been substantially refined and updated to reflect the many new contributions that have been put forward in the decade since the first edition was published.

Lawyer-economists began studying procedure and evidence in earnest in the late 1960s and early 1970s. The earliest contributions include Landes (1971), Gould (1973), and Posner (1973) – all of which were influenced by Becker (1968). The issues raised in these early contributions became the chief focal points of the ensuing four decades of scholarship in the area. These issues are covered in detail in this volume. Thus, Andrew Daughety and Jennifer Reinganum's chapter, "Settlement", concerns the vast theoretical literature on pre-trial bargaining. Reflecting advances in this research area over time, Daughety and Reinganum frame their analysis within the general conceptual taxonomy of game theory, thus helping the reader to understand what does and does not distinguish bargaining in the litigation context from bargaining in other areas. Likewise, Avery Katz and Chris Sanchirico's chapter, "Fee Shifting", considers another classic issue: how varying rules for allocating the cost of litigation among the litigating parties affects potential plaintiffs' incentives to file suit and the likelihood that litigants will settle out of court. The entry presents the literature's main theoretical results and also digests some recent empirical findings. Lucian A. Bebchuk and Alon Klement contribute a chapter on "Negative-Expected-Value Suits", which describes a relatively new segment of the literature on filing incentives and settlement. These new papers attempt to solve the puzzle of why defendants sometimes seem to settle lawsuits with plaintiffs whose expected litigation costs exceed their expected trial winnings. Thomas Miceli's chapter, "The Social versus Private Incentive to Sue", considers the private decision to file suit from a normative rather than a positive perspective. The question he addresses – another classic in this area – is whether the configuration of private incentives generates too many or too few lawsuits from a social perspective. Keith Hylton and Haizhen Lin, in their chapter "Trial Selection Theory and Evidence", consider how out of court settlement filters disputes, causing those cases that are fully litigated to differ from those that are filed. This has long been of concern to legal scholars, whose analytical methods include the study of published opinions and often rely implicitly on the assumption that such opinions are representative of the underlying population of disputes.

These are the central issues considered by the extant economic research on procedure and evidence. However, they are not necessarily comprehensive of the central issues of concern to litigators and policy makers. A number of the entries in this volume directly address questions that are important to the institution of litigation, but have not thus far received the same intensity of attention from economics-oriented researchers. These may be organized roughly according to where they appear along the litigation timeline. Robert Bone's chapter, "Class Action", reviews research on a device for initiating and prosecuting suit that, although anciently rooted, has gained prominence and sparked intense controversy over the last half century. Robert Bone also contributes a chapter on "Discovery", an institutional frame for pre-trial fact finding that appears to be far more central to actual civil litigation than to economic research thereon. Erin O'Hara O'Connor and Larry Ribstein's chapter, "Conflict of Laws and Choice of Law", concerns how courts decide which substantive law governs when a dispute involves parties, property or events located in more than one jurisdiction. O'Hara O'Connor and Ribstein also consider the enforcement of private contractual provisions that specify which substantive law is to govern the parties' dealings. How the organization of the courts affects judicial decision making is the subject of Lewis Kornhauser's chapter on "Judicial Organization and Administration". Kornhauser's related chapter on "Appeal and Supreme Courts" examines the implications of the hierarchal structure of the court system. Lastly, the chapter, "Preclusion", by Robert Bone focuses on how court decisions affect future litigation.

Several of the chapters in the volume reflect new trends in research over the last decade. The bulk of these concern the nature and design of judicial fact finding. Chris Sanchirico's chapter, "Evidence: Theoretical Models", reviews the several formal approaches to the question of how fact finders do and should make decisions regarding factual, as opposed to legal, issues. Most economic research on litigation focuses on filing incentives and settlement, and accordingly provides only a cursory account of fact finding. Sanchirico's chapter reviews the several attempts to bring probability theory and game theory to bear on that which filing initiates and settlement averts. Sanchirico's chapter, "Detection Avoidance and Enforcement Theory", studies how accounting for violators' incentives to conceal and fabricate evidence alters the conventional economic model of enforcement. Luke Froeb and Bruce Kobayashi's chapter on "Adversarial versus Inquisitorial Justice" surveys the economic literature on a fundamental issue of evidentiary design: the degree to which the fact finder should play an active role in investigation and interrogation. Two chapters, one by Gillian Hadfield and Shmuel Leshem and one by Alex Stein, consider specific evidentiary questions that have been the subject of recent research. Both questions fall within the evidentiary subfield of privileges. Hadfield and Leshem's chapter, "Attorney-Client Confidentiality", reviews the economic literature on the privilege accorded to certain communications between lawyer and client. Stein's chapter, "Self-incrimination", considers economic approaches to the "right to silence", including the privilege accorded to criminal defendants to decline to testify.

Lastly, Thomas Miles' chapter "Criminal Procedure: Empirical Analysis", reflects the trend toward empirical research in modern law and economics. Empirical findings are reviewed in several of the other entries, but, representative of the field itself, the volume's entries are most heavily populated with theoretical contributions. Miles specifically reviews the empirical research on criminal procedure, including the statistical evidence on racial profiling, bail, plea bargaining, and racial disparities in sentencing.

References

Becker, G. (1968), "Crime and Punishment: An Economic Approach", *Journal of Political Economy*, 76 (2), 169–217.

Gould, J.P. (1973), "The Economics of Legal Conflicts", *Journal of Legal Studies*, 2 (2), 279–300.

Landes, W.M. (1971), "An Economic Analysis of the Courts", *Journal of Law and Economics*, 14 (1), 61–107.

Posner, R.A. (1973), "An Economic Approach to Legal Procedure and Judicial Administration", *Journal of Legal Studies*, 2 (2), 399–458.

1 Adversarial versus inquisitorial justice
Luke M. Froeb and Bruce H. Kobayashi

1. Introduction

This chapter is about the merits of the adversarial system relative to its implied alternative, the inquisitorial system. The adversarial and inquisitorial systems are the two basic procedural systems used to control disputes.[1] While there are many differences between the two systems, the primary difference between the two emphasized in the economic literature is whether the production of information is centrally controlled, or produced in a decentralized manner by the parties.[2] In an adversarial system, the parties to the litigation produce and present evidence and arguments to a judge or jury, who renders a verdict. Compared to the adversarial decision maker, the inquisitorial decision maker exerts greater control over the trial process, from the organization of the case to the gathering, presentation, and interpretation of evidence. As a result, the parties' role is diminished, as the judge in effect carries out his own independent investigation of the case. In reality, all procedural systems have elements of both systems, which can vary over time.[3] However, studying the extreme characteristics of the pure adversarial or pure inquisitorial system, as most economic analyses have done, can lead to insights regarding the relative merits of the two systems, and the potential effects that incremental changes in one direction or another can have.

On the policy side, many have suggested that the adversarial system of justice is an inefficient system.[4] Critics point to selective production of evidence, the use of unsophisticated and potentially biased decision makers, and its high cost and slow speed as problems. In its place, they propose a movement toward neutral non-adversarial proceedings and offer a variety of solutions that place more of the litigation under the control of judges or magistrates.[5] These reforms include increasing the power of judges to

---

[1] Tullock (1975), (1980, chapter 6).
[2] Parisi (2002) (discussing differences in the two systems).
[3] Tullock (1975), Parisi (2002).
[4] *Id.* See also Langbein (1985), Thibault et al. (1972).
[5] These devices include expanded use of summary judgment, summary juries, and expanded use of directed verdicts. For a discussion of these issues, see Cecil et al. (1991) at 736–8.

prevent issues from reaching the jury and the elimination of the right to a jury trial in complex civil cases.[6] They also include expanded discovery rules to include mandatory disclosure of information to make it harder for parties to hide evidence,[7] and the use of more sophisticated decision makers, including court-appointed experts or special masters who would not have to rely on evidence produced by self-interested parties.[8] Indeed, much of the policy debate about the relative merits of the two systems has focused on the role of scientific or statistical evidence in the courts and on the role of experts in the courtroom.[9] In this setting, the problems facing a potentially unsophisticated decision maker are exacerbated because he is not trained to evaluate scientific or statistical evidence. Implicit in much of the criticism is the thought that a movement towards a neutral, non-adversarial proceeding, like that of an inquisitorial system, would lead to better and less costly decision making.

On the other hand, the adversarial system may give parties incentives to produce more information.[10] While an inquisitor may not have to

---

[6] For arguments in support of a complexity exception to the Seventh Amendment (the right to a trial by jury in civil cases), see Campbell (1988) and Campbell and LePoidevin (1980). But see Arnold (1980) (arguing that such an exception is not necessary).

[7] See Sobel (1989), Cooter and Rubinfeld (1994) (providing an economic analysis of mandatory disclosure); Brazil (1978), Schwarzer (1989) (advocating use of mandatory disclosure). But see Bell et al. (1992), Easterbrook (1989) (criticizing mandatory disclosure). Dissatisfaction with discovery under the adversarial process led to amendments to Rule 26 of the Federal Rules of Civil Procedure which controls discovery in the federal courts. The most controversial part of the amendments enacted in 1993 was a provision that required early disclosure of both favorable and unfavorable information. See the 1993 Amendments to the Federal Rules of Civil Procedure, Rule 26(a)(1). However, this provision was repealed in 2000 in favor of a rule that required the disclosure of favorable information only. See FRCP 26(a)(1) (2009).

[8] Court appointment of expert witnesses is provided for under Rule 706 of the Federal Rules of Evidence. Special "reference" masters can be appointed under "exceptional conditions" under Rule 53(b) of the Federal Rules of Civil Procedure. However, use of court-appointed experts and non-pretrial special masters has been rare. See Cecil and Willging (1994a, 1994b) and Farrell (1994). For a recent discussion of this issue, see Bernstein (2008).

[9] See Bernstein (2008).

[10] For example, opposing litigants can have more or better information than even a sophisticated decision maker, and competition among the litigants forces them to reveal relevant information (see Milgrom and Roberts (1986); Froeb and Kobayashi (1996); Lipman and Seppi (1995), McChesney (1977). See generally Hayek (1945, 1948) and Demsetz (1969) (discussing the informational advantages of decentralized systems).

worry about the selective production of evidence by interested parties, he typically has less information than the parties, and may have biases and prejudices of his own.[11] Determining which system is better for resolving legal disputes in general, and for disputes involving scientific or statistical evidence in particular, is a matter of obvious policy importance, but the issue is much broader than that. It also has implications for the way that institutions choose to organize. In many cases, organizations deliberately set up incentives for members to advocate or defend a specific "cause" that differs from group welfare maximization. Examples include legislatures, whose members advocate for specific constituencies, rather than for all citizens; and regulatory bodies whose mandate is very narrow, like protecting the environment, which is often in conflict with other goals, like economic growth. Typically, each of these narrow "causes" will have its own advocates. The broader policy issue is whether competition between these advocates leads to good policy; or, if not good policy, then at least the production of information that would allow a decision maker to make an informed decision about the benefits and costs of various policy proposals.[12]

In this chapter, we survey economics articles that have tried to assess the benefits and costs of the adversarial and inquisitorial systems. Except for several experimental papers, all of the reviewed articles construct theoretical models of one or both systems in order to evaluate or compare their performance, typically measured by the quality of decision making, or by the creation or production of information, a prerequisite to informed decision making. We compare the systems based on their accuracy and costs, and the quality of the decisions they produce, but not on their deterrent effects. All of the reviewed articles take legal disputes as exogenously given, and model their resolution at trial. They ignore the question of whether a particular system would encourage or discourage further disputes. In other words, all of the articles present partial equilibrium models of the resolution of disputes, not full equilibrium models of the generation and resolution of disputes.[13]

Predictably, whether the benefits of the adversarial system outweigh its costs depends crucially on the models' assumptions. But this is to be expected. Economists use models, with their attendant assumptions, to isolate the effects of various components of competing systems. This makes it difficult to compare results across models because the articles

---

[11] Froeb and Kobayashi (2001).
[12] Dewatripont and Tirole (1999).
[13] For a discussion of this issue, see Sanchirico (2001b).

identify advantages of the adversarial system under one set of assumptions and the advantages of the inquisitorial systems under a different set of assumptions. Often, when an economist identifies an intriguing or significant theoretical result, he or she will test the robustness of the result by "rigging" the model's assumptions against it. So, for example, if an economist finds that the adversarial system does better than the inquisitorial, the model is purged of all assumptions that might favor the adversarial system, so that the economist can isolate the significant factor that leads to the result.

Whatever the assumptions, to be credible, any theoretical model must be able to explain several salient features of each system. The most obvious is that, under the adversarial system, the parties report only favorable evidence to the court. All of the surveyed articles rule out lying by assuming that the decision maker can verify the truthfulness of reported evidence. Instead, they allow parties to withhold information that is unfavorable to their cause. This can be explained by adverse selection, that is, only parties with relatively good evidence choose to produce and present it; or by moral hazard – the parties produce evidence, and then report only favorable evidence. This raises two immediate follow-on modeling questions that must be addressed: (i) what happens to unfavorable evidence; and (ii) does the decision maker know about the potential existence of unfavorable evidence?

If he does, then the decision maker can learn as much from the evidence that is not reported at trial, as from that which is. In particular, if a party doesn't report evidence, a sophisticated decision maker can infer that it was adverse to this party's interests. In a criminal case, for example, a sophisticated decision maker learns something from the fact that a defendant chooses to exercise his Fifth Amendment rights. In a theoretical model, a sophisticated decision maker will update his beliefs in the usual way, so that the outcome of trial is a Bayesian equilibrium.[14]

As one might expect, this kind of sophistication turns out to be important for evaluating the merits of an adversarial versus an inquisitorial system of justice. A sophisticated decision maker mitigates some of the costs of the adversarial system because he is not fooled by the selective production of evidence. In fact, if the decision maker has good enough knowledge about what evidence could have been reported but wasn't, then the failure to report evidence can be just as informative as the actual evidence that is reported (for example, Shin (1998)). For this reason, this

---

[14] Harsanyi (1967).

chapter classifies articles using a taxonomy based on the sophistication of the decision maker.

The outline of the chapter is as follows. In the next section, we review two papers that we use to define and compare the adversarial and inquisitorial systems (Tullock (1975); Froeb and Kobayashi (2001)). Section 3 examines related articles on the performance of the two systems. In Section 3.1, we survey articles that assume the decision maker uses a naïve decision rule that does not take into account the fact that the litigants in an adversarial system may select the data that is produced and reported (Milgrom and Roberts (1986); Froeb and Kobayashi (1996)). We also examine a model that compares a hybrid system where both adversarial and inquisitorial evidence is produced (Parisi (2002)). Section 3.2 surveys four articles that assume a sophisticated decision maker, that is, one that takes into account the nature of the adversarial litigation and the evidence produced in its decision rule (Sobel (1985); Milgrom and Roberts (1986); Shin (1998); Dewatripont and Tirole (1999)). One article (Milgrom and Roberts (1986)) appears in both categories because it varies the sophistication of the decision maker. In Section 4, we examine the experimental literature that examines the performance of adversarial and inquisitorial systems. Two of the articles report experimental evidence used to "test" the assumption of sophisticated decision making (Block et al. (2001); Block and Parker (2004)). One article examines whether adversarial experts improve decision making, but does not compare the adversarial outcome with a single expert. In what follows, we discuss the articles and conclude with suggestions for future research.

2. Adversarial and Inquisitorial Regimes Defined and Compared

Tullock (1978) provided an early analysis comparing adversarial and inquisitorial procedural systems. In an adversarial system, evidence and arguments are produced by interested parties and transmitted to the decision maker, who decides which party will prevail. In contrast, in an inquisitorial system, the judge carries out an independent investigation of the case and gathers the evidence himself. Thus, the basic tradeoff between inquisitorial and adversarial systems can be viewed as one of centralized versus decentralized evidence production. In a mixed system, the decision maker can consider submissions by the parties in addition to conducting his own information gathering. Proponents of inquisitorial systems have stressed both the efficiency and neutrality of such systems. However, adversarial regimes can be superior to the extent that they take advantage of the superior information of the parties.

To compare the two systems, Tullock presents a model of litigation between two parties, Mr. Right and Mr. Wrong. In a pure adversarial system, the parties compete to alter the probability of obtaining a fixed prize D. Mr. Right and Mr. Wrong compete by spending resources R and W respectively to alter the probability of a victory by Mr. Right ($P(R,W)$). Tullock used a simple weighting function to model the probability that Mr. Right will prevail:[15]

$$P(R, W) = \frac{f(E)R}{f(E)R + W}. \tag{1.1}$$

The function $f(E)$ scales the effectiveness of R's expenditures depending on the evidence in the case (E). If $f(E) > (<) 1$, then Mr. Right is favored (disfavored) by the evidence. The two parties maximize the following functions:

$$V_R = DP(R, W) - R \tag{1.2}$$

$$V_W = D(1 - P(R, W)) - W. \tag{1.3}$$

Tullock notes that a noncooperative Nash equilibrium, (R^*, W^*) in the pure adversarial system is unlikely to be optimal for two primary reasons. First, there are Pareto-preferred litigation expenditure pairs ($R < R^*$, $W < W^*$) that yield the same outcome (that is, $P(R, W) = P(R^*, W^*)$). In addition, Tullock notes that if one assumes that it is socially optimal for Mr. Right to win, then the expenditures by Mr. Wrong are socially counterproductive.

To consider inquisitorial systems, Tullock modifies equation (1.1) so that

$$P(R, W) = \frac{f(E)R}{f(E)R + W} + g(F), \tag{1.4}$$

where F are resources invested in judging. The function $g(F)$ is assumed to increase the probability that Mr. Right prevails ($g'(F) > 0$). Under the assumption that it is socially optimal for Mr. Right to prevail, expenditures invested in F increase the probability that the socially preferred outcome occurs.

In a pure adversarial system, $F = 0$. As noted above, not only are the expenditures of the parties on litigation likely to be non-optimal, but in such adversary proceedings, "a great deal of the resources are put in by

---

[15] See generally, Dixit (1987) (discussing the use of similar functions in models of economic contests).

someone who is attempting to mislead."¹⁶ On the other hand, in a pure inquisitorial system, $R = W = 0$, so 100% of the resources F are committed to increasing P, thus moving the case in the socially proper direction. Tullock concludes that, based on this analysis, there is at least "a strong argument that the inquisitorial system is better."¹⁷

Critics of Tullock's analysis noted that his analysis ignored aspects of real world litigation that serve to mitigate the overinvestment implied by the noncooperative Nash equilibrium. These include the use of procedural devices such as discovery, and the use of settlements to avoid the costs of trial.¹⁸ Indeed, private settlements of legal disputes are ubiquitous, and economic models of the litigation/settlement decision predict settlement where there is little disagreement about the outcome.¹⁹ The critics also note the positive production of legal precedent as a benefit of adversarial systems.²⁰ Critics have also noted that adversarial systems may be more efficient in mitigating decision maker bias, and that inquisitorial systems can suffer from suboptimal incentives to produce information.²¹ Moreover, the assumption that a judgment for one of the litigants (Mr. Right) can be classified as a priori correct is also problematic. If this is not clear to the parties or the inquisitor ex ante, it is far from clear that expenditures on F will increase the probability that the correct or efficient outcome will occur. Moreover, even within Tullock's framework, one cannot conclude that the inquisitorial system is superior. The pure inquisitorial system will yield an unambiguously superior outcome only if it results in a higher probability that R will prevail at a lower cost. If the inquisitor is at a disadvantage vis-à-vis the parties in producing information, for example, if $g'(F)$ is small so that the equilibrium increase in $P(F)$, $g(F^*)$, is small, the pure inquisitorial system can in theory produce a lower probability that party R prevails with higher resource costs.²²

The possibility of this last outcome is demonstrated by Froeb and Kobayashi (2001). In their model, they characterize the relative advantages of adversarial versus inquisitorial regimes as one of centralized versus decentralized evidence production. That is, rather than characterize litigation in terms of right and wrong, they examine how centralized

---

16 Tullock (1980) at 96.
17 Tullock (1980) at 87.
18 McChensey (1977); Ordover and Weitzman (1977).
19 See generally, Kobayashi (1996).
20 McChesney (1977); Ordover and Weitzman (1977).
21 Zywicki (2008).
22 Ordover and Weitzman (1977).

and decentralized systems perform in terms of the production of evidence. Specifically, they examine the production of evidence consisting of draws out of a distribution $F(x)$ with mean μ and variance σ^2. In their analysis, the mean μ represents the value of the issue being litigated (for example, damages, the level of harm caused), and both the adversarial parties and inquisitor are interested in producing an estimate of the mean of X. The plaintiff seeks a high value of the estimated mean, while the defendant seeks to minimize the value of the estimated mean.

In a pure inquisitorial system, Froeb and Kobayashi presume that the sample mean, with its well-known optimality properties, would be used. Thus, if the inquisitor takes N_c draws, he will produce an unbiased estimate of the sample mean with variance σ^2/N_c.

In an adversarial regime, they assume that the decision maker is a passive, unsophisticated actor that takes the reports of the parties x_p and x_d and uses a naïve split-the-difference estimator:

$$x^* = (x_p + x_d)/2 \tag{1.5}$$

Each of the parties take draws from $F(x)$. Each draw costs c. As noted above, the plaintiff benefits from a high value of x^*, while the defendant benefits from a low x^*. To capture the selective use of evidence by the adversarial parties, Froeb and Kobayashi assume that parties report only the most favorable information to the court. If the plaintiff and defendant take N_p and N_d draws respectively, the parties report:

$$x_p = Max\{x_1, x_2, x_3, \ldots, x_{N_p}\} \tag{1.6}$$

$$x_d = Min\{x_1, x_2, x_3, \ldots, x_{N_d}\}. \tag{1.7}$$

The parties' payoff functions equal:

$$\pi_p = x^* - cN_p \tag{1.8}$$

$$\pi_d = -x^* - cN_d. \tag{1.9}$$

To capture the information advantage over the inquisitor, they assume that the parties know the distribution out of which they are drawing. Froeb and Kobayashi show that both parties use optimal stopping rules. In a dominant strategy equilibrium, the plaintiff stops producing evidence after a draw greater than υ_p and the defendant stops after a draw lower than υ_d. The stopping values υ_p and υ_d are defined by equating the marginal cost of a draw c to the marginal benefit of taking a draw:

$$c = \int_{v_p}^{\infty} (v_p - x) dF(x)/2 \qquad (1.10)$$

$$c = \int_{-\infty}^{v_d} (v_d - x) dF(x)/2. \qquad (1.11)$$

If the distribution $F(x)$ is symmetric, the stopping values will be symmetric around the mean of the distribution, and the court's split-the-difference estimator will be unbiased because the litigants are stopping equidistant from, but on either side of, the mean. Under these conditions, each party on average will take $N_d = N_p = 1/[1 - F(v_p)]$ draws. The variance of the split-the-difference estimator equals:

$$[Var(x|x > v_p) + Var(x|x < v_d)]/4 = Var(x|x > v_p)/2. \qquad (1.12)$$

Because both the sample mean used by the inquisitorial system and the adversarial split the difference estimator are unbiased, the estimators can be compared on the basis of variance and cost. The adversarial estimator will have a lower variance than the sample mean used by the inquisitor when:

$$Var(x|x > v_p)/2 < Var(x)/N_c. \qquad (1.13)$$

For equal cost estimators (that is, assuming that $N_c = N_d + N_p = 2/[1 - F(v_p)]$), the adversarial estimator will have a lower variance when:

$$Var(x|x > v_p) < Var(x)[1 - F(v_p)]. \qquad (1.14)$$

Satisfaction of condition (1.14) does not violate the Gauss-Markov theorem proving the optimality of the sample mean because the adversarial estimator does not belong to the class of linear estimators to which the theorem applies. Its potential superiority follows from the fact that, in the adversarial regime, the litigants know the properties of the distribution, and use this distribution to produce optimal stopping rules. Use of these optimal stopping rules can result in the adversarial estimator dominating the sample mean, depending upon the properties of the distribution.

For example, with a uniform distribution, Froeb and Kobayashi show that condition (1.14) is satisfied. Thus, holding the number of draws constant, the adversarial estimator will have a lower variance than the sample mean. This is because the large variance of a uniform distribution imparts

10   *Procedural law and economics*

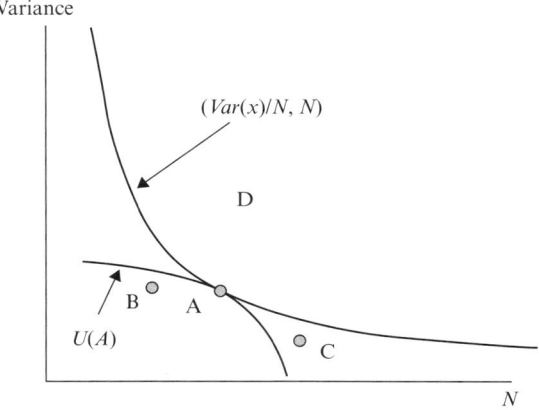

Figure 1.1   The tradeoff between cost and variance

a large variance on the sample mean, while simultaneously allowing the parties to move quickly to the endpoints of the distribution. In contrast, a double exponential distribution centered on μ generates the opposite result, as condition (1.14) never holds. Because of the memoryless characteristic of this distribution, the conditional variance does not decrease as the parties move out to the tails of the distribution. An intermediate case is the normal distribution. If the litigants stop near the mean of the distribution (for example, when c is large), the adversarial regime can dominate the sample mean for the same reasons as in the uniform case. For stopping values far from the mean, the adversarial regime throws away too much information to be efficient.

In addition, condition (1.14) is a necessary, but not sufficient, condition for the adversarial estimator to dominate the sample mean. Figure 1.1 plots the tradeoff between cost and variance offered by the sample mean. The horizontal axis is the number of draws (a proxy for the costs when the parties and the inquisitor have equal costs c). On the vertical axis is the variance of the estimator. The locus of points attainable in the inquisitorial system is the hyperbola $(Var(x)/N, N)$ in the figure. Assuming that society prefers both a lower variance and cost, society's indifference curves are concave toward the origin.[23] The indifference curve $U(A)$ represents the highest attainable societal indifference curve using the sample mean.

---

[23]   For a general discussion of the issue of accuracy in adjudication, see Kaplow (1994).

If condition (1.14) is not satisfied, then the adversarial estimator must lie in the inferior region D. If it is satisfied, the adversarial estimator can be preferred (as is the case for point B in the figure), or can be less preferred because of its high relative cost (as is illustrated by point C).

The feasibility of comparative analysis of two unbiased estimators depends on the assumption of a symmetric distribution $F(x)$ as well as other assumptions of the model. The effects of asymmetric distributions on equilibrium bias is examined by Daughety and Reinganum (2000), who find that differences in the cost of sampling or asymmetry in the sampling distribution can cause equilibrium bias. Their model considers only the performance of an adversarial system, and does not make a direct comparison with an inquisitorial system. A full consideration of the performance of adversarial and inquisitorial systems with equilibrium bias would consider trading off cost and two dimensions of accuracy, bias and variance.

3. Theoretical Literature on Adversarial and Inquisitorial Systems

In this section, we review the literature that has looked at the nature and performance of adversarial and inquisitorial system. In Section 3.1, we examine models that have looked at adversarial systems with a naïve decision maker. That is, the decision maker adopts a rule that interprets the evidence produced, without taking into account the fact that the parties select favorable evidence. Section 3.2 examine papers in which the decision maker's rule takes into account the selective or exaggerated reporting of evidence.

3.1 Naïve Decision Makers

Milgrom and Roberts (1986) find that even a naïve decision maker can reach a full information decision provided that the interests of the parties are sufficiently opposed, and evidence is costless to produce. Evidence not reported by one party, because it is unfavorable, will be reported by the other, and vice versa. While they do not explicitly consider the merits of an inquisitorial system, their results suggest an "equivalence" result between the two, in that the adversarial system produces a full information decision. This issue is also examined by Lipman and Seppi (1995) and Seidmann and Winter (1997).

This same theoretical result is extended to costly evidence production by Froeb and Kobayashi (1996) (see also McAfee and Reny (1992)), who model a naïve jury as using a simple proportional function to weight endogenously produced evidence. In their model, evidence consists of the favorable outcomes of draws from a binomial distribution (a coin flip). The probability the plaintiff prevails equals $p = H/(H + T)$. The parties produce selective evidence, that is, the plaintiff reports only the number of

12 *Procedural law and economics*

times he obtained an *H* outcome, but not the total number of flips taken. Similarly, the defendant reports only the number of *T* outcomes. Because a litigant disfavored by the probability distribution will require more costly flips to produce a given number of reportable (favorable) outcomes, such a party will be disadvantaged by the probability distribution. As a result, the party favored by the distribution produces more favorable evidence in equilibrium, and the naïve weighting function used by the jury reveals the truth. Furthermore, even when the jury has strong priors, the authors show that the adversarial system overcomes these priors as long as both parties produce evidence in equilibrium. Farmer and Pecorino (2000) examine the Froeb and Kobayashi result to consider other forms of jury bias. They find that the adversarial system does not eliminate this bias when the bias takes a multiplicative form rather than the additive bias considered by Froeb and Kobayashi. Moreover, they show that endogenous expenditures by adversarial litigants may not even reduce jury bias in some cases. They also consider how two-way fee shifting affects the equilibrium outcome, and find that use of such a system may exacerbate the effects of strong jury bias.

Parisi (2002) uses the same probability function to characterize the payoffs to the parties of producing evidence under an adversarial system, and finds, similar to the Tullock (1978) model discussed above, that parties in such a system produce "more" evidence than is socially optimal. In addition to the evidence produced by the parties, Parisi considers a "mixed" system where the court can produce its own evidence. In the mixed system, the court's decision is a weighted average of the decisions coming out of the two regimes. Parisi finds that by placing some weight on the adversarial regime, where the decision maker gathers evidence for himself, the incentives of the parties to produce evidence is reduced. Parisi also finds that a skeptical adversarial judge would reduce the wasteful production of evidence.

3.2 *Sophisticated Decision Makers*

Several models of the adversarial system analyze the role of sophisticated third party decision makers. An early example is Sobel (1985). In his model, litigants decide whether or not to withhold evidence in a setting where it is costly to report pre-existing evidence. Sobel's model treats the decision as a binary one. In his model, the decision maker is sophisticated in the sense that the judge who uses a mixed strategy maximizes social surplus by "favoring" one of the litigants with a lower burden of proof. He finds that if the burden of proof is lowered for the party with the low cost of evidence, this will lower the cost of evidence. On the other hand, placing the burden on the high-cost party will increase the cost of evidence, but will result in more informed decisions, as more evidence is produced. The optimal weights will depend on how the decision maker trades off the cost of evidence against the benefit of increased accuracy. Emons and Fluet (2007) also examine the tradeoff between cost of evidence and accuracy. They examine a setting where an arbiter chooses to hear from both parties, only one party, or no parties. In the last case, the arbiter decides the case on his priors. The decision maker in this model is sophisticated in that when only one party is allowed to present evidence, he rationally corrects for the biased information he receives from that party. In the two-party adversarial case, the arbiter uses a split-the-difference estimator. The optimal number of parties to submit evidence depends upon the costs of evidence, and the value of the information. Lower evidence costs favor hearing both parties, while the choice to hear only one party or not to hear from either party is rational at higher costs. Sanchirico (2001a) examines a setting where low burdens of proof or use of imperfect evidence are the result of an attempt by the fact finder to use less costly signals. In this setting, these burdens are not designed to elicit accurate fact finding, but rather are designed to create conditions under which meeting these burdens is more costly for one type of litigant.

In addition to naïvely credulous decision makers, Milgrom and Roberts (1986) also model decision makers who are sophisticated, in that they know (i) the preferences of interested parties, (ii) the kind of information to which the parties have access so that they know how to interpret a lack of evidence, and (iii) how to update beliefs following reports, or non-reports, from the parties. When the parties' interests are opposed, as in litigation, the first two of these restrictions can be relaxed because the sophisticated decision maker can count on at least one of the parties to divulge the information.

Shin (1998) compares adversarial and inquisitorial procedures in arbitration. As is the case in prior models, Shin examines a model where the arbiter can choose to hear from both parties and rely on this information exclusively (adversarial), or to rely on his own investigation exclusively (inquisitorial). The adversarial parties cannot submit false information, but can withhold information. He finds that the adversarial decision maker who receives reports from interested parties always receives more information than an inquisitorial decision maker who receives the signals directly, in the sense that the adversarial decision maker's posterior probabilities are less noisy. The advantage of the adversarial system derives from the case where neither party reports evidence (non-revelation) and where one of the parties is favored in its ability to produce evidence. The adversarial decision maker knows the party favored by the distribution and is able to allocate the burden of proof in an effective manner to extract information from the parties. As a result, the arbiter can learn more from a non-report than does a neutral inquisitorial decision maker who receives the signals directly.

Dewatripont and Tirole (1999) examines the problem of incentive alignment under adversarial and inquisitorial procedures. Unlike the authors of the other papers discussed, who implicitly assume that the agents of the two regimes (the advocates and the decision makers) act in the best interests of the principals, their model allows for agency costs. The authors find that, when effort is observable, the inquisitorial regime has an advantage because compensation of the inquisitor can be tied to observed effort. In the more realistic case when effort cannot be observed, the adversarial regime has an advantage because advocates' incentives can be tied to trial outcomes. This same kind of incentive compensation will not work for an inquisitorial regime because effort provision requires the inquisitor to be rewarded when the status quo is abandoned (to show he is not shirking). This will make the inquisitor reluctant to release conflicting pieces of evidence that make the status quo desirable. In a trial setting, the status quo can be thought of as favoring the defendant in either a criminal (innocent until proven guilty) or civil (preponderance of evidence) setting. Palumbo (2001) extends the Dewatripont and Tirole (DT) model where effort in information gathering is a continuous variable, and where agents can conceal evidence. She finds that when manipulation is possible, the costs of providing incentives to agents increase, and thus the conditions under which an adversarial regime would be superior to an inquisitorial scheme are more restrictive than implied by the DT model.

4. Experimental Tests of Sophistication

The complexity of adversarial and inquisitorial systems and the lack of natural experiments have precluded serious empirical work on comparing adversarial and inquisitorial systems. One set of authors has applied the tools of experimental economics to test various theories and assumptions of the models of adversarial and inquisitorial systems. Block et al. (2001) (BPVD) attempt to recreate experimental conditions to test the Tullock (1980) hypothesis that inquisitorial systems will be superior to adversarial systems. In their experiments, two case scenarios were presented to the experimental subject that embodied Tullock's assumption of an unambiguously "right" and "wrong" party. The authors find that the inquisitorial system does better at uncovering the truth in an experimental setting when the parties have uncorrelated signals – that is, when Mr. Wrong is given private and asymmetric discrediting information; but that the adversarial system does better when their signals are correlated – that is, when both parties have access to hidden information.

Block and Parker (2004) use the data from the earlier BPVD experiments to test predictions of the Shin (1998) and DT (1999) models regarding decision making under conditions of non-revelation. Specifically, they examine the Shin hypothesis that the adversarial system will perform relatively better under these conditions, as the decision maker gains information when he observes non-revelation by the relatively informed party. Concentrating on a subset of the experimental data where non-revelation occurred, Block and Parker find that the decision makers are unsophisticated, in that they do not learn to interpret evidence as postulated in Shin when confronted with a lack of evidence. In addition, Block and Parker test the DT hypothesis that adversarial proceedings tend toward the status quo and inquisitorial proceedings tend toward extremism in the absence of the revelation of decisive facts. This is because, in the absence of such facts, DT hypothesize that the adversarial system tends to produce offsetting and neutralizing information that leads to a compromise or "split-the-difference" result. In contrast, a single inquisitorial decision maker is more likely to choose between the competing positions based on his prior beliefs. Block and Parker find evidence consistent with the DT non-revelation hypothesis, in that they find a tendency toward moderation in the absence of decisive facts in the adversarial setting, but not in the inquisitorial setting.

Finally, Boudreau and McCubbins (2008) examine the extent to which the use of competing experts improves decision making in an experimental setting. Subjects in the experiment are asked to solve binary math problems and are rewarded for correct responses. In the baseline setting, these subjects solve the problems without any help. In the treatments, the subjects solve the problems after they receive reports from two "experts." One expert is paid if the subject answers the problem correctly, and the other expert is paid if the subject answers the problem incorrectly. Boudreau and McCubbins find that the introduction of the adversarial experts improve decision making, as for the subjects that receive the experts' reports there is an increase in the percentage of correct responses. In part, decision making improves because the experts' payoffs (including penalties for lying in some of the experiments) result in the subjects receiving two correct reports from the competing agents more often that they receive two incorrect reports. The experiment in Boudreau and McCubbins, however, compares the adversarial setting to the baseline setting of no expert, and does not address the use and relative performance of a single inquisitorial expert. In the context of comparing adversarial and inquisitorial systems, extending the data to consider a single expert would be of great interest.

5. Conclusion and Directions for Future Research

Obviously, the importance of sophistication, and exactly what it means, is important for evaluating the benefits and costs of the adversarial and inquisitorial regimes. More or better tests of how decision makers process evidence and whether decisions are sophisticated are important for modeling the benefits and costs of the two systems. But as several of the articles point out, even if decision makers are unsophisticated, the competing incentives of the parties to produce evidence can offset some of the costs of the adversarial system. Tests of decision making in isolation from the competitive production of evidence would seem to rig the outcome in favor of the inquisitorial system, and neglect one of the benefits of the adversarial system.

It is ironic that economists have focused on sophisticated decision making by either the judge or jury as favoring the adversarial regime when legal systems often seem to rule this out. For example, decision makers are instructed or constrained to behave in an unsophisticated way, that is, not to draw an inference from the fact that evidence is not reported that could have been reported. If sophisticated decision making is important, figuring out how to integrate it into existing legal regimes seems like an important area of research.

Another intriguing area is the principal-agent problem highlighted by Milgrom and Roberts. Just as principal-agent models have opened up the "black box" of firm decision making and led to a number of important insights about firm behavior, opening up the black box of the relationships between the judiciary and their agents (judges, juries) and between the parties and their agents (attorneys, experts) might yield similar returns.

References

Arnold, Morris S. (1980), "A Historical Inquiry into the Right to Trial by Jury in Complex Civil Litigation," *University of Pennsylvania Law Review*, 128, 829–48.

Bell, Griffin B., Chilton Davis Varner, and Hugh Q. Gottschalk (1992), "Automatic Disclosure in Discovery – The Rush to Reform," 27, Georgia Law Review, 1–58.

Bernstein, David E. (2008), "Expert Witnesses, Adversarial Bias, and the (Partial) Failure of the Daubert Revolution," *Iowa Law Review*, 93, 451–89.

Block, Michael K. and Jeffrey S. Parker (2004), "Decision Making in the Absence of Successful Fact Finding: Theory and Experimental Evidence on Adversarial versus Inquisitorial Systems of Adjudication," *International Review of Law and Economics*, 24, 89–105.

Block, Michael K., Jeffrey S. Parker, Olga Vyborna, and Libor Dusek (2000), "An Experimental Comparison of Adversarial versus Inquisitorial Procedural Regimes," *American Law and Economics Review*, 2, 170–94.

Boudreau, Cheryl and Mathew D. McCubbins (2008), "Nothing but the Truth? Experiments on Adversarial Competition, Expert Testimony, and Decision Making," *Journal of Empirical Legal Studies*, 5, 751–89.

Brazil, Wayne D. (1978), "The Adversary Character of Civil Discovery: A Critique and Proposals for Change," *Vanderbilt Law Review*, 31, 1295–361.

Campbell, James S. (1988), "The Current Understanding of the Seventh Amendment," *Washington University Law Quarterly*, 66, 63–70.
Campbell, James S. and Nicholas LePoidevin (1980), "Complex Cases and Jury Trials: A Reply to Professor Arnold," *University of Pennsylvania Law Review*, 128, 965–85.
Cecil, Joe S., Valerie P. Hans, and Elizabeth C. Wiggins (1991), "Citizen Comprehension of Difficult Issues: Lessons from Civil Jury Trials," *American University Law Review*, 40, 727–74.
Cecil, Joe S. and Thomas E. Willging (1994a), "Court-Appointed Experts," in Federal Judicial Center, *Reference Manual on Scientific Evidence*, Colorado Springs, Col.: Shepard's McGraw-Hill.
Cecil, Joe S. and Thomas E. Willging (1994b), "Accepting Daubert's Invitation: Defining a Role for Court-Appointed Experts in Assessing Scientific Validity," *Emory Law Journal*, 43, 995–1070.
Cooter, Robert D. and Daniel L. Rubinfeld (1989), "An Economic Analysis of Legal Disputes and their Resolution," *Journal of Economic Literature*, 27, 1067–97.
Cooter, Robert D. and Daniel L. Rubinfeld (1994), "An Economic Model of Legal Discovery," *Journal of Legal Studies*, 23, 435–64.
Coulam, Robert and Stephen Fienberg (1986), "The Use of Court-Appointed Statistical Experts: A Case Study," in M.H. DeGroot, S.E. Fienberg, and J.B. Kadane, eds., *Statistics and the Law*, New York: Wiley.
Daughety, Andrew F. and Jennifer F. Reinganum (2000), "On the Economics of Trials: Adversarial Process, Evidence and Equilibrium Bias," *Journal of Law, Economics and Organization*, 16, 365–94.
Demsetz, Harold (1969), "Information and Efficiency: An Alternative Viewpoint," *Journal of Law and Economics*, 12, 1–22.
Dewatripont, Mathias and Jean Tirole (1999), "Advocates," *Journal of Political Economy*, 107, 1–39.
Dixit, A. (1987), "Strategic Behavior in Contests," *American Economic Review*, 77, 891–8.
Easterbrook, Frank H. (1989), "Discovery as Abuse," *Boston University Law Review*, 69, 635–48.
Emons, Winand and Claude Fluet (2007), "Accuracy versus Falsification Costs: The Optimal Amount of Evidence under Different Procedures," *Journal of Law, Economics and Organization*, 25, 134–56.
Farmer, Amy and Paul Pecorino (2000), "Does Jury Bias Matter?," *International Review of Law and Economics*, 20, 315–28.
Farrell, Margaret G. (1994), "Special Masters," in Federal Judicial Center, *Reference Manual on Scientific Evidence*, Colorado Springs, Col.: Shepard's McGraw-Hill.
Froeb, Luke M. and Bruce H. Kobayashi (1996), "Naïve, Biased yet Bayesian: Can Juries Interpret Selectively Produced Evidence?," *Journal of Law, Economics and Organization*, 12, 257–76.
Froeb, Luke M. and Bruce H. Kobayashi (2001), "Evidence Production in Adversarial vs. Inquisitorial Regimes," *Economics Letters*, 70, 267–72.
Harsanyi, John C. (1967), "Games with Incomplete Information Played by 'Bayesian' Players, I-III," *Management Science*, 14, 159–82.
Hayek, F.A. (1945), "The Use of Information in Society," *American Economic Review*, 35, 519–30.
Hayek, F.A. (1948), "Individualism, True and False," in *Individualism and Economic Order*, Chicago: University of Chicago Press.
Kaplow, Louis (1994), "The Value of Accuracy in Adjudication: An Economic Analysis," *Journal of Legal Studies*, 23, 307–402.
Kobayashi, Bruce H. (1996), "Case Selection, External Effects, and the Trial/Settlement Decision," in David A. Anderson, ed., *Dispute Resolution: Bridging the Settlement Gap*, Greenwich, Conn.: JAI Press.
Langbein, J.H. (1985), "The German Advantage in Civil Procedure," *University of Chicago Law Review*, 52, 823–66.

Lipman, Barton L. and Duane J. Seppi (1995), "Robust Inference in Communication Games with Partial Probability," *Journal of Economic Theory*, 66, 395–421.
McAfee, R. Preston and Phillip J. Reny (1992), "Correlated Information and Mechanism Design," *Econometrica*, 60, 395–421.
McChesney, Fred S. (1977), "On the Procedural Superiority of a Civil Law System: A Comment," *Kyklos*, 30, 507–10.
Milgrom, Paul and John Roberts (1986), "Relying on the Information of Interested Parties," *RAND Journal of Economics*, 17, 18–32.
Ordover, J.A. and Phillip Weitzman (1977), "On the Efficient Organization of Trials: A Comment," *Kyklos*, 30, 511–16.
Palumbo, Giuliana (2001), "Trial Procedures and Optimal Limits on Proof-Taking," *International Review of Law and Economics*, 21, 309–27.
Parisi, Francesco (2002), "Rent-Seeking through Litigation: Adversarial and Inquisitorial Systems Compared," *International Review of Law and Economics*, 22, 193–216.
Sanchirico, Chris W. (2001a), "Relying on the Information of Interested – and Potentially Dishonest – Parties," *American Law and Economics Review*, 3, 320–57.
Sanchirico, Chris W. (2001b), "Character Evidence and the Object of Trial," *Columbia Law Review*, 101, 1227–311.
Schwarzer, William W. (1989), "The Federal Rules, the Adversary Process, and Discovery Reform," *University of Pittsburgh Law Review*, 50, 703–23.
Seidmann, D.J. and E. Winter (1997), "Strategic Information Transmission with Verifiable Messages," *Econometrica*, 65, 163–9.
Shin, Hyun Song (1998), "Adversarial and Inquisitorial Procedures in Arbitration," *RAND Journal of Economics*, 28, 378–405.
Sobel, Joel (1985), "Disclosure of Evidence and Resolution of Disputes: Who Should Bear the Burden of Proof?," in Alvin E. Roth, ed., *Game Theoretic Models of Bargaining*, Cambridge: Cambridge University Press.
Sobel, Joel (1989), "An Analysis of Discovery Rules," *Law and Contemporary Problems*, 52, 133–59.
Thibault J., L. Walker, and E.A. Lind (1972), "Adversary Presentation and Bias in Legal Decisionmaking," *Harvard Law Review*, 86, 386–402.
Tullock, Gordon (1975), "On the Efficient Organization of Trials," *Kyklos*, 28, 745–62.
Tullock, Gordon (1980), *Trials on Trial: The Pure Theory of Legal Procedure*, New York: Columbia University Press.
Zywicki, Todd J. (2008), "Spontaneous Order and the Common Law: Gordon Tullock's Critique," *Public Choice*, 135, 35–53.

2 Appeal and supreme courts
Lewis A. Kornhauser

1. Introduction

This chapter reviews the literature concerning several issues raised in the economic analysis of appeal and of supreme courts. These issues overlap with those considered in Chapter 11: "Judicial Organization and Administration". The overlap occurs in many dimensions. Most obviously, appeal constitutes an important dimension of judicial organization and administration. Appeal itself can be organized in a variety of different ways. This review thus addresses a variety of questions about the organization of appeal. Does the court system permit appeal? Should it permit appeal? Why do some systems permit appeal, while others do not? Assuming that a judicial system permits appeal, how many appeals is or should a litigant be permitted? How should appeal be organized? Should there be distinct appellate courts? Or should appeal be taken to another court at the same level? How many judges should hear an appeal? To what extent should appellate courts control their own docket? The legal-economic answers to these organizational questions are surveyed here.

Second, this chapter reviews the vast literature on how appellate *judges* behave. What explains how judges decide cases? Can we explain the precedential practices invoked by common law courts or by civil law courts? Do lower court judges comply with the rulings of higher courts? What explains the content of the opinions written by judges? When courts control their own jurisdiction, can we explain the set of cases chosen for review? This behavior, of course, will depend in part on the organization and administration of the courts. Some behavioral issues will arise in the review of Chapter 11 on "Judicial Organization and Administration". The discussion of judicial motivation in Section 2 of that review, particularly the discussion of policy preferences in Section 2.2, bears directly on the models of appeal.

Two further general comments about the literature are in order. First, most of the literature has focused on courts in common law countries. Indeed, most models that extend beyond the simplest features of adjudication do so in the context of the political system of the United States. This review consequently shares the parochial focus of the literature. Analyses of appeal in civil law systems and in the context of different political systems would greatly advance understanding of the subject, as they often present different institutional features. At least some civil law systems, for example, allow an appellate court to make an independent assessment of the facts of the case, a judgment denied common law courts. Similarly, the highest courts in some civil law jurisdictions hear substantially more cases than the highest courts in common law countries, a fact that may explain, or be explained by, differences in precedential practice and in the style and content of judicial opinions.

Second, most of the literature, particularly the literature from political science, has been heavily influenced by the positive political theory models developed for the study of legislation in general and of the United States Congress in particular. This influence has fostered significant advances in our understanding of judicial behavior and appellate organization, but it also has two distinct biases. Political scientists study politics and politics is often understood as conflicts of interests among actors. As a consequence, most models are *political* models in the sense that judicial behavior is analyzed and understood as a consequence of the conflicting interests of judges or of judges and other political actors. An alternative perspective, less represented in the literature, treats the judicial system as a *team* in the sense of Marschak and Radner (1972), a set of individuals with common interests. Teams must coordinate their efforts and the economic theory of teams studies these coordination problems. The theory of teams provides a distinct set of insights into judicial administration and behavior that helps clarify the role that conflict of interest plays in judicial behavior.

Use of the positive political theory model of legislation to study courts has had a second bias. Positive political theorists developed the model of legislation to illuminate legislative institutions. These institutions, of course, differ dramatically from judicial institutions. The use of the legislative model to study courts has sometimes diverted attention from the peculiar features of judicial institutions. Most importantly, legislatures enact statutes which are easily and appropriately understood as *policies*. Courts, by contrast, primarily decide *cases*. In the course of rendering judgment on the case, courts may also announce policy. The use of legislative models, however, has obscured questions of how case dispositions and policy announcements interact. Further differences are equally important. Legislatures generally control their own agendae; litigants set the judicial agenda. In addition, as the discussion of collegial courts underscores, the decision rules in legislatures are different from the decision rules in courts. These different procedures should, as positive political theory instructs, lead to different outcomes.

The discussion is organized around some simple "models" of judicial organization. First, I consider the literature on precedential practices of a single court. This literature generally assumes that each court consists of a single judge and considers the conflicts of interests (or coordination problems) that arise from a sequence of single-judge courts. Next, I consider collegial courts. On a collegial court, a panel of judges decides a case. The simplest model assumes a single court that consists of a fixed panel of immortal judges that decide all appeals in the jurisdiction. Most appellate courts in the world are collegial; cases are heard and decided by a panel of judges rather than by a single judge. Next, I survey the literature on hierarchy. Again, the cleanest model posits single-judge courts arranged hierarchically in one or more tiers. The literature then considers the conflicts of interest or coordination problems that arise in this hierarchical structure. Finally, I turn to models of the interaction of court and legislature. Again, the court is generally modeled as a unitary actor.

2. Precedential Practices

For purposes of this chapter, "precedent" refers to the body of previously decided case law in a particular judicial system. Different legal systems treat precedent differently. Economists and political scientists have studied the precedential practices of common law adjudication much more extensively than they have studied civil law practices. This survey reflects this bias in attention.

Common law precedential practices are quite complex. *Stare decisis* ("keep to what has been decided previously"), the most studied practice, requires that a court adhere to the decision in an "identical" prior case even when the court believes that the prior case was wrongly decided. *Stare decisis* in fact refers to a number of related practices. In this section, I shall focus on *horizontal stare decisis* which refers to how a court treats its *own* precedent, i.e. the body of cases previously decided by itself. I leave a discussion of vertical *stare decisis*, the common law practice that an inferior court must follow the decisions of a superior court, to the discussion of hierarchy below. Moreover, I treat horizontal *stare decisis* as a unitary practice, though, arguably, its parameters differ with respect to cases arising under the common law, under statutes, and under a constitution. Finally I discuss the literature on the related common law practices of overruling and distinguishing.

2.1 Theoretical Models of Stare Decisis and other Common Law Precedential Practices

Stare decisis refers to a set of practices peculiar to Anglo-American courts in which one court adheres to its own prior decisions or to the decisions of a higher court. For a fuller discussion of the legal aspect of these practices, references to the legal literature and the modeling questions they present, see Kornhauser (1998).

Several models of horizontal and vertical *stare decisis* have appeared in the literature. In this section, I shall focus primarily on models of horizontal *stare decisis* in which a court follows its own prior decisions. Discussions of vertical *stare decisis* are implicit or explicit in most political models of hierarchy because these models pose as one of the key questions the extent to which lower courts comply with the rulings of higher courts. Vertical *stare decisis* in a team model is discussed in both Kornhauser (1995) and Cameron and Kornhauser (2005, 2006). Kornhauser (1995) argues that vertical *stare decisis* arises because of the benefits presented by specialization of labor between fact-finding and law-making and for error-correction reasons. Cameron and Kornhauser (2005a, 2006) investigate the error-correction justification in detail.

Early models of horizontal *stare decisis* suggest a number of different justifications for, or explanations of, the practice. Heiner (1986) argues that *stare decisis* arises because courts only observe the "correct" answer to specific cases with error. A judge might then do better to announce a decision that is best "on average" (for some class of cases) and adhere to that decision rather than to make a series of errors on a case-by-case basis.

Kornhauser (1989) characterized horizontal *stare decisis* as a practice in which a court adheres to a decision it believes to be wrong. He offers two informal models based on two distinct justifications for the practice. The first model applies to a "panel court" in which each case is decided by one or more judges drawn from a larger bench. If judges have different views of the law, then *stare decisis* serves to reduce legal uncertainty faced by actors governed by the legal rule. The second model assumes a unitary court with an unchanging social objective; the court, however, faces a world in which the optimal behavior (as viewed from its perspective) changes because some underlying parameters change. Kornhauser's model modifies that in Blume and Rubinfeld (1982), in which the court, through its announcement of standards of care, seeks to minimize the costs of accidents and the costs of adjustment to new standards. In the Blume and Rubinfeld model, the court does not adopt a practice of *stare decisis*; rather, as the technology of care shifts, the court adjusts gradually towards the standards that would be optimal in an unchanging world with the new technology. In Kornhauser's version, a court must announce standards of care in a world in which the technology of accident care is improving at a known rate. The court adheres to *stare decisis* as long as the standards of care optimal under the new technology are not too far from the old standards. Otherwise, it announces new standards that overshoot those currently optimal.

Later models are more technically sophisticated and fall roughly into two classes: those that rely on imperfect information and those that do not. Rasmusen (1994) presents a political model for horizontal *stare decisis*. Rasmusen's model provides a formal justification for an argument implicit in O'Hara (1993). The court consists of a single judge who decides $n + 1$ cases and is then replaced by another judge who also decides $n + 1$ cases. Each judge has preferences over the outcomes of all cases and these preferences differ. Assume that only one of these $n + 1$ cases is a case of first impression. Under a practice of *stare decisis*, each judge would adhere to the n prior decisions governing n of his cases and n subsequent judges would adhere to the decision he announces in his case of first impression. Rasmusen shows that a practice of *stare decisis* is one equilibrium to this game.

In Rasmusen's model, the judge adheres to precedent in order to insure that his own decisions are followed; *stare decisis* thus rests on the structure of the judge's preferences over policies. Miceli and Cosgel (1994) identify conditions under which *stare decisis* emerges in equilibrium for a different structure of preferences. In their model, judges have preferences over policies and a concern for their reputation. If the concern for reputation is sufficiently strong, a judge adheres to the prior decision even when it deviates from his own ideal decision.

Daughety and Reinganum (1999) is an early information-based explanation of horizontal *stare decisis*. They consider a set of appellate courts, all inferior to the same supreme court. Each has private information about the Supreme Court's interpretation of the law. When an appellate court observes a prior decision of another appellate court, it updates its prior about the view of the Supreme Court. In this setting, an informational cascade is possible in which all courts follow the lead of a prior court and, possibly, endorse the wrong view. In their interpretation, the model is one of persuasive precedent, as one appellate court is not bound to follow a ruling by a different appellate court. A different interpretation would yield a model closer in spirit to the practice of *stare decisis*. Suppose the best legal rule depends on the state of world, about which the courts are uncertain. Consider a sequence of judges on a single court. Each judge gets a signal about the state, as well as observing the decisions of the judges who preceded her on the bench. A similar informational cascade may result.

Stone (2008) offers a different informational story. Here a court must choose between two rules to apply to a case. For society, the optimal rule is contingent on the state of the world. Some judges are also neutral, but others have an ideological preference for one rule over the other. Judges, however, also prefer to have a reputation for neutrality. When a case comes before the court, the judge gets a signal of the true state of the world. Here there are a multiplicity of equilibria, in some of which judges adhere to *stare decisis*.

Gennaioli and Shleifer (2007a) also consider the role of bias in a model of the related practice of distinguishing. Their model lies in a two-dimensional "case space" – the idea of case space was introduced in Kornhauser (1992b). A policy, in this formulation, is simply a partition of case space. Judges want to maximize social welfare, but they are constrained in the set of rules they can announce. Given the constraint, some judges prefer rules biased towards plaintiffs, other judges prefer rules biased towards defendants, and a third group are neutral. When the first case arises, the court can announce only a simple partition that is conditional on only one of the two facts. When a second case arises, the next judge may "distinguish" the first case by conditioning liability on the second factual dimension. They show that the ability to distinguish improves the efficiency of the law.

Gennaioli and Shleifer (2007b) consider the practice of overruling precedent in the same model. Overruling, unlike distinguishing, has negative effects because only ideologically extreme judges have an interest in overruling; but that interest leads to oscillation in the law.

Fernandez and Ponzetto (2008) also work in the Gennaioli and Shleifer framework. They, however, do not restrict the class of rules that the judge may announce. They study the evolution of the law and show that, if the judiciary is sufficiently polarized ideologically, the efficient rule will be announced. The intuition is straightforward. Polarization is necessary because there is a cost to changing the law. On the other hand, efficiency is achieved because all judges rank the welfare-maximizing rule highest; their ideological disagreements are only second-order disagreements.

Whitman (2000) further studies the model of Miceli and Cosgel (1994). A sequence of judges must decide an infinite sequence of cases. The case is governed by one of two rules and the decision in a case identifies the applicable rule. Each judge takes the decision of the prior judge as "precedent"; he must decide whether to follow precedent or to replace the prior rule with the second. Judges have policy preferences and preferences for reputation, i.e., that their decision be followed. In this model, the system converges to a single rule when a sufficiently high proportion of judges agrees on a particular rule as best. If a third compromise rule is added to the model, convergence to the compromise rule is most likely when ideological division over the other two rules is sufficiently high.

2.2 Empirical Studies of Stare Decisis

Several studies have attempted to determine the extent to which justices of the US Supreme Court in fact adhere to *stare decisis*. Segal and Spaeth (1996, Spaeth and Segal 1999) trace the sequelae of prominent decisions of the Supreme Court of the United States. On their view, a justice of the Supreme Court adheres to *stare decisis* if (a) he voted against the result in

Prior Case and (b) accepts the rule or standards of the majority in Prior Case in his decision in Subsequent Case. They examined 346 votes in 146 progeny of 54 landmark cases. Their definition of *stare decisis* requires that they consider the votes only of justices who dissented in the initial case. They found that justices voted according to their revealed preferences in the landmark cases roughly 91% of the time; hence they conclude that Supreme Court justices do not adhere to a practice of *stare decisis*.

This study has several flaws. Brenner and Steir (1996) followed a similar procedure to study the behavior of four moderate justices on the Warren Court. They included memorandum and per curiam opinions that Segal and Spaeth had excluded. They find that these justices adhered to precedent 47% of the time. Moreover, this percentage increased if progeny decided in the same term were excluded; on progeny decided later, the justices adhered to precedent 64% of the time. The methodology of Brenner and Steir thus paints a very different picture.

Songer and Lindquist (1996) argue that the coding of data in Segal and Spaeth leads to an underestimate of the effect of *stare decisis*. A vote in a subsequent case to limit the precedent is coded as a violation of *stare decisis* even though it acknowledges the authority of the case. In fact, this argument points out a difficulty in assessing the role of *stare decisis* in judicial decision, particularly at the Supreme Court level. The subsequent case before the Supreme Court is rarely identical and clearly governed by Prior Case; subsequent case generally raises a new issue. Hence, it is the practice of distinguishing rather than of *stare decisis* that is most relevant. The norms governing legal reasoning, however, are too imprecise and poorly understood for us to determine whether a court has inappropriately distinguished, rather than followed, a prior case.

Lim (2000) follows a procedure similar to Segal and Spaeth, but he embeds his analysis in a more structured random utility model; in addition, he restricts his analysis to four natural courts between 1986 and 1994. He analyses 600 progeny cases and finds that precedent has a significant effect on the decision-making of each judge.

2.3 Precedent in Civil Law Legal Systems

In civil law systems, no single judicial decision has authority; it does not bind other courts or the rendering court in the future. These systems, however, have developed a precedential practice called, in France, *jurisprudence constante*, that gives a sufficiently uniform mass of decisions authority to bind. The legislature sets some parameter T in the interval $[0,1]$ that indicates the threshold degree of uniformity that must exist in decisions governing a particular issue for that body of law to bind other courts. This precedential practice differs greatly from that in common law systems. Unfortunately, it has been little studied by economists and political scientists.

Fon and Parisi (2006) provide the only formal model of this process. They consider a set of disputes in which decisions for defendant imply that plaintiffs have no cause of action, while decisions for plaintiff establish her legal right. On this account, the body of precedent lies in one of three regions: either the percentage P of cases decided for plaintiff exceeds the threshold T and subsequent courts should decide in favor of plaintiff, or P decided against plaintiff is greater than T and subsequent courts should decide in favor of defendant, or P lies between T and $1 - T$ and the case law is unsettled.

Fon and Parisi assume that a court has some probability p of deciding for plaintiff. This probability depends on the recent history of decisions for plaintiff, with the weighted difference between the rate of decision for plaintiff and against plaintiff called $F(t)$ and on the entire history of decisions with the weighted difference between the rate of decision for and against plaintiff called $H(t)$. They then specify the motion of the system as a function of these variables. They show, not surprisingly, that as T increases, the region of legal uncertainty increases.

3. Collegiality

Generally, an appeal is decided by a panel of judges rather than a single judge. In the United States, the three-judge panels that sit on federal intermediate appeals courts are drawn from a larger bank of judges, while the nine justices of the Supreme Court sit en banc. The inverted pyramidal structure of the federal hierarchy in the United States, in which the size of the panel deciding a case increases as the case rises through the system, is a nearly universal feature of court systems. The highest courts in some civil law countries (e.g., the Cour de Cassation in France), however, function similarly to the federal intermediate courts, with each case decided by a panel drawn from a larger bench.

Collegiality presents several puzzles. First, why are appellate courts collegial and why does the number of judges increase as one proceeds up the hierarchy? Second, what consequences for adjudication does collegiality have? The economic literature began with Easterbrook (1983), which addressed the second question. Prior to addressing these questions, I set out a baseline model that underlies much of the political science literature.

3.1 A Baseline Model: One-Dimensional Spatial Preferences in Policy Space

Much of the political science literature on courts simply adapted the positive political theory models developed to study legislation generally and

Congress in particular. For collegial courts, only minimal changes to this model were made. Thus, the literature to a large extent treats a collegial court as a legislature operating under an open rule. (This contrasts with the adaptation made to study the separation of powers, discussed below, which assumed that the court operated on a closed rule.) Again, if one continues to import ideas from the literature on legislation, one assumes that a collegial court, in choosing a policy, uses a Condorcet-consistent procedure on a one-dimensional policy space. Then, one concludes that the court will adopt the policy of the median justice on the court.

We know, from the literature on electoral competition, that this result is reasonably robust, particularly if one assumes, as much of the literature on collegial courts does, that the justices have perfect information about the ideal points of the other justices. The literature has been rather imprecise in specifying the games that the justices play to arrive at the median justice conclusion (see e.g., Hammond et al. (2005) in which two of three "models" support the median justice hypothesis), but the oral tradition generally acknowledges that result.

This strategy of adaptation, though initially fruitful, leaves much judicial behavior on collegial courts unexplained and ignores the institutional structures that distinguish courts from legislatures. For the moment, maintain the assumption that justices have preferences over policies only and that they announce only policies. The median voter model implies that the policy announced by the court is independent of the judge who writes the opinion. Moreover, the role for dissents and concurrences is unclear. The implicit model of voting presumably precludes such practices because allowing them suggests, again from the electoral competition literature, that the court might announce a non-median policy.

Most obviously, courts decide cases, as well as announce policy. The legislative model ignores this and the models do not admit the possibility that a judge might vote strategically with respect to the disposition of a case in order to induce the court to announce a policy closer to his ideal point.

Moroever, evidence in Cameron and Clark (2006) suggests that the location of opinions depends not only on the location of the median justice but also on the ideological location of the chief justice. Theoretical approaches to the location of opinions is discussed below.

3.2 Why are Appellate Courts Collegial?
Posner (1985 at 12) offered several reasons for the existence of collegiality on the Supreme Court: (a) multiple judges reduces the costs of poor appointments; (b) multiplicity of judges reduces the power of any single judge on a court which has vast power; (c) a multiplicity of judges allows

the court to benefit from deliberation; and (d) a multiplicity of judges permits the division of the labor of opinion drafting and hence increases the productivity of the court.

Kornhauser and Sager (1986) provided a more systematic analysis of the reasons for collegiality. First, they distinguished two conceptions of adjudication: the rendering of judgment and the rendition of preferences. They then suggested three different models of collegial adjudication, each of which identified a distinct standard against which to measure judicial performance. (1) One might view collegial courts as engaged in the aggregation of the preferences of the judges on the court and one would measure the quality of the court by its *authenticity*, the extent to which the court's judgment correctly reflects the preferences of the judges. (2) One might view collegial courts as engaged in the aggregation of judgments and one would evaluate the court's procedures in terms of their *accuracy*, i.e., their ability to "get the right answer" however one defines the right outcome. (3) One might view collegial courts as representative institutions that seek to reach the outcome that the represented body would have reached had they deliberated and voted. This representative model suggests two different evaluative measures: *fit*, which is simply the tendency to arrive at results that the represented group would have reached and *reliability*, which is the absence of bad surprises.

Kornhauser and Sager reject preference aggregation as an appropriate understanding of adjudication. This eliminates authenticity as an evaluative measure. They then argue that increasing the numbers of judges improves accuracy, fit and reliability. They focus specifically on accuracy and rely on the Condorcet Jury Theorem.

Good and Tullock (1984) offer a representation model of Supreme Court collegiality. The justices of the Supreme Court are treated as a representative sample of the population of competent lawyers. Good and Tullock calculate the probability $p(r,s)$ that a case decided by a vote of r to s will fit the decision of the represented group. They determine that $p(5,4) = 0.62304$ and $p(9,0) = 0.99902$.

3.3 Policy Choice on Collegial Courts

Collegial courts present many questions for scholars of courts. First, do they yield a stable policy outcome? If so, what outcome do they yield? Does the outcome vary with the opinion writer?

I start first with the question of stability. We have already seen the answer when judges have spatial preferences in a one-dimensional policy space and they vote over policies in a "legislative" way: the policy of the median judge prevails.

What happens in a multi-dimensional space? We might address this question in two different ways: we might either remain in policy space or we might shift to "case" or "fact" space, introduced in Kornhauser (1992a). Fact space reflects an important institutional feature of adjudication: judges decide cases, either prior to or in tandem with the announcement of policies. A case is simply a vector of all "relevant" facts in disputes. From this perspective, a policy is simply a partition of the fact space; it divides the fact space into two sets: the set of those cases in which plaintiff prevails and the set of those cases in which defendant prevails. Fact space has very high dimensionality. Lax (2007) shows that, as long as each judge has preferences over policies that are separable in cases – or, equivalently, preferences over case dispositions that are separable – then, a stable majority policy exists. This policy assigns the majority disposition to each case. Moreover, the policy (or rule) of the court may not coincide with the ideal policy of any judge on the court. Anderson and Tahk (2007) prove a similar result in a multi-dimensional policy space in which judicial preferences are separable over policy dimensions and where judges vote dimension by dimension. These results are not surprising as separability is a very strong assumption. Kornhauser (1992a) had shown that, in a sequence of single-judge courts, a stable, unique policy existed if preferences were separable over cases. He also showed that, under a practice of strong *stare decisis*, the resulting policy was stable but path dependent.

Most models concerning policy choice on collegial courts model the Supreme Court of the United States. As noted earlier, the simple transfer of the legislative model to the context of collegial courts yields the median justice result. That result rests on several assumptions. First, it assumes competition among opinions. Second, it assumes that the court adopts a Condorcet-consistent procedure when it determines which policy to enact. Schwartz (1992) was an early model that rejected the second premise by assuming that the court essentially operated under a "closed rule" that limited its choices to a status quo and an arbitrarily identified alternative.

Lax and Cameron (2007) reject the second premise. They offer a model that identifies an opinion writer who may face an entering, competing opinion for another justice. This potential competition prevents the opinion writer from announcing her own ideal point because that might not garner enough votes. In addition, without the expenditure of effort, the actual policy implemented under the opinion is random. More precisely, an opinion written at policy p is understood as a random variable with mean p and variance q which is a function of the (costly) effort expended by the opinion writer. Judges have *ex post* preferences that are separable in the realized opinion location and effort; *ex ante* each judge faces a quadratic loss from policies not at her ideal point. In the sequential game, the court has a straw vote to determine the initial majority, the "chief justice" then assigns the opinion, the assignee then writes an opinion, then any other judge may write a competing opinion. They identify conditions under which the opinion writer chooses a location and quality of opinion that blocks entry from other opinions. They also investigate the incentives facing the chief justice who chooses the opinion writer. In general, the chief justice has an incentive to assign to "experts" who have low costs of writing or to extremists.

Lax and Rader (2007) try to distinguish empirically between various models of opinion assignment, including the median justice rule, the Lax and Cameron theory discussed above and a "median of the majority" theory. They argue that the evidence rejects the median justice theory and supports the Lax and Cameron model.

Cameron and Kornhauser (2010) investigate a general model that questions both the first and second premises of the median voter rule. Their model is firmly located in case space so that each judge has complex preferences with several parameters. First, the judge values an opinion that disposes of the case as she would under her ideal rule. Second, she has spatial preferences so that she values opinions closer to her ideal policy. Third, she cares about the "clarity" of the opinion; the more votes garnered by an opinion, the more value it has in fixing the law; for some parameters, however, the value of an opinion with more support declines when the opinion is sufficiently far from the judge's ideal point. Finally, the judge has an additional expressive value for joining an opinion at her ideal point. In this context, they first consider "monopoly" models in which a randomly assigned opinion writer offers the *only* opinion. They then consider models with entry in which the plurality opinion serves as the "winning" opinion for purposes of determining judicial utility.

As the general model is too complex to solve, they consider special cases in which various of the parameters are set to zero. In all, the location of the case is important because it determines which judges get the dispositional value of the case. This feature also implies the existence of another form of strategic behavior by judges: a judge may vote against her preferred disposition in order to give a "good" opinion more "clarity". In their analysis of the cases with entry, they exploit models of electoral politics among candidates with policy preferences to derive a mean voter result and to show that the policy of the median judge is not always the equilibrium.

3.4 Panel Effects
Revesz (1997), in his study of environmental decisions by the DC circuit, tested for effects of panel composition on the voting behavior of individual judges. In particular, he asked whether the reversal rate of a judge depended on whether she was in the minority or a majority on the panel.

He identified judicial policy preferences with the party of the appointing president and found substantial differences between the voting behavior of judges in an ideological minority on a panel from those in an ideological majority. Numerous subsequent studies – see, for example, Sunstein et al. (2004), Hettinger et al. (2006), Fischman (2008) – confirm this result. Fischman (2008) provides a particularly illuminating study as he estimates a structural model to determine the costs of dissent.

Cross and Tiller (1998) studied how the grounds on which the lower court rested its decision affected the behavior of panels. They found that ideology governed on homogeneous panels but that, on ideologically heterogeneous panels, the minority position would prevail when supported by doctrine.

3.5 Consistency and Coherence
In the first model of collegiality, Easterbrook (1983) relied on simple social choice arguments to argue that one could not expect the Supreme Court of the United States to generate a consistent body of case law. Easterbrook assumed that each case presented the Court with a choice between two legal rules to govern a particular doctrinal realm. When more than two legal rules were possible and no rule was a Condorcet winner, the Court's case law would cycle as successive cases challenged the prevailing rule with an alternative that a majority of the Court preferred.

Kornhauser and Sager (1986) distinguished between *consistent* and *coherent* patterns of decisions. A court that decides cases consistently will decide identical cases identically. The definition of coherence was less clear; a court that decides coherently creates a body of law that exhibits the quality of conceptual unity. They then argued that a panel of judges, each of whom had a consistent view of the law, would produce a consistent body of law; but a panel of judges, each of whom had a coherent conception of the law, need not yield a coherent body of decisions.

Kornhauser (1992a) extended this analysis. Kornhauser identified three different bases of judicial decision: result-bound, rule-bound, and reason-bound decision. In a result-bound decision process, the court is obligated to respect the results of the prior decisions of the court; in a rule-bound process, the court is obligated to respect the rule announced in prior cases, while a reason-bound court respects the reasons provided in prior decisions. He then argued that, with a rule of strict *stare decisis*, law in a result-bound judicial system will generally be path dependent and consistent.

Stearns (1995) offered an analysis of the development of the law in a collegial court that contained elements of both Easterbrook's and Kornhauser and Sager's analysis. Stearns, like Easterbrook, viewed adjudication as rule-bound, though he abandoned Easterbrook's assumption that a case presented only two rules. Stearns, however, emphasized the role of both *stare decisis* and standing doctrine in ameliorating any cycling problems.

Landa and Lax (2007) provide a more formal and compelling analysis. They characterize a class of "coherent" rules from which the rules of the sitting judges are drawn. They identify conditions under which the rule resulting from case-by-case majority decision will be among the set of coherent rules.

3.6 Actual Voting protocols on Collegial Courts

3.6.1 The doctrinal paradox Kornhauser and Sager (1986) noted a paradoxical feature of collegial adjudication which later attracted extensive comment. Specifically, they considered a case that presented two distinct issues for decision. Legal doctrine determines the relation between the decisions on each issue and the decision on the case. In some circumstances, the procedure the court adopts for aggregating votes will determine the outcome of the case. They discussed two procedures: *case-by-case* adjudication, in which each judge registers her view of how the *case* should be decided and the court aggregates these votes to reach a majority judgment. Alternatively, each judge may register her view on how each *issue* in the case should be decided; the court then aggregates the votes on each issue and applies the legal doctrine to the issue-by-issue results to reach a judgment in the case.

Kornhauser (1992b) named this conflict "the doctrinal paradox" and extended this analysis in several ways. A single judge decides a case by deciding each legal issue in each cause of action. To prevail on a cause of action, plaintiff must prevail on each issue; to prevail in the case, she must prevail on at least one cause of action. On a multi-member court, the two different aggregation methods may lead to different results. Kornhauser showed that the doctrinal paradox was distinct from the Condorcet cycle. When the judges' orderings of outcomes (described as the vector of outcomes on each issue) yield a Condorcet cycle, issue-by-issue and case-by-case voting might not conflict. Conversely, when the judges' orderings produce a Condorcet winner over outcomes, the issue-by-issue result might differ from the case-by-case result. Finally, he analyzed several actual instances in which the doctrinal paradox arose.

Rogers (1991) examined and classified all plurality opinions of the United States Supreme Court. He counted approximately 150 such cases. Of these he identified only eight cases in which the vote of one or two justices effectively resulted in a court aggregation of votes on an issue-by-issue, rather than a case-by-case, basis. He argued further that the limited doctrinal incoherence of case-by-case aggregation was normatively preferable to the inconsistency and indeterminacy that may result from issue-by-issue adjudication. Leonard (1984) found a similar paucity of instances of issue-by-issue aggregation in a study of decisions in criminal cases by the highest courts of Alabama, California, Indiana, and New York. Rogers based his argument for case-by-case voting on the grounds that issue-by-issue adjudication may lead to unfair results.

Post and Salop (1992) argued that collegial courts should always aggregate votes issue-by-issue. They did so on several grounds. First, they disputed the unfairness of case-by-case aggregation. Second, they argued that case-by-case aggregation led to path dependent decision-making; framed more positively, they argued that an aggregation procedure should yield the same results regardless of the order in which cases arrive before the court. Third, issue-by-issue aggregation promotes collegial deliberation by inducing the judges to join issue. Post and Salop (1996) expand and clarify their argument in favor of issue-by-issue voting. They note that issue-by-issue voting clarifies the law more quickly than case-by-case voting.

Kornhauser and Sager (1993) then extended their earlier analysis of the doctrinal paradox. They emphasized the peculiar nature of actual Supreme Court practice, which permitted each judge to count votes as he wished and which suppressed discussion of the aggregation procedure. They argued that the Court should justify its decision on whether to resolve cases issue-by-issue or case-by-case because the appropriate decision procedure was context-dependent.

Rogers (1996), Stearns (1996) and Post and Salop (1996) then recapitulated the debate over the appropriate aggregation method. Rogers noted importantly that issue-by-issue voting required the Court to identify a set of issues on which each judge should vote and illustrated the complexity of this task. Stearns (1996) argues that in fact agreement on issues is not as difficult as Rogers suggests. Post and Salop (1996) also argue that the identification of issues is less problematic than Rogers asserts.

Bonnefon (2007) designed an experiment to test how individuals resolved this experiment. Using roughly 1000 subjects, he found that subjects thought case-by-case decision-making was simpler and hence, *ceteris paribus*, preferable; that subjects prefer issue-by-issue voting when they believe that all issues are rarely resolved favorably, and finally, that subjects preferred the protocol that produced the more "lenient" outcome.

Chapman (1998, 2003) has argued that the problems presented by different results are in fact resolved by a sequential decision procedure used by courts. This procedure reflects the structure of legal reasoning.

Discussions of the doctrinal paradox have led to an extensive formal literature on judgment aggregation, a generalization of social choice theory that shows that there are no procedures that do not lead to paradoxical outcomes. An introduction to the theory and the literature appears on Christian List's website at http://personal.lse.ac.uk/list/doctrinalparadox.htm.

3.6.2 Sincere versus sophisticated voting Analysis of the doctrinal paradox assumed that each judge voted "sincerely" on each issue regardless of the method of aggregation of the votes on the court. (Defining "sincerity" in the context of multiple issue cases presents difficulties that are addressed in a different voting context in Benoit and Kornhauser (1995).) An assumption of sincerity comports well with a team model; it does not easily fit into a political model. In a political model, a self-interested, rational judge should foresee the results of sincere votes that might be detrimental to the realization of her interests.

Spiller and Spitzer (1995) ask whether judges are voting sincerely or with sophistication. They assume a court with one sincere judge and show how that judge can be manipulated by sophisticated judges. In their model, the judges and the legislature play a two-stage game. In stage 1, the court interprets a statute and in stage 2, the legislature decides whether to overrule the court's interpretation. All judges and legislators have preferences over a one-dimensional policy space. The model predicts that (1) the legislature will frequently overrule the court and (2) coalitions of extremes will often form. They then contend that, as these phenomena are not observed, one should assume that all judges vote with sophistication.

4. Hierarchy

4.1 Why Does Hierarchy Occur?
Appeal, and supreme courts, only arise in court systems which are organized hierarchically. Why does hierarchy occur? Posner (1985) suggested that the primary function of a supreme court was law creation and the insurance of uniformity of application of law among the lower courts. In addition, he argued that, in the United States, concerns about unreviewable power implied that trial courts would be subject to some supervision. These ideas have not been much elaborated in the literature. Rather, two distinct research strategies have emerged from two different models of adjudication. The "team" model assumes that all judges in the system share a common objective function – to maximize the number of "correct" decisions rendered by the system. Hierarchy emerges because it somehow promotes the goal of error minimization. The "political" (or "principal-agent") model assumes that judges differ in their objective functions.

Hierarchy arises in this model so that the small set of politically dominant judges can enforce their views on recalcitrant judges lower in the hierarchy.

Kornhauser (1995) provides an informal team model that explicitly addresses the question of the optimal organization of n judges into a judicial system. Judges share the goal of minimizing the number of errors; the likelihood of a correct decision depends on the amount of effort the judge invests in deliberation on the case. Moreover, deliberation on a specific case also provides a signal about the correct resolution of "nearby" cases. Because the court faces a resource constraint, the question of optimal organization of judges arises. Kornhauser argues that, in appropriate circumstances, a hierarchy will emerge in which there is (a) division of labor between trial judges who find facts and appellate judges who determine the law; and (b) strict vertical *stare decisis* so that lower court judges will always adhere to the decisions of higher court judges. Models of hierarchy that emphasize the need for consistency, as in Rogers (1995) and Dorf (1995), are team models in which the "correct decision" requires consistency.

Political models generally justify appellate review in terms of lawmaking. They do this in large part because the structure of the model requires that interpretation. Each court usually has preferences over policy space. Thus, to decide a case is to announce a policy, or put differently, to announce a new legal rule.

4.2 Lower Court Compliance with Higher Courts

Hierarchy serves a variety of functions. It permits a division of labor among tiers: usually trial courts find the facts, intermediate appellate courts correct errors, and high courts make law. Several questions about the relation of courts across tiers arise. How do higher courts in fact monitor lower courts, given the costs of such monitoring? What explains the number of tiers? The following subsections address these issues.

4.2.1 Doctrine Doctrine constitutes the central focus of much traditional legal scholarship, but it has, until recently, played little role in the social scientific study of adjudication. Doctrine may be understood as a managerial tool that higher courts use to guide and control lower courts. It is thus distinct from a number of precedential practices such as horizontal *stare decisis*. This subsection reviews some attempts to address doctrine formally.

Courts in common law systems do more than announce an outcome "upheld" or "reverse" to an appeal. An opinion offers a rationale for the decision and it is this rationale which guides the decisions of lower courts. To study appeal, then, the analyst must model this "doctrinal" structure.

The literature reveals two distinct approaches to modeling doctrine, approaches that have already been alluded to in the prior discussion. The importance of the issue, however, merits a brief exposition of the two approaches.

One approach, first set forth in Kornhauser (1992b), describes a case as a vector of fact characteristics. Kornhauser then defines a cause of action as a pair (**S**,**f**), where **S** is a class of subsets S of the fact space and **f** is a collection of functions f_S from each subset S into a two-element set that might be interpreted as proven (unproven) or for plaintiff (for defendant). Each S in **S** is an issue. A case is then a collection of causes of action. For plaintiff to prevail on a case, she must prevail in at least one cause of action; to prevail in a cause of action, the plaintiff must prevail on every issue. The approach models doctrine essentially in terms of a partition on the fact space and sees the development of the law in terms of changes in this partition. The approach has been followed in Kornhauser (1995), Cameron and Kornhauser (2005a, 2006) and Cameron, Segal, and Songer (2000).

The second approach, which adapts the framework of Ferejohn and Shipan (1990) and has been employed by Schwartz (1992), Cohen and Spitzer (1994) and McNollgast (1995), assumes that the Supreme Court has preferences over a two-dimensional space. One dimension remains the policy space in the original political model. The second dimension, variously called "deference" or "precedent", explicitly measures the judge's level of tolerance for deviation from her optimal policy choice. In one sense, this modeling strategy parallels that of the first approach; it also yields a partition of the policy space. More fundamentally, however, this second approach remains inherently "political" and non-legal; it makes no reference to the facts of a case or features of legal discourse that appear in an opinion.

Gely and Spiller (1990) offer a variant of this political model of doctrine that acknowledges some of the structure captured in the legal model. In their model, justices (and other political actors) have preferences over a multi-dimensional policy space. They seek to explain the Court's choice of grounds – constitutional or non-constitutional – for the Court's review of agency action. They argue that a constitutional decision restricts the discretion of the agency (or of other political actors) by lowering the dimensionality of the policy space from which the agency may choose a policy. This ingenious idea captures the effect of doctrine without requiring that one model the legal attention to facts and explicit doctrinal structure.

In political models, "doctrine" generally serves to explain the extent of discretion granted to lower courts (or administrative agencies). Thus, Cohen and Spitzer (1994) argue that the amount of discretion is a function of the ideological alignment of the Supreme Court relative to other political actors. McNollgast (1995) prove that, as the number of cases in a particular area increases, the amount of discretion granted lower courts never decreases and it may increase.

Schwartz (1992) presents a political model of "doctrine" in which each justice acts in a strategic manner. "Doctrine" here refers to a feature of vertical precedent: the probability that a lower court will respect the Supreme Court's policy announcement in the case. Thus, in this model, justices have preferences over a two-dimensional space. Each justice has an ideal policy; the second dimension measures the degree of precedent that the justice attaches to the policy. The justice's preferences are for less strict precedent the more distant the announced policy is from his ideal policy.

Each case presents the Court with a choice between two policy alternatives. The sequence of the game is as follows. First, the justices vote in reverse order of seniority for one of the two policy alternatives. Second, the senior member of the majority designates an opinion writer who voted for that alternative; the senior member of the minority also designates an opinion writer. Third, each opinion writer drafts an opinion that specifies a level of precedent for the proposed policy. In the fourth stage, the justices vote between the two policy/precedent pairs represented by the two opinions. The majority vote determines the outcome.

Schwartz restricts his analysis to the case in which the Court initially divides five to four between the two policy alternatives. He calculates the range of precedent that is invulnerable to invasion by the minority. The senior member of the majority can then pick an opinion writer that will draft an opinion with the optimal level of precedent from the senior member's point of view. Schwartz then illustrates his analysis through a discussion of some reapportionment cases.

Other early models of doctrine treat doctrine in a similarly schematic way. In McNollgast (1995), courts determine around an "ideal point". This discretionary range provides a safe harbor for lower courts. If they locate their decisions within this area, they escape review. Tiller and Spiller (1999) analyze a model in which a court may choose among different grounds on which to rest a decision. Some instruments provide greater protection from reversal and the lower court chooses strategically.

Richards and Kritzer (2002) consider "jurisprudential regimes" as a set of case-relevant facts that structure judicial inquiry and affect the outcome. Using logistic regression, they argue that these jurisprudential regimes have substantial effects on judicial decision.

A number of papers have studied the extent to which a lower court complies with the doctrinal dictates of higher courts. These studies generally focus on a particular doctrinal area. Gruhl (1980) studied libel law; Songer and Haire (1992) studied obscenity cases, and Songer, Segal, and Cameron (1994) studied search and seizure cases. These cases generally find a substantial degree of compliance, though it is difficult to distinguish compliance induced by fear of reversal from compliance induced by respect for the law.

The quantitative study of courts has relied primarily on standard regression tools, either ordinary least squares or logit or probit analyses. These are not obviously well designed to study doctrine as it is difficult to capture doctrinal structure within this framework. One might, for example, consider fact pattern analysis – see Kort (1957) for an early example – as an investigation into doctrinal structure. This procedure will generate a set of "weights" for the decision-relevant facts. It adopts, in some sense, a realist view of adjudication as it ignores the logical structure of doctrine.

Kastellec (2007b), in order to remedy this failing, introduced an estimation technique known as classification and regression trees or CART that sought the logical structure that best approximated the sorting actually done by the facts. Cameron and Kornhauser (2005) also argued in favor of this estimation technique, at least for doctrines that, unlike balancing tests, relied on explicit rules to determine liability. CART, however, has some liabilities. The estimation technique finds the tree that provides the best fit, not the tree that the courts actually use. This distinction is important because the use of CART on Supreme Court cases applies the technique to a set of cases that reflect the shifting boundaries of doctrine rather than the settled core of analysis. This selection bias is apt to distort the estimated tree away from the doctrine that the lower courts must apply.

4.2.2 Political agency models Cameron (1993) presents the political model of review in its starkest form. There is one Supreme Court and *n* lower courts. Each court has spatial preferences over a one-dimensional policy space. There is complete information so that each lower court knows the Supreme Court's ideal point and the Supreme Court knows the location in policy space of the decision of each lower court. Each lower court seeks to maximize its utility, which depends only on the final decision in the case it decides; the Supreme Court wants to maximize its utility, which is a function of the decisions in all cases. The game has two stages: in stage 1, each lower court issues a decision; in stage 2, the Supreme Court selects at most only one case for review. There is a unique equilibrium to this game in which each lower court decides its case by announcing the ideal policy point of the Supreme Court as its decision and the Supreme Court reviews no case because it has already achieved its optimum utility. No other pattern of lower court decisions is an equilibrium because, in any other pattern, the lower court that will be reversed on appeal has an incentive to alter its strategy.

McNollgast (1995) offer a more elaborate political model. They focus on conflicts in the policy views of the Supreme Court, the legislature and the lower courts. To enforce its views the Supreme Court must both induce lower courts to adhere to its "doctrine" and avoid reversal through legislation. McNollgast extend the model of Cohen and Spitzer (1994). They consider a three-stage game in which the Supreme Court first identifies the range of acceptable decisions in policy space. In stage 2, the lower courts decide whether to adhere to Supreme Court "doctrine." In stage 3, the Supreme Court reviews some subset of the lower court decisions; the number of cases reviewed is determined by the Supreme Court's budget. Each case presents a single issue in a K-dimensional policy space. Each judge has separable, spatial preferences over this policy space, an assumption that reduces a decision in any given case to the framework outlined in Cameron. That is, each judge's preferences can be represented by an ideal point in each dimension such that she prefers any decision closer to that ideal point to one further away. The Supreme Court has preferences defined over the outcomes of all cases decided within the system but each lower court has preferences defined over its case load only. Moreover, the Supreme Court does not know either the ideal point of any specific court nor the actual decision rendered by a lower court. The Supreme Court does know the distribution of ideal points of lower courts and it does know whether a lower court has complied with Supreme Court doctrine. It will thus choose to review some random sample of non-complying lower courts; upon review it will learn their actual decisions. Several results flow from this model. First, in general, some but not all lower courts will comply with Supreme Court doctrine; compliance, however, results from the threat of enforcement. Second, the game has a unique Bayesian equilibrium. Third, as the costs of enforcement rise, the Supreme Court may expand the range of acceptable lower court decisions.

4.2.3 Team models of error correction Shavell (1995) is the earliest formal model of error correction. Shavell assumes that the state must decide first, whether to establish both trial and appellate courts or trial courts only; and second, how many resources to devote to each level of court that it establishes. The probability of correct decision by a court increases with increased allocation of resources to that court. The state seeks to minimize social costs which consist of the costs of the judicial system and the costs created by wrongly decided cases. A trial court is characterized by the probability (as a function of state resources) that it will render the wrong decision. Litigants know for certain whether a court has correctly decided their case. An appellate court is characterized by two probabilities (as functions of state resources devoted to appeal): the probability $q(y)$ that an incorrect trial decision will be reversed on appeal and the probability $r(y)$ that a correct trial decision will be reversed on appeal. Litigants know with certainty whether the court has rendered a correct decision. Litigants face a cost to appeal. It is straightforward to see that, if $q(y) > r(y)$ and if the court can impose fees or give subsidies for appeal, then the state can insure that only cases wrongly decided at trial will be appealed.

Shavell then characterizes the state's optimal strategy by showing when appellate courts should be created and how resources should be divided between trial and appellate levels. He also shows that litigant selection of cases is superior to the random review of trial court decision. When a court undertakes random review of lower court cases, it unnecessarily uses resources to reconsider some correctly decided cases; under litigant selection (with the appropriate subsidies and fees), by contrast, only cases that should be reconsidered are in fact reviewed.

Cameron and Kornhauser (2006) offer a more strategic model of error correction that formalizes a portion of the argument in Kornhauser (1995). Their paper divides into two distinct parts. First, they identify conditions under which it would be desirable to add an additional level of appeal to a court structure. They define the selectivity of a process as the ratio of the proportion of wrongly decided cases that would be appealed to a new tier to the proportion of correctly decided cases that would be appealed to a new tier. They define the error-correction ratio as the ratio of the probability that the new appellate court would reverse a wrongly decided case on appeal to the probability that the new appellate court would uphold a rightly decided case on appeal. They prove that an additional tier of review is desirable if the appeals process is sufficiently selective or sufficiently error correcting.

The second part of Cameron and Kornhauser's argument considers a particular technology of review. The correct decision of a case depends on the defendant's type, which, initially, is known to the defendant but not to the plaintiff. At trial, the plaintiff, but not the court, becomes fully informed about the defendant's type. A court's ability to discriminate among defendant types is a function of the effort it invests in the case. Litigants incur a cost each time they appeal. Judges seek first to maximize the number of correct decisions; in addition, a judge prefers not to be reversed. Cameron and Kornhauser show that, when litigants select cases for appeal, the hierarchy will have three tiers. They also study the process when the appellate courts select cases for review. In Cameron and Kornhauser (2005a), they extend the toy model to an environment in which the plaintiff has incomplete information about the liability of the defendant. Trial now produces both a public signal, as before, and a private signal to the plaintiff. They prove a similar result that one never needs more than three tiers to minimize error. In this environment, however, equilibria require that judges on at least one lower tier adhere to a rule that, in the presence of an uninformative public signal, places liability on the defendant in order to exploit her superior information.

4.3 Discretionary Review

The United States Supreme Court has a largely discretionary jurisdiction. This discretion cannot be explained in a team model of error correction when litigants select which cases to appeal, for, as Cameron and Kornhauser (2006) show, the optimal hierarchy will have only three tiers and the highest tier will hear no cases. Discretionary review, however, might be explained in a team model in which the Supreme Court has lawmaking powers.

Cameron, Segal, and Songer ("CSS") (2000) use a political model to study the Supreme Court's certiorari procedure. They assume that the Supreme Court serves only to correct error. As is typical in political models, both higher and lower courts have preferences over a one-dimensional policy space. As in Cameron and Kornhauser (2006), each case is characterized by a single parameter and each court is characterized by an ideal point so that defendant should prevail if the value of the case parameter is less than the court's ideal point. For ease of exposition, CSS assume that the ideal point of the Supreme Court lies to the right of the lower court's ideal point. Consequently, the two courts disagree about the appropriate resolution of the case if its parameter lies in the interval between the two ideal points. The Supreme Court has discretionary authority to review, but it decides to review the lower court decision on the basis of an index of the parameter rather than the true value which is both known to the lower court and would be revealed to the Supreme Court in the course of a review on the merits. Each court wants to maximize the number of correct decisions (from its point of view); lower courts get disutility from reversal and the Supreme Court incurs cost in the event it decides to review a case on the merits. CSS characterize the equilibrium strategies of both lower court and Supreme Court. They then present an exploratory analysis of Supreme Court certiorari practice in search and seizure cases between 1972 and 1986.

Discretionary review in the US Supreme Court employs a submajority rule of four of the nine justices to trigger review. This submajority review raises interesting legal and strategic questions concerning the behavior of the justices themselves. Revesz and Karlan (1988) presented a largely legal analysis of this rule (and a "Rule of Three" governing the granting of stays), but their analysis raises a number of issues for economic analysis. They argue that the rule of four creates a legal process with less stable precedent than a process in which discretionary review required a majority.

Lax (2003) extends the model in Cameron, Segal and Songer to provide significant insight into the rule of four. The model replaces uncertainty with spatial preferences over the "facts", as facts diverge from the cutpoint in CSS, the value of the correct disposition increases for the Laxian judge. With this preference structure, one can deduce the zone of compliance that is assumed in such doctrinal articles as McNollgast (1995), discussed above.

Lax shows how the zone of compliance alters with the rule of four. Indeed, he proves that lower court compliance with the doctrine favored by the median justice increases when the median justice will not vote for certiorari. In addition, all nine justices prefer a rule of four to a majoritarian rule. Finally, Lax shows that the justices on each side of the median justice act strategically; they signal more extreme preferences to the lower courts in order to induce more compliance.

5. Separation of Powers Models

5.1 Models of Adjudication Embedded in a Constitutional System

Many, if not most, cases on the appellate docket do not present common law issues; rather they raise issues of statutory or constitutional interpretation. The decisions of the courts thus rely on, and affect, the decisions of other political actors, including administrative agencies, legislatures and the executive. Most applications of the political model to adjudication have concerned these institutional relations.

Marks (1989), in a Ph.D. dissertation, first applied positive political theory to the study of the interaction of court and congress. The paper, though it has spawned a large literature, is not easily accessible. The two earliest, published applications to adjudication appear to be Ferejohn and Shipan (1990) and Gely and Spiller (1990). Specifically, Ferejohn and Shipan assumed that all political actors had preferences over a one-dimensional policy space, while Gely and Spiller assumed that institutional actors had preferences over a multi-dimensional policy space. I set out the Ferejohn and Shipan model here because of its simplicity and because most subsequent models exploit their formulation. Gely and Spiller (1990) is discussed in Section 4.2.1 in the context of its interesting model of doctrine.

Ferejohn and Shipan analyze the effects of judicial review on the activities of administrative agencies. In addition to the assumption of a one-dimensional policy space, their results depend critically on the sequence in which the institutions act. In their model, the agency acts first. It is then subject to judicial review. The court, in turn, is subject to potential legislative overrides. (They study both the case of overrides that require a presidential veto and those that do not.) They show that judicial review may shift the equilibrium policy towards the policy preferred by the legislature.

Eskridge and Ferejohn (1992a, 1992b) use the model in Ferejohn and Shipan to analyze the balance of powers in the US Constitution in general and the effect of *INS v Chadha*, 462 US 919 (1983) on that balance of power. *Chadha* ruled that legislative vetoes of administrative action were unconstitutional. According to Eskridge and Ferejohn, this ruling shifted power to the agencies; put differently, the decision made Congressional delegations of power to administrative agencies less desirable.

The literature employing variants of this political model has proliferated. For instance, Gely and Spiller (1992) present a three-stage game in which, in the first stage, an administrative agency announces an interpretation of a statute; in the second stage, the court reviews the agency interpretation; and in the third stage, the legislature decides whether to overrule the Supreme Court and announce its own policy outcome. Note that, in each stage, the interpretation is an announcement of a policy. Each actor has spatial preferences over a one-dimensional policy space. The model predicts that the Court will always pick that policy that is best for it and just avoids legislative overruling. Gely and Spiller investigate several variants of this structure in which the legislature is modeled somewhat differently. They then test their model on data from the United States National Labor Relations Board and subsequent review.

Cohen and Spitzer (1994) apply this political model to the analysis of the effects of another Supreme Court decision, *Chevron USA Inc. v Natural Resources Defense Council Inc*, 467 US 837 (1984), which required courts to grant more deference to an administrative agency's own interpretation of statutes it implemented. They assume political actors have preferences over policy-deference pairs. They then show that the Supreme Court's rulings on deference respond to the relative pattern of policy preferences among the other institutional actors: President, Congress, and the appellate court.

Toma (1991, 1996) have argued that the Congressional budgetary process serves as a means to control the decisions of the Supreme Court by signaling approval or disapproval of the Court's behavior. Again, both justices and Congress have spatial preferences over policy space. She examines two time series of decisions of the Supreme Court of the United

States: one consists of civil liberties cases decided from 1946 through 1988 and the other of economic liberties cases decided over the same time period. She determines the "average degree of liberality" of each of these two-yearly portfolios of decisions and similarly takes the average ADA rating of the members of the judiciary subcommittee of the Senate and House appropriations committees. For each group of cases, she then regresses the size of the yearly Supreme Court budget on the divergence between the judicial and Congressional liberality ratings; she finds a statistically significant pattern, with the budget rising when Supreme Court opinions conform more closely to the views of Congress. She then regresses the liberality of the judicial portfolio against the Supreme Court budget, the parameter of which is also statistically significant

Spiller and Tiller (1997), Tiller (1998) and Tiller and Spiller (1999) study the extent of review adopted by the court. The court has preferences over policies and costs of review. Less costly review is less intensive but leaves the agency with greater discretion so that the court does not achieve as good a policy outcome as it would under more intensive review. In these models, the agency may alter its choice of regulatory instrument in order to avoid more intensive review

Shipan (2000) introduced a prior stage to the separation of powers game. Judicial power over agency action is only in part constitutional. It is, to a large extent, controlled by the legislature, which may determine the extent of the court's jurisdiction or the nature of review in which it engages. Shipan considers a six-stage game. In stage 1, a legislative committee decides whether to recommend a bill that authorizes agency action subject to judicial review or not subject to review. If judicial review is recommended, the legislature decides whether to accept judicial review or not. The agency then chooses a policy. When subject to review, the court reviews the agency choice of policy. The legislative committee may decide whether to introduce legislation to reverse the judicial decision. The legislature then acts under an open rule on the committee recommendation, if any. Shipan concludes that legislative discretion to include judicial review is weakly superior to the absence of discretion.

Huber and Gordon (2007) study an interesting variant of the separation of powers game. They consider sentencing decisions of state judges and study how the legislature may act to constrain or control judicial exercise of that power. In an interesting twist, they also consider the electoral incentives faced by many judges. In their model, they find that legislators who value proportionality in sentencing increase the level of judical descretion as punishment increases. They note also that voter ignorance about the extent of statutory discretion in sentencing granted to judges and of judicial preferences for re-election limit electoral control of judges.

Stephenson (2004) introduces an electorate into the separation of powers game. There are three players: the legislature, the courts and the voters. The legislature enacts a policy and the courts may then declare the policy illegal or legal. The legislature then may acquiesce in this decision or not. The voters may then punish the legislature or not. The voter has incomplete information about the preferences of the legislature and the judiciary. Stephenson shows that legislative acquiescence in judicial review will arise when the judicial ruling of illegality is more informative about the quality of the policy than the fact that the legislature enacted it.

5.2 Empirical Studies of Separations of Powers
This separation of powers model provoked controversy among the community of political scientists who study "judicial politics". The attitudinal model that had dominated the literature assumed that high court judges simply voted their preferences unconstrained by the other branches. Segal (1997, 1998), a leading attitudinalist, tested the degree to which the US Supreme Court is in fact constrained by Congress. He examines statutory decisions between 1947 and 1992 and concludes that the Supreme Court was rarely constrained.

Bergara et al. (2003) re-estimated Segal's dataset using a maximum likelihood method from Gely and Spiller (1992). Contrary to Segal's finding, they concluded that the US Supreme Court was constrained in roughly one-third of its decisions in the 46 years under study.

Smith (2007) studies empirically the model in Cohen and Spitzer (1994). Smith analyzed cases decided by the United States Supreme Court between 1969 and 1999. He considers two hypotheses: (1) following the strategic analysis of Cohen and Spitzer, the first hypothesis states that justices will be more likely to vote in favor of deference to administrative agencies when they are ideologically closer to the sitting president; and (2) following the attitudinal model, the second hypothesis states that justices will be more likely to vote in favor of deference when the judges are ideologically closer to the President at the time the agency acted. Smith finds support for the attitudinal hypothesis, but not for the strategic hypothesis.

A number of other studies, perhaps spurred by Eskridge (1991), have sought to understand Congressional responses to Supreme Court review.

6. Concluding Remarks
The study of judicial organization in general and the nature and function of appeal in particular is in its infancy. Though analysts have begun to investigate the reasons for hierarchy, the nature of the interaction among courts and other political branches, and the internal workings of the courts themselves, most questions remain open or even unaddressed.

Bibliography

Anderson, Robert and Tahk, Alexander (2007), "Institutions and Equilibrium in the United States Supreme Court," *American Political Science Review*, 101, 811–25.

Bar Niv, Moshe and Safra, Zvi (2006), "On the Desirability of Appellate Courts," *Review of Law and Economics*, 2, 381–96.

Benesh, Sara C. and Reddick, Maria (2002), "Overruled: An Event History Analysis of Lower Court Reaction to Supreme Court Alteration of Precedent," *Journal of Politics*, 64, 534–50.

Benoit, Jean-Pierre and Kornhauser, Lewis A. (1995), "Assembly-Based Preferences, Candidate-Based Procedures, and the Voting Rights Act," *Southern California Law Review*, 68, 1503–44.

Bergara, Mario, Richman, Barak, and Spiller, Pablo T. (2003), "Modeling Supreme Court Strategic Decision Making: The Congressional Constraint," *Legislative Studies Quarterly*, 28, 247–80.

Blume, Larry and Rubinfeld, Daniel (1982), "The Dynamics of the Legal Process," *Journal of Legal Studies*, 11, 405–19.

Bonneau, Chris W., Hammond, T., Maltzman, F. and Wahlbeck, P.J. (2007), "Agenda Control, the Median Justice, and the Majority Opinion on the U.S. Supreme Court," *American Political Science Review*, 51, 890–905.

Bonnefon, Jean-François (2007), "How do Individuals Solve the Doctrinal Paradox in Collective Decisions? An Empirical Investigation," *Psychological Science*, 18, 753–5.

Brenner, Saul and Steir, Marc (1996), "Retesting Segal and Spaeth's Stare Decisis Model," *American Journal of Political Science*, 40, 1036–48.

Brent, James (2003), "A Principal-Agent Analysis of US Courts of Appeals Responses to Boerne," *American Politics Research*, 31, 557–70.

Bueno de Mesquita, Ethan and Stephenson, Matthew (2002), "Informative Precedent and Intrajudicial Communication," *American Political Science Review*, 96, 755–66.

Cameron, Charles M. (1993), "New Avenues for Modeling Judicial Politics," University of Rochester Wallis Institute of Political Economy Working Paper.

Cameron, Charles M. and Clark, Thomas S. (2006), "The Macropolitics of the Supreme Court," Working Paper.

Cameron, Charles and Kornhauser, Lewis A. (2005a), "Decision Rules in a Judicial Hierarchy," *Journal of Institutional and Theoretical Economics*, 161(2), 264–92.

Cameron, Charles and Kornhauser, Lewis A. (2005b), "Modeling Law: Theoretical Implications of Empirical Models," mimeo.

Cameron, Charles and Kornhauser, Lewis A. (2006), "Appeals Mechanisms, Litigant Selection, and the Structure of Judicial Hierarchies," in Jon Bond, Roy Flemming, and James Rogers (eds.), *Institutional Games and the Supreme Court*, Charlottesville, VA: University of Virginia Press, 173–204.

Cameron, Charles M. and Kornhauser, Lewis A. (2010), "Modeling Collegial Courts 3: Adjudication Equilibria," mimeo.

Cameron, Charles M., Segal, Jeffrey A. and Songer, Donald R. (2000), "Strategic Auditing in a Political Hierarchy: An Informational Model of the Supreme Court's Certiorari Decisions," *American Political Science Review*, 94, 101–16.

Chapman, Bruce (1998), "More Easily Done than Said: Rules, Reason and Rational Social Choice," *Oxford Journal of Legal Studies*, 18, 293–329.

Chapman, Bruce (2003), "Rational Choice and Categorical Reason," *Pennsylvania Law Review*, 151, 1169–210.

Cohen, Linda and Spitzer, Matthew (1994), "Solving the *Chevron* Puzzle," *Law and Contemporary Problems*, 57, 65–110.

Cross, Frank (2005), "Appellate Court Adherence to Precedent," *Journal of Empirical Legal Studies*, 2, 369–405.

Cross, Frank B. (2007), *Decision Making in the U.S. Courts of Appeals,* Palo Alto, CA: Stanford University Press.

Cross, Frank B. and Tiller, Emerson H. (1998), "Judicial Partisanship and Obedience in

Legal Doctrine Whistleblowing on the Federal Courts of Appeals," *Yale Law Journal*, 107, 2155–76.
Daughety, Andrew and Reinganum, Jennifer (1999), "Stampede to Judgment: Persuasive Influence and Herding Behavior by Courts," *American Law and Economic Review*, 1, 158–89.
Daughety, Andrew and Reinganum, Jennifer (2000), "Appealing Judgments," *RAND Journal of Economics*, 31, 502–25.
Daughety, Andrew and Reinganum, Jennifer (2006), "Speaking Up: A Model of Judicial Dissent and Discretionary Review," *Supreme Court Economic Review*, 1–41.
Dorf, Michael C. (1995), "Prediction and the Rule of Law," *U.C.L.A. Law Review*, 42, 651–715.
Easterbrook, Frank (1983), "Ways of Criticizing the Court," *Harvard Law Review*, 95, 802–32.
Eisenberg, Theodore and Johnson, Sheri Lynn (1991), "The Effects of Intent: Do We Know How Legal Standards Work?," *Cornell Law Review*, 76, 1151–97.
Epstein, Lee, Martin, Andrew, Segal, Jeffrey A., and Westerland, Chad (2007), "The Judicial Common Space," *Journal of Law, Economics and Organization*, 23, 303–25.
Epstein, Richard A. (1987), 'Judicial Review: Reckoning on Two Kinds of Error," in Dorn, James A. and Manne, Henry G. (eds.), *Economic Liberties and the Judiciary*, Fairfax, VA: George Mason University Press, 39–46.
Eskridge, William N. (1991), "Overriding Supreme Court Statutory Interpretation Decisions," *Yale Law Journal*, 101, 331–455.
Eskridge, William N. and Ferejohn, John (1992a), "The Article I, Section 7 Game," *Georgetown Law Journal*, 80, 523–64.
Eskridge, William N. and Ferejohn, John (1992b), "Making the Deal Stick: Enforcing the Original Constitutional Structure of Lawmaking in the Modern Regulatory State," *Journal of Law, Economics and Organization*, 8, 165–89.
Farhan, Sean and Wawro, Gregory (2004), "Institutional Dynamics on the US Court of Appeals: Minority Representation under Panel Decision Making," *Journal of Law, Economics and Organization*, 20, 299–330.
Ferejohn, John and Shipan, Charles (1990), "Congressional Influence on Bureaucracy," *Journal of Law, Economics and Organization*, 6, 1–20 (Special Issue).
Fernandez, Patricio A. and Ponzetto, Giacomo A.M. (2008), "Stare Decisis: Rhetoric and Substance," mimeo, March.
Fischman, Joshua B. (2006), "Uniformity of Interpretation in a Hierarchical Court," Working Paper, January 14.
Fischman, Joshua B. (2008), "Decision-Making under a Norm of Consensus: A Structural Analysis of Three-Judge Panels,." 1st Annual Conference on Empirical Legal Studies Paper.
Fon, Vincy and Parisi, Francesco (2006), "Judicial Precedent in Civil Law Systems: A Dynamic Analysis," *International Review of Law and Economics*, 26, 519–35.
Gely, Rafael and Spiller, Pablo T. (1990), "A Rational Choice Theory of Supreme Court Statutory Decisions with Applications to the *State Farm* and *Grove City* Cases," *Journal of Law, Economics and Organization*, 6, 263–300.
Gely, Rafael and Spiller, Pablo T. (1992), "The Political Economy of Supreme Court Constitutional Decisions: The Case of Roosevelt's Court Packing Plan," *International Review of Law and Economics*, 12(1), 45–67.
Gennaioli, Nicola and Shleifer, Andrei (2007a), "The Evolution of the Common Law," *Journal of Political Economy*, 115, 43–68.
Gennaioli, Nicola and Shleifer, Andrei (2007b), "Overruling and the Instability of Law," *Journal of Comparative Economics*, 35, 309–28.
George, Tracey and Solimine, Michael E. (2001), "SC Monitoring of the US Courts of Appeals en banc," *Supreme Court Economic Review*, 9, 171–204.
George, Tracey E. and Yoon, Albert H. (2003), "The Federal Court System: A Principal-Agent Perspective," *St. Louis University Law Journal*, 47, 819.

George, Tracey E. and Yoon, Albert H. (2007), "Chief Judges: The Limits of Attitudinal Theory and Possible Paradox of Managerial Judging," Vanderbilt Law and Economics Discussion Paper No. 07–24.

Good, I.J. and Tullock, Gordon (1984), "Judicial Errors and a Proposal for Reform," *Journal of Legal Studies*, 13, 289–98.

Groseclose, Tim and Schiavoni, Sara (2001), "Rethinking Justices' and Committees' Strategies in Segal's Separation of Powers Game," *Public Choice*, 106, 131–5.

Gruhl, John (1980), "The Supreme Court's Impact on the Law of Libel: Compliance by Lower Federal Courts," *Western Political Quarterly*, 33, 502–19.

Hammond, Thomas H., Bonneau, Chris and Sheehan, Reginald (2005), *Strategic Behavior and Policy Choice on the US Supreme Court*, Stanford, CA: Stanford University Press.

Hammond, Thomas H., Bonneau, Chris and Sheehan, Reginald (2006), "A Court of Appeals in a Rational-Choice Model of Supreme Court Decision-Making," in James R. Rogers, Roy B. Flemming, and Jon R. Bond (eds), *Institutional Games and the U.S. Supreme Court*, Charlottesville, VA: University of Virginia Press.

Heiner, Ronald (1986), "Imperfect Decisions and the Law: On the Evolution of Legal Precedent and Rules," *Journal of Legal Studies*, 15, 227.

Hettinger, V.A., Lindquist, S.A., and Martinek, W.L. (2003), "Separate Opinion Writing on the United States Courts of Appeal," *American Politics Research*, 31, 215–50.

Hettinger, Virginia A., Lindquist, Stefanie A., and Martinek, Wendy L. (2006), *Judging on a Collegial Court: Influence on Federal Appellate Decision Making*, Charlottesville, VA: University of Virginia Press.

Hettinger, Virginia A. and Zorn, Christopher (2005), "Explaining the Incidence and Timing of Congressional Responses to the U.S. Supreme Court," *Legislative Studies Quarterly*, 30, 5–28.

Huber, Gregory A. and Gordon, Sanford C. (2007), "Directing Retribution: On the Political Control of Lower Court Judges," *Journal of Law, Economics and Organization*, 23, 386–420.

Huxtable, Philip A. (1994),"Incorporating the Rules Committee: An Extension of the Ferejohn/Shipan Model," *Journal of Law, Economics and Organization*, 10, 160–67.

Ignagni, Joseph, Meernik, James, and King, Kimi Lynn (1998), "Statutory Construction and Congressional Response," *American Politics Quarterly*, 26, 459–84.

Iossa, Elisabetta and Palumbo, Giuliana (2007), "Information Provision and Monitoring of the Decision-Maker in the Presence of an Appeal Process," *Journal of Institutional and Theoretical Economics*, 163, 657–82.

Jacobi, Tonja and Tiller, Emerson H. (2007), "Legal Doctrine and Political Control," *Journal of Law, Economics and Organization*, 23, 326–45.

Kastellec, Jonathan P. (2007a), "Panel Composition and Judicial Compliance on the US Courts of Appeals," *Journal of Law, Economics and Organization*, 23, 421–41.

Kastellec, Jonathan P. (2007b), "The Structure of Legal Rules and the Analysis of Judicial Decisions," SSRN Working Paper, January.

Kastellec, Jonathan P. and LAX, Jeffrey R. (2008), "Case Selection and the Study of Politics," SSRN Working Paper, November, forthcoming *Journal of Empirical Legal Studies*, 5, 407–46.

Klein, David E. and Hume, Robert J. (2003), "Fear of Reversal as an Explanation of Lower Court Compliance," *Law and Society Review*, 37, 579–606.

Koppen, P.J. van (1990), "Cassatieadvocaten en de selectiekamer" [Cassation Lawyers and the Chamber of Selection], *Nederlands Juristen Blad*, 14–26.

Kornhauser, Lewis (1989), "An Economic Perspective on Stare Decisis," *Chicago-Kent Law Review*, 65, 63–92.

Kornhauser, Lewis A. (1992a), "Modeling Collegial Courts I: Path Dependence," *International Review of Law and Economics*, 12(2), 169–85.

Kornhauser, Lewis A. (1992b), "Modeling Collegial Courts. II. Legal Doctrine," *Journal of Law, Economics and Organization*, 8(3), 441–70.

Kornhauser, Lewis (1995), "Adjudication by a Resource-Constrained Team: Hierarchy and Precedent in a Judicial System," *Southern California Law Review*, 68, 1605–30.
Kornhauser, Lewis (1998), "Stare Decisis," in Peter Newman (ed.), *New Palgrave Dictionary of Economics and the Law*, volume 3, Basingstoke: Palgrave Macmillan, 509–14.
Kornhauser, Lewis A. and Sager, Lawrence G. (1986), "Unpacking the Court," *Yale Law Journal*, 96, 82–117.
Kornhauser, Lewis and Sager, Lawrence (1993), "The One and the Many: Adjudication in Collegial Courts," *California Law Review*, 81, 1–59.
Kort, Fred (1957), "Predicting Supreme Court Decisions Mathematically: A Quantitative Analysis of the Right to Counsel Cases," *American Political Science Review*, 51, 1–12.
Landa, Dimitri and Lax, Jeffrey R. (2007), "Legal Doctrine on Collegial Courts," Working Paper, March.
Landes, William M. and Posner, Richard A. (2001), "Harmless Error," *Journal of Legal Studies*, 30, 161–92.
Langer, Laura (2003), "Strategic Considerations and Judicial Review: The Case of Workers' Compensation Laws in the American States," *Public Choice*, 116, 55–78.
Lax, Jeffrey (2003), "Certiorari and Compliance in the Judicial Hierarchy: Discretion, Reputation and the Rule of Four," *Journal of Theoretical Politics*, 15(1), 61–86.
Lax, Jeffrey R. (2007), "Constructing Legal Rules on Appellate Courts," *American Political Science Review*, 101, 591–605.
Lax, Jeffrey R. and Cameron, Charles M. (2007), "Bargaining and Opinion Assignment on the US Supreme Court," *Journal of Law, Economics and Organization*, 23, 276–302.
Lax, Jeffrey R. and McCubbins, Mathew D. (2006), "Courts, Congress, and Public Policy, Part II: The Impact of the Reapportionment Revolution on Urban and Rural Interests," *Journal of Contemporary Legal Issues*, 15(1), 199–218.
Lax, Jeffrey R. and Rader, Kelly (2007), "Tactical Opinion Assignment on the Supreme Court," Columbia Working Paper.
Leonard, David P. (1984), "The Correctness Function of Appellate Decision-Making: Judicial Obligation in an Era of Fragmentation," *Loyola of Los Angeles Law Review*, 17, 299–304.
Lim, Youngsik (2000), "An Empirical Analysis of Supreme Court Justices' Decision Making," *Journal of Legal Studies*, 29, 721–52.
Luse, Jennifer, McGovern, Geoffrey, Martinek, Wendy L. and Benesh, Sara C. (2007), "Such Inferior Courts. . .: Compliance by Circuits with Jurisprudential Regimes," 2nd Annual Conference on Empirical Legal Studies Paper.
Marks, Brian Andrew (1989), "A Model of Judicial Influence on Congressional Policymaking: Grove City v. Bell," unpublished Ph.D. thesis.
Marschak, Jacob and Radner, Roy (1972), *Economic Theory of Teams*, New Haven: Yale University Press, available at http://cowles.econ.yale.edu/p/cm/m22/index.htm.
Martin, Andrew D. (2007), "Assessing Preference Change on the US Supreme Court," *Journal of Law, Economics and Organization*, 23, 365–85.
McCubbins, Mathew D. and Lax, Jeffrey R. (2006), "Courts, Congress, and Public Policy, Part I: The FDA, the Courts, and the Regulation of Tobacco," *Journal of Contemporary Legal Issues*, 15(1), 163–98.
McNollgast (1995), "Politics and the Courts: A Positive Theory of Judicial Doctrine and the Rule of Law," *Southern California Law Review*, 68, 1631–83.
Mialon, H.M., Rubin, P.H. and Schrag, J.L. (2004), "Judicial Hierarchies and the Rule-Individual Tradeoff," Law and Economics Research Paper 05–5, Emory.
Miceli, Thomas J. and Cosgel, Mitan (1994), "Reputation and Judicial Organization," *Journal of Economic Behavior and Organization*, 23, 31–51.
O'Hara, Erin (1993), "Social Constraint or Implicit Collusion? Toward a Game Theoretic Analysis of Stare Decisis," *Seton Hall Law Review*, 24, 736–78.
Posner, Richard A. (1982), "Toward an Economic Theory of Federal Jurisdiction," *Harvard Journal of Law & Public Policy*, 6, 41–50.

Posner, Richard A. (1985), *The Federal Courts: Crisis and Reform*, Cambridge, MA: Harvard University Press.
Post, David and Salop, Steven (1992), "Rowing against the Tidewater: A Theory of Voting by Multi Judge Panels," *Georgetown Law Journal*, 80, 743–1086.
Post. David and Salop, Steven (1996), "Issues and Outcomes, Guidance, and Indeterminacy: A Reply to Professor John Rogers and Others," *Vanderbilt Law Review*, 49, 1049–85.
Rasmusen, Eric (1994), "Judicial Legitimacy as a Repeated Game," *Journal of Law, Economics and Organization*, 10, 63–83.
Revesz, Richard L. (1997), "Environmental Regulation, Ideology, and the D.C. Circuit," *Virginia Law* Review, 83, 1717–22.
Revesz, Richard L. and Karlan, Pamela (1988), "Non Majority Rules and the Supreme Court," *University Pennsylvania Law Review*, 136, 1067–133.
Richards, Mark J. and Kritzer, Herbert M. (2002), "Jurisprudential Regimes in Supreme Court Decision Making," *American Political Science Review*, 96, 305–20.
Rogers, John M. (1991), "'I Vote this Way Because I'm Wrong,': The Supreme Court Justice as Epimenides," *Kentucky Law Journal*, 79, 439–75.
Rogers, John M. (1995), "Lower Court Application of the 'Overruling Law' of Higher Courts," *Legal Theory*, 1, 179–204.
Rogers, John (1996), "'Issue Voting' by Multi Member Appellate Courts: A Response to Some Radical Proposals," *Vanderbilt Law Review*, 49, 997–1039.
Rogers, James R. (2001), "Information and Judicial Review: A Signaling Game of Legislative-Judicial Interaction," *American Political Science Review*, 45, 84–99.
Schanzenbach, Max M. and Tiller, Emerson H. (2007), "Strategic Judging under the United States Sentencing Guidelines: Positive Political Theory and Evidence," *Journal of Law, Economics and Organization*, 23, 24–56.
Schwartz, Edward P. (1992), "Policy, Precedent, and Power: A Positive Theory of Supreme Court Decision Making," *Journal of Law, Economics and Organization*, 8(2), 219–52.
Scott, Kevin M. (2006), "Understanding Judicial Hierarchy: Reversals and the Behavior of Intermediate Appellate Judges," *Law and Society Review*, 40, 163–91.
Segal, Jeffrey A. (1997), "Separation-of-Powers Games in the Postive Theory of Congress and the Courts," *American Political Science Review*, 91, 1225–49.
Segal, Jeffrey A. (1998), "A Correction to Separation-of-Powers Games in the Postive Theory of Congress and the Courts," *American Political Science Review*, 91, 1225–49.
Segal, Jeffrey A. and Spaeth, Harold J. (1996), "The Influence of Stare Decisis on the Votes of U.S. Supreme Court Justices," *American Journal of Political Science*, 40, 971–1003.
Shavell, Steven (1995),"The Appeals Process as a Means of Error Correction," *Journal of Legal Studies,* 24(2), 379–426.
Shavell, Steven (2006), "The Appeals Process and Adjudicator Incentives," *Journal of Legal Studies,* 35(1), 1–29.
Shipan, Charles R. (2000), "The Legislative Design of Judicial Review: A Formal Analysis," *Journal of Theoretical Politics*, 12, 269–304.
Smith, J.L. (2007), "Presidents, Justices, and Deference to Administrative Action," *Journal of Law, Economics and Organization*, 23, 346–64.
Songer, Donald R. and Haire, Susan (1992), "Integrating Alternative Approaches to the Study of Judicial Voting: Obscenity Cases in the U.S. Courts of Appeals," *American Journal of Political Science*, 36, 963–82.
Songer, Donald R., Segal, Jeffrey A., and Cameron, Charles M. (1994), "The Hierarchy of Justice: Testing a Principal Agent Model of Supreme Court–Circuit Court Interactions," *American Journal of Political Science*, 38, 673–86.
Songer, Donald, R. and Lindquist, Stefanie A. (1996), "Not the Whole Story: The Impact of Justices' Values on Supreme Court Decision Making," *American Journal of Political Science*, 40, 1049–63.
Spaeth, Harold and Segal, Jeffrey (1999), *Majority Rule or Minority Will: Adherence to Precedent on the U.S. Supreme Court*, Cambridge: Cambridge University Press.

Spiller, Pablo and Spitzer, Matthew (1992), "Judicial Choice of Legal Doctrines," *Journal of Law, Economics and Organization*, 8, 8–46.
Spiller, Pablo and Spitzer, Matthew (1995), "Where is the Sine in Sincere? Sophisticated Manipulation of Sincere Judicial Voters (With Applications to Other Voting Environments)", *Journal of Law, Economics and Organization*, 11, 32–63.
Spiller, Pablo T. and Tiller, Emerson H. (1997), "Decision Costs and the Strategic Design of Administrative Process and Judicial Review," *Journal of Legal Studies*, 26, 347–70
Spitzer, Matthew L. and Talley, Eric (2000), "Judicial Auditing," *Journal of Legal Studies*, 29, 649–83.
Stearns, Maxwell (1995), "Standing Back from the Forest: Justiciability and Social Choice," *California Law Review*, 83, 1309–413.
Stearns, Maxwell (1996), "How Outcome Voting Promotes Principled Issue Identification: A Reply to Professor John Rogers and Others," *Vanderbilt Law Review*, 49, 1045–67.
Stephenson, Matthew C. (2004), "Court of Public Opinion: Government Accountability and Judicial Independence," *Journal of Law, Economics and Organization*, 20, 379–99.
Stith, Kate (1990), "The Risk of Legal Error in Criminal Cases: Some Consequences of the Asymmetry in the Right to Appeal," *University of Chicago Law Review*, 57, 1–61.
Stone, Rebecca (2008), "Following Precedent to Signal Ideological Neutrality," mimeo.
Sunstein, Cass R., Schkade, David, and Ellman, Lisa M. (2004), "Ideological Voting on the Federal Courts of Appeal: A Preliminary Investigation," *Virginia Law Review*, 90, 301–54.
Sunstein, Cass R., Schkade, David, Ellman, Lisa M., and Sawicki, Andres (2006), *Are Judges Political? An Empirical Analysis of the Federal Judiciary*, Washington, DC: Brookings Institution.
Tiller, Emerson H. (1998), "Controlling Policy by Controlling Process: Judicial Influence on Regulatory Decisionmaking," *Journal of Law, Economics and Organization*, 14, 114–35.
Tiller, Emerson H. and Cross. Frank B. (2006), "What is Legal Doctrine?," *Northwestern University Law Review*, 100, 517–33.
Tiller, Emerson H. and Spiller, Pablo T. (1999), "Strategic Instruments: Legal Structure and Political Games in Administrative Law," *Journal of Law, Economics and Organization*, 15, 349–77.
Toma, Eugenia (1991), "Congressional Influence and the Supreme Court: The Budget as a signaling device," *Journal of Legal Studies*, 20, 131–46.
Toma, Eugenia (1996), "A Contractual Model of the Voting Behavior of the Supreme Court: The Role of the Chief Justice," *International Review of Law and Economics*, 16, 433–47.
Vanberg, George (2001), "Legislative-Judicial Relations: A Game-Theoretic approach to Constitutional Review," *American Journal of Political Science*, 45, 346–61.
Whitman, Douglas Glen (2000), "Evolution of the Common Law and the Emergence of Compromise," *Journal of Legal Studies*, 29, 753–81.

3 Attorney-client confidentiality
Gillian K. Hadfield and Shmuel Leshem

1. Introduction

The protection of information generated and shared in the attorney-client relationship is a fundamental attribute of Anglo-American legal systems. In such systems, otherwise characterized by extensive efforts such as liberal discovery rules and broad subpoena powers to increase the information available to courts, regulators and opposing litigants, attorneys generally cannot be compelled to disclose either what they have told to or been told by their client (attorney-client privilege) or what facts or ideas they have generated in preparation for litigation (work-product doctrine).[1] Nor, as a result of professional ethics regulation, can they voluntarily choose or threaten to disclose such information against their clients' wishes. (We will refer to these three distinct forms of protection collectively as attorney-client confidentiality.) Protection of the confidentiality of attorney-client communications and legal efforts on behalf of a client has direct effects on the cost and welfare implications of litigation through its impact on the production and sharing of information. It also has substantial indirect effects on the economics of legal markets as a result of the role of confidentiality in the design of legal professional regulation. Protection of attorney-client confidentiality is the core traditional rationale for several distinctive and arguably non-competitive features of legal markets, including regulatory prohibitions on the corporate provision of legal services and non-lawyer ownership, financing, or management of legal providers.

In this chapter, we review the disparate threads in the literature that address attorney-client confidentiality either directly or implicitly, providing a framework that attempts to organize this literature in such a way as to identify what might be addressed by an integrated analysis of the costs and benefits of confidentiality.

---

[1] The attorney-client privilege protects only communications between attorney and client and is generally difficult to overcome unless the advice is in furtherance of a criminal or fraudulent act. The work product doctrine protects, in addition to attorney-client communications, documents or testimony obtained from others in the course of preparing for potential litigation and is generally thought easier to overcome by a showing of necessity.

2. The Existing Literature: Legal Advice and Strategic Revelation

The traditional professional rationale for the protection of attorney-client confidentiality outside of the criminal context (where protection can be seen as an extension of constitutional rights against self-incrimination and to the effective assistance of counsel) is squarely economic in character: critical protection is seen as essential to preserve the incentive of clients to seek out legal advice and information about the law and to disclose information to their attorneys.[2] And yet despite the fact that attorney-client confidentiality is a core tenet of legal ethics and is offered as the central rationale for the distinctive regulatory structure of legal markets, the law and economics literature on attorney-client confidentiality is both thin and disconnected. Rarely is the question of attorney-client confidentiality addressed head on. We attempt here to connect the literatures that are relevant to a coherent analysis of confidentiality.

The existing literature has largely focused on the impact of confidentiality protections on the incentives to produce or transmit legally relevant information in several different channels: client disclosures of known facts to an attorney, attorney provision of legal information to clients, attorney investment in research into facts and legal theories, disclosure of information to opposing parties in litigation, and transmission of information to courts or other decisionmaking bodies. From a social welfare perspective, there are two basic settings: before potentially sanctionable action is taken and during litigation caused by an action. In the first setting, the question is whether confidentiality, by increasing the quantity and value of information available to actors, induces them to better align their conduct with social welfare. In the second setting, the question is whether or not confidentiality improves the efficiency of legal rules by increasing the amount and/or reliability of information reaching courts and thus improving the accuracy of judicial decisionmaking. In both cases, the social value of confidentiality protections depends on whether more and/or more reliable information flows are generated in these different channels as a result of confidentiality and on the social value of information in these channels. (As we will discuss below, the existing literature by and large does not systematically address the other potential welfare impacts of confidentiality on the cost of litigation: the likelihood of settlement, or the dynamic evolution of legal rules.) The multiple steps in the normative chain linking

---

[2] The ABA Model Rules of Professional Conduct in its preamble, for example, states the claim that "a lawyer can be sure that preserving client confidences ordinarily serves the public interest because people are more likely to seek legal advice, and thereby heed their legal obligations, when they know their communications will be private."

54 *Procedural law and economics*

confidentiality with social welfare explains in part why the literature is largely disconnected: researchers have addressed different pieces of the puzzle, but few have integrated them systematically and formally to address the ultimate question of the net social effect of confidentiality protection. We see three strands in the existing literature.

2.1 Confidentiality of Information Shared between Attorney and Client Prior to a Contemplated Act

The most sustained attention in the literature has been to the question of the incentive to acquire legal advice and the social welfare impacts of legal advice. Shavell (1988) presented the first economic analysis of the provision of legal advice to parties before they act and the impact of confidentiality. This analysis focuses explicitly on the information (about legal rules and sanctions) flowing from attorney to client; implicitly, it also applies to information flowing from client to attorney about the client's plans and alternatives.

Shavell showed that the social welfare effect of confidentiality in a relatively simple model is not unambiguously positive. There is no effect in the case in which the motivation to acquire legal information is to comply with a legal rule and incur no risk of an enforcement action: confidentiality has no value to those who act so as to avoid future litigation. The effect is also nil if the party would choose to violate the rule in any event (in which case the party has no incentive to pay for legal information in the first place). In the case in which legal information is probabilistic and hence even those who seek to conform their conduct to the legal rule and reduce their risk of sanctions contemplate the potential for future litigation, the effect of confidentiality depends on the optimality of the underlying legal rule. If the rule is optimal in the sense that expected sanctions equal expected harms, then improved information about the rule will increase its capacity to produce desired behavior; confidentiality will improve information and thus social welfare. But if legal rules are sub-optimal, then increased information may or may not improve behavior. Suppose, for example, that agents believe that expected sanctions are high when in fact they are low relative to expected harms. Then ignorance of the law moves deterrence in a welfare-improving direction. Similarly, if the law in fact is overdeterring but actors underestimate the legal consequences of their actions, social welfare is not improved by relieving them of their miscalculation. Bundy and Elhauge (1993) emphasized that because of the generality of legal rules, even when they are optimally designed and implemented, courts will make both type 1 and type 2 errors, that is, deterring some desirable conduct (overdeterrence) and failing to deter some undesirable conduct (underdeterrence). Moreover, beliefs about legal rules are heterogeneous:

some will overestimate and some will underestimate the true probabilities of sanction. This makes the ambiguity of the welfare implications of legal advice obtained in contemplation of an action, and thus confidentiality of that advice, pervasive. (Bundy and Elhauge, however, argue that empirically the effect is likely to be on balance positive.)

Shavell's analysis assumes that if the act of obtaining legal advice or the information disclosed to the attorney (about the range of contemplated acts, for example) is observable to third parties such as potential plaintiffs or enforcement officials, then the expected sanctions for conduct in violation of a rule increase. (This might occur if, for example, plaintiffs, regulators, or prosecutors are more likely to investigate potential rule violations if they learn that a putative defendant has sought legal advice. It might also occur if a legal rule explicitly makes a defendant's state of knowledge about legal consequences an element of the rule (knowing infringement of a patent, for example, is subject to greater sanction than inadvertent infringement) or, as will often be the case, as a practical matter, judges and juries are more likely to find liability and/or impose harsher penalties if they learn that a defendant acted knowingly, even if the underlying legal rule does not distinguish between knowing and inadvertent violations.) This assumption links the analysis of the impact of confidentiality about advice obtained before acting to the impact of confidentiality in the event of litigation over actions that have been taken.

2.2 Confidentiality of Information Shared between Attorney and Client or Generated by an Attorney during Litigation over Completed Acts

Kaplow and Shavell (1989, 1990) analyze the welfare impact of affording confidentiality to the information shared between attorney and client, or generated by an attorney, during litigation over a completed act. The primary private value for legal advice during litigation, they claim, is found in the ability of the attorney to make expert strategic choices about what information to disclose and what information to withhold from a tribunal. If discovery by opposing parties is otherwise imperfect, meaning that not all the information that a client discloses to an attorney or that the attorney can generate through investigation of third party sources and documents can be obtained at reasonable cost by the other side, then confidential communications between attorney and client and confidential attorney work product must weakly improve expected litigation outcomes for a litigant. Focusing on defendants, they argue that this has a negative impact on social welfare if the expected sanctions in the absence of strategic disclosure to the tribunal would deter undesirable conduct: confidential legal advice reduces expected sanctions and thus diminishes the deterrence that would otherwise obtain. Allen et al. (1990) counter this conclusion by focusing on defendants who have potentially valid defenses, particularly contingent defenses such as contributory negligence. Such defenses, they claim, require defendants to concede what they might perceive as unfavorable facts, such as their own negligence, which defendants are likely to lie about in court and mistakenly withhold from their attorney unless they believe their communication with their attorney is confidential. Increasing the flow of this information to attorneys can increase its flow to courts and while indeed reducing expected sanctions, this effect is on net welfare-promoting.

Although Kaplow and Shavell draw an important analytical distinction between information exchanged before and after actions are taken – drawing out that confidentiality has different effects depending on whether it changes primary activity decisions or not – Shavell's (1988) analysis undermines the sharpness of the distinction. As we noted above, Shavell's analysis depends on the assumption that information exchanged between attorney and client prior to the client's action will remain confidential during litigation and thus not alter expected sanctions. Thus his result on the positive effect of confidentiality on action choices when legal rules are optimal requires that during litigation parties are able to strategically and effectively withhold information about what advice was obtained or information revealed when they made the decision to act. Suppose, for example, that a legal rule formally or in practice subjects a knowing violation of a legal rule (such as patent infringement) to higher penalties than an inadvertent violation. Or that the relevant evidence that might be introduced in litigation includes information known to the client at the time it took an action (such as information about the relative performance of employees who are candidates for a promotion in an employment discrimination suit). Shavell's (1988) result on the desirability of confidentiality of advice obtained in contemplation of an action depends on the capacity to suppress in later litigation what the client was told by the attorney about the legality of an action (in the first example) or what the attorney was told by the client about the alternatives under consideration at the time an action was taken (in the second example). Kaplow and Shavell's (1989, 1990) analysis, however, would appear to treat the advice to withhold the information obtained prior to acting as litigation advice and hence would conclude that confidentiality is generally undesirable. Moreover, as Bundy and Elhauge (1993) emphasize, in practice and particularly for organizational clients that retain in-house or regular outside legal counsel, the distinction between advice given before a contemplated action is undertaken and later during any litigation generated by that action is difficult to discern. For ongoing activities – such as product design or employment practices or contractual behavior – advice given during litigation over past conduct is also effectively advice about future conduct. In addition, Bundy and Elhauge point out that, like primary conduct, evidentiary conduct (compliance with discovery obligations for example) is also subject to legal rules and thus advice during litigation is effectively advice about contemplated actions potentially subject to legal sanction.

What Kaplow and Shavell's distinction does bring to the fore, however, is the recognition that confidentiality affects welfare through its impact on the behavior of multiple actors: clients, attorneys, opposing litigants, and judicial decisionmakers. This helps us to see that an integrated analysis of confidentiality requires incorporating the decisions of all of these actors.

2.3 Confidentiality and the Strategic Revelation of Information to Courts
Kaplow and Shavell's analysis emphasizes that the private value of expert legal advice during litigation lies in the capacity to make strategic decisions about what information to reveal and notes that the ambiguity of the impact of confidentiality on social welfare arises in some settings because it is difficult to say what the net effect of withholding bad information and revealing good information is on judicial inferences about the facts. They recognize that the welfare implications of attorney-client confidentiality depend on whether the expected sanctions in court are adjusted to take into account the withholding of unfavorable information that is likely to result from strategic legal advice, but they do not expressly model the strategic interaction between litigants and the court. There is a relatively developed literature in economics, however, that analyzes the strategic revelation of information to decisionmakers (Milgrom and Roberts 1986, Froeb and Kobayashi 1996, Shavell 1989b, Shin 1998, Daughety and Reinganum 2000), albeit without express attention (with the exception of Che and Severinov 2008, discussed in Section 3, below) to the role of lawyers and confidentiality protections. These analyses all presume that a litigant who either has information on hand when litigation is initiated or who can search for information during trial preparation can costlessly choose which information to disclose and which information to suppress. These economic models assess the extent to which competitive efforts between adversaries who can suppress information can nonetheless result in accurate inferences about the underlying facts by judges who may or may not be sophisticated Bayesian decisionmakers. Milgrom and Roberts (1986) show, for example, that even in the absence of sophisticated decisionmakers in some settings competition between symmetrically informed agents vying for a decision in their favor can lead to full revelation of information. (These results build on Milgrom (1981) and Grossman (1981), who show that a sophisticated decisionmaker who implements a skeptical strategy of making the worst inference possible if an interested

party not facing competition fails to produce favorable information can thus elicit full disclosure of the information available to the interested party. Relatedly, Shavell (1989a) shows that a court can elicit full revelation from an agent by employing a sanctioning function that punishes the failure to provide evidence.) Their model is intended to capture a much wider range of decisionmaking settings than court (including market competition and political lobbying), but in application to judicial settings the information structure raises subtle questions. The fact that full information can be produced by competition between interested parties who are symmetrically informed could, on the one hand, suggest a role for expansive discovery and subpoena power. Attorney-client confidentiality destroys the symmetry discovery would otherwise produce unless all relevant information is obtained from a source other than the attorney or as a result of search at the direction of someone other than the attorney. With attorney-client privilege, then, Milgrom and Roberts' basic result about the capacity of competition to induce full revelation of information to a decisionmaker has less relevance to the judicial setting.

Shin (1998) and Daughety and Reinganum (2000) relax the symmetry assumption. Shin (1998) shows that an adversarial procedure in which the parties have the capacity to suppress unfavorable information before a judge is on average more likely to reach the truth than an inquisitorial procedure in which the judge rather than the parties conducts his or her own investigation, even if the judge has on average as good a chance as the parties do of observing the truth. In this model, a Bayesian judge in an adversarial setting with potential reports from two observers is able to exploit asymmetries in the likelihood that the litigants have evidence of the truth to reduce the cost imposed by strategic suppression of evidence and gain an advantage, on average, over the inquisitorial judge who has only one observation to work with. Daughety and Reinganum (2000) analyze a model of strategic sequential search for evidence from a pool that is available to both sides but where parties can strategically suppress unfavorable search results. They show that asymmetries in search costs, the sampling distribution, stakes, and the role of litigants (plaintiffs initiate cases) lead to systematic biases in the capacity of rule-based (non-Bayesian) courts to reach accurate decisions. Other models in this literature, varying such elements as the cost of generating evidence and the specification of judicial inference (Froeb and Kobayashi 1996, Farmer and Pecorino 2000), reach different results about the capacity of courts to reach accurate results in light of strategic withholding of evidence by adversarial litigants.

The strategic revelation literature thus provides a rich set of results about how suppression of evidence affects judicial accuracy – the issue that animates but is not formally analyzed in the debate in the law literature on the impact of confidential legal advice. But it does so without attention to the role of discovery and attorney-client confidentiality – which the law literature recognizes are policy variables – in establishing the information structure that underpins the strategic revelation game in court. Integrating the strategic revelation literature and the policy-oriented legal advice literature is thus a central task in evaluating the professional claim that confidentiality ultimately serves social welfare by improving the capacity of courts to reach accurate decisions and for law to more effectively guide behavior.

3. The Welfare Effects of Legal Information Production and Exchange: Analyzing Attorney-Client Confidentiality

In this concluding section, we consider how the disparate threads in the law and economics literature might be connected and what unanswered questions remain if we are to reach a better understanding of the welfare implications of attorney-client confidentiality.

3.1 Accuracy and Primary Activity Incentives

The focus of the existing literature is on the impact of confidentiality on the accuracy of judicial decisions and on primary activity incentives. As we have seen, to evaluate the welfare implications of attorney-client confidentiality as a limit to otherwise expansive discovery, however, there is a need for models that analyze the strategic interaction of multiple players: those engaged in primary activities subject to potential liability or sanction, prospective plaintiffs and prosecutors who initiate litigation, attorneys who may advise clients about primary activity decisions and litigation decisions and who may conduct investigations on behalf of clients both before and during litigation, and decisionmakers such as judges and juries. The equilibrium decision whether and how to use legal services, with or without attorney-client confidentiality, cannot be assessed without more careful modeling of the strategic revelation games in courts; the equilibria of strategic revelation games are informative about the policy question of whether and how much to protect attorney-client confidentiality only if the underlying information structure (who is informed and at what cost) is endogenized.

A recent paper by Che and Severinov (2008) makes some progress in this direction, as the first model to analyze the social welfare impact of lawyers and legal advice on the strategic revelation game in courts. Like the rest of the strategic revelation literature, they assume parties can costlessly suppress unfavorable information, but they also expressly consider the incentive to hire a lawyer who has better information about the legal significance of a piece of information and hence the capacity to improve the client's decision about what to disclose and what to reveal. They show, however, that when courts respond strategically – whether they are Bayesian or not (their model is general enough to allow the sophistication of the decisionmaker's strategy to vary) – the impact of legal advice on the disclosure decision on social welfare is ultimately nil if advice is costless (the assumption we find in most of the law literature). This is because, even for non-Bayesian judges, the equilibrium inference given the different disclosure strategies of advised and unadvised litigants fully compensates. Che and Severinov then demonstrate that hiring a lawyer can have a positive impact on social welfare if lawyers are costly, but not because they improve disclosure decisions through their expert advice but because the availability of costly advice supports a signaling equilibrium in which clients who choose not to hire a lawyer disclose more information (which in some cases turns out to be unfavorable to them). They also show that lawyers can improve results for clients by developing a reputation for withholding *favorable* evidence (which makes the equilibrium judicial inference when no information is disclosed less damaging), but this reduces rather than increases social welfare. This paper thus sheds significant light on what comes from integrating the legal advice analysis with strategic revelation analysis. But what this work has not yet done is to incorporate the impact of discovery, allowing us to compare welfare with and without confidentiality exceptions in discovery.

Other potential directions for this work would include extending the impact of the strategic revelation game with and without legal advice in litigation backwards to the incentive to obtain confidential versus discoverable legal advice prior to acting. Clearly, confidentiality reduces the cost of obtaining legal advice about contemplated acts. Whether this will lead to increases in the amount of legal information sought by actors, however, depends on the consequences of remaining uninformed. If the costs of remaining uninformed outweigh the costs of becoming informed (including any increased exposure to legal sanctions), then actors will face no increased incentive to become informed by a reduction in the cost of information. Shavell (1988) investigates this question in a simple model in which actors can only choose whether to act and not how to modify actions that are too costly to forgo completely. The presumption of most of the deterrence literature in law and economics, however, contemplates that primary activity decisions are informed by legal rules in the first instance in order to select an optimal action from a continuum of choices, choosing, for example, an optimal level of investment in precautionary activities. If the naïve belief about the risk of choosing actions without legal advice is sufficiently high, then there is no need for the additional incentive of confidentiality.

This issue has been largely ignored in the literature. Wickelgren (2010) presents a model that investigates the incentive of a corporate client to investigate the potential harms of a contemplated act in light of the risks of uncovering information that would be unfavorable in a future civil lawsuit, but focuses on the impact of a right to silence – prohibiting a court from drawing negative inferences from the failure to provide evidence disproving liability – on the incentives to investigate. Wickelgren's analysis, building on insights from Shavell (1992), highlights the potential for overinvestment in the production of information relative to socially optimal levels because of the private benefit of potentially reducing expected sanctions; a right to silence, by diminishing the cost of remaining uninformed, can offset the incentive to overinvest. The model does not explicitly illuminate the question of attorney-client confidentiality, because it presumes that a defendant can costlessly suppress unfavorable information in litigation, but it makes clear that we cannot simply assume that in the absence of confidentiality there will be underinvestment in information about legal rules to inform primary activity choices.

In a strategic setting, it is also not clear that the risk of discovering unfavorable information will undercut incentives to investigate when litigation is under way. As Bundy and Elhauge (1993) note, for example, if the unfavorable information may be discovered independently by the other side, the incentive to investigate to learn unfavorable information, in order to prepare a defensive response, is enhanced. The strategic revelation models that incorporate the decision to search for information (Froeb and Kobayashi 1996, Farmer and Pecorino 2000, Daughety and Reinganum 2000) do not consider the value of discovering unfavorable information in order to prepare a defense in the event the other side discovers it as well; litigants search only in order to find favorable information. These considerations will be relevant to an analysis of the value of attorney-client confidentiality: if there is an incentive to search for unfavorable information as a defensive strategy, even at risk of increasing the likelihood that unfavorable information reaches the tribunal, protection of attorney-client confidentiality may have less effect on the total production of information than more informal analyses suggest.

None of the existing models address a further complication in the context of corporate or organizational actors, namely that the capacity to conceal information produced by an attorney creates an incentive to channel investigations through lawyers rather than through other agents. In anticipation of litigation (which is a routine event for most corporations of significant size), there is a choice about who will conduct investigations or collect information: the client or the attorney. In many cases, these investigations will optimally be conducted prior to acting – before introducing a new consumer product or establishing a branch office in another tax jurisdiction or completing a merger. If these investigations are conducted by the client (or other agents such as accountants or consultants), the results will be discoverable if litigation ensues; if conducted by the attorney, or at the direction of the attorney, they will (largely[3]) be protected. It seems reasonable to suppose that much of this information – the safety of a new product, the extent of foreign tax burdens, the impact of a merger on sales and profits, for example – would be conducted whether or not at the direction of counsel and hence work-product immunity only reduces and does not increase the amount of legally relevant information produced. Moreover, on the advice of counsel, many organizations may adopt document production, management, and retention practices that reduce the overall quantity of documentation available – avoiding the use of email or engaging in regular purges of email, for example. This may have an impact not only on the availability of information in litigation, but also on the efficiency of organization and information flows generally and the quality of decisionmaking both with respect to profits and with respect to harms caused to others. The implications of the pervasiveness of legal advice in modern corporations with in-house counsel for the analysis of the welfare effects of attorney-client confidentiality has not yet been explored in the literature.

We now turn to additional welfare implications of attorney-client confidentiality that have largely been ignored in the literature, going beyond the analysis of the accuracy of judicial decisionmaking and primary activity choices.

3.2 Litigation Costs

Although some in the literature have taken account of the fact that legal information – whether legal advice or factual investigation – is costly to obtain (Shavell 1988, Froeb and Kobayashi 1996, Farmer and Pecorino 2000, Che and Severinov 2008), the impact of attorney-client confidentiality on the overall costs of litigation has not been explored. But confidentiality generates both direct and indirect costs that need to be

---

[3] The question will be whether early investigations were in fact conducted in anticipation of litigation, at the direction of counsel, and not in the ordinary course of business. In US federal courts, if the testimony or documents contain facts only – and not the opinion of counsel – they may also be discoverable based on a showing of need by the other side. But even factual documents will be protected from discovery if producing them may reveal "the mental impressions, conclusions, opinions or legal theories of a party's attorney or other representative concerning the litigation." Fed. R. Civ. Proc. 26(b)(3)(B).

counterbalanced against the goals of accuracy and incentives for efficient primary activity choices.

Attorney-client confidentiality directly increases the cost of litigation by requiring opposing parties to duplicate efforts in investigation and legal analysis. In general, this increases the overall costs of the legal system. There may be some benefits from costly advice: Posner (1999), for example, argues that requiring duplicative effort could reduce frivolous litigation by requiring plaintiffs to incur costs to frame complaints that adequately allege the facts that support the action. Che and Severinov (2008) assume litigants can use litigation expenditures to signal the quality of a case or the credibility of evidentiary claims, but do not do a comparative analysis to assess whether any increased cost due to duplicative efforts in litigation is justified by any welfare gains.

Beyond duplication, however, attorney-client confidentiality may be a significant source of the rapidly increasing costs of discovery in Anglo-American legal systems. Before documents are released in discovery, they are routinely screened to determine whether they are protected by attorney-client privilege or work-product immunity. This requires significant and costly legal input. Moreover, disputes about what is and is not covered by attorney-client protections are a rich source of costly discovery disputes and delays. The benefits of these protections – which, as we have seen, may be ambiguous in terms of judicial accuracy and efficient activity incentives – need to be weighed against these potentially large costs.

Indirectly, too, attorney-client confidentiality can increase legal costs in both transactions and litigation. One channel through which this can occur is the distortion in information flows that may be caused in an organization in order to protect confidentiality in the event of litigation. This could include document avoidance or destruction practices and the routing of investigations and analyses through legal departments and costly outside legal providers.

A second indirect and potentially very important channel through which attorney-client confidentiality may increase costs is through the distortion confidentiality creates in the markets for legal goods and services. Because lawyers can offer secrecy benefits to their clients that other potentially competing providers cannot offer, the demand for legal services is enhanced and competition is reduced (Fischel 1998). More subtly, however, attorney-client confidentiality is a key plank in the justifications offered for the extensive regulation of legal markets by lawyers themselves, regulation that significantly limits the potential for competition and cost-reducing innovation in legal markets (Hadfield 2008). Concerns about protecting attorney-client confidentiality motivate in part the American

Bar Association's ongoing prohibition of multi-disciplinary practices and non-lawyer ownership or investment in legal providers.

Attorney-client confidentiality may also affect litigation costs by influencing the propensity for and timing of settlement. The effect here is via the impact on the scope of discovery. As the law and economics literature on discovery (Shavell 1989b, Cooter and Rubinfeld 1994, Hay 1994, 1995) demonstrates, the exchange of information prior to trial influences the likelihood of trial. By constricting discovery, attorney-client confidentiality thus may reduce the capacity for pre-trial beliefs to converge and for settlement negotiations to succeed. Hay (1995) explicitly considers the impact that attorney-client confidentiality – specifically confidentiality of the level of effort expended by attorneys in case preparation – may have on the persistence of asymmetric beliefs and hence the failure of settlement.

3.3 Dynamic Quality of Law

Missing entirely from the literature is analysis of the impact of attorney-client confidentiality and information production incentives in litigation on the evolution of legal rules. In all legal systems, but most obviously in common law systems, the evolution of legal rules and their dynamic quality (as distinct from their static accuracy and efficiency in a given case) depends significantly on the information ultimately supplied to courts by litigants. Litigant presentations are the only source of material available to common law courts in the process of interpreting and adapting rules to changes in the environment. This information accumulates (depending on the institutional attributes, such as opinion writing and publication practices, of the legal regime) as what Hadfield (2008) calls legal human capital. Legal human capital in turn determines judicial error and expertise and thus underpins assumptions about judicial competence, particularly the capacity for judicial inference in the face of incomplete and potentially biased evidence. Moreover, as Hadfield (2008) demonstrates, the incentives of parties to expend resources in collecting and presenting facts and legal analysis depend in part on the rate of judicial error (understood as the likelihood of reaching a socially optimal decision) in interpreting and applying evidence and argument. Nor are these incentives obvious: litigants with information that promotes socially optimal interpretation and adaptation of the law have reduced incentives to invest if little legal human capital has accumulated and judges are thus highly error-prone. Litigants with information that undermines socially optimal decisionmaking – who seek to introduce what is effectively disinformation – are, however, encouraged by low rates of judicial expertise. The quantity and composition of the information reaching and accumulating in legal systems should be an element of the economic analysis of attorney-client confidentiality.

The dynamic quality of law also depends on the level of complexity in law. If the information accumulated in litigation is excessive, law may become excessively complex. Complexity in law drives legal costs both directly in terms of the quantity of information and analysis necessary to implement complex rules and indirectly in terms of the potential for the market for legal services to be competitive (Hadfield 2000). Any evaluation of the impact of attorney-client confidentiality on the overall quantity of information produced to lawyers and ultimately to courts, then, must take into account not merely the value of increased information in the adjudication of a given case but also the external effects on the cost and complexity of the legal regime as a whole.

References

Allen, Ronald J., Mark F. Grady, Daniel D. Polsby and Michael S. Yashko (1990), "Positive Theory of the Attorney-Client Privilege and the Work Product Doctrine," *Journal of Legal Studies*, 19: 359–97.

Bundy, Stephen M. and Einer Elhauge (1993), "Knowledge about Legal Sanctions," *Michigan Law Review*, 92: 261–334.

Che, Yeon-Koo and Sergei Severinov (2008), "Lawyer-Advised Disclosure," Manuscript.

Cooter, Robert D. and Daniel L. Rubinfeld (1994), "An Economic Model of Legal Discovery," *Journal of Legal Studies*, 23: 435–61.

Daughety, Andrew F. and Jennifer Reinganum F. (2000), "On the Economics of Trials: Adversarial Process, Evidence and Equilibrium Bias," *Journal of Law, Economics and Organization*: 16: 365–94.

Farmer, Amy and Paul Pecerino (2000), "Does Jury Bias Matter?," *International Review of Law and Economics*, 20: 315–28.

Fischel, Daniel R. (1998), "Lawyers and Confidentiality," *University of Chicago Law Review*, 65: 1–33.

Froeb, Luke M. and Bruce H. Kobayashi (1996), "Naïve, Biased, yet Bayesian: Can Juries Interpret Selectively Produced Evidence?," *Journal of Law, Economics and Organization*, 12: 257–76.

Grossman, Sanford J. (1981), "The Informational Role of Warranties and Private Disclosure about Product Quality," *Journal of Law and Economics*, 24: 461–83.

Hadfield, Gillian K. (2000), "The Price of Law: How the Market for Lawyers Distorts the Justice System," *Michigan Law Review*, 98: 953–1006.

Hadfield, Gillian K. (2008), The Levers of Legal Design: Institutional Determinants of the Quality of Law," *Journal of Comparative Economics*, 36(1): 43–73.

Hay, Bruce L. (1994), "Civil Discovery: Its Effects and Optimal Scope," *Journal of Legal Studies*, 23: 481–515.

Hay, Bruce L. (1995), "Effort, Information, Settlement, Trial," *Journal of Legal Studies*, 24: 29–62.

Kaplow, Lewis and Steven Shavell (1989), "Legal Advice about Information to Present in Litigation: Its Effects and Social Desirability," *Harvard Law Review*, 102: 567–615.

Kaplow, Lewis and Steven Shavell (1990), "Legal Advice about Acts Already Committed," *International Review of Law and Economics*, 10: 149–59.

Milgrom, Paul (1981), "Good News and Bad News: Representation Theorems and Applications," *Bell Journal of Economics*, 12: 380–91.

Milgrom, Paul and John Roberts (1986), "Relying on the Information of Disinterested Parties," *RAND Journal of Economics*, 17: 18–32.

Posner, Richard A. (1999), "An Economic Approach to the Law of Evidence," *Stanford Law Review*, 51: 1477–546.

Shavell, Steven (1988), "Legal Advice about Contemplated Acts: The Decision to Obtain Advice, its Social Desirability, and Protection of Confidentiality," *Journal of Legal Studies*, 17: 123–50.

Shavell, Steven (1989a) "Optimal Sanctions and the Incentive to Provide Evidence to Legal Tribunals," *International Review of Law and Economics*, 9: 3–11.

Shavell, Steven (1989b) "Sharing of Information Prior to Settlement or Litigation," *RAND Journal of Economics*, 20: 183–95.

Shavell, Steven (1992), "Liability and the Incentive to Obtain Information about Risk," *Journal of Legal Studies*, 21: 259–70.

Shin, Hyun Song (1998), "Adversarial and Inquisitorial Procedures in Arbitration," *RAND Journal of Economics*, 29: 378–405.

Wickelgren, Abraham L. (2010), "A Right to Silence for Civil Defendants?," *Journal of Law, Economics and Organization*, 26: 92–114.

4 Class action
Robert G. Bone

1. Introduction[1]

The class action is a device that allows one or more parties, called "class representatives," to sue on behalf of many other similarly situated persons, called "absent class members" or "absentees." It traces its early roots to medieval forms of group litigation and its modern shape to the courts of equity of the seventeenth and eighteenth centuries (Yeazell 1989; Bone 1990).

The class action played a relatively minor role in American civil litigation through more than half of the twentieth century. In 1966, the federal class action rule, Rule 23 of the Federal Rules of Civil Procedure, was revised and expanded and ever since the class action has sparked intense controversy. Class action supporters celebrate its potential for achieving efficiency gains, redressing imbalances of litigating power, and enforcing the substantive law effectively. Class action critics condemn its potential for enriching class attorneys, pressuring risk-averse defendants to settle, and giving high damage plaintiffs only average recovery. Indeed, the class action has been called a "Frankenstein monster" and "legalized blackmail" (Miller 1979, at 665–6, noting the sharp rhetoric).

Although Rule 23 authorizes class actions for plaintiffs and defendants, virtually all class actions are brought on the plaintiff's side (Willging et al. 1996). The class need not have existed as a group prior to the litigation. Class members can be, and usually are, total strangers to one another, with nothing in common except the fact that they have all been injured by the same or similar legal wrong. For example, one or more persons harmed by a mass-marketed drug might seek to represent a class of all persons injured by the same drug, or one or more investors might seek to represent a class of all shareholders who held shares during a defined period and suffered loss as a result of the company's fraud.

The class action in effect functions as a complex preclusion device. It serves to adjudicate the claims of many plaintiffs in one proceeding and bind them all to the result. The specific structure of the class action reflects

---

[1] This entry is based on the treatment of the class action in Bone (2003a), at 259–98.

this goal. That structure seeks to strike an optimal balance between the benefits of preclusive class treatment, on the one hand, and the costs of aggregation, on the other, including the costs of binding parties who do not in fact participate or exercise meaningful control.

The following discussion analyzes the plaintiff class action from an economic perspective. It briefly surveys the benefits and costs and describes some of the more notable reform proposals. It is worth mentioning, however, that many class action scholars also worry about rights-based and fairness values. For example, the fact that the class action binds absent class members who have no meaningful opportunity to participate is said to intrude on the right to a personal day in court, and the fact that class settlements provide only average recovery to absentees with above-average claims raises concerns of compensatory fairness (Bone 2003b, at 487–9). These rights-based and fairness concerns are beyond the scope of this discussion.

2. The Benefits of Class Action Treatment

According to the available empirical evidence, most class actions seek damages (Willging et al. 1996). Nevertheless, classes are sometimes certified for injunctive and declaratory relief. These non-damage class actions raise fewer controversial issues, as their benefits are relatively clear and their costs much less serious than those associated with damage class actions.[2]

The remainder of this discussion focuses on the damage class action. There are two broad types of damage class action (Coffee 1987, at 904–6). The first type, called a large claim class action, consists mostly or entirely of plaintiffs with marketable claims, that is, plaintiffs who have enough at stake to justify hiring an attorney and suing individually. The second type, called a small claim class action, consists mostly or entirely of plaintiffs who have unmarketable claims, that is, plaintiffs with too little at stake to justify hiring an attorney and suing individually.

2.1 Large Claim Class Actions

There are two main benefits to the large claim damage class action. The most frequently cited benefit has to do with economies of scale achieved by litigating common issues of fact and law in one proceeding (e.g., Hensler

---

[2] These non-damage class actions achieve three main benefits: a remedial benefit in facilitating a group injunction, a heuristic benefit in focusing the judge on the group nature of the wrong, and a practical benefit in guaranteeing class-wide preclusion.

et al. 2000). Consider a mass tort class action in which class members all suffer serious personal injury from an allegedly defective drug. If the class members were to sue individually, each would have to prove that the particular drug can cause the general type of injury from which she suffers and that the drug is in fact defective given the risks and the information available to the defendant. With strict limits on nonparty preclusion, each plaintiff can litigate the common issues over again even if previous plaintiffs lost. In a large mass tort, repeated litigation of common issues generates substantial duplicative litigation costs, and the class action avoids these costs by aggregating all the related lawsuits in one proceeding.

Any evaluation of economies of scale, however, must count the litigation costs that the class action itself generates. A class action is a complex procedural device that invites more intensive litigation and requires much more judicial oversight and case management than an individual suit. The additional costs it creates must be subtracted from the costs it saves (Bernstein 1978).

The second benefit of the large damage class action has to do with reducing the asymmetry of litigation costs and stakes and equalizing litigation investment across the party line (Rosenberg 2000; Hay and Rosenberg 2000 and 2002a; Note 2004). The first thing to note is that the class action eliminates a cost asymmetry that can skew the error risk in the defendant's favor when suits are brought individually. In a class action, all the plaintiffs invest only once in preparing common questions compared to duplicative investments in separate suits. This gives the class plaintiffs the same cost advantage as the common defendant, which helps to even out litigating power and avoid skewed error.

The class action also reduces the pernicious effect of asymmetric stakes on error risk. Suppose that in our drug example, there are 1000 plaintiffs in the class, P-1 to P-1000, and that each plaintiff has one million dollars at stake. If P-1 sues alone, the defendant D has much more at stake than P-1. D knows that it faces preclusion or *stare decisis* in future suits if it loses on the common issue in P-1's suit. Thus, the outcome in P-1's suit will affect D in future suits, and D invests accordingly. By contrast, P-1 has only his own suit at stake and thus invests less than D. When one side invests more than the other, the party investing more is more likely to win, all other things equal. Thus, individual litigation creates a condition of asymmetric stakes, which generates asymmetric litigation investment and produces outcomes skewed in favor of the defendant.

The class action reduces the asymmetry and with it the skewed error risk. In our drug example, an attorney representing the class who takes the case on a contingency expects to receive a percentage of the total class recovery as a fee. Since his fee depends on total recovery, the attorney will consider the stakes for all plaintiffs in the class and invest up to the point where the marginal benefit in terms of an enhanced fee just equals the marginal cost.[3] This result does not necessarily equalize litigation investment across the party line, as the class attorney receives only a fraction of the total class recovery while the defendant pays it all (Coffee 1987). However, it does reduce the asymmetry and thus the skewed error risk.

These two benefits – achieving economies of scale and mitigating the effects of skewed error – assume that the class action is litigated all the way through trial. However, virtually all class actions settle (Willging et al. 1996; Bohn and Choi 1996; Garth 1987). The prospect of settlement reduces the economy-of-scale benefits of the class action, since cost savings are less when issues are not litigated. However, it does not necessarily reduce the error-reduction benefits, since litigation asymmetry affects settlement as well as trial. When parties anticipate a probability of trial success skewed in defendant's favor, they are likely to settle for an amount skewed in the same direction. Insofar as the class action reduces this asymmetry, it also produces settlements less tainted by skewed incentives and closer to the optimal amount for deterrence.[4]

2.2 Small Claim Class Actions

Because a small claim class action, by definition, includes claims too small to justify individual suits, authorizing a class action creates litigation where none would exist otherwise. Thus, the small claim class action is

---

[3] This assumes substantial agency costs; in other words, it assumes that the attorney runs the class action with the exclusive goal of maximizing his own fee. Agency costs in the class action setting are discussed in Section 3.1 below.

[4] This is a highly simplified analysis. A more complete treatment should consider effects on settlement rate and settlement amount. As for settlement rate, if the class action increases total litigation investment, it also increases the potential surplus from settlement. Depending on the circumstances, a larger surplus can increase the likelihood of settlement by enlarging the range of feasible settlement allocations, or reduce the likelihood by encouraging strategic bargaining over the larger settlement stakes. The effect on settlement amount can be seen by considering a simple settlement model where p is the probability of success at trial, w is the expected trial award conditional on success, and C_P and C_D are the expected trial costs for each side. Assuming both sides agree on values for these variables and there is equal bargaining power, the settlement range is $[pw - C_P, pw + C_D]$, and the likely settlement is at the midpoint of this range, i.e., $pw + (C_D - C_P)/2$. If class treatment elicits greater relative investment from the plaintiffs, it should increase p, which increases the settlement amount all other things equal. But insofar as class treatment aligns litigation investments more closely across the party line, it reduces $C_D - C_P$, which reduces the settlement amount. Without more information, it is not possible to determine which of these opposing effects dominates.

not about litigation cost savings or asymmetry-reducing benefits. Instead, it is about empowering parties as private attorneys general to enforce the substantive law and deter wrongdoing, where the legal violation systematically creates small harms for large numbers of geographically dispersed victims. Kalven and Rosenfeld (1941) and Dam (1975) provide classic treatments of this justification (see also Wright 1969). And numerous commentators since 1980 have examined it in more detail (Macey and Miller 1991; Rubenstein 2006).

The central idea is that small stakes disable private enforcement through individual lawsuits, and geographical dispersion coupled with free riding incentives makes voluntary organization and collective action virtually impossible. As a result, there would be no lawsuits if victims were limited to individual suits or voluntary joinder. The class action overcomes the collective action barriers and enables private lawsuits that internalize the costs of legal violations. The result is enhanced deterrence.

As an example, consider a company that fails to disclose material information to its investors. Most of the defrauded investors own too little stock in the company to warrant individual litigation, and transaction costs and free-rider obstacles stand in the way of their organizing a litigating group on their own. With the class action, however, an attorney can sue on behalf of all the investors, with one or more shareholders acting as class representatives, and obtain a large aggregate recovery and a large fee. Suppose there are 500,000 defrauded investors in the class and the average loss for each investor is $100. Also, suppose an attorney considering whether to take the class action expects a settlement of $20 million. If, as is usually the case, class attorneys receive fees roughly equal to 25% of class recovery (Alexander 1991; Eisenberg and Miller 2004b), the attorney can expect a fee of about $5 million, an amount sufficient to attract skilled counsel.

However, even a perfectly functioning small claim class action generates costs of its own. These include the costs of litigating claims that would not otherwise be brought and the delay and opportunity costs for other lawsuits. These costs must be balanced against the class action's deterrence benefits (Bernstein 1978). Moreover, given the class action's enforcement goals, striking the optimal balance must also take account of public enforcement mechanisms. The Securities and Exchange Commission, for example, enforces the federal securities laws; the Federal Trade Commission and the Department of Justice enforce the federal antitrust laws, and various agencies enforce consumer protection laws. From an economic perspective, the goal must be to coordinate public and private enforcement in an overall scheme that minimizes social costs.

Indeed, the problem is particularly acute because of the serious risk that private enforcement through the class action can produce overdeterrence (Rosenberg and Sullivan 2006). For example, many private antitrust class suits follow on the heels of public enforcement actions. If public enforcement already achieves deterrence, the class action might end up overdeterring, especially with the threat of treble damages and high litigation costs.

The literature includes very little systematic treatment of this coordination problem. A notable exception is Rosenberg and Sullivan (2006) which offers an interesting approach. The authors' complex proposal, which they apply to antitrust enforcement, has three main features. First, it vests initial and exclusive enforcement authority in a public enforcer. Second, it requires the public enforcer to auction the class action to prospective private enforcers, with the public enforcer retaining an option to buy back the class action at the winning bid price. Third, it requires that the class action be a mandatory-litigation class action, meaning that it is automatically certified and must go to trial if it does not settle and no class members can opt out. Rosenberg and Sullivan argue that this procedure produces the optimal mix of private and public enforcement.

3. The Costs of Class Action Treatment

As already mentioned, class actions create high litigation costs for courts and parties, and by generating additional litigation, the small claim class action creates delay costs for other litigants. This section examines other types of cost, including costs associated with agency problems, adverse selection and opt out, and frivolous litigation.[5]

3.1 Agency Costs

There is a vast economic literature analyzing the principal-agent problem in many different settings. Miller (1987) gives the classic treatment for litigation in general, and numerous scholars have analyzed agency problems for the class action in particular (e.g., Dam 1975; Coffee 1987; Macey and Miller 1991; Hay and Rosenberg 2000; Klement 2002). Class agency problems take two principal forms: conflict of interest between the class attorney and the class, and conflict of interest between class representatives and other class members. The first is the more serious of the two.

It is well accepted that the class attorney controls class litigation. This has led many to analyze class actions as a type of "entrepreneurial litigation" with the attorney as the litigating entrepreneur (Coffee 1987). The dominance of the class attorney is most obvious for the small claim class

---

[5] There are other costs as well. For example, Che (2002) shows how class action plaintiffs can exploit informational asymmetries in settlement bargaining.

action, in which representative plaintiffs function as little more than "figureheads" (Macey and Miller 1991). Few class members have enough at stake to justify monitoring class counsel and those who do normally lack expertise to perform the task effectively. Indeed, the class attorney is often the one who seeks out the named representatives and he is likely to choose representatives who are willing to comply with his wishes.[6]

The situation is much the same for the large claim class action. Although in these cases there are class members with enough at stake to justify monitoring class counsel, very little monitoring in fact occurs. There are several reasons for this. One has to do with lack of expertise and limited access to information about attorney performance. These problems also exist in ordinary litigation, but they are particularly serious for the class action because of its broad impact. The second reason for inadequate monitoring has to do with free riding. Monitoring is a public good that benefits the class as a whole, so each class member has an incentive to free ride on the monitoring efforts of others. The result is suboptimal investment in monitoring. Judges sometimes make incentive payments to class representatives to counteract the free-rider effect (Eisenberg and Miller 2006). But there are limits to what judges can do (Silver and Dinkin 2008).

As a result, the class attorney has wide latitude to run the class action for her own private gain. The most problematic result is the so-called "sweetheart settlement." A sweetheart settlement is a settlement in which the class attorney and the defendant collude to maximize their respective gains at the expense of the class. The defendant agrees to pay the class attorney a large fee, and the class attorney agrees to accept a small settlement for the class. In effect, the class attorney trades a low class recovery for a high fee[7] (Coffee 1987; Macey and Miller 1995; Coffee 2000; Hay and Rosenberg 2000; Klement 2002).

---

[6] As discussed below, the Private Securities Litigation Reform Act (PSLRA) tries to address this problem for securities fraud class actions in federal court by creating a procedure to select as class representatives large institutional investors who have the incentive and wherewithal to monitor class counsel (Cox and Thomas 2006; Silver and Dinkin 2008).

[7] Attorneys often compete for the class fee by filing separate and overlapping class actions aimed at the same wrongdoing. The idea is to race to be the first to secure a settlement and with it the class fee. (A settlement in one class action usually precludes class members from pursuing other class actions.) Defendants can exploit these incentives by pitting attorneys against one another in a "reverse auction." The defendant in effect shops for an attorney willing to accept a settlement on defendant's terms. For a discussion of the reverse auction, see Coffee (1995). For an analysis of overlapping class actions in general, see Miller (1996).

The social costs of sweetheart settlements differ somewhat between small and large claim class actions. Since class members in a small claim class action have too little at stake to make compensation significant, the most salient cost is the adverse effect on deterrence (Bone 1994; Gilles and Friedman 2006). In a large claim class action, such as a mass tort suit, a sweetheart settlement impairs compensation as well as deterrence. Suboptimal compensation for class members can have adverse effects on risk-bearing costs, investment in primary activity, and insurance choices.

One has to be careful, however, when assessing these costs. In the case of a small claim class action, it is possible that public enforcement might make up for any deterrence shortfall. Thus, the important question is not whether the class action itself achieves optimal deterrence, but how much of a deterrence gap remains after taking account of all enforcement methods (public and private). Moreover, for large claim class actions, one should compare the costs of class action settlement with the costs of settlement in the absence of a class action. This is significant because experience shows that nonclass settlements of informal aggregations are tainted by agency problems similar to those that plague the class action (Erichson 2000).

Trial judges are supposed to control opportunistic behavior on the part of class attorneys, but they often lack the necessary information to make an evaluation. Furthermore, faced with congested dockets and intense pressure to resolve cases quickly, judges have incentives to overlook attorney self-dealing when a class settlement promises to resolve a large number of cases at once (Coffee 1987; Macey and Miller 1995; Hensler et al. 2000). This judicial tendency is consistent with empirical findings that show a correlation between docket congestion and the size of the fee award judges are willing to approve (Helland and Klick 2007).

Moreover, sweetheart settlements can be structured in ways that conceal the true relationship between the class settlement and the fee award. One relatively simple way to do this involves making side payments to class counsel.[8] A more complicated method involves structuring nonmonetary

---

[8] In mass tort cases, for example, class counsel will often have a large inventory of individual clients in addition to those in the class. By structuring the class action to exclude the inventory clients, the class attorney and the defendant can enter into a deal in which the defendant settles the class claims for a small amount and the inventory claims for large amounts. In this way, class counsel receives a substantial fee from the inventory settlements without disclosing the amount to the judge reviewing the class settlement. In the past, this technique was used as part of a strategy for achieving global class settlements of future claims (Coffee 1995, at 1373–5). Congress targeted this practice in the Class Action Fairness Act of 2005,

relief so it appears as though the settlement is much larger than it actually is. Nonmonetary settlements can make class members better off, but they can also compound agency problems and make class members worse off (Miller and Singer 1997).[9] For example, antitrust and consumer class action settlements often include coupon distributions. Typically, the defendant and the class attorney urge the reasonableness of the fee as a proportion of the total face value of the coupons, all the while expecting the redemption rate to be low and thus the real cost to the defendant and the real value to the class to be small.[10] The Class Action Fairness Act of 2005 (CAFA) targeted this practice in federal court by requiring the class attorney's percentage fee to be based on the value to class members of the coupons *actually redeemed* by consumers. However, it is not clear how much of an effect this reform has had, and it is worth noting that CAFA does not reach coupon settlements in state court.[11]

3.2 Intra-Class Conflict: Adverse Selection and Opt Out

In large claim class actions, such as those arising from mass torts, the class attorney has an incentive to make the class as large as possible because a larger class supports a larger fee. Since there is a limit to the number of strong claims, the likely result is a class heavily stocked with plaintiffs who have weak or moderate claims. Furthermore, because settlement is designed to avoid the costs of determining individual claim values, compensation must be calculated on an average basis and the settlement distributed pro rata (perhaps subdivided by injury category). As a result, class members with above-average claims receive only average recovery.

---

which requires parties to disclose all side agreements when the judge reviews a class settlement. The same requirement is also imposed by the 2003 revisions to Rule 23 of the Federal Rules of Civil Procedure. But it is not clear how effective these reforms have been.

[9] See also Durand (1981) for an economic analysis of fluid recovery remedies, which distribute class damages in ways only roughly matching individual harm.

[10] There are other problems with coupon settlements. The effect of coupons on price can leave consumers as a group no better off (Borenstein 1996), and the effect of coupons on demand can create deadweight loss (Polinsky and Rubinfeld 2008).

[11] Also, CAFA does nothing to address the reversionary fund settlement, another popular way to disguise sweetheart settlements. In a reversionary fund settlement, the defendant creates a large settlement fund for the class and pays the class attorney a large fee. The large fee appears reasonable as a percentage of the total settlement fund. However, the attorney and the defendant collude to minimize the number of class members claiming on the fund, and the amount of the fund left after a specified period reverts to the defendant.

In effect, the class action transfers wealth from those with above-average claims to those with below-average claims.

To illustrate with a simple example, suppose a mass tort class includes 100 plaintiffs with strong cases, each of whose claims has an expected trial value of $500,000, and 100 plaintiffs with weak cases, each of whose claims has an expected trial value of only $10,000. The defendant understands the class attorney's incentives and expects the class to be stocked with weak claims, which should depress the amount of any settlement. Suppose the class action settles for $20 million and the settlement is distributed pro rata to all 200 class members, so each receives $100,000. Those class members with weak claims end up with ten times the expected value of their claims, and those class members with strong claims end up with only one-fifth.

This averaging creates an adverse selection problem. Rule 23 gives each class member in (b)(3) damage class actions a right to opt out of the class.[12] Armed with this right, class members with high value claims will have an incentive to opt out to avoid damage averaging, while class members with low value claims will stay in.[13] The result is a class action that adversely selects for low value claims.

Che (1996) shows that there are limits to adverse selection when plaintiffs are privately informed about damages. In the equilibrium of his signaling model, some low value plaintiffs leave the class in order to pool with exiting high value plaintiffs and to signal (falsely) that they too have high value claims. Moreover, some high value plaintiffs remain in the class. Still, a significant adverse selection effect remains.[14]

Adverse selection is costly for two reasons. First, it undermines the efficiency of the class device by encouraging class members to litigate separately and by diverting social resources to compensate low value

---

[12] Rule 23(c)(2). In addition, class counsel must give the best practicable notice to the class, including individual notice to all class members who can be reasonably identified, so that class members can decide whether to exercise their opt-out right.

[13] A high value plaintiff has an incentive to opt out when individual litigation or joinder in a nonclass aggregation promises a larger net recovery. In theory, a class action could unravel completely at the high end, as the expected settlement and pro rata share decline with exiting high value plaintiffs. The incentive to opt out, however, depends on a number of factors, including how much the plaintiff knows about the strength of her claim, the additional cost of litigating separately, and the degree of risk aversion.

[14] Friedman (1996) proposes a mechanism for generating damage payments to class members that reflect the strength of their individual cases. His mechanism extrapolates from trial verdicts in a sample of cases drawn from the class after giving the defendant an opportunity to choose the sample.

claims. Second, adverse selection exacerbates agency problems by driving high value plaintiffs out of the class and making it even less likely that the remaining class members will have enough at stake to monitor the class attorney.

There are other ways in which the interests of class members can conflict (Morawetz 1993), and when they do, there is always a risk that powerful parties will prevail over weaker parties. One solution to this problem involves dividing the class into subclasses with separate representatives and separate attorneys. Subclassing, however, reduces the benefits of class-wide adjudication and raises the transaction costs of settlement bargaining. Miller (2003b) analyzes intra-class conflict and proposes an approach based on hypothetical *ex ante* consent.[15] (See also Morawetz 1993, examining theories of distributional fairness to guide measures for handling intra-class conflict, and Dana 2006, using hypothetical consent as a standard for determining the permissibility of collateral attack.) Kornhauser (1983) offers a framework based on cooperative game theory and the solution concept of the core to analyze the fairness of a class settlement in the presence of interest conflict.

3.3 Frivolous and Weak Class Action Suits

Some observers of the class action worry that the settlement leverage created by class certification might pressure defendants to settle frivolous and weak class action suits. Commentators disagree about the precise magnitude of this risk. Some commentators believe it is at least serious enough to justify some kind of merits review at the certification stage (Bone and Evans 2002; Priest 1997). Others are more skeptical (Silver 2003).

Those who see a potentially serious problem point to several contributing factors, such as the way the class action magnifies stakes and complexity thereby compounding defendant's litigation, risk-bearing, and reputation costs (Bone and Evans 2002; see also Note 2005, discussing the effect of risk preferences on class action litigation). The judicial tendency to push for settlement only makes matters worse, as do cost and informational asymmetries (Coffee 1986) and the practice in federal court of reviewing the merits of class claims in only a very limited way (Bone and Evans 2002).[16]

---

[15] For a critical analysis of hypothetical consent arguments generally in procedure, see Bone (2003b).

[16] In recent years, some courts have been willing to investigate the merits more closely at the certification stage, although the inquiry is confined only to those merits issues relevant to certification standards. *See, e.g.*, In Re Hydrogen

4. The Special Case of the Settlement Class Action

The settlement class action is particularly susceptible to agency problems. In a settlement class action, the parties enter into a settlement before filing suit and file a class action not to litigate, but to obtain judicial approval of the settlement so they can bind the entire class. The most notorious examples of settlement class actions involve mass torts. In several highly publicized asbestos cases, defendants tried to use the settlement class action to obtain global peace by binding everyone, including those with future claims.

Coffee (1995, 2000) provides an extensive discussion of the agency problems and sweetheart settlement risks of mass tort settlement class actions. These include the incentives of class counsel to negotiate particularly large fees and the incentives of defendants to play lawyers off against one another in reverse auctions to obtain the most attractive settlement arrangement.

5. Reform Proposals

There are many reform proposals designed to improve the class action's cost-benefit balance. Some have been implemented; others are only suggestions. The following, while hardly comprehensive, discusses some of the more salient proposals.

5.1 Improving the Monitoring of Class Counsel

One set of proposals aims to reduce agency costs by improving the monitoring of class counsel. The Private Securities Litigation Reform Act (PSLRA) implements this approach for securities fraud class actions in federal court. After filing a securities class action, the would-be lead plaintiff must publish notice inviting other class members to apply for the lead plaintiff role. The district judge considers all the applicants and chooses as lead plaintiff the one "most capable of adequately representing the interests of class members." The PSLRA creates a presumption in favor of appointing the investor or group of investors with the "largest financial stake in the relief sought." Once appointed, the lead plaintiff selects and retains class counsel, sets the terms of the fee award, and (ideally) monitors counsel's performance throughout the litigation.

Securities fraud classes often include a few large institutional investors who have enough at stake to justify monitoring class counsel. The goal of the PSLRA is to attract these institutional investors to the role of lead

---

Peroxide Antitrust Litigation, 552 F.3d 305 (3d Cir. 2008); Initial Public Offering Securities Litigation, 471 F.3d 24 (2d Cir. 2006).

plaintiff, thereby improving the monitoring of class counsel. Weiss and Beckerman (1995) proposed this idea and Congress implemented it in the PSLRA.

Cox and Thomas (2006) review anecdotal and empirical evidence bearing on the success of the PSLRA in attracting institutional investors to the role of lead counsel. They find a very low (though increasing) rate of participation. They also find that institutional investors produce larger class settlements, which offers some support for an improved lead-plaintiff-as monitor approach. (See Choi (2011) for a review of the empirical literature and a study of the PSLRA's impact on agency costs.)

Silver and Dinkin (2008) explain why private institutional investors (as opposed to public and union funds) are reluctant to volunteer for the lead plaintiff role, and they propose compensation mechanisms, including a bidding scheme, to attract them.[17] Klement (2002) also proposes a bidding scheme to select the monitor, but in his proposal bidders do not have to be class members or involved in the class suit in any way other than as monitors. The winning bidder selects counsel and receives a percentage of the class recovery to compensate for its monitoring efforts.

5.2 *Bolstering Judicial Review of Class Settlements*

One way to guard against sweetheart settlements is to bolster trial judge review of proposed settlements. Reviewing settlements is problematic in part because no one in the litigation has an incentive to identify problems. Both class counsel and the defendant want the judge to approve the settlement. Absent class members can raise objections, but data show that they seldom take advantage of the opportunity (Eisenberg and Miller 2004a). Judges sometimes appoint a guardian *ad litem* to advocate on behalf of the class or a special master or court monitor to assist in settlement review. But compensation issues and other problems complicate these appointments, and there is at least some risk of collusion among the appointed agent, the defendant, and class counsel.

The Class Action Fairness Act implements a different approach. CAFA requires that the court inform public authorities of the pendency of a class

---

[17] Kobayashi and Ribstein (2004) discuss a special problem that arises when the attorney who prepares the complaint and initiates suit is not the attorney chosen as lead counsel. In such a case, the selected attorney is able to free ride on the efforts of the originating attorney, and this undermines *ex ante* incentives to investigate, research, and file class action suits. Kobayashi and Ribstein propose that the originating attorney receive special consideration in the appointment of lead or co-lead counsel and be compensated for his efforts by receiving a portion of the class fee.

80   *Procedural law and economics*

action settlement. This is supposed to facilitate the involvement of state and federal government officials, who can advocate for the public interest and the interests of the class.

5.3   Adjusting Fee Award Rules
There is a very large literature investigating fee award rules as a way to align the incentives of class counsel with the interests of the class and with the public interest in optimal deterrence.[18] Proposals abound. For example, Macey and Miller (1995) recommend that the fee award be calculated on a percentage-of-recovery basis, so counsel has an incentive to maximize class recovery. Hay and Rosenberg (2000) and Hay (1997b) propose a fee formula that equalizes the fee that class counsel expects from settling with the fee that he expects from going to trial. The idea is to eliminate the incentive to enter into sweetheart settlements by making it impossible to buy off the lawyer with a larger fee. Klement and Neeman (2004) use mechanism design theory to derive a fee schedule that awards a fixed percentage for recoveries above a specified threshold.

Some commentators have proposed auctioning the role of class counsel, and the auction approach has actually been used in a few securities class action cases. Prospective attorneys for the class submit bids with proposed fee schedules, and the judge chooses the lowest bidder subject to quality constraints. There are, however, serious problems with this approach. For a review of the cases and the critique, along with a novel auction proposal, see Harel and Stein (2004).

One particularly ambitious variant on the auction idea involves auctioning the entire class claim. Macey and Miller (1991) first proposed this idea for securities class actions and derivative litigation, and Macey and Miller (1995) generalize it to include mass tort class actions as well. The idea is to eliminate divided ownership and internalize the costs and benefits of litigation in the party who controls the lawsuit. Thomas and Hansen (1993) apply insights from auction theory to criticize this proposal.

5.4   Screening Frivolous or Weak Class Action Suits
There are several reform proposals specifically addressed to screening frivolous and weak class actions suits. One approach adopted by the PSLRA involves strengthening sanctions for frivolous filings. Another approach, tentatively suggested by Hensler and Rowe (2001), would apply a modified

---

[18]   For an empirical study of class action fee awards, see Eisenberg and Miller (2004b).

version of the British Rule to shift some portion of the winner's attorney's fee to the losing side.

A third approach would have the trial judge conduct a preliminary merits review at the class certification stage and grant certification only if the plaintiffs can demonstrate some significant probability of success on the merits (Bone and Evans 2002). Although this proposal is likely to increase process costs and erroneous denials of class certification, it will reduce erroneous grants and, according to its supporters, is likely to produce more benefits than costs.

The fourth proposal, by Hay and Rosenberg (2000), aims to reduce the effects of defendant risk aversion in pressuring settlement and attracting frivolous and weak class action suits. Hay and Rosenberg (2000) propose that the judge "hold multiple class trials and base its judgment on some suitable weighted combination of the class verdicts" (at 1382). This approach reduces the defendant's risk-bearing costs by avoiding the all-or-nothing quality of a single class trial.

Bibliography

Alexander, Janet Cooper, *Do the Merits Matter? A Study of Settlements in Securities Class Actions*, 43 STAN. L. REV. 497 (1991).

Alexander, Janet Cooper, *Contingent Fees and Class Actions*, 47 DEPAUL L. REV. 347 (1998).

Bernstein, Roger, *Judicial Economy and Class Actions*, 7 J. LEGAL STUD. 349 (1978).

Bohn, James and Stephen Choi, *Fraud in the New Issues Market: Empirical Evidence on Securities Class Actions*, 14 U. PA. L. REV. 903 (1996).

Bone, Robert G., *Personal and Impersonal Litigative Forms: Reconceiving the History of Adjudicative Representation*, 70 B.U. L. REV. 213 (1990).

Bone, Robert G., *Rule 23 Redux: Empowering the Federal Class Action*, 14 REV. LITIG. 79 (1994).

Bone, Robert G., THE ECONOMICS OF CIVIL PROCEDURE 259–98 (2003a).

Bone, Robert G., *Agreeing to Fair Process: The Problem with Contractarian Theories of Procedural Fairness*, 53 B.U. L. REV. 485 (2003b).

Bone, Robert G. and David S. Evans, *Class Certification and the Substantive Merits*, 51 DUKE L.J. 1251 (2002).

Borenstein, Severin, *Settling for Coupons: Discount Contracts as Compensation and Punishment in Antitrust Lawsuits*, 39 J.L. & ECON. 379 (1996).

Che, Yeon-Koo, *Equilibrium Formation of Class Action Suits*, 62 J. PUBL. ECON. 339 (1996).

Che, Yeon-Koo, *The Economics of Collective Negotiations in Pre-Trial Bargaining*, 43 INT'L ECON. REV. 549 (2002).

Choi, Stephen J., *Motions for Lead Plaintiff in Securities Class Actions*, 40 J. LEG. STUD. 205 (2011).

Coffee, John C., Jr., *Understanding the Plaintiff's Attorney: The Implications of Economic Theory for Private Enforcement of Law Through Class and Derivative Actions*, 86 COLUM. L. REV 669 (1986).

Coffee, John C., Jr., *The Regulation of Entrepreneurial Litigation: Balancing Fairness and Efficiency in the Large Class Action*, 54 U. CHI. L. REV. 877 (1987).

Coffee, John C., Jr., *Class Wars: The Dilemma of the Mass Tort Class Action*, 95 COLUM. L. REV. 1343 (1995).

Coffee, John C., Jr., *Class Action Accountability: Reconciling Exit, Voice, and Loyalty in Representative Litigation*, 100 COLUM. L. REV. 370 (2000).

Cohen, George, *The "Fair" is the Enemy of the Good: Ortiz v. Fibreboard Corporation and Class Action Settlements*, 8 SUP. CT. ECON. REV. 23 (2000).
Cox, James D. and Randall S. Thomas with Dana Kiku, *Does the Plaintiff Matter: An Empirical Analysis of Lead Plaintiffs in Securities Class Actions*, 106 COLUM. L. REV. 1587 (2006).
Dam, Kenneth W., *Class Actions: Efficiency, Compensation, Deterrence, and Conflict of Interest*, 4 J. LEGAL STUD. 47 (1975).
Dana, David, *Adequacy of Representation after Stephenson: A Rawlsian/Behavioral Economics Approach to Class Action Settlements*, 55 EMORY L.J. 279 (2006).
Dewees, Donald N., J. Robert, S. Pritchard and Michael J. Trebilcock, *An Economic Analysis of Cost and Fee Rules for Class Actions*, 10 J. LEGAL STUD. 155 (1981).
Durand, Anna L., *Note, An Economic Analysis of Fluid Class Recovery Mechanisms*, 34 STAN. L. REV. 173 (1981).
Edelman, Paul H., Richard A. Nagareda and Charles Silver, *The Allocation Problem in Multiple-Claimant Representations* 14 SUP. CT. ECON. REV. 95 (2006).
Eisenberg, Theodore and Geoffrey Miller, *The Role of Opt-Outs and Objectors in Class Action Litigation: Theoretical and Empirical Issues*, 57 VAND. L. REV. 1529 (2004a).
Eisenberg, Theodore and Geoffrey Miller, *Attorney Fees in Class Action Settlements: An Empirical Study*, 1 J. EMPIR. LEGAL STUD. 27 (2004b).
Eisenberg, Theodore and Geoffrey Miller, *Incentive Awards to Class Action Plaintiffs: An Empirical Study*, 53 UCLA L. REV. 1303 (2006).
Erichson, Howard M., *Informal Aggregation: Procedural and Ethical Implications of Coordination among Counsel in Related Lawsuits*, 50 DUKE L.J. 381 (2000).
Friedman, David, *More Justice for Less Money*, 39 J.L. & ECON. 211 (1996).
Garth, Bryant, *Civil Litigation through the Class Action*, 62 IND. L. J. 497 (1987).
Garth, Bryant, Eileen Nagel and Sheldon Plager, *The Institution of the Private Attorney General: Perspectives from an Empirical Study of Class Action Litigation*, 61 S. CAL. L. REV. 353 (1988).
Gilles, Myriam and Gary Friedman, *Exploding the Class Action Agency Costs Myth: The Social Utility of Entrepreneurial Lawyers*, 155 U. PA. L. REV 103 (2006).
Hamdani, Assaf and Alon Klement, *The Class Defense*, 93 CAL. L. REV. 685 (2005).
Harel, Alon and Alex Stein, *Auctioning for Loyalty: Selection and Monitoring of Class Counsel*, 22 YALE L. & POL'Y REV. 69 (2004).
Hartman, Raymond and Michael J. Doane, *The Use of Hedonic Analysis for Certification and Damage Calculations in Class Action Complaints*, 3 J.L. ECON. & ORG. 351 (1987).
Hay, Bruce L., *Asymmetric Rewards: Why Class Actions (May) Settle for Too Little*, 48 HASTINGS L.J. 479 (1997a).
Hay, Bruce L., *The Theory of Fee Regulation in Class Action Settlements*, 46 AM. U. L. REV. 1429 (1996).
Hay, Bruce L. and David Rosenberg, *"Sweetheart" and "Blackmail" Settlements in Class Actions: Reality and Remedy*, 75 NOTRE DAME L. REV. 1377 (2000).
Helland, Eric and Jonathan Klick, *The Effect of Judicial Expedience on Attorney Fees in Class Actions*, 36 J. LEGAL STUD. 171 (2007).
Hensler, Deborah R., Nicholas M. Pace, Bonita Dombey-Moore, Beth Giddens, Jennifer Gross and Erik K. Moller, CLASS ACTION DILEMMAS: PURSUING PUBLIC GOALS FOR PRIVATE GAIN (2000).
Hensler, Deborah R. and Thomas D. Rowe, Jr., *Beyond "It Just Ain't Worth It": Alternative Strategies for Damage Class Action Reform*, 64 LAW & CONTEMP. PROBS. 137 (Spring/ Summer 2001).
Johnson, John and Gregory K. Leonard, *Economics and the Rigorous Analysis of Class Certification in Antitrust Cases*, 3 J. COMPETITION L. & ECON. 341 (2007).
Kalven, Harry, Jr. and Maurice Rosenfeld, *The Contemporary Function of the Class Suit*, 8 U. CHI. L. REV. 684 (1941).
Klement, Alon, *Who Should Guard the Guardians? A New Approach for Monitoring Class Action Lawyers*, 21 REV. LITIG. 25 (2002).

Klement, Alon and Zvika Neeman, *Incentive Structures for Class Action Lawyers*, 20 J.L. ECON. & ORG. 102 (2004).
Kobayashi, Bruce A. and Larry E. Ribstein, *Class Action Lawyers as Lawmakers*, 46 ARIZ. L. REV. 733 (2004).
Kornhauser, Lewis A., *Control of Conflicts of Interest in Class-Action Suits*, 41 PUB. CHOICE 145 (1983).
Leslie, Christopher, *The Significance of Silence: Collective Action Problems and Class Action Settlements*, 59 FLA. L. REV. 71 (2007).
Lynk, William J., *The Court and the Market: An Economic Analysis of Contingent Fees in Class-Action Litigation*, 19 J. LEGAL STUD. 247 (1990).
Macey, Jonathan R. and Geoffrey P. Miller, *The Plaintiff's Attorney's Role in Class Action and Derivative Litigation: Economic Analysis and Recommendations for Reform*, 58 U. CHI L. REV. 1 (1991).
Macey, Jonathan R. and Geoffrey P. Miller, *A Market Approach to Tort Reform via Rule 23*, 80 CORNELL L. REV. 909 (1995).
Marceau, Nicolas and Steve Mongrain, *Damage Averaging and the Formation of Class Action Suits*, 23 INT'L. REV. L. & ECON 63 (2003).
Miller, Arthur R., *Of Frankenstein Monsters and Shining Knights: Myth, Reality and the "Class Action" Problem*, 92 HARV. L. REV 664 (1979).
Miller, Geoffrey P., *Some Agency Problems in Settlement*, 16 J. LEGAL. STUD. 189 (1987).
Miller, Geoffrey P., *Overlapping Class Actions*, 71 N.Y.U. L. REV 514 (1996).
Miller, Geoffrey P., *Competing Bids in Class Action Settlements*, 31 HOFSTRA L. REV. 633 (2003a).
Miller, Geoffrey P., *Conflicts of Interest in Class Action Litigation: An Inquiry into the Appropriate Standard*, 2003 U. CHI. LEGAL. F. 581 (2003b).
Miller, Geoffrey P., *Review of the Merits in Class Action Certification*, 33 HOFSTRA L. REV. 51 (2004).
Miller, Geoffrey P. and Lori Singer, *Nonpecuniary Class Action Settlements*, 60 LAW & CONTEMP. PROBS. 97 (Autumn 1997).
Morawetz, Nancy, *Bargaining, Representation and Fairness*, 54 OHIO ST. L.J. 1 (1993).
Note, *The Rule 23(b)(3) Class Action: An Empirical Study*, 62 GEO. L.J. 1123 (1974).
Note, *Locating Investment Asymmetries and Optimal Deterrence in the Mass Tort Class Action*, 117 HARV. L. REV. 2665 (2004).
Note, *Risk-preference Asymmetries in Class Action Litigation*, 119 HARV. L. REV. 587 (2005).
Polinsky, A. Mitchell and Daniel L. Rubinfeld, *The Deadweight Loss of Coupon Remedies for Price Overcharges*, 56 J. INDUS. ECON. 402 (2008).
Priest, George L., *Procedural versus Substantive Controls of Mass Tort Class Actions*, 26 J. LEGAL STUD. 521 (1997).
Resnik, Judith, Dennis Curtis and Deborah Hensler, *Individuals within the Aggregate: Relationships, Representation, and Fees*, 71 N.Y.U. L. REV. 296 (1996).
Rosenberg, David, *Class Actions for Mass Torts: Doing Individual Justice by Collective Means*, 62 IND. L.J. 561 (1987).
Rosenberg, David, *Mass Tort Class Actions: What Defendants Have and Plaintiffs Don't*, 37 HARV. J. ON LEGIS. 393 (2000).
Rosenberg, David, *Avoiding Duplicative Litigation of Similar Claims: The Superiority of Class Action vs. Collateral Estoppel vs. Standard Claims Market*, Harvard Law School, Public Law Research Paper No. 44; Harvard Law and Economics Discussion Paper No. 394 (2002a).
Rosenberg, David, *Mandatory-Litigation Class Action: The Only Option for Mass Tort Cases*, 115 HARV. L. REV. 831 (2002b).
Rosenberg, David and James P. Sullivan, *Coordinating Private Class Action and Public Agency Enforcement of Antitrust Law*, 2 J. COMP. L. & ECON. 159 (2006).
Rosenfield, Andrew, *An Empirical Test of Class Action Settlements*, 5 J. LEGAL STUD. 113 (1976).

Rowe, Thomas D., *Beyond the Class Action Rule: An Inventory of Statutory Possibilities to Improve the Federal Class Action*, 71 N.Y.U. L. REV. 186 (1996).
Rubenstein, William, *Why Enable Litigation?: A Positive Externalities Theory of the Small Claims Class Action*, 74 UMKC L. REV. 709 (2006).
Silver, Charles, *"We're Scared to Death": Class Certification and Blackmail*, 78 N.Y.U. L. REV. 1357 (2003).
Silver, Charles and Sam Dinkin, *Incentivizing Institutional Investors to Serve as Lead Plaintiffs in Securities Fraud Class Actions*, 57 DEPAUL L. REV. 471 (2008).
Thomas, Randall and Robert Hansen, *Auctioning Class Action and Derivative Lawsuits: A Critical Analysis*, 87 NW. U. L. REV. 423 (1993).
Weiss, Elliott J. and John S. Beckerman, *Let the Money Do the Monitoring: How Institutional Investors Can Reduce Agency Costs in Securities Class Actions*, 104 YALE L.J. 2053 (1995).
Willging, Thomas E., Laural L. Hooper and Robert J. Niemic, EMPIRICAL STUDY OF CLASS ACTIONS IN FOUR FEDERAL DISTRICT COURTS: FINAL REPORT TO THE ADVISORY COMMITTEE ON CIVIL RULES (Federal Judicial Center, 1996).
Wright, Gerald A. *The Cost Internalization Case for Class Actions*, 21 STAN. L. REV. 383 (1969).
Yeazell, Stephen, FROM MEDIEVAL GROUP LITIGATION TO THE MODERN CLASS ACTION (1987).
Yeazell, Stephen, *Collective Litigation as Collective Action*, 43 U. ILL. L. REV. 43 (1989).

5 Conflict of laws and choice of law
Erin O'Hara O'Connor and Larry E. Ribstein

1. Introduction

When a legal dispute involves parties, property or events located in more than one government jurisdiction, and the substantive laws of those jurisdictions differ, whose substantive laws govern the rights and obligations of the parties? As barriers to migration and trade between jurisdictions fall, choice of law increasingly complicates transaction and litigation planning and provides new opportunities for private ordering.

Until approximately fifty years ago, all courts in the United States applied the territorial rules roughly embodied in the First Restatement of Conflicts when they resolved inter-jurisdictional disputes. The rules, which address most litigation subjects, are premised on a 'vested rights' theory. A party's rights vest, if at all, at a particular place and point in time. Only that state has the power to create the rights relied on by the plaintiff (Beale, 1935; Brilmayer, 1995). Tort issues, for example, are governed by the law of the 'place of the wrong', which is defined for a variety of tortious activities. Contract validity, necessary forms, and substantial performance issues are treated according to the law of the place of contracting, while details of performance are governed by the place of performance. Property issues are resolved according to the law of the *situs* of the property (Restatement (First) Conflict of Laws, 1934). Accordingly, although an interstate dispute is litigated in a Massachusetts court, the court might apply the substantive law of another state to resolve that dispute.

Several decades ago, however, conflicts scholars began increasingly to criticize the territorial approach to choice of law. The First Restatement Rules were condemned as arbitrary (Brilmayer, 1995). Indeed, conflicts scholars searched the case law for places where the choice of law under the First Restatement led to intuitively unsatisfying results (Cavers, 1933; Currie, 1958a, 1958b; Ehrenzweig, 1956). Tort immunities as applied to common domiciliaries is one such place (Ely, 1981). Under the First Restatement, a husband's ability to recover for an injury caused by his wife's negligence while they were on vacation in another state is governed by the law of the place of the injury, even though the marital domicile is the only state which really has an interest in compensating this husband or preserving this family's harmony. As another example, some have advocated a place-of-sale rule for products liability cases to better enable manufacturers to charge customers for the varying standards of care and liability levels present in differing places. Because products can be moved anywhere, the First Restatement's place-of-injury rule ends up causing customers in states with lesser tort protections to help pay for the increased tort protections of customers in other states (Kozyris, 1987; McConnell, 1988; O'Hara and Ribstein, 1997; Solimine, 1989).

Defenders of the First Restatement dismissed these occasional unsatisfying results and instead focused on the general benefits of rules. Rules promote predictability, uniformity, ease of application, and judicial restraint, while discouraging forum-shopping (Reese, 1972; Rosenberg, 1968). In reality, however, a number of 'escape devices' sometimes enabled courts to avoid First Restatement rules. One method found in every rule-based system is characterization (North and Fawcett, 1992): how the forum court characterized a case, as one of tort or contract for example, determines the choice of law. Where ambiguities arose, judges were free to choose a more preferred governing law. In addition, a public policy exception in the First Restatement permitted courts to avoid applying any foreign law that violated the public policy of the forum. Critics argued that these and other escape devices deprived the First Restatement rules of the very benefits they purported to confer (Brilmayer, 1995). As discussed later in this section, however, subsequent empirical studies cast some doubt on the strength of critics' claims.

In any event, critics argued that courts should replace the rule-based approach with a more sensible basis for choosing governing law. As detailed later in this section, some advocated maximizing the ability of states to give effect to important policies, while others promoted the use of the better or more 'progressive' states' laws. Still others proffered personal rights-based approaches to choice of law. Most of the critics favored standard over rule-based approaches. As a consequence of widespread First Restatement criticism, a significant majority of US state courts have abandoned the traditional approach in favor of one of several alternative approaches to choice of law. As of 2009, only fourteen US states purported to follow the First Restatement in the areas of torts, contracts, or both (Symeonides, 2009), and each of the others has adopted one of at least four alternative approaches. Consensus has clearly disappeared.

Part A will consider four questions regarding choice of law when the parties have not effectively chosen their governing law by contract. First, why do courts ever apply anything other than the law of the forum? Second, if a court sometimes applies foreign law, is a rule-based or standard-based approach to its choice preferable? Third, why have so many states abandoned rule-based approaches in favor of standard-based ones? Finally, is there any real practical difference between the First

Restatement and modern approaches? After all, if the standard-based choices do not differ systematically in practice from the First Restatement, the academic debate seems irrelevant. Moving to contractual choice of law, Part B discusses the costs and benefits of enforcing parties' choice of law. Permitting parties to choose the governing law that best fits their transactions and future private disputes can enhance jurisdictional competition and help restore predictability to the conflicts of law problem. On the other hand, enabling party choice can hinder legitimate state efforts to regulate conduct. We propose allowing party choice except when legislatures pass statutes specifically limiting the enforcement of choice-of-law clauses in a given context.

As indicated in this Introduction, we focus on choice of law by US states. The same basic economic principles apply, of course, to international choice of law. Although a detailed examination is beyond the scope of this chapter, we note some international comparisons and implications at relevant points in our chapter. We also note at the outset that choice of law within the US may have very different implications from choice of law in Europe given legal harmonization under European Community directives and regulations (O'Hara and Ribstein, 2008).

Nor do we discuss arbitration. An arbitration clause in an agreement is a type of forum selection. The choice of law governing the agreement may be as significant as choice of law in other contexts. On the other hand, the arbitrator may not be bound to apply any specific body of law, especially under the European approach of 'de-localised' arbitration (Dicey, 1980: pp. 583–5). On the other hand, arbitration enhances party choice because arbitrators typically are obligated to apply the law chosen by contracting parties (Ware, 1999; O'Hara and Ribstein, 2009).

A. THE CONFLICT OF LAWS PROBLEM

2. Forum Law: The Costs and Benefits

Forum law has at least two efficiency advantages over applying foreign law. First, it is easier to ascertain. Because the judges and lawyers who are licensed to practice in the jurisdiction have previously made significant capital investments learning the details of forum law, the costs of applying that law to any given case are generally lower than the alternatives. Second, the precedent created by applying forum law provides valuable information to primary actors as well as courts and litigators regarding future legal treatment of the issues. In contrast, an investment in foreign law is less valuable locally because foreign precedent is less binding and therefore less important in guiding local conduct or judicial decisions (Thiel, 1996).

An interesting question thus arises: why should a court ever apply the laws of another state? One reason is to enhance predictability. If actors can rely on the application of the law of a particular state, they can structure transactions and other activities and avoid inappropriate or inefficient laws. This, in turn, forces states to internalize the costs of inferior laws, thereby promoting competition among jurisdictions for more efficient substantive rules (O'Hara and Ribstein, 1997). *Ex ante* reliance on Delaware corporations law, for example, is only attainable if New York courts commit themselves to applying Delaware law to the internal affairs of a Delaware corporation. A *lex fora* approach to choice of law therefore impedes pre-litigation predictability. Conflicts scholars have, however, questioned the benefits of predictability by doubting whether people respond to differing legal standards in such contexts as accidents and child abuse (Sterk, 1994; Symposium, 1997). If governing laws do not provide marginal deterrent value in these contexts, then *ex ante* predictability is not sufficiently valuable to justify the increased costs of applying foreign law. On the other hand, empirical evidence indicates that governing tort standards do affect aggregate behavior (Bruce, 1984; Landes, 1982; Landes and Posner, 1987). In particular, repeat players, including manufacturers and insurance companies, pay careful attention to differing laws. Moreover, the actual uncertainty created when the plaintiff can forum shop for the applicable law is debatable. Actors can predict that disputes will likely be governed by the most plaintiff-favoring law in the set of possible fora for disputes. And, even if parties cannot be certain which forum will ultimately be chosen, in the event of litigation they can proceed with probabilistic expectations. Although the outcome of a plaintiff's forum shopping law may not be very predictable *ex ante* in many circumstances, it is often not clearly less predictable than anticipating what law a court will apply under default choice-of-law standards which, as discussed below, can be vague and open-ended.

Another disadvantage to a forum law rule is that it encourages forum shopping which can produce inefficiencies. Differing substantive laws create disparities across jurisdictions regarding plaintiffs' expected gains from litigation. Forum shopping is generally regarded as skewing the litigation process toward plaintiffs and distributing litigation unevenly across jurisdictions (Sterk, 1994). Jurisdictions with more plaintiff-favoring laws or procedures (LoPucki, 2005) end up being swamped with litigation, while lawyers in states with relatively more defendant-protecting laws and procedures face a lower demand for their services.

A third reason for applying foreign law is to take advantage of foreign jurisdictions' comparative regulatory advantages (Posner, 1992; O'Hara and Ribstein, 1997). Suppose, for example, that a South Carolina driver collides with a Florida driver in New York City. Presumably New York adopts traffic and tort laws to encourage an optimal level of care in New York. If a defendant is sued in South Carolina and the court applies South Carolina traffic and tort laws to the suit, then the effectiveness of New York's laws are watered down, given that drivers from all over the country traverse the streets of New York. If everyone is subject to New York standards of liability, then New York can better tinker with its own laws to encourage the standard of care it seeks.

Brilmayer (1995: 15) describes the tendency of courts across the world to sometimes consider foreign law as 'virtually universal'. In the US, only two states, Kentucky and Michigan, explicitly embrace a *lex fora* approach (Solimine, 1989). Indeed, the United States Supreme Court has held that application of forum law is unconstitutional if the forum has no substantial interest or connection to the litigation (*Home Insurance Co. v. Dick*). This result is supported by our conclusion that the benefits of predictability, regulatory efforts and jurisdictional competition probably outweigh the costs of applying forum law in many interstate contexts.

3. Rule versus Standard-Based Approaches

Assuming that a court should sometimes apply foreign law, should choice-of-law decisions be based on rules or a standard? Rules provide predictability, enhance planning and help ensure uniform treatment of similarly situated litigants. In contrast, standards are often better at generating just results in individual cases. Because the costs of overdeterrence and underdeterrence can differ according to the context, rules may be preferable in some areas, while standards may be preferable in others.

As mentioned earlier, the First Restatement rules seemed arbitrary in some contexts. But does a standard-based approach improve choice of law overall? And if a standard-based approach is preferable, what should the governing standard be? States that have abandoned the First Restatement have usually adopted one of three alternative standards: (1) Leflar's 'better law'; (2) interest analysis; or (3) the 'most significant relationship' test. Leflar (1966a, 1966b) says that courts should give significant weight to the 'better law' when faced with the choice, and the better law is generally the one that achieves the most justice, which is courts' primary obligation.

Interest analysts advocate that choice of law should advance state policies behind their laws. Each state thinks its laws are 'better' in general. Consequently, courts should determine which states have an interest in applying their laws to this dispute, given the domiciles of the parties and the location of property and events leading to litigation. As originally conceived by Brainard Currie, states intend to protect or compensate only their own domiciliaries with their laws, not foreign residents. And a state has a regulatory interest in conduct occurring only within its borders. Currie argued that the forum always should apply its own law when it is 'interested' in the outcome of the dispute. If no state has an interest in the outcome, the forum should still apply its own law because it is cheaper than applying foreign law. Foreign law should be applied only when the foreign state is interested and the forum state is disinterested (Currie, 1959). Baxter (1963), offered an alternative 'balance of state interests' approach. Under this approach, courts should use interest analysis to maximize the joint effectuation of state policies. If two or more states are 'interested' in the outcome of a dispute, a court should determine which state stands to lose most if its policies are ignored, and then apply the law of that state. In other words, in the face of a conflict, Baxter proposed that courts minimize social costs, as those costs are perceived by the individual interested states.

The drafters of the Second Restatement took a third approach. They concluded that courts should apply the law of the state with 'the most significant relationship' to the parties, property and events involved in the dispute. In making this determination, courts should consider a number of factors, including 'the needs of the interstate and international systems'; 'the relevant policies of the forum'; 'the relevant policies of other interested states and the relative interests of those states in the determination of the particular issue'; 'the protection of justified expectations'; 'the basic policies underlying the particular field of law'; 'certainty, predictability and uniformity of result'; and 'ease in the determination and application of the law to be applied' (Restatement (Second) Conflict of Laws, 1971). This test approach is similar to the 'most significant relationship' test used in Europe, except that the latter provides somewhat more guidance in selecting the applicable jurisdiction (Scoles and Hay, 1992: 45–7).

Each of the three standards used in American courts has significant problems. Leflar's approach allows judges significant leeway for application of outcome-determinative choice-of-law rules. Moreover, judges' varying preferences undermine predictability. The same can be said of the Second Restatement test, which gives no indication of how much weight to give to each of the numerous factors (Brilmayer, 1995).

Interest analysis is more complicated. The narrow range of state interests recognized by Currie fails adequately to promote the purported goal of the standard. A state's substantive goals reach far beyond compensating its plaintiffs or protecting its defendants. Often a state is attempting to achieve a sensitive balance between competing interests. Viewing the state's interests behind its substantive laws ignores important choice-of-law concerns such as protecting party expectations and interstate harmony and preventing forum shopping (Brilmayer, 1980). On the other hand, while modern interest analysts advocate considering the state's true interests behind its laws (Kramer, 1990, 1991a, 1991b), this reduces any predictability the approach might otherwise provide (Brilmayer, 1995) since many factors can motivate state decision making. Moreover, the idea of state interests becomes problematic from a public choice perspective (O'Hara and Ribstein, 1997). States are not monolithic entities. Individual legislators vote for very different reasons, and the state government officials, including judges, who influence the application of the laws have their own concerns. Interest groups that lobby for laws are often trying to achieve purposes very different from the 'public policies' stated by the legislators themselves.

Baxter's comparative impairment approach to interest analysis further complicates the choice. Baxter advocates applying the law of the state with the most to lose if its laws are ignored. However, this calculation is often impossible. Suppose, for example, that two states have interests in applying their laws to a contract dispute. Under State A's laws, spendthrifts can void their contracts. Under State B's laws, spendthrifts contracts are enforceable against the spendthrifts. C, a spendthrift from State A, borrows money from D, a creditor from State B. C fails to repay the loan and D sues to enforce the loan contract. Under interest analysis, State B has an 'interest' in compensating its creditor, while State A has an interest in protecting its spendthrift. Which state's policy suffers greater impairment if its laws are ignored? If such conflicts arise frequently, at least one of the states necessarily will end up having difficulty protecting its residents (Allen and O'Hara, 1999).

The standard-based approaches have proved unsatisfying. A better solution might be to retain the First Restatement rules with periodic modifications to avoid frequent arbitrary results. Indeed, Posner (1992) has argued that the First Restatement, for all its faults, had the virtue of enabling states to exercise their comparative regulatory advantages. For example, by defining and then applying the 'place of the wrong' to tort suits, states usually could apply their laws to tortious conduct within their states, and could therefore ensure that actors took optimal levels of care. The First Restatement *situs* rule for property enabled the state where the land was located to regulate its use. Title questions are also resolved by the law of the place of property, a clear rule easing the tracking of titles and therefore facilitating the transfer of property to its highest valued use. Finally, contract validity issues are governed by the place of contracting, and the detailed rules tended to protect those who contract within their own borders. Those who reached across borders were on notice of being subject to the differing protections outside their states. The rule minimized the costs of gathering personal and legal information for those, such as consumers, who transacted business locally. Details of performance were governed by the state with the greatest regulatory concern, where those details were to be performed.

The choice between rules and standards also may be viewed from a contractual perspective. Part B, below, discusses the enforcement of express choice-of-law clauses. A related issue is the appropriate default rules to supply in the absence of express contract in order to facilitate private bargaining. Standards provide 'tailored' defaults that fit specific situations, while rules provide 'untailored' defaults that apply across a range of cases (Ayres, 1993). In general, untailored rules can reduce contracting costs by decreasing uncertainty as to the rule applied in the absence of contracting. Tailored defaults, by attempting to anticipate the parties' actual preferences, can reduce the need for costly customized contracting (Whincop and Keyes, 1998a: 525–6). But untailored *choice-of-law* rules, because they only choose legal systems rather than specific rules, may actually do a good job of anticipating the parties' preferences in the usual case, as distinguished from the odd cases courts actually decide (Whincop and Keyes, 2001, Ch. 3).

Any choice-of-law approach should take into account concerns for harmonizing state interests, protecting party expectations, minimizing costs of legal information, as well as allowing states to exercise their comparative regulatory advantages. But a rule-based system under which the drafters take these concerns into account to the extent feasible also could promote uniformity and thereby minimize forum shopping. Compared to the standard-based alternatives that have received court attention, the First Restatement likely provides much greater predictability despite its escape devices, and would be even better if these devices were narrowed.

4. Coordination Problems with Rule-Based Approaches

If the First Restatement approach to choice of law is so superior, why have most states abandoned it? In other words, why have the states been unable in recent decades to coordinate choice of law to achieve increased uniformity and predictability? Unless the states collectively adopt or retain choice-of-law rules, the primary benefits of those rules are lost. A few conflicts scholars have advocated a return to a rule-based approach that would yield net benefits across states, perhaps with legislative encoding of a new Restatement to foster cooperation (Rosenberg, 1981; Scoles and Hay, 1992). But individual rules do not always benefit the state or judge that is supposed to follow them, and interstate enforcement problems may have led to the breakdown of choice-of-law rules. In other words, courts face an unresolved prisoner's dilemma in the choice-of-law context.

In general, as the late Judge Breitel once explained in an unpublished speech (Sterk, 1994), judges first ask themselves who deserves to win. Then they assess how much cost to jurisprudence is likely imposed if they manipulate the system to get that outcome. If costs will be borne by future worthy litigants, judges will apply rules with less preferred outcomes for the present litigants. In other words, future litigants constrain judges in the present case to a general application of rules, including procedural ones. Judges who are nevertheless tempted to violate the precedents of other judges are constrained by reputational sanctions imposed by colleagues and higher courts (O'Hara, 1993).

But choice of law is different. Issues arise in many factual contexts involving people and events from different places, and sufficiently infrequently that the specific issue seldom arises again. Because the precedential value of a given choice-of-law decision is quite limited, costs to future litigants of reduced predictability in that factual context are slight. And colleagues and higher courts are much less likely to attempt to vigilantly protect choice-of-law precedents than they are to protect precedents that shape forum substantive law.

Even if rules are generally preferred to standards, formulating a comprehensive set that leaves all states better off than they are under choice-of-law anarchy might prove difficult to formulate (Sterk, 1994). Perhaps more importantly, judges are always tempted to defect from individual rules in favor of local litigants (Hay, 1992), or to apply more easily ascertained local laws. While other states may suffer as a consequence, they are unlikely to pressure the deciding state to prevent these defections. The classic tit-for-tat enforcement strategies (Axelrod, 1984) would be difficult to implement, especially because monitoring of other states' choice-of-law decisions is costly. Even with monitoring, escape devices allow states in some contexts to defect while feigning cooperation under the rules. When defections are difficult to detect, enforcement becomes much more difficult, and bargains are likely to unravel for at least a while (Friedman, 1971; Green and Porter, 1984). Moreover, it might be years before an interstate dispute arises in the disadvantaged state enabling retaliation against the state that originally defected. Larger plaintiff-favoring states, which were the first to abandon the First Restatement, have more opportunity to defect because they handle a larger volume of interstate litigation.

In a few areas where cooperation among the states really matters, interstate compacts have been formed on a piecemeal basis. For example, state taxation of corporations and child custody disputes are now treated with relatively uniform choice-of-law provisions. Where cooperation is important but has proven unsuccessful, Congress can step in and federalize the substantive law, as it has done, for example, regarding both bankruptcy and products liability for vaccine manufacturers. For better or worse, choice-of-law problems are mooted once the federal government imposes uniform federal laws. Finally, private parties can enhance predictability and uniformity to some extent with choice-of-law provisions in their contracts (Kobayashi and Ribstein, 1998). What is left may not be worth coordinating, at least on the grand scale of a new Restatement.

Some coordination may persist in smaller rural states. The First Restatement states are clustered together in the south, including Maryland, Virginia, West Virginia, Tennessee, Alabama, North Carolina, South Carolina and Georgia (Solimine, 1989). These states share a relatively distinct economy and culture that may limit a majority of interactions to people and events in one of the other First Restatement states, perhaps enhancing cooperation. Alternatively, coordination in these states may have more to do with a shared conservative legal culture. In any event, it is not surprising that the First Restatement broke down across a majority of states as legal realism permeated the law, beginning with the larger, plaintiff-favoring states. The benefits to achieving preferred results in individual cases outweighed the costs to individual judges' preferences of ignoring the settled choice-of-law rules.

5. Do the Choice-of-Law Approaches Matter in Practice?

The academic debate over choice of law loses relevance if court decisions do not vary significantly under the alternative regimes. Some commentators have suggested that the approaches to choice of law followed within the US make no difference in the end. Sterk (1994), for example, argues that courts care about ensuring that deserving parties win their cases. In contrast, the choice-of-law theorists concern themselves with a host of issues that do not concern the courts. The courts therefore cannot be expected to take any of the approaches seriously. In fact, Leflar (1977) points out his casual impression that courts often make a choice-of-law determination, and then rely on the choice-of-law theories that support the court's conclusion.

Even assuming that each state is committed to a single choice-of-law approach, systematic differences in chosen law between the modern approaches might be difficult to detect, if the modern approaches leave judges effectively unconstrained. One might predict, then, that results differ between First Restatement states and states adopting modern approaches, but not among states that have adopted each of the modern approaches. Alternatively, if First Restatement escape devices also leave judges unconstrained, then no differences among states would be found based on choice-of-law approach. It has also been suggested that the modern approaches are more pro-resident, pro-forum, and pro-recovery in principle than the relatively neutral First Restatement (Brilmayer, 1980) and that, because each of the modern approaches rests on theoretically distinct grounds, some of the modern approaches display these biases more than others (Borchers, 1992).

Three empirical papers have attempted to test for systematic differences across states according to choice-of-law approaches for torts. Solimine (1989) studied 227 cases retrieved from a Westlaw computer search of all published US state supreme court and federal court of appeal cases that explicitly reviewed choice-of-law determinations in torts. He compared those decisions made according to the First Restatement with those decided according to one of the modern theories. Solimine found that the modern theories resulted in choices of law that were more likely to favor residents, recovery and forum law than did the First Restatement.

It may seem surprising that Solimine would find differences across jurisdictions, at least with regard to recovery-favoring rules. After all, Priest and Klein (1984) demonstrated convincingly that disputes that are actually litigated are biased toward those that are on the margin. Plaintiff win rates should tend toward 50 percent. Even if they vary due to asymmetric information or stakes, win rates should not vary systematically across courts. But choice-of-law questions might be sufficiently inexpensive and preliminary in the litigation process that results may vary at the margin across jurisdictions.

Borchers (1992) followed with a more extensive study, and ascertained confidence intervals to test the significance of variations across choice-of-law methodologies. Borchers classified each state by choice-of-law approach, and then collected 800 published state and federal cases, including those reported at both the trial and appellate level. In the First Restatement states, he retrieved every case found on-line from 1960. In the modern approach states, he retrieved all cases found subsequent to the shift in methodology. Borchers attempted to ascertain the differences both between the First Restatement and modern states as a group and among the specific methodologies applied in the modern states. When the modern states taken together were compared with the First Restatement states, Borchers' results confirmed Solimine's. The modern approach states were significantly more pro-recovery, resident and forum favoring in their choice of laws. However, Borchers found essentially no statistically significant variations across the modern approaches. He found significant variation only with respect to recovery-favoring rules. The Second Restatement and Leflar states were statistically distinguishable from each other, with the Leflar states generating more recovery-favoring outcomes. Borchers' results were seriously qualified, however, by the fact that neither the Second Restatement nor the Leflar states produced choices statistically distinguishable from interest analysis. Borchers concluded (p. 379),

'Courts do not take the new approaches seriously. Because all of the competitors to the First Restatement start from different analytic premises, if courts were faithful to their tenets they would inevitably generate different result patterns. Yet in practice the outcomes are largely indistinguishable.'

Thiel (1996), a trained econometrician, criticized Borchers' methodology for lacking a regression analysis that could control for legal culture. Pro-recovery and pro-plaintiff results can come partly from the modern choice-of-law approach, but could also be affected by systematic differences in the general legal culture of the First Restatement and modern approach states. At the same time, the states that have adopted the same choice-of-law methodology might have positively correlated legal cultures. To separate out these influences on choice-of-law decisions, Thiel used Borchers' state classifications, and remeasured the differences, using variables that might control the estimates for the influence of legal culture.

Thiel found that while the modern approach states clearly apply forum law more often than do states using the First Restatement, there was little difference at the margin between the two groups of states with respect to recovery-favoring choice-of-law determinations. Thiel believes that the results indicate that plaintiffs push lawsuits to where their prospects of prevailing on choice-of-law rulings are about equal in all states. Thiel's most interesting results are found in comparing states according to modern methodology. Unlike Borchers, Thiel's regressions produced statistically significant variations across the modern approaches with respect to forum and recovery-favoring choice of law. As predicted by theoretical analyses of modern methodologies (Borchers, 1992), the point estimates of the differences indicate that the Leflar states are relatively strongest in their generosity to plaintiffs and preference for forum law. The interest analysis states also show a strong bias toward choice of forum law, and are relatively strongest in favoring local parties.

More empirical studies could help clarify the choice-of-law debate. In the conflicts field, as least as much as any other, legal academics make bald statements claiming that various approaches or rules will work in particular ways or have specific effects on primary behavior. Those statements are supported at best with slight anecdotal evidence. The field is ripe for empiricists who can cut through the legal and academic thicket to view the landscape. Recent, more narrowly focused empirical investigations in the area of choice of law include Borchers (1997, 2000a, 2000b).

B. CONTRACTUAL CHOICE OF LAW

Law and economics scholars increasingly have focused on the interests of contracting parties rather than solely those of states (O'Hara and

Ribstein, 2000; Guzman, 2002a; Whincop and Keyes, 2001). Since conflicts problems typically arise in the context of private disputes, it makes sense for courts to apply the law that would maximize the joint value of the parties' transactions. Given courts' difficulty of determining which of two or more laws enacted by co-equal sovereigns should apply in a case, it also makes sense to give the parties the option to choose the law that they think best suits their relationship. Enforcing clauses in contracts that select the applicable law has several possible benefits (O'Hara and Ribstein, 2009; Ribstein, 1993; Whincop and Keyes, 2001, Ch. 3).

6. Benefits of Enforcing Contractual Choice of Law

Eliminating Inconsistency
The parties may contract for choice of law in order to eliminate problems that arise when inconsistent mandatory rules otherwise might be applied to different aspects of or parties to the contract, such as shareholder voting rules and the rights of franchisees.

Clarifying the Applicable Law
Contracting for choice of law enables the parties easily to determine what law governs the transaction. Uncertainty about the applicable law that results from the choice-of-law default rules discussed above prevents the parties from easily determining the standard of conduct to which they should conform or how to price contract rights and duties. Uncertainty at the time of litigation can increase both the costs and frequency of litigation. In particular, the uncertainty may increase the parties' gains from litigating rather than settling (Priest and Klein, 1984). This is not only privately more costly for the parties, but also imposes costs on the judicial system that are borne by taxpayers generally.

Jurisdictional Competition
Enforcing contractual choice of law is particularly useful in fostering jurisdictional competition for more efficient laws across states (O'Hara and Ribstein, 2009; Kobayashi and Ribstein, 1998; Ribstein 1993). Competition works both by encouraging states to develop new terms to attract new legal business, and by encouraging states to retain legal business by efficiently revising their laws. Jurisdictional competition was first observed with regard to corporations, where a clear choice-of-law rule, the internal affairs rule in the US, compels application of the law of the state of incorporation (see Section 8, below). This rule encourages corporations to select the applicable law. Commentators have debated whether this process is a 'race to the bottom' in which the states attract incorporation

business by exploiting principal-agent problems resulting from the separation of ownership and control (Cary, 1974) or a 'race to the top' that is disciplined by efficient capital markets (Winter, 1977). For empirical evidence favoring the race to the top hypothesis, see Carney (1993), Romano (1985), Dodd and Leftwich (1980). For studies of the role of jurisdictional competition in the transition from special chartering to general incorporation, see Shughart and Tollison (1985) and Butler (1985).

This jurisdictional competition in effect creates a market for governing laws. This "law market" potentially functions in a wide variety of areas in addition to corporate law (O'Hara and Ribstein, 2009). Specific examples include unincorporated firms (Kobayashi and Ribstein, 2009), electronic commerce (Kobayashi and Ribstein, 2002a), employment law (Kobayashi and Ribstein, 2002b), insurance (Butler and Ribstein, 2008), marriage and family law (Buckley and Ribstein, 2001), and trust and property law (Sitkoff and Schanzenbach, 2005; Bell and Parchomovsky, 2005).

The operation of the law market is an application of basic federalism principles (Kobayashi and Ribstein, 2007). As Tiebout recognized, the ability of people and firms to exit jurisdictions whose policies they do not like motivates governments to reflect voters' preferences (Tiebout, 1956; Frey and Eichenberger, 1995; Gerken, 1995; Kerber and Vanberg, 1995). Thus, the demand side of jurisdictional competition requires, among other things, that actors are mobile (Easterbrook, 1983; Tiebout, 1956; Fischel, 1987). For example, with regard to business associations, mobility costs include foreign registration fees. Larger firms may lack incentives to incur these costs because they can get most of what they want by adapting the default provisions of their resident-state's law (Ayres, 1992a). But jurisdictional competition may work even in this context, at least above the level of the smallest firms (Kobayashi and Ribstein, 2009). Clearly large multistate firms easily can absorb the costs of shopping for law because they pay these costs anyway in all but one state in which they transact business and have scale economies that can absorb the costs.

The supply side of state competition requires that states have incentives to compete for formation business (Daniels, 1991). The states provide their law free of charge at taxpayers' expense. If states cannot internalize the benefits from efficient contract rules, they may have inadequate incentives to devote legislative and judicial resources to developing and maintaining efficient contract rules. The standard explanation of the state competition for corporate law is based on the states' incentives to earn franchise and related fees from incorporating firms (Romano, 1985). They can also earn revenue if enforcing choice of law attracts firms' operations to the state. Either of these mechanisms would, in effect, give the state property rights in application of its law.

In analyzing the supply side of state competition, it is necessary to disaggregate the 'state' and determine what motivates politicians to compete. Contracting parties' ability to exit the state is a necessary but not sufficient basis for efficient competition. It is also necessary that this exit be translated into incentives for politicians. Whatever the benefits to states of participating in interstate competition, it is not clear that taxpayers can motivate state legislators to draft state-of-the-art legislation solely in order to maximize state revenues, particularly given legislators' costs of producing this legislation. No individual taxpayers can capture enough benefits from legislative action to justify expending resources on legislation. Also, legislators may not be able to capture benefits from engaging in the competition because other jurisdictions easily can free-ride on their efforts by copying successful legislation (Rose-Ackerman, 1980). At the same time, legislators incur costs in competing to provide state law. In particular, because legislators can earn contributions and other support from affected parties by brokering changes in mandatory rules, they do not have strong incentives to lead the movement toward more enabling rules. Third, legislators face an unfavorable balance of risks and rewards. They take the risk that the legislation will fail to accomplish its objectives or will alienate groups that otherwise would have supported them, while their successes can be copied easily by other states. For discussions of legislators' weak incentives to innovate, see Rose-Ackerman (1980), Ayres (1992b), Carney (1993), MacIntosh (1993), Ribstein and Kobayashi (1996).

State competition to supply law could be driven by lawyers rather than legislatures, however (Ribstein, 1994, 2003). Lawyers not only wield the conventional power of a cohesive interest group but, in most states, draft complex business statutes. Lawyers have an incentive to make their state a standard for commercial contracts in order to attract more litigation business to the state's courts and increase the value of advice on and expertise in the state's law. This could help explain competition for non-corporate business associations, which appears to exist even without the motivation of franchise fees (Kobayshi and Ribstein, 2009). However, as the price for assisting in the competition of state laws, lawyers may reduce the demand for these rules by pressing for rules that favor lawyers, such as by offering open-ended default rules that discourage settlement and increase litigation (Macey and Miller, 1987; White, 1992; Priest and Klein, 1984). Accordingly, lawyers may have an interest in preventing the parties from simplifying choice of law by contracting in advance to be governed by a particular law. On the other hand, lawyers are constrained by jurisdictional competition. In general, lawyers would support rules that reduce demand for law up to the point that the reduction in demand exceeds their benefits from the rules. Demand may be reduced by inefficient legal rules that cause parties to move their legal business to other states, federal courts and arbitrators.

The extent to which states compete to supply non-corporate law depends significantly on whether interest groups in those states can protect their benefits from mandatory rules from erosion by state competition. Under standard interest group theory, state legislation is determined by the relative strength of the various groups that the legislation helps and hurts (Olson, 1965; McCormick and Tollison, 1981; Tollison, 1988). To be sure, states can successfully compete only by making their underlying legal rules generally attractive to contracting parties. Thus, a state could not win a competition to attract, say, franchise law business simply by adopting a pro-franchisee law. However, the state might be able to help franchisees by imposing retroactive burdens on existing franchise contracts. Groups helped by such laws might oppose vigorous choice-of-law competition. On the other hand, there is evidence that franchise regulation drives franchises out of regulating states, thereby injuring in-state groups such as employees (Klick, Kobayashi and Ribstein, 2006). States' incentives to compete therefore depend on how well organized are groups that favor mandatory rules, the costs and benefits to competing groups of applying contract-friendly enabling rules rather than protective mandatory rules, and the effect of exit of regulated firms on lawyers and other groups in the regulating states (O'Hara and Ribstein, 2009). Thus, for example, Delaware may be in a good position to compete to supply law in part because it has a highly organized commercial bar but no well-organized competing groups (Ribstein and O'Hara, 2008).

The quantity and quality of state competition ultimately depend on the legal rules regarding contractual choice of law. Politicians may protect themselves by, for example, restricting enforcement of contractual choice of law. While the courts may have considerable discretion to interpret the legislature's statutes, they can do little in the face of a statute that explicitly invalidates choice-of-law clauses. Even if the statute does not invalidate exit by choice of law, judges may have their own incentives to maximize the value of interest group deals by protecting them from dilution by party choice of law. After all, judges clearly have some incentive to respond to legislators' interests to the extent that the latter control judges' salary and tenure. If so, judges can be expected to act to increase the durability and value of legislators' interest group deals by enforcing them within the state (Anderson et al., 1989; Crain and Tollison, 1979; Landes and Posner, 1975).

Although legislators and judges may attempt to block contractual choice of law, contracting parties to some extent have the last say. They may, among other things, choose the fora in which disputes are decided and completely exit jurisdictions that are hostile to contractual choice of law. These moves, in turn, put pressure on courts and legislators to enforce contractual choice (Kobayashi and Ribstein, 1998; O'Hara and Ribstein, 2009).

Jurisdictional Competition and Evolutionary Theories
Contractual choice of law may lead to a process of legal evolution. As to legal evolution generally, see Benson (1995); Kerber and Vanberg (1995). Alchian (1950) observed that a study of the 'adaptive mechanism' of the market may be more fruitful than that of 'individual motivation and foresight'. Under this theory, individuals and firms who have an incentive to minimize their transaction and information costs and an ability to choose legal regimes that accomplish this goal will cause the law to move toward efficiency. For example, corporate law evolved from the sale of corporate charters by state legislators to largely enabling statutes and alternative forms of limited liability business forms because of the pressure of jurisdictional competition (Butler, 1985; Shughart and Tollison, 1985). There is also evidence of such evolution with respect to the demand for statutory forms (Ribstein, 1995a) and the demand for uniform statutory provisions (Kobayashi and Ribstein, 1996). This evolutionary theory suggests that the conditions for efficiency may exist even if this outcome could not be predicted *ex ante* based on a study of the incentives of legislators or other key actors.

It may be indeterminate whether the mechanisms for efficient competition are in place, and therefore impossible to determine *ex ante* whether competition among unknown alternatives will produce more efficient results than applying a centralized rule. Nevertheless, it may be more efficient to facilitate jurisdictional competition by enforcing contractual choice of law in order to promote a process of discovering more efficient alternatives (Hayek, 1948; Vihanto, 1992; Kobayashi, Parker and Ribstein, 1994; Gerken, 1995). Contractual choice of law is also likely to be superior to other alternatives, such as the adoption of uniform or national laws, precisely because differing state laws foster experimentation (Ribstein and Kobayashi, 1996; Kobayashi and Ribstein, 1996). Moreover, diverse environments may suggest differing optimal rules, and choice of law enables parties to choose the rule that fits best with their contracting situation (Posner and Scott, 1980; Easterbrook, 1983; Baysinger and Butler, 1985; Romano, 1985).

On the other hand, enforcing contractual choice of law might not lead to efficient competition if state legislators engage in 'herd' behavior by ignoring their private information generated by other states' experiences and simply adopting prior laws. (For theoretical treatments of herd behavior, see Banerjee, 1992; Bikhchandani, Hirshleifer and Welch, 1992; Scharfstein and Stein, 1990.) However, evidence from the evolution of statutory forms for closely held firms indicates that legislators do not simply follow the leader but rather apply new information in adopting legislation (Ribstein, 1995a).

7. Costs of Contractual Choice of Law

Notwithstanding the above arguments, there are also reasons why enforcing contractual choice of law may lead to inefficient results (Ribstein, 1993).

Evasion of Mandatory Rules

Enforcing contractual choice of law can be problematic where it permits contracting parties to evade mandatory rules that are intended to address specific bargaining problems that lead to suboptimal or misunderstood contract terms. This may be the case, for example, where the parties are attempting to escape prohibitions on contract terms such as fiduciary duty waivers, usurious interest rates, termination-at-will, or noncompetition provisions.

The argument against enforcing the contractual choice of law in these situations may seem to be precisely the same as that supporting the mandatory rule itself. However, there are several reasons for permitting the parties to opt out of locally mandatory rules by contractually choosing the applicable law or forum. First, where several jurisdictions' laws may apply, the parties' choice of law is not obviously less appropriate than any other basis for selecting the applicable law.

Second, evasion of mandatory rules is constrained by the fact that avoidance requires applying a state law rather than solely the voluntary act of contracting parties. That the chosen state's law applies to its own residents reduces state legislators' incentives to engage in this sort of conduct. Accordingly, this danger of enforcing contractual choice of law exists mainly where most victims live outside the state.

Third, the enacting legislature may not have intended to preclude contracting for the applicable law or forum. In particular, a mandatory rule may not make sense to the extent that it precludes efficient bargains. The parties arguably indicate that the mandatory rule is costly when applied to them by their willingness to incur the costs of contracting for choice of law. Thus, courts generally should enforce contractual choice of law or forum even to the extent that it overrides a locally mandatory rule (Whincop and Keyes, 2001, Ch. 4). States could usefully clarify when their policy is important enough to justify non-enforcement of choice-of-law clauses by enacting a statute providing for the prohibition (O'Hara and Ribstein, 2000; O'Hara and Ribstein, 2009).

Information Asymmetry and Protecting Contracting Parties
Enforcing contractual choice of law arguably may lead to externalization of costs because the party responsible for the term is probably more well-informed concerning the chosen law. Indeed, such information asymmetries may skew interstate competition because states may tailor their rules to suit the more informed party. However, information asymmetry is arguably not a problem where the effect of the law-selection clause is to choose a legal regime that literally enforces the contract; in long-term contracts negotiated by sophisticated and knowledgeable parties who have the ability and incentive to read the contract carefully or hire an attorney to do so; or where firms are subject to market incentives to disclose and to constraints on cheating (Kobayashi and Ribstein, 2002a; Schwartz and Wilde, 1979). In any event, regulators could minimize information costs by mandating disclosure of unusual and significant law-selection terms in some circumstances.

Similarly, enforcing contractual choice of law is arguably inefficient where the choice-of-law clause can be characterized as an 'adhesion' contract imposed by one party on another. This argument also has been used to justify broad regulation of corporate governance. However, this is not the case merely because of the parties' acceptance of a standard term, particularly where the contract chooses the entire local law of a particular jurisdiction. A state's entire law as to a complex contract probably will not operate unfairly against one of the parties on all or most of the many issues that could arise in the future. Here again, state prohibitions on the enforcement of choice-of-law clauses should be enacted through clearly worded statutes.

8. Enforcement of Contractual Choice of Law

This section considers the extent to which choice-of-law provisions are enforced in United States courts.

Common Law
The common law, as summarized in Second Restatement (1971), § 187(1), provides for enforcement of the parties' contractual choice of law as to interpretation issues the parties could have resolved by contract. Under Second Restatement § 187(2), the contract is not enforced as to issues such as validity, where choice of law matters most, if:

(a) the chosen state has no substantial relationship to the parties or the transaction and there is no other reasonable basis for the parties' choice, or
(b) application of the law of the chosen state would be contrary to a fundamental policy of a state which has a materially greater interest than the chosen state in the determination of the particular issue and which, under

the rule of §188, would be the state of the applicable law in the absence of an effective choice of law by the parties.

Courts and commentators have not clearly articulated a rationale for these limitations on enforcement of contractual choice of law (Ribstein, 1993). The 'substantial relationship' test in subsection (a) seems problematic. For example, it is not clear why any mutually agreed choice would not be prima facie 'reasonable'. The test conceivably could be defended on the ground that it addresses externalization of costs by states whose law is applied. But even if the particular contract at issue does not relate to the contractually selected state, the state might still be subject to market discipline where the applied law has substantial application within the applying state. In other situations, such as corporate law, the state is otherwise subject to market discipline in formulating its law. With respect to the vague 'fundamental policy' exception in subsection (b), the Restatement gives as examples 'illegal' contracts or rules 'designed to protect a person against the oppressive use of superior bargaining power' (Restatement, 1971: 568). This appears to track potential concerns about bargaining power and information asymmetries (see Section 7, above). Alternatively, this ground for non-enforcement may just invite courts to determine and effectuate the underlying goal of the interest groups that promoted the law. In any event, this provision helps to ensure that contracting parties locate at least some of their activities and assets in states with desired laws, and that movement helps to facilitate jurisdictional competition for governing laws (O'Hara and Ribstein, 2009).

In general, courts applying the US Restatement (Second) rule have quite generally enforced contractual choice of law (Ribstein, 1993). A study of more than 700 reported cases indicates that the choice-of-law clause was enforced 80 percent of the time, and those cases all involved a fight over enforcement of the clause (Ribstein, 2003; O'Hara and Ribstein, 2009). In most litigation, enforcement is quiet and routine, so this 80 percent figure underestimates the enforceability of choice-of-law clauses. Thus, in practice, the US rule is close to the rule favoring enforcement articulated in the leading UK case of *Vita Food Products Inc. v. Unus Shipping Co*. That case enforced a provision applying English law, though there was nothing to connect the contract with England except the choice-of-law clause.

Statutory Law
Several states, including California, Illinois, Delaware, New York and Texas, have promulgated statutes that, to varying degrees, clarify the enforcement of choice-of-law clauses (Ribstein, 1994). These choice-of-law statutes provide some evidence both of jurisdictional competition to

supply law and of the determinants of such competition. The laws do not generate obvious gains for legislators. They do not generate franchise fee or other obvious income for the state. Nor do they even appear to benefit firms and individuals residing or doing business in the enacting states since such parties do not need the statute to secure jurisdiction in or to justify contractual enforcement of the law of the enacting states. However, the laws are understandable in light of the role of lawyers in promoting jurisdictional competition (see Section 6). Lawyers' role also helps explain differences among the four statutes. The broadest statute is in Delaware, where lawyers clearly dominate. In the larger commercial states such as Texas, other powerful interest groups clearly would want to protect local mandatory laws from erosion by interstate competition.

Corporate Internal Affairs Rule
In contrast to the rule applied to other contractual relationships, the parties' rights regarding the internal governance of a corporation usually are determined by the law selected by the parties – that is, the law of the state of incorporation (Restatement, 1971, § 302(2)). The conflicts rules that apply to corporations therefore differ substantially from those which apply to non-corporate contracts. This ignores the fact that corporations and other types of firms are fundamentally similar in the sense of being alternative devices for minimizing transaction costs (Williamson, 1985; Coase, 1937). Nor do the costs and benefits of applying contractual choice of law discussed above differ significantly according to whether corporate or non-corporate contracts are involved (Ribstein, 1993). For example, parties to non-corporate contracts, like those to corporations, would benefit from being permitted to shop for the applicable law, from the certainty of applying a contractually-selected law, and from applying the same law to all parties to interstate contracts. On the other side of the ledger, corporations present the same potential problems as other contracts regarding potential evasion of mandatory rules, as indicated by commentators such as Cary (1974) who have condemned interstate competition for corporate law as a 'race to the bottom'. Although corporations do clearly identify the applicable law through their centrally filed certificates or articles of incorporation, this does no more than justify analogous requirements for non-corporate contracts. The fact that corporate shares are traded on efficient securities markets that discount significant contract terms plainly does not justify a distinction between closely held corporations and other types of contracts. Indeed, there is evidence of an active jurisdictional competition for the law related to limited liability companies that resembles the corporate competition in some respects, including the dominant role played by Delaware (Kobayashi and Ribstein, 2009).

The different treatment of corporations and other types of contracts with regard to enforcement of contractual choice of law may be due at least partly to the long acceptance of the legal fiction that a corporation is a legal 'person' created and endowed with certain attributes by the chartering state (Ribstein, 1995b). This characterization is conducive to application of contractual choice of law because it seems to give greater weight to the parties' jurisdictional choice than would characterizing the corporation as a mere contract. The entity theory helped create a legal momentum toward enforcement of contractual choice of law in corporations that has never been opposed by coordinated interest groups. In other words, the special choice-of-law rule for corporations, which has been instrumental in ensuring efficient state default rules and enforcement of contracts in firms, ironically may be attributable to the fact that the corporation traditionally has been viewed as a legal person rather than an ordinary contract.

Despite superficial differences between choice of law for corporations and non-corporate contracts, there are also fundamental similarities. Not only has jurisdictional competition developed in both areas, but the forces underlying this development have been shown to be similar – that is, firms' exit from states that refuse to enforce contractual choice of law and the role of groups affected by this exit (Ribstein and O'Hara, 2008).

There is a potential tension between the corporate internal affairs rule and the choice-of-law statutes discussed above. Those statutes arguably permit the parties to a corporation to select the law *other than* of the state of incorporation. This raises the question of whether states should be able to, in effect, bundle their lawmaking and adjudication services by insisting that their corporate law applies only to parties who have formally incorporated in the state and, therefore, paid the franchise tax (Ribstein, 1994). Fees and taxes arguably play a role in giving states an incentive to compete to provide law, depending on the role of lawyers in promoting this competition (see Section 6, above).

Constitutional Law
The federal government in a federal system has an important role with respect to contractual choice of law. For broad-based discussions of the economics of federalism, see Hayek (1948), Riker (1964), Shapiro (1972), Rose-Ackerman (1980, 1981), Cover (1981), Kitch (1981), Macey (1990) and Carney (1993). This section discusses Constitutional provisions that mandate enforcement of choice-of-law clauses. Other potential effects of federal law are discussed below.

The commerce clause of the US Constitution, § 8, cl. 3, provides in part that Congress has the power '[t]o regulate Commerce . . . among the several states'. The 'negative implication' of this clause is that *only* Congress, and not the individual states, can regulate such commerce (see *Cooley v. Board of Wardens*). The Supreme Court has endorsed an exportation-of-costs theory of the commerce clause which holds that if the costs of state regulation fall mostly on interest groups outside the state while the benefits accrue to those within it, the legislature lacks incentives to consider both costs and benefits in enacting laws (Posner, 1992: 638–44; Fischel, 1987; Levmore, 1983). From an efficiency standpoint, cost exportation subverts interest group interaction within the enacting jurisdiction that otherwise would cause laws to tend toward Kaldor-Hicks efficiency.

The cost-exportation theory arguably justifies invalidation under the commerce clause of state statutes to the extent that they prevent enforcement of choice-of-law clauses. This targets a particular application of state law that generally tends to benefit concentrated in-state groups, while imposing costs on out-of-state firms or interest groups (Ribstein, 1993). It is significant in that regard that such clauses tend not to be enforced when they are in form contracts that are used on a national scale rather than within a single state (Ribstein, 1993). This theory is arguably supported by two Supreme Court cases on state anti-takeover laws, *Edgar v. Mite Corp.* and *CTS Corp. v. Dynamics Corp. of America*. *Edgar* struck down on Commerce Clause grounds a state law which imposed conditions, including approval by a state agency, on interstate tender offers, while *CTS* held under the Commerce Clause that an interstate tender offer *could* be regulated by the law of the state of incorporation. These cases are best rationalized on the basis that regulation of a corporate contract which is inconsistent with the law of the contractually selected state – that is, the law of the state of incorporation – is invalid under the Commerce Clause.

Even if the Commerce Clause technically applies in this situation, its application may be unnecessary in the long run. Costs ultimately may be borne inside the state even if they initially fall on nonresidents (Kitch, 1981), and laws that hurt out-of-state groups invite retaliation by other states (Levmore, 1983).

The Full Faith and Credit Clause, US Constitution art. IV, § 1, provides in part that 'Full Faith and Credit shall be given in each State to the public Acts, Records, and judicial Proceedings of every other State'. This requires states to respect the laws of other states at least to the extent of having a principled basis for refusing to follow the law in a particular case (see *Allstate Insurance Co v. Hague*). However, this principle does not directly protect individuals' rights to freedom of contract.

Some early 'Full Faith and Credit' cases involving fraternal benefit associations held that the association's formation state law or charter must apply in order to ensure that a single legal regime applies to all association members (see, for example, *Supreme Council of the Royal Arcanum v. Green*, enforcing increase in assessment rate pursuant to association's constitution). However, given the limited objectives of the Full Faith and Credit Clause discussed above, it is unlikely that this authority would be broadly applied today to compel enforcement of choice-of-law clauses. At most, these cases might justify applying a single rule, such as the law of the one state that has overwhelming contacts with the transaction even if this is not the law the parties selected.

Federal Law
Congress is explicitly empowered under the Full Faith and Credit and Commerce Clauses to regulate choice of law. A federal choice-of-law rule could preserve state power and reinforce private contracts similar to Commerce Clause protection of contractual choice of law. However, any Congressional action would have to emerge from a competition among interest groups. There is probably no group that would gain enough from a general rule validating choice-of-law clauses to organize support for such a law. Congress may fail to act only to avoid negative interest group pressure (Macey, 1990) rather than because action would be inefficient. This suggests that it may be better to rely on the Supreme Court's power under the Constitution to lift state burdens on interstate commerce.

Bibliography

Allen, William H. and O'Hara, Erin A. (1999), 'Second Generation Law and Economics of Conflict of Laws', **51** *Stanford Law Review*, 1011 ff.

Anderson, Gary M., Shughart, William F. and Tollison, Robert D. (1989), 'On the Incentives of Judges to Enforce Legislative Wealth Transfers', **32** *Journal of Law and Economics*, 215 ff.

Ayres, Ian (1992a), 'Judging Close Corporations in the Age of Statutes', **70** *Washington University Law Quarterly*, 365 ff.

Ayres, Ian (1992b), 'Making a Difference: The Contractual Contributions of Easterbrook and Fischel', **59** *University of Chicago Law Review*, 1391 ff.

Ayres, Ian (1993), 'Preliminary Thoughts on Optimal Tailoring of Contractual Rules', **3** *Southern California Interdisciplinary Law Journal*, 1 ff.

Bainbridge, Stephen M. (1984), 'Trade Usages in International Sales of Goods: An Analysis of the 1964 and 1980 Sales Conventions', **24** *Virginia Journal of International Law*, 619 ff.

Bainbridge, Stephen M. (1986), 'Comity and Sovereign Debt Litigation: A Bankruptcy Analogy', **10** *Maryland Journal of International Law and Trade*, 1 ff.

Basedow, Jurgen and Kono, Toshiyuki (eds) (2006), *An Economic Analysis of Private International Law*, Tübingen: Mohr Siebeck, Max Planck Institute.

Baxter, William F. (1963), 'Choice of Law and the Federal System', **16** *Stanford Law Review*, 1 ff.

Beale, Joseph H. (1935), *A Treatise on the Conflict of Laws*, Cambridge, MA: Harvard University Press.

Bell, Abraham and Parchomovsky, Gideon (2005), 'Of Property and Federalism', **115** *Yale Law Journal*, 72 ff.

Benson, Bruce L. (1992), 'Customary Law as a Social Contract: International Commercial Law', **2** *Constitutional Political Economy*, 1 ff.

Benson, Bruce L. (1995), 'Competition Among Legal Institutions: Implications for the Evolution of Law', in Gerken, Luden (ed.), *Competition among Institutions*, London: Macmillan, 153 ff.
Borchers, Patrick J. (1992), 'The Choice of Law Revolution: An Empirical Study', **49** *Washington and Lee Law Review*, 357 ff.
Borchers, Patrick J. (1997), 'Courts and the Second Conflicts Restatement: Some Observations and an Empirical Note', **56** *Maryland Law Review*, 1232 ff.
Borchers, Patrick J. (2000a), 'Empiricism and Theory in Conflicts Law', **75** *Indiana Law Journal*, 509 ff.
Borchers, Patrick J. (2000b), 'Louisiana's Conflicts Codification: Some Empirical Observations Regarding Decisional Predictability', **60** *Louisiana Law Review*, 1061 ff.
Boyd, James (1996), 'Environmental Liability Reform and Privatization in Central and Eastern Europe', **3** *European Journal of Law and Economics*, 39 ff.
Brilmayer, Lea (1980), 'Interest Analysis and the Myth of Legislative Intent', **78** *Michigan Law* Review, 392 ff.
Brilmayer, Lea (1995), *Conflict of Laws*, Boston, MA: Little Brown.
Bruce, Christopher J. (1984), 'The Deterrent Effects of Automobile Insurance and Tort Law: A Survey of the Empirical Literature', **6** *Law and Policy*, 67 ff.
Buckley, Francis H. and Ribstein, Larry E. (2001), 'Calling a Truce in the Marriage Wars', *University of Illinois Law Review*, 561 ff.
Butler, Henry N. (1985), 'Nineteenth-Century Jurisdictional Competition in the Granting of Corporate Privileges', **14** *Journal of Legal Studies*, 129 ff.
Butler, Henry N. and Ribstein, Larry E. (2008), 'The Single-License Solution', **31(4)** *Regulation*, 36 ff.
Carney, William J. (1993), 'The ALI's Corporate Governance Project: the Death of Property Rights?', **61** *George Washington Law Review*, 898 ff.
Carney, William J. (1997), 'The Political Economy of Competition for Corporate Charters', **26** *Journal of Legal Studies*, 303 ff.
Cary, William L. (1974), 'Federalism and Corporate Law: Reflections upon Delaware', **83** *Yale Law Journal*, 663 ff.
Cavers, David (1933), 'A Critique of the Choice-of-Law Problem', **47** *Harvard Law Review*, 173 ff.
Coase, Ronald H. (1937), 'The Nature of the Firm', **4** *Economica*, 386 ff.
Cover, Robert M. (1981), 'The Uses of Jurisdictional Redundancy: Interest Ideology and Innovation', **22** *William and Mary Law Review*, 639 ff.
Crain, W. Mark and Tollison, R.D. (1979), 'Constitutional Change in an Interest Group Perspective', **8** *Journal of Legal Studies*, 165 ff.
Currie, Brainard (1958a), 'Survival of Actions: Adjudication versus Automation in the Conflict of Laws', **10** *Stanford Law Review*, 205 ff.
Currie, Brainard (1958b), 'Married Women's Contracts: A Study in Conflict-of-Laws Method', **24** *University of Chicago Law Review*, 227 ff.
Currie, Brainard (1959), 'Notes on Methods and Objectives in the Conflict of Laws', **1959** *Duke Law Journal*, 171 ff.
Daniels, Ronald J. (1991), 'Should Provinces Compete: The Case for a Competitive Corporate Law Market', **36** *McGill Law Journal*, 130 ff.
Dezalay, Yves and Garth, Bryant G. (1995), 'Merchants of Law as Mortal Entrepreneurs: Constructing International Justice from the Competition for Transnational Business Disputes', **29** *Law and Society Review*, 27 ff.
Dicey, Albert Venn (1980), *Dicey and Morris on the Conflict of Laws*, London: Stevens.
Dodd, Peter and Leftwich, Richard (1980), 'The Market for Corporate Charters: Unhealthy Competition versus Federal Regulation', **53** *Journal of Business*, 259 ff.
Easterbrook, Frank H. (1983), 'Antitrust and the Economics of Federalism', **26** *Journal of Law and Economics*, 23 ff.
Ehrenzweig, Albert (1956), 'Parental Immunity in the Conflict of Laws: Law and Reason versus the Restatement', **23** *University of Chicago Law Review*, 474 ff.

Ely, John Hart (1981), 'Choice of Law and the State's Interest in Protecting Its Own', **23** *William and Mary Law Review*, 173 ff.
Fischel, Daniel R. (1987), 'From MITE to CTS: State Anti-Takeover Statutes, the Williams Act, the Commerce Clause, and Insider Trading', **47** *Supreme Court Review*, 47 ff.
Frey, Brumo S. and Eichenberger, Reiner (1995), 'Competition among Jurisdictions: The Idea of FOCJ', in Gerken, Luden (ed.), *Competition among Institutions*, London: Macmillan, 209 ff.
Green, Edward J. and Porter, Robert H. (1984), 'Noncooperative Collusion Under Imperfect Price Information', **52** *Econometrica*, 87 ff.
Guzman, Andrew T. (2002a), 'Choice of Law: New Foundations', **90** *Georgetown Law Journal*, 883 ff.
Guzman, Andrew T. (2002b), 'Public Choice and International Regulatory Competition', **90** *Georgetown Law Journal*, 971 ff.
Hay, Bruce L. (1992), 'Conflicts of Laws and State Competition in the Product Liability System', **80** *Georgetown Law Journal*, 617 ff.
Henry, Sherrye P. and Bainbridge, Stephen M. (1984), 'Nationalizations – Standard of Compensation', **24** *Virginia Journal of International Law*, 993 ff.
Joustra, Carla (1992), 'Cross Border Consumer Complaints in Private International Law', **15**(4) *Journal of Consumer Policy*, 431 ff.
Kitch, Edmund W. (1981), 'Regulation and the American Common Market', in Tarlock, A. Dan (ed.), *Regulation, Federalism and Interstate Commerce 9*, Cambridge, MA: Oelschlager, Gunn & Hain.
Klick, Jonathan, Kobayashi, Bruce H. and Ribstein, Larry E. (2006), 'The Effect of Contract Regulation: The Case of Franchising', George Mason Law & Economics Research Paper No. 07-03; 2nd Annual Conference on Empirical Legal Studies Paper; FSU College of Law, Law and Economics Paper No. 07/001, http://ssrn.com/abstract=951464.
Kobayashi, Bruce H., Parker, Jeffrey S. and Ribstein, Larry E. (1994), *The Process of Procedural Reform*, George Mason University Law and Economics Working Paper, 96-5.
Kobayashi, Bruce H. and Ribstein, Larry E. (1996), 'Evolution and Spontaneous Uniformity: Evidence from the Evolution of the Limited Liability Company', **34** *Economic Inquiry*, 464 ff.
Kobayashi, Bruce H. and Ribstein, Larry E. (1998), 'Contract and Jurisdictional Competition', in Buckley, F.H. (ed.), *Fall and Rise of Freedom of Contract*, NC, Duke University Press.
Kobayashi, Bruce H. and Ribstein, Larry E. (1999), 'Uniformity, Choice of Law, and Software Sales', **8** *George Mason University Law Review*, 261 ff.
Kobayashi, Bruce H. and Ribstein, Larry E. (2002a), 'State Regulation of Electronic Commerce', **51** *Emory Law Journal*, 1 ff.
Kobayashi, Bruce H. and Ribstein, Larry E. (2002b), 'Privacy and Firms', **79** *Denver University Law Review*, 526 ff.
Kobayashi, Bruce H. and Ribstein, Larry E. (eds) (2007), *Economics of Federalism*, Cheltenham, UK and Northampton, MA, USA: Edward Elgar.
Kobayashi, Bruce H. and Ribstein, Larry E. (2009), *Delaware for Small Fry: Jurisdictional Competition for Limited Liability Companies, 2010*, University of Illinois Law & Economics Research Paper No. LE09-017, 53, http://ssrn.com/abstract=1431989.
Kötz, Hein (1986), 'Rechtsvereinheitlichung – Nutzen, Kosten, Methoden, Ziele (Law Harmonization – Benefits, Costs, Methods, Goals)', **50** *Rabels Zeitschrift für Ausländisches und Internationales Privatrecht*, 483 ff.
Kozyris, John P. (1987), 'Choice of Law for Products Liability: Whither Ohio?', **48** *Ohio State Law Journal*, 377 ff.
Kramer, Larry (1990), 'Rethinking Choice of Law', **90** *Columbia Law Review*, 277 ff.
Kramer, Larry (1991a), 'Return of the Renvoi', **66** *New York University Law Review*, 979 ff.
Kramer, Larry (1991b), 'More Notes on Methods and Objectives in the Conflict of Laws', **24** *Cornell International Law Journal*, 245 ff.

Leflar, Robert (1966a), 'Choice-Influencing Considerations in Conflicts Law', **41** *New York University Law Review*, 267 ff.
Leflar, Robert (1966b), 'Conflicts Law: More on Choice Influencing Considerations', **54** *California Law Review*, 1584 ff.
Leflar, Robert (1977), 'Choice of Law: A Well-watered Plateau', **41** *Law and Contemporary Problems*, 10 ff.
Levmore, Saul (1983), 'Interstate Exploitation and Judicial Intervention', **69** *Vanderbilt Law Review*, 568 ff.
LoPucki, Lynn M. (2005), *Courting Failure: How Competition for Big Cases is Corrupting the Bankruptcy Courts*, Ann Arbor: University of Michigan Press.
Macey, Jonathan R. (1990), 'Federal Deference to Local Regulators and the Economic Theory of Regulation: Toward a Public Choice Explanation of Federalism', **76** *Vanderbilt Law Review*, 265 ff.
Macey, Jonathan R. and Miller, Geoffrey P. (1987), 'Toward an Interest-Group Theory of Delaware Corporate Law', **65** *Texas Law Review*, 469 ff.
MacIntosh, Jeffrey G. (1993), *The Role of Interjurisdictional Competition in Shaping Canadian Corporate Law: A Second Look*, University of Toronto Law and Economics Working Paper Series, WPS 18.
Malysiak, James T. (1973), 'Toward a Substantive Private International Law of Trademarks: The Lessons of the Carl Zeiss Litigation', **82(5)** *Yale Law Journal*, 1072 ff.
McConnell, Michael W. (1988), 'A Choice of Law Approach to Products-Liability Reform', in Olson, Walter (ed.), *New Directions in Liability Law*, New York: The Academy of Political Science.
Michaels, Ralf (2008), 'Economics of Law as Choice of Law', **71** *Law and Contemporary Problems*, 73 ff.
Nagel, Bernhard (1992), 'Von der Lex Mercatoria zur Lex Laboris, zur Rechtlichen Bewältigung der Internationalen Arbeitsbeziehungen (Lex Mercatoria and Lex Laboris: On the Legal Analysis of International Work Relations)', in Däubler, Wolfgang, Bobke, Manfred and Kehrmann, Karl (eds), *Festschrift für Albert Gnade*, Köln: Bund-Verlag.
North, P.M. and Fawcett, J.J. (1992), *Cheshire and North's Private International Law*, London: Butterworths.
O'Hara, Erin Ann (2000), 'Opting Out of Regulation: A Public Choice Analysis of Contractual Choice of Law', **53** *Vanderbilt Law Review*, 1551 ff.
O'Hara, Erin Ann (2002a), 'Economics, Public Choice and the Perennial Conflict of Laws', **90** *Georgetown Law Journal*, 941 ff.
O'Hara, Erin Ann (2002b), 'The Jurisprudence and Politics of Forum-Selection Clauses', **3** *Chicago Journal of International Law*, 301 ff.
O'Hara, Erin Ann (2005), 'Choice of Law for Internet Transactions: The Uneasy Case for Online Consumer Protection', **153** *University of Pennsylvania Law Review*, 1883 ff.
O'Hara, Erin Ann (ed.) (2007), *The Economics of Conflict of Laws*, Cheltenham, UK and Northampton, MA, USA: Edward Elgar (2 volumes).
O'Hara, Erin and Ribstein, Larry E. (1997), 'Interest Groups, Contracts and Interest Analysis', **48** *Mercer Law Review*, 765 ff.
O'Hara, Erin A. and Ribstein, Larry E. (2000), 'From Politics to Efficiency in Choice of Law', **67** *University of Chicago Law Review*, 1151 ff.
O'Hara, Erin Ann and Ribstein, Larry E. (2008), 'Rules and Institutions in Developing a Law Market: Views from the United States and Europe', **82** *Tulane Law Review*, 2147 ff.
O'Hara, Erin A. and Ribstein, Larry E. (2009), *The Law Market*, New York: Oxford University Press.
Parisi, Francesco (1995), 'Toward a Theory of Spontaneous Law', **6** *Constitutional Political Economy*, 211 ff.
Parisi, Francesco (1996a), 'Normative Knowledge and Self-Enforcing Rule in International Law', **2** *International Legal Theory*, 27 ff.
Parisi, Francesco (1996b), 'Law as a Voluntary Enterprise', in Ratnapala, S. and Moens, G. (eds), *The Jurisprudence of Liberty*, London: Butterworths, 111 ff.

Parisi, Francesco (1997), 'The Economics of Customary Law: Lessons From Evolutionary Socio-Biology', in Ott, Claus and von Wangenheim, Georg (eds), *Essays in Law and Economics IV*, Antwerpen: Maklu.
Parisi, Francesco (1998a), 'Customary Law', in Newman, Peter (ed.), *The New Palgrave Dictionary of Economics and the Law*, London: Macmillan.
Parisi, Francesco (2000a), 'The Cost of the Game: A Topology of Social Interactions', **6** *European Journal of Law and Economics*, **9**, 99 ff.
Parisi, Francesco (2000b), 'Spontaneous Emergence of Law: Customary Law', in De Geest, Gerrit, *Encyclopedia of Law and Economics*, Cheltenham, UK and Northampton, MA, USA: Edward Elgar and University of Gent.
Reese, Willis (1972), 'Choice of Law: Rules or Approach', **57** *Cornell Law Review*, 315 ff.
Ribstein, Larry E. (1993), 'Choosing Law by Contract', **18** *Journal of Corporation Law*, 245 ff.
Ribstein, Larry E. (1994), 'Delaware, Lawyers and Choice of Law', **19** *Delaware Journal of Corporate Law*, 999 ff.
Ribstein, Larry E. (1995a), 'Statutory Forms for Closely Held Firms: Theories and Evidence from LLCs', **73** *Washington University Law Quarterly*, 369 ff.
Ribstein, Larry E. (1995b), 'A Critique of the Uniform Limited Liability Company Act', **25** *Stetson Law Review*, 313 ff.
Ribstein, Larry E. (1995c), 'The Constitutional Conception of the Corporation', **4** *Supreme Court Economic Review*, 95 ff.
Ribstein, Larry E. (2003), 'From Efficiency to Politics in Contractual Choice of Law', **37** *Georgia Law Review*, 363 ff.
Ribstein, Larry E. and Kobayashi, Bruce H. (1995), 'Uniform Laws, Model Laws and Limited Liability Companies', **66** *University of Colorado Law Review*, 947 ff.
Ribstein, Larry E. and Kobayashi, Bruce H. (1996), 'Economic Analysis of Uniform State Laws', **25** *Journal of Legal Studies*, 131 ff.
Ribstein, Larry E. and O'Hara, Erin Ann (2008), 'Corporations and the Market for Law', **2010**, *University of Illinois Law Review*, 661 ff.
Riker, William H. (1964), *Federalism: Origin, Operation, Significance*, Boston, MA: Little Brown.
Romano, Roberta (1985), 'Law as Product: Some Pieces of the Incorporation Puzzle', **1** *Journal of Law, Economics, and Organization*, 225 ff.
Rose-Ackerman, Susan (1980), 'Risk Taking and Reelection: Does Federalism Promote Innovation?', **9** *Journal of Legal Studies*, 593 ff.
Rose-Ackerman, Susan (1981), 'Does Federalism Matter? Political Choice in a Federal Republic', **89** *Journal of Political Economy*, 152 ff.
Rosenberg, Maurice (1968), 'Comments on Reich v. Purcell', **15** *UCLA Law Review*, 641 ff.
Rosenberg, Maurice (1981), 'The Comeback of Choice-of-Law Rules', **81** *Columbia Law Review*, 946 ff.
Rubin, Paul H. (1993), 'Private Mechanisms for the Creation of Efficient Institutions for Market Economies', in Somogyi, Laszlo (ed.), *The Political Economy of the Transition Process in Eastern Europe*, Cheltenham, UK and Northampton, MA, USA: Edward Elgar.
Rubin, Paul H. (1994), 'Growing A Legal System in the Post-Communist Economies', **27** *Cornell International Law Journal*, 1 ff.
Ruhl, Giesela (2006), 'Methods and Approaches in Choice of Law: An Economic Perspective', **24** *Berkeley Journal of International Law*, 801 ff.
Santagata, Walter (1995), 'Istituzioni per il Mercato dell'Arte: Artisti e Mercanti tra Regole, Convenzioni e Allocazioni dei Diritti (Institutions for the Market of Works of Art: Artists and Merchants among Rules, Conventions and Allocation of Rights)', *Economia Publica*, 87 ff.
Schenk, Karl-Ernst (1978), 'Grenzüberschreitende Unternehmensformen in den Ost-West-Wirtschaftsbeziehungen (Transnational forms of Enterprises in East-West Economic Relations, with A. Wass von Czege)', in Schiller, Karl (ed.), *Technologietransfer durch*

Ost-West-Kooperation, Ökonomische Studien aus den Institut für Außenhandel und Überseewirtschaft, Bd. 27, Stuttgart/New York: Fischer, 1 ff.

Schenk, Karl-Ernst (1988), 'Technologietransfer, Joint Ventures und Transaktionskosten. Möglichkeiten und Grenzen strategischer Allianzen von Unternehmen in und zwischen Ost und West (Transfer of Technologies, Joint Ventures and Transaction Costs: Opportunities and Boundaries of Strategic Alliances by Enterprises of East and West)', in Dürr, E. and Sieber, H. (eds), *Weltwirtschaft im Wandel: Festgabe für E. Tuchtfeldt*, Bern-Stuttgart: P. Haupt, 595 ff.

Schenk, Karl-Ernst (1991), 'Internationale Kooperationen und Joint Ventures. Theoretische und strategische Grundlagen ((International Cooperations and Joint Ventures: Theoretical and Strategical Foundations)', in Schoppe, S.G. (ed.), *Kompendium der Internationalen Betriebswirtschaftslehre*, München-Wien: R. Oldenberg, 153 ff.

Schmidt Trenz, Hans Jorg (1990), *Außenhandel und Territorialität des Rechts. Grundlegung einer Neuen Institutionenökonomik des Außenhandels* (Trade and Territoriality of Law), Baden-Baden: Nomos.

Schmidtchen, Dieter (1993), 'Neue Institutionenökonomik internationaler Transaktionen (New Institutional Economics of International Transactions)', in Schlieper, Ulrich and Schmidtchen, Dieter (eds), *Makro, Geld and Institutionen*, Tübingen: J.C.B. Mohr, 57 ff.

Schmidtchen, Dieter (1995), 'Territorialität des Rechts, Internationales Privatrecht und die privatautonome Regelung internationaler Sachverhalte. Grundlagen eines interdisziplinären Forschungsprogramms (Territoriality of Law, International Private Law, and Private Autonomous Order of International Relations)', **59(1)** *Rabels Zeitschrift für Ausländisches und Internationales Privatrecht*, 56 ff.

Schmidtchen, Dieter and Schmidt-Trenz, Hans-Jorg (1990), 'The Division of Labor is Limited by the Extent of the Law: A Constitutional Approach to International Private Law', **1(3)** *Constitutional Political Economy*, 49 ff.

Scoles, Eugene and Hay, Peter (1992), *Conflict of Laws*, St. Paul, Minn.: West Publishing Co.

Shapiro, Martin M. (1972), 'Toward a Theory of Stare Decisis', **1** *Journal of Legal Studies*, 125 ff.

Shughart, William F., II and Tollison, R.D. (1985), 'Corporate Chartering: An Exploration in the Economics of Legal Change', **23** *Economic Inquiry*, 585 ff.

Sitkoff, Robert H. and Schanzenbach, Max (2005), 'Jurisdictional Competition for Trust Funds: An Empirical Analysis of Perpetuities and Taxes', **115** *Yale Law Journal*, 356 ff.

Solimine, Michael E. (1989), 'An Economic and Empirical Analysis of Choice of Law', **24** *Georgia Law Review*, 49 ff.

Solimine, Michael E. (2002). 'The Law and Economics of Conflict of Laws', **4** *American Law and Economics Review*, 208 ff. (review of Michael J. Whincop and Mary Keyes, *Policy and Pragmatism in the Conflict of Laws*, Ashgate Publishing, 2001).

Stephan, Paul B. (2000), 'Choice of Law and its Consequences: Constitutions for International Transactions', **26** *Brooklyn Journal of International Law*, 211 ff.

Stephan, Paul B. (2002), 'The Political Economy of Choice of Law', **90** *Georgetown Law Journal*, 957 ff.

Sterk, Stewart E. (1994), 'The Marginal Relevance of Choice of Law Theory', **142** *University of Pennsylvania Law Review*, 949 ff.

Streit, Manfred E. and Voigt, Stefan (1993), 'The Economics of Conflict Resolution in International Trade', in Friedmann, D. and Mestmäcker, E.J. (eds), *Conflict Resolution in International Trade*, Baden-Baden: Nomos, 39 ff.

Symeonides, Symeon C. (2009), 'Choice of Law in the American Courts in 2008: Twenty-Second Annual Survey', **57** *American Journal of Comparative Law*, 269 ff.

Symposium (1997), 'Choice of Law: How It Ought to Be', **48** *Mercer Law Review*, 623 ff.

Thiel, Stuart E. (1996), 'Choice of Law and the Home Court Advantage: Evidence', (Unpublished Manuscript).

Trachtman, Joel P. (1994), 'Conflict of Laws and Accuracy in the Allocation of Government Responsibility', **26** *Vanderbilt Journal of Transnational Law*, 975 ff.

Trachtman, Joel (2001), 'Economic Analysis of Prescriptive Jurisdiction', **42** *Virginia Journal of International Law*, 1 ff.
Vihanto, Martti (1992), 'Competition between Local Governments as a Discovery Procedure', **148** *Journal of Institutional and Theoretical Economics*, 411 ff.
Voigt, Stefan (1992), *Die Welthandelsordnung zwischen Konflikt und Stabilität – Konfliktpotentiale und Konfliktlösungsmechanismen* (The World Trade System between Conflict and Stability), Freiburg: Haufe.
Ware, Stephen J. (1999), 'Default Rules from Mandatory Rules: Privatizing Law through Arbitration', **83** *Minnesota Law Review*, 703 ff.
Watson, Alan (1974), *Legal Transplants: An Approach to Comparative Law*, Cambridge, MA: Harvard University Press.
Whincop, Michael (1999), 'The Recognition Scene: Game Theoretic Issues in the Recognition of Foreign Judgments', **23** *Melbourne University Law Review*, 416 ff.
Whincop, Michael (2000), 'Three Positive Theories of International Jurisdiction', **24** *Melbourne University Law Review*, 379 ff.
Whincop, Michael J. and Keyes, Mary (1997), 'Putting the "Private" Back into Private International Law: Default Rules and the Proper Law of the Contract', **21** *Melbourne University Law Review*, 515 ff.
Whincop, Michael J. and Keyes, Mary (1998a), 'Statutes' Domains in Private International Law: An Economic Theory of the Limits of Mandatory Rules', **20** *Sydney Law Review*, 435 ff.
Whincop, Michael and Keyes, Mary (1998b), 'Economic Analysis of Conflict of Laws in Tort Cases: Discrete and Relational Torts', **22** *Melbourne University Law Review*, 370 ff.
Whincop, Michael J. and Keyes, Mary (1999), 'The Market Tort in Private International Law', **19** *Northwestern Journal of International Law and Business*, 215 ff.
Whincop, Michael J. and Keyes, Mary (2001), *Policy and Pragmatism in the Conflict of Laws*, Aldershot: Ashgate Publishing.
White, Michelle J. (1992), 'Legal Complexity and Lawyers' Benefit from Litigation', **12** *International Review of Law and Economics*, 381 ff.
Williamson, Oliver E. (1985), *The Economic Institutions of Capitalism*, New York: Free Press.
Winter, Ralph A. (1977), 'State Law, Shareholder Protection, and the Theory of the Corporation', **6** *Journal of Legal Studies*, 251 ff.

Other References

Alchian, Armen A. (1950), 'Uncertainty, Evolution, and Economic Theory', **58** *Journal of Political Economy*, 211 ff.
Axelrod, Robert (1984), *The Evolution of Cooperation*, New York: Basic Books.
Banerjee, Abhijit (1992), 'A Simple Model of Herd Behavior', **107** *Quarterly Journal of Economics*, 797 ff.
Baysinger, Barry D. and Butler, Henry N. (1985), The Role of Corporate Law in the Theory of the Firm', **28** *Journal of Law and Economics*, 179 ff.
Bikhchandani, Sushil, Hirshleifer, David and Welch, Ivo (1992), 'A Theory of Fads, Fashion, Custom, and Cultural Change as Informational Cascades', **100** *Journal of Political Economy*, 992 ff.
Friedman, James (1971), 'A Non-cooperative Equilibrium for Supergames', **28** *Review of Economic Studies*, 1 ff.
Gerken, Luder (1995), 'Institutional Competition: An Orientative Framework', in Gerken, Luder (ed.), *Competition among Institutions*, Basingstoke: Palgrave Macmillan, 1 ff.
Hayek, F.A. (1948), *Individualism and Economic Order*, Chicago: University of Chicago Press.
Kerber, Wolfgang and Vanberg, Viktor (1995), 'Competition among Institutions: Evolution without Constraints', in Gerken, Luder (ed.), *Competition among Institutions*, Basingstoke: Palgrave Macmillian, 33 ff.
Landes, Elisabeth (1982), 'Insurance, Liability and Accidents: A Theoretical and Empirical Investigation of the Effect of No-Fault Accidents', **25** *Journal of Law and Economics*, 49 ff.

Landes, William M. and Posner, Richard A. (1975), 'The Independent Judiciary in an Interest Group Perspective', **18** *Journal of Law and Economics*, 875 ff.
Landes, William M. and Posner, Richard A. (1987), *The Economic Structure of Tort Law*, Cambridge, MA: Harvard University Press, 14 ff.
McCormick, R. and Tollison, R. (1981), *Politicians, Legislations and the Economy: An Inquiry into the Interest-Group Theory of Government*, Boston, MA: Nijhoff-Kluwer.
O'Hara, Erin (1993), 'Social Constraint or Implicit Collusion: Toward A Game Theoretic Analysis of Stare Decisis', **24** *Seton Hall Law Review*, 736 ff.
Olson, Mancur (1965), *The Logic of Collective Action*, Boston, MA: Harvard University Press.
Posner, Richard A. (1992), *Economic Analysis of Law*, 4th edn, Boston, MA: Little Brown.
Posner, Richard A. and Scott, Kenneth (1980) (eds), *Economics of Corporation Law and Securities Regulation*, Boston, MA: Little Brown.
Priest, George and Klein, Benjamin (1984), 'The Selection of Disputes for Litigation', **13** *Journal of Legal Studies*, 1 ff.
Restatement (First), Conflict of Laws (1934).
Restatement (Second), Conflict of Laws (1971).
Scharfstein, David and Stein, J. (1990), 'Herd Behavior and Investment', **80** *American Economic Review*, 465 ff.
Schwartz, Alan, and Wilde, Louis A. (1979), 'Intervening in Markets on the Basis of Imperfect Information: A Legal and Economic Analysis', **127** *University of Pennsylvania Law Review*, 630 ff.
Tiebout, Charles M. (1956), 'A Pure Theory of Local Expenditure', **64** *Journal of Political Economy*, 416 ff.
Tollison, Robert (1988), 'Public Choice and Legislation', **74** *Virginia Law Review*, 339 ff.

Cases

Cooley v. Board of Wardens, 53 U.S. 299 (1851)
Supreme Council of the Royal Arcanum v. Green, 237 U.S. 531 (1915)
Home Insurance Co. v. Dick, 281 U.S. 397 (1930)
Vita Food Products Inc. v. Unus Shipping Co., A.C. 277 (1939)
Allstate Insurance Co v. Hague, 449 U.S. 302 (1981)
Edgar v. Mite Corp., 457 U.S. 624 (1982)
CTS Corp. v. Dynamics Corp. of America, 481 U.S. 69 (1987).

6 Criminal procedure: empirical analysis
Thomas J. Miles

1. Introduction

The criminal justice system in the United States has two prominent features. The first is that the system is enormous. A common measure of its size is the number of persons currently subject to criminal punishment. For example, in 2007, US prisons and jails held nearly 2.3 million people, and another 5 million were on probation or parole (Bureau of Justice Statistics 2007). But, this stock of punished persons underestimates the number of people who flow through the preliminary stages of the criminal justice system. For example, in 2003 police made more than 13.7 million arrests (Bureau of Justice Statistics 2003), and although an exact figure is not known, the number of people stopped and questioned by police is surely a multiple of arrests.[1] The second important fact about the American criminal justice system is its sharp racial disparities. For example, nearly 20% of black men born between 1965 and 1969 served time in prison by their early thirties, compared to only 3% of whites (Pettit and Western 2004).

The stunning magnitudes of these figures raise difficult questions about what determines how much punishment the criminal justice system delivers, to whom the system metes it out, and whether these choices are the right ones. Regarding the positive questions of the aggregate amount of punishment and its distribution, the content of substantive criminal law and the level of funding for enforcement are surely crucial factors. But, another often-overlooked influence is the law of criminal procedure.

Criminal procedure, the law governing the process of investigating and adjudicating criminal cases, influences the allocation and distribution of punishment in society by affecting the cost of bringing prosecutions. Easterbrook (1983) referred to criminal procedure as a market system that helps set the "price" of committing crimes. By determining how many resources the government must invest in order to obtain a conviction, criminal procedure affects both the level of enforcement and the choice of which crimes to enforce. Legal scholars who usually perceive criminal procedure as mainly pertaining to constitutional protections of individual

---

[1] One study of stops by police in New York City showed that only 15% of stops resulted in arrests (Fagan and Davies 2000).

rights may view the economist's attempt to understand it in terms of costs and benefits as inapposite. But, to the extent that criminal procedure influences the allocation and distribution of punishment, economics is a useful mode of examining criminal procedure.

This chapter surveys the sizable empirical literature on the economic analysis of criminal procedure. It is a diverse literature in which contributions are sometimes not expressly identified as pertaining to criminal procedure. Only rarely have economists attempted to probe the consequences of specific constitutional decisions that safeguard rights in the criminal process. Instead, economists have typically addressed a specific aspect of the criminal justice system or the behavior of a particular actor in that system. As a result, economic work in the area typically focuses on specific subtopics, such as prosecutorial discretion, racial profiling, or sentencing outcomes.

The variety of studies is likely due to absence of a single conceptual framework and limitations on available data. A single conceptual model does not unify empirical studies of criminal justice institutions in the same way that Becker's (1968) model of deterrence guides the economists' study of criminal behavior. The Beckerian framework is a model of offending behavior that largely abstracts from the criminal justice system. Legal institutions are relevant to the economic model of crime to the extent that they influence the expected penalty through the probability of punishment or the magnitude of the penalty. In contrast, empirical studies of particular criminal justice institutions typically do not test the deterrence hypothesis. Nor has legal scholarship provided a single conceptual framework. Some legal scholars, such as Stuntz (2001, 2006), have considered the systemic relationships between criminal procedure, substantive criminal law, and crime rates. But, empirical work by economists on criminal justice has not examined these macro-level relationships. Rather, their studies consider the operation of specific legal institutions, actors, or procedures. In lieu of a single unifying conceptual model, these studies typically present a behavioral framework specific to the particular inquiry. The models often lack wider application and are tailored to the particular data set that a researcher possesses.

In addition, a lack of readily available data hampers economic studies of the criminal justice system. No government agency assembles annual data on criminal prosecutions, sentences, and appeals at the state or local level. Although the US Sentencing Commission makes available data on the sentences of federal defendants, many important variables, including the identity of the judge, are not collected. Moreover, federal policies lack the natural cross-sectional variation of state policies, and the absence of cross-state variation hampers identification of causal effects. Economists interested in empirical analysis of state criminal courts often engage in costly data collection. The use of different data sets limits the comparability of their results even when studies address similar research questions.

In view of these limitations, two important questions are how empirical studies of criminal justice by economists differ from inquiries on similar topics by criminologists and how they differ from economic studies of civil justice. With respect to criminology, the economic approach is distinguished by its use of the rational actor model to develop and test hypotheses about the behavior of particular actors within the justice system. Moreover, some of the economic contributions in this area are effectively studies of specific labor markets that exist within the justice system. Also, economists generally give greater attention to the identification of causal directions than other social scientists. With respect to the economic analysis of civil disputes, these models have much in common with the economic approach to criminal justice because both topics involve adjudication through litigation and importantly the possibility of settlement before trial. But, the criminal context is distinct because the litigants' objectives are more uncertain than in civil litigation where the parties' concerns are typically monetary. For example, it is unclear whether a defendant facing the loss of liberty would behave in the same way as a defendant facing even a large damage award.

The remainder of the chapter is organized largely around specific actors in the criminal justice system. Section 2 discusses police behavior, with particular attention to racial profiling and the exclusionary rule. Section 3 reviews research on pretrial release and bail. Section 4 examines prosecutors, their charging decisions, and their career concerns. Section 5 considers judges and their decisions in sentencing criminal defendants. Section 6 concludes.

2. Police Discretion and the Regulation of Investigations

2.1. Racial Profiling

Most economic analyses of police have focused on whether increases in the size of police forces reduce crime. These studies consider the level of policing to be a proxy for the probability of apprehension, and whether the number of police employed affects crime is then a test of Becker's (1968) deterrence hypothesis. Levitt and Miles (2007) provide a review of these studies. In contrast, criminologists have given less attention to the level of police and instead have given more attention to the efficacy of various policing strategies, such as community policing, "hot spot" policing, and crackdowns. Nagin (1998) and Sherman (2002) review this literature. Economists have infrequently examined which policing strategies or methods are most effective, but a few exceptions exist. Grogger (2002) studied gang ordinances in Los Angeles and found that violent crime fell substantially in neighborhoods subject to them relative to other neighborhoods. Miles (2005) examined the impact of a specific apprehension device, publicity, and reported that fugitives exposed to it experienced quicker apprehension times.

Other than its effect on offending, the aspect of policing that economists have studied most closely is the racial disparity in enforcement. For example, in city-level data, Donohue and Levitt (2001) found a correlation between the racial composition of police forces and arrests. They reported that increases in the number of minority police officers tracked increases in the arrests of whites, but not the arrests of minorities. Similarly, increases in the number of white police officers correlated with increases in the arrests of minorities, but not the arrests of whites. Both the causes and effects of these patterns were unclear. The estimates suggested that higher own-race policing reduced property crime, but had no appreciable effect on violent crime.

An aspect of the racial disparity in policing that received much attention in recent years is that police disproportionately stop and search black motorists. This fact has led to litigation alleging "racial profiling," or the use by police of a driver's race as a criterion in choosing whether to stop or to search, a practice that violates the Equal Protection Clause of the 14th Amendment, such as *Chavez v. Illinois State Police*, 251 F.3d 612 (7th Cir. 2001).

Racial profiling could arise at both the stop and the search margins. The probability that police stop a minority motorist may be higher than that for a white motorist, and conditional on stopping a motorist, the likelihood police search a minority motorist may be higher than that for a white motorist. A difficulty in assessing whether racial profiling occurs with respect to stops is that researchers do not observe the racial distribution of the population at risk of being searched. That is, the racial distribution of motorists, or in statistical terms the risk set, is not observed. The racial composition of the jurisdiction in which stops occur is a poor measure of the risk set because of racial differences in automobile ownership and travel patterns.

Grogger and Ridgeway (2006) proposed a solution to this problem. They compared the racial incidence of stops occurring at night and during the day. Police are less likely to observe the race of a motorist at night than during the day, and a comparison of the racial distribution of stops occurring during the day and at night is a test for the existence of racial profiling in motorist stops. The test requires the racial distribution of travel to be the same during the day as it is at night, an assumption which may not be valid. A refinement of their test that addresses this objection exploits the variation in hours of daylight over the seasons. By limiting attention to twilight hours, Grogger and Ridgeway (2006) sought to hold constant the racial distribution of travel, while varying the exposure to daylight. They tested these predictions using data from Oakland, California, and their results did not support the presence of racial profiling in traffic stops. If police engaged in racial profiling, the rate at which police stop minority motorists should be higher during the day than at night, and Grogger and Ridgeway (2006) found the opposite is true. When the sample was limited to twilight hours, the difference was modest, but its direction remained contrary to what the presence of racial profiling would predict.

With respect to the margin of searches, economists sought to distinguish the two economic theories of discrimination. Becker's (1957) model describes racial prejudice as the decision-maker's preference for treating members of a particular race less favorably. In contrast, the decision-maker in Arrow's (1973) model of "statistical discrimination" has no preference for discrimination, but race predicts an outcome of interest. The predictive power of race prompts the decision-maker in Arrow's model to treat minorities less favorably while maximizing the outcome of interest.[2]

Knowles et al. (2001) developed a model to test whether police were Beckerian or Arrowian discriminators in conducting motor vehicle searches. The model distinguished whether racial prejudice or the goal of maximizing the number of successful searches explained the racial disparity in motor vehicle searches. The central prediction of the Knowles et al. (2001) model was an "outcomes" test. It compared the rates at which searches of the two racial groups yielded contraband. If police were not racially prejudiced and merely maximized the number of successful searches, the rate at which the marginal white motorist was found to be carrying contraband should have been equal to that for the marginal black motorist. But, if police had a preference for discrimination, they would tolerate a lower rate of successful searches among the disfavored group.

This prediction shifted empirical attention away from the differential treatment of racial groups toward differences in outcomes. Prior research commonly estimated regressions on the likelihood of search as a function of race and other characteristics, and the test for the presence of discrimination was whether the coefficient on race was nonzero. A difficulty of this approach is that researchers cannot be confident that their equations

---

[2] It is worth noting that the economic theory of discrimination is irrelevant to whether the police practice violates the Equal Protection Clause. Either form of discrimination would be illegal.

include all variables used by officers in choosing whether to search, and if variables are missing, the estimated coefficient on race may suffer from omitted variable bias.

An innovation of Knowles et al. (2001) was to direct attention to outcomes rather than treatments. But, their key prediction of equality in hit rates pertains to the marginal motorist who is searched. Absent the full information set of the officers, the researcher cannot identify the marginal motorist and can test only average hit rates. This presents the so-called infra-marginality problem: that average hit rates may differ from marginal rates. A second contribution of Knowles et al. (2001) was to incorporate in their model the motorist's decision to carry contraband and to show that, in the equilibrium of their model, average and marginal hit rates would be equal. The outcome test for discrimination could then be conducted using average hit rates.

Knowles et al. (2001) tested their hypothesis on a data set obtained from ACLU litigation. The data contained all vehicle searches along an interstate highway in Maryland over a four-year period. The authors could not reject that the rates at which police found contraband during searches were equal across racial groups. They also could not reject equality across racial groups in the rates of successful searches within subsamples of the data, such as age of the vehicle, whether the vehicle is a luxury model, and whether the search occurred during the day or at night. These patterns were consistent with statistical discrimination rather than racial prejudice. Persico and Todd (2006) applied on extended version of the Knowles et al. (2001) model to data from vehicle searches in Wichita, Kansas. In those data, the hypothesis that hit rates were equal across racial groups, age groups, racial groups stratified by age, and gender could not be rejected. These patterns were also consistent with statistical discrimination.

Several economists criticized the Knowles et al. (2001) finding. Dharmapala and Ross (2004) argued that in a more generalized model including varying offenses levels and imperfect observability of offenders, the appropriate test requires stratifying the data by offense severity. Dharmapala and Ross (2004) concluded that, in the absence of these variables, the Knowles et al. (2001) data could not distinguish the presence of discrimination, reverse discrimination, or the absence of discrimination. Harcourt (2007) offered another criticism. He showed that when police are assumed to prefer to minimize crime rather than maximize hit rates, the equilibrium outcome may not be unequal search rates and equal hit rates. Dominitz and Knowles (2006) develop a more formal model of this idea and argue that the extraction of information from hit rates may still be valid under certain assumptions about the joint distribution of criminality by race.

122 *Procedural law and economics*

Antonovics and Knight (2009) extended the Knowles et al. (2001) framework to include officers belonging to two racial groups. They predicted that if officers were statistical discriminators who maximized hit rates, the incidence of search should not correlate with an officer's race. But, they found in data from the Boston Police Department that officers were more likely to search members of the opposite race. The finding is consistent with Donohue and Levitt (2001). Antonovics and Knight (2009) excluded the possibilities that the assignment of officers to different neighborhoods and officers' ability to search members of their own racial group explained the results. Rather, they attributed the patterns to preference-based discrimination.

Anwar and Fang (2006) further explored whether officers of different races varied in their search behavior. They developed a model centering on whether officers were "monolithic" in their search behavior, meaning that officers of different races searched white motorists at the same rate. Their model predicted that if officers were monolithic, officers of each race would search motorists of a given race at the same rate, and the officers would have the same hit rates in searching motorists of a given race. Anwar and Fang (2006) tested these predictions using two years of data from the Florida Highway Patrol that included information on officer characteristics. They rejected that officers of different races were monolithic in their search behavior. White officers searched motorists of all racial groups more often than black officers did, but white officers had lower hit rates with motorists of all races than black officers did.

As these contributions illustrate, the literature on outcome tests as applied to racial profiling has grown rapidly. Each new article features a model with more sophisticated conceptions of police and motorist behavior and articulates empirical predictions requiring more elaborate data sets. Persico and Todd (2006) present models with officers who are heterogenous in their tastes for discrimination and in their costs of searching and in which motorists can adjust their characteristics in response to monitoring. The methods developed for examining racial profiling are likely to have useful application in the study of racial disparities elsewhere in the criminal justice system.

2.2. The Exclusionary Rule
For lawyers and legal academics, the phrase "criminal procedure" typically refers to the law governing criminal investigations, searches and seizures, and the trial process. The core of the subject is the criminal justice process leading to the adjudication of guilt or innocence. The stages of the criminal process occurring after conviction, such as sentencing, appeals and habeas corpus, also involve complex procedures, are

often not covered in standard "criminal procedure" courses or treatises. Rather, they are cast as specialized, advanced topics. In addition, criminal procedure is effectively a subcategory of constitutional law, because the individual rights secured in the Bill of Rights largely determine how police, prosecutors, and judges must treat criminal defendants or individuals suspected of criminality.

For economists who have studied procedural aspects of the criminal justice system, it is nearly the opposite: the bulk of their work has focused on sentencing rather than the earlier stages of the criminal justice process, and when they have studied other aspects of that process, they have given little attention to the constitutional nuances. Economic research on racial profiling, described above, illustrates the latter pattern. The empirical analysis there sought to distinguish differing economic theories of discrimination. While empirical evidence on this question was illuminating, it may not directly inform the legal question of whether the police's conduct violated the requirement of equal protection of the law. Thus, inquires of legal academics have not always aligned with interests of lawyers or the legal questions facing courts.

Two exceptions to this pattern are the modest bodies of work on the exclusionary rule and *Miranda* rights. The exclusionary rule refers to the remedy for the government's obtaining evidence in violation of an individual's Fourth Amendment right against unreasonable searches and seizures. Such evidence is not admissible at trial, and instead, it must be suppressed or excluded. The purpose of the rule is to safeguard the rights of individuals and to dissuade police from collecting such evidence. A common criticism of the rule is that when incriminating evidence is excluded, the government often cannot carry its burden of proof and must abandon the prosecution. Thus, the guilty defendants escape punishment, the opportunity for incapacitation and deterrence are lost, and crime rates rise.[3]

A small body of research has tried to measure these hypothesized social costs of the exclusionary rule. Early empirical scholarship on the rule tried to tabulate the frequency with which evidence was excluded under the rule and prosecutions were consequently dropped. Oaks (1970) and Spiotto (1973) examined motions to suppress made in preliminary hearings and at trials in the criminal courts of Chicago in 1969–70 and

---

[3] For example, in a dissent from a subsequent decision, Chief Justice Warren Burger wrote, "Some clear demonstration of the benefits and effectiveness of the exclusionary rule is needed to justify it in view of the high price it extracts from society – the release of countless guilty criminals." *Bivens v. Six Unknown Named Agents*, 403 U.S. 388, 416 (1971) (Burger, C.J., dissenting).

1971, respectively. Both found wide variation across offense categories in the rates at which motions were made, and generally high rates at which motions were granted. For example, Spiotto reported that over 70% of such motions were granted at the preliminary hearing and 20% at the trial stage. Both of these authors noted the high grant rate was likely attributable at least in part to the practical absence of any screening of cases by Chicago's prosecutors before the preliminary hearing during that period. A decade later, Nardulli (1983) examined a sample of nine midsize counties, and concluded the impact of the rule was "marginal." He found that motions to exclude physical evidence, identifications, and confessions occurred in fewer than 8% of cases and that these motions infrequently succeeded. Moreover, in cases in which the court suppressed evidence, the government did not necessarily drop its prosecution. Nardulli (1983) concluded that less than 0.6% of cases were lost due to the exclusionary rule. Davies (1983) provided a thorough review of prior studies and in particular criticized the National Institute of Justice's estimates of the cases lost in California. According to data he separately collected for that state, Davies (1983) found that only 0.8% of felony arrests in California were lost due to the exclusionary rule, and the rate was highest (2.4%) in drug cases.

More recently, a pair of economists attempted to measure the effect of the exclusionary rule on crime rates. Atkins and Rubin (2003) observed that in the early part of the twentieth century, states varied in whether they applied some form of exclusionary rule, and in a 1961 decision, *Mapp v. Ohio*, 367 U.S. 643 (1961), the Supreme Court held that the exclusionary rule applies to state criminal proceedings in addition to federal ones. These variations allowed Atkins and Rubin (2003) to compare crime rates in states before and after they adopted the exclusionary rule relative to states experiencing with no change in the rule. In other words, it afforded the opportunity to estimate the effect of the exclusionary rule using differences-in-differences. Atkins and Rubin's (2003) main results came from a panel of state crime rates covering the years 1947–1967, and their estimates were sizable. For example, robbery and property crime rates rose by 4% to 8% following the adoption of the exclusionary rule. When these estimates are compared to earlier research showing that lost cases were a relatively rare occurrence, one cannot help but wonder whether such large estimates reflect omitted variable bias. This important legal and public policy question needs further empirical investigation by economists.

A second procedural doctrine that has received significant empirical study is the Supreme Court's decision in *Miranda v. Arizona*, 384 U.S. 436 (1966). The popularity of innumerable detective-themed entertainments has made the four warnings of *Miranda* well known: the right to silence; the possibility that statements will be used against the speaker; the right to counsel; and if the defendant is indigent, the provision of counsel by the state. Under *Miranda*, these warnings are needed to dispel the Court's presumption that statements made by defendants while in police custody are compelled. Exclusionary rule furnishes the remedy for a violation of the *Miranda*'s framework: the defendant's statements are inadmissible at trial. Unsurprisingly, the same criticisms that were made of the exclusionary rule were also made of *Miranda*. Namely, that it would permit some guilty defendants to escape punishment and thus increase crime.[4]

Miranda immediately inspired a flurry of studies that attempted to measure its effect of police behavior. The first generation of empirical scholarship of *Miranda* sought to measure whether the decision altered how police conducted interrogations and whether defendants invoked the right to silence. Cassell (1996), Schulhofer (1996), and Thomas and Leo (2002) provide convenient guides to this large literature, which consists of direct observations of police interrogations, surveys of interrogators and the interrogated, and reviews of case files. The findings of Wald et al. (1967) and Leiken (1970) are typical of this literature. They observed that police tended to follow the commands of *Miranda* and that suspects, despite receiving the warnings, usually spoke with investigators in the absence of legal counsel. These patterns do not appear to have changed in subsequent decades. Leo (1996, 1998) summarizes more recent studies showing that police faithfully recite the *Miranda* warnings while still persuading over 80% of suspects to waive their rights.

As with the early studies of the exclusionary rule, there have been attempts to calculate the number of convictions lost due to *Miranda*. Cassell (1996) asserted that *Miranda* caused a 3.8% decline in the number of convictions. He arrived at this figure by claiming that *Miranda* lowered the incidence of confession by 16% and nearly 24% of cases depended upon confessions. Schulhofer (1996) challenged these calculations and claimed that a more accurate figure was a loss of only 0.78% of criminal cases. Schulhofer believed that the number of cases in which a confession was instrumental was 19%, but more crucially, he believed *Miranda* lowered confessions by only 4.1%. In addition, Schulhofer hypothesized

---

[4] *Miranda*, 384 U.S. at 542–3 ("In some unknown number of cases the Court's rule will return a killer, a rapist or other criminal to the streets and to the environment which produced him, to repeat his crime whenever it pleases him. As a consequence, there will not be a gain, but a loss, in human dignity . . . There is, of course, a saving factor: the next victims are uncertain, unnamed, and unrepresented in this case") (White, J., dissenting).

that these declines were temporary because over time police learn techniques that elicit confessions despite *Miranda*'s warnings.

Cassell and Fowles (1998) examined another metric of law enforcement performance, clearance rates or the ratio of arrests to reported offenses. They regressed a national time series of annual clearance rates on a set of control variables, including an indicator variable for the years 1966 through 1968. The estimated coefficient on that indicator variable was negative and statistically significant for robbery and property offenses, and they claimed that it captured the social cost of *Miranda*. This approach is less convincing than the differences-in-differences estimates of, for example, Atkins and Rubin (2003), because estimates from national time series may be biased by unobserved, contemporary events. Donohue (1998) and Feeney (2000) describe this and many other criticisms in detail. Further study by empirical economists could do much to advance our understanding of the consequences of the Fourth Amendment's protections.

3. Bail and Pretrial Release

Bail and conditions on a defendant's pretrial release (such as electronic monitoring) are the primary mechanisms that ensure the defendant's appearance at trial. A long-standing policy question is what amount of bail and which conditions are appropriate. A difficulty in relating bail to the risk of flight is the endogeneity of pretrial release conditions. Judges are likely to require those with the greatest risk of flight to post the largest amounts of bail or be subject to the most restrictive bail conditions, and ordinary least squares estimates of bail on outcomes such as re-arrest or failure to appear will be biased toward zero.

The first studies by economists of bail and pretrial release often came to conflicting conclusions about the impact of bail on defendant flight because of this endogeneity. For example, Landes (1973) in studying a sample of criminal defendants in New York City found that offense type and bail amounts correlated with the likelihood of jumping bail. But, Clarke et al. (1976) in their study of defendants in Charlotte, NC, reached a different conclusion. According to their estimates, offense type and demographic characteristics were not significantly correlated with the defendant's failure to appear. Yet, they also found that the strictness of supervision during release and court delay were strongly related to flight risk. Myers (1981) showed that estimates of the effect of bail were sensitive to plea bargaining, and this is perhaps not surprising as a defendant on pretrial release may be reluctant to accept a plea bargain which requires incarceration. In studying New York defendants, Myers (1981) found that after controlling for plea bargains, the risk of flight correlated weakly with court delay, but it was strongly and negatively related to larger bail amounts. Helland and Tabarrok (2004) demonstrated that bounty hunters are much more effective than public law enforcement in reducing bail jumping and catching those who skip bail.

Abrams and Rolfs (2011) attempted to overcome the endogeneity problem by studying a randomized experiment in bail setting in Philadelphia in 1981. The experiment required a group of judges to follow a set of bail-setting guidelines that had the effect of lowering the amounts of bail required, and when combined with the random assignment of cases to judges, the experiment induced plausibly random variation in bail amounts. The resulting estimates implied that bail reduced the probability of re-arrest by a greater degree than was apparent in cross-sectional comparisons. Using these estimates, Abrams and Rolfs (2011) calculated that the average defendant would be willing to pay roughly $1,000 for 90 days of freedom, and they concluded that judges set bail amounts close to the socially optimal levels even in the absence of bail guidelines.

Just as they have examined the influence of race in other parts of the criminal justice system, economists have made careful study of racial disparities in bail. Ayres and Waldfogel (1994) studied criminal defendants in New Haven, Connecticut, and found that bail amounts for African-American and Hispanic men were substantially higher than for whites and women, even after controlling for observable characteristics. Their estimates also indicated that African-Americans and Hispanics paid significantly lower interest rates on their bail bonds. Ayres and Waldfogel (1994) argue that because bond dealers willingly accepted lower interest rates from minorities for use of their capital, the possibility that minorities pose greater flight risks could not justify their higher bail amounts. The approach here – asking whether racial differences in flight risk justify the racial disparity in bail amounts – is an early example of the sort of "outcome analysis" that was subsequently developed in the racial profiling literature. Ayres and Waldfogel (1994) concluded their estimates were initial evidence of racial prejudice in setting bail.

4. The Behavior of Prosecutors

The seminal model of prosecutorial behavior is Landes (1971), in which prosecutors maximized the sum of expected sentences of cases subject to a resource constraint. Prosecutors and defendants differed in their expectations of victory at trial, and Landes derived conditions for settlement and the amount of resources invested in trial. Using several years of state and federal court data, Landes tested these predictions, and found that trials were more common in jurisdictions where defendants more often secured pre-trial release and where a defendant's legal fees were subsidized.

A sizable theoretical literature has extended Landes' model (see, e.g., Grossman and Katz 1983; Reignanum 1988; Bjerk 2007). In addition, it inspired a flurry of early empirical investigations into the determinants of prosecutor behavior and plea bargaining. Rhodes (1976) reported that in federal courts the frequency of plea bargains correlated positively with the leniency of sentencing offers. Forst and Brosi (1977) found in data from the District of Columbia trial court that the length of time prosecutors left a case pending was positively related to the strength of the evidence against the defendant. Weimar's (1978) estimates from a California court showed that the sentence prosecutors offered in plea negotiations rose with a proxy for the expected sentence at trial. Also, he found that the likelihood that the defendant insisted on a trial fell with the magnitude of the discount offered in a plea.

More recent empirical economic studies have given close attention to the effect of harsher penalties on prosecutorial behavior. These studies are highly relevant to policy because many legislatures recently passed mandatory minima in an effort to impose tougher penalties and to constrain judicial discretion. Under Landes' conception of prosecutorial behavior, mandatory minimums should raise the length of the average sentence. But prosecutors may not favor higher penalties in all instances. The cost to a prosecutor of obtaining a conviction may be higher when a larger penalty induces a defendant to litigate rather than plea. Also, Tonry (1996) claimed that some prosecutors perceive mandatory sentences as unduly harsh and prosecutors avoid them by charging offenses that are similar but do not trigger application of the mandatory sentence. This response highlights a particular form of plea bargaining, called "charge bargaining," in which prosecutors agree to seek conviction for an offense carrying a lesser penalty rather than offering a reduced penalty on the originally charged offense. Discretion to charge bargain gives prosecutors the opportunity to avoid large penalties and particularly mandatory minima.

Yet, several recent studies find that when penalty enhancements are enacted, punishments increase. This pattern suggests that either prosecutors' discretion is not so wide that they can ignore the higher penalties, or that they prefer to impose higher penalties. Kessler and Piehl (1998) studied the consequences of California's Proposition 8, a referendum passed in 1982 that imposed mandatory minimum sentences for particular violent offenses. Kessler and Piehl (1998) compared sentences before and after the passage of the referendum for three groups of defendants: those convicted of offenses subject to the mandatory minimum; those convicted of offenses factually similar but not subject to the mandatory minimum; and those convicted of offenses factually different and not subject to the mandatory minimum. Among their findings was that the average sentence for robbery, a crime subject to the mandatory minimum, increased by 50% following the referendum. In contrast, the average sentence for grand larceny, which was factually similar to robbery but not subject to a mandatory minimum, increased slightly. The crime of drug possession provided a still sharper contrast. It is a crime that is factually different than robbery, and it is not subject to the mandatory minimum. Following passage of the referendum, its average sentence fell slightly. Kessler and Piehl saw their results as evidence that prosecutorial discretion is not as unconstrained as some thought and that when prosecutors exercise their discretion, they do so to raise rather than reduce sentences.

In the 1990s, several states passed three-strikes laws, which are statutes imposing enhanced penalties on repeat offenders. The cross-sectional variation in the presence of these laws and the differential timing among states that adopted them permitted Bjerk (2005) to employ a differences-in-differences methodology to estimate their effect on sentencing. He found that when an eligible defendant was arrested on a felony charge requiring application of the third-strike enhancement, prosecutors were roughly twice as likely to charge a misdemeanor instead. But, because relatively few defendants were eligible for the third strike, the fraction of cases in which prosecutors exercised this discretion remained modest. Despite these mitigating decisions by prosecutors, the three-strike law increased the average sentence of defendants eligible for the penalty enhancement. Bjerk (2005) discussed other evidence suggesting that his estimates reflected the moderating decisions of prosecutors rather than resource constraints or the behavior of other actors in the criminal justice system.

Kuziemko (2006) studied the reintroduction of the death penalty in New York in the mid-1990s. Using a difference-in-differences methodology, she found that death-eligible felony defendants accepted more severe plea bargains after the death penalty was re-established. But, the frequency of plea bargains did not change. Kuziemko interpreted these results as indicating that the presence of the death penalty altered the terms of trade in plea bargains. Her results also showed that prosecutors did not completely undo this increase in the potential penalty by declining to charge death-eligible offenses.

Piehl and Bushway (2007) examined how prosecutors exercise discretion in response to sentencing guidelines rather than enhanced penalties. Numerous legal scholars have observed that sentencing guidelines reallocate the discretion to determine sentences from judges to prosecutors. Piehl and Bushway (2007) predicted that prosecutors have greater power to charge bargain when the guidelines are mandatory for judges and when the sentencing grid of the guidelines has narrower ranges. To capture this, they measured the reduction in sentence from a charge bargain rather than the incidence of charge bargains, and they compared sentences in two states: Maryland, which had voluntary guidelines with wide sentencing ranges and Washington, which had mandatory guidelines with narrow ranges. The results were complicated by the fact that Washington used incarceration less frequently than Maryland. But after controlling for this difference, the guidelines in Washington had a larger impact on sentencing outcomes in plea bargaining than those in Maryland. The estimates are consistent with the view that prosecutors exercised more discretion in the state with the mandatory, narrow guidelines.

These studies might leave the impression that discretion is inevitable in the criminal process, that it may be shifted between actors in the system but not eliminated. Wright and Miller (2002) examined the district court in New Orleans, where a local prosecutor implemented an early screening process in selecting which cases to prosecute. The screening process also sought to reduce charge bargaining by discouraging changes in charges once they had been made. Although the article is not a test of an economic model, the empirical patterns were pronounced. Wright and Miller (2002) found that, under the policy, prosecutions were declined more often and plea bargains occurred less often. Consequently, the incidence of trials rose slightly, and defendants pled guilty to the initial charge more often. The results suggest that prosecutorial offices can adopt policies that limit the discretion of their line prosecutors.

Economists have increasingly given attention to broader aspects of prosecutorial preferences, such as career concerns and their productivity. These studies examine prosecutors as actors in a broader labor market rather than examine the effect of a specific criminal procedure on prosecutors. Glaeser et al. (2000) compared the characteristics of prison entrants in the federal and state systems to learn which cases prosecutors preferred. They found that federal defendants were on average older and more highly educated and that they were more likely to be female, white, Hispanic, and married. Federal defendants were also more likely to have experience in managerial or technical employment and less likely to have a prior conviction. They were more often charged with drug distribution rather than possession and hired private attorneys with greater frequency. These patterns suggest that prosecutors gained valuable human capital from prosecuting cases involving more sophisticated defendants and more complex offenses.

Boylan (2005) evaluated federal prosecutors' career patterns by assessing how their performance in office related to success in their subsequent careers. In a sample of former US Attorneys who served between 1969 and 2000, a federal judgeship was the most preferred career outcome. The length of prison sentences correlated positively with later career success, but conviction rates did not. Boylan's (2005) evidence supports the Landes (1971) view that prosecutors maximize expected sentence lengths. Boylan and Long (2005) examined the career paths of line prosecutors in the federal system. They found that federal prosecutors were more likely to take a case to trial in districts where private attorneys received higher salaries. They hypothesized that lawyers seek positions as federal prosecutors in order to obtain trial experience that is valued in private practice. They documented that turnover among prosecutors was higher in districts with higher private compensation, and that departing prosecutors in higher income districts were more likely to take positions with large law firms.

The variation in experience and career paths that Glaeser et al. and Boylan and Long documented suggests that attorneys differ in their ability. Abrams and Yoon (2007) attempted to measure attorney ability in criminal cases by exploiting the random assignment of defense attorneys to cases in the Las Vegas public defender's office. They observed wide variation in outcomes for clients that was uncorrelated with the case characteristics. But, it correlated with some attorney characteristics. Perhaps most importantly, there appeared to be returns to experience. They estimated that a public defender with ten years of experience reduced the average client's sentence by 17% relative to a public defender in her first year on the job. Although they found no effects of gender or quality of legal education, Hispanic attorneys secured shorter sentences on average than other attorneys. The estimates of Abrams and Yoon (2007) provide strong support that the quality of lawyering can affect outcomes in criminal cases.

5. The Imposition of Punishment

5.1. The Regulation of Judicial Discretion

The central issue in sentencing policy over the past two decades has been the efficacy and desirability of sentencing guidelines. Before the advent of guidelines in the 1980s, sentencing judges had wide discretion to sentence defendants to terms falling anywhere within the statutory range, which often encompassed not only the length of sentence, but also the choice between probation and prison. The advantage of discretionary sentencing was that it afforded judges the opportunity to tailor sentences to individual defendants and to extend leniency where appropriate. But, discretionary sentencing had two prominent disadvantages. Broad judicial discretion risked compromising the principle of equal treatment under law by producing dissimilar treatment of similar defendants (Frankel 1973). Under discretionary sentencing, the sentences of defendants convicted of the same offense and having similar criminal histories exhibited wide variation. In addition, these variations were often correlated with race.

Minority defendants received more severe sentences than whites convicted of similar crimes and with similar criminal histories.

In response to these problems, states and the federal government introduced sentencing guidelines, which in many jurisdictions (including at the federal level) were mandatory rather than mere recommendations. Sentencing guidelines attempted to restrain judicial discretion in sentencing while retaining sufficient flexibility to permit individual sentences in each case (Breyer 1988; Stith and Cabranes 1998). At the federal level, the guidelines narrowed the range of permissible sentences and allowed deviations from those ranges only for a certain specified reasons. Under the guidelines, a grid largely determines sentences (US Sentencing Commission 2003). The vertical axis measures the severity of the defendant's criminal history, and the horizontal axis measures the severity of the current offense. A complex set of rules governs calculation of the criminal history category and offense level. Each box on the grid contains a sentencing range that is much narrower than the range of punishment prescribed in the corresponding criminal statute. A judge may "depart" from the guidelines, or impose a sentence outside the range specified on the grid, only in an atypical case that presents factors or circumstances that the guidelines do not consider. By establishing this formal process for determining a defendant's sentence, guidelines sought to reduce the influence of the identity of the sentencing judge and the demographic characteristics of the defendant in the determination of the sentence.

Criminologists and sociologists have developed a large empirical literature on sentencing, and the topic drew the interest of economists only since the enactment of sentencing guidelines at the federal level in 1989. Albonetti (1997), Hofer et al. (1999), and Bushway and Piehl (2001) provide extensive reviews of the earlier literature. Economists have generally been interested in empirically evaluating whether the guidelines succeeded in their stated goals. Much of the work by economists on sentencing falls into two categories: examinations of whether the guidelines reduced inter-judge disparities in sentencing and tests of whether they eliminated racial disparities. Recently, a third category has arguably emerged, and it analyzes whether judicial ideology influences sentences.

With respect to inter-judge disparity, a threshold question is how to measure it. Although the principle that judges should impose similar sentences in similar cases is intuitively clear, it is difficult to express in practice. Most studies take as the benchmark the average sentence conditional on offense of conviction and criminal history within a district and year. But, researchers take different approaches to calculating this disparity. Anderson et al. (1999) measure it as the mean difference in prison sentences for each judge relative to the mean prison sentence in the district in a given year. In contrast, Hofer et al.'s (1999) metric of inter-judge disparity was the proportion of the total variation in sentences attributable to judges, as measured by whether the R-square statistic rises when the regression on sentence lengths includes fixed-effect controls for the identity of each judge.

The studies typically evaluate whether inter-judge disparity has fallen by using the introduction of guidelines as source of "before and after" variation in judicial discretion. But, the studies differ in their samples. Waldfogel (1998) examines a single federal court in California, LaCasse and Payne (1999) study two federal courts in New York, Payne (1997) analyzes two federal courts in New York and one in Pennsylvania, and Hofer et al. (1999) and Anderson et al. (1999) examine national samples of federal courts. Perhaps because of their different metrics and samples, the studies did not reach similar conclusions about the amount of inter-judge disparity and whether it fell following the introduction of guidelines. Waldfogel (1998) estimated that 9% of the variation in discretionary sentences was attributable to inter-judge disparity, but Payne (1997) found that it was only 5%. Anderson et al. (1999) estimated that the expected difference in sentence between any two judges was 17% or 4.9 months before the guidelines and 11% or 3.9 months, after the implementation of the guidelines. In contrast, LaCasse and Payne (1999) found that the amount of variation in sentences attributable to the identity of the judge did not change for plea bargains and even rose for cases that proceeded to trial. Payne (1997) described the reduction in inter-judge disparity after the introduction of the guidelines as "negligible," but observed that the effect varied by district.

A criticism of the before-after comparisons is that they cannot control for contemporaneous but unobserved changes in the distribution of cases. A specific concern is that the introduction of sentencing guidelines at the federal level occurred at the same time as the establishment of mandatory minima for many drug crimes, which were then the most commonly prosecuted offenses in federal courts. For example, Anderson et al. (1999) found that over their study period, the average sentence rose from 24 to 35 months. Payne (1997) observed an increase in the length of drug sentences subject to mandatory minima and little change in sentence length for other offenses. The increase in the average sentence length makes it difficult to evaluate whether the reduction in inter-judge disparity was socially meaningful. For instance, Hofer et al. (1999) found that 2.32% of the variation in sentences was attributed to judge identity before the guidelines, and that this proportion fell by 1.08% after the guidelines. In terms of sentence length, the reduction was modest. The portion of the sentence attributable to judge identity was 7.87 months in the pre-guidelines period, and it was 7.61 months in the post-guidelines period.

Another important policy change that was contemporaneous (or nearly so) with the introduction of sentencing guidelines was the abandonment of indeterminate sentencing. Previously, parole boards rather than judges determined the actual length of time served by defendants. Many states switched to fixed-sentence regimes by adopting so-called truth-in-sentencing laws, and the federal government eliminated parole when it adopted its sentencing guidelines. Economists have given relatively less attention to this institutional change, and in the few instances when they have, their interest has been in its effect on the incidence of crime rather than the behavior of other actors in the criminal justice system.

Shepherd (2002) examined the effect of truth-in-sentencing laws by exploiting differential timing in the adoption of these laws across states. She concluded that determinate sentencing substantially reduced violent crimes, but caused increases in burglary and motor vehicle theft. Kuziemko (2007) used micro-level data and variation in Georgia's parole system to estimate the impact of parole across several margins. She found that longer prison terms reduced recidivism, and that restrictions on a parole board's discretion led inmates to decrease investments in rehabilitative activities and to experience higher rates of recidivism. Her evaluation implied that the social benefits of parole exceed its costs.

The second major line of inquiry in criminal sentencing by empirical economists has been whether "extrajudicial factors," specifically race of the defendant, influenced judges in assigning sentences.[5] Hagan (1974) and Kleck (1981) surveyed the very large criminological literature on this question, and a small number of economists have recently made contributions. Rather than drawing pre- and post-comparisons as much of the literature on inter-judge disparities does, these economists have examined whether a defendant's race correlates with his sentence even during the post-guidelines period. The key prediction is that it should not, but Mustard (2001) and Bushway and Piehl (2001) found that it did.

Mustard (2001) analyzed the most comprehensive data set of federal sentences in the literature and tested whether a host of demographic characteristics correlated with sentences, even after controlling for the defendant's criminal history and offense severity. Mustard found that males, blacks, non-citizens, and persons with less than high school education received longer sentences. The sentences of drug-trafficking defendants exhibited the widest variation. The disparities resulted principally from

---

[5] Data limitations prevent these studies from examining whether the race of the defendant and the race of the victim interact in influencing the sentence in the manner found by Baldus et al. (1983) in death penalty cases.

"departures" from the guidelines rather than within-range adjustments. A departure occurs when a judge decides that the sentence recommended by the guidelines fails to take into consideration an aggravating or mitigating factor and chooses to impose a sentence different than the guidelines recommendation. Mustard (2001) found that black defendants were significantly less likely to receive downward departures. Moreover, in an equation for whether a defendant received an upward departure, the estimated coefficient was positive, implying that a black defendant had a greater likelihood of receiving an upward departure, but this difference was not statistically significant.

Bushway and Piehl (2001) studied sentences in the state courts of Maryland, a state with sentencing guidelines analogous to the federal system. These authors described in great detail the numerous differences in functional form among studies in the literature, such as whether sentence length should be estimated separately from the decision to incarcerate and whether the non-linearities in the sentencing grid warrant expressing sentence length in logarithms (and hence percentages) rather than levels. They also provided a more elaborate test of how legal and extra-legal factors influence sentencing.

The primary test in Mustard (2001), for example, was whether the coefficients on extra-judicial variables, such as the defendant's race, were zero, and he controlled for the defendant's recommended sentence by including a series of fixed effects for the defendant's position in the sentencing grid. In contrast, Bushway and Piehl (2001) included the recommended sentence as a control variable, and predicted that if judges followed the guidelines, the coefficient on the recommended sentence should be unity. Their estimate for this coefficient exceeded one, which implied that as the recommended sentence increased, judges in their discretion punished these offenders more severely. In some specifications, these authors constrained its coefficient to equal one in order to help isolate the behavior of the sentencing judge from that of other actors in the criminal justice system. The choice to constrain this coefficient made little difference on the coefficient for race. They found that African-Americans receive sentences 20% longer after controlling for the sentence recommended under the guidelines. This estimate meant that although judges tended to sentence defendants with longer recommended sentences more harshly and although black defendants tended to have longer recommended sentences, race continued to exert a significant direct influence on the sentence received.

Studies of this type have two important limitations. The first is that by focusing on the post-guidelines period, these studies do not provide any insight into whether the guidelines have reduced racial disparities in sentencing. They convincingly demonstrate that race continues to influence sentencing even under a set of mandatory guidelines, and in so doing, they provide evidence that the guidelines are not a complete success. But, they do not reveal whether racial disparities were worse before the imposition of the guidelines, and thus, they do not speak to whether the guidelines achieved partial success along that dimension.

A second criticism is that these analyses of sentence lengths are analogous to the first-generation studies of racial profiling in policing. Unless the researcher possesses all of the information of the sentencing judge, a condition which is unlikely to be satisfied, estimates of the effect of race may suffer from omitted variable bias. In addition, sentence lengths are a sort of "treatment" the judge imposes, and recidivism may be, to a substantial degree, the outcome that concerns the judge. For these reasons, a likely next step in economic studies of racial disparities in sentencing is to apply outcome tests of the sort used in the racial profiling and bail literatures to sentencing, with recidivism as perhaps the relevant outcome. A possible prediction would be that a judge engaging in statistical discrimination would impose longer sentences on minority defendants than white defendants, and recidivism rates of white and black offenders would be equal. In contrast, a judge with a preference for discrimination would impose longer sentences on minority defendants despite their lower recidivism rates. These predictions await further development and testing.

Recently, a third category of sentencing studies by economists has emerged. These articles are more closely related to the political science literature on judicial politics in that they examine not just whether judges vary in their sentencing patterns, but also whether particular judicial characteristics predict their sentencing patterns. Schanzenbach and Tiller (2007, 2008) predicted that judges differ in their policy preferences with regard to criminal cases, and consistent with that view, they found that Republican-appointed federal judges gave longer sentences on average for many crimes than Democratic appointees. Also, they predicted that the legal basis on which a judge sets a sentence will partly depend on the political composition of the appellate court that reviews the sentences for compliance with existing law. In their model, a judge chooses between rendering a decision on the basis of law or fact. Law-based decisions have precedential effect, but appellate courts review them *de novo*. Fact-based decisions have little or no precedential effect, but appellate courts review them with some deference. Schanzenbach and Tiller (2007, 2008) predicted that, when the majority of the appellate court shares a judge's political affiliation, the risk of reversal is lower, and she will render the sentence on the basis of law in order to influence future cases. But when the majority of the appellate court does not share a judge's political affiliation, the risk of reversal is higher, and she will render the sentence on the basis of fact.

In a large sample of federal sentencing cases, Schanzenbach and Tiller (2007, 2008) found evidence to support this strategic prediction. Under the federal sentencing guidelines, a judge may alter a sentence by making an adjustment, which is based on the facts of the case and has few implications for future cases, or by making a departure, which is based on law and has precedential effect for future cases. Schanzenbach and Tiller (2007, 2008) found that when a judge's political party aligned with that of the majority of the appellate court, the judge moved the sentence in her preferred policy direction by more often making departures, a law-based criterion. But when a judge's political party did not align with that of the majority of the appellate court, she was more likely to move the sentence in her preferred policy direction by making adjustments, a fact-based criterion.

The strategic theories of judging show that the strictness of appellate review is a potentially important constraint on a judge's discretion in sentencing. Fischman and Schazenbach (2011, forthcoming) present further evidence on this point. They hypothesize that differences between the sentences assigned by Republican and Democratic appointees should be greater when appellate review is more deferential. Since the passage of the federal Sentencing Guidelines, the Supreme Court and Congress clarified (or outright changed) the standard of review for criminal sentences several times, and Fischman and Schazenbach (2011, forthcoming) used the fluctuations in the standard to test their hypothesis. They found that the average gap between the sentences assigned by Democratic and Republican appointees was smaller when appellate courts conducted a (stricter) *de novo* review rather than a (more lenient) review for an abuse of discretion. Their results suggested that standards of review constrained judicial discretion in federal sentencing.

An interesting caveat on their finding was that judges who were appointed to the bench before the passage of the Sentencing Guidelines were more likely to depart from the Guidelines and were not responsive to changes in the standard of review. The latter of these two patterns suggests that judges vary in their sensitivity to the threat of appellate review and that the ability of standards of review to cabin judicial discretion may be limited in some circumstances. The reasons for the variation in judges' responsiveness to the standard of review remain an area for future research.

Perhaps the most important development in sentencing since the passage of the federal Guidelines has been a series of decisions which culminated in the Supreme Court rendering the Guidelines advisory. These decisions have inspired a burst of empirical research by economists on whether advisory rather than mandatory guidelines constrain the decisions of judges, and these studies represent a fourth potential category of sentencing literature by economists. The first of these decisions, *Apprendi v.*

138 *Procedural law and economics*

New Jersey, 530 U.S. 466 (2000), held that any fact, other than the fact of a prior conviction, that raised a criminal penalty above the statutory maximum must be proven to a jury beyond a reasonable doubt or admitted by the defendant. Most commentators believed that the ruling would benefit criminal defendants by raising the cost of bringing a prosecution, and others thought that juror hostility toward criminal defendants implied *Apprendi* would not favor defendants. Prescott (2010) hypothesized that defendants with longer criminal histories would be closer, all else equal, to an applicable statutory maximum under the Guidelines and thus the *Apprendi* decision was more likely to affect their sentences. He compared the sentences received by these defendants to a group of defendants with less extensive criminal histories in the three years before and the three years after *Apprendi*. His differences-in-differences estimates showed that the expansion of jury trial rights under the *Apprendi* decision reduced the average sentence of a defendant with a lengthy criminal history by about 5% or put differently, about six months. This result supports the view that stronger jury trial rights favor defendants.

In *United States v. Booker*, 543 U.S. 220 (2005), the Supreme Court applied the principle of *Apprendi* to the federal Sentencing Guidelines and concluded that the Guidelines violated the Sixth Amendment right to a jury trial because the Guidelines permitted a judge to find a fact (other than a prior conviction) that would raise a sentence above an otherwise applicable Guideline maximum. The remedy for this constitutional problem was to make the Guidelines effectively advisory rather than mandatory.

The *Booker* decision provided another opportunity for researchers to examine whether Guidelines succeeded in reducing the overall variation in sentences and in the disparity of sentences across judges. If mandatory guidelines had constrained judicial discretion, variation in the sentences should increase following *Booker*. Pfaff (2006) predicted that *Booker* would not produce a return of disparities of the same degree that existed before the implementation of the Guidelines. Pfaff based this prediction on the experience of state courts with voluntary guidelines in the years before *Booker*. Over the period of Pfaff's study, 1989–2000, several states adopted mandatory or voluntary guidelines, and this legal variation permitted the use of a differences-in-differences identification strategy. According to Pfaff's estimates, the adoption of mandatory guidelines reduced the variation in state sentence lengths by roughly 55% for both violent and property offenses, relative to sentences in states without any guidelines. In states that adopted voluntary guidelines, these declines were 35% for violent offenses and 21% for property offenses. Pfaff gave three possible explanations for the constraining effect of voluntary guidelines: they furnish a useful metric for judges, they represent an implicit threat from the legislature to impose mandatory guidelines, or that they provide a safe-harbor for judges fearing appellate reversal. The validity of these intriguing explanations awaits further investigation.

In the years since the *Booker* decision, enough data on federal sentences have accumulated to permit statistical analysis, and initial studies are finding increases in inter-judge disparities. For example, Scott (2010) examined the variation in sentences before and after *Booker* in a single federal district, Massachusetts, where the identities of individual judges could be determined. The analysis did not include many of the control variables that are now standard in the literature, such as offender demographics and criminal history. Still, the results suggested that the identity of the judge influences criminal sentences and that this effect has become larger since *Booker*. According to Scott's (2010) estimates, the identity of the judge explained 31% of the variance in sentence lengths before *Booker* and 6.1% in late 2007 and early 2008. These percentages imply that the average sentence given by the most lenient judge differs from that of the most severe judge by more than two years. More empirical scholarship on the implications of *Booker* is sure to follow in the years to come.

5.2. Post-conviction Litigation

With a stock of more than seven million people currently subject to criminal supervision and a large flow of new felony convictions in state and federal courts in recent years, appeals are likely to be an important feature of the criminal justice system. Systematic data on criminal appeals in state courts are not available, but data from the federal system indicates that there has been a substantial growth in criminal appeals mirroring the upward trend in prison populations. In 1980, there were 4,405 appeals in criminal cases in federal courts, and by 1990, this figure had more than doubled to reach 9,493. It peaked at 16,060 in 2005, and in 2010, the latest year for which figures are available, 12,797 criminal appeals were filed in federal courts (Bureau of Justice Statistics, 2010).[6] These figures represent 25% to 30% of the federal appellate courts' annual caseload.

Despite their substantial growth and their importance in the workload of the courts, empirically-inclined economists and legal scholars have given scant attention to criminal appeals. Heise (2009) made an initial examination of criminal appeals in federal courts. He observed that appeals filed in 2006 had a reversal rate of about 12% and that his rate was lower than the corresponding rate for civil appeals in federal courts

---

[6] These figures do not include prisoner petitions, such as habeas petitions or suits over prison conditions.

(18%) and much lower than the rate for civil appeals in state courts (32%). He also noted that the overall reversal rate masked substantial geographic variation across federal circuits. Reversal rates ranged from a low of less than 6% in one circuit to a high of just over 20% in another.

Other researchers have closely studied the reversal rates in a particular class of cases: death penalty cases. Leibman et al. (2000) gathered information on more than five thousand death sentences imposed after 1973 and reviewed by 1995. They traced the rates at which courts reversed death sentences at three different stages of appeal: direct appeal in state courts, post-conviction in state courts, and federal habeas appeal.

Cumulatively, the reversal rate for cases in which the defendant received a capital sentence was 68%. Gelman et al. (2004) examined an updated version of the Leibman et al. (2000) data and estimated the probability a capital sentence is reversed as a function of local demographic characteristics and the court's workload. Among their findings was that reversal was more likely where death sentences were imposed more often and where the rate of incarceration per FBI Index crime was lower.

Recently, empirical scholars have also investigated the determinants of federal court civil lawsuits by jail and prison inmates. Schlanger (2003) presented a detailed portrait of prison inmate litigation and offered initial evidence that the Prison Litigation Reform Act (PLRA) of 1996 greatly reduced the volume of such litigation. Piehl and Schlanger (2004) predicted that the volume of litigation on a per-inmate basis would rise with the number of inmates as more crowding could worsen conditions. They also hypothesized that the filing rate would rise more quickly with prison populations than with jail populations in part because the flow of inmates is faster through jails, which reduces opportunities for grievances to arise. Examining a panel of states covering 1981–2001, Piehl and Schlanger (2004) found support for these predictions. They also observed that the PLRA weakened the relationship of the filing rate to prison populations but had little effect on its relationship to jail populations.

Future scholarship will likely uncover other regularities about criminal appeals and inmate litigation, and it is probable that that the study of these forms of litigation will eventually involve testing behavioral theories about various actors and institutions in the criminal justice system.

6. Conclusion

This chapter surveyed the diverse and growing empirical literature by economists on the criminal justice system and the law of criminal procedure in particular. Empirical economics may on first impression have little relationship to criminal procedure because it is a topic primarily concerned with individual rights that are not well suited to quantification.

But when procedure's influence in setting the amount and distribution of criminal punishment is seen, empirical economics offers new insights into questions such as racial profiling, plea bargaining, and sentencing.

References

Abrams, David S. and Christopher A. Rolfs (2011), "Optimal Bail and the Value of Freedom: Evidence from the Philadelphia Bail Experiment", *Economic Inquiry*, 49(3): 750–770.

Abrams, David S. and Albert H. Yoon (2007), "The Luck of the Draw: Using Random Case Assignment to Investigate Attorney Ability", *University of Chicago Law Review*, 74(4): 1145–77.

Albonetti, Celesta (1997), "Sentencing under the Federal Sentencing Guidelines: Effects of Defendant Characteristics, Guilty Pleas, and Departures on Sentencing Outcomes for Drug Offenses, 1991–1992", *Law & Society Review*, 31(4): 789–822.

Anderson, James M., Jeffrey R. Kling, and Kate Stith (1999), "Measuring Interjudge Sentencing Disparity: Before and After the Federal Sentencing Guidelines", *Journal of Law and Economics*, 42(1): 271–307.

Antonovics, Kate and Brian Knight (2009), "A New Look at Racial Profiling: Evidence from the Boston Police Department", *Review of Economics and Statistics*, 91(1): 163–75.

Anwar, Shamena and Hanming Fang (2006), "An Alternative Test of Racial Prejudice in Motor Vehicle Searches: Theory and Evidence", *American Economic Review* 96(1): 127–51.

Arrow, Kenneth J. (1973), "The Theory of Discrimination", in: Orley Ashenfelter and Albert Rees, eds., *Discrimination in Labor Markets*, Princeton, NJ: Princeton University Press, 3–33.

Atkins, R.A. and P.H. Rubin (2003), "Effects of Criminal Procedure on Crime Rates: Mapping out the Consequences of the Exclusionary Rule", *Journal of Law and Economics*, 46(1): 157–80.

Ayres, Ian and Joel Waldfogel (1994), "A Market Test for Race Discrimination in Bail Setting", *Stanford Law Review*, 46(5): 987–1048.

Baldus, David C., Charles Pulaski, and George Woodworth (1983), "Comparative Review of Death Sentences: An Empirical Study of the Georgia Experience", *Journal of Criminal Law and Criminology*, 74(3): 661–753.

Becker, Gary S. (1957), *The Economics of Discrimination*, Chicago: University of Chicago Press.

Becker, Gary S. (1968), "Crime and Punishment: An Economic Approach", *Journal of Political Economy*, 76(2): 169–217.

Bjerk, David (2005), "Making the Crime Fit the Penalty: The Role of Prosecutorial Discretion under Mandatory Minimum Sentencing", *Journal of Law and Economics*, 48(2): 591–627.

Bjerk, David (2007), "Guilt Shall Not Escape or Innocence Suffer: The Limits of Plea Bargaining When Defendant Guilt is Uncertain", *American Law and Economics Review*, 9(2): 305–29.

Boylan, Richard T. (2005), "What Do Prosecutors Maximize? Evidence from the Careers of U.S. Attorneys", *American Law and Economics Review*, 7(2): 379–402.

Boylan, Richard T. and Cheryl X. Long (2005), "Salaries, Plea Rates, and the Career Objectives of Federal Prosecutors", *Journal of Law and Economics*, 48(2): 627–71.

Breyer, Steven (1988), "The Federal Sentencing Guidelines and the Key Compromises on which they Rest", *Hosftra Law Review*, 17(1): 1–50.

Bureau of Justice Statistics (2003), *Sourcebook of Criminal Justice Statistics*, Washington, DC: Government Printing Office.

Bureau of Justice Statistics (2007), *Correctional Populations in the United States*, Washington, DC: Government Printing Office.

Bureau of Justice Statistics (2010), *Sourcebook of Criminal Justice Statistics*, Washington, DC: Government Printing Office.

Bushway, Shawn and Anne Morrison Piehl (2001), "Judging Judicial Discretion: Legal Factors and Racial Discrimination in Sentencing", *Law & Society Review*, 35(4): 733–64.

Cassell, P.G. (1996), "*Miranda's* Social Costs: An Empirical Reassessment", *Northwestern University Law Review*, 90(2): 387–499.

Cassell, P.G. and R. Fowles (1998), "Handcuffing the Cops? A Thirty-Year Perspective on *Miranda's* Harmful Effects on Law Enforcement", *Stanford Law Review*, 50(4): 1055–145.

Clarke, Stevens H., Jean L. Freeman, and Gary G. Koch (1976), "Bail Risk: A Multivariate Analysis," *Journal of Legal Studies*, 5(2): 341–86.

Davies, Thomas Y. (1983), "A Hard Look at What We Know (And still Need to Learn) about the 'Costs' of the Exclusionary Rule: The NIJ Study and Other Studies of 'Lost' Arrests", *American Bar Foundation Research Journal*, 8(3): 611–90.

Dharmapala, Dhammika and Stephen Ross (2004), "Racial Bias in Motor Vehicle Searches: Additional Theory and Evidence", *Contributions to Economic Analysis & Policy, Berkeley Electronic Press*, 3(1): Article 12.

Dominitz, Jeff and John Knowles (2006), "Crime Minimisation and Racial Bias: What Can We Learn from Police Search Data", *The Economic Journal*, 116(515): F368–F384.

Donohue, J.J., III (1998), "Did *Miranda* Diminish Police Effectiveness?", *Stanford Law Review*, 50(4): 1147–80.

Donohue, John J. III and Steven D. Levitt (2001), "The Impact of Legalized Abortion on Crime", *Quarterly Journal of Economics*, 116(2): 379–420.

Easterbrook, Frank H. (1983), "Criminal Procedure as a Market System", *Journal of Legal Studies*, 12(2): 289–332.

Fagan, Jeffrey and Garth Davies (2000), "Street Stops and Broken Windows: Terry, Race and Disorder in New York City", *Fordham Urban Law Journal*, 28(2): 457–504.

Feeney, F. (2000), "Police Clearance: A Poor Way to Measure the Impact of *Miranda* on Police", *Rutgers Law Review*, 32(1): 1–114.

Fischman, Joshua and Max Schanzenbach (2011, forthcoming), "Do Standards of Review Matter? The Case of Federal Criminal Sentencing", *Journal of Legal Studies*.

Forst, Brian and Kathleen B. Brosi (1977), "A Theoretical and Empirical Analysis of the Prosecutor", *Journal of Legal Studies*, 6: 177–91.

Frankel, Marvin (1973), *Criminal Sentences: Law without Order*, New York: Hill & Wang.

Gelman, Andrew, James S. Leibman, Valerie West, and Alexander Kiss (2004), "A Broken System: The Persistent Patterns of Reversals in Death Sentences in the United States", *Journal of Empirical Legal Studies*, 1(2): 209–61.

Glaeser, Edward L., Daniel P. Kessler, and Anne Morrison Piehl (2000), "What Do Prosecutors Maximize? An Analysis of the Federalization of Drug Crimes", *American Law and Economics Review*, 2(2): 259–90.

Grogger, Jeffrey T. (2002), "The Effects of Civil Gang Injunctions on Reported Violent Crime: Evidence from Los Angeles County", *Journal of Law and Economics*, 45(1): 69–90.

Grogger, Jeffrey and Greg Ridgeway (2006), "Testing for Racial Profiling in Traffic Stops from Behind a Veil of Darkness", *Journal of the American Statistical Association*, 101(475): 878–87.

Grossman, Gene M. and Michael L. Katz (1983), "Plea Bargaining and Social Welfare", *American Economic Review*, 73(4): 749–57.

Hagan, John (1974), "Extra-legal Attributes and Criminal Sentencing: An Assessment of a Sociological Viewpoint", *Law & Society Review*, 8(3): 357–83.

Harcourt, Bernard H. (2007), *Against Prediction: Profiling, Policing, and Punishing in an Actuarial Age*, Chicago: University of Chicago Press.

Heise, Michael (2009), "Federal Criminal Appeals: A Brief Empirical Perspective", *Marquette Law Review*, 93(2): 825–43.

Helland, Eric and Alexander Tabarrok (2004), "The Fugitive: Evidence on Public versus Private Law Enforcement from Bail Jumping", *Journal of Law and Economics*, 47(1): 93–122.

Hofer, Paul J., Kevin R. Blackwell, and R. Barry Ruback (1999), "The Effect of the Federal Sentencing Guidelines on Inter-judge Sentencing Disparity", *Journal of Criminal Law and Criminology*, 99(1): 239–306.

Kessler, Daniel P. and Anne Morrison Piehl (1998), "The Role of Discretion in the Criminal Justice System", *Journal of Law, Economics and Organization*, 14(2): 256–76.

Kleck, Gary (1981), "Racial Discrimination in Criminal Sentencing: A Critical Evaluation of the Evidence with Additional Evidence on the Death Penalty", *American Sociological Review*, 46(6): 783–804.

Knowles, John, Nicola Persico, and Petra Todd (2001), "Racial Bias in Motor Vehicle Searches", *Journal of Political Economy*, 109(1): 203–32.

Kuziemko, Ilyana (2006), "Does the Threat of the Death Penalty Affect Plea Bargaining in Murder Cases? Evidence from New York's 1995 Reinstatement of Capital Punishment", *American Law and Economics Review*, 8(1): 116–42.

Kuziemko, Ilyana (2007), "Going Off Parole: How the Elimination of Discretionary Prison Release Affects the Social Cost of Crime", National Bureau of Economic Research Working Paper, No. 13380, September.

LaCasse, Cantale and A. Abigail Payne (1999), "Federal Sentencing Guidelines and Mandatory Minimum Sentences: Do Defendants Bargain in the Shadow of the Judge?", *Journal of Law and Economics*, 42(1): 245–69.

Landes, William M. (1971), "An Economic Analysis of the Courts", *Journal of Law and Economics*, 14: 61–107.

Landes, William M. (1973), "The Bail System: An Economic Approach", *Journal of Legal Studies*, 2(1): 79–106.

Leiken, L.S. (1970), "Police Interrogation in Colorado: The Implementation of *Miranda*," *Denver Law Journal*, 47(1): 1–53.

Leo, R.A. (1996), "Inside the Interrogation Room", *Journal of Criminal Law and Criminology*, 86(2): 266–303.

Leo, R.A. (1998), "*Miranda* and the Problem of False Confessions", in: R.A. Leo and G.C. Thomas III, eds., *The Miranda Debate: Law, Justice, and Policing*, Boston: Northeastern University Press, 271–82.

Levitt, Steven D. and Thomas J. Miles (2007), "The Empirical Study of Criminal Punishment", in A. Mitchell Polinsky and Steven Shavell, eds., *The Handbook of Law and Economics*, Oxford, UK: North-Holland, 453–95.

Liebman, James S., Jeffrey Fagon, Valerie West, and Jonathan Lloyd (2000), "Capital Attrition: Error Rates in Capital Cases, 1973–1995", *Texas Law Review*, 78: 1839–65.

Miles, Thomas J. (2005), "Estimating the Effect of *America's Most Wanted*: A Duration Analysis of Wanted Fugitives", *Journal of Law and Economics*, 48(2): 281–306.

Mustard, David B. (2001), "Racial, Ethnic, and Gender Disparities in Sentencing: Evidence from the U.S. Federal Courts", *Journal of Law and Economics*, 44(1): 285–314.

Myers, Jr., Samuel L. (1981), "Economics of Bail Jumping", *Journal of Legal Studies*, 10(2): 381–96.

Nagin, Daniel S. (1998), "Criminal Deterrence Research: A Review of the Evidence and a Research Agenda for the Outset of the 21st Century", in: Michael Tonry, ed., *Crime and Justice: An Annual Review of Research*, Chicago: University of Chicago Press, 23: 1–42.

Nardulli, Peter F. (1983), "The Societal Cost of the Exclusionary Rule: An Empirical Assessment", *American Bar Foundation Research Journal*, 8(3): 585–609.

Oaks, Dallin H. (1970), "Studying the Exclusionary Rule in Search and Seizure", *University of Chicago Law Review*, 37(4): 665–757.

Payne, A. Abigail (1997), "Does Inter-judge Disparity Really Matter? An Analysis of the Effects of Sentencing Reforms in Three Federal District Courts", *International Review of Law and Economics*, 17(3): 337–66.

Persico, Nicola and Petra Todd (2006), "Generalising the Hit Rates Test for Racial Bias in Law Enforcement, with an Application to Vehicle Searches in Wichita", *Economic Journal*, 116 (515): F351–F367.

Pettit, Becky and Bruce Western (2004), "Mass Imprisonment and the Life Course: Race and Class Inequality in U.S. Incarceration", *American Sociological Review*, 69(2): 151–69.

Pfaff, John F. (2006), "The Continued Vitality of Structured Sentencing Following *Booker*: The Effectiveness of Voluntary Guidelines", *UCLA Law Review*, 54(1): 236–307.

Piehl, Anne Morrison and Margo Schlanger (2004), "Determinants of Civil Rights Filings in Federal District Court by Jail and Prison Inmates", *Journal of Empirical Legal Studies*, 1(1): 79–109.
Piehl, Anne Morrison and Shawn D. Bushway (2007), "Measuring and Explaining Charge Bargaining", *Journal of Quantitative Criminology*, 23(2): 105–25.
Prescott, J.J. (2010), "Measuring the Consequences of Criminal Jury Trial Protections", University of Michigan Law School, Working Paper, November.
Reiganum, Jennifer F. (1988), "Plea Bargaining and Prosecutorial Discretion", *American Economic Review*, 78(4): 713–28.
Rhodes, William M. (1976), "The Economics of Criminal Courts: A Theoretical and Empirical Investigation", *Journal of Legal Studies*, 5(2): 311–40.
Schanzenbach, Max and Emerson Tiller (2007), "Strategic Judging under the United States Sentencing Guidelines: Positive Political Theory and Evidence", *Journal of Law, Economics, and Organization*, 23(1): 24–56.
Schanzenbach, Max and Emerson Tiller (2008), "Reviewing the Sentencing Guidelines: Judicial Politics, Empirical Evidence, and Reform", *University of Chicago Law Review*, 75(2): 715–60.
Schlanger, Margo (2003), "Inmate Litigation", *Harvard Law Review*, 116(6): 1555–706.
Schulhofer, S.J. (1996), "*Miranda's* Practical Effect: Substantial Benefits and Vanishingly Small Social Costs", *Northwestern University Law Review*, 90(2): 500–563.
Scott, Ryan W. (2010), "Inter-Judge Sentencing Disparity after *Booker*: A First Look", *Stanford Law Review*, 63(1): 1–66.
Shepherd, Joanna (2002), "Police, Prosecutors, Criminals, and Determinate Sentencing: The Truth about Truth-in-Sentencing Laws", *Journal of Law and Economics*, 45(2): 509–34.
Sherman, Lawrence W. (2002), "Fair and Effective Policing", in James Q. Wilson and Joan Petersilia, eds, *Crime*, San Francisco, CA: Institute for Contemporary Studies, 388–412.
Spiotto, James E. (1973), "Search and Seizure: An Empirical Study of the Exclusionary Rule and its Alternatives", *Journal of Legal Studies*, 2(1): 243–78.
Stith, Kate and Jose A. Cabranes (1998), *Fear of Judging*, Chicago, IL: University of Chicago Press.
Stuntz, William J. (2001), "The Uneasy Relationship between Criminal Procedure and Criminal Justice", *Yale Law Journal*, 107(1): 1–76.
Stuntz, William J. (2006), "The Political Constitution of Criminal Justice", *Harvard Law Review*, 119(3): 780–851.
Thomas, G.C. and R.A. Leo (2002), "The Effects of *Miranda v. Arizona*: 'Embedded' in Our National Culture?", in: M. Tonry, ed., *Research in Crime and Justice*, Chicago, IL: University of Chicago Press, 203–271.
Tonry, Michael (1996), *Sentencing Matters*, New York: Oxford University Press.
United States Sentencing Commission (2003), *Guidelines Manual*, Washington, DC: Government Printing Office.
Wald, M. (1967), "Interrogations in New Haven: The Impact of *Miranda*", *Yale Law Journal*, 76: 1519–648.
Wald, Michael, Richard Ayres, David W. Hess, Mark Schantz and Charles H. Whitebread, II (1967), "Interrogations in New Haven: The Impact of *Miranda*", *Yale Law Journal*, 76(8): 1519–649.
Waldfogel, Joel (1998), "Does Inter-Judge Disparity Justify Empirically Based Sentencing Guidelines?", *International Review of Law and Economics*, 18(3): 293–304.
Weimar, David L. (1978), "Plea Bargaining and the Decision to Go to Trial: The Application of a Rational Choice Model", *Policy Sciences*, 10(1): 1–24.
Wright, Ronald and Marc Miller (2002), "The Screening/Bargaining Tradeoff", *Stanford Law Review*, 55(1): 29–118.

7 Detection avoidance and enforcement theory
Chris William Sanchirico

1 Introduction

The subject of evidentiary foul play – inclusive of fabricated testimony, document destruction, and myriad other modes of detection avoidance – is underrepresented in both legal and law and economic scholarship on procedure and evidence. Judges and practitioners report that evidentiary misdeeds are commonplace (though systematic evidence is scarce). Explicit scholarly analysis of evidentiary misbehavior, however, is relatively uncommon.

This chapter considers attempts to add evidentiary misconduct to the conventional economic model of enforcement (Becker (1968) and others). In such context, evidentiary misconduct is typically referred to generically as "detection *avoidance*." Another chapter in this volume, *Evidence: Theoretical Models*, reviews the chief formal approaches to legal evidence. To varying extents the models reviewed in that chapter also take on the issue of evidentiary foul play, though in a different manner.

This chapter begins in Section 2 with a brief overview of the rather complex legal landscape that covers evidentiary misconduct. This is followed in Section 3 with a description of how the economic framework conventionally employed in studying enforcement must be expanded to accommodate detection avoidance activities. Section 4 examines a particular consequence of this expansion in the case in which detection avoidance activities are not themselves sanctioned – namely, that maximal sanctions may no longer be optimal. Sections 5 and 6 consider the sanctioning of detection avoidance activities themselves. Section 6 also examines the difficult problems for a sanctioning approach that are caused by the recursive nature of detection avoidance. Section 7 considers the alternative "technological" approach to detection avoidance.

2 Brief Overview of Legal Landscape

Two kinds of legal rules regulate evidentiary conduct. The first consists of penalties for misconduct. The second consists of what might be called "technological" measures: roughly, policies that decrease the effectiveness of effort and expense devoted to detection avoidance.

2.1 Penalties for Misconduct

Penalties for evidentiary foul play are imposed by a complex and overlapping set of statutes, procedural rules, precedents, judicial practices, and professional codes.[1]

First, three kinds of statutes criminalize evidentiary foul play: obstruction of justice, criminal contempt, and perjury. Criminal sanctions include fines and imprisonment. Second, when the underlying case is itself a criminal action, a convicted defendant who attempted to avoid conviction by means of evidentiary misconduct may face a stiffer sentence. US Federal Sentencing Guidelines, for example, provide for a sentencing enhancement for obstructing the investigation, prosecution, and sentencing of underlying offenses. Third, the court hearing the underlying case may impose sanctions for evidence tampering under either procedural rules (such as the US Federal Rules of Civil Procedure) or its "inherent power" to regulate process. Such sanctions include striking the offending party's pleadings, entering a default judgment against the party, dismissing a party's claims, forcing the party to pay her opponent's attorneys' fees, and providing a jury instruction in regard to what may be deduced from the fact that evidence has been destroyed. Fourth, a small number of jurisdictions allow private tort suits for evidentiary misconduct. Fifth, lawyers involved in evidentiary misconduct may be fined or disbarred under rules concerning professional responsibility.

Two regularities may be identified in the tangle of laws and rules penalizing evidentiary misconduct.[2] First, sanctions for evidentiary misconduct generally apply only to conduct that occurs far downstream in the litigation flow from primary activity through filing, discovery, and trial.[3] For example, in the US, Federal Rule of Civil Procedure 37, which sanctions discovery misconduct, only comes into play after the complaint has been filed; perjury can only be committed under oath; and the so-called omnibus obstruction of justice provision, section 1503, requires that a proceeding be pending. Moreover, with regard to the exercise of the court's "inherent power" to regulate its own proceedings – a term used to describe uncodified, though precedent-bound sources of judicial authority – a careful reading of the cases indicates that the courts have

---

[1] These are reviewed in detail in Gorelick et al. (1989), Koesel et al. (2000), and Sanchirico (2004a).

[2] Sanchirico (2004a) identifies this regularity in the context of Federal Civil Procedure in the US.

[3] Sanchirico (2004a) suggests that this structure may well be justifiable given that the private efficiency of detection avoidance increases as litigation proceeds and the identity of decisive items of evidence comes into clearer view.

been reluctant to exercise such powers to sanction pre-filing destruction. This reluctance is all the greater when no specific plaintiff looms on the horizon. *A fortiori*, firms' "document retention policies" that are not specifically directed at destroying potentially damaging records appear to remain largely effective as a means of insulating document destruction from inherent power sanctioning. Even section 1512(c), a new obstruction of justice provision, which makes general obstructive behavior criminal when there is no pending proceeding, may not extend to defendants who destroy evidence as part of routine document retention policies, or who, more generally, do not have a specific suit with a specific opponent in mind.

Second, even in the downstream reaches of the litigation flow wherein tampering is punished, the farther downstream the tampering, the more far reaching the prohibition. Of the two US federal perjury statutes, for example, section 1623, which prohibits lying only in judicial proceedings and depositions, is in other respects broader in scope than its counterpart section 1621, which applies any time a statement is made under oath. A similar pattern emerges from the untidy array of procedural and evidentiary sanctions. Here US Federal Rule of Civil Procedure 37(b) and inherent powers stand out as the main sources of sanctioning authority in practice. A court order to compel discovery under Rule 37 is only issued at the insistence of the opposing party. But if that order is later violated, penalties will be summarily and almost certainly imposed. If the court wishes to punish tampering somewhat farther upstream, it must use its inherent powers. The imposition of sanctions under this authority is hardly summary. The court must find that the offender had a "duty" to preserve the evidence, an inquiry which implicates the "reasonableness" of the destruction as well as the nexus between the destruction and the litigation. Moreover, as compared to the list of sanctions laid out in Rule 37(b), the typical inherent powers sanction is relatively lenient – an adverse inference instruction, which would seem to place the spoliator in the same position she would be in if she had not spoliated.

2.2 "Technological" Measures

In addition to penalizing evidentiary misconduct, certain aspects of investigation and evidentiary procedure may discourage such misconduct and/or render it less effective. These measures are helpfully categorized according to whether they exploit limits of human cognition or the limits of human cooperation. These two categories are discussed in more detail in Section 7.3.

3 How the Framework of the Enforcement Model Changes when Detection Avoidance is Incorporated

The probability that wrongs and offenses are detected is a central feature of the conventional economic model of enforcement. But the conventional model is starkly asymmetric regarding the determinants of this probability. It takes into account the government's efforts at detecting violations, but it ignores violators' efforts at avoiding detection. After briefly describing the conventional enforcement model, this section examines how incorporating detection avoidance activities changes the model.

3.1 The Conventional Approach (in Brief)

The conventional approach to enforcement – grounded in the work of Beccaria (1764), Bentham (1789) and Becker (1968) – has two essential characteristics: (1) its account of the basic "machinery" of deterrence, and (2) its description of the social cost-benefit analysis that ought to be conducted in making policy choices regarding public enforcement.[4]

3.1.1 Deterrence mechanics in the conventional approach Under the conventional approach to enforcement, the deterrent force exerted by law is viewed as the conjunction of two factors: the probability p that violations[5] are "detected"[6] and the magnitude of the sanction S imposed in the event of detection.[7] The potential violator[8] chooses to commit the violation if the expected sanction pS is less than her net private benefit b from committing the violation. The expected sanction pS may thus be regarded as the "level of deterrence." In order to avoid unrealistic binary outcomes in which either everyone or no one commits the violation, potential violators are usually assumed to have heterogeneous private benefits. If the cumulative distribution function $F(b)$ describes the population distribu-

---

[4] The account provided here is necessarily cursory. For more complete descriptions of the conventional approach – and its many variants – see Garoupa (1997), Polinsky and Shavell (2007), and Franzoni (2000).

[5] Unless otherwise noted, I shall be assuming throughout this discussion that violating the law is a binary choice. An important exception is the analysis in Section 4.2.

[6] Unless otherwise noted, I shall be assuming that individuals who choose not to violate the law are never mistakenly sanctioned. A more general model produces results that are qualitatively similar to those discussed in this entry.

[7] All variables that are not probabilities are expressed in terms of dollars. Concepts that are not natively measured in currency are implicitly converted to their dollar equivalents.

[8] Unless otherwise noted, I shall be assuming that individuals are fully rational and risk neutral.

tion of the private benefits from violation b, then $1 - F(pS)$ is the fraction of the population of potential violators that actually violates the law. If N is the size of the population of potential violators, then $N(1 - F(pS))$ is the number of violators.

3.1.2 Social cost-benefit analysis in the conventional approach The basic machinery of deterrence described in Section 3.1.1 immediately above can be configured in many ways. For example, the size of the sanction, the nature of the sanction, and the frequency of detection are all subject to policy choice.

Under the conventional model, a particular cost-benefit analysis guides these policy choices.

The social benefits of deterrence are taken to be the benefits of reduced violations, including the benefits to those who would otherwise be victimized. Thus, the social benefit of establishing the level of deterrence pS derives from the fact that some portion of potential violators is induced not to commit the violation. If h is the level of aggregate net private harm imposed upon victims by each violation,[9] and if it is assumed that the private benefits of violations are regarded as socially cognizable, then the net social benefit of the level of deterrence pS equals $NF(pS)(h - E[b|b < pS])$, where $E[b|b < pS]$ is the (unrealized) average private benefit of violations among potential violators who choose not to violate the law. In this expression $NF(pS)$ is the number of violations that do not occur and $h - E[b|b < pS]$ is the average net social savings for each.

The social *costs* of deterrence are typically parsed into two categories, corresponding to the two factors in the conventional approach to deterrence mechanics, as described in Section 3.1.1 above. First, there are "detection costs," the publicly incurred cost of investigating and prosecuting violations, as manifest in budgeting for regulatory enforcement divisions, police departments, and court systems. Thus, the probability of detection p is regarded as an increasing function, $p(d)$, of such detection costs d. Second, there are "sanctioning costs," $c(S)$, the cost of imposing sanctions when violations lead to conviction or liability, including, for example, the operating costs and opportunity costs of keeping convicts in prison. The cost of sanctions depends not just on the magnitude but also on the nature of the sanction. Prison time is costly, and more prison time is more costly. Fines are, however, generally regarded as costless transfers between individuals and the government; for fines $c(S)$ is constant at zero.

---

[9] Unless otherwise noted, it is assumed throughout that h is uniform across violations.

3.2 The Conventional Enforcement Model with Detection Avoidance Added[10]

3.2.1 The importance of adding detection avoidance Although detection activities and their social cost play an important role in the conventional approach to enforcement, the conventional approach generally does not take into account detection *avoidance* activities and their costs.[11] This asymmetry is difficult to justify. Although systematic statistical evidence is scarce,[12] casual empiricism points to the conclusion that violators are more than mere spectators. Just as the state invests in detecting their violations, they invest in avoiding that detection. The investigation and prosecution of crimes and regulatory violations, it would seem, is not an exercise in orienteering, but a chase, consisting of a pursuit and a flight.

When detection avoidance activity is added to the conventional model of enforcement, both deterrence mechanics and social cost-benefit accounting are altered. I consider these effects in turn.

3.2.2 The effect of detection avoidance on deterrence mechanics Under the conventional approach, the degree to which underlying violations are deterred depends on the sanction and the detection probability. Detection avoidance complicates this simple mechanic in four ways. These four ways may be grouped into two categories.

3.2.2.1 THE EFFECT ON THE LEVEL OF DETERRENCE FOR THE UNDERLYING ACTIVITY

3.2.2.1.1 FIRST EFFECT First, and most obviously, detection avoidance activities reduce the probability that underlying violations will be detected.[13] To this extent, such activities reduce the level of deterrence of underlying violations. Thus, the probability of detection must now be written as $p(d,a)$. The probability of detection is still an increasing function of the

---

[10] This account derives from Sanchirico (2006a, 2006b).
[11] This fact is apparent in the surveys listed in note 4.
[12] Sanchirico (2004a) critically reviews the systematic empirical evidence on detection avoidance activities. Such evidence includes Pepe (1983), Brazil (1980), Arther and Reid (1954), and Beckenstein and Gabel (1982).
[13] From the assumption that non-violators are never wrongfully sanctioned (see note 6), and the additional assumption, here adopted, that individuals know this fact, it follows that only violators engage in detection avoidance activity.

state's detection efforts d. But it is now also a decreasing function of violators' detection avoidance spending, a.[14]

An equivalent way of saying the same thing is as follows: positive detection avoidance activity increases the public detection cost of generating any given level of detection probability. Given that $p(d,a)$ increases in d, to say that positive detection avoidance activity a reduces the probability of detection $p(d,a)$ for any level of public detection effort d, is also to say that, given greater detection avoidance activity a, any (still attainable) level of detection probability p requires greater public detection effort d.

3.2.2.1.2 SECOND EFFECT Second, and counter to the first effect, detection avoidance activities are costly for those who engage in them, and such costs constitute, in effect, an additional component of the effective sanction for the underlying violation. Thus, although detection avoidance activities reduce the probability that violations will be detected, as just noted, the resulting reduction in deterrence is mitigated by the violator's detection avoidance costs.

Formally, if a potential violator chooses to violate the law and, accordingly, engages in detection avoidance activity at the level of a, her "*effective expected sanction*" is $p(d,a)S + a$. This expression, or rather its minimized value with respect to the potential violator's violation-contingent choice of a, is what the potential violator compares to the private benefit b of an underlying violation in determining whether to commit the violation. Accordingly, the "level of deterrence" provided by the system is no longer the expected sanction $p(d)S$, but rather the effective expected sanction $p(d,a^*)S + a^*$, where a^* minimizes $p(d,a)S + a$.

3.2.2.1.3 FIRST AND SECOND EFFECTS COMPARED It has been observed that the first and second effects just described are countervailing. It is thus worth asking: how do they compare in magnitude? This question must be answered separately with respect to (a) the total effect of detection avoidance activities on deterrence and (b) the marginal effect of such activities on deterrence.

The total effect of the violator's optimally chosen detection avoidance activity on the level of deterrence can only be to lower her effective expected sanction for the underlying violation. That is, the dollar value of

---

[14] In what follows I shall assume that p is twice continuously differentiable, $p_a < 0$, $p_d > 0$, $p_{aa} > 0$, $\lim_{a \to 0} p_a = -\infty$, $\lim_{a \to \infty} p_a = 0$. These assumptions guarantee that $p(d, a)S + a$ is minimized at a strictly positive value of a, and that there is only one such minimizing value of a.

the reduction in the probability of detection (the first effect identified in this subsection) must be at least as great as what the violator is spending on that reduction (the second effect identified in this subsection). Were this not true, the violator could, and would, improve her expected payoffs by engaging in no detection avoidance.

Formulaically, if a^* is the violator's optimal choice of detection avoidance activity, then $p(d,0)S - p(d,a^*)S$, the total reduction in the expected sanction due to privately optimal detection avoidance activity, must be at least as great as the private cost of detection avoidance a^*. This is the same as saying that $p(d,0)S$ must be at least as great as $p(d,a^*)S + a^*$. Were $p(d,0)S$ strictly less than $p(d,a^*)S + a^*$, the violator could do better by choosing $a = 0$.

By contrast, *marginal* changes from an optimally chosen amount of detection avoidance expenditure have no impact on the effective sanction for the underlying violation. This follows from the fact that an optimal amount of detection avoidance activity must satisfy the first-order condition for an interior minimum of $p(d,a^*)S + a^*$ with respect to a: $p_a(d,a^*)S + 1 = 0$. That is, the chosen level of detection avoidance cannot be optimal if it is possible to lower marginally the effective sanction $p(d,a)S + a$ by marginally increasing a (as when $p_a(d,a^*)S + 1 > 0$) or by marginally decreasing a (as when $p_a(d,a^*)S + 1 < 0$). Thus, on the margin, the amount by which additional detection avoidance reduces the expected sanction pS is precisely equal to its cost to the violator, and the two countervailing effects on deterrence are precisely offsetting.

If marginals add to totals, how is a zero marginal reduction compatible with a positive total reduction? The claim is not that the marginal effect of detection avoidance on the effective expected sanction is zero everywhere, only that it is zero at the privately optimal level of detection avoidance. As detection avoidance is increased "step-by-step" from zero up to the optimal level, the marginal impact of each "step" will generally be to reduce positively the effective expected sanction. This can be shown formally using the fundamental lemma of calculus. Although $p_a(d,a)S + 1 = 0$ when $a = a^*$,

$$\int_0^{a^*} (p_a(d,\tilde{a})S + 1)d\tilde{a} = (p(d,a^*)S + a^*) - p(d,0)S,$$

is negative.

3.2.2.2 POLICIES DIRECTED AT DETECTION AVOIDANCE ITSELF

3.2.2.2.1 THIRD EFFECT Third, adding detection avoidance to the story raises the possibility that detection avoidance itself can be sanctioned (a possibility, oddly, that is ignored by a fair portion of the small literature on detection avoidance).

Such "second-order sanctions" – on detection avoidance, rather than on the underlying violation – increase the level of deterrence *for the underlying violation*. As with the direct costs a of detection avoidance activities, whose effect was discussed in Section 3.2.2.1 above, this legally constructed cost counteracts the fact that detection avoidance reduces the detection probability for the underlying violation.

Thus, let S_1 be the sanction *for detection avoidance*. Let $p_1(a)$ be the probability that *detection avoidance* activity a will be detected, an increasing function of a.[15] (And, for the moment, assume that the detection of "first-order" detection avoidance cannot itself be avoided with "second-order" detection avoidance – an issue discussed in detail below in Section 6.) Then the effective sanction for underlying violations, and the level of deterrence for such underlying violations, is $p(d,a^*)S + a^* + p_1(a^*)S_1$, where a^* is chosen to minimize this triple sum. For reasons described in the next paragraph, the derivative of this expression with respect to the sanction S_1 for detection avoidance activities is simply $p_1(a^*) > 0$. Therefore, increasing S_1 increases the level of deterrence for the underlying activity.

How can the derivative of $p(d,a^*)S + a^* + p_1(a^*)S_1$ with respect to S_1 be simply $p_1(a^*)$, when S_1 also affects a^*, and a^* is a separate argument in $p(d,a^*)S + a^* + p_1(a^*)S_1$? Marginal changes in S_1 will indeed inspire marginal changes in detection avoidance a^*. But the effect of this responsive change in detection avoidance on the level of deterrence, $p(d,a^*)S + a^* + p_1(a^*)S_1$ will be nil. The reasoning is the same as in Section 3.2.2.1.3 above: if changes in the privately optimal level of detection avoidance did have a net marginal effect on the effective expected sanction $p(d,a^*)S + a^* + p_1(a^*)S_1$, the current level of detection avoidance would not be optimal for the violator. The proposition that one can ignore responsive behavioral changes when judging the impact on optimized payoffs of marginal parameter changes is referred to as the "envelope theorem."

3.2.2.2.2 FOURTH EFFECT Fourth, as discussed in more detail in Section 7, accounting for detection avoidance turns government detection effort itself into a more complex policy variable. Accordingly, the range of alternative detection policies expands. With detection avoidance in the model, violators themselves can affect the probability of detection, at cost. Thus, given the government's choice of detection activity d, the government

---

[15] I shall assume that p_1 is twice continuously differentiable, $p_{1a} > 0$, $p_{1aa} < 0$, $\lim_{a \to 0} p_{1a} = \infty$, $\lim_{a \to \infty} p_{1a} = 0$.

154 *Procedural law and economics*

effectively presents to the violator not a single probability of detection, $p(d)$, but a "menu" of detection probabilities, $p(d,.)$ one for each of her possible choices a of detection avoidance intensity. Section 7 describes how, by adjusting the shape of this menu, the state can affect both violators' detection avoidance choices and their decision whether to violate the law in the first place.

3.2.3 The effect of detection avoidance on social cost accounting Adding detection avoidance to the model alters not only the deterrence mechanics of the conventional enforcement model, but also its social cost-benefit accounting. Recall from Section 3.1.2 that the conventional approach to enforcement, which ignores detection avoidance, focuses on the publicly incurred cost of "detecting" underlying violations, as well as the direct social cost of sanctions like imprisonment. To these two costs, three new costs must be added. These new costs fall naturally into two groups.

3.2.3.1 THE PRIVATE COST OF DETECTION AVOIDANCE The first necessary addition to social cost-benefit accounting is the private cost of detection avoidance: expenses incurred by private parties in hampering investigation and fighting prosecution. In the model laid out above (in which, implicitly, violators differ only in their private benefits from underlying violations), every violator engages in the same level of detection avoidance: that which minimizes $p(d,a^*)S + a^* + p_1(a^*)S_1$. The number of violators is thus $N(1 - F(p(d,a^*)S + a^* + p_1(a^*)S_1))$. Detection avoidance costs are thus $N(1 - F(p(d,a^*)S + a^* + p_1(a^*)S_1)) \, a^*$.[16]

3.2.3.2 THE COSTS OF SANCTIONING DETECTION AVOIDANCE The other two costs that must be added to the analysis arise to the extent that detection avoidance is itself subject to sanction. They are merely the counterparts to the two costs – of detection and of sanctioning – that are emphasized in the conventional paradigm.

First, there is the public cost of detecting detection avoidance. Perjury, for example, must also be investigated and prosecuted. Thus, the probability that detection avoidance is detected is not actually $p_1(a^*)$, as above, but rather $p_1(d_1,a^*)$, where d_1 is the public cost of detecting detection avoidance.

Second, there is $c(S_1)$, the direct cost of imposing the sanction S_1 on detection avoidance, such as the costs of imprisonment.

---

[16] See notes 6 and 13: in this model, non-violators do not engage in detection avoidance because they are never wrongfully sanctioned.

4 The Effect on Detection Avoidance Activity of Sanctioning the Underlying Activity

It was noted above that increasing the sanction on detection avoidance increases the level of deterrence for the underlying violation and thus reduces commission of the underlying violation. An important segment of the literature on detection avoidance focuses on the reverse direction of causation: the effect of sanctioning *the underlying activity* on the incidence of detection avoidance.

Malik (1990), which is perhaps the first systematic account of detection avoidance in the context of the conventional economic enforcement model, recognizes that raising the sanction on the underlying activity inspires the expenditure of additional private resources on detection avoidance. (See also Snyder 1990.) When the government raises a fine, for instance, it increases not only the pain of detection for the violator, but also her relief from avoiding detection.[17] Were the fine $100,000, a detection avoidance activity that reduced the chance of detection by one percentage point would be worth $1000 to the violator. Doubling the fine to $200,000 doubles the value of that activity to $2000.

That increasing the sanction on the underlying activity increases detection avoidance can be seen in terms of the model introduced in Section 3.2. Assuming that detection avoidance is not itself sanctioned (as does Malik 1990), the violator's chosen level of detection avoidance satisfies the first-order condition $p_a(d,a^*)S + 1 = 0$, where, the reader will recall, $p_a < 0$. Applying the implicit function theorem to this first-order condition,[18] we see that the marginal impact on detection avoidance of raising the sanction on the underlying violation is $da^*/dS = -p_a/Sp_{aa}$. This marginal impact is positive because detection avoidance reduces the probability of detection

---

[17] On close inspection, it appears that Tabbach and Nussim (2008) are making essentially the same point when they show how an increase in "ex post punishment *of detection avoidance*" may increase avoidance activities. In their model, an increase in the level of "ex post punishment for detection avoidance" also increases the sanction for the underlying activity.

[18] The (single-dimensional) implicit function theorem – which is applied repeatedly to first-order conditions throughout this chapter – says, roughly, that if $F(x,y) = 0$, $(dx/dy)|_{F=0} = -F_y/F_x$. The derivative $(dx/dy)|_{F=0}$ is the change in x that, per change in y, keeps F constant at 0. Intuitively, if x increases F at a rate of 2 to 1 ($F_x = 2$), and y increases F at a rate of 1 to 1 ($F_y = 1$), then decreasing x at half the rate at which y is increased keeps F constant. Among other things, the theorem assumes the condition $F_x \neq 0$, a condition that is usually satisfied in the context of first-order conditions by assuming the strict concavity (convexity) of the function to be maximized (minimized).

($p_a < 0$) at a decreasing rate ($p_{aa} > 0$).[19] Therefore, raising the sanction for the underlying activity raises the violator's chosen level of detection avoidance.[20]

Let us now consider the impact of this dynamic – first on deterrence mechanics, and then on social cost-benefit accounting.

4.1 The Effect of Responsive Increases in Detection Avoidance on Deterrence Mechanics

Given that raising the sanction for the underlying violation induces more detection avoidance, does this imply that raising the underlying sanction can actually induce more *underlying violations*? On an intuitive level, it might seem that the responsive increase in detection avoidance could so lower the probability of detection $p(d,a)$ as to outweigh the impact of raising the ex post sanction S – thus causing the expected sanction to fall and inducing more underlying violations.

This intuition is problematic, however. It fails to account for the fact that increasing detection avoidance is costly for the violator. It specifically ignores the fact that, as described above in Section 3.2.2, marginal changes in detection avoidance away from the privately optimal level thereof have no marginal impact on the effective expected sanction because the reduction in the probability of detection is precisely offset by the increase in private detection avoidance costs.

Formally, the effective expected sanction for the underlying activity is $p(d,a^*)S + a^*$ (given that detection avoidance itself is not sanctioned). By the envelope theorem,[21] the derivative of this expression with respect to S is simply $p(d,a^*)$, which is positive. Thus, increasing S does indeed increase the effective expected sanction for the underlying violation, thus lowering its incidence – all this despite the responsive increase in detection avoidance.

The problematic intuition described above focuses on the change in $p(d,a^*)S$ due to changes in a^* that are inspired by changes in S. But the effective expected sanction is $p(d,a^*)S + a^*$ not $p(d,a^*)S$. And the effect on the effective expected sanction of the responsive change in detection avoidance is $p_a(d,a^*)S + 1$, which, the reader will recall, must be zero at optimally chosen a^*.

---

[19] See note 14. Note that a necessary condition for a minimum is $p_{aa} \geq 0$. Therefore, da^*/dS can never be finite negative or negative infinity, even if the assumption $p_{aa} > 0$ is abandoned.
[20] See note 14.
[21] See Section 3.2.2.2.1 above.

4.2 Extension: The Effect of Responsive Increases in Detection Avoidance on Deterrence Mechanics when Violation is a Continuous Variable

The same principle applies if the underlying violation is not a binary variable, but rather a continuous variable, so that there are varying degrees of violation. If the violator optimizes detection avoidance based in part on her chosen level of underlying violation, then responsive adjustments in detection avoidance due to changes in the sanction for that level of underlying violation have no impact on the effective expected sanction for that level of underlying violation.

The model can be (temporarily) extended to make this point formally. Let detection effort d be fixed and implicit. Let v be the level of underlying violation. Let $S(v,B)$ be a violation-contingent sanction, where B is a parameter that we shall use to adjust the sanction as a function of v. Let $a^*(v,B)$ be optimal violation-contingent detection avoidance for the violator. Then $p(v,a^*(v,B))S(v,B) + a^*(v,B)$ is the effective expected sanction *for the underlying violation level v*.

For any given level of underlying violation, v, the marginal change in the effective expected sanction with respect to sanctioning parameter B is, by the envelope theorem, $p(v,a^*(v,B))S_B(v,B)$. Just as in the binary violation model discussed in the preceding section, responsive changes in detection avoidance, $a^*_B(v,B)$, do not appear directly in this expression. Responsive changes in detection avoidance do not directly affect the marginal impact of B on the effective expected sanction for underlying violation level v. [22]

This basic point must be kept in mind when interpreting Nussim and Tabbach (2009), a recent contribution on this issue. Nussim and Tabbach's main assertion is that, in a model with detection avoidance, increasing the underlying sanction can actually induce an *increase* in the level of underlying violations *due to responsive increases in detection avoidance*. In a representative passage, they say:

> [H]arsher punishments may . . . result in more crime. . . . [C]onsider how a small additive, constant increase in punishment across all levels of criminal activities will affect the behavior of offenders . . . Such an increase will have no direct effect on the choice of crime, since it does not alter marginal expected punishment. Yet, *since total punishment is now higher, the marginal benefit from avoidance is greater, thus inducing offenders to invest more in avoidance. But once offenders invest more in avoidance, the probability of punishment falls, and*

---

[22] Again, this is a result of the fact that the marginal impact of already optimized detection avoidance on the expected sanction $p_a(v,a^*(v,B))S(v,B)$ must balance with its marginal cost, which is 1. That is, the fact that $p_a(v,a^*(v,B))S(v,B) + 1 = 0$ implies that the derivative of $p(v,a^*(v,B))S(v,B) + a^*(v,B)$ in B via B's inclusion in $a^*(v,B)$ (i.e., holding $S(v,B)$ constant) is zero.

marginal expected sanctions [*i.e., the derivative of expected sanction with respect to the level of the underlying violation*] *fall as well. This complementary effect increases crime levels.*[23]

It appears that Nussim and Tabbach may have misconstrued their model. Using the notation introduced above, the effective expected sanction for violation level v in Nussim and Tabbach's hypothetical is $p(v,a^*(v,B))(S(v) + B) + a^*(v,B)$. Notice that in this expression B is indeed a "constant increase in punishment across levels" of the underlying violation. Notice also that $a^*_B(v,B)$ is indeed positive – that is, it is true that "since total punishment is . . . higher [when B is increased], the marginal benefit from avoidance is greater, thus inducing offenders to invest more in avoidance." And because $p_a < 0$, it is indeed true that "once offenders invest more in avoidance, the probability of punishment falls." However, it would be a non sequitur to conclude from this, as Nussim and Tabbach seem to, that "marginal expected sanctions fall as well." By the envelope theorem-based reasoning described above, the responsive change in detection avoidance inspired by the increase in B has no direct impact on the effective expected sanction at each level of v, $p(v,a^*(v,B))(S(v) + B) + a^*(v,B)$. Therefore, the response change in detection avoidance also has no direct impact on "*marginal* expected sanctions:" that is, it also has no impact on the *derivative* of $p(v,a^*(v,B))(S(v) + B) + a^*(v,B)$ in v.

To more clearly identify the logical problem, consider the following special case. Suppose that sanctions are initially uniform, $S(v) = S$. Assume, also (like Nussim and Tabbach) that the probability of detection p is not a function of the level of the violation v, so that $p(v,a^*(v,B)) = p(a^*(v,B))$. Given these two assumptions, contingently optimal detection avoidance, and so the probability of detection, are the same across all possible choices for v. That is, for all v, $a^*(v,B) = a^*(B)$ and $p(a^*(v,B)) = p(a^*(B))$. Increasing B still increases detection avoidance – $a_B^*(B)$ is still positive. Thus Nussim and Tabbach's premise holds. However, Nussim and Tabbach's conclusion does not; increasing B provides no additional inducement to increase the level of the violation. The effective expected sanction was formerly the same at every v, namely $p(a^*(B = 0))S + a^*(B = 0)$. After increasing B, it is still the same at every v, namely $p(a^*(B))S + a^*(B)$. Thus the marginal effective expected sanction was and is zero.

This is not to deny that increasing the underlying sanction may inspire a greater level of the underlying violation. But this is for different reasons than Nussim and Tabbach provide. Returning to the setting in the

---

[23] Nussim and Tabbach (2009: 315) (emphasis added).

paragraph before last, the change in the effective sanction at each level of v is, by the envelope theorem, simply $p(v,a*(v,B))$. Thus, when sanctions are increased by the same amount across the board, the effective expected sanction at any given v increases according to the initial probability of detection at v. As a result, the increase in the expected effective sanction will be greater at levels of the violation that are initially more likely to be detected. If, in particular, greater levels of the underlying violation are more likely to be detected, then the uniform increase in the sanction will increase the sanction by a greater amount at greater levels of the underlying violation and so induce a decrease in the level of the underlying violation. If, on the other hand, lower levels of the underlying violation are more likely to be detected, then the uniform increase in the sanction will induce an increase in the level of the underlying violation – thus generating the perverse result that Nussim and Tabbach highlight.

What does this have to do with detection avoidance? In one sense, it has nothing to do with detection avoidance. More precisely, the perverse result that Nussim and Tabbach represent to be a consequence of detection avoidance may arise in a model without detection avoidance. In such a model, the increase in the expected effective sanction at v due to increasing B would again be the probability of detection at v, now simply $p(v)$. Thus the increase in the expected sanction would be greater for lower levels of v, if lower levels of v were more likely to be detected.

Yet the question then arises: why would the probability of detection ever be greater for lower violations than for greater violations? And here detection avoidance activity may have a role to play. Suppose (as do Nussim and Tabbach) that the probability of detection is solely a function of detection avoidance. Assume, not unreasonably, that initial sanctions are increasing in the level of the violation. Then contingently optimal detection avoidance is greater for higher levels of the underlying violation than for lower. Accordingly, the probability of detection – assumed to be a function solely of detection avoidance – is greater for lower levels of the underlying violation than for higher. Therefore, a uniform increase in the sanction induces an increase in the underlying violation.

There are, however, two caveats, both having to do with the fact that the probability of detection is not in fact solely a function of detection avoidance. First, the level v of the underlying violation probability has a direct impact on the probability of detection. It is not implausible to suppose that greater levels of the underlying violation emit greater amounts of evidence, leading, all else the same, to a v-increasing detection probability. Second, the probability of detection is also a function of the government's detection effort: detection is not just a flight, it is also a pursuit. It is not implausible that authorities will investigate and prosecute larger violations with greater vigor, again leading, all else the same, to a v-increasing detection probability. In the end, therefore, the question is how the combination of these three factors – variation in detection effort, variation in detection avoidance effort, and variation in the nature of the violation – determines the variation in detection probabilities across levels of underlying violation.[24]

A second point about Nussim and Tabbach's (2009) analysis concerns the structure of the ex post sanction. The last several paragraphs have considered the case in which the increase in the sanction is the same at every level of v. This was solely for analytical convenience. The authorities might instead increase the ex post sanction to a greater extent for larger violations. Doing so could eliminate the perverse effect that Nussim and Tabbach highlight. Returning to the more general analysis at the beginning of this section, the change in the effective expected sanction at any given v due to any increase in B is $p(v,a^*(v,B))S_B(v,B)$. Because $S_B(v,B)$ is generally a function of v, the relative impact on the effective expected sanction at high and low underlying violations is under the control of the authority setting the sanctioning structure. Even if $p(v,a^*(v,B))$ were decreasing in v, the authority could structure the sanction increase so that $S_B(v,B)$ increased in v at a rate that exceeded the rate at which $p(v,a^*(v,B))$ decreased in v. This would be sufficient to guarantee that the product $p(v,a^*(v,B))S_B(v,B)$ increased in v. And this would mean that the v-increasing increase in the sanction induced a reduction in the level of the underlying violation.

What then is the takeaway point from Nussim and Tabbach (2009)? Perhaps it is this: the existence of detection avoidance is most likely to make $p(v,a^*(v,B))$ less v-increasing than it would otherwise be, and possibly even v-decreasing. Consequently, an increase in the ex post sanction that would otherwise be sufficiently v-increasing to induce a reduction in the level of the underlying violation may not be so by virtue of detection avoidance activity. Nussim and Tabbach (2009) provide an example in which the ex post sanction is $S(v,B) = Bv$, as if B were the price of crime. In this case, the marginal increase in the sanction at v due to an increase in B is v itself, and so is increasing in v. Nussim and Tabbach then provide a condition on the probability of detection function $p(a)$ under which this manner of increasing the sanction would still induce an increase in the

---

[24] Both of the effects identified in this paragraph also call into question the joint assumption in the previous paragraph that detection avoidance activity, all else the same, increases with the level of the underlying violation and acts to make the probability of detection greater for lower levels of underlying violation.

Detection avoidance and enforcement theory 161

underlying violation. They also identify a specific probability function, based on the logarithm, which would fulfill their condition.[25]

4.3 The Effect of Responsive Increases in Detection Avoidance on Social Cost-Benefit Accounting

The responsive change in detection avoidance has important implications for social cost-benefit accounting. The main point of Malik (1990) itself is that this dynamic effectively adds an additional component to the cost of underlying sanctions, and thus generates (yet another) qualification to Becker's (1968) famous prescription – crafted in a model without detection avoidance – that it is generally best to generate any desired level of deterrence with large monetary fines and small detection probabilities. Several subsequent contributions, discussed below, have qualified Malik's qualification. As elsewhere in enforcement theory,[26] Becker's prescription has been the chief concern of most research on detection avoidance.

4.3.1 Malik's qualification to Becker Under Becker's analysis (much simplified), a monetary fine is merely a transfer of resources from the offender to the government and a virtually costless means of generating additional deterrence. That is, if S is a fine, $c(S) = 0$ for all S. By contrast, increasing the chance that violations are detected diverts labor and capital away from other productive activities. Best then, concludes Becker, to lower detection effort, only rarely catching offenders, and to compensate by imposing large fines upon those few who are caught. That is, any level of deterrence $p(d)S$ may be generated with lower public costs by lowering

---

[25] Nussim and Tabbach (2009: 317). Nussim and Tabbach draw this example and its analysis from a referee report received on an earlier draft.

[26] The literature qualifying Becker's prescription is extensive and begins shortly after Becker's article was published in 1968. For example, Stigler (1970) focuses on cross-offense incentives and argues that if all fines are set to the same maximum level, offenders will choose serious rather than minor offenses, at least if detection probabilities cannot be appropriately adjusted across offenses. Polinsky and Shavell (1979) incorporate additional risk-bearing costs borne by risk-averse offenders when sanctions are increased. Bebchuk and Kaplow (1992) find that increasing sanction multiplies the effect of individuals' errors in judging probability of detection and thus exacerbates over- and underdeterrence. Bebchuk and Kaplow (1993) find that lowering the fine and perhaps raising the detection probability facilitates imposition of effectively separate expected sanctions according to individuals' heterogeneous ability to avoid detection, thus preventing over- or underdeterrence. Kahan (1997) notes that "if individuals infer widespread criminality from a low probability of apprehension, the power of social influence could more than offset any efficiency gains from this tradeoff." See also the list of qualifications described in the surveys listed in note 4.

162 *Procedural law and economics*

d (thus reducing public detection costs) and raising the level of the fine S (which has no impact on public sanctioning costs) by enough to make up for the reduction in $p(d)$.[27]

Yet, as Malik (1990) points out, although raising the fine may not incur the expenditure of additional public resources on detection, it does inspire the expenditure of additional private resources on detection avoidance. Consequently, monetary fines and detection probabilities are placed on more equal footing with respect to how efficiently they generate deterrence, and one can no longer claim that the monetary fines should carry all (or even more) of the weight.

Formally, the level of deterrence, which is the level of the effective expected sanction, is $p(d,a^*(S))S + a^*(S)$, where it is implicitly assumed that $p_{da} = 0$, so that the violator's level of detection avoidance is a function solely of the ex post sanction. If S is a fine, so that $c(S) = 0$, then the expected social cost of generating this effective expected sanction is $a^*(S) + d$. Now repeat Becker's maneuver: raise S and lower d so as to keep the level of deterrence, $p(d,a^*(S))S + a^*(S)$ the same (which now requires accounting for the sanctioning role of detection avoidance). In Becker's model, in which there is no detection avoidance, social costs are simply d, and the maneuver lowers such costs by decreasing d. In Malik's model, the increase in S causes an increase in $a^*(S)$, and it is not generally possible to say whether the sum $a^*(S) + d$ increases or decreases.

4.3.2 Innes' qualification to Malik Innes (2001) shows that Becker's prescription is restored – even in the presence of costly detection avoidance – if the government invites violators to self-report and charges them a self-reporting sanction equal to the effective expected sanction for non-self-reporting. That is (assuming again that detection avoidance is not sanctioned), the government sets the sanction for self-reported violations equal to (a small amount less than) $p(d,a^*)S + a^*$, and this induces all violators to self-report. The result is that deterrence is maintained and no detection avoidance costs are actually incurred. Therefore, actually incurred detection avoidance costs (which are zero) are not sensitive to the combination of d and S which is used to create the (never carried out) threat of $p(d,a^*)S + a^*$. (In Innes' model, even with self-reporting, the

---

[27] Becker also finds that even if the sanction is socially costly to impose (contrary to the monetary fines considered in this paragraph), it will still be efficient to increase the sanction and lower the detection probability if the social cost elasticity of sanctions is no greater than one. A similar issue arises in Tabbach (2010) discussed below in Section 4.3.5. For more on the conventional model of enforcement, see Garoupa (1997), Polinsky and Shavell (2007), and Franzoni (2000).

government must still actually incur public detection costs d.) It follows that it is optimal to create such threat in a manner that minimizes the sum of d and $c(S)$, just as in Becker (1968). Thus, Becker's prescription is restored.

As Innes notes, this stark result depends, *inter alia*, on an assumed uniformity across violators of $p(d,a^*)S + a^*$, the effective expected sanction for non-reporting. In his model, as in the model that is being carried along in this entry, violators differ only in their private benefits b for violating the law, and not in any other way. In particular, violators do not differ in their detection avoidance opportunities or efficiencies. If violators did so differ, and such differences were not fully observable by the government, any self-reporting sanction structure would generate infra-marginal detection avoiders – violators who choose not to self-report and who, accordingly, actually incur detection avoidance costs. In this case, detection avoidance costs would again be a factor in determining the optimal enforcement structure.

Arguably, Innes' assumption that violators are homogeneous in detection avoidance creates a problematic asymmetry in his analysis. On the one hand, the detection avoidance problem itself is in large measure created by the fact that, *on the level of the underlying violation*, it is assumed that there is sufficient heterogeneity to ensure the existence of infra-marginal violators. These infra-marginal violators are the ones whom we would expect to incur the greatest detection avoidance costs. On the other hand, the solution to the detection avoidance problem that Innes studies is in large measure dependent on the fact that, *on the level of detection avoidance*, there is sufficient *homogeneity* to ensure the *non-existence* of infra-marginal detection avoiders. Presumably, the general principle that justifies heterogeneity on the level of the underlying violation also justifies heterogeneity on the level of detection avoidance.

Nonetheless, we may take from Innes (2001) the following general lesson: self-reporting can economize not only detection costs (as was already known), but also, and for similar reasons, detection avoidance costs.

4.3.3 Langlais' first qualification to Malik Langlais (2008) considers the case in which public detection effort and private detection avoidance effort are "strategic complements:" when the authorities increase the level d of detection, violators are inspired to increase the level of their detection avoidance. This phenomenon arises when $p_{da} < 0$, so that the change in the probability of detection brought about by an increase in detection avoidance, $p_a < 0$, is of greater (negative) magnitude the greater is public detection effort. The situation is not implausible, at least over some ranges.

164 *Procedural law and economics*

Consider that if there is no detection effort at all, then detection avoidance is irrelevant: the probability of detection is zero in any event. Likewise, if the authorities have devoted sufficient resources to check every file, then there is a greater expected benefit to the violator herself from going through each and every file, destroying that which is incriminating.

Now consider the Beckerian maneuver of raising the fine and lowering the detection probability. Raising the fine inspires an increase in costly detection avoidance, as Malik (1990) emphasizes in arguing such maneuver is not always beneficial. However, when detection and detection avoidance are strategic complements, the simultaneous reduction in detection effort inspires violators to reduce detection avoidance. If this reduction in detection avoidance caused by the reduction in detection exceeds the increase in detection avoidance caused by the increase in the fine, then the beneficial character of Becker's maneuver is restored.[28]

4.3.4 Langlais' second qualification to Malik   Langlais (2009) considers a different kind of violator activity, which he calls "dissembling." Dissembling refers to efforts by violators to prevent the disgorgement of illegal benefits. In Langlais' model, violators who are caught must disgorge their apparent illicit benefits and pay an additional "punitive" fine. Violators may choose to expend effort dissembling in order to hide their benefits, and these efforts are socially costly. Increasing the punitive portion of the fine in this model does not induce additional dissembling effort, because the benefits of dissembling do not depend on the punitive part of the sanction. Accordingly, Langlais finds, in his central case, that the punitive fine should be maximal, as in Becker. The upshot is that not all types of avoidance activities are the same, and some do not lead to the effects highlighted by Malik (1990).

4.3.5 Tabbach's qualification to Malik   Malik (1990) studies the case of fines, wherein the social cost of imposing ex post punishment S is zero: $c(S) = 0$. In contrast, Tabbach (2010) studies the case in which the social cost of imposing ex post punishment S exceeds the punishment itself: $c(S) > S$.[29] Tabbach's case might arise where the ex post punishment is generated solely by imprisonment and imprisonment incurs social costs over and above those borne by the imprisoned violator. Tabbach specifically considers the subcase in which $c(S)$ is linear, taking the form cS so that c is

---

[28] Langlais (2008) also presents several results concerning changes in the maximal fine in the case that the maximal fine is optimal (pp. 377–8).
[29] In Tabbach's notation, S is "αS" and $c(S)$ *is* "$(\alpha + \gamma)S$".

the social "price" of imposing a dollar's worth of ex post sanction on the violator. Tabbach shows (in effect) that when $c > 1$, Becker's prescription to maximize S is restored despite detection avoidance costs.

One way to present the argument is this. The effective expected sanction is, as in Malik (1990), $p(d,a^*(S))S + a^*(S)$.[30] But expected social costs are now $p(d,a^*)cS + a^* + d = cp(d,a^*)S + a^* + d$. Consider the following modified Becker maneuver: raise S and lower d in such manner that the effective expected sanction $p(d,a^*)S + a^*$ remains constant. The maneuver causes a^* to increase (by raising S). Thus, the maneuver must cause $p(d,a^*)S$ to decrease by an equal amount (by lowering d sufficiently). Therefore – and this is the key step – given that $c > 1$, the maneuver causes $cp(d,a^*)S$ to decrease by *more* than a^* increases. Therefore, $cp(d,a^*)S + a^*$ decreases. Thus, expected social costs, $cp(d,a^*)S + a^* + d$, decrease: the maneuver decreases not only detection costs d, but also "non-detection expected social costs" $a^* + cp(d,a^*)S$.

If, on the other hand, the social price of imposing a dollar of ex post sanction on the violator was any amount less than \$1,[31] then, in the key step, $cp(d,a^*)S$ would decrease by *less* than $a^*(S)$ increases. Consequently, although Becker's maneuver would still decrease d, it would increase non-detection expected social costs, $cp(d,a^*)S + a^*$.

The intuition for these results may be stated as follows:[32] Ignore detection costs d, and focus on non-detection expected social costs, $a^* + cp(d,a^*)S$. In performing Becker's maneuver – which effectively raises a^* while keeping $p(d,a^*)S + a^*$ constant – society is effectively replacing dollars of effective expected sanction in the form of $p(d,a^*)S$ with dollars of effective expected sanction in the form of detection avoidance costs a^*. The social cost of creating effective expected sanctions with detection avoidance costs is one-to-one. If the social cost of creating effective expected sanctions through $p(d,a^*)S$ is anything greater than one-to-one – if $c > 1$ – then the substitution effected by the Becker maneuver reduces non-detection expected social costs. If, on the other hand, the social cost

---

[30] As in Malik (1990) and Tabbach (2010), the assumption is that $p_{da} = 0$, so that a^* is a function solely of S.

[31] This case is largely implicit in Tabbach (2010). See, however, the last paragraph of the article's text (p. 285).

[32] The following intuition is provided in Tabbach (2010: 268–9): "The reason is simple. Without avoidance, increasing imprisonment and reducing its probability so as to leave the expected sanction unaltered saves on enforcement costs without affecting the costs of punishment. With avoidance, increasing imprisonment provides another type of benefit because it induces more avoidance, which substitutes for costlier punishment, thereby saving not only enforcement but also punishment costs."

of creating effective sanctions through $p(d,a^*)S$ is anything less than one-to-one – if $c < 1$ – then the substitution effected by Becker's maneuver increases non-detection expected social costs.

Some remarks on the condition $c > 1$ are in order.

First, the condition is sufficient for restoration of Becker's maximum sanction result, but not necessary, since detection costs d also decrease.

Second, despite some indications to the contrary in the introduction to Tabbach (2010),[33] $c > 1$ does not automatically hold whenever sanctions fail to be purely monetary. Indeed, mixing in a small fine – small relative to the size of the additional social cost of non-monetary fines – can cause the condition to fail. This is because fining delivers dollars of effective expected sanction at a cost of *zero*-to-one, and so mixing fines into S quickly brings down the average cost of creating effective expected sanctions through S.

Suppose, for example, that 40% of the dollar value to the violators of ex post sanctions S came in the form of monetary transfers to the government (or to plaintiffs) and 60% came in the form of imprisonment. Suppose further that each dollar of the portion of the ex post sanction that is generated by imprisonment (such portion being $0.6S$) costs society $1.50 *in addition to* the cost, $1, borne by the violator. Then the cost $c(S)$ of the ex post sanction S would be the violator's cost of imprisonment $0.6S$ plus the society's additional cost of imprisonment $1.5(0.6S)$. This totals $0.9S$. Thus, c would equal 0.9, and it would not be possible to conclude that Becker's maneuver lowered non-detection expected social costs.

More generally, if f is the fraction of S generated by monetary sanctions, and m is the *additional* social cost per dollar value of imprisonment cost to the violator, then $c = f0 + (1-f)(1 + m)$. Thus, $c \leq 1$ – and the condition fails – so long as the proportion of the total ex post sanction that is monetary, f, is greater than or equal to the proportion of the total social cost of imprisonment that is not borne by the violator, $m/(1 + m)$. Notice that, as the latter proportion, m, goes to zero, so does the threshold fraction of f for the condition $c \leq 1$.

---

[33] According to the introduction of Tabbach (2010), "Th[e] article shows that Malik's (1990) argument against maximal sanctions applies if and only if sanctions are monetary or more generally have no social costs above and beyond the costs incurred by offenders" (p. 268). Further, we read that "if optimality requires utilizing fines and imprisonment, Malik's (1990) argument again does not apply, whereas Becker's (1968) result holds" (p. 269).

Compare these introductory statements to the last section, and in particular, the last text paragraph of the article (p. 285), which is consistent with the analysis in this entry.

Third, as Tabbach (2010) makes clear, the restoration of Becker's result presumes that the government is constrained to use sanctions for which $c > 1$. If sanctions with $c < 1$ are available, optimization over sanctioning form will require using these instead, and Malik's qualification will again apply.

Fourth, the relationship between imprisonment and the case that $c > 1$ may be less clear than it first appears. It certainly seems plausible that imprisonment requires government outlays over and above the dollar sanction borne by the violator. But, on the other hand, imprisonment may in some cases also generate social benefits in the form of incapacitation. These social benefits are not enjoyed by the violator, and so they act to reduce m (in the notation above) and so c. Indeed, there might be cases in which $m < 0$ – that is, in which the social benefit of incapacitation exceeds the non-privately borne costs of imprisonment. In this case, $c < 1$ even if the fraction of monetary sanctions, f, is zero.

Fifth, it should be noted that despite the substantive law focus of the root article in this area, Becker (1968), the detection avoidance dynamic identified in Malik (1990) applies in the regulatory context and in civil litigation,[34] where monetary fines are dominant.

Sixth, if the social cost of the ex post sanction $c(S)$ is nonlinear, the relevant condition is more complicated than the mere analogue to $c > 1$, which would be $c(S) > S$. The curvature of $c(S)$ also becomes important. Referencing the key point identified above, the fact that the maneuver causes $p(d,a^*)S$ to decrease by the same amount that a^* increases, does not imply that $p(d,a^*)c(S)$ decreases by *more* than a^* increases, even if $c(S) > S$. If $c(S)$ increases at an increasing rate, then a change that raised S but left $p(d,a^*)S$ constant – which constitutes a mean-preserving spread of the distribution of the ex post sanction (viewed as a random variable) – would *increase* convex $c(S)$ (by Jensen's inequality).[35] This effect would work against the fact that, in Becker's maneuver, $p(d,a^*)S$ is not held constant, but decreases.

5 Sanctioning Detection Avoidance – Assuming No Recursivity

5.1 The Importance of Considering Sanctions for Detection Avoidance

Several of the papers discussed in Section 4 immediately above – Malik (1990), Innes (2001), Nussim and Tabbach (2009), for example – assume that it is not possible to sanction detection avoidance itself.[36] The

---

[34] See, for example, the analysis of decoupling in Choi and Sanchirico (2004).
[35] Indeed, Becker (1968) itself analyzes this issue.
[36] Tabbach (2010) discusses sanctioning detection avoidance when $c > 1$ (see

assumption is occasionally supported by arguing that sanctioning detection avoidance is infeasible because, for example, such activities are unobservable by the enforcement authority. This defense is problematic both conceptually and empirically.

On a purely conceptual level, it would be difficult to argue successfully that detection avoidance activities are categorically more difficult for the government to detect and sanction than underlying violations. Each category houses a diverse variety of activities. Moreover, certain underlying violations (such as fraud, insider trading, slander, etc.) resemble detection avoidance, while certain detection avoidance activities (e.g., witness intimidation) resemble underlying violations.

On an empirical level, detection avoidance – in the form of lying to investigators, obstruction of justice, perjury, discovery misconduct, etc. – is in fact detected and sanctioned. Indeed, some commentators decry the fact that prosecutors will too often abandon prosecution of the underlying crime in favor of pursuing sanctions for various forms of derivative detection avoidance.[37] It is said that prosecutors often do this because detection avoidance crimes are *easier*, not harder, to prosecute.

5.2 The Potentially Decisive Impact of Adding Sanctions for Detection Avoidance

As discussed in Section 4.3, Malik (1990) shows that accounting for detection avoidance can overturn Becker's conventional prescription to generate deterrence via large fines and low detection probabilities. Several authors have since provided the literature with a list of conditions – concerning self-reporting, strategic complementarities, and sanctioning costs – that restore Becker's prescription despite the dynamics of detection avoidance. However, the very possibility of sanctioning detection avoidance itself restores Becker's prescription – at least if it is assumed, as it shall be in this section (but not in the next, Section 7), that the detection of detection avoidance activity cannot itself be avoided.

Section 4.3.5), but the article's actual results are more limited than they appear from verbal descriptions in the introduction and elsewhere. In Tabbach's model, the condition $c > 1$ also applies to sanctions for detection avoidance. But detection avoidance activity, at any level, is always detected and always sanctioned by the same amount (p. 277). Consequently, decreases in detection avoidance activity do not lower the expected cost of sanctioning detection avoidance. In this special setting, the article provides two specific results. These results reject, respectively, the two extreme outcomes for detection avoidance sanctioning: (1) the sanction for detection avoidance should not be zero (p. 278); and (2) the sanction for detection avoidance should not be so large as to deter completely detection avoidance (p. 279).

[37] See, for example, Griffin (2009) and Richman and Stuntz (2005).

Recall that Becker's prescription is to lower public detection costs d and raise the fine S in such manner as to maintain deterrence, the sole result being a reduction in social costs. Recall also Malik warning that raising the fine increases the private cost of detection avoidance. But the private cost of detection avoidance may be kept in check by simultaneously, and costlessly, raising the fine S_1 *on detection avoidance*.

Thus, after lowering public detection costs d à la Becker, instead of raising only the fine on the underlying violation, S, let the government raise both S and S_1 together. Let it do so at relative rates that guarantee that the positive impact of raising S on detection avoidance is precisely cancelled by the negative impact on detection avoidance of raising S_1. (The next paragraph describes how such relative rates may be determined.) Let this relatively calibrated joint increase in S and S_1, which induces no change in detection avoidance activity, be itself calibrated to offset the reduction in deterrence of the underlying violation due to the reduction in d.[38] The end result is a reduction in public detection costs, no change in the level of deterrence for the underlying violation, *and no increase in detection avoidance*.

Formulaically, imagine that violators choose detection avoidance a to minimize an effective expected sanction that includes a sanction for detection avoidance: $p(d,a)S + a + p_1(a)S_1$, as discussed in Section 3.2.3.1. Then, per Section 4, the implicit function theorem may be applied to the first-order condition for the effective expected sanction-minimizing level of a^* in order to establish that the change in detection avoidance due to the increase in the fine on the *underlying violation* is $da^*/dS = -p_a/(Sp_{aa} + S_1 p_{1aa}) > 0$.[39] Also by the implicit function theorem, the change in detection avoidance due to an increase in the fine *on detection avoidance*, is $da^*/dS_1 = -p_{1a}/(Sp_{aa} + S_1 p_{1aa}) < 0$. Thus, increasing the fine on the underlying violation increases detection avoidance, while increasing the fine on detection avoidance decreases it. Specifically, marginally increasing S, while simultaneously marginally increasing S_1 at the relative rate of $dS_1/dS = -p_a/p_{1a} > 0$, has, in total, no marginal impact on a^*.[40]

Nevertheless, this coordinated increase in both sanctions causes the effective expected sanction for the underlying violation to increase by $p(d,a^*) + (-p_a/p_{1a})p_1(a^*) > 0$. (This follows from applying the envelope theorem to the derivative of $p(d,a^*)S + a^* + p_1(a^*)S_1(S)$ with respect to S, when S_1 is treated as a function of S whose derivative is $dS_1/dS = -p_a/p_{1a}$.)

---

[38] Note that, as discussed in Section 3.2.2.2., the increase in S_1 also adds to underlying deterrence.
[39] See notes 14 and 15.
[40] That is, $-p_a/(Sp_{aa} + S_1 p_{1a}) + (-p_a/p_{1a})(-p_{1a}/(Sp_{aa} + S_1 p_{1a})) = 0$.

Given that S and S_1 are fines, such increase in the expected effective sanction does not incur additional sanctioning costs: $c(S) = c(S_1) = 0$ for all S and all S_1. Therefore, the coordinated increase in the two fines can play the role played by increasing the fine for the underlying violation in Becker's (detection avoidance-free) argument for high fines and low detection probabilities.

Thus, the fact that existing models leave out the possibility that detection avoidance may itself be sanctioned is decisive for the literature's main results. It must be reiterated, however, that this analysis assumes that detection of detection avoidance is not itself avoidable, a possibility discussed in the next section.

6 The Recursivity of Detection Avoidance[41]

One might be tempted to regard detection avoidance as just another hidden action to which the vast literature on incentives[42] – inclusive of the conventional enforcement model – may be brought to bear. But a fundamental and differentiating characteristic of detection avoidance is that it is a recursive activity. Thus, in the context of the conventional enforcement model, sanctioning any activity – *including detection avoidance* – generates additional effort to avoid detection of that activity. The recursivity of detection avoidance thus spins out a potentially infinite sequence of ever greater orders of detection avoidance. Sanctioning the underlying offense encourages "first-order" detection avoidance. Sanctioning first-order detection avoidance encourages "second-order" detection avoidance. Sanctioning second-order detection avoidance encourages third-order. Sanctioning third encourages fourth. And so on.

The recursivity of detection avoidance was first pointed out and analyzed in Sanchirico (2006a, 2006b). This section of the chapter first discusses the practical import and conceptual nature of detection avoidance's recursivity. It then considers how such recursion effects the efficacy of sanctioning detection avoidance.

6.1 The Practical Import of Detection Avoidance's Recursivity

Is it plausible that violators engage in, say, detection avoidance four times removed? Arguably, it is conditionally plausible and that is all it needs to be. Fourth-order detection avoidance is plausible, that is, if it is assumed that the government can identify, sanction, and thereby discourage

---

[41] This section is drawn from Sanchirico (2006a) and the corresponding formal analysis in Sanchirico (2006b).
[42] Kreps (1990), chapter 16, describes this literature.

detection avoidance *three* times removed – which is the only case in which the plausibility of fourth-order detection avoidance matters. The effectiveness of the sanction on third-order detection avoidance presupposes that third-order detection avoidance is a discernible activity in the minds of violators. And, at that point, the pedigree of the activity becomes irrelevant: it is just an activity and it will be covered up like any other that is also subject to sanction.

It is thus important to keep in mind that the real impact of detection avoidance's recursivity lies not in the full conceptual stretch to infinity. It lies, rather, in the fact that detection avoidance always grows another head, and so remains one order greater than the last effective order of sanction.

6.2 The Nature of Detection Avoidance's Recursivity

It is also important to distinguish the recursivity of detection avoidance from the well-recognized policy pitfall of ignoring substitution effects: as when limiting boat size induces fishermen to use better equipment with little effect in reducing harvest; or as when rewarding for high student test scores quashes the teaching of unobservable attributes like creativity.[43] In these cases, a single activity is effectively taxed (respectively, subsidized), and the corresponding reduction (respectively, increase) in that activity makes an alternative activity more (respectively, less) productive. The interactive mechanism is a "cross effect" in the violator's optimization problem – a substitution effect to be precise.

The recursivity of detection avoidance does not describe a situation in which lower-order detection avoidance is taxed and thereby causes a substitution into higher. (Indeed, as discussed below, orders of detection avoidance are likely to be complements rather than substitutes.) Rather, what is happening is that the tax on lower-order detection avoidance simultaneously acts as a subsidy on higher-order avoidance. An additional dollar of sanction on $n - 1$th-order avoidance is in effect an additional dollar of reward for nth. Thus the interactive mechanism across orders of detection avoidance comes not from cross-effects in the violator's effective expected sanction minimization problem, but rather from the fact that the policy instrument – the sanction on $n - 1$th-order avoidance – has two points of impact on that minimization problem.

Formulaically,[44] allowing for infinite orders of detection avoidance and sanctions thereon, the effective expected sanction for the underlying

---

[43] See, for example, Holmstrom and Milgrom (1991).
[44] The technical material that follows is derived from Sanchirico (2006b).

172 *Procedural law and economics*

violation is the minimized value of $(p_0S_0 + a_1) + (p_1S_1 + a_2) + (p_2S_2 + a_3)$ ..., or more precisely,

$$\min_{a_1,a_2,\ldots} \underbrace{p_0\left(\overset{+}{d_0};\overset{-}{a_1},\overset{-}{a_2},\ldots\right)S_0}_{\text{expected sanction for underlying violation}} + \underbrace{\sum_{i=1}^{\infty} p_i\left(\overset{+}{d_i},\overset{+}{a_i};\overset{-}{a_{i+1}},\overset{-}{a_{i+2}},\ldots\right)S_i}_{\text{expected sanction for }i\text{th-order detection avoidance}} + \underbrace{\sum_{i=1}^{\infty} a_i}_{\substack{\text{spending} \\ \text{on }i\text{th-} \\ \text{order} \\ \text{detection} \\ \text{avoidance}}}$$

In this expression, a_i is the potential violator's ith-order detection avoidance expenditure, p_0 is the probability that the underlying violation is detected, p_i is the probability that the violator's ith-order detection avoidance is detected, d_0 is public expenditure on detection of the underlying violation, d_i is public expenditure on detection of ith-order detection avoidance, S_0 is the ex post sanction on the underlying activity, and S_i is the ex post sanction on ith-order detection avoidance.

The pluses and minuses in the expression show the assumed signs of first derivatives.[45] For example, the probability p_0 that the underlying violation is detected increases in public detection effort d_0 and decreases in first-order detection avoidance effort, as well as higher-order detection avoidance efforts. For another example, the probability p_2 that second-order detection avoidance is detected increases in second-order detection avoidance itself a_2 and in detection effort d_2 directed at second-order detection avoidance, and decreases in third-order detection avoidance a_3 as well as higher orders of detection avoidance.

The contradictory effect of sanctioning a given order of detection avoidance can be seen from this expression. Consider the addend in the middle summation for some arbitrary counting order $i' \geq 1$. Sanctioning i'th-order detection avoidance "taxes" i'th-order detection avoidance – according to the amount that such i'th-order detection avoidance increases the chance that i'th-order detection avoidance itself is detected. But sanctioning i'th-order detection avoidance also "subsidizes" all orders of detection avoidance that are higher than i' – according to the amount that such higher orders of detection avoidance decrease the chance that ith-order detection avoidance is detected.

What effect does the tax/subsidy which is S_i have on various orders

---

[45] I shall make assumptions regarding all p_i that are analogous to those made for p and p_1 in notes 14 and 15. In particular, I shall assume that $p_{i-k,a_i} > 0$ for all positive k such that $i - k$ is not less than zero. Thus, higher-order detection avoidance *decreases* the probability of all lower-order detection at a decreasing rate.

of detection avoidance? The answer is potentially complicated by cross-effects of the form $p_{ja_ka_i}$. Because of such cross-effects, one cannot say whether detection avoidance of any given order will increase or decrease as a result of increasing the sanction of any given order.[46] Let us, therefore, assume that such cross-effects are negligible. (For a further discussion of cross-effects see Section 6.4.) Then the left-hand side of the first-order condition for any given order i of detection avoidance, which is

$$\overset{+}{\overbrace{p_{ia_i}}} S_i + \sum_{j=0}^{i-1} \overset{-}{\overbrace{p_{ja_i}}} S_j + 1 = 0 \tag{7.1}$$

is independent of the level of all other orders $k \neq i$ of detection avoidance. The implicit function theorem may, therefore, be individually applied to each order of detection avoidance. And it may thereby be determined that the effect on ith-order detection avoidance of raising the ith-order sanction itself is negative:

$$\frac{\delta a_i}{\delta S_i} = -\overset{+}{\overbrace{p_{ia_i}}} \bigg/ \left(\overset{+}{\overbrace{p_{ia_ia_i}}} S_i + \sum_{j=0}^{i-1} \overset{+}{\overbrace{p_{ja_ia_i}}} S_j \right) < 0,$$

while the effect on ith detection avoidance of raising a sanction *of order less than i* is positive: for all $i > k \geq 0$,

$$\frac{\delta a_i}{\delta S_k} = -\overset{-}{\overbrace{p_{ka_i}}} \bigg/ \left(\overset{+}{\overbrace{p_{ia_ia_i}}} S_i + \sum_{j=0}^{i-1} \overset{+}{\overbrace{p_{ja_ia_i}}} S_j \right) > 0.$$

To answer the initial question regarding the impact of increasing a particular $S_{i'}$ on various orders of detection avoidance, we can turn the foregoing analysis around and fix the sanctioning order rather than the order of detection avoidance. Assuming small cross-effects, increasing the i'th-order sanction $S_{i'}$ decreases i'th-order detection avoidance, but increases all higher orders of detection avoidance $i > i'$.

6.3 Sanctioning Hierarchies

It was shown in Section 5.2 that adding sanctions for first-order detection avoidance can restore Becker's maximal fine prescription *when higher orders of detection avoidance are ignored*. More generally, it was shown that the simultaneous sanctioning of underlying violations and detection

---

[46] The ambiguity caused by cross-effects is a common phenomenon in economic theory.

avoidance can counteract the positive effect on detection avoidance of increasing the sanction for the underlying violation. The question then arises: does the same idea carry over to a model that acknowledges the recursivity of detection avoidance?

It is true that, in such a model, there are more orders of detection avoidance to be counteracted. But it is also true that there are also more orders of sanction to be applied. Thus, although there is always yet another order of detection avoidance no matter how far out sanctions extend, there is always another higher order of sanction to be imposed. Thus, perhaps sanctioning all orders simultaneously would have an effect analogous to that described for the single order case in Section 6.2.

Sanchirico (2006a, 2006b) studies this question. He begins with the point that *uniformly* sanctioning all orders of detection avoidance – that is, imposing the same sanction on all orders of detection avoidance – is likely to increase, not decrease, detection avoidance – and at every order. He then shows that the kind of variable sanctioning structure that would be required to reduce detection avoidance is ever increasing across orders of detection avoidance, and so, he concludes, impractical. These findings are reviewed in the remainder of this section.

6.3.1 Uniform sanctions hierarchies Consider, first, a uniform sanction for all orders of detection avoidance as well as the primary violation: that is, for all $i = 0,1,2,3, \ldots S_i = S > 0$. Such a sanctioning structure resembles several aspects of the law as written[47] (if not all aspects, and if not as such law-enforced): all orders of perjury, including perjury about perjury about perjury about perjury, are potentially perjury and are sanctioned, in theory, to the same degree. The same holds for all orders of obstruction of justice.

The first-order condition for choice of ith-order detection avoidance, (7.1), simplifies to

$$\left(\overset{+}{\overrightarrow{p_{ia_i}}} + \sum_{j=0}^{i-1} \overset{-}{\overrightarrow{p_{ja_i}}} \right) S + 1 = 0.$$

The first addend is the marginal net *increase*, due to ith-order detection avoidance, of the effective expected sanction. The second addend, 1, is the marginal cost of ith-order detection avoidance. Given fulfillment of the first-order condition, the first addend must be negative, which is to

---

[47] Section 2.1 describes laws regulating evidentiary foul play. See also Sanchirico (2004a).

say that the violator must be choosing ith-order detection avoidance at a level such that marginal ith-order detection avoidance further reduces the effective expected sanction. More specifically, marginal ith-order detection avoidance must reduce the expected sanction *per dollar of S*:

$$p_{ia_i} + \sum_{j=0}^{i-1} p_{ja_i} < 0. \tag{7.2}$$

It follows that, even though S, the sanction that applies to all orders of detection avoidance, is both a sanction and reward for ith-order detection avoidance, raising S *raises*, on net, the marginal benefit to the violator of ith-order detection avoidance. This, in turn, implies that S raises the level of ith-order detection avoidance.

Formally, applying the implicit function theorem to the first-order condition (continuing to assume that cross-effects are negligible) and using (7.2) to sign the numerator, we have:

$$\frac{\partial a_i}{\partial S} = -\frac{\overbrace{p_{ia_i} + \sum_{j=0}^{i-1} p_{ja_i}}^{-}}{\left(\overbrace{p_{ia_ia_i}}^{+} + \sum_{j=0}^{i-1} \overbrace{p_{ja_ia_i}}^{+}\right)S} > 0.$$

Note that the sign of this derivative is positive for all orders i of detection avoidance. Therefore, all orders of detection avoidance increase as a result of increasing the uniform sanction.[48]

As an aside, consider, by contrast, the effect *on the underlying violation* of increasing the uniform sanction. By the envelope theorem, the effective expected sanction increases by the sum of the detection probabilities, $p_0() + \Sigma_{i=1}^{\infty} p_i > 0$. Thus, although all orders of detection avoidance increase, fewer underlying violations occur. Why the contrary effect on the underlying violation? The underlying violation is different than all orders of detection avoidance. In the case of the underlying violation, and only in the case of the underlying violation, there is no lower-order sanction that the underlying violation helps to avoid. Hence, there is no lower-order sanction whose increase acts to encourage more of the underlying violation.

6.3.2 Variable sanctioning hierarchies So far, we have considered only uniform sanctioning hierarchies, wherein $S_i = S$, for all i. And we have

---

[48] Sanchirico (2006a) provides a more detailed description of the intuition behind this result.

176 *Procedural law and economics*

seen that increasing the uniform sanction S may well encourage all levels of detection avoidance. In theory, however, the government can adjust the sanctioning hierarchy so as to increase the effective expected sanction for the underlying violation without also increasing detection avoidance of order i. To do so, it must raise the sanction for order i at a faster rate than it raises the sanction on lower orders of detection avoidance (including the primary violation as order 0). More precisely, and as shown below, the rate of increase in ever higher-order sanctions must be greater than a particular weighted average of the rate of increase at lower orders of sanction.

Imposing an increasing sanctions hierarchy corresponds to the fix described in Section 5.2 for the case of a single order of detection avoidance. However, as discussed below, imposing an ever increasing sanctions hierarchy is unlikely to be feasible in practice.

6.3.2.1 THE THEORETICAL POSSIBILITY OF PREVENTING INCREASES IN SOME OR ALL ORDERS OF DETECTION AVOIDANCE Given numbers dS_i for all i, write

$$S_i(\beta) = S_i + \beta dS_i,$$

for all i. Changing the parameter β changes the sanctioning hierarchy in a particular direction defined by the given sequence of dS_i. The violator's first-order condition for ith-order detection avoidance, (7.1), can then be rewritten as

$$\overset{+}{\overbrace{p_{ia_i}}} S_i(\beta) + \sum_{j=0}^{i-1} \overset{-}{\overbrace{p_{ja_i}}} S_j(\beta) + 1 = 0. \tag{7.3}$$

Continuing to assume negligible cross-effects, the implicit function theorem applied to the parameter β then implies

$$\frac{\delta a_i}{\delta \beta} = -\left(p_{ia_i} dS_i + \sum_{j=0}^{i-1} p_{ja_i} dS_j \right) \bigg/ \left(\overset{+}{\overbrace{p_{ia_i a_i}}} S_i + \sum_{j=0}^{i-1} \overset{+}{\overbrace{p_{ja_i a_i}}} S_j \right),$$

where this derivative is evaluated at $\beta = 0$.

Our question is this: for which sequences of dS_i is the foregoing derivative non-positive. Assuming, as we shall throughout, that $S_k > 0$ for all k, this is the same as asking: for which sequences is the term in parentheses in the numerator non-negative,

$$p_{ia_i}dS_i + \sum_{j=0}^{i-1} p_{ja_i}dS_j \geq 0 \Leftrightarrow p_{ia_i}dS_i \geq - \sum_{j=0}^{i-1} p_{ja_i}dS_j. \quad (7.4)$$

Now, from the first-order condition, (7.3), we have

$$p_{ia_i}S_i + 1 = \sum_{j=0}^{i-1} \overbrace{-p_{ja_i}}^{+} S_j.$$

Both sides of this equality are positive. Dividing both sides of (7.4) by the respective side of such equality yields:

$$\left(\frac{p_{ia_i}S_i}{p_{ia_i}S_i+1}\right)\frac{dS_i}{S_i} \geq \sum_{j=0}^{i-1}\left(\frac{\overbrace{-p_{ja_i}}^{+} S_j}{\sum_{j=0}^{i-1}\overbrace{-p_{ja_i}}^{+} S_j}\right)\frac{dS_j}{S_j}.$$

The right hand-side of this inequality is a weighted average (with positive weights adding to one) of the dS_j/S_j from $j = 0$ to $j = i - 1$. These are the percentage increases in the sanction at orders of detection avoidance below i (including the underlying violation). Each such lower order is weighted by its contribution to the marginal reduction in the effective expected sanction caused by increasing a_i. This weight represents the relative importance of such lower order in the benefit to the violator of increasing ith-order detection avoidance, that benefit being the reduction in lower-order expected sanctions.

Thus, writing α_j for the importance-weight corresponding to lower-order j, the condition is fulfilled *if and only if*

$$\frac{dS_i}{S_i} \geq \left(1 + \overbrace{\frac{1}{p_{ia_i}S_i}}^{+}\right)\sum_{j=0}^{i-1}\alpha_j\frac{dS_j}{S_j}. \quad (7.5)$$

This condition implies that in order to prevent the sequence dS_i of sanction changes from causing an increase in ith-order detection avoidance it is necessary that the percentage increase in the sanction at i exceed or equal the importance-weighted average of the percentage increases in the sanction at all orders lower than i. Furthermore, it is sufficient for preventing an increase in ith-order detection avoidance that the percentage change in S_i be $100 \times 1/(p_{ia_i}S_i)$ percent greater than such weighted average of lower-order percentage changes.

Extrapolating, in order for the sequence of sanction changes not to cause an increase in *any* orders of detection avoidance $i \geq 1$, it is necessary and sufficient that condition (7.5) hold for all $i \geq 1$.

178 *Procedural law and economics*

Consider, for example, the special case in which a_i affects only p_{i-1}, the probability of detection of the adjacent lower order, and not the detection probability at other even lower orders such as $i-2$, $i-3$ etc. Then condition (7.5) reduces to

$$\frac{dS_i}{S_i} \geq \left(1 + \overbrace{\frac{1}{p_{ia_i}S_i}}^{+}\right) \sum_{j=0}^{i-1} \overbrace{\alpha_j}^{=1,\ \text{if}\ j=i-1}_{=0,\ \text{otherwise}} \frac{dS_j}{S_j} \Leftrightarrow \frac{dS_i}{S_i} \geq \left(1 + \overbrace{\frac{1}{p_{ia_i}S_i}}^{+}\right) \frac{dS_{i-1}}{S_{i-1}}.$$

Thus, the percentage increase in the sanction must be $100 \times 1/(p_{ia_i}S_i)$ percent greater at each successively greater order of detection avoidance.

Suppose, for example, that the initial sanctioning structure is uniform across orders at the value $S = 100$. Further, suppose that for all i, the marginal impact of ith-order detection avoidance on its detection probability is $p_{ia_i} = 0.10$. Then, in order to avoid increasing detection avoidance at any order, the percentage increase in the sanction at order i (which equals the absolute increase given $S = 1$) must grow at a rate of 10% in i. It follows that the increase in the sanction on eighth-order detection avoidance must be twice that for the underlying sanction, the increase in 25th-order detection avoidance must be ten times that for the underlying sanction, and so on.

6.3.2.2 PRACTICAL ASSESSMENT Imposing ever increasing sanctions across higher and higher orders of detection avoidance supposes that the state can reliably distinguish between such orders. This seems unlikely, especially given the incentive that is thereby created for perpetrators to portray their higher-order avoidance activities as being of lower order – yet another form of detection avoidance. (Note that the problem here is not an inability on the part of the government to observe detection avoidance activities. Rather the problem is the government's inability to determine whether a particular instance of detection avoidance that it observes is of order i rather than order j.)

Indeed, there is some reason to believe that the best the state can do as a practical matter is a decreasing hierarchy of sanctions. Arguably, higher orders of detection avoidance are more likely to get lost in the crowd of daily activity. Indeed, in US Federal law, despite the fact that obstruction of justice of any order is technically obstruction of justice, higher orders of obstruction are, in fact, unlikely to result in separate charges, and are more likely to be punished with sentencing enhancements for the lower-order activity. These sentencing enhancements produce in effect a decreasing sanctions hierarchy. By one reading of the Federal sentencing guidelines, for instance, first-order obstruction is punished by 18 months in prison, second-order by six, and third-, fourth-, fifth-, etc. by zero.[49]

Therefore, the practical prospects for controlling detection avoidance by means of sanctioning – even sanctioning that in principle extends to all orders of detection – seem dim. A somewhat weaker but still decisive claim, considered in Section 7, is that sanctioning detection avoidance is a relatively *inefficacious* way of controlling it, given the possibility of alternative "technological" approaches.

It must be reiterated, however, that such conclusions have been derived under the assumption that cross-effects are small. Let us now turn to a discussion of cross-effects.

6.4 Accounting for Complementarities Across Orders of Detection Avoidance

In previous subsections it was assumed that there were no cross-effects across orders of detection avoidance. As Sanchirico (2006a) notes,[50] however, higher and lower orders of detection avoidance are likely to be "complements." More of either increases the productivity of the other. More cover-up of the cover-up, that is, makes the underlying cover-up itself more productive. Conversely, more cover-up makes covering up the cover-up more productive.

The fact that orders of detection avoidance are complementary in the sense just described complicates, but does not fundamentally alter, the conclusion that sanctioning detection avoidance is relatively inefficacious.

Taking account of complementarities across orders of detection avoidance, consider sanctioning *only* first-order detection avoidance. This has two countervailing effects on second-order detection avoidance. First, as already discussed, the sanction on first-order detection avoidance acts as a reward for second-order detection avoidance. Second, because sanctioning first-order detection avoidance discourages first-order detection avoidance itself, and because first- and second-order detection avoidance are complementary, sanctioning first-order detection avoidance will, through this second channel, act to discourage second-order detection avoidance.

Thus, the direct effect of the first-order sanction – operating through the first-order sanction's other role as a second-order reward – is to encourage second-order cover-up, while the indirect effect of the first-order

---

[49] For details, see Sanchirico (2004a, 2006a).
[50] Following Sanchirico (2006a, 2006b), Nussim and Tabbach (2009) also make reference to complementarity. Nussim and Tabbach only consider such complementarity between the primary violation (zero-order detection avoidance) and first-order detection avoidance.

180 *Procedural law and economics*

sanction – operating through complementarities – is to discourage second-order cover-up. Either effect may predominate. Thus, incorporating complementarities, it is not possible to say whether sanctioning first-order cover-up will increase or decrease second-order cover-up.

However, *any* measure that reduces first-order detection avoidance – whether that measure be a sanction on first-order cover-up or a technological restructuring of evidentiary process, as discussed in Section 7 immediately below – benefits from the indirect reduction in second-order detection avoidance that operates through complementarity. The difference between the technological approach, described in the next section, and the sanctioning approach is that the technological approach gives this benefit free reign, while the sanctioning approach hampers it by simultaneously subsidizing second-order detection avoidance, as has just been described.

7 Technological Approaches to Detection Avoidance

As pointed out in Section 3.2.2.2.2, sanctioning is not the state's only means of dealing with detection avoidance. Given the state's choice of detection activity d, the government effectively presents to the violator not a single probability of detection, $p(d)$, but a "menu" of detection probabilities, $p(d,.)$ one for each of her possible choices a of detection avoidance intensity. By adjusting the shape of this menu (by the means described below), the state can affect both violators' detection avoidance choices and their decision whether to violate the law in the first place.

Sanchirico (2006a, 2006b) points out the existence of this alternative policy instrument and further argues that such a "technological approach" to detection avoidance may be a more efficient and effective means of reducing detection avoidance than sanctioning.

7.1 The Mechanics of the Technological Approach

A simple diagram from Sanchirico (2006b) helps to clarify the nature and effect of technological approaches to detection avoidance. Thus, suppose that we wish to reduce detection avoidance and imagine, for simplicity, that there are no pre-existing sanctions on detection avoidance.

The horizontal axis in Figure 7.1 depicts (first-order) detection avoidance effort a (in dollars). The vertical axis depicts the expected sanction per se for the underlying violation, the product of the probability of detection for the underlying violation $p(a)$ and the sanction for the underlying violation S. (Note that this "expected sanction per se" does not account for private detection avoidance costs.) The downward sloping line(s) (focus on the lower one for now) shows the inverse relationship between detection avoidance spending a and the expected sanction per se: the more the individual spends on detection avoidance, the lower the

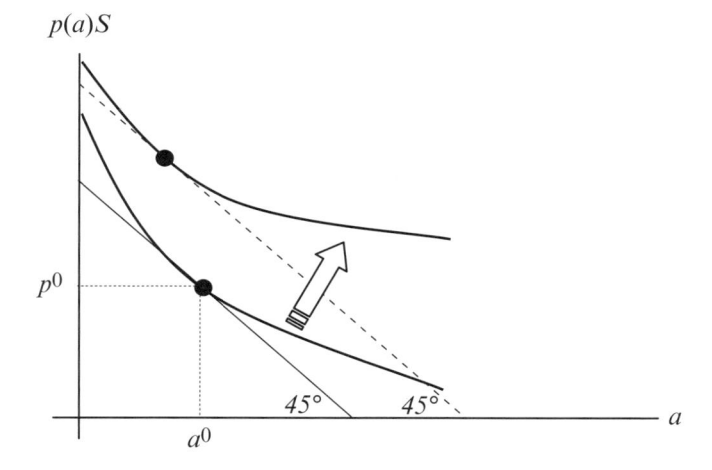

Figure 7.1   A technological approach to detection avoidance

probability of detection, and so the lower the expected sanction per se. This is the menu of detection probabilities presented to the violator by the state.

This curve can also be thought of as the violator's "production function" for detection avoidance. Put another way, it describes the "technology" of detection avoidance in the same way that a firm's production function describes its technology of production. In the technology of avoidance, detection avoidance is the costly input, and a reduced expected sanction per se is the output.

Notice that detection avoidance is assumed to reduce the expected sanction at a decreasing rate (an assumption that I have imposed throughout[51]). This reflects the assumption that detection avoiders employ the most productive avoidance measures first and must reach deeper down into the barrel (or higher up into the fruit tree) as they expend more and more effort and expense on avoidance.

As in the analysis in Section 3.2.2.1 above, the violator, who wishes to minimize $p(a)S + a$, the sum of the expected sanction per se and the cost of the avoidance, will choose a so that the marginal reduction in the expected sanction $-p_a(a)S$ equals the marginal cost of an additional dollar of detection avoidance spending, which is one dollar by definition. Therefore, she will choose her detection avoidance activity at a point where the slope of

---

[51]   See, for example, note 14.

the curve $p(a)S$ equals -1. For the lower curve, this is the point corresponding to a^0 on the horizontal axis and p^0 on the vertical.

A technological approach to reducing detection avoidance shifts the technology of detection avoidance. Specifically, ideally implemented, it shifts the expected sanction per se curve according to two requirements: (1) it uniformly reduces the marginal productivity of detection avoidance activity; and (2) it does not lower the probability of detection in the absence of avoidance activity (i.e. at $a = 0$). It therefore flattens the curve describing the relationship between avoidance and expected sanction without lowering (and possibly even raising) its level at $a = 0$. Such "upward flattening" is depicted by movement from the lower curve to the upper curve in the figure.

This upward flattening has two effects. First, violators spend less on detection avoidance. The slope of the upper curve flattens to a slope of -1 at a lower level of detection avoidance expenditure. Second, the probability of detection of the underlying activity is greater. This implies that deterrence of the underlying activity has increased.[52] (As in Section 3.2.2.1 above, the envelope theorem dictates that marginal adjustments to detection avoidance activity a have no effect on deterrence.)

Therefore, the technological approach decreases detection avoidance costs while increasing deterrence of the underlying activity. (As discussed in Section 7.2 below, it may also increase the public costs of detection.)

It is important to recognize that the technological approach is not merely a matter of "making detection avoidance harder." That is, requirement (1) above is not merely a matter of increasing the cost to the violator of reducing the probability of detection by an additional percentage point. Doing just this may lead violators to try harder, and thereby to increase, rather than decrease, the expenditure of resources on detection avoidance. Rather, the first requirement of the technological approach requires something more: that the productivity of avoidance effort and expenditure be reduced. To reduce the productivity of detection avoidance is to reduce the number of percentage points by which an additional dollar of detection avoidance reduces the probability of detection. As Sanchirico (2006a, 2006b) shows, this second requirement implies, but is not implied by, an increase in the cost of reducing the probability of detection.

---

[52] Following Sanchirico (2006a, 2006b), Nussim and Tabbach (2009) identify the same two effects.

7.2 Public Detection Costs and the Comparison to Sanctioning

Reducing the productivity of detection avoidance is likely to come at the price of additional public costs. Decreasing the effectiveness of the detection avoidance dollar may, for example, require more costly surveillance systems or more lengthy and numerous interrogation sessions.

Yet if the issue is relative efficacy, such public costs cannot be considered in isolation, but must be compared with the public costs of the sanctioning approach. The sanctioning approach to detection avoidance requires additional, costly processes, which may be quite substantial. Perjury and obstruction also must be investigated and prosecuted.

Therefore, the sanctioning approach and the technological approach to detection avoidance are similar along two dimensions in the social calculus, but quite different along a third. They both increase primary activity deterrence and they both incur public costs. But because the technological approach is not prone to the recursivity that plagues sanctioning, the technological attack is more effective at reducing private detection avoidance costs.

7.3 Implementing the Technological Approach

How can the marginal productivity of detection avoidance be reduced (while also not increasing its total product)?

Merely devoting additional public resources to detecting violations will not suffice. Simply questioning yet another witness, for example, will not necessarily decrease the productivity of detection avoidance spending. If, without coaching, a witness's answers will increase the violator's chance of having to pay a $100,000 sanction by ten percentage points, but with $5000 of "preparation" this can be wholly prevented, then interrogating an additional witness will most likely increase, rather than decrease, the productivity of detection avoidance spending. Rather, to implement the technological approach, public detection spending must be specifically channeled so that each dollar and each unit of effort spent avoiding detection buys less of a reduction in the probability of detection. This is essentially a matter of making detection avoidance more difficult at each step – so that, for example, $5000 of witness coaching only partially prevents the witness's positive impact on the probability of detection.

Sanchirico (2006a) suggests accomplishing this by designing evidentiary process so as to exploit and amplify the difficulties generally encountered in all human endeavors. Two difficulties – of cognition and of cooperation – are already exploited by current evidentiary process and may hold further potential.

An earlier paper, Sanchirico (2004b), reviews in detail how the law of evidentiary procedure exploits cognitive limitations. Imagine, for example, that the offender wishes to reduce the probability of detection by supplying a witness to swear falsely that the offender did not commit the underlying crime. Exploiting the witness's cognitive limitations, the law takes several steps to reduce the productivity of time and effort spent preparing this witness. Consider three specific aspects of how testimony, depositions, and interrogations generally proceed. First, the witness will usually not see the questions in advance. Time spent preparing answers to the questions that one can anticipate is thereby less productive for the fact that such preparation may well be rendered much less valuable with a few poorly improvised answers to questions that were unexpected. Second, the questioner need not commit to her questions ahead of time, but may rather adjust the subject or tenor of additional questions based on what she perceives to be uncertainties and inconsistencies in the answers provided to previous questions. This renders preparation less productive because the witness is largely denied the opportunity of playing the odds that particular topics will not be "tested." The test is not written ahead of time. If it becomes apparent that the witness is less prepared for a particular line of questioning, the questioner may shift course and emphasize that line of questioning. Conversely, if it becomes apparent that the witness has prepared for a given line of questioning, the questioner can choose to move on to other topics. Preparation time is thus generally rendered less productive. Lastly, interrogations and depositions exploit the very real effects of fatigue. The difficult task of fabricating testimony becomes all the more difficult as the fabricator tires. While interrogators and deposers may substitute in and out during questioning, the witness is on her own. Hours of preparation can be rendered virtually ineffective by a few unguarded answers in the last few moments of a long day of questioning.

Game theorists have long recognized the possibility of exploiting the difficulties and fragilities of coordination and cooperation among multiple agents. These lessons apply to the state's efforts to reduce the productivity of detection avoidance activity. Detection avoidance, like any human activity, often requires or is facilitated by coordination among several individuals, especially if it is effected on a large scale. The state can play these individuals against each other by structuring interrogation and prosecution to amplify the temptation to break ranks. Specific practical techniques employed by law enforcement in this area include, first, the hearsay exception for statements of a co-conspirator. Statements made by a co-conspirator (during the pendency of the conspiracy and in furtherance thereof) may be used substantively against a party even if they are not made for the purpose of testifying in the current case. Other devices include prosecutorial immunity, plea agreements, no prosecution agreements, special protection for whistleblowers, and rewards for informants. All of these make cooperation in detection avoidance harder to maintain and thus reduce the usual productivity gains from teamwork.

8 Conclusion

The state's efforts to detect violations play a leading role in the conventional model of economic enforcement. Violators' efforts to avoid detection, on the other hand, are barely alluded to. Yet the best data available suggest that, in reality, detection and detection avoidance share the stage — that they are indeed yin to each other's yang. Law and economics has just begun to bridge this important gap between the way it understands enforcement and the way that enforcement actually proceeds. More work remains to be done — especially with regard to policy tools, such as sanctions or technological adjustments to legal process, that are directed at detection avoidance itself.

Bibliography

Arther, R.O. and J.E. Reid (1954), "Utilizing the Lie Detector Technique to Determine the Truth in Disputed Paternity Cases", *Journal of Criminal Law, Criminology and Police Science*, 45 (2), 213–21.

Bebchuk, L.A. and L. Kaplow (1992), "Optimal Sanctions when Individuals are Imperfectly Informed about the Probability of Apprehension", *Journal of Legal Studies*, 21 (2), 365–70.

Bebchuk, L.A. and L. Kaplow (1993), "Optimal Sanctions and Differences in Individuals' Likelihood of Avoiding Detection", *International Review of Law and Economics*, 13 (2), 217–24.

Beccaria, Cesare (1764), "Of Crimes and Punishments", in Alessandro Manzoni, *The Column of Infamy; Prefaced by Cesare Beccaria's Of Crimes and Punishments*, reprinted Kenelm Foster and Jane Grigson (trans.) (1964), London: Oxford University Press.

Beckenstein, A.R. and H.L. Gabel (1982), "Antitrust Compliance: Results of a Survey of Legal Opinion", *Antitrust Law Journal*, 51 (4), 459–516.

Becker, G.S. (1968), 'Crime and Punishment: An Economic Approach', *Journal of Political Economy*, 76 (2), 169–217.

Bentham, Jeremy (1789), *An Introduction to the Principles of Morals and Legislation*, reprinted J.H. Burns and H.L.A. Hart (eds.) (1970), London: Athlone Press.

Brazil W.D. (1980), "Civil Discovery: Lawyers' views of its Effectiveness, its Principal Problems and Abuses", *American Bar Foundation Research Journal*, 1980 (4), 787–902.

Choi, A. and C.W. Sanchirico (2004), "Should Plaintiffs Win What Defendants Lose? Litigation Stakes, Litigation Effort, and the Benefits of Decoupling", *Journal of Legal Studies*, 33 (2), 323–54.

Chu, C.Y.C. and Y. Qian (1995), "Vicarious Liability under a Negligence Rule", *International Review of Law and Economics*, 15 (3), 305–22.

Cooter, R. and W. Emons (2003), "Truth-Revealing Mechanisms for Courts", *Journal of Institutional and Theoretical Economics*, 159 (2), 259–79.

Emons, W. (2005), "Perjury versus Truth Revelation: Quantity or Quality of Testimony", *Journal of Institutional and Theoretical Economics*, 161 (3), 392–410.

Franzoni, Luigi A. (2000), "Tax Evasion and Tax Compliance", in Boudewijn Bouckaert and Gerrit de Geest (eds.), *Encyclopedia of Law and Economics* 4, Cheltenham, UK and Brookfield, MA, US: Edward Elgar, pp. 52–94.

Friehe, T. (2010), "On Avoidance Activities after Accidents", *Review of Law and Economics*, 6 (2), Article 3.

Garoupa, N. (1997), "The Theory of Optimal Law Enforcement", *Journal of Economic Surveys*, 11 (3), 267–95.

Gorelick, Jamie S., Stephen Marzen, and Lawrence Solum (1989), *Destruction of Evidence*, New York: Wiley, cumulative supplement Jamie S. Gorelick et al. (2010), New York: Aspen Publishers, updated version available at http://westlaw.com (ID and password required).

Griffin, L.K. (2009), "Wanting the Truth: Comparing Prosecutions of Investigative and Institutional Deception", *International Commentary on Evidence*, 7 (1), Article 4.

Holmstrom, B. and P. Milgrom (1991), "Multitask Principal-Agent Analyses: Incentive Contracts, Assets Ownership, and Job Design", *Journal of Law, Economics, and Organization*, 7 (Special Issue), 24–52.

Innes, R. (2001), "Violator Avoidance Activities and Self-Reporting in Optimal Law Enforcement", *Journal of Law, Economics, and Organization*, 17 (1), 239–56.

Kahan, D.M. (1997), "Social Influence, Social Meaning, and Deterrence", *Virginia Law Review*, 83 (2), 349–95.

Koesel, Margaret M., David A. Bell, and Tracey L. Turnbull (2000), *Spoliation of Evidence: Sanctions and Remedies for Destruction of Evidence in Civil Litigation*, Chicago, IL: Tort and Insurance Practice Section, American Bar Association, updated version available at http://westlaw.com (ID and password required).

Kreps, David M. (1990), *A Course in Microeconomic Theory*, Princeton, NJ: Princeton University Press.

Langlais, E. (2008), "Detection Avoidance and Deterrence: Some Paradoxical Arithmetic", *Journal of Public Economic Theory*, 10 (3), 371–82.

Langlais, E. (2009), "On the Ambiguous Effects of Repression", *Annals of Economics and Statistics*, 93–4 (April/June), 349–62.

Malik, A.S. (1990), "Avoidance, Screening and Optimum Enforcement", *RAND Journal of Economics*, 21 (3), 341–53.

Nussim, J. and A.D. Tabbach (2008), "(Non)Regulable Avoidance and the Perils of Punishment", *European Journal of Law and Economics*, 25 (3), 191–208.

Nussim, J. and A.D. Tabbach (2009), "Deterrence and Avoidance", *International Review of Law and Economics*, 29 (4), 314–23.

Pepe, S.D. (1983), "Standards of Legal Negotiations: Interim Report and Preliminary Findings", unpublished manuscript.

Polinsky, A.M. and S. Shavell (1979), "The Optimal Tradeoff between the Probability and Magnitude of Fines", *American Economic Review*, 69 (5), 880–91.

Polinsky, A. Mitchell and Steven Shavell (2007), "The Theory of Public Enforcement of Law", in A. Mitchell Polinsky and Steven Shavell (eds.), *Handbook of Law and Economics*, Amsterdam, Boston: Elsevier, pp. 403–54.

Richman, D.C. and W.J. Stuntz (2005), "Al Capone's Revenge: An Essay on the Political Economy of Pretextual Prosecution", *Columbia Law Review*, 105 (2), 583–639.

Sanchirico, C.W. (2004a), "Evidence Tampering", *Duke Law Journal*, 53 (4), 1215–336.

Sanchirico, C.W. (2004b), "Evidence, Procedure, and the Upside of Cognitive Error", *Stanford Law Review*, 57 (2), 291–365.

Sanchirico, C.W. (2006a), "Detection Avoidance", *New York University Law Review*, 81 (4), 1331–99.

Sanchirico, C.W. (2006b), "Detection Avoidance: Web Appendix", available at http://www.cstone.net/~csanchir.

Snyder, E.A. (1990), "The Effect of Higher Criminal Penalties on Antitrust Enforcement", *Journal of Law and Economics*, 33 (2), 439–62.

Stigler, G.J. (1970), "The Optimum Enforcement of Laws", *Journal of Political Economy*, 78 (3), 526–36.

Tabbach, A.D. (2010), "The Social Desirability of Punishment Avoidance", *Journal of Law, Economics, and Organization*, 26 (2), 265–89.

Tabbach, A.D. and J. Nussim (2008), "Controlling Avoidance: Ex Ante Regulation Versus Ex Post Punishment", *Review of Law and Economics*, 4 (1), Article 4.

8 Discovery
Robert G. Bone

1. Introduction[1]

Discovery is the process by which parties obtain information from one another and from otherwise uncooperative third parties. The United States is unusual among the nations of the world for the extremely broad scope of discovery it allows (Subrin 1998). For example, the Federal Rules of Civil Procedure (FRCP) authorize discovery in federal court cases "regarding any matter, not privileged, that is relevant to the claim or defense of any party" and state that "relevant information need not be admissible at the trial if the discovery appears reasonably calculated to lead to the discovery of admissible evidence" (Rule 26). The FRCP also furnish a powerful set of discovery tools, including requests for production of documents (Rule 34); interrogatories (Rule 33); oral depositions (Rule 30); requests for admissions (Rule 36); and physical or mental examinations (Rule 35).

Broad discovery was first introduced into American litigation in 1938 as one of the most important innovations of the Federal Rules of Civil Procedure. Its purpose, as conceived by the FRCP drafters, was to resolve cases on the facts and evidence and avoid trial surprise (Subrin 1998). Broad discovery elicited few complaints for the first 40 years of its operation, but in the 1970s, judges, lawyers, and commentators began to criticize the system (Brazil 1978). Critics today complain that parties use broad discovery excessively and also sometimes abusively to impose costs on their opponents and leverage more favorable settlements.

Although there is anecdotal evidence to support these charges, reliable empirical evidence is limited (Easterbrook 1989; Mullenix 1994). According to several studies, serious discovery problems seem to be confined to a small set of complex, multi-party cases involving high stakes (Mullenix 1994; Willging et al. 1997; Kakalik et al. 1998; Garth 1998). For example, in a 1997 study based on a survey of about 1200 attorneys nationwide, the Federal Judicial Center found that "high levels of discovery problems and high expenses were more likely to occur in cases with high stakes, high levels of contentiousness, high levels of complexity, or

---

[1] This chapter is based on the treatment of discovery in Bone (2003) at 200–31.

high volumes of discovery activity" (Willging et al. 1997, at 2). Even so, this same study also found that investment in discovery constituted 50% of total litigation costs for those cases that had some discovery, and 90% of total costs for the top 5% of most expensive cases[2] (Willging et al. 1997).

The following discussion reviews the economic literature on discovery. It first evaluates the benefits of discovery, then examines the costs, and concludes with a brief survey of some reform proposals.

2. The Social Benefits of Discovery

Proponents of broad discovery cite benefits for the quality of settlements and trial outcomes, for filing and other litigation incentives, and for incentives to comply with the substantive law. Before analyzing each of these benefits, it is first necessary to examine what, if any, information would be disclosed voluntarily in the absence of formal discovery. This initial inquiry defines the information-disclosure baseline against which the effects of discovery can be evaluated.

2.1. Voluntary Disclosure

Parties frequently share information voluntarily. For example, 46% of attorneys in the Federal Judicial Center's study reported informal exchange in cases where no formal discovery or disclosure took place[3] (Willging et al. 1997, at 13–14). The following discussion surveys the literature on voluntary disclosure, first relative to favorable information and then relative to unfavorable information.

2.1.1. Voluntary disclosure of favorable information The economics literature contains numerous articles examining the voluntary revelation of private information in general (Milgrom and Roberts 1986), and the law-and-economics literature contains studies of voluntary disclosure incentives in litigation (Shavell 1989). One result is relatively obvious: a party will tend to disclose information favorable to its side early in the litigation, absent countervailing factors (Shavell 1989). Disclosing favorable information corrects for an opponent's excessive optimism, which increases the likelihood of a successful settlement that is more favorable to the disclosing party. If the defendant discloses favorable information,

---

[2] It is important to note that a low rate of observed discovery does not necessarily indicate the absence of discovery problems, even in those cases with little discovery. Little or no discovery can be part of a settlement equilibrium supported by credible threats to engage in abusive discovery.

[3] In addition, 62% of attorneys reported some informal exchange of information in cases where formal discovery or disclosure also took place.

for example, the plaintiff should reduce her estimate of likely trial success and thus her minimum demand. This drives the midpoint of the settlement range down, which, all other things equal, should yield a settlement more favorable to the defendant.

Three factors complicate this simple result. First, the opposing party must believe that the disclosure is truthful. However, disclosing parties have obvious incentives to exaggerate or misrepresent. Aware of these incentives, the opposing party will discount the truthfulness of disclosures he is unable to verify, and disclosing parties, who anticipate this response, will be less inclined to disclose when disclosure is costly (Hay 1994).

Second, in a world without formal discovery, parties might conceal favorable information to exploit the benefits of surprise at trial. But given the high costs of trial and the likelihood of settlement in any event, it is reasonable to suppose that the benefit of an early settlement will often exceed the expected benefit of trial surprise.

Third, the settlement benefits from voluntary disclosure depend on the receiving party processing information rationally. However, as the bounded rationality literature demonstrates, parties and their lawyers do not always behave with perfect rationality (Lowenstein et al. 1993; Korobkin and Guthrie 1994). For example, the self-serving bias causes parties to interpret information in ways that reinforce their pre-existing beliefs. Thus, a party who receives a disclosure might construe the information as less favorable to the disclosing party than a perfectly rational person would. This reduces the benefit from disclosure and thus the incentive to disclose in the first place.

Even so, it seems reasonable to assume that incentives to disclose favorable information voluntarily remain strong in a wide range of cases despite obstacles to verification, trial benefits from concealment, and bounded rationality effects.

2.1.2. Voluntary disclosure of unfavorable information   Although somewhat counterintuitive, there is reason to believe that a party will voluntarily disclose even unfavorable information when disclosure is needed to convince an opponent that the party is not as bad as the opponent assumes he is (Shavell 1989; Hay 1994). For example, an accomplice to a robbery and murder might confess to his role in the robbery in order to convince police that he did not commit the murder.

These disclosure incentives can produce an "unraveling effect," whereby parties disclose all their private information, both favorable and unfavorable (Hay 1994). Consider the following simple example. Suppose that D has private information about liability. Suppose as well that the strength of a case can vary from 1 (the weakest for P) to 5 (the strongest for P) and that the different types are uniformly distributed over the interval. Assume P knows these facts but does not know D's private information about liability in P's particular case.

Given the uniform distribution, a P who knows nothing else will estimate the strength of her case as 3 (the mean of the uniform distribution). If D has information showing that the case is actually weaker than 3 (i.e., 1 or 2), D will disclose that information in order to convince P of that fact and obtain a better settlement. P knows that D will do this, so if D remains silent, P will infer that the case is a 3, 4 or 5 (since D would have disclosed otherwise). Thus, P will revise her estimate of case strength upward to 4 (the mean of the uniform distribution over the new interval [3, 5]). Anticipating this response from P, D will disclose its information if it shows that case strength is less than 4 (i.e., a 3). Thus, if D remains silent, P will infer the case is a 4 or 5 and revise her estimate of case strength upward to 4.5.

This dynamic repeats itself indefinitely until the only D remaining silent is the D in a case that is strongest for P. All the parties know this will happen, so in equilibrium the pool completely unravels and the defendant immediately reveals all his private information, favorable and unfavorable, in order to convince the plaintiff that the case is in fact weaker than the plaintiff thinks it is.

There are limits to unraveling (Shavell 1989; Hay 1994). For one thing, it works best only if the parties make truthful disclosures, but parties have obvious incentives to mislead. Although the litigation system includes sanctions and other mechanisms to encourage truthful disclosure and parties can sometimes detect deception on their own, there is still room to mislead. In addition, the costs of voluntary disclosure and trial limit the extent of unraveling. And in the absence of discovery, a privately informed party will not disclose information that the party knows will never be revealed at trial. Thus, the risk of deception, coupled with disclosure costs and other factors, reduces the efficacy of unraveling (Cooter and Rubinfeld 1994).

In sum, theory predicts that parties will sometimes disclose favorable and unfavorable information in the absence of discovery, and this prediction is confirmed by empirical evidence showing a significant amount of informal information exchange. The benefits of adding discovery must be evaluated against this baseline.

2.2. Benefits for Settlement
The available data show that less than 6% of filed cases in federal court are actually tried. Given this, the benefits of discovery for settlement loom particularly large. These benefits fall into two broad categories: increasing settlement rate and improving settlement quality.

192 *Procedural law and economics*

2.2.1. Settlement rate According to the standard argument, pre-trial discovery increases the settlement rate by reducing informational asymmetry (Cooter and Rubinfeld 1994). Formally, assume that P and D each have private information about the case. For example, P might have private information about damages (w) while D has private information about liability (p). Let $x = pw$ be the expected trial award, and let x_π be plaintiff's subjective estimate of x and x_Δ be defendant's subjective estimate of x. According to the standard settlement model, settlement is feasible only if $x_\pi - x_\Delta \leq c_\pi + c_\Delta$, where c_π and c_Δ are P's and D's expected costs of litigating the case through trial, respectively. Suppose the parties are mutually optimistic about x. This means x_π is high and x_Δ is low, so the difference, $x_\pi - x_\Delta$, is large. The larger $x_\pi - x_\Delta$ is, the more likely it is to exceed $c_\pi + c_\Delta$, rendering settlement impossible. Discovery corrects the informational asymmetry, which reduces $x_\pi - x_\Delta$ and makes it more likely that the settlement feasibility condition, $x_\pi - x_\Delta \leq c_\pi + c_\Delta$, is satisfied.

One problem with this standard argument is that it ignores the voluntary disclosure baseline. The change in the settlement rate with the addition of discovery depends in part on the mix of favorable and unfavorable information that would have been disclosed in the absence of discovery. For example, suppose the baseline is that parties voluntarily disclose favorable information but not much unfavorable information without discovery. Adding discovery could actually reduce the equilibrium settlement rate (Cooter and Rubinfeld 1994). Discovery will force the disclosure of information unfavorable to the disclosing party, which should make each side more optimistic about its chance of success compared to the baseline. As a result, x_π should increase and x_Δ decrease, making it less likely that the settlement feasibility condition, $x_\pi - x_\Delta \leq c_\pi + c_\Delta$, is satisfied. (This ignores discovery's benefits for settlement quality, which are discussed in Section 2.2.2 below.)

A more complex analysis of voluntary disclosure incentives and the effect of adding discovery must take account of strategic effects. Shavell (1989), for example, models information revelation with privately informed plaintiffs and take-it-or-leave-it settlement offers made by defendants. Adding discovery (which Shavell assumes is costless) reduces the frequency of trials (which occur when some plaintiffs are unable to reveal their private information credibly) and also assures that all plaintiffs who can credibly disclose do so and obtain settlements equal to the expected value of their claims (rather than the mean value over a non-disclosing group).[4]

---

[4] One interesting feature of the model is that the beneficial effect on the trial rate results not from parties disclosing and settling when they would otherwise

Sobel (1989) models discovery with two-sided incomplete information and lets the plaintiff make a take-it-or-leave-it counteroffer following the defendant's initial settlement offer. Unlike Shavell, Sobel assumes that disclosure is costly for the disclosing party. The result is that defendants have no incentive to reveal their private information (since disclosure is costly and the plaintiff can capture the entire settlement surplus with her final offer), and some cases go to trial. The benefit of discovery is that it reduces the equilibrium probability of trial by forcing disclosure.[5]

Farmer and Pecorino (2005) expand on these models. They assume that the plaintiff has private information and can make a voluntary disclosure. If the plaintiff does not voluntarily disclose, the defendant can take discovery. They also assume that voluntary disclosure is costly for the disclosing party and that discovery is costly for both sides. They model both a screening game (defendant makes the offer) and a signaling game (plaintiff makes the offer). In the screening game, discovery takes place in equilibrium when it is not too costly; otherwise, voluntary disclosure takes place. Still, it is the credible threat of mandatory discovery that makes the plaintiff voluntarily disclose. In the signaling model, discovery never takes place, but voluntary disclosure does. As a result, the discovery option reduces trial frequency and thus trial costs. (Of course, it adds discovery and voluntary disclosure costs, which are considered below.)

Other game-theoretic models of the discovery process yield varying results depending on the model's specifications and the solution concept employed (see, e.g., Mnookin and Wilson 1998). However, all confirm the potential benefit of discovery in increasing the settlement rate and reducing the frequency of trial.

2.2.2. Settlement quality According to the standard argument, discovery improves settlement quality by reducing informational asymmetry and producing settlements that reflect the true merits of the case (Cooter and Rubinfeld 1994). What is less obvious is that discovery need not actually take place in order to reap at least some of these benefits.

To illustrate, assume that the defendant has private information which, if revealed, would help the plaintiff prove liability at trial and that the defendant would not disclose this information voluntarily. With

---

have gone to trial. Rather, those forced to disclose in the model are parties who would have settled anyway.

[5] In Sobel's model, discovery also benefits plaintiffs by producing higher settlement offers compared to a regime with no disclosure at all.

discovery available to the plaintiff, defendant must consider that the information will be revealed if the case goes to trial. As for the plaintiff, she does not know the precise information that the defendant possesses, but she does know the kind of information defendants of the same type usually possess and can estimate the expected value of that information for her case.

The defendant anticipates that the plaintiff will make this estimate, so the defendant increases its maximum offer above where it would have been without the availability of discovery. So too, the plaintiff increases its minimum demand (at least if the expected cost of discovery to obtain the information is not too high). Assuming that litigation costs are equal across the party line, the likely result is a larger settlement for the plaintiff when discovery is available. More important, the settlement will be closer to the expected trial judgment with complete information (which can be considered an ideal) because the prospect of discovery forces the defendant to take account of its private information when bargaining (although in a limited way).[6] To repeat, it is the credible threat of discovery that produces this result even if no discovery actually takes place.

The result can change, however, if the costs of discovery are distributed unequally between the parties. For example, if the plaintiff can credibly

---

[6] Suppose the plaintiff's estimate of the probability of establishing liability at trial without the private information is p. Suppose that the probability of success increases to $p + \alpha$ with the private information (i.e., α measures the value of the private information). If w is the expected trial award conditional on establishing liability, then $(p + \alpha)w$ is the ideal settlement. Let c be the cost to each side of going to trial without any discovery and let $c + k$ be the cost to each side of going to trial with discovery (i.e., k is the cost of discovery for each side). Since the plaintiff has a credible threat to take discovery and obtain the private information, the defendant knows that if the case does not settle, the information will be revealed and its expected loss from trial will be $(p + \alpha)w + c + k$. The plaintiff does not know the private information but can take an expectation over all possible private information scenarios. Suppose that the plaintiff estimates its trial success at $p + \beta$, where β is the plaintiff's estimate of the expected value of the private information ($\beta < \alpha$). Since we assume that costs are the same for both sides, the plaintiff's minimum demand will be $(p + \beta)w - c - k$. Assuming that the settlement bargaining process does not signal defendant's private information in any way, the defendant, while willing to offer up to $(p + \alpha)w + c + k$ if necessary, will behave as though its maximum offer is $(p + \beta)w + c + k$, aware that the plaintiff does not know any better. (This assumes no unraveling.) Now let's calculate the likely settlements with and without discovery assuming equal bargaining power (so the Nash bargaining solution predicts an equal division of the surplus). With discovery, the settlement will be $(p + \beta)w$. Without discovery, the settlement will be pw. Recall that the ideal settlement is $(p + \alpha)w$. Obviously, the settlement with discovery is closer to the ideal than the settlement without.

threaten to seek discovery that would be much more costly for the defendant to provide than for the plaintiff to seek (and the defendant has no credible threat to reciprocate in kind), then the prospect of costly discovery skewed against the defendant could lead to a settlement skewed in that same direction.

Thus, introducing formal discovery has two countervailing effects. First, it reduces informational asymmetry, which can improve settlement quality. Second, it sometimes creates a cost asymmetry across the party line, which can reduce settlement quality.

2.3. Benefits for Trial Outcomes

Proponents of broad discovery often cite its value in producing better trial verdicts, understood as verdicts more in line with the parties' substantive entitlements. This is especially true if discovery forces disclosure of information that would never be revealed otherwise (Hay 1994). Cooter and Rubinfeld model this effect by focusing on the distribution of trial error (Cooter and Rubinfeld 1994, at 446). Let x^* denote the accurate trial outcome when the court has complete information about the facts and the law. Cooter and Rubinfeld suppose that the court observes x^* with some error, ε. The court's observation is unbiased if $E(\varepsilon) = 0$. In this model, pre-trial discovery can be socially beneficial in two possible ways: (1) by reducing bias in the ε distribution, that is, by shifting $E(\varepsilon)$ closer to 0, and (2) by reducing variance in the ε distribution.

There are two ways that discovery achieves these benefits. First, it changes the timing of disclosure. Before the Federal Rules of Civil Procedure instituted broad discovery, much information was revealed for the first time at trial, and this gave the opposing party very little time to prepare a response. By requiring disclosure before trial, discovery avoids surprise and allows each side to prepare more effectively. Even so, more time to prepare does not always improve the outcome. As many have noted, advanced preparation sometimes produces equivocal and even deceptive answers under circumstances where a spontaneous question would have elicited a more direct and truthful response. For discovery to improve outcomes by shifting disclosure to an earlier stage, it must be the case that the value of preparation exceeds the value of spontaneity.

The second way that discovery reduces bias and variance is by forcing disclosure of information that would never be revealed at trial (Hay 1994). The magnitude of this benefit depends on how much information is actually disclosed through discovery and how much more is disclosed than would be voluntarily revealed without discovery. These points are discussed in Section 2.2 above.

2.4. Benefits for Filing Incentives

At first glance, it might seem obvious that discovery would filter out many weak and frivolous suits. If the plaintiff knows that the weak merits of her case will be revealed before trial, she should assign a very low probability to success and refrain from filing suit in the first place. The problem with this analysis is that it assumes discovery actually takes place and succeeds in revealing the plaintiff's private information to the defendant. But parties sometimes settle before the discovery stage is complete. Indeed, one reason why frivolous suits succeed is that the plaintiff can leverage the high cost of discovery to obtain a pre-discovery settlement (Bone 2003).

2.5. Benefits for Primary Activity Incentives

The availability of discovery can also have beneficial effects on incentives in the real world outside the courtroom. One way it does this is by improving the accuracy of trial verdicts and aligning settlements more closely with the expected trial value of the underlying claims. More accurate outcomes improve compliance with the substantive law.

Discovery can affect primary activity incentives in another, more direct way. Consider a rational party, D, choosing whether to comply with the substantive law. D knows that she might be sued whether she complies or not, but that she is more likely to be sued and pay damages if she does not comply. The cost of discovery itself adds an extra inducement to compliance by boosting the expected cost of a lawsuit. Moreover, suppose that the cost of discovery is higher when D does not comply with the substantive law than when D does (but is sued anyway). For example, a noncomplying D might fight hard to prevent discovery of damaging evidence. This discovery cost differential adds to compliance incentives. Noncompliance under these conditions produces higher discovery costs in two ways: by increasing the likelihood of suit (and thus the likelihood of having to invest in discovery) and by increasing the cost of discovery conditional on suit being filed.

However, the precise relationship between discovery and deterrence is more complicated. More discovery does not necessarily produce greater deterrence. For one thing, the deterrent effect of additional discovery depends on the cost of precautions necessary to comply with the substantive law (Hay 1994, at 502–9). Moreover, a system of broad discovery that deters when it is actually used might not deter if parties routinely settle before the discovery stage. This is important because broader discovery is more costly and thus more likely to pressure settlements in advance. When discovery is not actually undertaken, guilty defendants can pool with innocents and receive the same settlement in equilibrium (Hay 1994, at 513).

Finally, even if broader discovery enhances deterrence, it might not be socially optimal if its costs are too high. These costs include the expense of those extra precautions that added deterrence induces *plus* the cost of the broader discovery itself.

3. The Social Costs of Discovery

Discovery is extremely costly. The Federal Judicial Center study found that discovery consumed about half of total litigation costs for the 85% of sampled cases that had some significant discovery and about 90% of total costs for the top 5% of most expensive cases (Willging et al. 1997, at 3–4). Discovery costs appear to be particularly high in large, multi-party lawsuits with high stakes. The large amount of private information makes discovery vital and the high stakes invite strategic abuse (Willging et al. 1997; Garth 1998). Moreover, these costs have increased markedly with the advent of electronic discovery.

Concerns about the cost of discovery take two forms. First, some critics focus on party incentives to engage in *excessive discovery*, defined as discovery beyond the point where marginal benefit equals marginal cost. Second, some critics focus on party incentives to engage in *abusive discovery*, defined as discovery aimed not at obtaining information, but at gaining a strategic advantage by threatening the imposition of costs.

Before discussing each of these concerns, it is important to emphasize that the costs of discovery must be evaluated relative to the costs of information acquisition in the absence of discovery. This is important because parties without access to discovery might use more expensive self-help techniques to obtain the information they need, such as hacking into computers, relying on spies, bribing employees, and the like. Firms faced with these risks are likely to adopt countermeasures to deter disclosure. The result can be an escalating and wasteful "arms race" if those seeking information use increasingly sophisticated and costly acquisition techniques and those possessing information respond with sophisticated and costly countermeasures. Formal discovery reduces the reliance on self-help and thus prevents the arms race.

3.1. Excessive Discovery

The incentive to engage in excessive discovery results from the fact that the party requesting discovery does not have to pay the costs of responding. Cooter and Rubinfeld (1994) analyze this externality and argue for making the requesting party pay the responding party's costs of response beyond a certain threshold level. Hay (1994) criticizes the Cooter-Rubinfeld argument by pointing out that discovery beyond the point where marginal private cost exceeds marginal benefit might sometimes be desirable from a social point of view. The reason is that private parties do not internalize all the benefits and costs of litigation (Shavell 1982), and in particular all the deterrence benefits and public costs of discovery. In other words, discovery that is excessive in terms of private costs and benefits might not be excessive in terms of social costs and benefits.

Other factors besides cost externalization contribute to excessive discovery. For example, lawyers hired on a fee-for-services basis have an incentive to run up discovery costs in order to pad their fees (Frankel 1993, at 258–9). Also, risk-averse young associates in large law firms, who are often left to handle discovery on their own, have incentives to err on the side of too much discovery out of fear that they might miss something significant and incur a partner's wrath.

3.2. Abusive Discovery

Discovery is abusive when it is conducted not for its informational value, but rather for its strategic value in imposing costs on an opposing party and leveraging a more favorable settlement (Easterbrook 1989; Setear 1989). Several scholars model discovery abuse as a Prisoners' Dilemma (PD) game (Setear 1989; Gilson and Mnookin 1994; Bone 2003). In a PD game, each side engages in abusive discovery out of fear that the other side will do so and they will end up a "sucker."

More specifically, if it costs the requesting party less to make the request than it costs the responding party to respond, the requesting party can gain an advantage by serving a discovery request. If the responding party chooses to settle rather than respond, the resulting settlement will be skewed in the requesting party's favor. If the responding party simply ignores an abusive request, the requesting party can file a motion to compel, and assuming a sufficiently high probability of a (mistaken) grant, the responding party will take the motion seriously. Thus, an abusive discovery request has teeth insofar as it can be backed up by a credible threat to compel, and in that case the responding party has an incentive to settle rather than incur the high cost of a response.

In the PD game, both sides make abusive discovery requests in order not to be left at a cost disadvantage in settlement. These strategies, however, leave the parties in the same position relative to settlement if the strategies cancel one another out. However, when the discovery requests are actually enforced (which must happen sometimes in order to have a credible threat), the parties end up worse off than they would have been if they both had avoided abusive discovery completely.

The PD game has some plausibility, but it might not be the best way to model abusive discovery. Sanchirico (2007) argues, following Katz (1988), that parties are not likely to engage in mutual aggression in the way the

PD game predicts. Instead, one side is likely to respond to aggression with aggression (strategically complement), while the other side is likely to respond with retreat (strategically substitute). As a result, one side acts more aggressively than the other in equilibrium. These equilibrium strategies make intuitive sense. When A adopts a strategy of retreat in the face of aggression, B will act less aggressively, since A's retreat reduces the marginal benefit to B of additional aggression. And less aggression by B makes A better off. Shepherd's empirical study supports the existence of this equilibrium (Shepherd 1999). He finds that defendants respond to discovery aggression by acting aggressively and that plaintiffs respond by retreating.

This equilibrium does not generate the same level of wasteful litigation costs as the equilibrium of the PD model. It is possible, however, that the equilibrium systematically skews settlement in favor of the more aggressive party, thereby distorting the incentive effects of the substantive law.

4. Discovery Reforms

The current system relies primarily on sanctions to control discovery costs, but critics complain that obstacles to enforcement and judicial reluctance to sanction render sanctions less than optimally effective. The following discussion briefly discusses some other methods.

4.1. Mandatory Disclosure

In a system of mandatory disclosure, parties are required at the outset of the litigation to disclose certain core information without a formal discovery request, such as key documents and witness testimony.[7] Proponents argue that mandatory disclosure saves the cost of discovery requests and reduces the need to rely on formal discovery later in the suit. Critics argue that formal discovery will be used anyway. Each party knows that the other party is not likely to disclose all required information, especially information that is particularly damaging. As a result, the parties will use formal discovery to check the completeness of the mandatory disclosures (Issacharoff and Loewenstein 1995).

Proponents of mandatory disclosure also cite its benefit in encouraging early settlement by forcing information exchange at the beginning of the lawsuit. Critics argue that reducing the need for formal discovery

---

[7] For example, Rule 26(a) of the Federal Rules of Civil Procedure imposes a duty to disclose certain categories of information, but limits the duty to information favorable to the disclosing party. Parties are then free to conduct formal discovery later in the litigation.

reduces the settlement surplus, which in turn reduces the incentive to settle (Issacharoff and Loewenstein 1995). This effect offsets to some extent the settlement benefits of early information exchange.

4.2. Discovery Limits

Another way to limit discovery costs is to limit the number of discovery requests. Quantitative limits can make parties better off by facilitating pre-commitment and avoiding the perverse effects of the Prisoners' Dilemma (Bone 2007, at 2006–11). To do so effectively, discovery limits should often be strict rather than presumptive.[8] Strict limits support pre-commitment more strongly and avoid the strategic abuse that presumptive limits invite. In a system of presumptive limits, parties can take discovery up to the limit and then threaten to drag their opponents through a costly battle to obtain more.

Strict limits, however, suffer from the same defects as strict rules more generally. A strict limit is set based on the needs of the average case and as such can get discovery wrong for cases that depart from the average. For example, a strict limit will furnish less discovery than is optimal for particularly complex and information-dense cases and too much discovery for particularly simple and information-sparse cases. Thus, the objective from an economic perspective must be to devise a system of discovery limits that optimally balances the benefits and costs.

Moss (2007) examines a different approach to limiting discovery, so-called proportionality limits that authorize the trial judge to deny additional discovery when the marginal costs exceed the marginal benefits.[9] Using the federal e-discovery rules as his principal target, he argues that judges will find it difficult to strike the optimal cost-benefit balance without the information that discovery would reveal.[10]

---

[8] The Federal Rules of Civil Procedure, for example, employ presumptive limits, such as a presumptive limit of ten depositions and a presumptive limit of 25 interrogatories. A presumptive limit can be overcome by showing that more discovery is needed.

[9] Rule 26(b)(2)(C)(iii) of the Federal Rules of Civil Procedure gives the judge power to deny burdensome discovery requests when the marginal costs of the additional discovery exceed the marginal benefits for the case.

[10] The Federal Rules of Civil Procedure were amended in 2006 to add new provisions regulating discovery of material in electronic digital format. Rule 26(b)(2)(B) states that a party need not furnish discovery of electronic information in response to a discovery request when that information is not reasonably accessible because retrieval involves undue burden or cost. However, the judge can allow such discovery if the party seeking it shows good cause considering, among other things, the cost-benefit proportionality standard.

4.3. Cost Shifting

Cooter and Rubinfeld (1994) argue that insofar as excessive discovery is an externality problem, the solution is to make the requesting party pay the opponent's response costs. They add a requirement that the judge approve the reasonableness of the response costs in order to prevent the responding party from running up those costs.

There is, however, a problem with a simple cost-shifting rule. When private information is asymmetrically distributed, the party with less information has greater need for discovery and as a result will incur higher discovery costs, especially when it must pay for response costs as well as request costs. This cost asymmetry can produce settlements ex ante that are skewed against the party with less private information and a greater need for discovery. Cooter and Rubinfeld (1994) recognize this problem and try to deal with it by proposing a two-stage cost-shifting rule. Their proposal makes the responding party pay its response costs up to a certain point and then shifts those costs to the requesting party beyond that point. The switching point is set to roughly equalize the discovery costs for both sides.

There are problems with the switching-point proposal and with cost shifting more generally. Still, an approach that combines rule-based limits on discovery with some version of cost-shifting holds promise and is worth exploring further.

Bibliography

Barkai, John and Gene Kassebaum, *The Impact of Discovery Limitations on Cost, Satisfaction, and Pace in Court-annexed Arbitration*, 11 U. HAW. L. REV 81 (1989).
Bone, Robert G., ECONOMICS OF CIVIL PROCEDURE 232–58 (2003).
Bone, Robert G., *Who Decides? A Critical Look at Procedural Discretion*, 28 CARDOZO L. REV. 1961 (2007).
Brazil, Wayne, *The Adversary Character of Civil Discovery: A Critique and Proposals for Change*, 31 VAND. L. REV. 1295 (1978).
Cooper, Edward, *Discovery Cost Allocation: Comment on Cooter and Rubinfeld*, 23 J. LEGAL STUD. 465 (1994).
Cooter, Robert and Daniel Rubinfeld, *An Economic Model of Legal Discovery*, 23 J. LEGAL STUD. 435 (1994).
Cooter, Robert and Daniel Rubinfeld, *Reforming the New Discovery Rules*, 84 GEO. L. J. 61 (1995).
Easterbrook, Frank H., *Discovery as Abuse*, 69 B.U. L. REV. 635 (1989).
Farmer, Amy and Paul Pecorino, *Civil Litigation with Mandatory Discovery and Voluntary Transmission of Private Information*, 34 J. LEGAL STUD. 137 (2005).
Frankel, Lawrence M., *Disclosure in the Federal Courts: A Cure for Discovery Ills?*, 24 ARIZ. ST. L.J. 249 (1993).
Garth, Bryant G., *Two Worlds of Civil Discovery: From Studies of Cost and Delay to the Markets in Legal Services and Legal Reform*, 39 B.C. L. REV. 597 (1998).
Gilson, Ronald J. and Robert H. Mnookin, *Disputing through Agents: Cooperation and Conflict between Lawyers in Litigation*, 94 COLUM. L. REV. 509 (1994).
Hay, Bruce, *Civil Discovery: Its Effects and Optimal Scope*, 23 J. LEGAL STUD. 481 (1994).

Inglis, Laura, Kevin McCabe, Steve Rassenti, Daniel Simmons, and Erik Tallroth, *Experiments on the Effects of Cost-shifting, Court Costs and Discovery on the Efficient Settlement of Tort Claims*, 33 FLA. ST. U.L. REV. 89 (2005).

Issacharoff, Samuel and George Loewenstein, *Unintended Consequences of Mandatory Disclosure*, 73 TEX. L. REV. 753 (1995).

Jost, Peter J., *Disclosure of Information and Incentives for Care*, 15 INT'L. REV. L. & ECON. 65 (1995).

Kakalik, James S. et al., DISCOVERY MANAGEMENT: FURTHER ANALYSIS OF THE CIVIL JUSTICE REFORM ACT EVALUATION DATA (RAND, 1998).

Kaplow, Louis, *The Value of Accuracy in Adjudication: An Economic Analysis*, 23 J. LEGAL STUD. 307 (1994).

Katz, Avery, *Judicial Decisionmaking and Litigation Expenditure*, 8 INT'L. REV. L. & ECON. 127 (1988).

Korobkin, Russell and Chris Guthrie, *Psychological Barriers to Litigation Settlement: An Experimental Approach*, 93 MICH. L. REV. 107 (1994).

Lowenstein, George, Samuel Issacharoff, Colin Camerer, and Linda Babcock, *Self-serving Assessments of Fairness and Pretrial Bargaining*, 22 J. LEG. STUD. 135 (1993).

McKenna, Judith and Elizabeth Wiggins, *Empirical Research on Civil Discovery*, 39 B.C. L. REV. 785 (1998).

Milgrom, Paul R. and John Roberts, *Relying on the Information of Interested Parties*, 17 RAND J. OF ECONOMICS 18 (1986).

Mnookin, Robert and Robert Wilson, *A Model of Efficient Discovery*, 25 GAMES & ECON. BEHAVIOR 219 (1998).

Moss, Scott A., *Litigation Discovery Cannot be Optimal But Could be Better: The Economics of Improving Discovery Timing in a Digital Age*, 58 DUKE L. J. 889 (2009).

Mullenix, Linda S., *Discovery in Disarray: The Pervasive Myth of Discovery Abuse and the Consequences for Unfounded Rulemaking*, 46 STAN. L. REV. 1393 (1994).

Sanchirico, Chris William, *Harnessing Adversarial Process: Optimal Strategic Complementarities in Litigation* (Feb. 2007).

Schrag, Joel L., *Managerial Judges: An Economic Analysis of Judicial Management of Legal Discovery*, 30 RAND J. ECON. 305 (1999).

Setear, John K., *The Barrister and the Bomb: The Dynamics of Cooperation, Nuclear Deterrence, and Discovery Abuse*, 69 B.U. L. REV. 569 (1989).

Shapiro, David L., *Some Problems of Discovery in an Adversary System*, 63 MINN. L. REV. 1055 (1979).

Shavell, Steven M., *The Social versus Private Incentives to Bring Suit in a Costly Legal System*, 11 J. LEGAL STUD. 33 (1982).

Shavell, Steven M., *Sharing Information Prior to Settlement or Litigation*, 20 RAND J. ECON. 183 (1989).

Shepherd, George B., *An Empirical Study of the Economics of Pretrial Discovery*, 19 INT'L REV. L. & ECON. 159 (1999).

Sobel, Joel, *Disclosure of Evidence and Resolution of Disputes: Who Should Bear the Burden of Proof?*, in GAME THEORETIC MODELS OF BARGAINING (A. E. Roth ed., 1985).

Sobel, Joel, *An Analysis of Discovery Rules*, 52 L. & CONTEMP. PROBS. 133 (1989).

Subrin, Stephen N., *Fishing Expeditions Allowed: The Historical Background of the 1938 Federal Discovery Rules*, 39 B.C. L. REV. 691 (1998).

Willging, Thomas E., John Shapard, Donna Stienstra, and Dean Miletich, DISCOVERY AND DISCLOSURE PRACTICE, PROBLEMS, AND PROPOSALS FOR CHANGE: A CASE-BASED NATIONAL SURVEY OF COUNSEL IN CLOSED FEDERAL CIVIL CASES (Federal Judicial Center, 1997).

9 Evidence: theoretical models
Chris William Sanchirico

1. Introduction

Few legal disputes are solely a matter of how the law should be interpreted. The parties to a legal dispute are rarely in complete agreement regarding who did what, when, to whom, under what circumstances. Thus, courts – acting through professional judges or juries of citizens – routinely generate "findings of fact," as opposed to "findings of law." Such factual determinations are the subject of the field of law called "evidence."

The fundamental questions of legal evidence are these: First, how do "fact finders" (judges or juries, as the case may be) make deductions about factual issues? Second, how *should* fact finders make such deductions?

Legal scholars and social scientists have taken varying approaches to these questions. This entry specifically concerns models of legal evidence, where the word "model" is defined to encompass any approach explicitly grounded in, and making abundant use of, mathematical reasoning. Most of the entry concerns theoretical contributions, although occasional reference is made to pertinent empirical findings. Models of legal evidence appear chiefly in three overlapping scholarly literatures: the legal literature on evidence, the law and economics literature, and the economics literature on game theory and mechanism design.

Section 2 situates models of evidence within the larger context of models of litigation. This discussion helps to clarify the boundaries of the entry. It also explains why evidence models, which are far outnumbered by nonevidentiary models of litigation, fill an important gap in the literature.

Sections 3 to 6 describe the four main approaches taken in modeling evidence.

Section 3 discusses "pure probabilistic deduction." The fact finder in these models interprets the evidence it receives using Bayes' rule (defined within), but usually without accounting for the strategic interests of the party supplying the evidence. This is the dominant modeling approach in the legal literature on evidence.

Section 4 discusses the dominant approach to evidence in the economics literature on game theory and mechanism design, "omission models." This approach explicitly accounts for strategic interests of the parties who supply the evidence. However, it exogenously limits the means that parties have to pursue those interests. Parties in these models may omit to report all that they know, but they may not lie or fabricate evidence.

The third approach, "endogenous cost signaling," which appears in the law and economics literature on evidence, is discussed in Section 5. These models view evidence as a form of differential cost signaling, an approach that encompasses both omission and fabrication. These models also link evidence production to the out-of-court activities that form the basis of the suit ("primary activities"). Such models allow for the possibility that the evidence used by the fact finder is such that its cost to the party presenting it is at least probabilistically determined by ("endogenous" to) the party's primary activity choices. By means of this linkage, the secondary activity of evidence production gains potential as a device for setting primary activity incentives.

Section 6 discusses a fourth and still largely nascent approach to legal evidence, "correlated private information." This approach – which has been extensively studied outside the evidence context in the economics literature on mechanism design and game theory – explores the potential benefits of playing parties off against each other, as when party A's evidence is used to reward or punish party B, and vice versa.

In preparing this chapter, I have not attempted to catalogue the full set of contributions on the topic. Rather, I have tried to describe several seminal and/or representative articles in enough detail to communicate not only their findings but also their reasoning. Furthermore, I have devoted a fair portion of the entry to comparing, contrasting and evaluating different approaches. My ultimate goal is to provide the reader with a template. The hope is that this template will facilitate the assimilation of not only those contributions discussed in the entry, and not only the many worthwhile existing contributions that could not be discussed, but also the many contributions that are hopefully yet to come.

2. The Law and Economics of Evidence in the Larger Context of the Law and Economics of Litigation

Before reviewing the four modeling approaches to legal evidence, it is important to situate the full quartet of approaches within the subsuming context of models of litigation. Most of the vast literature on the law and economics of litigation, which is surveyed elsewhere in this volume,[1] is not primarily concerned with how the fact finder does or should make deductions from evidence. From an evidentiary point of view, these nonevidentiary models may be sorted into "p models" and "$p(x, y)$ models."

---

[1] See, for example, the chapters on Settlement, Fee Shifting, and Negative-Expected-Value Suits.

2.1. p Models

The vast majority of contributions to the law and economics of litigation focus on parties' incentives to initiate lawsuits and to settle them out of court. The main event that filing leads towards, and that settlement avoids – that is, the fact finding process – is not explicitly modeled in these studies. Rather, the fact finding process is summarized by an exogenous probability p of plaintiff or prosecutor victory – a modeling structure dating back to Becker (1968).

For example, in Gould's (1973) and Posner's (1973) seminal analyses of settlement in civil lawsuits, the plaintiff[2] will accept nothing less from the defendant in settlement of the case than the amount $p_p W - c_p$, where p_p is the plaintiff's assessment of the probability that she will prevail at trial, W is the amount she will receive from defendant if she wins and c_p are the costs she incurs if the case proceeds to trial. Similarly, in Shavell's (1982) analysis of potential plaintiffs' incentives to file suit given the anticipated possibility of future settlement, the plaintiff files suit if and only if $p_p W > c_p$.[3] In both of these models, the outcome of trial (or rather the plaintiff's belief regarding such) is summarized with a single number between zero and one, "p_p." This number is not derived within the model, but is rather an exogenous parameter.

Many other more recent models of litigation, too numerous to mention, also employ this fixed exogenous probability structure. In such models, the institution of legal fact finding is perfunctorily depicted as a kind of "one-arm bandit." The parties drop their "coins" into the fact finding machine (i.e., they pay their respective trial costs), the lever is pulled (fact finding occurs), and a number is generated (i.e., the amount that the defendant owes the plaintiff, or the criminal penalty to which the defendant is subjected). The internal mechanics of the fact finding machine are not examined. The focus is rather on the plaintiff's right to force the defendant to pay and play (the incentive to file suit) and the prior negotiations that may occur between the parties for the purpose of avoiding having to feed coins into the machine (settlement).

2.2. $p(x, y)$ Models

In some models of litigation the probability of plaintiff victory is not a fixed number, but rather a fixed function – in particular, a fixed function

---

[2] Throughout this entry, all actors are assumed to be risk neutral unless otherwise noted.

[3] This is the condition when the rule is that both parties must pay their own legal costs.

mapping scalar measures of the amount of effort exerted by each litigating party in preparing and arguing her case onto the chance that the plaintiff will win the case.

These functions are specific examples of what are often called "contest success functions," and litigation, when modeled in this way, is an example of a more general game theoretic phenomenon referred to as a "contest:" "a game in which the players compete for a prize by exerting effort so as to increase their probability of winning" (Skaperdas 1996: 283). Contest models have also been used to study, among other things, rent-seeking, elections, lobbying, research and development races, and sports. See Corchón (2007) for a recent survey of contest theory.

Within the literature on litigation, for instance, consider Posner's (1973) seminal model of litigation expenditure, in which the plaintiff's probability of prevailing is given by $p(x, y) = ex/(x + y)$, where x and y are the plaintiff's and defendant's litigation spending/effort, respectively, and e is a parameter representing the relative effectiveness of plaintiff spending. Katz (1988), and Bernardo, Talley, and Welch (2000) analyze a similar probability function. Katz (1988), Braeutigam, Owen and Panzar (1984), and Rubinfeld and Sappington (1987) analyze a more general, but nevertheless fixed, probability function.[4]

From the perspective of legal evidence, positing an exogenous probability function is similar to positing an exogenous probability number. To return to, and expand the "one-arm bandit" analogy, the parties may now vary how many coins they drop into their respective slots, and the relative amounts will affect the readout after the lever is pulled, but the mechanics are still hidden inside the box. The structure of the exogenous probability function $p(x, y)$ is, by definition, not derived within the model, but is rather a parameter that is imposed upon the model. The papers in this branch of the literature generally do not supply a positive theory to justify their choice of the probability function that the fact finder is assumed to deploy. Nor is their choice of functional form generally accompanied by a normative analysis of what such a function *should* look like given some set of societal objectives. Rather, as Skaperdas (1996: 283) notes, "a considerable majority of the papers in the contest literature [including its subliterature on litigation] has been employing specific functional forms . . . without any particular reason other than analytical convenience."

---

[4] In Rubinfeld and Sappington (1987), the productivity of (hidden) trial effort by the defendant depends on whether she is (exogenously) innocent or guilty. In Bernardo, Talley, and Welch (2000), which is discussed in Section 5.2.2.3 below, productivity of trial effort depends on an earlier chosen primary activity action, similar to Sanchirico (1995, 2000, 2001b).

Furthermore, litigation effort in these models is a single-dimensional variable. No description is provided regarding how parties can, do, or should direct their litigation effort within the multidimensional space of evidence production. No story is told regarding how different manifestations of effort should be differently interpreted by the fact finder.

2.3. Assessment

The law and economics of litigation – inclusive of legal evidence – has only rarely stepped beyond the two kinds of reduced form models just described, and it is worth noting that this state of affairs was not entirely to be expected. Several subfields of economics seem particularly well suited to the study of legal fact finding per se, including game theory, information economics, and mechanism design. These overlapping fields, which have been fruitfully applied to such diverse areas as taxation, regulated industries, and auction design, concern themselves with problems that arise from the combination of hidden actions, hidden information and conflicting interests – precisely the kinds of issues that would seem to be implicated by adversarial fact finding. Yet the potential for applying and extending these fields to encompass legal fact finding remains largely untapped.

Notwithstanding this general trend in litigation modeling, a relatively small group of papers takes a complementary approach. Rather than modeling fact finding in reduced form so as to focus on filing and settlement, these papers eschew a detailed analysis of filing and settlement in favor of a more explicit and in depth account of fact finding. I now turn to a review of the four main approaches that can be found in this sub-literature.

3. Pure Probabilistic Deduction

The first approach to fact finding is "pure probabilistic" deduction, as typified and advanced by Finkelstein and Fairly (1970) and Lempert (1977).[5] This approach analogizes fact finding to the probabilistic deductions of an unbiased researcher examining data in the laboratory or in the field. The approach may be normative or positive.

This part of the entry first describes the basic structure of the pure probabilistic deduction model. Next, it reviews some salient applications of the model. Lastly, it describes several criticisms that have been leveled against the approach.

---

[5] This approach is also discussed in Posner (1999).

208 *Procedural law and economics*

3.1. Basic structure
Readers who are already familiar with conditional probability and Bayes' rule may want to skip to Section 3.2.
The basic elements of the pure probabilistic deduction approach can be grasped by examining the following simple hypothetical.

Charged with deciding whether to hold the defendant guilty of the crime charged (or liable for damages), a fact finder has two tasks. The first is to determine the likelihood of guilt. The second task is to decide on a verdict. Consider first the fact finder's task of determining the likelihood of guilt.

3.1.1. Bayes' rule On seeing a given piece of evidence, the fact finder modifies her belief regarding guilt – just as one might change one's beliefs regarding the speed of a horse on seeing it win a race. Beliefs, before and after evidence is observed, are represented as probabilities and are accordingly assumed to be subject to the mathematical properties thereof. One of those properties, Bayes' rule, provides a formula for updating beliefs upon receiving new evidence.

3.1.1.1. THE ODDS FORMULATION There are several equivalent statements of Bayes' rule. The "odds formulation" of Bayes' rule is generally the most convenient to express and deploy. Let G be the event that the defendant is guilty. Let I be the event that the defendant is innocent. Let E be a particular, arbitrarily chosen body of evidence that may be observed by the fact finder. Let $P(G)$, a number between zero and one, be the prior probability of guilt – the probability that the fact finder places on the defendant's being guilty before the evidence has been seen.[6] Let $P(I)$ be the prior probability of innocence. The prior odds of guilt are defined to be $P(G)/P(I)$. If, for example, the prior probabilities of guilt and innocence are both 0.5, then the prior odds of guilt equal one, in which case we might say that the odds of guilt are "one to one." Conversely, if the prior odds of guilt are two – "two to one," that is – then the prior probability of guilt must be two-thirds and the prior probability of innocence must be one-third.

What value should be placed on the prior odds of guilt in this framework? One might argue that, as a descriptive matter, the prior odds of guilt are given by the fact finder's knowledge that the defendant has been arrested or indicted. (As discussed in Section 3.2.2 below, Lempert, Gross, and Liebman (2000) emphasize this point in their analysis of character

---

[6] Except as otherwise noted, I shall assume that all events encountered in the following analysis have non-zero probability.

evidence.) Or one might argue normatively that the fact finder must act as if the prior odds of guilt are one, so that the fact finder is "unbiased." Or perhaps the prior odds of guilt should be less than one: to give content to the "presumption of innocence."

The probability of guilt conditional on having seen the evidence, the "posterior probability" of guilt is denoted $P(G|E)$. In general, the probability of event A conditional on (positive probability) event B is defined as follows: $P(A|B) = P(A \cap B)/P(B)$, where $A \cap B$ is the conjunctive event that both A and B occur. The probability of event A conditional on event B may thus be viewed as the proportion of all possible "states of the world" where B occurs that are also states of the world in which A occurs.

The posterior probability of innocence is denoted $P(I|E)$ and is similarly defined. Note that $P(I|E) = 1 - P(G|E)$. That is, if the probability of guilt conditional on the evidence E is 0.6, then the probability of innocence conditional on the evidence E must be 0.4. Conditional probabilities add to one over all possible outcomes, just like unconditional probabilities.

The posterior *odds* of guilt (cf. the *prior* odds of guilt and the posterior *probability* of guilt) are defined to be $P(G|E)/P(I|E)$.

It is easy to confuse the probability of guilt conditional on having seen the evidence, $P(G|E)$, as just defined, with $P(E|G)$, the probability *of seeing evidence E* conditional on *the defendant's being guilty*. (See the discussion of "base rate neglect" in Section 3.2.1 below.) These two conditional probabilities are not generally equal to each other. The probability of clouds given rain (very high, if not one) is not the same as the probability of rain given clouds (not as high). Similarly, let E be the subset of adults in some group of adults and children, and let G be the subset of the same group of adults and children that are over six feet tall. Assign equal probability to each person in the overall group – so that probabilities correspond to population frequencies. The probability that an adult in the group is over six feet tall, $P(G|E)$, is not the same as the probability that a person over six feet tall in the group is an adult, $P(E|G)$. It may be that half the adults are over six feet ($P(G|E) = \frac{1}{2}$), but that no children in the group are over six feet tall so that every person over six feet is adult ($P(E|G) = 1$).

The conditional probability $P(E|I)$ is similarly defined, and should be similarly distinguished from $P(I|E)$.

The probabilities of the evidence conditional on each of the possible underlying truths, $P(E|I)$ and $P(E|G)$, play an important role in Bayes' rule. The ratio of the probability of the evidence conditional on guilt to the probability of seeing the same evidence conditional on innocence, $P(E|G)/P(E|I)$ is called the "likelihood ratio" (*of* or *for* the evidence E *relative to* the event of guilt). This likelihood ratio is discussed in more detail in Section 3.1.1.2 immediately below.

210   *Procedural law and economics*

Bayes' rule, in its odds formulation, expresses a simple relationship among the three ratios that have just been defined – the prior odds of guilt, the posterior odds of guilt, and the likelihood ratio:

$$\underbrace{\frac{P(G|E)}{P(I|E)}}_{\text{posterior odds}} = \underbrace{\frac{P(E|G)}{P(E|I)}}_{\text{likelihood ratio}} \times \underbrace{\frac{P(G)}{P(I)}}_{\text{prior odds}}. \tag{9.1}$$

Thus, the posterior odds of guilt equal the prior odds of guilt multiplied by the likelihood ratio. The derivation of this equation is provided below the line.[7] A numerical example is provided in Section 3.1.1.2 immediately below. The process of deducing posterior odds from a given piece of evidence is called "(Bayesian) updating."

Information about the *probabilities* (as opposed to the odds) of guilt before and after the evidence is observed is easily recovered from the odds formulation of Bayes' rule. Using the two equations, $P(I|E) = 1 - P(G|E)$ and $P(I) = 1 - P(G)$, Bayes' rule can be rewritten to show how (a particular strictly increasing function of the) *probability* of guilt conditional on the evidence depends on (the same strictly increasing function of) the prior *probability* of guilt:

$$\underbrace{\frac{P(G|E)}{1-P(G|E)}}_{\substack{\text{strictly increasing} \\ \text{function of prob} \\ \text{of guilt conditional} \\ \text{on evidence}}} = \underbrace{\frac{P(E|G)}{P(E|I)}}_{\text{likelihood ratio}} \times \underbrace{\frac{P(G)}{1-P(G)}}_{\substack{\text{strictly increasing} \\ \text{function of prob} \\ \text{of guilt}}}. \tag{9.2}$$

Given a number for $O(G|E) = P(G|E)/(1 - P(G|E))$, for example, one recovers $P(G|E)$ algebraically or, what is the same, by means of the general relation $O = P/(1 - P) \Leftrightarrow P = O/(1 + O)$.

---

[7] The odds formulation of Bayes' rule may be derived from the definition of conditional probability (as discussed in the text in this section) as follows:

$$P(A|B) = \frac{P(A \cap B)}{P(B)}, \; P(B|A) = \frac{P(A \cap B)}{P(A)} \text{ and } P(-A|B) = \frac{P(\neg A \cap B)}{P(B)},$$

$$P(B|\neg A) = \frac{P(\neg A \cap B)}{P(\neg A)} \Rightarrow P(A|B)P(B) = P(B|A)P(A) \text{ and}$$

$$P(\neg A|B)P(B) = P(B|\neg A)P(\neg A) \Rightarrow \frac{P(A|B)\cancel{P(B)}}{P(\neg A|B)\cancel{P(B)}} = \frac{P(B|A)P(A)}{P(B|\neg A)P(\neg A)},$$

where $\neg A$ denotes the event that A does not occur, the logical complement of A.

3.1.1.2. THE LIKELIHOOD RATIO The key to using and understanding Bayes' rule is the likelihood ratio: the probability of seeing the evidence were the defendant truly guilty divided by the probability of seeing the evidence were the defendant truly innocent.

The likelihood ratio's role in Bayes' rule embodies the following intuition: The evidence E may be quite likely to arise when the defendant is guilty. And one may be tempted to conclude from this fact alone that E indicates guilt. But if E is also quite likely to arise when the defendant is *innocent*, E will not be (or rather should not be regarded as) particularly informative of guilt. That is, in the latter case, posterior beliefs of guilt generated upon seeing the evidence according to Bayes' rule will not deviate markedly from prior beliefs of guilt.

Conversely, the evidence E may be quite *unlikely* to arise when the defendant is guilty. But if it is *even less* likely to arise when the defendant is innocent, it *will* be particularly informative of guilt. That is, the posterior odds of guilt will indeed be markedly higher from the prior odds.

What matters, therefore, is the likelihood that the evidence would arise given guilt *relative* to the likelihood that it would arise given innocence. The word "relative" is given precise content in Bayes' rule: what specifically matters is the *ratio* of these likelihoods – that is, what matters is the likelihood ratio.

If, for example, the prior odds are one, and the evidence is twice as likely to arise given guilt than it is given innocence, then the posterior odds are 2, meaning that guilt is twice as likely as innocence (after the evidence has been observed), or that the posterior probability of guilt is $2/(1 + 2) = 2/3$.

3.1.2. Iterated application of Bayes' rule Conditional probabilities are themselves probabilities and Bayes' rule may be applied to them as well, as though they were prior probabilities. The iterated application of Bayes' rule will be useful in interpreting "trial selection bias," as discussed in Section 3.2.2 below.

Thus, after seeing evidence E, the posterior odds of guilt – where "posterior" is defined relative to E – are, as already discussed, $P(G|E)/P(I|E)$. If additional evidence F is then observed, the E-posterior odds of guilt may be further updated by treating $P(G|E)/P(I|E)$ as the prior odds relative to F. This results in the formula:[8]

---

[8] The following formula is easily verified by replacing each conditional probability with its definition. It is then seen that both sides of the equation reduce to

$$\frac{P(G|E\cap F)}{P(I|E\cap F)} = \frac{P(F|G\cap E)}{P(F|I\cap E)} \times \frac{P(G|E)}{P(I|E)}.$$

The left-hand side of this equation represents the odds of guilt given that evidence E and F have both been observed. On the far right-hand side appear the "medial" odds of guilt, the odds of guilt given that evidence E has been observed; there are as yet no observations either way regarding event F. The other ratio on the right is the relevant likelihood ratio for the second round of updating, $P(F|G\cap E)/P(F|I\cap E)$.

It is important to notice that the likelihood ratio for second-round updating takes into account that evidence E has already been observed. In general, $P(F|G)/P(F|I)$, which does not account for E's prior occurrence, is not the same as $P(F|G\cap E)/P(F|I\cap E)$. For instance, a witness' sighting of the defendant on the block where the murder took place (F) means something different if the defendant establishes that his elderly mother happens to reside on that block (E).

The updating process may then be repeated again for additional evidence G using $P(G|E\cap F)/P(I|E\cap F)$ as prior odds, and so on.

3.1.3. The loss function Having updated her beliefs on all the evidence, the fact finder's second task is to decide on a verdict. Here she considers not just her posterior assessment of guilt, but also her view of the relative harm of wrongful conviction versus wrongful acquittal. Let W_C be the cost of wrongful conviction and let W_A be the cost of wrongful acquittal. Letting E now represent the conjunction of all evidence, the fact finder chooses to convict if $P(I|E)W_C < P(G|E)W_A$, that is, if the expected cost of wrongful conviction exceeds the expected cost of wrongful acquittal. (Here we are taking E to be the totality of the evidence presented in the case.) If, for instance, the cost of wrongful conviction exceeds the cost of

---

$P(G\cap E\cap F)/P(I\cap E\cap F)$.

In interpreting the formula as an iterated application of Bayes' rule, note that conditioning on an event E and then on a second event F is the same as conditioning once on the event which is the intersection of E and F. To wit, the initial act of conditioning on event E generates a new probability measure, $P(\ |E)$ that may be used to form probabilities of G (or I) conditional on F. That is, $P(G|F|E) \equiv P(G\cap F|E)/P(F|E)$. We then have $P(G|F|E) = P(G\cap F|E)/P(F|E) = (P(G\cap E\cap F)/P(E))/(P(E\cap F)/P(E)) = P(G\cap E\cap F)/P(E\cap F) = P(G|E\cap F)$. By similar reasoning, $P(F|G\cap E) = P(F|G|E)$. It follows that the formula may be written as

$$\frac{P(G|F|E)}{P(I|F|E)} = \frac{P(F|G|E)}{P(F|I|E)} \times \frac{P(G|E)}{P(I|E)}.$$

wrongful acquittal, then conviction will not follow even if the fact finder assesses the probability of guilt to be greater than 50%. The elevated reasonable doubt standard of proof in criminal cases is sometimes justified in this way.

3.2. Applications
Bayes' rule has proven useful in clarifying and assessing various theories and empirical findings regarding fact finder error.

3.2.1. Base rate neglect A large literature within evidence scholarship combines the prescriptive aspect of Bayes' rule with experimental evidence[9] to argue that fact finders are prone to misinterpret evidence. In particular, individuals are said to "neglect base rates" in drawing inferences from evidence. For instance, they know or are told that if the defendant were guilty, the evidence they are being shown would arise with 90% probability, and they incorrectly deduce from this that, having seen such evidence, they should regard the probability that the defendant is guilty as 90%. In making this improper deduction the fact finder, it is sometimes said, neglects the fact that the percentage of guilty individuals in the overall population – the "base rate of guilt" – is very low. Other times it is said that the fact finder is neglecting the base rate of the evidence itself. Still other times it is simply said that the finder is "neglecting base rates."

Bayes' rule helps uncover the precise nature of the mistake described in the example in the immediately preceding paragraph. It is also useful in describing how precisely the mistake deserves the name "base rate neglect" – that is, how the mistake is logically related to the base rate for guilt and/or evidence.

The fact finder's mistake corresponds to confusing $P(G|E)$ with $P(E|G)$. As discussed in Section 3.1.1.1 above, the fact that $P(E|G)$ is 90% does not imply that $P(G|E)$ is also 90%. As is evident from the version of Bayes' rule presented in equation (9.2), the reason that the probability of guilt conditional on the evidence $P(G|E)$ does not necessary equal the probability of the evidence conditional on guilt $P(E|G)$ is that the former depends on two other things besides $P(E|G)$. It depends on the base rate of guilt, $P(G)$ (as manifest in the prior odds of guilt). And it depends on $P(E|I)$, the probability that the evidence would arise were the defendant innocent.

---

[9] Base rate neglect has its roots in Kahneman and Tversky (1973) and Nisbett et al. (1976). The literature applying these ideas to legal decision making is quite large. For a recent discussion, see Guthrie, Rachlinski, and Wistrich (2007).

214 *Procedural law and economics*

It is thus apparent that the mistake is not solely a matter of neglecting the base rate of guilt. It is also not solely a matter of neglecting the base rate of the evidence. The unconditional probability of the evidence may be written as a weighted average of the two conditional probabilities:[10]

$$P(E) = P(E|G)P(G) + P(E|I)(1 - P(G)). \qquad (9.3)$$

If the fact finder, given $P(E|G)$, also took into account $P(E)$, but nothing else besides these two quantities, she would still not be able to determine $P(G|E)$. In terms of the analysis in the previous paragraph, some algebraic manipulation shows that the fact finder would not be able to determine $P(E|I)$ and $P(G)$ from this limited information.[11] (However, it is easier to see that $P(G|E)$ could not be so determined by examining equation (9.4) below.)

Yet, the simultaneous neglect of both base rates – that of guilt and that of the evidence – does adequately describe the fact finder's mistake. This can be seen in two ways. First, from equation (9.3), it is clear that combining $P(E|G)$ with both $P(G)$ and $P(E)$ makes it possible to recover $P(E|I)$. This latter quantity, along with $P(G)$ and $P(E|G)$ can then be taken to Bayes' rule to determine $P(G|E)$.

Second, and more directly, we may use the definition of conditional probability to write

$$P(G|E) = P(E|G)\frac{P(G)}{P(E)}. \qquad (9.4)$$

Thus, in order to "reverse the roles" of conditioning and conditioned events, it suffices to know the base rate of both guilt and the evidence. Conversely, to mistake $P(E|G)$ for $P(G|E)$ is to neglect either the base rate of guilt or the base rate of the evidence, or both.

More precisely, as (9.4) makes clear, to reverse conditioning and conditioned events it is not necessary to know the separate values of the two base rates. It suffices to know their ratio. Thus, a more informative (if not more appealing) label for the fact finder's mistake might be "*ratio of* base rates neglect."

---

[10] The validity of this formula may be confirmed by substituting from the definition of conditional probability. Specifically, $P(E|G)P(G) + P(E|I)P(I) = P(E \cap G) + P(E \cap I)$, which equals $P(E)$ because events G and I are mutually exclusive and mutually exhaustive.

[11] More precisely, the fact finder would not be able to determine the quantity $(1/P(E|I))(P(G)/(1 - P(G)))$, which is multiplied by $P(E|G)$ to determine $P(G|E)$.

3.2.2. Trial selection bias and past crimes evidence Another application of Bayes' rule concerns the propriety of admitting evidence of the defendant's past crimes. Lempert, Gross, and Liebman (2000)[12] argue against admitting past crimes evidence on the following basis: although past crimes evidence may be probative of guilt among the general population, it will not be as probative of guilt (and may even be probative of innocence) among the set of defendants whose cases actually make it to trial. Lempert, Gross, and Liebman (2000) offer several reasons why this phenomenon might arise. Most famously, they suggest that it is rooted in the tendency of the police to "round up the usual suspects."

The trial selection bias argument can be formalized using an iterated application of Bayes' rule, as described above.[13] As we shall see, the exercise of formalizing the argument brings to the fore some potential weaknesses.

Fix an individual and an alleged crime. Let R be the event that the individual has a criminal record and let T be the event that he stands trial for the crime. The trial bias argument concerns the manner in which the individual's past record affects the odds of guilt *given* that the individual now stands trial for the crime. We are thus interested in a statement of Bayes' rule that shows how the existence of a past record converts the odds of guilt *given just trial* into the odds of guilt given *both* trial *and* a past record. This may be written as:

$$\frac{P(G|R \cap T)}{P(I|R \cap T)} = \frac{P(R|G \cap T)}{P(R|I \cap T)} \times \frac{P(G|T)}{P(I|T)}, \qquad (9.5)$$

Thus, accounting for trial, the likelihood ratio of a past record of guilt is $L_T^R = P(R|G \cap T)/P(R|I \cap T)$. This likelihood ratio appears similar to the likelihood ratio of a past record, not accounting for trial, $L^R = P(R|G)/P(R|I)$. The difference however, is that this new likelihood ratio represents the information value of a past record for determining guilt among defendants *who appear at trial*, rather than among all potential defendants. As noted in the example presented in Section 3.1.2 above (involving the defendant and his elderly mother), these values may differ substantially.

The claim of the trial selection argument is that a past record, though generally informative of guilt, is not as informative of guilt – and may be informative of innocence – when such evidence is presented in the context of trial. Thus, the trial bias hypothesis is that while L^R may well be larger

---

[12] The argument originally appeared in Lempert and Saltzburg (1982).
[13] The following analysis is taken from Sanchirico (2001a).

than one, L_T^R is less than L^R, and possibly even less than one. What does this require? It is easy to confirm that the two likelihood ratios – describing the information value of a past record with and without trial – are related as follows:

$$L_T^R = \left[\frac{\frac{P(T|G \cap R)}{P(T|G)}}{\frac{P(T|I \cap R)}{P(T|I)}} \right] L^R.$$

The trial selection bias argument is thus equivalent to the assertion that the double ratio in brackets in the immediately preceding equation is less than one (and possibly even less than $1/L^R$). This double ratio is less than one if and only if its denominator exceeds its numerator:

$$\frac{P(T|I \cap R)}{P(T|I)} > \frac{P(T|G \cap R)}{P(T|G)}.$$

This inequality is perhaps more easily interpreted if rewritten in more compact notation:

$$\frac{P_I(T|R)}{P_I(T)} > \frac{P_G(T|R)}{P_G(T)}. \tag{9.6}$$

Inequality (9.6) is a math-symbolic statement of the key condition for the existence of the kind of trial bias that has been proposed: having a past record must increase the individual's chance of standing trial for the crime by a greater proportion if the individual is innocent, than if he is guilty.

Given that (9.6) is its key condition, the trial selection bias argument against past crimes evidence is arguably more fragile and problematic than it may at first appear. Condition (9.6) concerns a difference in differences. The issue is *not* whether having a past record increases the individual's chance of standing trial. The issue is whether having a past record increases the individual's chance of standing trial *more* if the individual is innocent, than if he is guilty. That a past record makes a difference for appearance at trial seems reasonably clear. How this difference *differs* across innocent and guilty defendants is far from certain and would seem to vary greatly across circumstances.

At the very least, the explanations that have thus far been provided for trial bias seem inadequate as justifications for the real condition, (9.6). In particular, trial bias cannot be solely a matter of the tendency of the police to round up the usual suspects. Such a tendency implies that having a past record increases the individual's chance of standing trial, period – both when the individual is innocent and when she is guilty. The usual suspects dynamic, by itself, is essentially silent on whether the increased chance of standing trial due to having a record is greater for the innocent than for the guilty.[14]

3.2.3. Across-person hindsight bias and its rational twin Several authors have investigated the possibility that fact finders are subject to across-person hindsight bias: namely, "in hindsight, people consistently exaggerate what could have been anticipated in foresight . . . People believe that others should have been able to anticipate events much better than was actually the case."[15] Experimental evidence has been offered to establish that across-person hindsight bias exists.

Across-person hindsight bias has important legal ramifications when a litigant's knowledge at the time of her alleged action or omission is at issue in the case. The bias may, for example, cause fact finders to misjudge whether due care was exercised under a negligence standard, whether warnings were adequate in product liability, or whether an accident was reasonably foreseeable under strict liability.

Yet, is it really a mistake to use knowledge that an event E has occurred in judging whether others should have or did in fact know that it was likely to occur ex ante? Bayes' rule can be used to show that is not incorrect in the case that one believes that (1) these others may have been in a position to know about the chance of events like E; and (2) the fact finder does not have access to full information regarding what these others knew.[16]

Thus, assume that it is common knowledge that the defendant took a particular action. Let A be the event that an accident occurred. Let I be the ex ante information observed only by the defendant prior to her decision to take the action regarding whether an accident would occur as a result.

From the perspective of the fact finder, the value of the information I received by the defendant is an uncertain variable. Thus, the defendant's various conditional probability assessments that are based on that information are, from the fact finder's perspective, random variables.

The fact finder is interested in whether, having seen the information I, whatever its value may have been, the defendant "knew" that the accident

---

[14] See Sanchirico (2001a) for a fuller analysis of trial selection bias.
[15] Fischhoff (1982). For an experimental design with legal attributes see e.g., Kamin and Rachlinski (1995).
[16] The analysis in this section is a formalization and generalization of Sanchirico (2004c).

would occur. More precisely, the fact finder must determine whether the defendant's assessment of the conditional probability of an accident exceeded some legally determined state of mind threshold k:

$$P_D(A|I) \geq k.^{17}$$

The subscript "D" indicates that the preceding probability represents the defendant's subjective beliefs. The value of the number $P_D(A|I)$ depends on I, which is uncertain from the fact finder's point of view. Thus, from the fact finder's perspective, $P_D(A|I)$ is simply a random variable and the question for the fact finder is whether this random variable exceeds k.

The above threshold condition may be restated in terms of the defendant's I-posterior assessment of odds of an accident:

$$\frac{P_D(A|I)}{P_D(\neg A|I)} \geq \frac{k}{1-k} \equiv o.$$

This odds ratio is, from the fact finder's viewpoint, also a random variable.

The fact finder directly observes whether A or $\neg A$ ("not A") occurs. The fact finder then uses this information to update her beliefs regarding whether the random variable $P_D(A|I)/P_D(\neg A|I)$ exceeds threshold o.

The question whether outcome information rationally changes the fact finder's assessment of defendant's knowledge may be formalized as follows: is it true that

$$P_F\left(\frac{P_D(A|I)}{P_D(\neg A|I)} \geq o \Big| A\right) > P_F\left(\frac{P_D(A|I)}{P_D(\neg A|I)} \geq o \Big| \neg A\right)? \qquad (9.7)$$

The subscript "F" indicates that the probability represents the fact finder's subjective beliefs.

In words, the issue is whether the rational fact finder's assessment of the probability that the defendant "knew an accident would occur" conditional on the defendant's having observed I, whatever I might have been, is greater when the fact finder observes that an accident did occur than when the fact finder observes that an accident did not occur.

---

[17] Here I am assuming that the fact finder has point beliefs regarding the probability measure that describes the defendant's prior beliefs over accident occurrence and signal value. The analysis can be generalized so that the fact finder has probabilistic beliefs regarding the defendant's prior beliefs.

Evidence: theoretical models 219

Substituting from the odds formulation of Bayes' rule (shown above), (9.7) becomes

$$P_F\left(\frac{P_D(I|A)}{P_D(I|\neg A)} \geq o'|A\right) > P_F\left(\frac{P_D(I|A)}{P_D(I|\neg A)} \geq o'|\neg A\right) \quad (9.8)$$

where $o' \equiv o(P_D(\neg A))/(P_D(A))$. Therefore, the question is whether the defendant's likelihood ratio for the information I – which information is probabilistic from the fact finder's point of view – should be considered more likely to have been above the (transformed) threshold o' when it is observed that an accident has occurred than when it is observed that an accident has not occurred.

Now, consider the special case in which I takes two values $\bar{I}$ and $\underline{I} < \bar{I}$.[18] To make the problem non-trivial, assume that the defendant's observation of $\bar{I}$ raises the defendant's assessed odds of an accident above the threshold, while the defendant's observation of $\underline{I}$ does not. That is, in terms of the transformed threshold o', assume

$$\frac{P_D(\bar{I}|A)}{P_D(\bar{I}|\neg A)} > o' > \frac{P_D(\underline{I}|A)}{P_D(\underline{I}|\neg A)} \quad (9.9)$$

Therefore, from the fact finder's perspective, the event that the defendant's random odds ratio $P_D(I|A)/P_D(I|\neg A)$ was greater than or equal to o' is equivalent to the event that the defendant saw $\bar{I}$. Thus, condition (9.8) reduces to the condition

$$P_F(\bar{I}|A) > P_F(\bar{I}|\neg A). \quad (9.10)$$

Condition (9.10) is the condition that the *fact finder's* likelihood ratio for the defendant's observation of $\bar{I}$ exceeds 1. This is the condition that, were the fact finder to have learned – prior to learning of the occurrence of an accident – that the defendant had observed $\bar{I}$, the *fact finder* would have raised her assessment of the odds that an accident would occur.

Condition (9.10) is satisfied if the fact finder has the same view as the defendant regarding what it means for the chance of an accident when the defendant sees $\bar{I}$. More formally, if the fact finder's likelihood ratios for the two values of the signal are ordered in the same manner as the defendant's – that is, if

---

[18] The example generalizes to signals with more than one possible value.

$$\frac{P_D(\bar{I}|A)}{P_D(\bar{I}|\neg A)} > \frac{P_D(\underline{I}|A)}{P_D(\underline{I}|\neg A)} \text{ implies } \frac{P_F(\bar{I}|A)}{P_F(\bar{I}|\neg A)} > \frac{P_F(\underline{I}|A)}{P_F(\underline{I}|\neg A)},$$

then condition (9.10) follows from condition (9.9):

$$\frac{P_D(\bar{I}|A)}{P_D(\bar{I}|\neg A)} > \frac{P_D(\underline{I}|A)}{P_D(\underline{I}|\neg A)}$$
$$\Rightarrow \frac{P_F(\bar{I}|A)}{P_F(\bar{I}|\neg A)} > \frac{P_F(\underline{I}|A)}{P_F(\underline{I}|\neg A)}$$
$$\Leftrightarrow \frac{P_F(\bar{I}|A)}{P_F(\bar{I}|\neg A)} > \frac{1 - P_F(\bar{I}|A)}{1 - P_F(\bar{I}|\neg A)}$$
$$\Leftrightarrow P_F(\bar{I}|A)(1 - \cancel{P_F(\bar{I}|\neg A)}) > P_F(\bar{I}|\neg A)(1 - \cancel{P_F(\bar{I}|A)})$$

Therefore, if the defendant received, prior to the accident, private information that determined her legal state of mind, and if the fact finder and defendant generally agree on the meaning of such information vis-à-vis the chance of accident, then, having observed that an accident did in fact occur, the fact finder should rationally increase her probability assessment of the event that the defendant had a culpable state of mind. In other words, when the fact finder cannot know all that the defendant knew, the fact finder's hindsight that an accident did occur is rationally informative of the defendant's foresight that an accident would occur.

Thus, something observationally similar to across-person hindsight bias is actually a rational response to outcome information. This does not, of course, imply that across-person hindsight bias is nonexistent. Nevertheless, many experimental designs that attempt to measure the unwarranted outcome adjustment of across-person hindsight bias do not appear to control adequately for the presence of the correlate rational adjustment. The result obtained from such experiments may thus overstate the magnitude of the irrational adjustment.

What if the fact finder also observes what the defendant observed, which is to say I? In this case, the occurrence of an accident is irrelevant for determining the defendant's state of mind.

To see this, return to the more general case in which the information may take many values. (The following analysis will also serve to explicate this more general case.) The question is again whether the following inequality holds for any given value of I:

$$P_F\left(\frac{P_D(I|A)}{P_D(I|\neg A)} \geq o' \Big| A \cap I\right) > P_F\left(\frac{P_D(I|A)}{P_D(I|\neg A)} \geq o' \Big| \neg A \cap I\right).$$

Let $\Im$ be the subset of information values I such that $P_D(I|A)/P_D(I|\neg A) > o'$. Then the inequality above reduces to $P_F(\Im|A \cap I) > P_F(\Im|\neg A \cap I)$. Using the definition of conditional probability, this may be restated as

$$\frac{P_F(\Im \cap A \cap I)}{P_F(A \cap I)} > \frac{P_F(\Im \cap \neg A \cap I)}{P_F(\neg A \cap I)}.$$

This condition is impossible. The left and right sides of this strict inequality are always equal. If $I \notin \Im$, then the numerators on both sides are zero, and so also the ratios. If $I \in \Im$, then the appearance of $\Im$ in the numerators is redundant, and both ratios are equal to one.

In words, if the fact finder knows what the defendant knew at the time of the defendant's decision, then the finder knows the defendant's state of mind at the time of the defendant's decision, and information regarding whether an accident later occurred is superfluous. Therefore, the rationality of using outcome information to determine state of mind relies on the (plausible) premise that the fact finder does not directly observe the information that was available to the defendant at the time of the defendant's decision.

3.3. Paradoxes and Criticisms

The pure probabilistic approach to fact finding accords with the conventional approach to decision making under uncertainty followed by probabilists, statisticians, and economists.[19] Even in these originating fields, however, it is not without detractors. Paradoxes such as those due to Allais (1953) and to Ellsberg (1961), for instance, call into question both its descriptive power and its normative validity.[20]

As a description of legal fact finding, in particular, it has been subject to a number of specific objections.[21] Two of these are clearly laid out in Allen (1986). A third leads naturally to a discussion of the next class of evidence models.

3.3.1. The conjunction problem The first is the "conjunction problem," itself the result of a conjunction of legal features. First, guilt or liability often turns on two or more findings of fact – as when a verdict requires findings regarding how the defendant acted, what harm she thereby caused, and whether she intended the consequences of her actions. Second, the law

---

[19] Savage (1954).
[20] Allais (1953), Ellsberg (1961).
[21] An early and often cited critique appears in Tribe (1971).

requires that each element of the charge, claim or defense be found to have obtained with a threshold probability, a "standard of proof" (commonly thought to be 50% in civil actions and something more than this, perhaps 90%, in criminal actions). The requirement that each element must individually be subject to a 50% threshold, say, implies a weaker requirement, possibly much weaker, for the probability of the *conjunction* of elements, which is to say the charge, claim or defense itself. In the extreme case in which the elements are statistically independent, the fact that each is more likely than not implies only that their conjunction is more likely than $0.5^n < 0.5$, where n is the number of components. Particularly troubling is the fact that the implied threshold probability for a charge, claim, or defense decreases (quite rapidly) in the number of elements it contains, a factor with uncertain relevance. With four independent elements, it is not 50%, but 6.25%.[22]

3.3.2. The gatecrasher paradox The second objection is implicated by the "gatecrasher paradox." Suppose that the defendant was in attendance with 1000 others at an event at which it is known that 499 attendees purchased tickets and 501 crashed the gate. Assuming no other evidence is available, could (should) a fact finder conclude that the defendant more likely than not failed to pay for his seat, and could (should) the law hold the individual liable for the ticket price? While probabilistic analysis appears to imply that the defendant should be held liable, some see this as strongly contrary to intuition.[23]

3.3.3. Accounting for the interests of the parties Allen (1986) is drawn from a watershed symposium held at Boston University on the benefits and drawbacks of applying probabilistic deduction to evidence law. (Symposium (1986).) Many of the other papers in the corresponding issue of the *Boston University Law Review* are also well worth examining. Taken as a whole, the symposium papers provide a comprehensive picture of evidence scholarship at the time regarding the utility of applying formal theories of probability, conventional and unconventional, to the problem of legal evidence.

Yet the symposium (as well as contemporaneous evidence scholarship) largely ignores an arguably more serious drawback of the pure

---

[22] Recent discussions of the conjunction problem appear in Levmore (2001), Stein (2001), and Allen and Jehl (2003).
[23] Kaye (1979) defends conventional probabilistic analysis from this troubling hypothetical. Allen (1986) comments on this defense.

probabilistic approach.[24] The approach gives short shrift to a fundamental and distinctive fact about legal evidence. Unlike experimental evidence generated in a chemist's laboratory or field evidence gathered in a macroeconomist's survey of inventories, legal evidence is provided by conscious, animate individuals with strong interests in what the fact finder decides and a strong possibility of influencing that decision.[25]

It is one thing to prescribe, as does the pure probabilistic approach, that the fact finder interpret evidence according to the relative likelihood of its production under alternative truths. It is another thing to explain how these relative likelihoods ought to account for the interests of the parties responsible for the production. And it is yet another thing to ask how fact finding should be structured to account for the necessity of this strategic accounting. If the defendant in a criminal case produces for us her oath-bound testimony that she is innocent, how do we evaluate the relative likelihood of observing such a performance if she really were innocent versus if she were in fact guilty? Wouldn't she claim innocence either way? If so, what constitutes convincing evidence of innocence?

4. Omission Models

Where then should one turn to gain a better understanding of how deductions from evidence are and ought to be made in light of the parties' interests? Within the discipline of economics, game theory – including the subfields of information economics and mechanism design – seems like a natural candidate. Much of game theory, after all, concerns the situation in which one individual or entity would like to make use of information in the possession of another whose interests differ from her own.[26] The theory of optimal auction design, for example, studies the tension between the seller's desire to learn – and charge – the maximum price that a bidder would be willing to pay, and the bidder's reluctance, anticipating this plan, to truthfully reveal this value. The theory of optimal taxation is similarly based on taxpayers' reluctance to truthfully reveal their immutable

---

[24] Indeed the problem is one that spans both the application of conventional probabilistic analysis, as described in Lempert (1977), as well as many alternative systems for representing and manipulating the phenomenon of likelihood, such as that laid out in Cohen (1977) and often cited in evidence scholarship.

[25] One can see evidence scholarship starting to bump up against this fact in analyzing the gatecrasher paradox. Kaye, in particular, suggests that the plaintiff's inability to provide anything other than the "naked statistical evidence" of seats filled versus seats purchased should itself be taken as evidence. See Kaye (1979).

[26] For a general review of these aspects of game theory, see, for example, Kreps (1990).

endowments and preferences – upon which the government would ideally base its tax system – if doing so would adversely affect their tax bill.

However, on the relatively limited number of occasions that economists have turned their attention to legal evidence, they have generally taken a more limited approach. Although economic models of legal evidence do account for litigants' incentive to manipulate the information reaching the fact finder, the account is typically incomplete. In most such models, parties may refrain from reporting to the fact finder all that they know. But they may not falsify, fabricate or forge. This stark omission (as it were) generates stark, but fragile, results.

This section of the chapter begins with a description of the basic structure of omission models. It then presents several interpretations of, and variations on, this basic structure. A third subsection describes extensions and applications of the model, and a fourth reviews several criticisms.

4.1. Basic Structure

The omission model approach to legal evidence is typified by Milgrom and Roberts (1986).[27] Milgrom and Roberts present both a single agent model and multiple agent model. The next two sections present each model verbally, provide a numerical example, and describe "precedents" in law and legal scholarship.

4.1.1. Single party model Milgrom and Roberts show how the fact finder may costlessly determine the true state of affairs from a nonetheless interested party who is known to be informed regarding that state of affairs under the assumption that the party may not and will not provide information that is inconsistent with her knowledge. In this case, the fact finder need only announce ahead of time that if the informed party supplies her with ambiguous information, she will assume the worst outcome for the party that is consistent with the information supplied.[28] It follows that the worst deduction for the party that is consistent with the information that she provides will in fact be the truth. This is because the party would always have an incentive to clear up any ambiguity as between the truth and any less favorable deduction.

---

[27] Other early contributions taking this approach include Sobel (1985) and Shavell (1989). More recent applications and extensions are discussed in Section 4.3.

[28] Within economics scholarship this result is referred to as "unraveling" and is usually jointly attributed to Grossman (1981) and Milgrom (1981). An early critical analysis appears in Farrell (1986). The separate, parallel (and older) pedigree of this idea within evidence law and scholarship is discussed below.

A simple numerical example will help to clarify the result and its logic. Suppose that the true state of the world is one of ten possibilities, each indexed with a number between 1 and 10. The fact finder (she) does not know the true state. The party (he) does know the true state, and the fact finder knows that the party knows. The fact finder would like to learn the true number (i.e., state of the world). The party would like the fact finder to think the number is as high as possible, and the fact finder knows this as well.

The party chooses what to report about the true number to the fact finder. (Other, "more evidentiary" interpretations of this game are presented in Section 4.2 below.) The fact finder makes a deduction about the true number based on this report.

The rules of the game are that the party may not lie. He may, however, omit to say all that he knows. That is, he may decline to report the exact number, providing instead a subset of numbers in which the true number lies. He might, for example, reveal that the number is odd (if in fact it is). Or that the number lies between 3 and 7 (if in fact it does).

Despite the party's ability to omit information, the fact finder can be assured of learning the true number by announcing that upon hearing the party report a subset of numbers, she will assume that the true number is the lowest in that subset. The party would in that case never find it in his interest to report a subset containing a number lower than the truth. He can always do better – that is, inspire the fact finder to deduce a greater number – by removing any number from his report that is lower than the truth. Therefore, the lowest number in the party's report, the number in fact chosen by the fact finder, will indeed be the truth. If, for example, the true state is 4, the party will never report the subset {2, 4, 6, 8, 10}. Doing so would cause the fact finder to deduce that the truth is 2. The party could do better by eliminating 2 from this report, whence the truth finder will deduce 4, which is the truth.

It is worth noting that the assume-the-worst rule used by the fact finder in Milgrom and Roberts is akin to an adverse inference from "spoliation,"[29] an ancient component of evidence doctrine dealing with a party's refusal or purposeful inability to supply evidence alleged to be under her control. In terms of the numerical example in the immediately preceding paragraph, an additional document in the party's possession

---

[29] "Spoliation" is a general term referring to evidentiary misconduct. But it is perhaps most often used to describe a party's failure to produce evidence when so required – either because the evidence has been destroyed or is being withheld. For a discussion of "spoliation" doctrine, see, for example, Sanchirico (2004b).

226 *Procedural law and economics*

might, for example, allow the fact finder to distinguish between state 2 and the subset of states {4, 6, 8, 10}. If the party refuses to provide the document – that is, if the party in effect reports {2, 4, 6, 8, 10} – the fact finder, under this rule, assumes that the truth is 2, the worst case for the party among the relevant possibilities.

Analysis of this kind of assume-the-worst rule also crops up in the legal scholarship on evidence preceding Milgrom and Roberts (1986). Indeed, the idea appears in attempts to resolve the gatecrasher paradox, as discussed in Section 3.3.2 above. Kaye (1979), for example, suggests that the plaintiff's failure to present any information beyond the naked statistical evidence of ticket sales and attendance may be taken to indicate that the rest of the evidence that is likely available to him would hurt his case.

4.1.2. Multiple Informed Parties with Conflicting Interests Milgrom and Roberts (1986) also put forward a related dual informed party model in which the parties' interests are in conflict. In this model, the fact finder again learns the truth. Indeed, this occurs no matter what rule the fact finder uses to choose among the set of states that are consistent with both parties' reports: the parties' conflict of interest substitutes for the fact finder's sophistication. If the parties have strictly opposing interests and each knows the truth, the fact finder will always end up learning the truth so long as she restricts her decision to the intersection of the parties' reports. (Again, the parties may omit information, but may not lie.) This is because whatever the fact finder's decision within that intersection, if it is not the truth, one party will prefer the truth and so will have an incentive to (and the ability to) refine her report.

Return to the subset reporting example presented above in which there were ten possible states. Imagine now that two parties know the truth and each reports a subset containing it. Suppose that one party wants the fact finder to think the number is as high as possible and the other as low as possible. Thus, the parties' interests are in conflict. Suppose that the fact finder (unthinkingly) takes as the true state the average (rounded up or down) of the numbers in the intersection of the parties' reports. Then, if the average of the points in the intersection of reports is not the truth, one party or the other will prefer the truth to this average and thus have an incentive to report the truth as a singleton. If, for example, the truth is 4, one party says "3 or greater" and the other "7 or less," then the intersection of reports is 3 through 7, the average is 5 and the party that prefers lower numbers to high has an incentive to refine her report to "4."

The logic of this result resonates with earlier less formal discussions within case law and evidence scholarship regarding the relative benefits of adversarial procedure.³⁰ According to the US Supreme Court, "the very premise of [the] adversarial system . . . is that partisan advocacy on both sides of a case will best promote the ultimate objective that the guilty be convicted and the innocent go free."³¹

4.2. Four Interpretations/variants of the Omission Model
Several interpretations/variants of the two games discussed above appear in the omission literature. I will discuss these with reference to the single agent model in Section 4.1.1.

4.2.1. Subset reporting The first interpretation is "subset reporting," which was described above and is the main interpretation offered by Milgrom and Roberts (1986). The logic of truth revelation is clearest under this interpretation. Yet, as a description of actual evidence production, it might be regarded as too abstract.

4.2.2. Truth-consistent presentation The "truth-consistent presentation" interpretation is somewhat more representational of actual legal evidence. Under this interpretation, rather than directly reporting to the fact finder a particular subset of states, the informed party makes an evidentiary presentation that is commonly known to correspond to a particular subset of states.

Thus, imagine that each state s is associated with a subset of evidentiary presentations or "messages," $E(s) \subset E$. The subset $E(s)$ represents the evidentiary presentations that are consistent with state s in some "natural" sense (which may not be fully specified). The association may be semantic. For instance, the state s may in part specify that the party paid a third person to supply him with a particular product. Several of the presentations in $E(s)$ may involve providing the fact finder with a signed contract whose language is consistent with that fact.

A given presentation $e \in E$ may be associated with more than one state: that is, there may exist two states s and s' such that $s \neq s'$ and $e \in E(s) \cap E(s')$. Thus, a signed contract may also be consistent with the state in which the party failed to pay for the product. Indeed, the null presentation (i.e., the choice to make no presentation), which is presumably an available option for the party, is consistent with all states.

Two assumptions are imposed upon this structure. First, the correspondence $E(.)$ is common knowledge between the party and fact finder.

---

[30] See, for example, Landsman (1984) and sources cited therein.
[31] *Herring v. New York*, 442 U.S. 853, 862 (1975).

228 Procedural law and economics

Table 9.1 Example illustrating the connection between subset reporting and truth-consistent presentation

		Documents							
		A	B	C	D	F	G	H	I
States	1	▓	▓	▓	▓			▓	
	2			▓	▓	▓	▓		
	3				▓		▓	▓	▓

Second, given true state s, the party may make any presentation in $E(s)$, but no presentation outside of $E(s)$. Thus, the party's presentation must be consistent with the true state, though it need not fully indicate the true state.

To understand the linkage between this structure and subset reporting, consider the following simple example: eight evidentiary presentations might be made, A, B, C, D, F, G, H, I, in each of *three* possible states, 1, 2, 3. Table 9.1, read row-by-row, shows for each state (row) the presentations (columns) that are naturally associated with that state. For example, presentations D, G, H and I are associated with state 3. The set $E(s)$ corresponds to the set of shaded boxes in the row corresponding to state s. Thus $E(3) = \{D, G, H, I\}$.

The key to linking this framework to the subset reporting model described above is to notice that the table can also be read column-by-column. Thus, given any evidentiary performance, the table tells us the subset of states with which such performance is naturally associated. For example, reading down column G, we see that performance G is associated with states 2 and 3. It follows that when the party makes a particular presentation to the fact finder, he is in effect truthfully reporting to the fact finder a subset of states, as in the subset reporting interpretation. When the party makes presentation G, for instance, he is in effect truthfully reporting to the fact finder that the true state lies in the subset $\{2, 3\}$. In general notation, on presenting evidence e, the fact finder is in effect reporting the subset $\{s | e \in E(s)\}$ of states.

The truth revelation result discussed above may be restated in terms of this new interpretation. Indeed, this interpretation serves to highlight both an implicit requirement and a generalization of such result.

The additional requirement is that the correspondence $E(s)$ be sufficiently "rich." To take an extreme example, if every cell in Table 9.1 were shaded – signifying that every available evidentiary presentation was consistent with every true state – truth revelation would be impossible. (In subset reporting terms, this would correspond to the party's somehow being unable to convey in language that the true state was in any subset other than the full set itself.)

Notice that quite contrary to this possibility, Table 9.1 has the following "extreme richness" property: every subset of states has at least one corresponding presentation in the sense that such subset precisely equals the subset of states consistent with such presentation. That is, for all subsets of states S there exists a presentation e such that $\{s | e \in E(s)\} = S$. For the singleton subset consisting solely of state 1, for instance, there are, in fact, two such presentations: A and B. For the subset of states $\{1, 2\}$, there is one, C. For the subset of states $\{1, 2, 3\}$ there is also one, D, and so on. Thus, just as in the subset reporting interpretation, every subset of states may, in effect, be reported.

Extreme richness is sufficient (but not necessary) for truth revelation. Recall that in the subset reporting interpretation, the fact finder announces that she will assume that the truth is the party's least favorite state among the states in the subset that the party reports to her. In the truth-consistent presentation interpretation, the fact finder announces that upon seeing a presentation A, B, C, . . ., or I, she will deduce that the true state is the party's least favorite state among those states that are consistent with the presentation. Suppose, for example, that the truth is 2 and that the party prefers higher states to lower. Given that the true state is 2, the party is able to present C, D, F, or G. If the party makes presentation C or F, the fact finder, using an assume-the-worst rule, will deduce that the true state is 2. If the fact finder makes presentation D or G, the fact finder will deduce that the true state is 3, which is worse than 2 for the party. Therefore, the party will present C or F and the fact finder will decide that the state is 2, which is the truth.

Conversely, extreme richness is not necessary for truth revelation – this is the generalization referred to above. The truth revelation result does not require that every subset of states be effectively reportable via some presentation. All that is required is that for every state there be at least one presentation which allows the party to rule out in the fact finder's mind those states that the party regards as worse than such state. Assuming the party prefers higher states to lower states, the requirement is that every state be the lowest state that is consistent with some presentation. Consider, for example, Table 9.2, which is a pared down version of Table 9.1. Notice that each state is the lowest that is consistent with some presentation. For example, state 2 is the lowest consistent with G. An assume-the-worst rule would also produce truth revelation under Table 9.2. Were state 3 the true state, for example, the party, who prefers higher states to lower states, would be able to report G, H, or I. But the party would never present G or H because, given the fact finder's assume-the-worst rule,

230 *Procedural law and economics*

Table 9.2 Example illustrating that extreme richness is not necessary for truth revelation

		Documents		
		G	H	I
States	1		■	
	2	■		
	3	■	■	■

the party could do better presenting I, in which case the fact finder's rule would lead it to the truth.

4.2.3. Feasible presentation The third interpretation, "feasible presentation," is similar in structure to truth-consistent presentation. The difference lies in the interpretation of the correspondence $E(.)$. Under the feasible presentation approach, $E(s)$ represents the presentations that are feasible for the party in any given state, rather than those that are naturally or semantically consistent with the true state. Interpreting Table 9.1 in this way, when the true state is state 3, presentations D, G, H, and I are the only presentations that the party is *able* to make. All other presentations are impossible.

The feasible presentations interpretation subsumes the truth-consistent presentation interpretation. Return for a moment to viewing Table 9.1 as a map of presentations that are naturally/semantically consistent with each state, as opposed to feasible under such state. If we layer on top of this the restriction that truthful presentations, and only truthful presentations are possible, Table 9.1 becomes also a representation of the set of feasible messages.

Conversely, the feasible presentations interpretation is conceptually broader than the truth-consistent presentations interpretation. The feasible presentations interpretation does not specify what the "technology" is that rules out certain presentations in certain states. An exogenous legal prohibition on untruthful presentation may well be doing some or all of the work. Physical impossibility or prohibitive cost may also be important factors.

4.2.4. Infinite or zero cost A fourth interpretation, which is actually a gloss on the first three, merely replaces "feasible/permitted" with "of zero/negligible cost" and "infeasible/not permitted" with "infinitely/prohibitively costly." In the subset reporting interpretation, with this gloss, the cost of reporting any subset containing the true state is zero, while the cost of reporting any subset not containing the true state is infinite. In the truth-consistent presentation interpretation, all evidentiary performances in $E(s)$ have zero cost when the true state is s, while all performances outside $E(s)$ have infinite cost. The source of infinite cost is presumably sanctions for truth-inconsistent reporting. The adjustment in the feasible presentation interpretation is similar: "feasible" becomes "of zero cost," "infeasible" becomes infinitely costly. The source of costs is left unspecified and may be legal, technological, economic, or some combination thereof.

This third "binary cost" interpretation will be useful in comparing omission models with the endogenous cost signaling models discussed in Section 5.1 below.

4.3. Applications and Extensions

In this section, I discuss a selection of the many applications and extensions of the basic omission models described above in Section 4.1.

4.3.1. Strategic search models and the possibility of pro-plaintiff or pro-defendant bias in the litigation system
The strategic search model of evidence production is a variant of the omission model that in effect combines the logic of the omission model with the logic of contest models of litigation, as discussed in Section 2.2. In strategic search models of litigation, parties sample from an exogenous distribution for "pieces of evidence," deciding both when to stop sampling and what of their accumulated sample to show the court. Each time a party draws a sample she incurs a cost. Parties may decline to report elements of their accumulated sample to the court, but, as in Milgrom and Roberts (1986), they may not fabricate observations.

Froeb and Kobayashi (1996) use a strategic search model to show in effect that Milgrom and Robert's (1986) two-party result, described above, extends to the case in which evidence is costly to acquire and the decision maker may be biased. The fact that evidence is costly to acquire does not prevent a correct decision because, all else the same, the party in the right, being favored by the distribution of evidence from which parties draw, ends up presenting more favorable evidence to the fact finder. Moreover, the litigation system automatically compensates for any decision maker bias because the party favored by such bias reacts, in Froeb and Kobayashi's model, by slacking off on evidentiary effort.

Daughety and Reinganum (2000) generalize Froeb and Kobayashi's model and emphasize the dependence of Froeb and Kobayashi's results on symmetries in sampling costs and sampling distributions. Daughety and Reinganum suggest that, all told, the adversarial system favors defendants.

Froeb and Kobayashi (2000), discussed in Section 4.3.2 immediately below, is another example of this type of model.

4.3.2. Adversarial versus inquisitorial procedure Omission models have been employed to compare the relative merits of adversarial process (wherein litigating parties compete before a spectator/fact finder) and inquisitorial process (whereby the parties are restrained and the fact finder investigates and questions).[32] Shin (1998) argues that inquisitorial process generates less information than adversarial process even when the inquisitor's investigative ability is as good as that of each adversary (taken individually). In Shin's model, as in Milgrom and Roberts (1986), parties can suppress evidence but cannot fabricate it. Shin shows, in essence, that the downside of adversarial process – the fact that evidence may be manipulated – can be significantly alleviated by the kind of assume-the-worst-of-omission deductions studied in Milgrom and Roberts (1986). With this downside mitigated, the upside of adversarial process – the fact that it offers multiple sources of evidence – becomes decisive in comparing systems.

Froeb and Kobayashi (2000) employ a strategic search model of evidentiary sampling similar to that in Froeb and Kobayashi (1996). Under adversarial process, each party decides first, how many times to draw from a given distribution of evidence and second, what of her sample to present in court. Once again, parties cannot fabricate any portion of their sample. The fact finder "averages" the evidence placed before her. This induces each party to present only the single piece of evidence in her sample that most favors her case. Under inquisitorial process, on the other hand, the inquisitor herself samples from the distribution and averages *all* the data. Which system does better? If the parties face the same sampling costs, both systems leave the fact finder with the same assessment on average, namely the true mean of the distribution. In other words, whether one takes the average of extreme draws in each case or the average of all draws in each case, one's average assessment over all cases will equal the true mean of the sampled distribution: both estimating procedures are "unbiased." However, the two estimators differ in their variance – a proxy for their degree of error.[33] Which system has less error is indeterminate. The

---

[32] The Anglo-American system of fact finding relies for evidence on the adversarial efforts of the parties. The continental European system, by contrast, assigns the judge a more active role in investigating the case and questioning witnesses. The latter is often referred to as "inquisitorial procedure." (On this issue, see Chapter 1 in this volume on Adversarial versus Inquisitorial Justice.)

[33] The variance of each system depends on the size of each sample. The authors

Evidence: theoretical models 233

outcome depends on the shape of the underlying distribution and the cost of sampling.

4.3.3. Link to primary activities Bull and Watson (2004) adopt a variant of the feasible presentation interpretation discussed above. They link evidence production in a later phase of the model to action choice in an earlier phase: action choice determines the set of feasible evidentiary presentations.[34] In particular, Bull and Watson study how the prospect of transfers based on evidence production affects contracting and contractual performance. Their main result characterizes kinds of actions that are implementable under this endogenous evidentiary structure.

4.3.4. Partial provability in a multi-party context Consider again the example from Section 4.1.2 in which each of two informed parties with conflicting interests reports to the uninformed fact finder something true, but perhaps not complete, about the actual state of the world, where the state of the world is indexed by the numbers between one and ten. In that example, the conflict of interest between the two parties implied that, whatever the fact finder's rule for choosing among elements in the intersection of the parties' reports, if the truth would differ from the fact finder's determination, one of the parties would prefer to refine her report to precisely indicate truth. An implicit assumption in that analysis was that the party who preferred to refine her report was also able to do so.

What if the parties were not always able to precisely communicate the true state? What if, for example, both parties were able to report the true state precisely in all states except state 5, in which the *only* report that either side could make was the subset {2, 4, 5, 6}. How would this situation arise? Perhaps (to shift momentarily to the feasible or truth-consistent evidentiary presentation interpretation), the evidentiary presentations available to the parties in state 5 are simply "inconclusive:" everything the parties could show or do in front of the fact finder in state 5 might also be shown or done in states 2, 4 and 6.

Would the truth revelation result fall apart? This is the main question addressed by the sub-literature on partial or limited "provability."

Section 4.2.2 discussed partial provability in the context of the single

---

compare the same amount of sampling: the inquisitor samples as many times as the two adversaries combined.

[34] In so endogenizing evidence production, Bull and Watson (2004) follows Sanchirico (1995, 2000, 2001b) discussed below. Bull and Watson (2007) is a technical companion to Bull and Watson (2004).

party model. This remainder of this section discusses partial provability in the context of the multi-party conflict of interest model.

4.3.4.1. GENERAL DISCUSSION   Let us begin by establishing that limits on provability may indeed be sufficient to prevent truth revelation, even in a model with two parties that have conflicting interests. This is certainly the case if the fact finder is unsophisticated, as in Milgrom and Roberts' (1986) multi-party model. If, for example, the fact finder's rule is to average (and round down) the intersection of reports, then, in the example from the last paragraph, the fact finder will incorrectly deduce "4" when, the true state being 5, she hears "{2, 4, 5, 6}" from both parties.

Even when the fact finder is both sophisticated and fully aware of the limitations on provability, partial provability may prevent her from being able to deduce the truth. Suppose, for example, that {2, 4, 5, 6} was *also* the only report that each party could make when the truth was 6. Then the fact finder would be unable to distinguish states 5 and 6 based on the parties' reports.

Conversely, it is equally clear that full provability is unnecessary for truth revelation (just as in the single party case discussed in Section 4.2.2). If, to use the same example, the precise state may be reported in all states except 5, in which only {2, 4, 5, 6} may be reported, then the fact finder will deduce the truth by adopting any rule which chooses from within the intersection of reports, and in which "{2, 4, 5, 6}" heard from both parties is interpreted as "5." If the state is not 5, one of the parties will prefer the true state to 5, and be able to report the true state precisely. Thus, the fact finder will hear "{2, 4, 5, 6}" from both parties when and only when the truth is 5.

The question(s) then arise: given a set of assumptions about the sophistication and knowledge of the fact finder, and the degree of conflict in the parties' interests, how partial can provability be without defeating the fact finder's ability to learn the truth? One version of this question is considered by Lipman and Seppi (1995) ["LS"].[35]

4.3.4.2. LIPMAN AND SEPPI (1995)   LS consider partial provability with conflict of interest and sophisticated fact finders who are fully aware of the restrictions on provability. In LS all players face the same restrictions on

---

[35] Okuno-Fujiwara, Postlewaite, and Suzumura (1990) is another important contribution in this area. These authors analyze an augmented asymmetric information model in which agents can announce their private information beforehand. They provide conditions for the full revelation of agents' private information when some of the agents' announcements are exogenously "certifiable."

provability. Furthermore, LS model reporting as a sequential game, rather than a simultaneous game.[36]

Although LS is a very technical paper, much of its complexity arises from the authors' consideration of the case in which there are more than two parties. The two-party case, once it is culled from LS' more general technical analysis (which itself is not easy), is not particularly difficult to grasp.

Nevertheless, a proper explanation will require some development, and some readers may wish to skip to the next section.

Thus, suppose that the two parties each move once in sequence, reporting in effect a subset of states.[37] Consider the state 5 and all the subsets of states, each containing 5, that may be reported when the truth is 5. Suppose one of these subsets is {2, 4, 5, 6} and suppose that the report {2, 4, 5, 6} has the following property: if the truth is 2 and not 5, a subsequent subset report could be made that includes 2 and not 5; similarly, if the truth is 4 and not 5, a subsequent report could be made that includes 4 and not 5; and if the truth is 6 and not 5, a subsequent report could be made that includes 6 but not 5. That is, for every state in the report aside from 5 itself, a subsequent report could be made that rules out 5. The subset of even numbers, for example, would simultaneously work as such a report for 2, 4, and 6.

Suppose then that the fact finder were to announce a decision rule in which, inter alia, she would provisionally believe 5 if she heard "{2, 4, 5, 6}," but would change her mind if the second reporter subsequently reported a subset not containing 5. Then, by hypothesis, if the true state were not 5, this falsity could be effectively "communicated" by the second reporter. The second reporter's report would not necessarily, on its face, communicate, even in conjunction with the first report, the precise identity of the true state. But it would refute the fact finder's provisional belief that the true state were 5. Thus, {2, 4, 5, 6}, if taken to mean "5," acts as a subsequently/potentially "refutable" report of "5." And, therefore, we may say that state 5 "has" (at least one) refutable report.

Let us now imagine that for every state there is at least one such refutable report. In this case, the message space taken as a whole is, in LS' terms, "weakly refutable."[38] LS prove that, in the context of their model, weak refutability (plus a "rich language condition" to be discussed) are sufficient for the existence of a decision rule for the fact finder that lands on the true

---

[36] This is to insure the existence of pure strategy equilibria. See LS note 13 at 382.
[37] LS actually cast their analysis in terms of feasible presentation interpretation, discussed above in Section 4.2. More on this below.
[38] See LS' proposition 7, Corollary 3, and the discussion surrounding these results, all at 389–90.

state no matter what it might be, so long as the parties' interests are in conflict (and even if the decision maker knows only this about their preferences).[39]

Here is the argument. Imagine that the fact finder begins to construct the following decision rule (which LS refer to as a "believe-unless-refuted" rule): The fact finder wishes first to assign to each possible state a refutable report. But she wishes to do so on a one-to-one basis, so that each state has its own refutable report. Given the assumption of weak refutability, each state has at least one refutable report. In the example above, 5 has {2, 4, 5, 6}. But, does each state have *its own unique* report?

In the subset reporting framework in which parties simply report subsets, the answer is "not necessarily." However, LS adopt the feasible presentation interpretation described in Section 4.2.3. The feasible presentation interpretation, like the truth-consistent presentation interpretation (see the last point in Section 4.2.2), allows for the possibility that there may be several different ways to effectively report a subset of states. LS specifically assume (their "rich language condition") that for any given subset of states, there are at least as many different ways to report such subset as there are elements in the subset. It is as if such reports of subsets are made in writing with crayons and there are as many crayon colors to choose from as there are elements of the subset being reported.[40]

(To show fulfillment of LS' rich language condition in Table 9.1 (which has only three states) we would need at least $3 + 3 \times 2 + 1 \times 3 = 12$ columns. Alternatively, we could imagine that each column/presentation may be made in any one of three colors.)

If we impose LS' rich language condition, then each state does have its own report by the following argument. Suppose that, without the crayons, {2, 4, 5, 6} is the only refutable report for both 5 *and* 6. This subset having four elements, there must be at least four colors in which it might be reported. Therefore, it is possible for the fact finder to announce a rule that assigns, say, {2, 4, 5, 6} *in red* to 5 and {2, 4, 5, 6} in blue to 6, and so on.

Given this unique assignment of refutable reports to states, the fact finder announces that she will provisionally believe that a state is true if she hears its uniquely assigned refutable report. For example, if the fact finder receives {2, 4, 5, 6} in red from the first reporter, she provisionally believes that the true state is 5.

Now move to the second party's report, assuming that {2, 4, 5, 6} in red has been reported and is interpreted to mean "5." If 2, 4, or 6, and not 5, is

---

[39] LS also prove that weak refutability is *necessary* for the existence of the particular type of truth revealing rule discussed below. See 389–90.

[40] See LS, p. 376.

in fact not the truth, then by the assumed refutability of the message space, there must in each case be another subset containing, respectively, 2, 4, or 6, and not 5 that the second reporter could report. If any one of these subsets were reported, 5 would be refuted. But what would the fact finder *then* believe? If there existed three *distinct* reports refuting 5, one consistent with each of 2, 4, and 6, the answer would be simple. The fact finder would believe 2 upon hearing the distinctive report for 2, 4 on hearing the distinctive report for 4, and so on. But what is to guarantee that the 5-refuting reports for 2, 4 and 6 are distinct? Again, LS' rich language condition solves the problem. Even if the only refuting report for each of 2, 4, and 6 is, for instance, "the even numbers," the rich language condition implies, in effect, that this one report could be made in as many different colors as there are even numbers. *A fortiori*, the fact finder can associate "the even numbers" *in yellow* with 2, "the even numbers" in green with 4, and "the even numbers" in purple with 6. The upshot is this: there is a way for the second reporter to correct the finder's decision, when after the first round, the combination of the fact finder's decision rule and the report she receives causes the fact finder to be mistaken.

Given this, imagine that the fact finder finishes the construction of her decision rule by adopting the following subsidiary rule for the second move: continue to believe the state associated with the first report, unless the second reporter reports a refuting subset/color, in which case believe the single state pre-associated with that subset/color.

It then follows that the fact finder will learn the truth. For consider what happens when it is the second reporter's turn. Let's imagine (although the fact finder need not know this) that the first mover prefers higher states to lower, and the second mover, lower states to higher.

One possibility is that the first reporter "reports the truth." Suppose, for example, that the truth is 5, and that the first reporter reports the subset/color pre-assigned to 5: namely, {2, 4, 5, 6} in red. In that case, the second reporter cannot refute 5. As in the rest of the literature on omissions, all of the second reporter's reports must correspond to the true state 5. In terms of the feasible presentations interpretation (see Section 4.2.3), when the true state is 5, the second reporter cannot, by definition, make a report that is not feasible in state 5. Therefore, given the fact finder's believe-unless-refuted rule, the fact finder correctly decides that 5 is the true state.

For future reference note that, because every state is so reportable according to the fact finder's association of subset-colors and states, the first reporter always has the option of obtaining truth-telling payoffs. Therefore, she will never choose a report that is projected to provide her with lower payoffs than this.

A second possibility is that the first reporter makes the report associated with a given state even though that state is not the truth. For example, the first reporter might make the report associated with 5, {2, 4, 5, 6}, in red, even though the truth is not 5, but is 2, 4, or 6. Note that the fact that {2, 4, 5, 6} in red has been associated with state 5 does not change the fact that it is also feasible when the true state is 2, 4, or 6. Note also that if {2, 4, 5, 6} in red is reported, the true state cannot be anything other than 2, 4, 5, or 6.

The first subsidiary case of this second possibility is that the truth is higher than the fact finder's interpretation of the first reporter's report (recall that the first reporter prefers higher states). Suppose, for example, that the true state is 6. Then, the second reporter, who prefers lower states, may or may not choose to refute the first reporter's report of 5 (i.e., {2, 4, 5, 6} in red). But if she does, this would only be to make the fact finder believe that the truth is *even lower than* 5. Therefore, the *first* reporter, who prefers higher states, and can guarantee herself truth payoffs from 6, will never present the report for 5. In general, the first reporter will never communicate any state that is lower than the truth.

The second subsidiary case is that the truth is lower than the state assigned to the first reporter's report. For example, suppose the truth is 4 even though the first reporter reported {2, 4, 5, 6} in red, which is pre-associated with 5. The second reporter, who prefers lower numbers, would prefer the truth, 4, to a decision that the state is 5. Moreover, the second player has the ability to communicate that the state is 4, by, for example, stating in green that the true number is even, if that is the report pre-associated with 4. Indeed, the second player *may* even be able to refute 5 by making a report that is interpreted as a state even lower than 4. Perhaps the second reporter can state *in yellow* that the true state is even, and this will be taken to mean 2. In any event, the fact finder will end up deciding on something that is either the truth or lower than the truth. If it is the truth, we are done. If it is lower than the truth, then the first reporter, anticipating all this, would not have gotten herself into such a position in the first place; she would have made a report that would have been taken to mean the true state, 4.

Therefore, anticipating the second reporter's move, the first reporter has no incentive to make any report other than that pre-assigned to the true state, which message the second reporter cannot refute. And, conversely, in the only cases in which the first reporter has no *affirmative* incentive to make the report that *is* assigned to the true state, the second reporter has an affirmative incentive to make any necessary corrections.[41]

---

[41] For another application of the omission approach – in this case to expert witnesses – see Yee (2008). See also Deneckere and Severinov (2003).

4.4. Assessment of Omission Models

This section critically appraises the literature on omission models and in doing so sets the stage for the third approach to modeling legal evidence, which is described in Section 5 below.

4.4.1. The no-lying assumption in the subset-reporting and truth consistent presentation interpretations Truth revelation results for omission models are precariously balanced on the assumption that agents cannot fabricate evidence. If, for instance, we remove the restriction on lying from the one-through-ten example used to explain Milgrom and Roberts' (1986) single agent result in Section 4.1, the fact finder's assume-the-worst rule merely induces the single agent to report her favorite outcome, "10," regardless of the true state. Likewise, if we remove the no-lying restriction from the two agent conflict-of-interest example presented in Section 4.1.2, one agent will respond to the fact finder's intersection rule by reporting "1," and the other by reporting "10." The fact finder's decision rule will not lead to truth revelation. Indeed, the rule, which specifies a way of choosing from the intersection of the parties' reports, will not even function: the agents' reports will not intersect.

It is thus worth asking whether the no-lying assumption is justified, at least as an approximation of reality.

Many contributors to the omissions literature motivate the no-fabrication assumption by pointing out that lying in court is illegal by virtue of statutes criminalizing perjury, obstruction of justice and similar transgressions. This defense is problematic in several respects.

First, let us accept for purposes of argument the premise that behavior that has been rendered illegal is not an issue for the analysis of legal evidence. The problem for the omissions literature, then, is that much of the behavior that this literature would characterize as "omission," rather than fabrication, is also illegal – by virtue of subpoena enforcement, compelled discovery, and statutes on obstruction of justice and contempt.[42] Furthermore, instances of omission that are not now illegal might be made so. Thus, if illegality does (or can) rule out behavior, the omissions literature itself is left without a problem to solve. (Alternatively, it must explain why making omission illegal is not the best policy – see the fourth point below.)

Second, the implicit premise that illegal behavior is not an issue for evidence is troublesome. The illegality of fabrication does not rule it out,

---

[42] See Sanchirico (2004b: 1247–86) for a description of the laws governing evidentiary misconduct in US federal civil cases.

either in practice or in principle. As a matter of theory, the detection-probability-discounted penalty for lying may not outweigh the potential gains from doing so. As a matter of empirics, despite the fact that fabrication in court is often illegal, what limited data exist suggests that it is a regular occurrence.[43]

Third, one is justified in asking why, if the no-lying assumption is legitimate in the context of judicial process, it is so rarely deployed by economists in other more frequently studied settings in which the government is also the principal. There is no corresponding no-fabrication assumption in the literature on optimal taxation, or in large swaths of the literature on optimal regulation. Perjury and related crimes, like lying to investigators and tax fraud, apply in these settings as well. If the existence of such sanctions justify the no-lying assumption in omission models, why does it not justify assuming that the optimal tax authority can observe wage rates as opposed to just labor earnings?

Fourth, and perhaps most importantly, by assuming that agents cannot lie, the omissions literature on evidence effectively assumes away one of its most fundamental challenges and, correspondingly, blocks off one of its chief sources of potential utility. Crucial and interesting questions central to the practical design of evidentiary procedure are shunted aside. How precisely do laws regarding perjury and obstruction function? Are such laws effective? Are they efficient? Are they effective and efficient in some settings and not in others? What are the alternatives to such laws for system design? More generally, what is the best way to structure litigation if we do not take as already solved the elemental problem that parties have an incentive to falsify their testimony and forge their tangible evidence?[44]

4.4.2. Lingering problems in the feasible presentation interpretation The assumption, in subset reporting, that a party may not lie, becomes, in truth-consistent presentation, the assumption that the party may not make a presentation that is inconsistent with the true state, where the

---

[43] See Sanchirico (2004b), which surveys in Part I the empirical evidence on evidentiary misconduct.

[44] The relative efficacy of perjury and obstruction laws is studied in Sanchirico (2006), which emphasizes that the cost of (recursive) detection avoidance is a drawback of relying too heavily on such policies. Sanchirico (2004b) studies the optimal structure of such laws in a primary activity incentive-setting context and finds that the middling enforcement intensity that is seen in practice may well be justified. Cooter and Emons (2003, 2004) propose an alternative to perjury and obstruction laws: parties post bonds that they later forfeit if their testimony turns out to be false.

correspondence $E(.)$, as represented by Table 9.1, defines consistency. Presumably, in both of these interpretations, some external legal prohibition defines and enforces these reporting restrictions.

In feasible presentation, the no-lying assumption is transmuted into the bare assumption that the party's choice of presentation is constrained by the table – for reasons that are not specified. Thus, assume that the true state is 1. In subset reporting, the party is prohibited from lying and reporting that the true state is in the subset {2, 3}. In truth-consistent presentation, the party is prohibited from making presentation G, which is consistent with 2 and 3, but not 1. In feasible presentation, G is simply designated as impossible. G may be impossible because it is semantically inconsistent with the truth and truth-inconsistent presentations are legally prohibited. Or it may be somehow technologically or economically impossible, without the aid of legal prohibition. That is, G is the kind of presentation that, for whatever reason, cannot be faked when the truth is neither 2 nor 3.

Arguably, eschewing the explicitly truth-semantic subset reporting and truth-consistent presentations interpretations in favor of the feasible presentation interpretation does little to solve the problem identified in the preceding subsection. Rather, the feasible presentations interpretation appears merely to relocate the problem. In lieu of wondering why the defendant/surgeon could not lie about her performance during the seven-hour operation, the reader is left to wonder why there should exist an evidentiary performance that would be possible (at zero cost) for the surgeon if she had mindfully followed best practices, and impossible if she had not. If the response to the reader's inquiry relies on the assertion that the surgeon is legally prohibited from presenting evidence that semantically contradicts the truth, then we are back to the problem with the explicit no-lying assumption. If the response relies on the assertion that there exists a kind of evidentiary presentation that is physically/technologically/economically impossible when the surgeon has not followed best practices, the question then becomes: where can such evidence be found? The time, expense, and endemic, lingering ambiguity of actual litigation suggest that, even if this unicorn exists, it is rarely discovered and harnessed by litigants.

Put another way, in the feasible presentation interpretation, the richness condition takes on added importance and correspondingly requires greater scrutiny. By contrast, with truth-consistent presentation, it is not difficult to imagine that there exists a presentation that is truth consistent with each given subset of states. As noted, simply reporting the subset of states is, after all, a presentation. What is perhaps difficult to imagine in truth-consistent presentation is the absolute prohibition on lying. In the feasible interpretation, we are not specifically asked to imagine an absolute prohibition on lying. Rather, we are asked to imagine that for (not all, but) a key collection of subsets of true states, it is possible to find an evidentiary presentation that would be effectively impossible in any state outside that state. This may be likely true for some subsets of states. But is it true for enough subsets of states to make possible the level of discernment that the fact finder requires? Is the evidentiary space rich enough?

For example, in one possible presentation, the party may appear before the fact finder missing a leg. This presentation is effectively impossible in a number of possible states. For example, the fact finder may be effectively certain that the true state is one of those in which the party has no leg. Moreover, the fact finder may be effectively certain that the true state is one of those in which party's leg was involuntarily severed. Yet, this presentation tells the fact finder little about *how* the leg was severed. Was it caused by an accident? If so, who was the injurer? Was the injurer negligent? Was the party herself contributorily negligent? How will missing a leg impact the party economically? Mentally and emotionally? The fact finder may be interested in these issues as well, and it seems unlikely that the evidentiary space is rich enough to contain unfakeable presentations for all, or even most of what will be at issue in the case.

4.4.3. The illusory solution of adopting the infinite or zero cost interpretation Recall that a fourth interpretation replaces "feasible/permitted" with "of zero/negligible cost" and "infeasible/not permitted" with "infinitely/prohibitively costly." Arguably, this cost-based interpretation adds little to the omission model besides, perhaps, rhetorical appeal. After all, one could argue that economics as a field is partly defined in opposition to the mistake of regarding as predetermined variables that are actually subject to choice by self-interested agents. Could it be that the binary cost interpretation absolves omissions models of this mistake with respect to fabrication and lying? If so, then presumably any model that exogenously prohibits an action might improve itself by specifying that actors, with finite budgets, may indeed choose the action, so long as they pay an infinite price.

Indeed, in some respects, the binary cost interpretation makes the omission model look less appealing. Recasting the model in terms of binary costs places in stark relief the questionable binary nature of permissibility/feasibility. Under the cost interpretation, all evidentiary performances inside $E(s)$ are equally (un)costly. For instance, an evidentiary performance e that pinpoints the state – i.e., $E^{-1}(e) = \{s\}$ – costs as much to present, namely zero, as an evidentiary performance e' that communicates nothing about the state $E^{-1}(e') = \{1, \ldots, 10\}$. Furthermore, all evidentiary performances outside $E(s)$, regardless of whether they merely spin the truth or turn it fully on its head, are equally (prohibitively) costly.

Accordingly, the cost difference between any performance in $E(s)$ and any performance outside $E(s')$ is always the same: it is always infinite.

4.4.4. The partial solution of partial provability Allowing for only partial provability, as do Lipman and Seppi (1995), does weaken the no-lying/infeasibility assumption and so restores some degree of plausibility to the omission model. But, relative to the substantial distance separating omissions models from the basic outlines of real litigation, the improvement seems negligible. Lipman and Seppi's truth revelation result requires, inter alia, that it be impossible for the second mover to falsely refute the true state. If the first mover/defendant/surgeon has actually taken adequate care and makes a presentation that is contingently so interpreted, and if a given presentation by the second mover/plaintiff/patient would be interpreted as a refutation of the surgeon's assertion, such presentation must be, in the state of adequate care, infinitely costly for the plaintiff.

Moreover, for truth revelation to work, any allowance for paucity in the evidence available to the second mover must be compensated for by additional richness in the evidence available to the first mover. Whenever there is no means for the second mover to distinguish state s from state s' (that is, whenever every feasible second mover report that contains s also contains s'), there must be a first mover report that is of zero cost when the true state is s and of infinite cost when the true state is s'. Thus, if the patient cannot distinguish best practice and negligence, there must (again) be a report that is feasible for the surgeon if she followed best practice and impossible for the surgeon if she was negligent.

4.4.5. Other problems There are other drawbacks to omission models in addition to the severity of the no-lying assumption. Several important issues are masked by the extreme binary nature of evidence costs, as discussed in Section 4.4.3 above. For instance, the manner in which the structure of evidence costs determines the range of supportable rewards and punishments is hidden from view. In an omission model, the stakes of the case are never so large as to inspire the production of false evidence; the cost of false evidence is infinite. Furthermore, all evidence that is actually presented in an omissions model is of zero cost (or at least constant cost), and so the question of how to design efficiently evidentiary process – taking account of the potential tradeoff between detail and certainty, on the one hand, and the deadweight cost of investigation and presentation, on the other – is simply not encountered in this literature.

These points will resurface in Section 5.2.1 when the omission model is compared to the costly signaling model.

5. Evidence as Endogenous Cost Signaling

Responding in part to the drawbacks of omission models, Sanchirico (1995, 2000, 2001b) analyzes the production and interpretation of legal evidence in a world in which parties can and will attempt to mislead the fact finder whenever it is in their interest to do so, and in whatever manner furthers those interests. This allowance necessitates viewing evidence production – to the extent that one believes it is at all effective – as a form of differential cost signaling, as described below.

These papers also take the additional step of explicitly linking evidence production to social goals beyond litigation per se. To the extent that legal evidence production is effective at the specific task of setting ex ante incentives in the "primary activity" – incentives to, for instance, refrain from physical violence, take adequate precaution, adopt safe product designs, comply with environmental regulations, disclose material adverse information, or fulfill contractual promises – the signaling costs of legal evidence must be endogenous to parties' primary activity decisions.[45]

These two elements of the endogenous cost signaling approach – costly signaling and the primary activity-endogeneity of signaling costs – are discussed in sequence in the next two subsections.

5.1. Exogenous cost signaling

5.1.1. In general The idea of exogenous cost signaling is often attributed to Spence (1974), who models educational attainment as a signal of natural ability. It is, in fact, also the basis of Mirrlees' (1971) optimal income tax model.[46] Almost 40 years after publication of these papers, costly signaling remains a commonly deployed mechanic in economic modeling generally. Yet it is oddly uncommon in the economics literature on legal evidence, for which it is arguably perfectly suited.

Spence's approach was roughly this: Suppose an employer would be willing to pay higher wages to individuals of higher ability if only she knew

---

[45] A fair portion of the economics analysis of procedure also grounds itself in primary activity incentives. However, this literature does not consider how claims are proven. Instead, it assumes exogenous probabilities (or probability functions) for various trial outcomes and focuses instead on filing, settlement, and fee shifting provisions. See Section 2 above.

[46] In some quarters, it is regarded as important to distinguish "signaling" from "screening." By "signaling" I mean the phenomenon whereby different types find it in their interest to take different observable actions, without regard to whether such phenomenon arises "naturally" or is in response to a menu of choices laid out ahead of time by a principal.

who these individuals were. Merely asking job candidates whether they are of high ability won't do: given the prospect of a higher wage, many candidates would answer "yes" whatever the truth. A candidate's possession of a college degree might, however, act as a more reliable signal. Even though individuals of all abilities could conceivably raise their wage by earning a degree, this might be cost justified only for individuals of high ability, for whom earning the degree is less arduous.

One may agree or disagree with this account of education. But Spence's (1974) general point regarding credible information transmission has resonance: an individual's action reliably "signals" that she is of a particular "type" – i.e., has particular characteristics or knows particular information – when it would not have been in her interest to take that action were she some other type. In other words, talk is cheap and actions speak louder than words.

5.1.2. Applied to legal evidence In the case of legal evidence, parties' "types" are what they know about the event or condition in question, or how they acted in the primary activity. The relevant actions/signals are parties' "performances" before the fact finder. This includes whether they present documents and things that are difficult to forge, as well as whether the witnesses they offer give consistent, detailed, robust and coordinated testimony. Focusing on the role of cognitive limitations, Sanchirico (2004a) explains why these "performances" might be more costly for some "types" than for others.

Assuming that such cost differences exist – at least probabilistically – their role is illustrated by the following example. Suppose that some piece of evidence cost $10 to produce when it is real and $100 when it is fake. If it is understood that production of this piece of evidence increases the party's payoffs at litigation by some amount strictly between $10 and $100, then the evidence would be worth producing only when it is real. That is, the fact finder may reliably deduce that the evidence is real from the fact that it is produced, because it would not have been in the party's interest to produce it otherwise.

One could question whether evidence is reliably more expensive to fake than to truthfully present. One could also question whether litigation payoffs can be reliably calibrated to separate the truthful from the untruthful (though we shall see that separation is not necessary). Yet, arguably, something like the dynamic in this (albeit stark) example must be at work if evidence production is to have value in a world of interested parties and hidden information.[47]

---

[47] Rubinfeld and Sappington (1987) appear to model legal evidence as

Table 9.3 Omission model version

State	Present evidence	Do not present evidence
1	0	0
2	∞	0

Table 9.4 Costly signaling version

State	Present evidence	Do not present evidence
1	$10	$0
2	$100	$0

5.1.3. Comparison to omission models   Before moving on to endogenous cost signaling, it is worth comparing exogenous cost signaling with the zero/infinite cost interpretation of omission models (see Section 4.2.4). It could be said that exogenous cost signaling smoothes the cost structure relative to this interpretation of omission models. Whereas the cost of an evidentiary performance must be either zero or infinite in omissions models, it may have some middling value in exogenous cost evidence models. Alternatively, one can say that omissions models rule out the choice to lie and fabricate (what is possible at infinite cost is, in fact, not possible), whereas exogenous cost signaling models incorporate such choices into the analysis. Moreover, exogenous cost signaling models recognize even truth-consistent evidentiary presentations are expensive, which raises several interesting issues of system design.

Tables 9.3 and 9.4 show the omission model version and the costly signaling version, respectively, of the numerical example in the previous section. These tables help to clarify the difference between the two approaches.

Under the omissions model, if the state is 1, no matter how small the (positive) "reward" for presenting the evidence, the party always presents it. Moreover, when she presents it, the social cost is zero. On the other hand, if the state is 2, then no matter how large the reward for presenting the evidence, the party never presents it.

---

differential cost signaling. A closer look, however, reveals that their model is an exogenous probability function model, as discussed above in Section 2.2.

Under the "smoothed" costly signaling version, if the true state is 1, the agent presents the evidence if and only if the reward is greater than $10, and this cost (which includes the cost of investigation and presentation) is added to the social cost of litigation. Notice that even though the evidence is true, the party will not present it, if the reward for doing so is insufficient. On the other hand, if the state is 2, then the agent presents the evidence if and only if the reward exceeds $100, and this larger amount is added to the social cost of litigation. Even though the evidence is false, the party will still present it, if the stakes are high enough.

Two issues arise naturally in the costly signaling model that are absent from the omission model.

First, notice that, in the costly signaling version, the agent's payoff in state 1 cannot be more than $90 greater than her payoff in state 2. In state 2, the agent always has the option of paying an additional $90 in evidence costs to achieve the reward (or lesser punishment) that is available to her in state 1. Thus, the structure of evidence costs imposes limits on implementable payoff differences across states. This phenomenon does not arise in omission models.

Second, suppose there was another evidentiary performance whose costs were $5, $50 rather than $10, $100. This new evidentiary performance imposes lower costs on society, but is only capable of producing a payoff difference of $45, as opposed to $90. Thus, a potential tradeoff arises between the size of the payoff difference that is implemented and the deadweight cost of evidence production. This phenomenon also does not arise in omission models.

The second phenomenon suggests another drawback of omission models. Section 4.4 criticized the assumption in omission models that there exists evidence that is of infinite (or prohibitive) cost when the state that it is taken to represent is not true. The tradeoff discussed in the last paragraph points to the fact that existence is not the only issue. Even if effectively-impossible-to-fake evidence did exist, it might be woefully inefficient. Suppose it were true that evidence that was extremely expensive when false was also quite expensive, though less so, when true. Perhaps the many witnesses, documents, and things that make the performance so difficult to fake, also make it difficult to present truthfully. Thus, imagine that there is another piece of evidence in the example above that costs $1,000,000 (which we will regard as effectively infinite) to present when false, and $10,000 to present when true. If system design requirements were such that the payoff difference need only be $85, it would be much more efficient to use the $10, $100 evidence. The latter is sufficiently difficult to forge, and much cheaper when truthfully presented. These kinds of cost considerations are very real; they are frequently cited in evidence case law and in the history of evidentiary rule-making. (See, for example, Federal Rule of Evidence 403.)[48]

5.2. Endogenous cost signaling

5.2.1. Basic structure Sanchirico (1995, 2000, 2001b) ties the idea of evidence as a costly signal directly to the creation of primary activity incentives by positing that parties' evidence costs are not exogenous but rather endogenous to their behavior in the primary activity. The gist of the model is apparent in the following simple example.

A regulator wishes to induce firms to comply with a particular regulation, despite the fact that compliance costs firms an additional $100,000. The regulator requires that at the end of the period each firm appear before a review board to "present evidence" of its compliance. Based solely on this evidence, the review board then decides whether and how much to fine the firm.

In order for the regulator to induce compliance in this setting, it is both necessary and sufficient that it identify some form of presentation or performance before the review board, some "evidence," whose production costs for the firm vary appropriately with the firm's compliance activity.

To illustrate that the appropriate production cost differences can be *sufficient*, suppose that compliance happens to lower the firm's cost of a particular presentation from $140,000 to $20,000. Let the regulator announce prior to the firm's compliance decision that it will fine the firm $130,000 unless it presents this evidence before the review board. How does the firm react? First, consider its choice of what to present to the review board contingent on whether it has complied. If the firm has complied, the presentation would cost $20,000, but save $130,000 in fines; hence, the firm's "best case" would be to present the $20,000 evidence and avoid the fine. If the firm has not complied, the presentation would cost $140,000 to produce, which is more than it would save in fines. The firm's "best case" would now be to simply show up and pay the fine. Therefore, the firm's prospective payoffs at the review board hearing will be $-\$20,000$ if it complies, and $-\$130,000$ otherwise. Consequently, compliance increases the firm's prospective hearing payoff by $110,000. Stepping back to the firm's choice

---

[48] Compare the preceding two points (from Sanchirico 1995, 2000 and 2001b) to the later analysis in Deneckere and Severinov (2003), which claims to achieve zero cost implementability with small cost differentials. Deneckere and Severinov assume the existence of a zero cost message across which separation is effected. Moreover, the cost differentials they refer to are for per period costs in a model allowing any number of periods.

in the primary activity, we see that this $110,000 benefit outweighs compliance's $100,000 direct cost, and so the firm chooses to comply.

To illustrate that such endogenous cost differences are necessary for incentive setting, suppose the regulator made avoiding the $130,000 fine dependent on a form of evidence whose presentation cost was always $50 regardless of the firm's compliance behavior. Then the firm would always present the evidence at the hearing, regardless of its compliance choice, and its prospective payoffs at the hearing would always be −$50. The hearing would then be irrelevant to its compliance choice, and so it would make this choice solely according to compliance's $100,000 direct cost – i.e., it would choose not to comply. The same problem crops up if the designated evidence always costs the firm $1,000,000. In this case, the firm would never present the evidence and would always lose $130,000 at the hearing, regardless of its compliance activities; the hearing would again be irrelevant to its compliance decision. What is important is not that the evidence be costly to present, but that presentation costs tend to be lower following compliance.

5.2.2. Implications and applications

5.2.2.1. TRUTH REVELATION VERSUS PRIMARY ACTIVITY INCENTIVE SETTING In most scholarship on legal evidence, finding out what really happened between the parties is taken to be the objective of trial. Consider the widespread use of the phrase "fact finding" to describe the central activity of trial. And recall that the chief issue in the literature on omission models is whether there is truth revelation. In an endogenous cost signaling model, by contrast, the reason to have trials is to create primary activity incentives. Importantly, truth finding is neither sufficient nor even necessary for this task. What is important for truth finding is some separation in evidentiary actions. What is important for primary activity incentive setting is sufficient separation in evidentiary payoffs. In an endogenous cost signaling model, either of these may occur without the other.

It is fairly clear that truth finding is insufficient for incentive setting – that some separation in evidentiary actions does not imply sufficient separation in litigation payoffs. In the example that was provided above to illustrate the basic mechanic of endogenous cost signaling, imagine dividing all the dollar figures by 1000 – except compliance costs, which remain at $100,000. The firm still presents the evidence (now costing either $140 or $20) if and only if it has complied. Therefore, the regulator still learns the truth about compliance. However, compliance increases the firm's prospective hearing payoff by only $110, which is insufficient to the additional $100,000 primary activity cost of compliance.

To see that truth finding is unnecessary – that sufficient separation in evidentiary payoffs is possible without any separation in evidentiary actions – consider again the example from above with all numbers restored to their original magnitudes. Recall that the regulator announced that it would fine the firm $130,000 unless it presented the evidence costing either $140,000 or $20,000. With this reward structure, only the compliant firm presents the evidence. Thus, the regulator learns whether the firm has been compliant. But the fact that the regulator learned the truth from the evidence was purely collateral. What mattered was the fact that the hearing payoffs were sufficiently higher for the compliant firm than for the noncompliant firm. And since evidence production costs differ, this does not require that compliant and noncompliant firms present different evidence. Suppose, for example, that the regulator instead announced that the firm would be fined $150,000 if it did not present the evidence. Then both compliant and noncompliant firms would find it worthwhile to present the evidence, and the regulator would never learn whether a given firm had been compliant or not. On the other hand, the hearing payoffs for both firms would now consist solely of presentation costs, and the difference in these costs (between $140,000 and $20,000) would still be enough to overcome the additional $100,000 cost of compliance in the primary activity.[49]

---

[49] This phenomenon should be distinguished from other differences between primary activity incentive setting and truth finding that have been identified in the literature.

First, Schrag and Scotchmer (1994) show (Propositions 1 and 2) that the optimal threshold quantum of evidence for guilt is generally lower when the object is taken to be error minimization, rather than deterrence maximization. Assuming false convictions and false acquittals are equally weighted, trial error is proportional to $P(I|C)P(C) + P(G|A)P(A)$, where I is true innocence, G is true guilt, C is conviction and A is acquittal. Deterrence, on the other hand, is proportional to the difference between the probability of conviction given true guilt and the probability of conviction given true innocence: $P(C|G) - P(C|I)$. Using $P(C|G) = 1 - P(A|G)$ and the definition of conditional probability (see Section 3.1 above), this difference may be written as

$$1 - \left(\frac{P(I|C)P(C)}{P(I)} + \frac{P(G|A)P(A)}{P(G)} \right).$$

Now, choosing x to maximize $1 - f(x)$ is the same as choosing x to minimize $f(x)$. Thus, maximizing this set-off expression immediately above is different from minimizing $P(I|C)P(C) + P(G|A)P(A)$ if (and only if) $P(I) \neq P(G)$. In particular, if $P(G) < P(I)$, as in Schrag and Scotchmer (1994), then deterrence

Evidence: theoretical models 251

5.2.2.2. QUESTIONING THE EMPHASIS ON "VERIFIABILITY" IN CONTRACTS SCHOLARSHIP Contract theorists sometimes suggest that it is optimal for contracts to condition obligations only on contingencies that can be "verified" to a court (see, e.g., Hart and Moore 1988; Schwartz 1992). One implication of this principle, it would seem, is that an optimal contract should not specifically induce parties to fabricate evidence should a legal dispute arise.

Yet, to most contracting parties, verifiability is an intermediate goal. Adjudication creates value primarily through its ex ante effect on performance incentives. Anticipating the judicial resolution of future disputes, contracting parties are likely to be interested in the likelihood or cost of judicial truth finding only to the extent that the court's ability to discern the truth efficiently improves contract incentives and the gains from trade.

Indeed, Sanchirico and Triantis (2008) argue that the parties themselves might prefer to permit evidence fabrication as part of a conscious contracting strategy that emphasizes efficient performance incentives over accuracy or fairness in the resolution of disputes.

The authors make their point using a probabilistic endogenous cost

---

maximization puts more weight than error minimization on reducing $P(G|A)P(A)$, the incidence of false acquittals.

Second, Kaplow and Shavell (1996) assert that accuracy in the assessment of damages has zero impact on incentives. The specific claim is that in a world in which there is perfect information about whether or not an accident has occurred, and precautionary choice is binary (reasonable care or not), there is no incentive difference between charging the injurer with the harm that she expected to cause or the harm that she actually did cause, even though the later assessment of damages is in a sense "more accurate." The more general point, implicit in Kaplow and Shavell (1996), is that, when implementing a hidden action with a noisy signal, some of the information in the signal may be superfluous. This will occur when the dimensionality of the signal space exceeds the dimensionality of alternative actions. A similar issue arises in Section 6 below.

Third, Sanchirico's (2001a) analysis of character evidence hinges on the fact that evidence can be informative of conduct and yet not be affected by such conduct. "Trace" evidence such as fingerprints and eyewitness recollections are both informative of the act and are byproducts of conduct. In contrast, "predictive evidence" (e.g., character evidence), though it may rationally change the fact finder's assessment of the likelihood that defendant acted in a particular way, is the same whether or not defendant actually did act in that way. If the object is to guess whether the defendant engaged in the conduct, then both types of evidence are useful. But if the object is to affect whether the defendant engages in the conduct, only trace evidence of that conduct is useful. Only trace evidence changes with conduct. Thus, keying penalties and rewards to the production of trace evidence is the only way to make penalties and rewards change with conduct. And making penalties and rewards change with conduct is the only way to create incentives.

signaling model of evidence. A buyer and a seller design a sales contract in which they seek to motivate the seller to "perform" (e.g., deliver a good or service of a particular quality within a particular time frame). In particular, they wish to induce the seller to perform while incurring the lowest possible prospective litigation costs.

The buyer can sue under the contract to collect damages and, in litigation, can present either true or fabricated evidence.[50] An "evidentiary state" is defined to be the quantum of truly existing evidence of nonperformance, and the probability of a given evidentiary state is endogenous to whether the seller in fact performed. True evidence of nonperformance is costly for the buyer to present, and the buyer can choose to present all or part of the existing quantity of such evidence. Importantly, the buyer may also choose to present a quantum of evidence that exceeds the quantity of existing evidence. That is, the buyer may also fabricate evidence of nonperformance. The marginal cost of fabricated evidence is higher than that of true evidence.

Because the parties care about litigation costs, and because fabricated evidence is more expensive, the parties would prefer – all else the same – to induce seller performance without inducing the buyer to go beyond the quantity of truly existing evidence of nonperformance. Were this factor the only consideration, the parties would indeed wish to avoid the circumstance in which the reward that the buyer receives for evidence of nonperformance is so great that it induces the buyer to fabricate. Avoiding this circumstance would effectively bound the seller's liability (which equals the buyer's reward for evidence) in each state.

However, all else is not the same. The effect on the seller's ex ante performance incentive of increasing the seller's liability in any given evidentiary state depends in part on the difference between the probability that the state will occur if the seller performs (p) and the probability that the state will occur if the seller does not perform (q). Moreover, the effect on ex ante litigation costs of the buyer's presentation of a given unit of evidence of nonperformance depends not only on the ex post cost of such unit of evidence, but also on the ex ante likelihood that such state will occur (r). Thus, ignoring for a moment the difference in cost between truthful and fabricated evidence, the parties can reduce the cost of achieving any given

---

[50] Bull (2008b) studies implementability in an extension of this model that allows both sides to present evidence. That paper emphasizes that costly evidence can facilitate Nash implementation by enabling the principal to punish one side without rewarding the other, even when the transfer function is assumed to be zero-sum.

performance incentive by increasing the seller's sanction in states in which the ratio $r/(q-p)$ is low and reducing it where such ratio is high.

The consideration described in the immediately preceding paragraph constitutes a second factor in optimal contract design, and it is independent of the difference in cost between truthful and fabricated evidence. Importantly, this second factor may well be decisive. Specifically, where the ratio $r/(q-p)$ ranges widely across different evidentiary states – and so is much greater in some states than in others – the parties may prefer to increase the seller's liability in states with low ratios even if that requires paying the greater evidentiary costs of the fabrication by the buyer that is thereby induced in those states.

5.2.2.3. "PRESUMPTIONS" AND LITIGATION-PRIMARY ACTIVITY FEEDBACK Bernardo, Talley, and Welch [BTW] (2000) apply the idea of endogenous evidence costs (Sanchirico 1995, 2000, 2001b) to study the effect of legal "presumptions." The definition and real impact of legal presumptions is a complex and unresolved issue in evidence scholarship. In BTW (2000), the effect of legal presumptions is interpreted as a parameter in the kind of exogenous probability function studied in Posner (1973), as discussed in Section 2.2.[51]

The theoretical analysis in BTW (2000) concerns the positive effect of presumptions on litigation and primary activity behavior. Normative issues regarding the optimal design of litigation are also analyzed, but the analysis is confined to numerical simulations. BTW apply their findings to three substantive law areas: private securities litigation, the business judgment rule in Corporations law, and fiduciary duties to lenders in financially distressed firms.

The remainder of this discussion concerns BTW's positive findings and the structure of the BTW model.

BTW's positive findings center on the counterintuitive consequences of feedback effects from litigation design to primary activity behavior. The authors highlight the possibility that shifting "presumptions" in favor of defendants may increase, rather than decrease, plaintiff filings and may even result in a larger, rather than a smaller, frequency of plaintiff victory among filed cases. These effects can be explained by imagining that the changes induced by modifying the presumption occur in sequence.

The shift in the presumption initially increases the (potential) defendant's

---

[51] In BTW (2000), the system designer is effectively constrained to choose a liability-per-evidence schedule from within the parameterized class of contest success functions that BTW consider.

litigation payoffs. This is true regardless of the defendant's marginal cost of evidence (which may be "high" or "low"; evidence costs are linear). Given BTW's functional form assumptions,[52] however, the increase in litigation payoffs is greater for high marginal evidence cost defendants. The defendant has high marginal evidence costs if and only if she has "shirked" in the primary activity. Thus, the favorable shift in the "presumption" increases the defendant's incentive to shirk. As a result, the defendant more often shirks. Therefore, given a "bad outcome" in the primary activity, the likelihood that this outcome is a result of the defendant's shirking – and not just bad luck – is now greater than it was before the shift in the presumption.[53]

When (and only when) there is a bad outcome, the (potential) plaintiff may choose to file suit against the (potential) defendant. The plaintiff chooses whether to file based on his expected litigation payoffs. These expected payoffs are determined in part on his assessment of the chance that the bad outcome has been caused by the defendant's shirking, and that the defendant thereby has high marginal evidence costs. (The plaintiff does not directly observe the defendant's evidence costs or primary activity choices.)

What impact does shifting the presumption in favor of defendants have on the number/frequency of filings? There are three effects.

The first effect is the most direct: conditional on a bad outcome, and conditional on the defendant's marginal evidence cost, the change in the presumption in favor of defendants lowers the plaintiff's expected litigation payoffs, and thereby acts to reduce filings.

Second, however, conditional on a bad outcome, the defendant is more likely to have shirked, and so more likely to have high marginal evidence costs. Hence, the defendant is more likely to present less evidence. This acts to increase the plaintiff's expected litigation payoff. Notice that this second effect is a result of litigation-primary activity feedback: litigation design influences primary activity behavior, which in turn influences litigation outcomes. If the second effect dominates the first, then there will be more filed cases *per bad outcome*. This is the possibility that BTW emphasize.

Third, because the defendant more often shirks, there will be more bad outcomes. This will also act to increase the number of filed cases. This third effect, another kind of litigation-primary activity feedback effect,

---

[52] As noted, BTW employ a kind of contest success function. See Section 2.2.
[53] The point in this sentence follows from the odds formulation of Bayes' rule, as presented in Section 3.1 above. Let G be the event "shirking," and let E be the event "bad outcome."

is not emphasized in BTW and has deep roots in the law and economics literature on litigation.

What is the impact of the shift in the presumption on the frequency of plaintiff victory at trial? Consider a filed case after the change in the presumption. Per the first effect identified above, the presumption has shifted against the plaintiff, which lowers the plaintiff's chance of victory. However, per the second effect, the defendant is more likely to have high marginal cost of evidence, and so more likely to present less evidence. This increases the chance of plaintiff victory given any level of plaintiff evidence. One possible result, therefore, is that the plaintiff more often wins filed cases – despite the fact that the litigation playing field has been tilted against him.

5.2.2.4. ALLOCATION OF PROOF BURDENS AND STRATEGIC COMPLEMENTARITIES IN EVIDENTIARY CHOICE   Sanchirico (2008) uses an endogenous cost signaling model of evidence to investigate the question of which party in litigation should be assigned the burden of proof. He finds some justification for the regularity in actual law that the burden of proof is assigned to the opponent of the party whose primary activity incentives are being set by the law in question – as when the plaintiff has the burden of proving the defendant's negligence and the defendant the burden of proving the plaintiff's contributory negligence.

Sanchirico (2005) generalizes these findings by considering the question of how optimal litigation design structures strategic complementarities between parties' evidentiary choices. The payoff structure of the adversarial litigation game is such that one party strategically complements (i.e., mimics her opponent's advances and retreats), while the other strategically substitutes (i.e., does the opposite of her opponent). Which party plays which role depends on how the litigation transfer function – the mapping from evidence onto liability – is structured. Since the litigation transfer function is a policy choice, the question arises: should litigation be designed to induce the plaintiff to strategically complement and the defendant to substitute, or vice versa? On the basis of an asymmetry derived from the envelope theorem, Sanchirico (2005) argues that the answer depends on whether and whose primary activity incentives are being set by the particular evidentiary contest in question. Within each subsidiary evidentiary contest, the "incentive target" should be induced to complement and her adversary to substitute. In some cases, the defendant will be the incentive target, as when the issue is the defendant's negligence or contractual breach. In other cases, the plaintiff will be the target, as when the defendant defends by claiming that the plaintiff has been "contributorily negligent."

256 *Procedural law and economics*

The analysis of the optimal allocation of proof burdens in Sanchirico (2008), cited above, is a special case of the general phenomenon described in Sanchirico (2005). As discussed in the former paper, the party who is *not* assigned the proof burden tends to be the one who strategically complements. Thus, to induce the incentive target to complement, per Sanchirico (2005), is to assign the proof burden to the opponent of the incentive target.[54]

6. Correlated Private Information
The potential for exploiting multiple agents' correlated private information has been extensively studied in the mechanism design literature, most notably in the context of auction design. See, for example, Crémer and McLean (1985, 1988); Hermalin and Katz (1991). In its simplest manifestation, the idea is to gather information about one agent's "type" (i.e., one agent's private information) from the report of a second agent regarding the second agent's own type. This is possible if the agents' types are not statistically independent. Moreover, if the second agent's type report is used only to set the first agent's payoffs, then the second agent has no affirmative incentive to misreport her type. The example below – specifically the discussion in Section 6.2.1 – illustrates this basic principle.

Sanchirico (2000) studies correlated private information in the context of legal evidence.[55] In that model, correlated private evidence works side by side with endogenous cost signaling (as discussed in Section 5) and a tradeoff between these two sources of information is identified and analyzed. This section begins with a general discussion, then provides an extended numerical/diagrammatic example, and lastly discusses an historical application.

6.1. General Discussion
Extracting useful information from interested parties by means of endogenous cost signaling, as described in Section 5, is a costly endeavor: the very signaling costs that give the evidence meaning are otherwise a deadweight loss to the system. This raises the question: why does the system not

---

[54] Bull (2008a) extends the analysis of endogenous cost evidence models by considering dynamic evidence production games with randomization and public messages.

[55] As discussed below, an important and novel wrinkle in this application of correlated types is that the rank of the opponents' joint signal is endogenous to the mechanism, since it depends on the collection of signals that inspire suit and the number of individuals involved in each suit.

garner all necessary information from (relatively) *uninterested* "parties" so as to reduce these evidence costs?

Employing the correlated type reports of uninterested parties has its own costs. The efficacy of such "third-party information" is endogenous to system design. It is tied to the breadth of circumstances triggering suit and the number of individuals participating in each litigation. Both of these factors go to what the mechanism design literature refers to as the "rank" of the information provided by third parties.[56] If, for instance, suit occurs in only one state of the world and there is only one third-party participant who makes a report that may take only one of two values, then the signal received by the court from this individual is of low rank, and will be of limited use in creating an incentive for the defendant to take a middling action – such as reasonable precaution, as opposed to negligence or extreme caution. This phenomenon is illustrated in the numerical example in Section 6.2 below – specifically, Section 6.2.2.

The fact that the efficacy of "third-party information" is tied to the breadth of circumstances triggering suit and the number of individuals participating in each suit implies that the cost of obtaining information in this manner accrues primarily in terms of the "fixed costs" of holding hearings – as opposed to the "variable costs" of the evidence therein "produced," which may be attributed to endogenous cost signaling. The more often suits are filed and the greater the number of participants per suit, the greater the imputed rent on the space used, the greater the salaries and wages of staff, and – most importantly – the greater the opportunity cost, in terms of lost production and leisure, of participation by the parties.

A fundamental tradeoff thus arises between the fixed costs of holding hearings and the variable cost of the evidence produced therein. Relying on interested parties necessitates costly evidence production. Relying instead on less interested observers necessitates more frequent hearings and/or greater attendance at each, and so greater fixed costs.

---

[56] See, e.g., Hermalin and Katz (1991). The term rank is used because the concept is directly related to the rank (per linear algebra) of a key matrix, the rows of which correspond to possible action choices and the columns of which correspond to states.

Unique to the model described in the text, the rank of the information provided by third parties is endogenous to the mechanism because it depends on the breadth of circumstances triggering suit and the number of parties involved in each, both of which are determined by system design.

258 *Procedural law and economics*

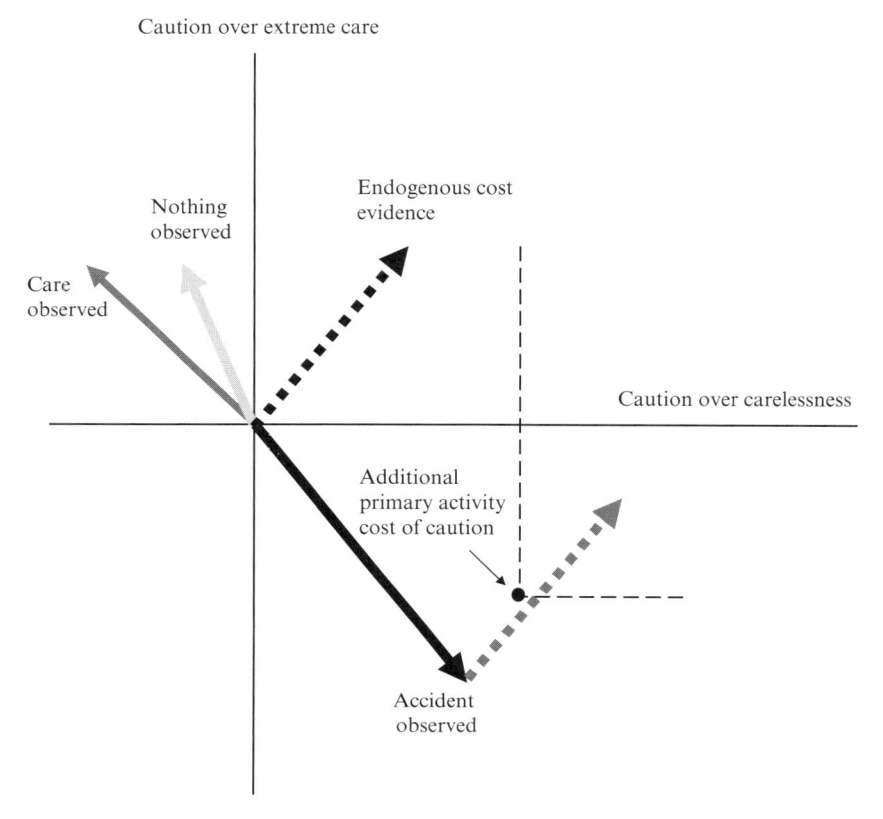

Figure 9.1 The basic mechanics of correlated private information

6.2. Numerical/Diagrammatic example

The following numerical example – whose essential structure is depicted in Figure 9.1 – illustrates the basic tradeoff between costly evidence production and third-party information.[57] The example describes two liability schedules that implement a middling action choice ("Caution"), the first having more frequent filings and less evidence production than the second. In order to keep the example manageable, let us assume that liability and award are "decoupled" (i.e., parties' awards and payments are not neces-

---

[57] This example is taken from Sanchirico (2000).

sarily zero sum),[58] and let us restrict attention to the effect of exogenous increases in the fixed costs of suits.

There are two agents, an "observer" (he) and a "caretaker" (she).

In the first phase of the model, the caretaker chooses one of three action levels in a tort-like primary activity, "Carelessness," "Caution," and "Extreme Care." All else the same, the caretaker prefers carelessness over caution and caution over extreme care.

The caretaker's primary activity choice probabilistically determines both the signal observed by the observer (the observer's "type") and the caretaker's (constant marginal) evidence costs (the caretaker's "type"). The caretaker's type is either low or high. The signal observed by the observer takes one of three values, "accident," "neutral," or "care" (that is, taken by the caretaker).

In the second phase of the model, after observing his signal, the observer decides whether to "file suit." If he files suit, a hearing occurs (there is no settlement in this model) and the caretaker and observer each incur a fixed cost F in attending this hearing.

During this hearing, the third phase of the model, the observer is given a chance to report her observation and the caretaker to present costly evidence. The principal then metes out monetary rewards and punishments based on this presentation. The principal does this according to a function that the principal announced and committed to before the caretaker made her primary activity choice.

The numerical details are as follows: The caretaker's possible actions, "carelessness," "caution," and "extreme care" impose primary activity costs on the caretaker of $60, $100, and $120, respectively. If the caretaker is a low type, her evidence cost for evidence level e is $$e$. If she is a high type, her evidence costs for e are $2e$. Table 9.5 shows the assumed joint and marginal probability distributions over the two agents' types, as determined by the caretaker's primary activity action choice. For example, if the caretaker chooses extreme care, then the probability that the observer sees neutral and that the caretaker's evidence costs are low is 0.20.

6.2.1. Implementing Caution without endogenous cost signaling This section illustrates the basic mechanic of correlated private information by showing how the middling primary activity action, caution, may be implemented (largely) without costly evidence production.

The caretaker's primary activity incentives – incorporating both primary

---

[58] Sanchirico (2000) discusses the impact of imposing the additional constraint that parties' transfers be zero sum.

Table 9.5 Joint and marginal probability distributions over agents' types for each possible primary activity choice of the caretaker

		Carelessness			Caution			Extreme Care		
		Caretaker's Type								
		Low Cost	High Cost	Marginal	Low	High	Marginal	Low	High	Marginal
Observer's Type	Accident	0	0.7	0.7	0.15	0.2	0.35	0	0.1	0.1
	Neutral	0.1	0.1	0.2	0.15	0.15	0.3	0.2	0.2	0.4
	Care	0.1	0	0.1	0.25	0.1	0.35	0.5	0	0.5
	Marginal	0.2	0.8		0.55	0.45		0.7	0.3	

activity costs and hearing payoffs – are depicted in Figure 9.1. The diagram may be interpreted as follows: consider the "basic" liability structure in which the "principal" (the evidence system designer) charges the caretaker $100 if the observer files suit and then reports "accident," and charges the caretaker $0 in all other circumstances. Assume for the moment that the observer files only when he sees accident, and then truthfully reports his observation at the hearing. (We shall relax this assumption below.) Then, based on the three marginal probabilities of accident, one for each of the three caretaker actions, as indicated by the three shaded boxes in Table 9.5, the caretaker's expected hearing payoffs from carelessness, caution, and extreme care are $-\$70 - F$, $-\$35 - F$, and $-\$10 - F$, respectively. For example, if the caretaker is careless, there is a 70% chance of an accident, and so a 70% chance that she will have to pay both the $100 charge and the fixed cost of hearing attendance.

Now, the caretaker is induced to choose caution if the amount (possibly negative) by which the expected hearing payoff from caution exceeds the expected hearing payoff from carelessness (resp. extreme care) is greater than the amount (possibly negative) by which the *primary activity cost* of caution exceeds the primary activity cost of carelessness (resp. extreme care). I shall refer to the first of these differences as the "hearing advantage" (possibly negative) of caution over carelessness (respectively, extreme care). These two hearing advantages for caution are measured along the x and y axes, respectively, in the figure. In the example we are now considering – given that the caretaker is charged $100 (in addition to having to pay F) if the observer files suit and reports "accident" and $0 otherwise, and given that the observer files suit and reports accident when and only when he in fact sees accident – the hearing advantage of caution over carelessness (resp. extreme care) is \$35 $(= (-\$35 - F) - (-\$70 - F))$ (resp. $-\$25$). This vector of hearing advantages for caution, (\$35, $-\$25$), is represented by the darkest solid arrow in the figure.

The other two solid vectors represent the hearing advantages for caution when analogous basic liability schedules are constructed from each of the two other observations, neutral and care. For example, the lightest solid vector represents the hearing advantages of caution given that the caretaker pays \$100 if the observer files suit and reports "neutral" and pays zero otherwise, and given that the observer only files suit and reports neutral when he actually sees neutral.

The space of all possible hearing advantages that can be created by conditioning solely on the (assumed-to-be-truthful) report of the observer is the set of all linear combinations of the three solid vectors – which is to say, the span of the three basic liability vectors. For example, if the caretaker is effectively "fined" \$50 for neutral observations and \$200 for accidents (and the observer files suit in these cases and then reports truthfully), the resulting hearing advantages for caution would correspond to the head-to-tail addition of (a) the vector for neutral shrunk to half its length and (b) the vector for accidents expanded to twice its size.

Now consider the dashed right angle. This angle has as its corner the point (40, -20). This is the caretaker's additional primary activity cost of caution over carelessness (\$100 $-$ \$60 $=$ \$40) and of caution over extreme care (\$100 $-$ \$120 $=$ $-\$20$), respectively. The set of points to the northeast of this point – that is, inside the corner – is the set of all points whose coordinates exceed (\$40, $-\$20$) respectively.

I now describe a liability structure that implements caution without (substantially) costly evidence production. The hearing advantage vectors for accident and neutral span the space in the figure. *A fortiori*, some linear combination of these two vectors enters the dashed right angle and therefore exceeds (\$40, $-\$20$) across both coordinates. It is thus possible to structure a liability schedule based entirely on the observer's report with the property that – assuming the observer is compliant – caution's hearing advantage over each alternative action choice exceeds caution's additional primary activity cost with respect to such action choice. If the principal sets the liability schedule in this way, and can otherwise ensure that the observer, first, files suit in these two circumstances only and, second, truthfully reports his observation, the principal will have induced the caretaker to take the middling activity level, caution.

How then can the principal insure that the observer behaves in this way? Here is one method. Augment the liability schedule discussed in the preceding paragraph as follows: First, given that the observer has filed suit, let the principal reward the caretaker (the negligible amount of) \$1 for presenting (the even more negligible amount of) evidence of $e = 0.90$. Since the caretaker will present $e = 0.90$ when and only when her evidence costs are low (i.e., are $\$e$ rather than $\$2e$), the caretaker's presentation will serve as a (negligibly costly) signal of the caretaker's type. And since the costs and payoffs involved in this extension of the liability schedule are small for the caretaker, the extension will not alter the caretaker's primary activity incentive to choose caution. Second, let the principal award the observer $F + \$1$ when the caretaker does not present the evidence $e = 0.9$ (and so is of high type), and $F - \$0.90$, otherwise.

How will this payoff structure influence the observer's decision of whether to file suit? One can calculate that, whatever the observer's prior beliefs with respect to the caretaker's primary activity choice, he will file suit only when he sees accident or neutral. For example, if the observer is sure that the caretaker has been cautious, but still observes an accident, then his posterior belief that the caretaker is of low type is, from Table 9.5, $0.15/0.35=0.43$.[59] Thus, his expected payoff from the hearing will be $0.57(F + \$1 - F) + 0.43(F - \$0.90 - F) = \$0.183 > 0$, and so he will file suit.

What about the incentive of the observer to truthfully report his type once he is at the hearing? Once at the hearing, the observer's payoffs do not turn on what he reports. Rather, his payoffs turn solely on whether the caretaker presents $e = 0.90$. Having no positive incentive to lie, we may assume that observer reports what he actually sees.[60]

6.2.2. Less frequent suits using endogenous cost signaling Alternatively, the principal can implement caution under a liability schedule in which the observer files suit only when he sees an accident – as opposed to when his observation is either accident or neutral. However, this will require that the principal also relies on the caretaker's presentation of substantially costly evidence.

Figure 9.1 illustrates why the principal cannot rely merely on knowing whether or not the observer has seen "accident." If the principal cannot distinguish between neutral and care – which the principal cannot if suits only arise when accidents occur – then the liability schedule for the caretaker must be constant (e.g., zero) across these observations. As the reader can confirm, any vector that is a linear combination of care and

---

[59] See Section 3.1 for a discussion of Bayes' rule.
[60] The observer can be given a strict incentive to tell the truth once at the hearing – again at negligible cost – if the model is extended to allow for the *observer's* presentation of (negligibly) costly evidence whose cost depends on the observer's type. This would be analogous to the payoff structure surrounding the caretaker's presentation of evidence $e = 0.90$, as discussed in the text.

neutral and that assigns the same coefficient to each of these vectors is a scalar multiple of the accident vector. (This is not a special feature of the numbers chosen for this example, but is a general consequence of the fact that the hearing advantage vectors are constructed from the probabilities of the three observations, which given any primary activity choice, must add to one.[61]) It is clear from the diagram that the principal cannot produce a vector that enters the dashed right angle solely by shrinking or expanding the accident vector.

The more general mathematical phenomenon at work here is this: a requirement that some subset of vectors all receive the same coefficients generally reduces the dimensions of the space spanned by the superset of vectors. Imposing such requirement may thereby render a given system of linear inequalities insoluble. Here there are two linear inequalities – that caution's hearing advantage exceed its additional primary activity costs with respect to both extreme care and carelessness.

Returning to the numerical example, I now explain how caution can be implemented if the caretaker's liability is made a function of both the observer's report of accident and the caretaker's endogenous cost evidence. It is best to begin with the caretaker's incentives (at the hearing and in the primary activity), assuming compliance by the observer. The explanation of the caretaker's incentives has two steps.

First, consider the dashed vector emanating from the origin labeled "endogenous cost evidence." The point of this vector is at ($15, $15), which represents caution's hearing advantages when (1) hearings are held only after the observer sees an accident, and (2) at those hearings, the caretaker receives $200 + F − $0.10 if she presents evidence of $e = 100$, and F otherwise. How so? Once the caretaker is at the accident hearing, she will present $e = 100$ if and only if she is a low type (i.e., has evidence costs $e, rather than $2e). Consequently, the low evidence cost caretaker ends up with hearing payoffs of (roughly) ($200 + F) − ($100 + F) = $100, and the high cost caretaker with payoffs of $F − F = 0. Thus, it is as if the principal rewards the caretaker with $100 in the *joint* event that the observer sees an accident *and* the caretaker is of low type. Now, as Table 9.5 shows, if the caretaker is cautious rather than careless, she increases the chance of this joint event by 0.15 (= 0.15 − 0). Thus, the hearing advantage of

---

[61] Given any primary activity choice a, the probability of accident plus the probability of neutral plus the probability of care must equal 1. That is $p_A(a) + p_N(a) + p_C(a) = 1$. Therefore, given any two primary activity choices, a and b, $(p_A(a) − p_A(b)) + (p_N(a) − p_N(b)) + (p_C(a) − p_C(b)) = 0$. It follows that the three hearing advantage vectors must sum to (vector) zero. Therefore, each hearing advantage vector is a scalar multiple (−1) of the sum of the other two.

caution over carelessness is $15. A similar calculation reveals that the hearing advantage of caution over extreme caution is also $15.

Second, combine the costly evidence scheme just described with a baseline punishment for the caretaker of $100, just for the fact that the observer has filed suit. Diagrammatically, the principal is adding, head to tail, the vector ($15, $15) to the vector for accident. The fact that the summed vector enters the dashed box indicates that caution's hearing advantages jointly exceed its additional primary activity costs. The caretaker thereby is induced to be cautious.

It remains only to ensure that the observer files only when he sees an accident and that he then reports this observation truthfully. The reader can confirm that this can be accomplished by rewarding the observer $2F + \$1$ if the caretaker fails to present evidence $e = 100$ (is of high type), and $0 if the caretaker does make the presentation. As can be gleaned from Table 5, whatever the observer believes regarding the caretaker's primary activity choice, if he sees accident, he believes that the caretaker is strictly more likely to be high than to be low, and if he sees anything else, he believes that the caretaker is no more likely to be high than to be low. Given that the observer incurs attendance costs of F if he files, and given that his reward is slightly less than $2F$ when the caretaker is of high type and zero otherwise, the observer will file suit only if he believes that the chance that the caretaker is of high type is strictly greater than the chance that the caretaker is of low type. Thus, the observer will only file when he observes accident.

All told, this second liability structure is as follows. If the observer files suit against the caretaker, and the caretaker fails to produce exonerating evidence ($e = 100$), the observer receives $2F + \$1$ and the caretaker pays $100 - F$. If the caretaker does produce the evidence, the observer gets nothing, whereas the caretaker pays nothing and is reimbursed $100 and F, for her evidence and attendance costs respectively. The caretaker, looking forward to the prospect of suit, including the possibility that she will be able to present evidence to save her from liability, decides that it is worthwhile to choose middling caution rather than carelessness or extreme caution.

6.2.3. Comparison Let us now compare the system costs of the two implementations. In the first implementation, the observer files suit in two circumstances, accident and neutral, the probabilities of which are determined by the fact that the caretaker chooses caution. Such probabilities sum to 0.65. Evidence production costs are *de minimis* in this first implementation. The expected social cost of this two-hearing implementation of caution is thus roughly $(0.65)2F = 1.5F$. Such cost consists solely of the expected fixed cost of hearings. In the second implementation, the agents appear before the court only when there is an accident. Given the caretaker's cautious behavior, this happens with probability 0.35. Therefore the expected fixed cost of hearings is $(0.35)2F = 0.7F$, which is substantially lower than in the first scheme. With probability 0.15, however, the caretaker will find herself in court (the observer having seen accident) and desirous of producing $100 of evidence (the caretaker being of low type). Expected evidence production costs – the expected variable costs of the hearing – are thus $15. Total costs for this second method then are $0.7F$ + $15.

Which is larger – $1.5F$ or $0.7F$ + $15? If the fixed costs of attending hearings are small, the least costly implementation will be the first, the one with hearings in two contingencies. If fixed costs are large, however, then the fact that the first implementation has more hearings will be decisive in making it less efficient. The best alternative will be to suffer the caretaker's evidence production costs in exchange for a reduction in the likelihood that a hearing will be held.

6.3. Application: Historical Evolution of the Jury's Role
The foregoing analysis suggests that increases in the opportunity cost of process, due to increases in labor productivity, were one factor in the gradual shift through English legal history from a system relying mostly on relatively disinterested observers to one relying mostly on costly evidence production by the parties themselves.

Crucial to this historical comparative static is the preliminary theoretical point that increases in both fixed and variable cost parameters have an asymmetric effect on system costs. Increases in the variable costs of producing evidence can be mitigated, in part or whole, by relying on different, less costly evidence. Suppose, for example, that the caretaker's cost of evidence in the numerical example above doubles, so that evidence of e units costs $\$2e$ dollars, rather than $\$e$ dollars, when the caretaker is a low type and $\$4e$, rather than $\$2e$, when the caretaker is a high type. Then the evidence costs and litigation payoff differences that were formerly generated by any level of evidence e are now generated by the level of evidence $\frac{1}{2}e$. Thus, if we now count as two units of evidence what were formerly counted as one, the example goes through in the same way. The same dynamic does not work with respect to the fixed costs of hearings. If the state tries to compensate for the increase in appearance costs by halving the frequency of trials or the number of individuals attending each, it effects a real reduction in the information content of third-party information.

From its origins in the 12th century up until perhaps the beginning of the 15th century, the English jury operated as a bank of witness/investigators: 12 "freemen" from the neighborhood in which the case arose, called upon either to employ their pre-existing knowledge of the matter at hand or to conduct their own investigation. By the 16th century, the jury had come to resemble more the blank-slate panel of modern day. During a late phase of the Industrial Revolution, an act of Parliament allowed parties to waive jury process and by 1900 juries were used in only half of the cases before the High Court. During World War I, the jury was abolished in civil cases due to lack of juror supply – the "temporary" change lasted well beyond World War I. A 1933 law allowed jury trials only by leave of the court; in practice, leave is almost never granted.

At least until 1750 the parties themselves, along with other "interested" persons, were prohibited from testifying or even from presenting documents of their own creation, however long ago they were drafted. Toward the end of the Industrial Revolution, however, amidst a flurry of legal reform spearheaded by Jeremy Bentham and others, restraints on interested parties' ability to testify in older common law procedure were lifted by acts of Parliament. In the modern era, parties' own presentation of costly evidence – including sponsored eyewitnesses, expert witnesses, plain testimony at risk of perjury, and media production – constitutes the main source of information for the English fact finder.

Thus, one may discern in English legal history a shift from reliance on the reports of disinterested third-party observers to reliance on evidence sponsored by the very parties who stood to gain or lose from the court's decision. The transformation is marked by punctuated changes in and around the time of the Industrial Revolution. The asymmetric impact of rising process costs may help to explain these changes. The productive activity that is sacrificed by collecting and preparing evidence and participating in court hearings is an important component of the social cost of legal process. Arguably, these opportunity costs increased, in broad trend, over the course of English legal history following the 13th century, with marked acceleration during the Industrial Revolution, concomitant with increases in labor productivity. The model discussed in this section predicts that an across-the-board increase in the opportunity costs of process would increase the relative cost-effectiveness of endogenous cost signaling as opposed to correlated private information. Such an increase in underlying cost-effectiveness may have been one force (among many) acting to shape actual system design.

7. Conclusion

For scholarly attempts to develop a formal, systematic, mathematically based account of legal evidence, the challenge has not been a lack of available tools. Probability theory, game theory, information economics, and mechanism design offer a wealth of serviceable principles and techniques. The challenge rather has been in determining which of these elements to employ, and in what combination. The pure probabilistic deduction approach to legal evidence makes extensive use of the algebra of conditional probabilities, but almost no use of strategic reasoning. Most of the literature that accounts for strategic considerations – the literature that develops and applies the omission model – seems path-dependently encumbered by assumptions that rule out defining features of legal evidence. Endogenous cost signaling and correlated private information – approaches that combine moral hazard models, asymmetric information models, and probability theory – hold some potential (in the opinion of this author). But such approaches, shadowed as they are by the bowers of pure probabilistic deduction and the omission model, have only begun to take root.

References

Allais, M. (1953), "Le Comportement de l'homme rationnel devant le risque: critique des postulats et axiomes de l'ecole américaine", *Econometrica*, 21 (4), 503–46.
Allen, R. (1986), "A Reconceptualization of Civil Trials", *Boston University Law Review*, 66 (3), 401–37.
Allen, R. and S.A. Jehl (2003), "Burdens of Persuasion in Civil Cases: Algorithms v. Explanations", *Michigan State Law Review*, 2003 (4), 893–944.
Becker, G. (1968), "Crime and Punishment: An Economic Approach", *Journal of Political Economy*, 76 (2), 169–217.
Bernardo, A.E., E. Talley, and I. Welch (2000), "A Theory of Legal Presumptions", *Journal of Law, Economics, and Organization,* 16 (1), 1–49.
Braeutigam, R., B. Owen, and J. Panzar (1984), "An Economic Analysis of Alternative Fee Shifting Systems", *Law and Contemporary Problems*, 47 (1), 173–85.
Bull, J. (2008a), "Mechanism Design with Moderate Evidence Cost", *The B.E. Journal of Theoretical Economics*, 8 (1), Article 15.
Bull, J. (2008b), "Costly Evidence Production and the Limits of Verifiability", *The B.E. Journal of Theoretical Economics*, 8 (1 (Topics)), Article 18.
Bull, J. and J. Watson (2004), "Evidence Disclosure and Verifiability", *Journal of Economic Theory*, 118 (1), 1–31.
Bull, J. and J. Watson (2007), "Hard Evidence and Mechanism Design", *Games and Economic Behavior*, 58 (1), 75–93.
Cohen, Laurence Jonathan (1977), *The Probable and the Provable*, Oxford: Clarendon Press.
Cooter, R. and W. Emons (2003), "Truth-revealing Mechanisms for Courts", *Journal of Institutional and Theoretical Economics*, 159 (2), 259–79.
Cooter, R. and W. Emons (2004), "Truth-bonding and other Truth-revealing Mechanisms for Courts", *European Journal of Law and Economics*, 17 (3), 307–27.
Corchón, L.C. (2007), "The Theory of Contests: A Survey", *Review of Economic Design*, 11 (2), 69–100.
Crémer, J. and R.P. McLean (1985), "Optimal Selling Strategies under Uncertainty for a Discriminating Monopolist when Demands are Interdependent", *Econometrica*, 53 (2), 345–61.
Crémer, J. and R.P. McLean (1988), "Full Extraction of the Surplus in Bayesian and Dominant Strategy Auctions", *Econometrica*, 56 (6), 1247–57.

Daughety, A.F. and J.F. Reinganum (2000), "On the Economics of Trials: Adversarial Process, Evidence, and Equilibrium Bias", *Journal of Law, Economics, and Organization*, 16 (2), 365–94.

Daughety, A.F. and J.F. Reinganum (2011), "Settlement", in Chris W. Sanchirico (ed.), *Procedural Law and Economics, Encyclopedia of Law and Economics*, 2nd edn (Gerrit De Geest, general ed.), Cheltenham, UK and Northampton, MA, USA: Edward Elgar.

Deneckere, R. and S. Severinov (2003), "Mechanism Design and Communication Costs", mimeo, Department of Economics, University of Wisconsin, Madison and Fugua School of Business, Duke University.

Ellsberg, D. (1961), "Risk, Ambiguity, and the Savage Axioms", *Quarterly Journal of Economics*, 75 (4), 643–69.

Farrell, J. (1986), "Voluntary Disclosure: Robustness of the Unraveling Result, and Comments on its Importance", in Ronald E. Grieson (ed.), *Antitrust and Regulation*, Lexington, Mass.: Lexington Books, pp. 91–103.

Finkelstein, M. and W. Fairly (1970), "A Bayesian Approach to Identification Evidence", *Harvard Law Review*, 83 (3), 489–517.

Fischhoff, Baruch (1982), "For those Condemned to Study the Past: Heuristics and Biases in Hindsight", in Daniel Kahneman et al. (eds.), *Judgment under Uncertainty*, Cambridge, UK and New York: Cambridge University Press, pp. 335–41.

Froeb, L.M. and B.H. Kobayashi (1996), "Naive, Biased, yet Bayesian: Can Juries Interpret Selectively Produced Evidence?", *Journal of Law, Economics, and Organization*, 12 (1), 257–76.

Froeb, L.M. and B.H. Kobayashi (2000), "Evidence Production in Adversarial vs. Inquisitorial Regimes", *Economic Letters*, 70 (2), 267–72.

Froeb, L.M. and B.H. Kobayashi (2011), "Adversarial versus Inquisitorial Justice", in Chris W. Sanchirico (ed.), *Procedural Law and Economics, Encyclopedia of Law and Economics*, 2nd edn (Gerrit De Geest, general ed.), Cheltenham, UK and Northampton, MA, USA: Edward Elgar.

Gould, J.P. (1973), "The Economics of Legal Conflicts", *Journal of Legal Studies*, 2 (2), 279–300.

Grossman, S.J. (1981), "The Informational Role of Warranties and Private Disclosure about Product Quality", *Journal of Law and Economics*, 24 (3), 461–89.

Guthrie, C.J., J. Rachlinski, and A. J. Wistrich (2007), "Blinking on the Bench: How Judges Decide Cases", *Cornell Law Review*, 93 (1), 1–43.

Hart, O. and J. Moore (1988), "Incomplete Contracts and Renegotiation", *Econometrica*, 56 (4), 755–85.

Hermalin, B. and M. Katz (1991), "Moral Hazard and Verifiability: The Effects of Renegotiation in Agency", *Econometrica*, 59 (6), 1735–53.

Kahneman, D. and A. Tversky (1973), "On the Psychology of Prediction", *Psychological Review*, 80 (4), 237–51.

Kamin, K.A. and J.J. Rachlinski (1995), "Ex Post ≠ Ex Ante: Determining Liability in Hindsight", *Law and Human Behavior*, 19 (1), 89–104.

Kaplow, L. and S. Shavell (1996), "Accuracy in the Assessment of Damages", *Journal of Law and Economics*, 39 (1), 191–209.

Katz, A. (1988), "Judicial Decisionmaking and Litigation Expenditure", *International Review of Law and Economics*, 8 (2), 127–43.

Katz, A. and C.W. Sanchirico (2011), "Fee Shifting", in Chris W. Sanchirico (ed.), *Procedural Law and Economics, Encyclopedia of Law and Economics*, 2nd edn (Gerrit De Geest, general ed.), Cheltenham, UK and Northampton, MA, USA: Edward Elgar.

Kaye, D. (1979), "The Paradox of the Gatecrasher and Other Stories", *Arizona State Law Journal*, 1979 (1), 101–9.

Kreps, David M. (1990), *A Course in Microeconomic Theory*, Princeton, NJ: Princeton University Press.

Landsman, Stephan (1984), *The Adversary System: A Description and Defense*, Washington, D.C.: American Enterprise Institute for Public Policy Research.

Lempert, R.O. (1977), "Modeling Relevance", *Michigan Law Review*, 75, 1021–57.
Lempert, Richard O., Samuel R. Gross, and James S. Liebman (2000), *A Modern Approach to Evidence: Text, Problems, Transcripts and Cases* (3rd ed.), St. Paul, Minn.: West Publishing. Co.
Lempert Richard O. and Stephen A. Saltzburg (1982), *A Modern Approach to Evidence: Text, Problems, Transcripts and Cases* (2nd ed.), St. Paul, Minn.: West Publishing Co.
Levmore S. (2001), "Conjunction and Aggregation", *Michigan Law Review*, 99 (4), 723–56.
Lipman, B. and D. Seppi (1995), "Robust Inference in Communication Games with Partial Provability", *Journal of Economic Theory*, 66 (2), 370–405.
Milgrom, P.R. (1981), "Good News and Bad News: Representation Theorems and Applications", *Bell Journal of Economics*, 12 (2), 380–91.
Milgrom, P.R., and J. Roberts (1986) "Relying on the Information of Interested Parties", *RAND Journal of Economics*, 17 (1), 18–32.
Mirrlees, J.A. (1971), "An Exploration in the Theory of Optimum Income Taxation", *Review of Economic Studies*, 38 (2), 175–208.
Nisbett, Richard E., Eugene Borgida, R. Crandall, and H. Reed (1976), "Popular Induction: Information is Not Always Informative", in John S. Carroll and John W. Payne (eds.), *Cognition and Social Behavior*, Hillsdale, NJ: Erlbaum Associates, pp. 227–36.
Okuno-Fujiwara M., A. Postlewaite, and K. Suzumura (1990), "Strategic Information Revelation", *Review of Economic Studies*, 57 (1), 25–47.
Posner, R.A. (1973), "An Economic Approach to Legal Procedure and Judicial Administration", *Journal of Legal Studies*, 2 (2), 399–458.
Posner, R.A. (1999), "An Economic Approach to the Law of Evidence", *Stanford Law Review*, 51 (6), 1477–546.
Rubinfeld, D. and D. Sappington (1987), "Efficient Awards and Standards of Proof in Judicial Proceedings", *RAND Journal of Economics*, 18 (2), 308–15.
Sanchirico, C.W. (1995), "Enforcement by Hearing: How the Civil Law Sets Incentives", *Columbia Economics Department Discussion Paper*, No. 95–9603.
Sanchirico, C.W. (2000), "Games, Information and Evidence Production: With Application to English Legal History", *American Law and Economics Review,* 2 (2), 342–80.
Sanchirico, C.W. (2001a), "Character Evidence and the Object of Trial", *Columbia Law Review*, 101 (6), 1227–311.
Sanchirico, C.W. (2001b), "Relying on the Information of Interested – and Potentially Dishonest – Parties", *American Law and Economics Review*, 3 (2), 320–57.
Sanchirico, C.W. (2004a), "Evidence, Procedure, and the Upside of Cognitive Error", *Stanford Law Review*, 57 (2), 291–365.
Sanchirico, C.W. (2004b), "Evidence Tampering", *Duke Law Journal*, 53 (4), 1215–336.
Sanchirico, C.W. (2004c), "Finding Error", *Michigan State Law Review*, 2003 (4), 1189–203.
Sanchirico, C.W. (2005), "Harnessing Adversarial Process: Proof Burdens, Affirmative Defenses, and the Complementarity Principle", *University of Pennsylvania Institute for Law and Economics Research Paper Series*, No. 05–01.
Sanchirico, C.W. (2006), "Detection Avoidance", *New York University Law Review*, 81 (4), 1331–99.
Sanchirico, C.W. (2008), "A Primary-activity Approach to Proof Burdens", *Journal of Legal Studies*, 37 (1), 273–313.
Sanchirico, C.W. and G. Triantis (2008), "Evidentiary Arbitrage: The Fabrication of Evidence and the Verifiability of Contract Performance", *Journal of Law, Economics, and Organization*, 24 (1), 72–94.
Savage, L.J. (1954), *The Foundations of Statistics*, New York: Wiley, 2nd ed. 1972, New York: Dover.
Schrag, J. and S. Scotchmer (1994), "Crime and Prejudice: The Use of Character Evidence in Criminal Trials", *Journal of Law, Economics, and Organization*, 10 (2), 319–42.
Schwartz, A. (1992), "Relational Contracts in the Courts: An Analysis of Incomplete Agreements and Judicial Strategies", *Journal of Legal Studies*, 21 (2), 271–318.

Shavell, S. (1982), "Suit, Settlement, and Trial: A Theoretical Analysis under Alternative Methods for the Allocation of Legal Costs", *Journal of Legal Studies*, 11 (1), 55–81.

Shavell, S. (1989), "Optimal Sanctions and the Incentive to Provide Evidence to Legal Tribunals", *International Review of Law and Economics*, 9 (1), 3–11.

Shin, H.S. (1998), "Adversarial and Inquisitorial Procedures in Arbitration", *RAND Journal of Economics*, 29 (2), 378–405.

Skaperdas, S. (1996), "Contest Success Functions", *Economic Theory*, 7 (2), 283–90.

Sobel, Joel (1985), "Disclosure of Evidence and Resolution of Disputes", in Alvin Roth (ed.), *Game-theoretic Models of Bargaining*, Cambridge, UK: Cambridge University Press.

Spence, A. Michael (1974), *Market Signaling*, Cambridge, Mass.: Harvard University Press.

Stein, A. (2001), "Of Two Wrongs that Make a Right: Two Paradoxes of the Evidence Law and their Combined Economic Justification", *Texas Law Review*, 79 (5), 1199–234.

Symposium (1986), "Probability and Inference in the Law of Evidence", *Boston University Law Review*, 66 (3–4), 377–952.

Tribe, L. (1971), "Trial by Mathematics: Precision and Ritual in the Legal Process", *Harvard Law Review*, 84 (6), 1329–93.

Yee, K.K. (2008), "Dueling Experts and Imperfect Verification", *International Review of Law and Economics*, 28 (4), 246–55.

Cases

Herring v. New York, 422 U.S. 853 (1975).

10 Fee shifting
Avery Wiener Katz and Chris William Sanchirico

1. Introduction

In most Western legal systems, a party who prevails in litigation is generally entitled to indemnification from the losing party for at least part of his or her economic costs of prosecuting the lawsuit. The amount of litigation expenditures that can be recovered, however, varies substantially both among and within individual regimes. In the United States, the predominant rule awards a prevailing litigant what are officially termed 'costs' – typically defined by statute to include filing fees, court reporter charges, printing, copying, and witness fees, and the like – but does not entitle him or her to recover expenditures on attorneys' fees, which are usually of far greater magnitude in the case. Consequently, US litigants can bear significant expense even when they are ultimately vindicated on the merits. In the other common-law countries, in contrast, and indeed in most of the rest of the Western world, winning litigants are entitled to recover attorneys' fees as well as other out-of-pocket costs of litigation.

The substantial increase in expenditures on litigation and dispute resolution in the United States over the last two decades has led both policymakers and scholars to advocate a variety of substantive and procedural reforms in the legal system. The rules for allocating attorneys' fees in civil litigation have drawn particular attention in this regard, with a number of influential commentators recommending a move in the direction of fuller indemnification – or what in the US is usually called, for historical reasons, the 'English' or 'British' rule. Such recommendations have had influence on both public and private lawmakers. In the mid 1990s one of the more prominent and widely supported provisions in the Republican Party's 'Contract with America' platform would have adopted a modified form of the English rule for federal cases brought under diversity jurisdiction. In the late 2000s, as part of the ongoing debate over health care reform, several commentators and policymakers have proposed adopting a 'loser pays' rule as a way to curb medical malpractice costs.

But the ongoing political debate over litigation costs in the US does not seem to have assimilated the main lesson of the economic literature on the topic – that the effects of cost shifting on the amount and intensity of litigation are substantially more complicated than a superficial consideration of the matter might suggest. Indeed, the current state of economic knowledge does not enable us reliably to predict whether a move to fuller indemnification would raise or lower the total costs of litigation, let alone whether it would better align those costs with any social benefits they might generate.

The reason for this agnosticism is straightforward. In short, fee shifting is too coarse a tool for the multifaceted problem that it is meant to solve.

The problem that fee shifting is meant to solve is, in essence, the existence of externalities in the litigation decision making. Most supporters of fee shifting focus on a single negative externality: the costs that plaintiffs impose on both defendants and the public at large in deciding to bring suit. But the allocation of legal costs influences a long list of decision points along the litigation flow, including the decision of how much effort to expend in preparing for and participating in trial, the choice between settlement and trial, the decision to initiate a lawsuit, and the choice to modify one's out-of-court behavior so as to avoid suit in the first place. At each of these decision points, an individual litigant's incentives do not generally conform to the interests of society as a whole. And such divergences of private and social interest vary both in magnitude and direction.

For example, the plaintiff's private decision to bring suit is itself the locus of several opposing externalities. A plaintiff's decision to sue imposes an obvious cost on the defendant and on taxpayers, who foot the bill for public legal institutions. Less obviously, the suit affects litigants in other filed cases by crowding the courts and delaying the resolution of other disputes in the system. The suit also affects these and future litigants by altering the state of legal precedent. Lastly, the suit affects the public at large – both potential violators and their potential victims – by influencing the perceived likelihood of sanctions for violating substantive legal duties.

The decision to pursue a lawsuit to trial rather than settling, as well as the decision to litigate more rather than less intensively, generate analogous external costs and benefits.

Litigation does not, therefore, present a single externality that might be corrected with a single policy tool. It presents a complex bundle of positive and negative externalities whose correction requires an array of policy instruments. Shifting legal fees may indeed repair some externalities but it will fail to address others, and some it may well exacerbate.

This chapter surveys the effects of legal fee shifting on a variety of decisions arising before and during the litigation process. Section 2 provides a brief survey of the practical situations in which legal fee shifting does and does not arise. Section 3 analyzes the effects of indemnification on the incentives to expend resources in litigated cases. Section 4 examines how indemnification influences the decisions to bring and to defend against suit, and Section 5 assesses its effects on the choice between settlement and trial. Section 6 addresses the interaction between the allocation of legal fees and the parties' incentives for efficient primary behavior. Section 7 considers two important variants on simple indemnification: rules that shift costs based on the parties' settlement negotiations (such as US Federal Rule 68 and the English practice of payment into court), and rules that shift costs based on the margin of victory (such as US Federal Rule 11 and the common-law tort of malicious prosecution). Section 8 reviews the empirical literature on legal cost shifting. Section 9 summarizes the discussion and offers conclusions.[1]

2. The Practical Extent of Legal Fee Shifting

This chapter does not attempt to survey the law governing fee shifting, either in the US or elsewhere. For a continually updated account of US state and federal law, see Martin (2005). It should be recognized, however, that there are significant areas of US legal practice that do not follow the traditional American rule. Most important among these are the various federal and state statutes that entitle a successful plaintiff, though not a successful defendant, to court-awarded attorneys' fees as part of a recovery. Similar 'one-way' fee-shifting policies have also been established in both federal and state courts through a combination of statutory interpretation and common-law development, though the scope for such interpretations at the federal level was substantially limited by the Supreme Court in *Alyeska Pipeline Service Co. v. Wilderness Society*. Such provisions and policies, which make up a central part of litigation practice in such fields as civil rights, consumer, and antitrust law, have only some of the effects of the traditional two-way English rule. Second, both federal and state courts have authority to award indemnification to parties who are victimized by abuse of process, though such authority is typically exercised only in response to egregious behavior. Examples include the provisions in Federal Rule of Civil Procedure 11 dealing with frivolous or improper pleadings, and those in Federal Rule of Civil Procedure 37 relating to discovery abuse. US practice also provides litigants with an 'offer-of-judgment' procedure under which a defendant can make a settlement offer to the plaintiff which, if rejected and filed with the court, creates a trigger for partial indemnification. Both of these specialized types of provisions

---

[1] The scholarly literature on fee shifting is vast and it is not possible to discuss every pertinent contribution. This entry describes the seminal papers on the topic as well as a sizable and representative sample of additional contributions.

– sanctions for abuse and offers of judgment – are discussed separately in Section 7 below.

Conversely, even in jurisdictions following the majority or 'English' rule, indemnification for legal costs is substantially less than complete. Court-awarded attorneys' fees obviously do not compensate for the nonmonetary and psychic costs of litigation. Even the monetary amounts awarded, furthermore, are limited by the judge's view of what expenditures are reasonable and, in some jurisdictions (for example, British Columbia), by statutory schedule. Such judicial and statutory caps can and often do hold fee awards below the going market rate for legal representation, forcing winning litigants to pay the difference out of anticipated recoveries or their own pockets (indeed, Leubsdorf 1984, presents evidence that such court-imposed price ceilings were responsible for the historical development of the American rule in the first place). Accordingly, the pure English and American rules discussed below should be understood as ideal polar cases, and the differences among actual jurisdictional practices as ones of degree along a spectrum ranging from lesser to greater indemnification.

Additionally, Donohue (1991b) points out that the American rule is a default rule rather than a mandatory one, in that parties are generally free to provide for indemnification through private contract – either at the time they begin their litigation or, for those disputes arising out of a consensual relationship, in their original agreement. He presents anecdotal evidence that such *ex ante* indemnification terms are widespread, though the provisions he cites seem primarily to be drawn from standardized form contracts and tend to operate asymmetrically in favor of the drafting party: for instance, apartment leases that indemnify landlords but not tenants for attorneys' fees in the event of a dispute over unpaid rent. The scope for fee shifting in the US, therefore, may be significantly greater than is ordinarily supposed. Conversely, there is no apparent bar in England or in the other jurisdictions following the English rule to a partial settlement or stipulation in which the litigants agree in advance to give up their rights to indemnification *ex post*.

Somewhat more problematic, however, are Donohue's further conjectures that such contractual terms are likely to be efficiency-enhancing and that the pattern of such terms will help reveal whether the English or American rule is more efficient. To the extent that indemnification is provided by a one-sided standardized term, there is no guarantee that it promotes the joint interests of the parties. The nondrafting party may fail to notice the indemnification provision at all; and if he does notice it, he may avoid raising it as an issue for fear of revealing himself as someone who anticipates a dispute. Even when such agreements arise out of arm's-length bargaining, furthermore, this does not imply that they are efficient.

As Bernstein (1993) and Shavell (1995) have observed in their respective analyses of alternative dispute resolution, because of the divergence of private and social incentives in litigation, the fact that a particular agreement is in the litigants' *ex post* interest does not necessarily mean that it is socially efficient. The fact that the parties have come to litigation in the first place, moreover, casts doubt on the presumption that they are bargaining in a Coasian fashion.

3. The Effect of Fee Shifting on Trial and Pretrial Expenditures

The standard economic theory of litigation, as developed by Landes (1971), Posner (1973), and Gould (1973), models litigating parties as rational actors who seek to maximize their returns from the litigation process. From this perspective, amounts spent on trial preparation can be seen as a type of private investment. An additional hour of legal research or argumentation is profitable, in this view, only if the marginal return, measured by the change in the expected outcome of trial or settlement, outweighs the cost of the attorney's time. Plaintiffs, accordingly, will choose to spend legal resources up to the point where their expected recoveries, net of expenses, are maximized; defendants will act so as to minimize total payouts. The precise outcome of this contest depends on how the parties react and adjust to each other's decisions. One simple and natural assumption is that the litigants reach a Nash equilibrium in expenditure; that is, that each takes the other's expenditure as given when choosing his own. Whatever the nature of the parties' strategic interaction, however, the parties' expenditures are determined in equilibrium by a host of economic and technological factors, including the stakes of the case, the marginal cost of legal resources, and the sensitivity of trial outcomes to the parties' individual efforts. In high-stakes cases in which the outcome is heavily dependent on the parties' work product, expenditures will be high; in petty cases where the outcome is largely predetermined by legal precedent, expenditures will be low.

As Braeutigam, Owen, and Panzar (1984) first proved, and Katz (1987) subsequently explained, it follows from the standard model that fee shifting encourages greater expenditure in litigated cases. The reasons are twofold.

First, fee shifting increases the stakes of the case by making legal expenditures part of the potential damages. Second, fee shifting lowers the expected marginal cost of legal expenditure: each party, when deciding whether to purchase an additional unit of legal services, will discount its cost by the probability with which she expects to win and to be reimbursed by her opponent.

More formally: if we let p denote the probability of liability, A the amount awarded if the plaintiff wins, and x and y the amounts spent by the plaintiff and defendant respectively, then under the American rule a plaintiff will expect to recover $p(x, y) A(x, y) - x$. Assuming risk-neutrality for the sake of simplicity, it follows she will choose x to satisfy the first-order condition, $p_x A + p A_x = 1$. The defendant, conversely, expects to pay out $pA + y$, and will select y to satisfy his first-order condition, $p_y A + p A_y = -1$.

Under the English rule, in contrast, the plaintiff's expected recovery is $pA - (1 - p)(x + y)$; so her first-order condition is $p_x(A + x + y) + pA_x = 1 - p$. Similarly, the defendant's expected payout is $p(A + x + y)$, and his first-order condition is $p_y(A + x + y) + pA_y = -p$.

In all of these equations, the left-hand side represents the marginal private benefit of expenditure, and the right-hand side its marginal cost. Inspection of the equations reveals that the marginal private cost of legal expenditure is lower for both parties under the English rule. If the parties' expenditure affects the probability of liability (that is, if p_x and p_y are positive), the marginal private benefit is also higher; if expenditure affects only the amount awarded, and not also the probability of liability, marginal benefit is unchanged. Other things being equal, therefore, the English rule makes expenditure more attractive.

It should be noted that the marginal-cost effect depends not on the actual probability of liability, but on its perceived probability. It follows that the increase in expenditure under the English rule will be greater the more optimistic are the litigants. In the extreme, parties who regard themselves as very likely to win will perceive litigation as virtually costless and will increase their expenditures accordingly. To the extent that such efforts increase the probability of prevailing, therefore, such optimism will be partially self-fulfilling.

Similarly, in other than even cases, the marginal-cost effect will be stronger for the party with the stronger probability of prevailing *ex ante*. For instance, if both parties regard the initial probability of liability as 90 percent, the plaintiff will discount the expected marginal cost of legal services to 10¢ on the dollar, while the defendant discounts it only to 90¢. Accordingly, if the English rule is adopted, the stimulus to the plaintiff's expenditure will be ten times greater than the stimulus to the defendant's. Thus, fee shifting reinforces the advantages of the party who is initially favored in litigation.

Because of the interaction between the parties' expenditure decisions, it is not possible to prove that both sides will increase their expenditures under the English rule. The reason for this ambiguity is that a marginal increase in one side's expenditure has an ambiguous effect on the other side's expenditures. A marginal increase in the spending by one side could either provoke the opponent to respond in kind, or intimidate him into reducing his own efforts.

Braeutigam, Owen, and Panzar, however, showed that in Nash equilibrium the sum of the parties' expenditures must increase. The extent of the increase depends on how sensitive p and A are to litigation expenditure, as Plott (1987) has demonstrated. Using a Nash equilibrium model and making some simplifying technical assumptions regarding functional form, Plott found that if the case outcome depends entirely on factors out of the litigants' control, the English rule has no effect on expenditure. If case outcome is determined solely by litigants' efforts, conversely, the English rule will cause expenditure to increase without limit.

Such effects are mitigated in regimes that limit the amount of fees that can be shifted. For example, under both English and US practice, indemnification is limited to reasonable expenditures. Hyde and Williams (2002) study partial fee shifting, allowing for uncertainty regarding the quantity of costs that will be deemed shiftable by the court.

Similarly, some recent US proposals provide that a losing party need not pay any indemnification in excess of his or her own litigation costs. Hughes and Woglom (1996) show that the English rule operates as a tax on the weaker party's expenditure, since increases in the weaker party's spending raise the cap on the indemnification potentially payable to the stronger party.

Furthermore, while most of the economic literature on litigation expenditure has assumed a Nash equilibrium, a few authors (for example, Hersch 1990) have argued that it is not reasonable to expect litigants to ignore the effect on the other side's expenditure when choosing their own. The Nash specification is most appealing when expenditure is simultaneous, when each side must choose how much to spend before learning the opponent's decision, or when the expenditure decision is largely determined by one's initial choice of an attorney; it is least appealing when one side can commit to a given level of expenditure and communicate that commitment to the opponent in advance. One can analyze the latter situation using the model of conjectural variations – so-called because it allows a party's decision to depend upon his conjectures regarding how the opponent's decision varies with his own. Formally, let v_x denote the rate at which the plaintiff expects the defendant to respond to her expenditures. This rate could be positive (in which case expenditure would be provocative), negative (in which case expenditure would be intimidating), or zero (as in the Nash model). The plaintiff's first-order condition then becomes $(p_x + v_x p_y)A + p(A_x + v_x A_y) = 1$ under the American rule, and $(p_x + v_x p_y)(A + x + y) + p(A_x + v_x A_y) = (1 - p)(1 + v_x)$ under the English rule. (The analysis for the defendant is symmetric and is omitted for the sake of brevity.) Comparing the first term of each of the equations, one can see that the stakes effect is still present. The direction of the marginal-cost effect, however, is now ambiguous. Under the English rule, if the plaintiff spends an additional dollar on legal services it will cost her only $1 - p$, after she discounts for the probability of prevailing. But if the plaintiff loses, she will also have to pay the defendant's costs, and the additional dollar of plaintiff spending induces the defendant to change his expenditures by v_x. If the plaintiff's expenditure is intimidating, this will lower her marginal cost even further. If her expenditure is sufficiently provocative, however, her marginal cost of legal resources will rise; if it is provocative enough to outweigh the stakes effect, her equilibrium expenditure will fall.

Lastly, most models of fee shifting and litigation expenditure assume that lawyer and client act as one. When this is not the case – when there are agency problems in the lawyer-client relationship – the effects of fee shifting on litigation spending become potentially subject to the nature of the contract for attorney services. Hyde (2006) studies the interaction between the fee allocation rule and two such contracts: contingent fee arrangements – wherein the victorious lawyer receives a percentage of the litigation award – and *conditional* fee arrangements – wherein a victorious lawyer is paid a multiple of the market value of her services.

The analysis in this section has focused on the amount of resources expended in litigated cases. Total expenditures on litigation, however, are the product of two factors: expenditures per litigated case, and the number of cases that are actually litigated. Fee shifting can influence the number of litigated cases in two ways: by influencing the decision to bring the dispute to court in the first place, and by influencing the parties' incentive to settle cases before trial. The next section of this chapter discusses the former effect, and Section 5 discusses the latter.

4. Effects of Fee Shifting on the Decisions to File and Contest Lawsuits

Consider the case of a consumer who has purchased a defective ballpoint pen and who is in theory entitled to a refund. Because the value of the pen is exceeded by even the most streamlined judicial proceeding, the consumer's threat to litigate is not credible; and absent procedural devices such as a class action that can allow aggregation of her claim with others, she will be forced to rely on nonlegal incentives such as the seller's interest in its reputation. If the consumer can recover legal fees along with the value of her refund, however, her threat to sue becomes credible.

4.1 Basic Model
Shavell (1982a), extending the work of Landes (1971) and Gould (1973) on the incentives to sue, generalized this argument to show that the English

rule, and indemnification in general, works to encourage lawsuits by plaintiffs with relatively small claims but relatively high *ex ante* probabilities of victory. The American rule, conversely, encourages plaintiffs with relatively large claims but lower probabilities of victory.

The formal logic of the argument is as follows: let p represent the probability of a plaintiff victory, A the expected award if the plaintiff wins, and c the cost of litigation for each litigant. (To simplify the argument, suppose that this cost is the same for both sides; this will affect the specific point at which the incentives switch, but not the basic intuition of the argument.) Under the American rule, litigation is profitable if (and only if) $pA > c$; thus, a plaintiff will bring suit if she views her chances as better than the threshold probability p_{US} c/A. Under the English rule, however, the plaintiff's expected litigation cost is not c but $(1 - p)2c$, since she pays no costs if she wins, but $2c$ if she loses. She will accordingly wish to litigate if $pA > (1 - p)2c$, or equivalently, if she views her chances at better than $p_{ENG} 2c/(A + 2c)$. Algebraic manipulation reveals that $c > A/2$ implies $p_{US} > p_{ENG} > ½$, and $c < A/2$ implies $p_{US} < p_{ENG} < ½$. Thus, when costs are high or stakes low, the English rule encourages some better-than-average suits that would be deterred under the American rule; when costs are low or stakes high, the English rule discourages some worse-than-average suits that would be brought under the American rule.

An identical line of argument shows the effect of indemnification on the incentives to defend against a lawsuit once it has been brought. If it costs the defendant c to put up a defense that will succeed with probability p, it is worthwhile to defend (rather than suffer a default) only if the expected savings pA exceed the expected costs of litigation. Under the American rule these expected costs are c, and under the English rule they are $(1 - p)2c$. The logic is as before; the American rule encourages long-shot defenses in high-stakes and low-cost cases, while the English rule encourages high-probability defenses in high-cost and low-stakes cases.

Such arguments lend support to the frequently expressed view that the English rule is superior on grounds of corrective justice, since the claims and defenses that it promotes are relatively meritorious ones – at least when viewed from an *ex ante* perspective. Similarly, as Rosenberg and Shavell (1985) and Farmer and Pecorino (1998) argue, indemnification can help discourage certain frivolous or 'strike' suits. Rosenberg and Shavell argue that indemnification emboldens defendants to put forward costly defenses against strike suits (assuming that the frivolous nature of the suit is common knowledge; as Katz (1990) argues, the English rule may do little to discourage strike suits that cannot be identified as such without a trial). Farmer and Pecorino argue that indemnification reduces the frequency of strike suits by dampening the incentive of plaintiffs' attorneys

280   *Procedural law and economics*

to develop a reputation for carrying out the threat of pursuing frivolous litigation.

But there is a cost to this ostensible increase in justice. The claim and defenses encouraged by the English rule are low stakes and high cost – that is, expensive to try relative to their importance. The claims and defenses encouraged by the American rule may be relative longshots on the merits, but they are relatively cheap to resolve. Moreover, some suits, including those brought to test or clarify the law or to settle matters of principle, may be socially desirable notwithstanding a low *ex ante* probability of success. Accordingly, legal policy in this area may present a tradeoff between justice and more narrow conceptions of efficiency.

Any conclusions regarding the effect of litigation fee shifting on incentives to sue must also take account of the litigants' expected response to risk. As has been widely recognized, the English rule magnifies the private risk arising from litigation by increasing both the returns from success and the losses from defeat. Thus, it tends to discourage risk-averse parties from bringing or defending lawsuits, regardless of the merits of their positions – a factor that has been stressed by partisans of the American rule. What has been less well recognized, however, is that this same increase in variance can encourage more litigation by the risk-neutral. The reason is that most lawsuits are divided into a series of procedural stages, at each of which it is possible to decide whether to continue depending on how the case is going. Because of this flexibility, as Cornell (1990) has shown, the decision to litigate can be interpreted as the purchase of an option. Just as financial options can sell for a positive price even if the probability of exercising them is low, the option value of litigation can make it profitable to put forward claims with negative expected value. Because the value of an option increases with its variance, the English rule, by increasing both the upside and the downside of litigation, intensifies this incentive. Indeed, if parties can drop arguments before trial without penalty, such enhanced option value could increase litigation even by the risk-averse.

4.2   Multi-phase Models

Additionally, as the previous section indicated, the English rule indirectly alters incentives to sue through its effects on the expected cost of the individual case. Because indemnification encourages parties to litigate their disputes more intensively, it increases the expected cost of bringing and defending suits *ex ante*. This increase in the *ex ante* expected cost of bringing suit will, in turn, affect parties' decisions regarding whether to pursue their cases – that is, whether to file suit, in the case of a plaintiff, or refrain from defaulting in the case of a defendant. Adding litigation intensity to the model may thereby affect conventional conclusions regarding the effect of fee allocation rules on the composition of cases that are jointly pursued.

A number of recent papers on fee shifting have combined litigation intensity, filing decisions, and default decisions in a single model. In Farmer and Pecorino (1999), the plaintiff first decides whether to file suit. If the plaintiff does file suit, the defendant next decides whether to simply pay the default judgment. If the defendant decides not to default, the two parties engage in the kind of litigation expenditure game described in Section 3. Farmer and Pecorino ask which rule, English or American, imposes lower litigation costs, and which results in more accurate dispositions. They emphasize that the answer depends on the shape of the exogenous litigation expenditure technology that is assumed to be in place – that is, on the shape of $p(x, y)$ and $A(x, y)$, as defined above in Section 3. They show that for *each* fee allocation rule, there exist technology parameter values under which plaintiffs file only meritorious claims, defendants always pay the default judgment, and litigation costs are zero.

Baye, Kovenock, and de Vries (2005) also combine filing, default, and litigation expenditure decisions, though in a different manner. In their two-phase model, the parties first simultaneously decide whether to concede. If neither party concedes, the parties next simultaneously decide how much to spend on litigation. Baye, Kovenock, and de Vries assume that the party with the highest quality case wins the case with probability one. Furthermore, the quality of each party's case is, in turn, a strictly increasing function of her litigation expenditure. Thus, the party spending the most wins the case with probability one. In this context – which resembles a first price auction as much as it does litigation – Baye, Kovenock, and de Vries study a wide variety of fee-shifting rules. With regard to the comparison of American and English rules, they obtain more definitive results than do Farmer and Pecorino. This is not, however, inconsistent with Farmer and Pecorino's general point that the effect of fee shifting is sensitive to assumptions made about the exogenous litigation technology. The definitiveness of Baye, Kovenock, and de Vries's results appears to be due in large measure to their having restricted attention to a specific litigation technology.

5. Effects of Fee Shifting on the Settlement of Litigation

Because the great majority of civil cases are settled rather than tried, and because trial substantially increases the cost of disputes, effects on settlement are a critical factor in any comparison of the English and American rules. As a result, the economic literature on fee shifting has focused on this issue more than any other. The conventional wisdom among practicing attorneys appears to be that a shift toward fuller indemnification would encourage settlement. The conclusions of the scholarly literature, however, cannot be said to offer strong support for this proposition; at best the effects are ambiguous.

5.1 Relative Optimism Models
As a first approximation, fee shifting magnifies the effect of litigants' optimism, making them less likely to settle. As Landes (1971) and Gould (1973) observed, since litigation is a negative-sum game *ex post*, parties who accurately assess their chances of victory have a strong collective incentive to avoid the costs of trial. Indeed, in a world of purely Coasian bargaining, there would be no trials at all, since full sharing of information would eliminate any differences of opinion. Because of random variations in information, judgment, and temperament, however, some fraction of litigants will inevitably overassess their chances, and it is these optimistic litigants who have an incentive to go to trial. Pessimistic or unbiased parties, in contrast, would prefer to settle. But the degree of optimism necessary for a trial to result depends on how litigation costs are allocated, as the following argument (suggested by Mause 1969, and formally demonstrated by Shavell 1982a) shows.

Under the American rule, a plaintiff who perceives the probability of liability as p_P, her stakes as A_P, and her costs as c_P will insist on receiving a settlement of no less than $S_P = p_P A_P - c_P$. Similarly, a defendant who perceives the probability of liability as p_D, his stakes as A_D, and his costs as c_D will be willing to pay no more than $S_D = p_D A_D + c_D$. (Notice for future reference that the parties' stakes, and not just the probability assessments, may differ in this formulation.) Settlement is thus possible if (and only if) $S_P < S_D$, or equivalently, if the total litigation costs, $c_P + c_D$, exceed the difference between the parties' reservation settlement values, $p_P A_P - p_D A_D$. Parties whose litigation costs are below this cutoff level, conversely, will prefer to go to trial.

Under the English rule, however, the plaintiff's reservation settlement value becomes $S_P = p_P A_P - (1 - p_P)(c_P + c_D)$, and the defendant's becomes $S_D = p_D (A_D + c_P + c_D)$. Now settlement is possible only if $c_P + c_D > (p_P A_P - p_D A_D)/(1 - p_P + p_D)$. If the plaintiff's probability estimate that she will win, p_P, exceeds the defendant's probability estimate that the plaintiff will win, p_D – that is, if the parties are optimistic relative to each other – the aggregate litigation cost minimum for settlement under the English rule is equal to that under the American rule divided by a number that is less than one. The aggregate litigation cost minimum under the English rule is thus greater than the aggregate litigation cost minimum under the Amerian rule. Settlements are thus less likely under the English rule.

Another way to see this is as follows: From the two expressions for the plaintiff's minimal acceptable settlement amount S_P, it is clear that changing to the English rule from the American rule causes S_P to increase by $-(1 - p_P)(c_P + c_D) - (-c_P) = p_P(c_P + c_D) - c_D$. This change in S_P is easily interpreted by triangulating with a hypothetical baseline in which the plaintiff pays both parties' costs. Relative to this plaintiff-pays-all rule, the English rule pays the plaintiff back aggregate costs in the event that the plaintiff wins, a payment with expected value $p_P(c_P + c_D)$. Relative to the plaintiff-pays-all rule, the American rule always pays her back the defendant's costs, c_D. Thus, switching from the American rule to the English rule increases the plaintiff's expected costs by $p_P(c_P + c_D) - c_D$, as claimed.

We can conduct the same analysis for the defendant. From the above equations, we see that changing from the American rule to the Engish rule causes the *defendant's maximum* acceptable settlement amount S_D to increase by $p_D(c_P + c_D) - c_D$. Thus, triangulating with respect to a hypothetical baseline in which the defendant pays neither party's costs, the English rule makes the defendant pay both parties' costs in the event that the plaintiff wins, while the American rule always makes him pay his own costs.

Now, if $p_P = p_D$, fee shifting causes the plaintiff's minimal acceptable settlement amount and the defendant's maximum acceptable settlement amount to increase by the same amount, and there is no change in the minimum aggregate litigation cost $c_P + c_D$ for settlement. But if $p_P > p_D$, then fee shifting causes the plaintiff's minimal acceptable settlement amount to increase by more than the defendant's maximum acceptable settlement amount, and the minimum aggregate litigation cost for settlement increases.

The economic intuition underlying this result is that indemnification internalizes one externality while creating another. Under the English rule, a litigant is forced to take into account the other side's litigation costs to the extent that she risks losing the case, making her more willing to settle. But conversely, she is freed of her own litigation costs to the extent that she hopes to win, making her less likely to settle. Since litigants are disproportionately drawn from the population of optimists (else they would settle however costs are allocated), the latter effect tends to outweigh the former. Indeed, in the limiting case when both parties are fully confident of winning, neither expects to pay any costs at all and settlement is impossible.

This line of argument, however, suggests an important exception to the basic result: in some cases, parties might choose to litigate due to a difference of opinion not over liability but over stakes. A plaintiff who regarded the stakes as sufficiently higher than did the defendant – for example, because she hoped to establish a favorable precedent that could be drawn on in later cases – might refuse all settlements even if the parties agreed on the probability of liability or were both relatively pessimistic. If the parties' relative optimism about the stakes were enough to outweigh their relative pessimism about probability, fee shifting would encourage settlement and discourage trial.

5.2 Structured Bargaining with Asymmetric Information

The Landes-Gould model of settlement bargaining (often called the 'optimism model' in subsequent literature) is open to the criticism that it assumes that each party knows the other's reservation value in settlement negotiations, whereas such values are more naturally assumed to be private information. Accordingly, subsequent writers have often preferred to base their analyses on models of asymmetric information bargaining. In this formulation, as first proposed by Cooter, Marks and Mnookin (1982), trials are caused not by optimism but by uncertainty over the opponent's reservation settlement value.

In most formal models of asymmetric information settlement bargaining (see, for example, Bebchuk 1984), one party has private information regarding the outcome of the case, and the other makes a single take-it-or-leave-it settlement offer. (In Reinganum and Wilde 1986, however, the offeror also has private information.) Thus, the offeror does not know whether her single offer will be accepted, and if it is not, she must pay the cost of trial. This generates a familiar tradeoff: a more generous settlement offer is more likely to be accepted, which is good, but, on the other hand, the acceptance itself is not as favorable to the offeror. The tradeoff is similar to that faced by the classic monopolist: lowering price increases purchases, but every purchase generates less revenue.

Whether cases settle in such a model depends on a number of factors, including the stakes in the case, the cost of litigation, and, most importantly, the extent of the offeror's uncertainty regarding the reservation value of her opponent. Roughly speaking, greater dispersion in the probability distribution of the offeree's reservation settlement values means a lower density at any given value, so that a decision by the offeror to take a marginally tougher position sacrifices fewer bargains. This increases the net marginal benefit of making a less generous settlement offer. If the effect is sufficiently uniform across the continnum of possible settlement offers, more uncertainty will mean less settlement.

Asymmetric information models of settlement bargaining tend to confirm the optimism model's conclusion that the English rule generally discourages settlement in disputes revolving around liability, but not in disputes revolving around stakes. The reason is that indemnification magnifies uncertainty in the former set of cases but not in the latter. More precisely, uncertainty about opponents' reservation values can stem from numerous sources: variations in the private cost and stakes of litigation, variation in attitudes toward risk and delay, and variation in private information relevant to the trial outcome. Differences in risk aversion, time preference and litigation stakes are not affected by fee shifting, but differences in private cost and in information relevant to liability are. Fee shifting thus increases the difference between the reservation values of parties with favorable private information and high litigation costs on the one hand, and parties with unfavorable information and low litigation costs on the other. This increase in uncertainty leads all types of parties to toughen their overall bargaining stance, thus lowering the probability of settlement. Ironically, as Polinsky and Rubinfeld (1997) point out, this implies that the English rule actually lowers the average quality of tried cases, since the marginal parties it sends to trial have relatively less favorable private information than those who would litigate absent the prospect of indemnification.

Even if fee shifting does not alter the probability of settlement, however, it can still influence its amount. As Cooter and Rubinfeld (1994) have argued in the context of legal discovery and Bebchuk and Chang (1996) have argued in the context of offers of judgment, fee shifting can, by equalizing the bargaining power of parties with asymmetric litigation costs, help to move the settlement amount closer to the expected trial outcome. To the extent that trial outcomes are deemed to be just, fee shifting thus may help promote equity; to the extent that trial outcomes reflect substantive legal norms, fee shifting helps promote incentives for proper primary behavior – a subject more fully explored in the following section.

In most asymmetric information models the subject of private information is the outcome of the case. But parties may also have private information regarding other variables, such as their own trial costs. Chopard, Cortade, and Langlais (2008) study this possibility (for the case of both one- and two-sided asymmetric information). They emphasize that changing the subject of private information markedly changes the predictions of the model.

5.3 Multi-phase Models

The foregoing discussion of both optimism and asymmetric information models of settlement bargaining has taken the cost of litigation as given. As previous sections have observed, however, indemnification generally raises litigation costs – through its effect on litigation intensity.

Recent research imbeds a model of settlement negotiation within a large multi-phase model of litigation that includes litigation intensity decisions. Doing so greatly complicates the analysis. Tractability is typically restored by adopting helpful function form assumptions.

Gong and McAfee (2000) combine a model of two-sided

asymmetric-information settlement negotiation with a model of litigation expenditure that is similar to that described in Section 3. In particular, for their litigation expenditure phase, Gong and McAfee adopt a simplified litigation technology in which the chance of plaintiff victory equals the plaintiff's proportional contribution to total evidence. Gong and McAfee's chief concern is the accuracy of the settlement amount. They find that the English rule shifts the settlement amount away from the best estimate of the proper settlement amount – where such estimate is based on aggregating the information that is privately received by each of the parties.

Chen and Wang (2007) also analyze a multi-stage model that includes both settlement negotiation and litigation spending. Chen and Wang's model differs from Gong and McAfee's in several important respects. First, Chen and Wang include the plainntiff's filing decision. Second, the settlement negotiation phase in Chen and Wang's model is the usual one-sided asymmetric model in which the uninformed party makes a take-it-or-leave-it offer. Lastly, the plaintiff's lawyer, who is paid on a contingency fee basis, makes all litigation decisions for the plaintiff's side. With the addition of several functional form assumptions, Chen and Wang find that the English rule results in fewer filed suits, higher settlement rates under certain distributional assumptions, greater trial costs, and a greater chance of defendant victory.

6. Effects of Fee Shifting on Substantive Behavior

The discussion thus far is in a fundamental sense incomplete, since it has focused largely on the procedural costs of litigation. If such costs were one's only concern, of course, they could be eliminated entirely by abolishing the legal system and all publicly enforceable rights to relief. A central purpose of having a public system of courts, however, is to redress wrongs and to encourage compliance with primary substantive norms such as taking precautions against accidents and keeping one's promises. Indemnity of legal fees, accordingly, must ultimately be judged on these latter criteria – or more accurately, on whether it increases the social value of substantive enforcement net of process costs.

Viewed from this perspective, the English rule initially appears attractive, since it tends to encourage high probability suits and discourage low probability ones. Assuming that the probability of liability is correlated with the actual violation of substantive norms, therefore, indemnification increases the net expected punishment for such violations and thus helps promote substantive compliance. This is easily seen in the case where courts' liability determinations are error-free, as Rose-Ackerman and Geistfeld (1987) and Polinsky and Rubinfeld (1988) have shown. Consider a potential tortfeasor who can take precautions against an accident that will cause an uncertain amount of damage. Suppose that the possible damage ranges from zero to A, and that the cost of establishing liability following an accident is c. Under the American rule, it follows that the tortfeasor will have inadequate incentives for precaution. In the event that damages turn out to be less than c, the victim will not sue, so the tortfeasor will escape responsibility for a portion of the damages caused. Under the English rule, however, the victim will always have the incentive to sue, so that all accident costs will be fully internalized. Under a rule of negligence as opposed to strict liability, indeed, complete cost internalization can be achieved without incurring any litigation costs at all: defendants will be induced to take optimal care by the threat of litigation, so plaintiffs will never actually have to sue. Conversely, under the American rule, defendants may rationally decide to take excess care – or to abstain from risky though optimal activities – in order to avoid the greater expense of having to defend their behavior in court. Indemnification protects them from such expenses, thus preventing overdeterrence.

This happy outcome, however, depends on the assumption that deserving plaintiffs and defendants always win their cases. In the presence of legal error, as P'ng (1987) and Polinsky and Shavell (1989) have shown, neither the American nor the English rule provides incentives that are first-best optimal. Optimal incentives, rather, require at least two separate policy instruments – one to motivate efficient substantive behavior, and another to promote an efficient amount of litigation. Polinsky and Che (1991) demonstrate that, in general, this means decoupling the amounts paid by losing defendants from those received by victorious plaintiffs. (Indeed, as Polinsky and Rubinfeld (1996) show, decoupling is generally necessary even to achieve the lesser goal of minimizing the litigation costs associated with achieving a given level of deterrence.) Devices combining fines, punitive damages, and taxes (positive or negative) on litigation accomplish such decoupling, but the English rule, which merely re-allocates costs between the parties in zero-sum fashion, does not. Furthermore, it is not even the case that the English rule is second-best efficient within the category of zero-sum policy instruments. Kaplow (1993) shows that damage multipliers, such as the treble damage provisions of US antitrust law, provide a cheaper method of achieving any given amount of deterrence. The reason is that damage multipliers provide incentives for private law enforcement to be undertaken by those plaintiffs whose litigation costs are lowest; fee shifting, in contrast, encourages plaintiffs to bring lawsuits without regard to their costs of litigation.

One might still ask whether the English rule does better than the American in promoting efficient substantive behavior, notwithstanding the potential availability of alternatives that are superior to both. The answer to this question, however, is ambiguous, as Gravelle (1993), Hylton (1993a, 1993b), and Beckner and Katz (1995) demonstrate in independent formal models. It is possible to draw generalizations regarding when the English rule improves matters, but they depend on the subtle interaction of a number of factors, including whether substantive precaution affects the magnitude of injury or just its probability, the extent to which precaution affects the probability of liability, whether damage awards are sufficient to compensate plaintiffs for their losses, and whether defendants have the opportunity to act strategically by taking just enough care to foreclose litigation. Hylton, for instance, concludes that a one-way fee-shifting rule operating in favor of plaintiffs would be best, but this conclusion depends upon several features of his model (including, perhaps most importantly, the assumption that plaintiff's care does not affect the expected cost of accidents). Applying such generalizations to individual cases or categories of cases is probably beyond the capacity of either courts or legislatures. As Gravelle concludes, '[i]t seems more promising to pursue other, more direct means of correcting the inefficient incentives for care provided by a costly and imperfect legal system'.

More recently, Choi and Sanchirico (2004) investigate the effects of decoupling the amounts paid by losing defendants from the amounts received by victorious plaintiffs when substantive behavior, filing incentives, and the intensity of spending are all at issue. In their model, the defendant first chooses a substantive action. The plaintiff next decides whether to file suit. Finally, the parties choose their level of effort at litigation. Choi and Sanchirico investigate the problem of minimizing the social cost of a given level of deterrence by adjusting three policy instruments: an upfront filing fee, the amount that victorious plaintiffs recover, and the amount that losing defendants pay. Contrary to earlier work by Polinsky and Che (1991), whose model does not include litigation spending decisions, Choi and Sanchirico find that what plaintiffs recover should be no lower than what defendants pay when the conjunction of two conditions obtains: defendants are not wealth-constrained and the potential harm from defendants' violations is sufficiently great. Choi and Sanchirico show that their analysis is invariant to whether the fee allocation rule is English or American.

Klement and Neeman (2005) investigate the effect of fee-shifting rules when the objective is to maximize the probability of settlement subject to the constraint that a given amount of deterrence is generated by the threat of litigation. Klement and Neeman model settlement negotiations, but not litigation spending decisions. They find that maximizing the probability of settlement requires adopting the English rule. The English rule creates the largest divergence between the trial payoffs of liable and non-liable defendants. It, therefore, allows the greatest amount of deterrence per trial and so the fewest number of trials for a given amount of deterrence.

7. Variations on Simple Fee Shifting
The foregoing discussion has been premised on the assumption that 'costs follow the event' – that is, that any fee shifting that takes place is based solely on who wins the case. Much recent discussion in policy and scholarly circles, however, has focused on two more complicated forms of indemnification.

7.1 Fee Shifting Conditioned on Offers Made in Settlement
Both England and a number of American jurisdictions provide a mechanism through which a defendant who would otherwise be obliged to pay for legal expenses can partially avoid the obligation by making a suitable offer of settlement. In England this procedure is called 'payment into court' and requires the defendant to actually deposit funds with a court officer; while in the United States, Federal Rule of Civil Procedure 68 and similar rules[2] merely require the formal filing of what is labeled an 'offer of judgment'. Under either provision, a defendant who makes such a formal offer is considered the prevailing party for purposes of cost allocation if the plaintiff rejects the offer and then is subsequently awarded a lesser amount at trial. In such an event, the defendant avoids having to pay any costs incurred by the plaintiff subsequent to the offer, and is entitled to indemnification for his own subsequent costs as well. By all accounts, defendants avail themselves of this procedure much more frequently in England than in the US – probably because the prospect of shifting liability for 'costs' is likelier under the broader English definition of the term to outweigh the disadvantages of making a settlement offer. Similarly, within the US, Rule 68 appears to be used more widely in disputes covered by one-way pro-plaintiff fee-shifting statutes such as Title VII, since the Supreme Court held in *Marek v. Chesny* that attorneys' fees shifted under such statutes are to be considered 'costs' under Rule 68.

Because of the relatively infrequent use of Rule 68 in US courts, a number of American critics have in recent years supported its expansion – either by extending its coverage to attorneys' fees generally, or by making the procedure available to plaintiffs as well as defendants. (It should be

---

[2] Under the US Internal Revenue Code, Sec. 7430, if a taxpayer makes an offer to the Internal Revenue Service to settle a claim for taxes allegedly owed, and if the Internal Revenue Service rejects the offer and later obtains a judgment against the taxpayer that is not greater than the taxpayer's offer, the taxpayer may be entitled to recover reasonable litigation costs, including attorneys' fees.

noted, however, that providing the procedure to plaintiffs is meaningless to the extent that they are already entitled to collect costs when they prevail; in such circumstances, the opportunity to make an offer of judgment can only advantage defendants.) The U.S. Republican Party's recent 'Contract with America', for example, would have established just such a generalized offer-of-judgment rule in federal diversity cases. Such proposals have commonly been supported by the claim that they will reduce expenditures on litigation by encouraging parties to make more reasonable settlement offers and to accept such offers when they are made. Their proponents have also argued that it is fairer to charge the costs of trial to the party who, by refusing a reasonable settlement, causes those costs to be incurred.

In general, the economic literature on offers of judgment is substantially less developed than that on pure indemnification, and many interesting questions remain to be fully investigated, including the effect of the procedure on strategic behavior in negotiations. The place to begin any analysis of the offer of judgment, however, is with the observation that it is essentially an option to convert disputes over damages into disputes over liability. To see this, compare two cases: one in which it is clear that the defendant has acted negligently but unclear whether the plaintiff's injuries are 1000 or 3000 (with the two possibilities being equally likely), and a second in which it is clear that damages are 4000, but an even gamble whether the defendant is liable at all. In both cases, expected damages are 2000, but absent an offer-of-judgment procedure, the plaintiff's position is stronger in the former. She is certain to prevail at trial and to recover some fraction of her costs, even if it is only court fees. In the latter case, she runs the risk of paying both her costs and a portion of the defendant's. Under Rule 68 or a similar procedure, however, the defendant can convert the former dispute into a partial settlement of 1000 combined with a dispute over whether the defendant is liable for an additional 2000. In this converted dispute, the defendant stands an even chance of avoiding liability for the plaintiff's costs and of recovering his own. This improves his expected position to what it would be in the case of pure liability, at the plaintiff's expense.

The example illustrates two lessons. First, a rule authorizing defendants but not plaintiffs to make offers of judgment redistributes wealth from plaintiffs to defendants in disputes that are entirely or partly over damages, as both Priest (1982) and Miller (1986) have suggested. Second, such offers have no effect in disputes that are purely over liability. If the only possible trial outcomes are verdicts of zero or 4000, for instance, there is no advantage to the defendant in making a Rule 68 offer of less than the full 4000. If he offers a lesser amount, he will be liable for costs in the event of a plaintiff's verdict and certain to receive costs in the event of a defendant's verdict – just as he would if he made no offer at all. Similarly, a less-than-full offer does not affect the possible payoffs for the plaintiff. The defendant could of course offer to settle for the full 4000, but the plaintiff should be happy to accept such an offer whether or not Rule 68 is in force.

The offer-of-judgment procedure, accordingly, cannot affect whether an offer is made or accepted in such cases.

With these points taken as caveats, the effects of offer-of-judgment rules are roughly analogous to those of indemnification in general. The possibility that costs will be shifted following a settlement offer both raises the stakes of the case and lowers the perceived marginal cost of legal expenditure, thus increasing incentives to expend resources at trial. The effect is less than under the pure English rule, however, since only post-offer expenditures are liable to be shifted. Similarly, the opportunity to make an offer of judgment increases expected payoffs for plaintiffs who expect to win large awards at trial, and lowers expected payouts of defendants who expect awards to be low, emboldening such parties to pursue litigation.

The effect of offers of judgment on the settlement decision depends, like the effect of indemnification generally, on the parties' attitudes toward risk and on the model of settlement that one thinks appropriate. Under the Landes-Posner-Gould optimism model, offers of judgment tend to lower the chances of settlement between risk-neutral parties, since, as Priest (1982) suggests and Miller (1986) and Chung (1996) confirm, such offers lower the reservation values of optimistic defendants more than they do those of optimistic plaintiffs, thus reducing the potential settlement range. Offers of judgment also increase the risk of litigation, though not as much as pure indemnification does; this encourages risk-averse parties to settle, but risk-preferring parties to litigate. Anderson (1994), who extends the optimism model to include the possibility of bargaining stalemate, reaches similar results. Within Bayesian models of settlement, the outcome appears more complicated. Cooter, Marks and Mnookin (1982) conjecture that an offer-of-judgment rule, by effectively taxing hard offers and subsidizing soft ones, should encourage settlement. Spier (1994), however, in a model in which defendants make offers to plaintiffs with private information, finds that the procedure leads to more settlement than the pure American rule in cases where the plaintiff's private information relates solely to the size of the award, less settlement than the American rule in cases where the plaintiff's private information relates solely to the probability of liability, and an ambiguous effect in other cases. She also demonstrates a similar result using a mechanism-design model that, instead of specifying any particular bargaining process, assumes that the parties use a Pareto-efficient trading mechanism in the style of Myerson and Satterthwaite (1983). As

292 *Procedural law and economics*

with pure indemnification, accordingly, the effect of offers of judgment on settlement probabilities appears to depend on the sources of the underlying dispute.

7.2 *Fee Shifting Conditioned on the Margin of Victory*

In the United States, a variety of statutory and judicially created rules allow courts to award partial or full indemnification in lawsuits in which the losing party's case is deemed after the fact to be of sufficiently low merit. Such rules include the common-law torts of barratry, abuse of process, and malicious prosecution, the traditional authority of courts of equity to exercise their discretion in the interests of justice, the sanctions for discovery abuse provided by Federal Rule of Civil Procedure 37, and the (just amended) provisions of the Internal Revenue Code requiring the government to pay a taxpayer's reasonable litigation costs upon a court finding that the government's position in a tax dispute was substantially unjustified. Similarly, as Pfennigstorf (1984) reports, indemnification awards in most other Western legal systems are likely to be more generous in cases where the loser's legal or factual position appears weak.

The possibility of tying indemnification to the merits of the losing case has attracted increased attention in recent years, in part as a response to the growth of litigation practice under US Federal Rule of Civil Procedure 11. This rule requires persons filing court papers to warrant that their filings are well grounded, and authorizes courts to impose monetary sanctions on parties whose filings are found to be frivolous, harassing, or made for purposes of delay. Limiting fee shifting to cases of particularly low merit has seemed to many commentators an attractive compromise between the English and American rules, since it protects clearly deserving litigants without imposing unnecessary risk on those who bring colorable claims in good faith.

As Bebchuk and Chang (1996) have pointed out, the effect of policies such as Rule 11 is to condition fee shifting on the winner's margin of victory; those who win in a rout receive indemnification, while those who win narrowly do not. They confirm the conventional wisdom in a formal model, showing that such policies, if designed properly, can do a better job than either the English or the American rule at encouraging meritorious suits (and by analogy, defenses) and discouraging frivolous ones. The reason is that such policies make use of the parties' private *ex ante* information regarding the merits of the case. A party who loses by a large margin is less likely to have believed *ex ante* that her case had merit; conversely, one who wins by a large margin is less likely to have believed that her case lacked merit. While the optimal fee-shifting rule depends on the distribution of judicial and litigant error, it is possible by altering the threshold for fee shifting to regulate the proportion of potential claims and defenses that are actually brought into the system. Because its effects are zero-sum, however, margin-based fee shifting is still less efficient than policies that decouple one side's payments from the other side's recovery (see generally Polinsky and Rubinfeld 1993). Policies that tax or subsidize individual parties based on the *ex post* quality of their case may be best of all; they may also, of course, be the most difficult to administer.

While other incentive effects of margin-based fee shifting have not been formally explored, it appears likely that it has analogous consequences to indemnification generally, though in lesser degree. These consequences recapitulate the discussion in earlier sections of this chapter and can be surveyed in brief. First, to the extent that such policies succeed in encouraging meritorious claims and defenses and discouraging frivolous ones, they will tend to improve incentives for primary substantive behavior. The complications described in Section 6 above, however, remain to be analyzed. It is possible, for instance, that the prospect of shifting litigation costs to the other side following a commanding victory will induce excessive caretaking *ex ante*, though the benefits of doing so are less than under the pure English rule.

Second, margin-based fee shifting will both raise the stakes of litigation and decrease its expected marginal cost, inducing the parties to intensify their efforts at trial. Schmalbeck and Myers (1986) argue that this effect will be relatively minor, since in a truly frivolous case there is little that the parties can do to change the outcome. Their argument is open to question, however, as the substantial amount of litigation effort under Rule 11 illustrates (see, for example, Kobayashi and Parker 1993, who discuss the incentive effects of recent amendments intended to reduce such 'satellite' litigation). While margin-based indemnification has little effect on cases that are clearly contestable or clearly frivolous, in many disputes the colorability of the losing case is less obvious. Parties in such intermediate cases, thus, will have an incentive to increase their expenditures in order to influence the size of the margin of victory.

Third, margin-based fee shifting will decrease the likelihood of settlement to the extent that the parties have a difference of opinion regarding the chances of indemnification. Optimistic parties will exaggerate the likelihood that they will win by a large margin and underestimate the likelihood that they will lose by a large margin. The prospect of indemnification will cause such parties to toughen their settlement demands, reducing the range for settlement. Since pessimistic and unbiased parties will have an incentive to settle in any event, the net consequence will be an increase in trials. Similarly, given private information regarding the probability of a one-sided outcome, margin-based fee shifting will increase the variance of

294 *Procedural law and economics*

the parties' reservation settlement values, encouraging tougher bargaining and hence fewer settlements. The increased risk of trial, however, works to counteract such effects for risk-averse litigants.

In sum, however, the case for at least some margin-based fee shifting appears stronger than the case for indemnification generally, on grounds of both fairness and efficiency. Parties who lose lawsuits decisively are probably more deserving of sanction than those who lose barely. The social value of litigation is probably higher in close cases, whether measured by the public benefits of legal precedent or by more libertarian considerations. And margin-based fee shifting seems to do a better job at providing improved incentives for primary behavior, and has lower costs in terms of incentives for increased expenditure at trial. In light of the relatively limited theoretical and empirical work on this particular topic, however, these conclusions must be regarded as tentative.

8. Empirical Evidence on the Effects of Fee Shifting

Given the complexity and ambiguity of the aforementioned considerations, it would plainly be desirable to have some hard empirical evidence to bring to the policy debate. Unfortunately, such evidence is sparse. What evidence exists on the effects of fee shifting falls into three categories: laboratory research on bargaining behavior by experimental subjects, numerical simulations of litigation behavior based on empirically obtained parameters, and econometric evidence primarily drawn from a single policy experiment: Florida's experience with the English rule in medical malpractice cases from 1980 through 1985.

8.1 Laboratory Experiments

Coursey and Stanley (1988) tested the effects of fee shifting within an experimental setting they designed to simulate the process of bargaining under threat of trial. They divided their subjects (students at the University of Wyoming) into pairs and instructed them to attempt to divide between themselves a number of tokens that were subsequently convertible into cash. If time expired before the subjects reached agreement, the tokens were divided through a random drawing, intended to represent an uncertain court award. To simulate rational expectations, the subjects were presented with the probability distribution of awards arising from the random drawing, and to simulate the costs of trial, the subjects were collectively fined an amount equaling 40 percent of the total value of the tokens in the event the drawing had to take place.

The experimenters conducted negotiations using three different cost allocation rules. Under the simplest procedure, the fine was divided between the two parties equally, in an intended simulation of the American rule.

A second group of subjects negotiated under a rule whereby the fine was paid entirely by the party who received the smaller portion of the tokens in a random drawing; this was intended to simulate the English rule. Yet a third group negotiated under an offer-of-judgment rule intended to simulate Rule 68: the plaintiff paid the entire fine if the draw awarded her an amount less than or equal to the defendant's last proposal; and the fine was otherwise split equally.

The result of this experiment was that subjects settled more frequently under the English than under the American rule. Under Rule 68 settlement was likeliest of all; and in addition, the plaintiff was much more likely to be the accepting party. The authors also found that settlements were more favorable to the defendant under Rule 68 than under the English rule, consistent with the theoretical predictions outlined in the previous section. The American rule was most favorable of all for the defendant, though the authors ascribed this result to the behavior of one especially risk-averse individual. These findings are consistent with theoretical models that predict increased settlement on the basis of simple risk aversion. Because the experimental design ruled out the possibility of optimism or private information, however, its results cannot be extrapolated to situations in which such phenomena, which could cause the English rule to reduce settlement, are present.

In a separate series of survey experiments, Rowe and various co-authors studied the effects of cost allocation rules on lawyers' and students' responses to a variety of bargaining situations presented by hypothetical tort and civil rights cases. While this experimental design suffered from the weakness that the subjects were not provided with any direct financial incentives, the more realistic nature of the problems and the subjects' professional status and experience provided at least some motivation to bargain seriously. The results of the experiments, however, were mixed. Rowe and Vidmar (1988) found that there was little difference between the American rule and a modified Rule 68 (enhanced to cover attorneys' fees and to allow plaintiffs as well as defendants to make offers) on law students' willingness to accept offers of settlement, although they did find an effect on the size of counteroffers, as well as a difference in plaintiff acceptance rates, between modified Rule 68 and a one-way pro-plaintiff rule. Anderson and Rowe (1996) replicated this experiment with practicing lawyers, also examining the subjects' behavior under an alternative fee-shifting rule in which the maker of a rejected offer had to pay the rejecting party's subsequent reasonable attorneys' fees. They found that while modified Rule 68 did not appreciably affect plaintiffs' minimum asks relative to the American rule, it did raise the maximum amounts that defendants were willing to offer. Finally, Rowe and Anderson (1996) considered the effects of a modified Rule 68 on hypothetical bargaining in civil rights cases otherwise governed by a pro-plaintiff rule. They found that replacing this one-way rule with an enhanced Rule 68 significantly lowered plaintiffs' minimum asks, as well as the gap between plaintiff asks and defendant offers. In all, these results suggest that fee shifting has its strongest effect when it is one-sided and when the favored side is risk averse or liquidity constrained.

More recently, Main and Park (2000) find that shifting between the English and American rules has no effect on the frequency of pretrial settlements, but that the English rule leads to greater settlement amounts when the probability of the plaintiff prevailing is relatively large. Their experimental data is derived from repeatedly and randomly pairing 14 undergraduate students to play a five-minute negotiating game in which bids were transmitted back and forth by intermediaries. The subjects were modestly compensated. Each pairing of undergraduates played several times under different rules, and one play was selected at random for purposes of determining payoffs. This experimental design allowed repeated play and learning without creating wealth effects. (However, it also diminished the impact of the monetary reward on each play.)

Main and Park (2002) present experimental data on the effect of a defendant-offer-of-judgment rule when such a rule is applied against the backdrop of the *English* rule for costs. Thus, in those circumstances in which the offer-of-judgment rule does not operate – as when the defendant does not make an offer or the plaintiff wins more than the offer – the losing side pays all costs. Main and Park find that an offer-of-judgment rule has no effect on the frequency of settlement but lowers the settlement amount. The experimental design in Main and Park (2002) is similar to that in Main and Park (2000). Thirty-eight university students were repeatedly and randomly paired. The researchers modestly compensated their subjects based on the rule-affected outcome of a three-minute computer-interactive negotiation game. Each pairing of subjects played several times under different rules, and one play was selected at random for purposes of determining payoffs.

8.2 Simulations
A number of authors have attempted to estimate the quantitative effects of fee shifting by numerically simulating the behavior of theoretical models. Katz's (1987) approach is illustrative. He developed algebraic formulas, based on a linear approximation to the standard model of litigation expenditure, that relate the difference in expenditure per case between the English and American rules to two empirical parameters: the ratio of total expenditure to the stakes of the case, and the elasticity with which parties

increase their expenditures in response to higher stakes. Using empirical estimates of these parameters taken from the University of Wisconsin's Civil Litigation Research Project (Trubek et al. 1983), he calculated the likely effects of switching from the American to the English rule, concluding that such a switch would increase expenditures per case in the neighborhood of 125 percent.

Such a large increase in cost per case, however, could be expected to lead to a reduction in the number of cases or to increased settlement. In an attempt to measure this anticipated reduction, Hause (1989) extended the Landes-Gould optimism model to allow for variable expenditure, and calculated its numerical behavior for a range of possible parameter values. He concluded that the increased costs per case under the English rule were sufficient to outweigh any effects of optimism, resulting on balance in an increased frequency of settlement. Hersch (1990) recalculated Hause's simulations under the assumption that trial expenditure is determined in a conjectural-variations rather than a Nash equilibrium. He found that both settlement and costs per case rose, though by a lesser amount than Hause had estimated. The parameter values Hause and Hersch used, however, were not based on any empirical data. Donohue (1991a) recalculated Hause's simulations using what he argued were more plausible parameter estimates, and concluded that the English rule would increase trials on balance.

Hylton (1993a, 1993b) used numerical simulation to estimate the effects of fee shifting on primary behavior. He concludes that while litigation is more frequent under the English than the American rule, levels of substantive compliance under the two rules would be similar. Best of all, according to his calculations, is one-way pro-plaintiff fee shifting, which leads to the highest level of compliance and least amount of litigation. These conclusions, however, depend both on the functional form used in his simulations, and on the specific assumptions of his theoretical model.

Watanabe (2006), which is described below, combines simulation techniques with econometric estimation in order to study the effects of litigation reform on settlement timing.

8.3 *Econometric Evidence of Actual Disputes*

Schwab and Eisenberg (1988) report on a 1976 statute that established one-way pro-plaintiff fee shifting in federal constitutional tort cases (that is, cases in which the federal government is sued for violating the plaintiff's constitutional rights). They find some evidence that the statute was followed by a decline in plaintiff success rates at trial and by an increase in trials relative to other federal civil actions, but little evidence of any increase in the number of lawsuits filed. These results suggest that the statute had its primary effect in encouraging plaintiffs to bargain more aggressively in settlement negotiations, consistent with Rowe et al.'s survey experiments, as well as with the theoretical predictions of the optimism and Bayesian settlement models discussed in Section 5 above. Because of the relatively low magnitude of their quantitative estimates, however, and because their observations were muddied by the fact that some courts shifted fees on a discretionary basis before the statute was passed, the authors present their findings as tentative.

Fournier and Zuehlke (1989) develop an econometric model of settlement behavior in which the plaintiff's settlement demand and the probability of settlement are jointly determined. Using nonlinear methods that correct for data censoring (that is, the fact that the amount of the demand is only observed when settlement takes place), they estimate their model using data from a nationwide survey of civil federal filings between 1979 and 1981. The data classify disputes according to the type of legal claim at issue (for example, tort, copyright, antitrust) and include information regarding the alleged damages and the number of litigants in each case, the mean and variance of trial awards in litigated cases within each subject-matter classification, and separately prepared estimates of government litigation costs in each case classification, which the authors argue serve as a reasonable proxy for private litigation costs. The coefficients of the resulting equations suggest, not surprisingly, that settlement demands are positively correlated with mean trial awards and alleged damages, and negatively correlated with litigation costs. More interestingly, they also suggest that settlement is more likely in cases and categories with high alleged damages, high mean and variance of trial awards, multiple parties, and low (!) litigation costs. These latter results are at odds with the theoretical predictions of most models of settlement, although the negative relationship between settlement and potential trial awards is consistent with a hypothesis of risk aversion.

Because a fraction of the sampled filings were subject to the English rule, Fournier and Zuehlke were able to estimate its effects as well. They find that fee shifting is negatively correlated with both the probability of settlement and the size of the settlement demand, although the latter effect is not statistically significant. This finding lends some support to the predictions of both the optimism and Bayesian models. The filings in their sample governed by the English rule, however, were few in number and concentrated in a few specialized areas, so this evidence cannot be regarded as especially strong. It is possible that this correlation reflects differences in the types of disputes covered by the rule, rather than effects of indemnification. The authors' unusual findings regarding the other determinants of settlement also call this result into question.

More instructive is Hughes and Snyder's research on Florida's experiment with the English rule in medical malpractice cases. The Florida statute, passed in 1980 with the support of the state medical association, also provided an offer-of-judgment procedure and exempted insolvent parties from the obligation to pay indemnification; it was repealed in 1985 with the support of its original proponents following a series of expensive and well-publicized plaintiff verdicts. In Snyder and Hughes (1990), the authors use a bivariate probit procedure to analyze insurance company data on closed claims filed before, during, and after the period in which the rule was in effect, and estimate the effects of indemnification on plaintiffs' decisions to drop claims, settlement, and defendants' expenditure on lawyers. Their findings lend support to several of the theoretical predictions outlined in previous sections of this chapter. Specifically, they find that in cases governed by the English rule, (1) a significantly higher percentage of claims were dropped at an early stage of the litigation, consistent with the proposition that fee shifting encourages risk-averse and low probability plaintiffs to exit the system; (2) defendants spent significantly more per case, in amounts consistent with Katz's simulations, in both settled and in litigated cases; (3) holding other case characteristics constant, the likelihood of litigation increased, consistent with the optimism model. Because dropped cases tended disproportionately to have characteristics that would have made them likelier to go to trial had they remained in the system, however, the authors conclude that the English rule decreased the frequency of litigation on balance. Because of greater expenditure per case, however, total expenditures on litigation still increased.

In a subsequent article analyzing the same data set (Hughes and Snyder 1995), the authors find that the English rule was associated with an increased frequency of plaintiff success rates at trial, increased jury awards, and larger out-of-court settlements. These increases were significant not just statistically but in absolute terms; for instance, the average judgment in litigated cases increased from $25,190 in cases governed by the American rule to $69,390 in cases governed by the English rule. These results appear to be driven by the case selection effects detailed in the first article. The authors suggest that their results vindicate the proposition that indemnification improves the quality of claims brought, although they admit the possibility of an alternative explanation that low-damage cases are merely being driven away by the higher costs of litigation. They conclude that fee shifting, contrary to the assertions of some legal practitioners, is not necessarily an antiplaintiff policy. Rather, it benefits plaintiffs with high-quality or high-damage claims at the expense of those with low-quality or low-damage claims, and possibly at the expense of defendants. These conclusions, if valid, would explain why the financial advantages expected by the Florida statute's original proponents did not appear to materialize;

they would also suggest that the statute improved the deterrent effect of civil liability. Whether such an improvement would be worth the increased litigation expenditures it occasioned, however, and whether it would be replicated in other areas of law with different substantive and procedural characteristics from medical malpractice, remain open questions.

Two recent empirical studies emphasize the impact of cost-shifting rules on the dynamics of litigation, and in particular, the timing of settlement.

Watanabe (2006) also analyzes Florida data, but from a time period following repeal of that state's experiment with the English rule. Watanabe studies the effect of the English rule on the timing of settlement and the costs of delayed resolution. He finds that the English rule results in longer and costlier disputes because, with more at stake, parties have a greater incentive to wait longer for new information regarding the merits of the plainitff's case before making the decision to settle.

Watanabe uses a methodology that combines econometric estimation and numerical simulation. His analysis proceeds in three steps.

First, he constructs a theoretical model of settlement dynamics. Potential litigants meet to discuss settlement after injury has been suffered, but before a suit has been filed. During this prefiling phase of settlement negotiations, the plaintiff may file suit, thus causing bargaining to enter a second, litigation phase. The pre-litigation phase is time-bound by the statute of limitations; the litigation phase is time-bound by the scheduled court date. The parties begin negotiations with different beliefs about the plaintiff's chance of prevailing at trial. They identically discount future costs and benefits, and they agree, and are certain regarding, what the plaintiff would recover should she prevail at trial. In each period of each phase of negotiation: (1) new information may arrive upon which the parties update their beliefs regarding the plaintiff's chance of winning at trial, (2) one (randomly selected) party makes a settlement offer, (3) the other decides whether or not to accept the offer, and (4) in the pre-litigation phase, the plaintiff decides whether or not to accelerate the process by filing suit. Plaintiffs have contingent fee arrangements with their attorneys under which the attorneys pay all costs. Thus, Watanabe's model is a kind of sequential bargaining model with non-common priors and exogenous learning.

Second, Watanabe estimates his model. To do so, Watanabe uses a data set on medical malpractice insurance claims in Florida for serious injuries or death that were closed between 1985 and 1999. The data set contains detailed information on the time, mode, cost, and terms of settlement, the occurrence and time of filing, and litigant characteristics. Using numerical methods (combined with functional form assumptions), Watanable determines the conditional probability distribution of observable variables that would result from each possible array of unobserved parameter values. He then estimates such unobserved parameter values by choosing the array of such values that assigns the maximum likelihood to the configuration of observable variables that are actually observed in the data.

Third, Watanabe conducts policy experiments on his so-calibrated model. Of particular relevance to the topic at hand, Watanabe finds that moving to a loser-pays-all allocation of legal fees would delay settlement and increase legal costs. Under the rule modification that Watanabe studies, the plaintiff herself, as opposed to her attorney, pays defendant's legal costs if the plaintiff loses. For each party, the English rule causes a greater divergence in each party's payoffs as between prevailing and losing. Watanabe describes the intuition for additional delay this way:

> [The] trade-off between [the] potential for learning new information and [the] extra legal cost due to delay determines the equilibrium of the model. [T]he value of learning increases with loser-pay-all legal fee allocation because [the] difference in payoff from winning and losing judgment is increased. Hence, settlement timing delays and legal costs increase.

Yoon and Baker (2006) obtain quite different results. They use insurance data on the disposition (including settlement) of filed cases in New Jersey to study the effect of New Jersey's expansion of its bilateral offer-of-judgment rule to allow the categorical recovery of unlimited attorneys' fees. (The unilateral federal rule allows recovery of attorneys' fees only in certain situations.)

Yoon and Baker obtained their data from an insurance company (whose name they are unable to disclose). The cases in Yoon and Baker's sample consist of suits by non-policyholders against the insurance company for injuries allegedly caused by policyholders. Most suits in the database arise from automobile and homeowners' insurance policies.

Yoon and Baker employ a "difference-in-differences" approach. Their treatment group consists of New Jersey litigants involved in suits before and after the offer-of-judgment rule was strengthened. Their control group consists of similarly situated litigants in surrounding states that did not experience a similar rule change. Yoon and Baker examine whether differences in relevant variables across the two time periods differ across their treatment and control groups. Importantly, Yoon and Baker argue that the New Jersey rule change that they study – because it was judicial and not legislative – was likely exogenous and not itself a reflection of underlying, unobservable differences between the treatment and control groups.

Yoon and Baker find that the New Jersey rule change reduced time to resolution by roughly 7 percent and reduced the insurance company's attorneys' fees by roughly 20 percent. They conclude that "a substantial cost-shifting mechanism would be an effective means of increasing the efficacy of offer-of-judgment rules."

Yoon and Baker hypothesize that their results are driven mainly by the effect of the rule change on settlement timing. They suggest that expanding the range of shiftable costs under the bilateral offer of judgment rule caused parties to reach settlement more quickly (though not more often, according to their data), and that this reduction in the duration of litigation, in turn, was the dominant force acting on attorneys' fees. Why did the rule change reduce time to settlement? Yoon and Baker postulate that, among many conflicting forces, the dominant effects of expanded cost shifting were these: (1) parties were induced to make more generous settlement offers, and (2) parties regarded trial as a less favorable prospect because the increased stakes implied a harmful escalation in spending.

In contrast, Watanabe (2006), discussed above, finds that moving to a loser-pays-all allocation of legal fees *delays* settlement and thereby increases legal costs. Several factors might explain the difference in the implications for settlement timing as between Watanabe (2006) and Yoon and Baker (2006). One possible factor, of course, is that the rule changes considered in each study are not identical: the expanded cost shifting in Yoon and Baker, but not in Watanabe, is conditional on the proposal and rejection of a settlement offer. However, it is unclear from existing theory what impact this difference might have on settlement timing.

Another possible factor concerns differences in case composition. While Watanable looks at medical malpractice cases, Yoon and Baker consider cases arising from automobile accidents and property damage. In Watanabe (2006), cases take longer to settle with a cost-shifting rule because, the stakes of the case being greater, parties are willing to wait longer for new information revealed in pretrial process. It is possible that this wait-to-learn dynamic is more pronounced in medical malpractice cases than in auto accident and property damage cases. Plausibly, the information flow in medical malpractice cases is both more substantial and more extenuated – given the more prominent role of scientific and medical expertise.

9. Conclusion

All in all, despite the substantial scholarly and popular attention that the question of indemnity for legal fees has attracted, the number of robust conclusions that can be drawn regarding its consequences are few. Fee shifting does appear to increase legal expenditures per case, in some cases significantly. It also encourages parties with poorly grounded legal claims to settle or to avoid litigating them in the first place, and has a similar effect on litigants who are averse to risk, regardless of the merits of their cases. Aside from these generalizations, most of the other propositions commonly asserted about fee shifting can be neither verified nor rejected. It is unclear whether fee shifting increases the likelihood of settlement, whether it decreases total expenditures on litigation or total payouts by defendants, or whether on balance it improves incentives for primary behavior. It is even unclear whether fee shifting makes it easier for parties with small meritorious claims to obtain compensation, in light of the increased costs per case that it induces. In this regard, the relative lack of systematic empirical investigation of these questions is particularly lamentable.

In light of this state of affairs, one is tempted to conclude that the amount of scholarly attention directed to this topic exceeds its actual social importance. The continued popular and political interest in fee-shifting rules, however, makes this conclusion problematic. While some support for fee shifting arises from its relative simplicity and its status as the international majority rule, much of its continued appeal undoubtedly stems from its association with deeply held notions of corrective justice – and specifically, from the idea that a party who is determined *ex post* to be in the right should be made financially whole. Counterarguments based on economic efficiency, or indeed on any *ex ante* perspective, can never entirely rebut this simple yet powerful intuition.

Whether the English rule is more just than the American rule, or whether its greater fairness justifies its incentive properties, cannot be settled by lawyers or economists alone. The citizenry as a whole must decide whether the principle of full compensation for victorious litigants outweighs the procedural values of providing citizens with an open forum for grievances and an opportunity to be heard, the uncertainty imposed on those who cannot predict the outcome of court decisions, and the political implications of regulating legal fees through a system of bureaucratic oversight rather than through private contract between attorney and client. Moreover, as Prichard (1988) and Hylton (1996) have observed, rules of cost allocation feed back through the selection of cases to influence the development of other areas of substantive and procedural law. Rules that encourage parties to raise relatively innovative claims and defenses help to break down precedent, while rules that penalize risk-taking and novel arguments help to preserve traditional formal categories. Given the pervasive influence of ostensibly procedural rules on substantive outcomes, it may not be possible to separate the policy of fee shifting from deeper questions of what the law should be.

Bibliography

Anderson, David A. (1994). 'Improving Settlement Devices: Rule 68 and Beyond', 23 *Journal of Legal Studies*, 225–46.
Baye, Michael R., Kovenock, Dan and de Vries, Caspar G. (2005), 'Comparative Analysis of Litigation Systems: An Auction-Theoretic Approach', 115 *The Economic Journal*, 583–601.
Bebchuk, Lucian Arye and Chang, Howard F. (1996), 'An Analysis of Fee Shifting Based on the Margin of Victory: On Frivolous Suits, Meritorious Suits, and the Role of Rule 11', 25 *Journal of Legal Studies*, 371–403.
Beckner, Clinton F. and Katz, Avery (1995), 'The Incentive Effects of Litigation Fee Shifting when Legal Standards are Uncertain', 15 *International Review of Law and Economics*, 205–24.
Bowles, Roger A. (1987), 'Settlement Range and Cost Allocation Rules: A Comment on Avery Katz's Measuring the Demand for Litigation', 3 *Journal of Law, Economics, and Organization*, 177–84.
Braeutigam, Ronald R., Owen, Bruce M. and Panzar, John C. (1984), 'An Economic Analysis of Alternative Fee Shifting Systems', 47 *Law and Contemporary Problems*, 173–85.
Chen, Kong-pin and Wang, Jue-Shyan (2007), 'Fee-shifting Rules in Litigation with Contingency Fees', 23 *Journal of Law, Economics, and Organization*, 519–46.
Choi, Albert and Sanchirico, Chris (2004), 'Should Plaintiffs Win What Defendants Lose: Litigation, Stakes, Litigation Effort, and the Benefit of Decoupling', 33 *Journal of Legal Studies*, 323–54.
Chopard, Bertrand, Cortade, Thomas, and Langlais, Eric (2008), 'Trial and Settlement Negotiations between Asymmetrically Skilled Parties', Manuscript, University of Paris X – Nanterre, Economix, available at http://economix.u-paris10.fr/docs/889/bte_bilateral(juillet_2008).pdf.
Chung, Tai-Yeong (1996), 'Settlement of Litigation under Rule 68: An Economic Analysis', 25 *Journal of Legal Studies*, 261–86.
Cooper, Edward H. (1994), 'Discovery Cost Allocation: Comment', 23 *Journal of Legal Studies*, 465–80.
Cooter, Robert D. and Rubinfeld, Daniel L. (1989), 'Economic Analysis of Legal Disputes and their Resolution', 27 *Journal of Economic Literature*, 1067–97.
Cooter, Robert D. and Rubinfeld, Daniel L. (1995), 'Reforming the New Discovery Rules', 84 *Georgetown Law Journal*, 61–89.
Coursey, Don L. and Stanley, L.R. (1988), 'Pretrial Bargaining Behavior within the Shadow of the Law: Theory and Experimental Evidence', 8 *International Review of Law and Economics*, 161–79.
Dewees, Donald N., Prichard, J. Robert S. and Trebilcock, Michael J. (1981), 'An Economic Analysis of Cost and Fee Rules for Class Actions', 10 *Journal of Legal Studies*, 155–85.
Dnes, Antony W. and Rickman, Neil (1998), 'Contracts for Legal Aid: A Critical Discussion of Government Policy Proposals', 5(3) *European Journal of Law and Economics*, 247–65.
Donohue, John J. (1991a), 'The Effects of Fee Shifting on the Settlement Rate: Theoretical Observations on Costs, Conflicts, and Contingency Fees', 54 *Law and Contemporary Problems*, 194–222.
Donohue, John J. (1991b), 'Opting for the British Rule; or, If Posner and Shavell Can't Remember the Coase Theorem, Who Will?', 104 *Harvard Law Review*, 1093–119.
Farmer, Amy and Pecorino, Paul (1998), 'A Reputation for being a Nuisance: Frivolous Lawsuits and Fee Shifting in a Repeated Play Game', 18 *International Review of Law and Economics*, 147–57.
Farmer, Amy and Pecorino, Paul (1999), 'Legal Expenditure as a Rent-seeking Game', 100 *Public Choice*, 271–88.
Fournier, Gary M. and Zuehlke, Thomas W. (1989), 'Litigation and Settlement: An Empirical Approach', 71 *Review of Economics and Statistics*, 189–95.
Geng, Jiong and McAfee, R. Preston (2000), 'Pretrial Negotiation, Litigation, and Procedural Rules', 38 *Economic Inquiry*, 218–38.

Gravelle, Hugh S.E. (1993), 'The Efficiency Implications of Cost Shifting Rules', **13** *International Review of Law and Economics*, 3–18.
Halpern, Paul J. and Turnbull, Stuart M. (1983), 'Legal Fees Contracts and Alternative Cost Rules: An Economic Analysis', **3** *International Review of Law and Economics*, 3–26.
Hause, John C. (1989), 'Indemnity, Settlement, and Litigation, or I'll be Suing You', **18** *Journal of Legal Studies*, 157–79.
Hersch, Philip L. (1990), 'Indemnity, Settlement, and Litigation: Comment and Extension', **19** *Journal of Legal Studies*, 235–41.
Hughes, James W. and Snyder, Edward A. (1995), 'Litigation and Settlement under the English and American Rules: Theory and Evidence', **38** *Journal of Law and Economics*, 225–50.
Hughes, James W. and Woglom, Geoffry R. (1996), 'Risk Aversion and the Allocation of Legal Costs', in Anderson, David A. (ed.), *Dispute Resolution: Bridging the Settlement Gap*, Greenwich, CT: JAI Press, 167–92.
Hyde, Charles E. (2006), 'Conditional versus Contingent Fees: Litigation Expenditure Incentives', **26** *International Review of Law and Economics*, 180–94.
Hyde, Charles E. and Williams, Phillip L. (2002), 'Necessary Costs and Expenditure Incentives under the English Rule', **22** *International Review of Law and Economics*, 133–52.
Hylton, Keith N. (1993a), 'Litigation Cost Allocation Rules and Compliance with the Negligence Standard', **22** *Journal of Legal Studies*, 457–76.
Hylton, Keith N. (1993b), 'Fee Shifting and Incentives to Comply with the Law', **46** *Vanderbilt Law Review*, 1069–128.
Hylton, Keith N. (1996), 'Fee-shifting and Predictability of Law', **71** *Chicago-Kent Law Review*, 427–59.
Kaplow, Louis (1993), 'Shifting Plaintiffs' Fees versus Increasing Damage Awards', **24** *Rand Journal of Economics*, 625–30.
Katz, Avery (1987), 'Measuring the Demand for Litigation: Is the English Rule Really Cheaper?', **3** *Journal of Law, Economics, and Organization*, 143–76.
Katz, Avery (1990), 'The Effect of Frivolous Lawsuits on the Settlement of Litigation', **10** *International Review of Law and Economics*, 3–27.
Klement, Alon and Neeman, Zvika (2005), 'Against Compromise: A Mechanism Design Approach', **21** (2) *Journal of Law, Economics, and Organization*, 285–314.
Kobayashi, Bruce H. and Parker, Jeffrey S. (1993), 'No Armistice at 11: A Commentary on the Supreme Court's 1993 Amendment to Rule 11 of the Federal Rules of Civil Procedures', **3** *Supreme Court Economic Review*, 92–152.
Leubsdorf, John (1984), 'Toward a History of the American Rule on Attorney Fee Recovery', **47(1)** *Law and Contemporary Problems*, 9–36.
Main, Brian G.M. and Park, Andrew (2000), 'The British and American rules: An Experimental Examination of Pre-trial Bargaining in the Shadow of the Law', **47** *Scottish Journal of Political Economy*, 37–60.
Main, Brian G.M. and Park, Andrew (2002), 'The Impact of Defendant Offers into Court on Negotiation in the Shadow of the Law: Experimental Evidence', **22** *International Review of Law and Economics*, 177–92.
Martin, Lucas D. (2005), 'Costs', in **20** *American Jurisprudence 2d.*, Eagan, MN: Thomson/West, 1–123. Pocket part (2008), 1–15.
Mause, Philip (1969), 'Winner Takes All: A Re-examination of the Indemnity System', **55** *Iowa Law Review*, 26–55.
Miller, Geoffrey P. (1986), 'An Economic Analysis of Rule 68', **15** *Journal of Legal Studies*, 93–125.
Note (1984), 'State Attorney Fee Shifting Statutes: Are We Quietly Repealing the American Rule?', **47** *Law and Contemporary Problems*, 321–46.
Pfennigstorf, Werner (1984), 'The European Experience with Attorney Fee Shifting', **47** *Law and Contemporary Problems*, 37–124.
Plott, Charles R. (1987), 'Legal Fees: A Comparison of the American and English Rules', **3** *Journal of Law, Economics and Organization*, 185–92.

Polinsky, A. Mitchell and Che, Yeon-Koo (1991), 'Decoupling Liability: Optimal Incentives for Care and Litigation', **22** *Rand Journal of Economics*, 562–70.

Polinsky, A. Mitchell and Rubinfeld, Daniel L. (1993), 'Sanctioning Frivolous Suits: An Economic Analysis', **82** *Georgetown Law Journal*, 397–435.

Polinsky, A. Mitchell and Rubinfeld, Daniel L. (1996), 'Optimal Awards and Penalties when the Probability of Prevailing Varies among Plaintiffs', **27** *Rand Journal of Economics*, 269–80.

Polinsky, A. Mitchell and Rubinfeld, Daniel L. (1997), 'Does the English Rule Discourage Low-probability-of-prevailing Plaintiffs?', **26** *Journal of Legal Studies*, 519–35.

Prichard, J. Robert S. (1988), 'A Systematic Approach to Comparative Law: The Effect of Cost, Fee and Financing Rules on the Development of the Substantive Law', **17** *Journal of Legal Studies*, 451–75.

Priest, George L. (1982), 'Regulating the Content and Volume of Litigation: An Economic Analysis', **1** *Supreme Court Economic Review*, 163–83.

Reinganum, Jennifer F. and Wilde, Louis L. (1986), 'Settlement, Litigation, and the Allocation of Litigation Costs', **17** *Rand Journal of Economics*, 557–66.

Rosenberg, David and Shavell, Steven (1985), 'A Model in Which Suits are Brought for their Nuisance Value', **5** *International Review of Law and Economics*, 3–13.

Rowe, Thomas D. (1984), 'Predicting the Effects of Attorney Fee Shifting', **47** *Law and Contemporary Problems*, 139–71.

Rowe, Thomas D. and Anderson, David A. (1996), 'One-Way Fee Shifting Statutes and Offer of Judgment Rules: An Experiment', **36** *Jurimetrics Journal*, 255–73.

Rowe, Thomas D. and Vidmar, Neil (1988), 'Empirical Research on Offers of Settlement: A Preliminary Report', **51** *Law and Contemporary Problems*, 13–39.

Schmalbeck, Richard L. and Myers, Gary (1986), 'A Policy Analysis of Fee-shifting Rules under the Internal Revenue Code', **6** *Duke Law Journal*, 970–1002.

Schwab, Stewart J. and Eisenberg, Theodore (1988), 'Explaining Constitutional Tort Litigation: The Influence of the Attorney Fees Statute and the Government as Defendant', **73** *Cornell Law Review*, 719–84.

Shavell, Steven (1982a), 'Suit, Settlement and Trial: A Theoretical Analysis under Alternative Methods for the Allocation of Legal Costs', **11** *Journal of Legal Studies*, 55–81.

Slater, Dan (2008), 'The Debate over Who Pays Fees when Litigants Mount Attacks', *Wall Street Journal*, December 23, A8.

Snyder, Edward A. and Hughes, James W. (1990), 'The English Rule for Allocating Legal Costs: Evidence Confronts Theory', **6** *Journal of Law, Economics and Organization*, 345–80.

Spier, Kathryn E. (1994), 'Pretrial Bargaining and the Design of Fee-Shifting Rules', **25** *Rand Journal of Economics*, 197–214.

Symposium on Attorney Fee Shifting (1984), **47** *Law and Contemporary Problems*, 1–354.

Symposium on Fee Shifting (1996), **71** *Chicago-Kent Law Review*, 415–697.

Talley, Eric (1996), 'Liability-based Fee Shifting Rules and Settlement Mechanisms under Incomplete Information', **71** *Chicago-Kent Law Review*, 461–503.

Tomkins, Alan J. and Willging, Thomas E. (1986), *Taxation of Attorneys' Fees: Practices in English, Alaskan, and Federal Courts*, Washington: Federal Judicial Center.

Trubek, David M., Grossman, Joel B., Felstiner, William L. F., Kritzer, Herbert M. and Sarat, Austin (1983), *Civil Litigation Research Project: Final Report*, Madison, Wisconsin: Institute for Legal Studies.

Watanabe, Yasutora (2006), 'Learning and Bargaining in Dispute Resolution: Theory and Evidence from Medical Malpractice Litigation', Unpublished Manuscript, Department of Management and Strategy, Kellogg School of Management, Northwestern University.

Yoon, Albert and Baker, Tom (2006), 'Offer-of-judgment Rules and Civil Litigation: An Empirical Study of Automobile Insurance Litigation in the East', **59** *Vanderbilt Law Review*, 155–96.

Other References

Anderson, David A. (ed.) (1996), *Dispute Resolution: Bridging the Settlement Gap*, Greenwich, CT: JAI Press.

Anderson, David A. and Rowe, Thomas D. (1996),'Empirical Evidence on Settlement Devices: Does Rule 68 Encourage Settlement?', **71** *Chicago-Kent Law Review*, 519–45.

Bebchuk, Lucian A. (1984), 'Litigation and Settlement under Imperfect Information', **15** *Rand Journal of Economics*, 404–15.

Bebchuk, Lucian A. and Chang, Howard F. (1996), 'The Effect of Offer-of-settlement Rules on the Terms of Settlement', Manuscript, University of Southern California.

Bernstein, Lisa (1993), 'Understanding the Limits of Court-connected ADR: A Critique of Federal Court Annexed Arbitration Programs', **141** *University of Pennsylvania Law Review*, 2169–259.

Cooter, Robert D., Marks, Stephen and Mnookin Robert (1982), 'Bargaining in the Shadow of the Law: A Testable Model of Strategic Behavior', **11** *Journal of Legal Studies*, 225–51.

Cooter, Robert D. and Rubinfeld, Daniel L. (1994), 'An Economic Model of Legal Discovery', **23** *Journal of Legal Studies*, 435–63.

Cooter, Robert D. and Rubinfeld, Daniel L. (1995),'Reforming the New Discovery Rules', **84** *Georgetown Law Journal*, 61–89.

Cornell, Bradford (1990),'The Incentive to Sue: An Option Pricing Approach', **19** *Journal of Legal Studies*, 173–87.

Gould, John P. (1973), 'The Economics of Legal Conflicts', **2** *Journal of Legal Studies*, 279–300.

Harsanyi, John C. and Selten, Reinhard (1972), 'A Generalized Nash Solution for Two Person Bargaining Games with Incomplete Information', **18** *Management Science*, 80–106.

Katz, Avery (1988), 'Judicial Decisionmaking and Litigation Expenditure', **8** *International Review of Law and Economics*, 127–43.

Landes, William M. (1971), 'An Economic Analysis of the Courts', **14** *Journal of Law and Economics*, 61–101.

Myerson, Roger B. and Satterthwaite, Mark A. (1983), 'Efficient Mechanisms for Bilateral Trading', **29** *Journal of Economic Theory*, 265–81.

P'ng, Ivan P.L. (1987), 'Litigation, Liability, and Incentives to Take Care', **34** *Journal of Public Economics*, 61–85.

Polinsky, A. Mitchell and Rubinfeld, Daniel L. (1988), 'The Welfare Effects of Costly Litigation for the Level of Liability', **17** *Journal of Legal Studies*, 151–64.

Polinsky, A. Mitchell and Shavell, Steven (1989), 'Legal Error, Litigation, and the Incentive to Obey the Law', **5** *Journal of Law, Economics, and Organization*, 99–108.

Posner, Richard A. (1973), 'An Economic Approach to Legal Procedure and Judicial Administration', **2** *Journal of Legal Studies*, 399–458.

Rose-Ackerman, Susan and Geistfeld, Mark (1987), 'The Divergence between Social and Private Incentives to Sue: A Comment on Shavell, Menell, and Kaplow', **16** *Journal of Legal Studies*, 483–91.

Shavell, Steven (1982b), 'The Social Versus the Private Incentive to Bring Suit in a Costly Legal System', **11** *Journal of Legal Studies*, 333–9.

Shavell, Steven (1995), 'Alternative Dispute Resolution: An Economic Analysis', **24** *Journal of Legal Studies*, 1–28.

Cases

Alyeska Pipeline Service Co. v. Wilderness Society, 421 US 240 (1975)
Marek v. Chesny, 105 S.Ct. 3012 (1985)

11 Judicial organization and administration
Lewis A. Kornhauser

1. Introduction

Economic analysis of substantive legal rules generally suppresses the adjudication of factual and legal disputes that a legal rule might engender. The nature of adjudication, however, will influence greatly both the content of the substantive law and the costs of dispute resolution. An understanding of the structure of adjudication is thus central to an understanding of the effects of legal rules on behavior and on the identification of socially desirable legal rules. In addition, adjudication is a complex task implemented through a set of central legal institutions that vary across time and jurisdiction.

Two distinct but related sets of questions about adjudication arise. First, what explains the structure of and variation among observed adjudicatory institutions? Court systems throughout the world and across time exhibit a number of similarities and differences. They are generally hierarchical, with appellate courts generally collegial. On the other hand, we observe variation in the selection, tenure, and dismissal practices across systems, differences in the degree of specialization, and differences in the nature of judicial output. Second, what explains the behavior of judges within a given court structure? Answers to this second set of questions, of course, will vary with the structure of the courts. After all, judges like other agents will respond to the incentives created by institutions. Moreover, different court systems require different behaviors from judges.

A vast literature in political science, economics, psychology, sociology and law have addressed these two sets of questions though far more attention has been devoted to questions of judicial behavior within institutions than to explanations of the structure of court systems. Even the literature in one of these disciplines defies succinct summary. In this review, and the review of "Appeal and Supreme Court" that addresses similar questions, I shall thus focus on rational choice approaches to courts and adjudication. Political scientists and economists introduced formal rational choice models of courts and adjudication in the 1980s. In the last decade, these models have proliferated in number and grown dramatically in power and sophistication, but there is as yet no agreement on the fundamentals of modeling.

The *Encyclopedia*'s division of topics into "Judicial Organization and

Administration" and "Appeal and Supreme Courts" is not an analytically satisfying one. The two questions outlined above suggest a more natural division between the explanations of the structure of judicial institutions we observe and explanations of behavior *within* observed institutions. Unfortunately, most of the literature on specific elements of court organization asks how specific institutions of, for example, judicial selection, affect the behavior of judges rather than on the explanation of why the specific structure was chosen. The two chapters thus adopt a somewhat arbitrary division of the literature. This chapter surveys the literature on court organization other than hierarchy, a feature inherent in the idea of appeal. Chapter 2 on "Appeal and Supreme Courts" surveys the literature on hierarchy and on judicial behavior more generally.

This division is not airtight as much of the literature on court organization investigates the effects of court structures on judicial behavior. Discussion of this literature thus also requires some basic background about judicial behavior. Thus, I shall begin with a brief survey of the literature on judicial motivation, as different assumptions about motivation radically influence one's understanding of court organization and of judicial behavior.

2. What do Judges Want?

Economic models of judicial behavior and of court organization require an assumption concerning the motivations of judges. This requirement presents the central challenge to the economic analysis of judicial behavior. Several approaches have been adopted, most of which are surveyed here. A related, supplementary discussion that emphasizes a distinction between "team" and "political" models of judges appears in Chapter 2 on "Appeal and Supreme Courts".

2.1 Non-ideological Judicial Preferences

The literature has focused primarily on adjudication in common law jurisdictions. Suggestions have thus been attuned to the institutional structures of these courts rather than the very different organizational structure of courts in civil law jurisdictions. More seriously, the discussion of motivation has focused on the motivation of judges within the federal system of the United States. The institutional structure there is particularly spare; the judges have life tenure; their salary cannot be reduced; and they face limited prospects of promotion to a higher court. This focus has implied that lawmaking is the judicial function that has received the most motivational attention.

In this context, the literature has advanced three different types of answers to the question of judicial motivation. First, various authors, following Posner (1973, 2008), have claimed that judges, like all other economic agents, are motivated by self-interest. They value income, leisure, their reputations, power, and, perhaps in addition, they have preferences over policies and for their craft. A menu of preferential factors differs from a precise specification of a utility function. Nevertheless, this menu has spurred efforts to measure how judges respond to typical economic incentives such as promotion or retention in those jurisdictions in which judges face electoral scrutiny.

Posner (1973) sketched an approach to the problem of identification of the preferences of judges. He assumed that judges were self-interested and then briefly examined different incentive structures from which he inferred the underlying preferences of the judges. In particular, he compared the structure in many states in which judges lack life tenure and aspire to higher political office to the structure of the federal courts in the United States in which the judges have life tenure. These themes were developed in the subsequent literature.

Second, one can assume that judges meet their obligations as articulated in some jurisprudential theory of adjudication. Put differently, judges "follow the law". In Posner's terms, such judges place predominant importance on their craft or their reputation among peers. Team models, discussed in Section 2 of Chapter 2, attempt to ground this adherence to norms in a more economic framework.

Third, one can assume, as the predominant approach in political science does, that judges have preferences over "policies". In political science, this approach has two variants. One, the "attitudinal model" (Segal and Spaeth 2002), adopts a behaviorist perspective, with the case serving as a stimulus and the judicial vote on the disposition of the case as the behavioral response dictated by an unobservable internal attitude. The second variant explicitly adopts an economic framework in which judges with preferences over policies act strategically. In fact, political science models generally assume that each judge has spatial preferences over a one-dimensional policy space, that is, each judge has an ideal policy X^* and she prefers policy X to policy Y if and only if X is closer to X^* than Y is. This formulation of preferences is discussed at greater length in the course of the review of the behavior of judges on collegial courts in Chapter 2.

A large number of studies consider the implications of these assumptions on preferences in the context of particular features of court organization. A few studies, however, address the question of motivation either theoretically or in a more direct, empirical fashion. I briefly review these few studies here.

Aranson (1990) surveys the political science literature that applies the spatial theory of voting to courts and compares it to law and economics

Judicial organization and administration 311

approaches to judicial motivation. He suggests three competing views of judicial motivation. The first, that it is rule governed, parallels the first strand mentioned above and is discussed at greater length in Section 2 of Chapter 2. The second, that judicial motivation is rent redistributing, and the third, that it is wealth maximizing, describe systemic tendencies rather than the motivation of particular judges. One might understand "rent redistribution" consistently with the political model discussed in Section 3 of Chapter 2. Wealth maximization, by contrast, assumes that Posner's claim that the common law maximizes wealth can be explained in terms of judicial success in pursuit of their common aim.

Landes and Posner (1980) argue, with the system of US federal courts in mind, that utility maximizing judges will primarily seek to maximize their power because their performance is too weakly linked to income and promotion for those concerns to have much effect on judicial behavior. They adopt the number of times a judge is cited in other cases as a measure of his power. They then argue that judges with higher salaries and more secure tenure will have greater power (and hence be cited more often) because higher salaries both attract more competent judges and reduce the judge's incentives to distort his decisions and because longer tenure reduces turnover and the influence of politics. They provide an ingenious test of their hypotheses. They create two samples of common law appellate opinions rendered in 1950. First, they look at all 246 tort, contract and property cases decided by the federal appellate courts under their diversity jurisdiction. Second, they draw a random sample of 241 tort, property or contract cases decided by state supreme courts in 1950. The number of cases drawn from a specific state matches the proportion of federal cases decided under the law of that state. They then compare the citation rates of state and federal decisions in the two systems. They find only weak support for their hypothesis concerning higher salary and more secure tenure. Federal decisions are more likely to be cited in the state supreme courts of "other" states (i.e., states other than the one of which the federal court applied the law) than the decisions of state courts.

Cooter (1983) adopts a procedure similar to that of Landes and Posner (1979). He develops a theory of behavior of private judges and uses that as a benchmark from which to infer the preferences of public judges. He argues that both public and private judges would care about their reputations among other judges and the bar.

Higgins and Rubin (1980) address the concern for promotion somewhat more directly. They argue that judges have preferences over policy "discretion" and wealth; these preferences are conditional on their age. They argue that a judge's ability to satisfy her preferences are constrained in two ways. First, the reversal rate depends on the judge's policy preferences and the policy preferences of the higher court. Second, wealth depends on the reversal rate (because that affects each judge's prospect of promotion) and age. They then derive a test for the relative effects of discretion and wealth.

They study two samples. The first sample consists of those active district court judges in the eighth federal circuit in 1974 who permitted the release of data on the total number of cases they decided in 1973 and 1974. The second sample consists of all active district court judges in the fifth federal circuit in 1966. They find that neither age nor seniority explained the reversal rates of the eighth circuit judges. They did find, however, that the estimated parameter on reversal rate had the predicted sign and was significant at the 10% level in a logit estimation of the probability of being promoted.

Greenberg and Haley (1986) argue, contrary to the conventional wisdom in general and to Posner (1985) in particular, that low judicial salaries are socially desirable because they signal a greater willingness to accept the non-pecuniary benefits of the judiciary; moreover, they argue that individuals who derive greater non-pecuniary benefits from judging make better judges.

Elder (1987) identifies two distinct mechanisms for monitoring judges: political and administrative mechanisms. These mechanisms create different incentives so that one should observe different behaviors in systems with different monitoring mechanisms. Without specifying the judicial objective function precisely, he nevertheless argues that judges deciding criminal cases will produce more trial verdicts under political monitoring than they would under administrative monitoring. He then tests this claim on 1977 data drawn from state criminal courts in 247 districts in seven states. His parameter estimates are consistent with his hypothesis.

Cohen (1992) follows up Elder's approach. He argues that Elder implicitly assumes that each judge sought to maximize his preferences defined in terms of minimizing his workload and his reversal rate. He argues that these preferences also imply that, when the penalty range increases, a judge will increase the penalty of those defendants who request a trial more than they increase the penalty of those who plead guilty. He also argues that judges will be concerned about promotion and that this too will influence the pattern of sentencing. He then considers a sample that consists of all federal antitrust indictments from 1955 through 1980. In 1974, Congress increased the maximum penalties for antitrust violations from $50,000 to $100,000. He finds that promotion concerns are explanatory with respect to fines but not with respect to incarceration.

Cohen (1991) exploits the data generated by a "natural experiment" presented by the adoption of new sentencing guidelines by the United States federal courts. He examines 196 decisions by federal district courts that considered the constitutionality of the guidelines. He estimates a probit model of the probability of upholding the guidelines as a function of judicial ideology, caseload, promotion potential and the number of prior decisions for constitutionality. Promotion potential is measured by an index that reflects the (per district court judge) number of open seats on the appellate circuit. He finds that the parameters on workload and promotion potential have the predicted sign and are highly significant.

Katz (1988) adopts a behavioral approach. He assumes that judges decide cases on the basis of the arguments presented to it. Each party offers arguments in its favor and the court decides in favor of the plaintiff if the plaintiff's arguments, in light of the "underlying" (or, perhaps, ex ante) merits of the case, outweigh the defendant's arguments and some random error. He then shows that, when cases are more evenly balanced ex ante, expenditures of each party on litigation rise; and, if judicial decision is more random or variable, each party's expenditures fall.

2.2 Policy Preferences

2.2.1 Measuring policy preferences As already noted, most models of judicial behavior in the political science literature assume that judges have preferences over policies. Empirical tests of these models have used a variety of increasingly sophisticated, though not clearly more reliable or accurate, measures of these policy preferences. The creation and evaluation of these measures has spawned a large literature – for example Segal and Cover (1989), Epstein and Mershon (1996), Segal (2007), Cameron and Clark (2008), Martin and Quinn (2002, 2005), Epstein et al. (2007), Harvey (2006). Given their importance and prevalence in the literature, a brief discussion of them is warranted.

All these measures assume that policies lie on a one-dimensional continuum and that preferences are spatial. As a consequence, a judge's preferences are completely described by the location of her "ideal point", the policy that she thinks best. The measurement problem thus reduces to identifying this ideal point.

The measures fall into two classes. One set of measures uses data from during the judicial selection process and produces a relatively crude indicator of policy; the second set uses the voting behavior of the judge to construct a more refined measure. As most empirical work studies the behavior of the justices of the United States Supreme Court or, less frequently, other judges, the first set of measures looks to the process of appointment of the judge to extract a measure of the judge's ideal point.

Federal judges in the United States are nominated by the President subject to the advice and consent of the Senate. Some measures thus attribute the "ideological" (or policy) position of the President to the appointed judge. This attribution may be more or less crude. It may simply identify the ideology in a binary way as either liberal or conservative, with Democratic presidents presumed to be "liberal" and Republican presidents presumed to be "conservative". Or the ideology of the president may be measured by scoring the President's announced position on roll call votes in the Congress which generates what is called a NOMINATE score that runs from -1 to 1. A refinement of these measures considers the composition of the Senate at the time of confirmation and attributes an ideological score to the judge on the basis of this composition of the Senate and the political affiliation of the President. A third measure, the Segal-Cover scores, relies on a content analysis of the editorials published in various newspapers in the United States prior to confirmation. Segal and Cover (1989) scale the ideology of justices on the unit interval, a score of -1 being most conservative and a score of 1 the most liberal. The Segal-Cover scores allow a more precise characterization of the "ideal point" of each justice and they have the additional advantage of relying on information that is exogenous to their voting behavior on the Court. A fourth measure, proposed in Cameron and Clark (2007), integrates the Segal-Cover score with a constructed NOMINATE score for each nominee.

The second set of measures constructs the ideal points of judges from their votes on cases. The most basic of these appears in Spaeth (2006), a comprehensive database of Supreme Court decisions that includes among its variables a dichotomous variable that designates each vote as "liberal" or "conservative". Harvey (2006) criticizes this measure by considering votes assessing the constitutionality of statues and assigning the ideology of the enacting Congress to the statute.

A more refined scale is produced by considering the votes of judges on many cases. One seeks a set of ideal points that best predicts the patterns of voting, as defined by the set of coalitions that form on the Court. These ideal points are then scaled, with one end identified as conservative and the other as liberal. Bailey and Chang (2001) and Martin and Quinn (2002, 2005) proceed in this fashion. Farnsworth (2007) provides a non-technical assessment of this literature, while Bafumi et al. (2005) offer a technical introduction and assessment.

Clark and Lauderdale (2010) adopt a different approach. They consider the opinions in a given area of law – in their case, religious expression – and count the favorable and unfavorable citations by the justices of those citations. This yields an ideology score for each justice that is in fact correlated with the Martin Quinn score.

Brace et al. (2000) have produced a measure of ideology for justices of supreme courts of several states. Their measure uses a measure of citizen ideology for justices of supreme courts in which such judges are elected and a measure of the ideology of the political "elite" in states in which supreme court justices are appointed.

2.2.2 Are judges ideological? As noted earlier, a significant part of the American political science literature on adjudication seeks to determine the effects of the "ideological" views of the judges on judicial decisions. This literature in general implicitly accepts the political model of adjudication and it generally finds at least some influence of "ideology" on outcome, where the judge's ideology is measured either by her political affiliation or by the affiliation of the appointing President. In this section, I consider some recent studies within the legal-economic framework.

The first study, Eisenberg and Johnson (1991), examine 118 federal district court opinions and 66 federal circuit court opinions in racial discrimination cases decided under the fourteenth amendment to the US Constitution. These opinions constituted all opinions on this issue published between 7 June 1976 and 6 February 1988. Eisenberg and Johnson found no effect of ideology, measured either by party of judge or of appointing President, on outcomes at either the district or appellate level. They attempted to evaluate the effects of the selection of cases for trial on their results by comparing trial success rates and success rates on appeal in the class of cases that they studied to these success rates in other classes of cases.

Ashenfelter, Eisenberg and Schwab (1995) ("AES") also found no effects of ideology. In a clever research design, they studied 2258 federal civil rights and prisoner cases filed in three federal districts courts in fiscal 1981. Unlike most prior studies, AES examine the effects of ideology not only on cases with published opinions but on all case dispositions. AES determined whether a case settled and, if it did not settle, which party prevailed. They also collected data, including party and party of appointing President, on each of the 47 different judges who sat on some case in the sample. AES then analyzed this data by district. This district analysis permitted them to exploit the federal practice of random assignment of cases to judges. Any observed differences in behavior across judges could be attributed to differences in judges rather than differences in cases. They found that judges had relatively little effect on case disposition. Moreover, "ideological" variables did not explain the small effects observed.

Revesz (1997) studied the industry and environmental challenges to EPA rulemaking in the 1970s and the late 1980s through early 1990s. This sample of cases has two features that make it a nearly ideal sample for analysis. First, all such challenges were heard in the Court of the Appeals for the District of Columbia. Second, virtually all challenges to EPA rulemaking are appealed. Given the legal context, there is no opportunity for the agency to settle with dissatisfied litigants. Following AES, Revesz focused on time periods in which a large number of judges had continuous tenure on the Circuit; he restricted his analysis to these judges. He measured the judge's policy preferences by the party of the appointing President, assuming that Republicans would favor industry challenges and disfavor environmental challenges relative to Democrats. For the late 1980s through early 1990s, he observed that ideology had a clear effect on industry challenges and a more ambiguous effect on environmental challenges. (A different statistical test, however, would likely reveal a stronger ideological effect in environmental challenges.)

Pinello (1999) conducts a meta-analysis of 84 studies that use party as an indicator of judicial ideology. He concludes that ideology explains 38% of the variation in decisions, though the explanatory effect of ideology varies across institutional settings. Thus, he argues that it is less successful an explanatory variable in state courts than in federal courts and that, within the federal system, it is most important in explanations of Supreme Court decisions.

Sisk and Heise (2005), however, argue that Pinello overstated the significance of ideology on Supreme Court decisions. In their analysis, ideology explains only 7% of the variation of federal judicial votes. Songer, Sheehan and Haire (2000) had earlier provided a similar estimate of the size of the effect for the federal intermediate courts of appeal.

Lindquist and Klein (2006) attempt to determine the role of both attitudinal or ideological factors and of jurisprudential factors in Supreme Court decision making. They model the role of "law" in terms of the Supreme Court's responsiveness to lower court rulings. To do so, they study cases that involve conflicts among the circuits. They find that the Court is more likely to adopt the majority position on a conflict; less likely to adopt positions that have attracted dissents or confusing concurrences below, and more likely to endorse the view of a prestigious lower court judge.

3. The Functions of Courts

3.1 What Do Courts Do?
We may answer this question at several different levels. We might ask it within a "legal" framework or more "globally". The first phrasing asks what differentiates courts from other political institutions such as legislatures and the executive. The second asks how courts facilitate societal success or welfare.

3.1.1 The legal functions of courts Adjudication resolves disputes. Dispute resolution itself consists of at least four different tasks. First, courts must determine the facts of the dispute. Second, they apply the law to those facts. Third, the court may, in some instances, enforce its judgment against one of the parties. Finally, in some instances, the court may have to compel one or more of the parties to submit to the jurisdiction of the court.

In some legal systems, the judicial function is limited to these four tasks; in others, courts also make law. In civil law theory, for example, courts simply apply the law announced by legislatures to resolve disputes. In practice, civil law courts do make law, but the theoretical fiction has consequences for the development of the law. Legal theorists in common law countries, by contrast, contend that courts resolve disputes through the application of law, but also promulgate new legal rules; courts thus play a lawmaking function as well.

This difference between civil and common law perceptions of adjudication, as well as various structural differences between the two systems, presents a challenge to economic analysts which has yet to be answered. The sequel in this review and in Chapter 2 tries to draw out these differences in specific areas.

Analyses of lawmaking and error-correction are generally addressed in a specific context and are addressed in various subsections below or in Chapter 2.

3.1.2 The social functions of courts In the last ten years, a vigorous debate has arisen about the role of courts in economic development. La Porta et al. (1998) triggered this debate with its claim that societies with common law judicial systems led to superior economic performance of financial markets than societies with civil law systems. This claim was then generalized to economic growth in Mahoney (2001). Moreover, legal origin has been used as an instrument for institutional differences across countries in studies such as Acemoglu et al. (2001). A more comprehensive survey of the literature appears in Levine (2005).

Three questions arise. First, is the claim true? Do common law systems in fact cause societies to grow more quickly than civil law systems? Second, if the claim is true, through what causal mechanism does the difference in legal regimes cause differential growth? Of course, to answer this question – indeed to answer the first – we need some characterization of the differences between the two systems. Third, what explains the emergence of different legal systems in England and France? I briefly address these questions in turn.

For several reasons, it is difficult to characterize the differences between civil law legal systems and common law systems. Conventionally, commentators point to four sets of institutional differences. First, in theory at least, courts in common law legal systems are a source of law, while courts have no such power in civil law legal systems. Second, common law processes are adversarial, while civil law systems are inquisitorial. Crudely, this distinction generally means that common law judges play a less active role in the production of the facts needed to resolve the dispute and that common law advocates play a larger role in developing legal arguments. Moreover, common law trials are primarily oral, while civil law trials are primarily written. Often, and almost always at their origins, juries found the facts in common law adjudication, while judges did so in civil law adjudication. (While juries continue to play an important role in the United States, they no longer find facts in many other common law jurisdictions.) Third, the judiciary in common law legal systems is drawn from the practicing bar, with lawyers ascending to the bench in the middle of or late in their careers, while the judiciary in civil law legal systems are government bureaucracies, with entry generally at the beginning of the jurist's career. Finally, Djankov et al. (2003) claim that civil law legal systems are more formalistic than common law ones.

Unfortunately, both systems are quite complex. An historical perspective aggravates this complexity. Much of the literature in this area identifies legal origins with the imperial power that governed a particular region four or five centuries ago. Common law institutions today differ dramatically from those of the sixteenth century. For instance, common law adjudication in the United States was much more formalistic in the nineteenth century that it is today. Civilian legal systems did not yet exist, as they are a creation of the French Revolution and the Napoleonic wars. The structure of legal systems within Europe prior to the spread of the Napoleonic codes may have varied greatly. While it may be true that the countries coded for common law legal systems generally had better economic performance than those coded for civil law legal systems (or Scandanavian legal systems), attributing the observed difference to the structure of the court system requires a giant inferential leap. Berkowitz et al. (2002), for example, argue that it is not the origin of the legal system that matters but the manner in which it was received; countries in which the shift was imposed fared worse than those that freely adopted the system.

Through what mechanism does the structure of the legal system operate? Most accounts of development contend that economic development requires secure property rights and effective enforcement of contract law. Why should common law systems provide more protection of property rights and better contract enforcement than civil law systems? Glaeser and Shleifer (2002) argue that common law systems are more decentralized than civil law systems largely because of the common law institution of the jury. They trace this divergence back to the origins of each legal system in the twelfth and thirteenth centuries. Klerman and Mahoney (2007) argue persuasively that, in fact, at their origins, the common law courts emerged in Britain as an institutional means of centralized law enforcement. The creation of royal courts served to displace adjudication from local, manorial courts. They note that the common law courts were centralized in the sense that both the judiciary and the bar were quite small; in France, by contrast, they note that the size of the judiciary presented severe monitoring problems. Moreover, they argue that juries did not serve a lawmaking function. Rather juries served as a collective form of testimony. Finally, they contend that, as jurors were chosen by a royal official, they were not in fact outside of royal control.

Lee (2003) offers a more plausible story. He characterizes the structure of a legal system with five variables: the status and power of judges (measured by the tenure of the judges of the highest court and by whether judicial systems serve as a source of law) and the structure of adjudication of "administrative claims" (or claims against the government) (measured by the tenure of the judges of the highest adminstrative court and by whether the administrative claims are adjudicated by a separate court system). He finds that unitary adjudication of administrative claims and judicial decisions as a source of law have the greatest effect on growth.

What explains the different evolution of the English and French legal structures? Glaeser and Shleifer (2002) argued that conflict between the barons and the King in Britain led to the institution of the jury trial in the thirteenth century in Britain. On their account, by contrast, the balance of power in France was different, with the King able to impose a centralized legal system. Klerman and Mahoney (2007) again contest this explanation. They argue rather that the English Civil War (and the subsequent Glorious Revolution) and the French Revolution were the central events that triggered the divergence in the structure of the common law and civil law legal systems.

Roe (2007) offers a different rebuttal of Glaeser and Shleifer. He attacks not the claim about the origins of the jury and the inquisitorial system; rather, he argues that juries are not central to the protection of investors' rights. Roe makes two distinct arguments. First, he notes that Delaware, a primary source of investor protection in the United States, decides corporate cases in a chancery court that operates without a jury. Second, he argues that Britain did not generally transplant the jury system to its colonies as that might have interfered with imperial policy in those locations.

3.2 Public versus Private Adjudication

Adjudication is commonly considered a quintessential function of government. In recent years, however, there has been a substantial privatization of at least some of these functions through a growing use of arbitration and other "private judges". This phenomenon has prompted scholars to study the extent to which government must supply judicial functions.

Landes and Posner (1979) provide one of the earliest inquiries into the choice between private and public provision of adjudicatory services. Working within a common law framework, they identify the judicial functions as both dispute resolution and rule generation. They argue that only the dispute resolution function is suitable for (partial) privatization. Some public provision of dispute resolution might be necessary because (1) enforcement of judgments might require public authority and (2) in some instances, public authority may be necessary to compel one or more parties to submit the dispute to adjudication in the first place. A private market in adjudicatory services, however, would meet all other requirements of a dispute resolution system. They argue that a competitive market would produce competent and impartial judges because both qualities would be necessary to induce all parties to a dispute to consent to adjudication of their dispute by a given judge. Cooter (1983) offers a similar argument.

Landes and Posner, however, argue that private provision of rules will not, in general, be desirable. Rule generation is a public good and a private judge who announces a rule will not capture all the benefits that the announcement of a rule creates. Therefore, in a system of private adjudication, rules will be undersupplied. In addition, competing judges may generate competing sets of rules. They do not, however, explain why rules cannot be adequately supplied by legislatures.

Shavell (1995) considers the choice of private dispute resolution in the context of an established public system of courts. He addresses two questions: why would parties resort to private dispute resolution and when is it socially desirable? He distinguishes ex ante invocation of private dispute resolution, in which the parties agree prior to the emergence of a dispute to resort to private resolution of their dispute, from ex post invocation of it, in which the resort to these private methods occurs after the dispute arises. He argues that ex ante invocation is socially desirable for three reasons: (1) it may lower the costs and risks of dispute resolution; (2) it may create better incentives to perform because of the greater accuracy of private resolution; and (3) it may reduce the number of litigated disputes. He argues that ex post invocation of private dispute resolution is not desirable.

4. The General Organization of Courts

Courts are complex organizations that form only one branch of government. This section addresses global questions about court organization. The first concerns the relation of courts to other branches; specifically I review the literature on judicial independence. This literature largely considers independence at a macro or systemic level. In Chapter 2, I consider the strategic implications for the behavior of judges deciding specific cases. The second question concerns the appointment and tenure of judges.

In this section, I discuss some of the issues raised by this variety of court organization. I begin, however, with a discussion of the question of judicial independence.

4.1 Independence of the Judiciary

Judicial independence is much praised and almost universally urged upon developing countries as a necessary precondition for economic and political development, though the experience of China suggests that this claim is false. The various definitions offered are not wholly consistent. Moreover, judicial independence is instrumentally, rather than intrinsically, valuable; we value judicial independence because of the benefits it provides. Three interrelated benefits are sometimes attributed to judicial independence. (1) An independent judiciary provides impartial adjudication of private disputes; (2) an independent judiciary prevents expropriation of wealth (or private property) by the government; and (3) an independent judiciary assures the civil and human rights of its citizens. Notice that these functions might be exercised in a jurisdiction without judicial review of legislation on a constitutional basis. British courts, for example, had no power of judicial review over parliamentary statutes, prior to the establishment of the European Union (EU).

Economic analysts have devoted much attention to explanations for, and implications of, "independent" judiciaries. An "independent" judiciary is one that is free from external, primarily, political influence. This conception of independence is somewhat at odds with the ascription of a political motivation to judges themselves because independence is generally seen as guaranteeing a more "objective" resolution of disputes. Though the literature has not attended much to this specific problem, there are suggestions that a more general model of constitutional structure might justify an independent branch of politically motivated judges.

Most industrialized countries assert the independence of their judiciaries, but the structures that guarantee "independence" differ greatly. In the federal system in the United States, for example, judges have life tenure and their (nominal) salaries cannot be decreased during their lifetime. In many states of the United States, however, judges serve for a term of years; moreover, in many states, they may be elected in either partisan or non-partisan elections. In both the state and federal systems, as in common law jurisdictions generally, judges are, however, drawn from the general bar. In many civil law countries by contrast, law graduates choose to enter practice or the judiciary at the outset of their career; a judicial bureaucracy then creates incentives for that judge. The insulation of that bureaucracy from "normal" politics then determines the extent of judicial independence. This institutional variation across jurisdictions permits a comparative study of judicial independence. As a consequence, studies of independence, unlike studies in other areas of judicial organization, have been primarily comparative in nature.

One might investigate judicial independence in at least two ways. One might consider it functionally and ask what features of polities lead to court systems that exhibit judicial independence. Alternatively, one might examine particular institutional structures – a particular selection, promotion and tenure scheme, for example – and whether it functions acceptably. Thus much of the discussion below concerning selection, promotion and tenure and of judicial review might be understood as discussions of judicial independence.

Landes and Posner (1975) offered the earliest explanation for the emergence of judicial independence. Their argument rests on the claim that an independent judiciary will, in statutory interpretation, enforce the original legislative understanding. Individual legislatures accede to this practice because they want to increase the time a statute prevails. Landes and Posner then claim that the degree of independence should increase with the size of the jurisdiction because larger jurisdictions provide broader scope for rent-seeking. They then attempt to test their theory on data concerning 97 statutes declared unconstitutional by the United States Supreme Court between 1789 and 1972.

Ramseyer (1994) extends the analysis of Landes and Posner (1975) by drawing on a comparison of Japan and the United States. Ramseyer defines judicial independence as the extent to which politicians do not manipulate careers of sitting judges. He asks why some politicians provide an independent judiciary and others do not. He claims that a political structure will provide for an independent judiciary if (i) politicians believe that elections will continue indefinitely and (ii) politicians believe that their prospects of continued victory are low. He then does three case studies: the United States, which satisfies both antecedent conditions and has an independent judiciary; contemporary Japan, which satisfies the first condition but not the second and does not have an independent judiciary; and imperial Japan, which satisfied condition (ii) but not condition (i) and did not have an independent judiciary.

Stephenson (2003) places Ramseyer's argument within a formal model. In his model, parties compete for control of the legislature. The winning party announces a policy. Then the courts rule on the legality of the policy. The legislature may then either ignore the ruling or amend the policy. Judicial independence exists if an equilibrium exists in which the legislature acquiesces in judicial rulings of illegality. Stephenson proves that an equilibrium exhibiting judicial independence exists if the partisan politics are sufficiently competitive, the judiciary uses a "moderate" rule in determining the illegality of legislative actions, and the competing parties are sufficiently risk averse and care enough about the future.

Hanssen (2004b) provides a formal model for the Ramseyer model. The model extends Maskin and Tirole's (2004) analysis of electoral accountability. There are three periods. In period 0, the ruling party chooses between two court structures – a dependent judiciary in which the ruling party can choose judges each period and an independent judiciary in which the initial party chooses judges for life. "Politics" occurs in periods 1 and 2. In each period, a "judge" must choose one of two policies a or b. There are two parties A and B with A preferring a to b and B preferring b to a. In period 1, the constitutional designer has the power to appoint a judge who will then implement a policy. There are three parameters to the model: the probability p that the party in power in either period can determine the policy preferences of his appointees, the probability x that the party in power in period 1 will be re-elected in period 2, and the distance d between the two policies a and b.

Hanssen proves two results. First, as the probability x of re-election increases, the higher the quality p of screening must be to make judicial independence desirable. That is, as elections grow less competitive, judicial independence becomes less desirable. Second, as the distance d between policies increases, the lower the quality p of screening must be to make judicial independence desirable. Hanssen then tests his model using data from the states of the United States.

Ramseyer and Rasmusen (2003) provide an extensive study of the case of contemporary Japan. They study the careers of roughly 790 judges who entered the Japanese judiciary between 1959 and 1968. As a measure of political ideology, they use membership in a leftist organization, the Young Jurist League. As those who become judges in Japan have foregone lucrative careers as private attorneys, Ramseyer and Rasmusen assume that the judges have preferences for successful careers, understood as rapid promotion through the bureaucratic ranks and postings to desirable cities. After controlling for quality of judge (with various measures of academic quality), they find that ideologically left judges have somewhat less successful careers than non-members of the Young Jurist League. Ramseyer and Rasmusen also identify classes of cases in which the ruling party in Japan, the LDP, would have a particular interest. They then compare the career paths of judges who rule against the LDP interest with the career paths of those who rule according to the LDP interest. They conclude that, in some instances, the judges who rule against the LDP interest have less successful careers. Ramseyer and Rasmusen (2006) extend their analysis to the era after the collapse of the political dominance of the LDP.

Haley (2007) argues that Ramseyer and Rasmusen's argument has a fatal gap. The Japanese judiciary, as Ramseyer and Rasmusen acknowledge, is governed by a Secretariat that makes all promotion and posting decisions. Haley contends that Ramseyer and Rasmusen have not excluded the hypothesis that the Secretariat acts disinterestedly to further the careers of the "best" judges.

Cooter and Ginsburg (1996) also deploy comparative data to study the question of judicial independence. They work with a different conception of independence than Ramseyer. Ramseyer's definition referred to the structure of appointment, pay, promotion and tenure in the judiciary. Cooter and Ginsburg have a more substantive view of independence; they look to the courts' ability to make law that diverges from the views of the legislature. They argue that the degree of judicial independence will depend on both political and constitutional features of a society. In particular, they argue that societies in which a cohesive party dominates politics will be less likely to have judicial independence. On the other hand, the more "legislative vetoes" that the constitution builds into its political process, the more independence the courts have. They asked experts in comparative law to rank the daringness of the judiciary of various countries. They then regressed daringness on the number of vetoes and the duration of the governing coalition. Despite the small sample size, the parameters on both independent variables had the predicted sign and were statistically significant; moreover, they explained a substantial part of the variance.

As noted at the beginning of this section, the meaning of judicial independence is clear. Feld and Voigt (2003, 2004) define judicial independence in terms of the absence of short-term political pressure on judges. They distinguish two "types" of judicial independence: *de jure* and *de facto*. They measure *de jure* judicial independence, however, in terms of structural features of the court system. They focus on the highest court within a state and then consider twelve structural features, such as constitutional standing for the highest court, the nature of the appointments process, the tenure of judges, and the extent of the Court's control over its docket. They measure *de facto* judicial independence in terms of eight "performance" variables, such as the actual average term length of justies, the frequency of removal, the constancy of judical salary, the frequency with which legal rules governing the court are changed. These two measures led to dramatically different rankings of court systems. The United States, for example, ranked 30th out of 75 on the *de jure* scale, while Switzerland ranked 67th. Moreover, the two measures led to very different rankings; no country ranked in the top ten under the *de jure* measures ranks in the top ten under the *de facto* measure. In the earlier study, they found no significant correlation of growth in GDP with the *de jure* measure of judicial independence, while the *de facto* measure of judicial independence was significantly correlated with GDP growth. In a larger data set used in their later article, they found GDP was significantly correlated with constitutionally specified selection procedures and powers.

Iaryczower et al. (2002) define judicial independence as "the extent to which judges can reflect their preferences in their decisions without facing retaliation measures by Congress or the President." In their model, the court evaluates the constitutionality of a piece of legislation and then, if the court strikes it down, the President, when he has Congressional support, may sanction the court. In equilibrium, the court upholds the legislation when its preferences correspond to the President's or when the President has control over the Congress. They test this model on data from the Argentine Supreme Court and find that the court is more independent than conventionally believed.

Helmke (2005) provides a model that challenges this definition. In her model, justices are forward-looking and they act in an uncertain world. In rendering decisions, they must determine whether the current government will remain in power; if it is likely to fall, then the justices have an interest in deciding according to the interests of the successor government.

Klerman and Mahoney (2005) suggest that judicial independence means that judges can make decisions based "on the law without fear of reprisal from the executive or the legislature." They then consider several structural features of court systems as indicia of judicial independence, among them tenure, a non-manipulable appointments procedure, and a relatively fixed jurisdiction. In an empirical study of eighteenth century England, they find that increased judicial independence, particularly as measured by "tenure during good behavior", was strongly correlated with growth of GDP.

4.2   Appointment and Tenure of Judges

The appointment, promotion and tenure prospects of judges vary greatly across court systems. The literature often takes the federal system of the United States as paradigmatic, but it is, in fact, rather unusual. In the federal system, judges have life tenure and limited prospects of promotion from the trial bench to the courts of appeal and even less prospect of promotion to the Supreme Court. Nevertheless, as the prior discussion on judicial motivation suggested, these modest prospects of promotion apparently affect judicial behavior.

The 50 states of the United States offer a wide variety of distinct appointments and tenure policies. Some states have institutions that parallel those of the federal government. Many elect judges; these elections are themselves conducted in a variety of ways. Some are contested, partisan elections. Others are contested non-partisan elections. Some have periodic, uncontested retention elections. Still other states have nomination procedures that appoint judges for some term.

In most of these states, as in most common law countries, the line between the judiciary and the bar is relatively fluid, with practicing lawyers often entering the judiciary for greater or lesser stays sometime in the middle of their career.

Civil law systems have a very different structure. In these systems, the judiciary is part of the state bureaucracy. Individuals thus choose at the outset of their careers whether to practice law or to serve in the judiciary. These judges face bureaucratic incentives quite distinct from the variety of incentives found in common law systems. The discussion of judicial independence in Japan in the prior subsection illustrated at least one consequence of this different incentive structure. Guarnieri (2004) provides a description of the court systems in these countries.

In this section, I briefly survey some of the literature on appointments, promotion and tenure. Again, this literature has been heavily influenced by US institutions, so much of it focuses on electoral mechanisms. The studies here might equally have been discussed in the section studying judicial motivation.

Substantial evidence suggests that judges respond to electoral pressures, at least in prominent cases. Shepherd (2007) studied the effects of retention elections on state supreme court justices. She found that judges who faced retention decisions by Republicans were more likely to vote for business litigants over individual litigants, for employers in labor cases, for defendants in medical malpractice and other tort cases and for the state in criminal cases. Judges facing retention decisions by Democrats had the reverse tendencies. The tendencies were greatest when judges faced partisan elections.

Helland and Tabarrok (2002) study the effect of partisan elections on the level of tort awards. Their study contrasts both awards in states with partisan elections to those with non-partisan elections and to awards by elected state judges versus appointed federal judges. They find that judges in states with partisan elections made higher awards than both federal judges and judges elected in non-partisan elections.

Choi, Gulati, and Posner (2007) measure the comparative performance of appointed versus elected judges. They measure the quantity of output by the number of opinions and quality by the number of citations. They find that, though appointed judges write higher quality opinions, elected judges write more opinions. Total influence is thus roughly the same. Moreover, they find that elected judges exhibit as much judicial independence as appointed ones.

Hanssen (2002) attempts to explain why some states appoint judges and others elect them. He argues, on the basis of empirical data, that merit appointment procedures are correlated with increased litigation. As lawyers prefer more litigation to less, he claims that this increase explains their support for merit appointment.

5. The Organization of Adjudication

Adjudication involves a number of distinct tasks. Courts must find facts. They must apply the law to the facts; if no law exists, they must make the law. Once judgment is rendered, courts may be asked to enforce that judgment. Each of these tasks might be further subdivided. Finding facts requires a trial procedure with rules governing what evidence may be presented, in what order, and with what burden of production of evidence and burden of proof. These questions of trial procedure are considered elsewhere in this volume.

These tasks might be organized in radically different ways that exhibit greater or lesser degrees of division of labor and specialization of functions. All functions might be entrusted to a single court or they might be divided among them. Such a division of labor might occur in a number of different ways. In common law countries, since the merger of law and equity, courts usually have general jurisdiction. A single court may hear cases almost regardless of subject matter. Even in this system, however, some specialization exists. Within state courts, for example, generally family matters (issues concerning divorce, custody of children, delinquency) and probate have distinct courts of first instance, though appeals are taken to the appellate courts of general jurisdiction. In the federal system, many administrative issues, such as immigration status, claims under the social security act, and labor disputes, are heard first by administrative judges, with appeal sometimes permitted from these administrative courts to the appellate courts of general jurisdiction. A distinct appellate court exists to hear intellectual property cases.

Civilian legal systems, by contrast, are much more specialized. In France, for example, distinct court systems exist for hearing cases arising from government administration and for ordinary civil and criminal matters. In addition, a separate body hears constitutional questions.

Courts hearing ordinary civil matters generally do not have general jurisdiction. Commercial cases and labor cases, for example, are heard in separate fora.

5.1 Jurisdiction

5.1.1 Case and controversy requirement Courts generally resolve disputes, but the dispute must generally be, in some way, "live" and "real". In the United States, this requirement for the existence of a real dispute is embodied in the "case or controversy" requirement of Article III of the Constitution. The requirement, however, is not a peculiarity of United States federal courts. With the exception of some constitutional courts, such as those of France and Germany, that have jurisdiction to issue opinions on the constitutionality of legislation prior to its enactment, most judicial systems require some similar trigger. Why should this be so? And who should be allowed to press a claim concerning a "real" dispute?

Jensen, Meckling, and Holderness (1986) address this latter question of who should be allowed to press a claim in a live dispute. They argue for limited rules of standing because, they claim, a liberal standing rule increases the costs of engaging in any rule-governed transaction.

Landes and Posner (1994) address the first question concerning the justification of a requirement for a concrete case to trigger the adjudicatory power. They extend to the question of the case or controversy requirement a model of legal advice developed by Shavell (1988, 1992) and Kaplow and Shavell (1992) to investigate questions concerning the use of attorneys. Landes and Posner focus on the distinction between type 1 and type 2 errors – the wrongful attribution of liability to defendants versus the wrongful excusal from liability of defendants. They argue that this distinction can be deployed to explain much of the observed pattern of exceptions to the case or controversy requirement. Specifically, they note that anticipatory adjudication, in violation of the concreteness requirement, increases both errors. They then examine in detail the institutions of declaratory judgments, res judicata, advisory opinions, and preliminary injunctions.

Stearns (1995, 1996) argues that the case or controversy requirement serves to restrict the occurrence of cycling that plagues institutions of social choice. For a fuller discussion, see the section on collegiality in Chapter 2 on "Appeal and Supreme Courts".

5.1.2 Specialized courts versus courts of general jurisdiction Over what disputes should a court have jurisdiction to decide? Two methods for defining the subject matter jurisdiction of courts predominate. First, and most commonly, a court might have jurisdiction over any dispute that arises within a specified geographic area. Virtually all court systems consist primarily of these courts of general jurisdiction. Second, a court might have jurisdiction over disputes with a specified subject matter. Notice that these organizational patterns could be applied to courts of first instance (that find facts as well as apply law) only, to appellate courts only, or to both courts of first instance and to appellate courts. Moreover, in a system with specialized courts of first instance but appeal to courts of general jurisdiction, one could limit appeal to a single general court of jurisdiction or one could allocate non-exclusive jurisdiction to a number of appellate courts. In the United States, one may understand the administrative law structure as establishing administrative agencies as specialized courts to determine the facts and make initial legal rulings that are then appealed to courts of general jurisdictions. Thus most labor disputes, welfare disputes, and immigration disputes are first heard in administrative agencies and then, if necessary, appealed to the federal courts of appeals. In these instances, each of the federal courts of appeal has jurisdiction to hear appeals from these specialized tribunals. Many environmental disputes, by contrast, may only be appealed to the US Court of Appeals for the DC Circuit. Finally, there are some specialized courts of appeal such as the tax court and the federal circuit for Court of Appeals for the Federal Circuit which has jurisdiction over patent and other intellectual property disputes. What is the appropriate way to allocate jurisdiction among courts?

Posner (1985) argues that specialized appellate courts are likely to be more ideological than courts of general jurisdiction because judges on specialized courts are likely to be more focused on the subject matter of their jurisdiction and hence more likely to be sensitive, and responsive, to controversy.

Revesz (1990) analyzes the desirability of vesting appellate authority over administrative agencies in specialized courts. His analysis emphasizes the effect of the nature of the appellate court's jurisdiction on legislative ability to control agencies. He argues that review by specialized courts reduces the effectiveness of congressional delegation to administrative agencies. He develops a simple principal-agent model in which Congress is the principal and the administrative agency the agent. They have different policy preferences because commissioners in agencies have terms that do not correspond to the terms of the commissioners and because there may be a divergence in preferences between Congress and the President who appoints the head of many agencies. Congress has three mechanisms for the control of agencies: it may overrule particular decisions, it may exercise oversight through one or more committees, and it may alter the agency's budget. Congress, however, might also use the courts to monitor the agency. Revesz argues that a court of general jurisdiction is a better monitor.

5.1.3 Constitutional courts In some political systems, courts have the power to declare legislative enactments and actions of the government executive unconstitutional. This power of judicial review may, as in the United States, be exercised by the courts of general jurisdiction. Or the power may, as in Germany or France, be exercised by a distinct body governed by its own jurisdictional and standing rules. In some instances, adjudication must occur prior to the legislation coming into force and only specific public actors may challenge the constitutionality of a rule. In other instances, standing may be broad and challenges may be brought at any time.

5.2 Court Congestion

Comparative law scholars have often noted the variation in "litigiousness" across countries. There is little economic literature that seeks to explain this cross-cultural variation, but there is a substantial literature analyzing the causes of "congestion" in the courts of one notably litigious society, the United States.

Virtually every proposal to reduce court congestion in the United States federal courts recommends the abolition of diversity jurisdiction, which grants federal courts the authority to resolve disputes between citizens of different states, even when they involve only questions of state law. One justification for diversity is that it prevents discrimination against out-of-state residents. Goldman and Marks (1980) tested this claim by looking at two samples of attorneys drawn from the US District Court for the Northern District of Illinois in 1976. They randomly sampled 200 attorneys tied to specific questions and asked them their reasons for litigating in federal court. They had a 62% response rate. In addition, they randomly sampled 205 attorneys from the law division of Cook County District Court in 1976; this court had a $15,000 amount a controversy minimum so that the cases within its jurisdiction were reasonably comparable to those within the jurisdiction of the federal court. This survey had only a 37% response rate. Only 40% of the attorneys in federal court listed local bias as a reason for choosing federal court. Attorneys drawn from state court cases were asked to consider a hypothetical case identical to the one litigated but in which their client was an out-of-state resident. Roughly 25% said they would file in federal court. Local bias thus had very little influence on the choice of forum.

Noam (1981) attempts to assess the social cost of court congestion by calculating the effects of congestion on criminal sentences and then on the crime rate. He argues that plea bargain reached between prosecutor and defendant will depend on the caseload of the court. The higher the caseload per judge, the lower the average sentence. Moreover, he argues that the per capita crime rate is a function of the average sentence. Using simple specifications of these functional relations, he derives an equation that represents the marginal effect of additional resources devoted to the criminal courts. He then estimates his equation using FBI data on crime rates for four types of crimes against property in the District of Columbia. This estimation yields very high marginal returns to increased investment in the court system.

6. Fact-Finding

To resolve disputes, courts must determine the facts. A substantial portion of procedural rules govern the fact-finding process. Each of these rules influences the structure of the judicial system because each influences the cost of litigation relative to the cost of settlement and to self-help remedies. (The literature on evidence and the choice between settlement and litigation are summarized elsewhere in this volume.) Some procedural rules play a more central role in the organization of court systems. In this section, I examine the structure of trials and the use of juries, a characteristic element of many but not all court systems.

6.1 Sequential versus Unitary Trials

Most disputes present more than one factual issue for resolution. Should these be resolved simultaneously or sequentially? In the United States, factual issues are generally resolved simultaneously, but often the question of liability and the question of remedy are decided sequentially, sometimes by different fact-finders.

Landes (1993) presents the primary investigation of this issue. He modifies his own, early model of the choice between settlement and litigation (see Landes 1971) to analyze several issues concerning the effect of trial structure on the settlement rate. The analysis rests on the insight that a sequential structure to the litigation reduces the expected cost of litigation. Hence, plaintiff's incentive to sue increases, which implies that the number of lawsuits will increase. Landes argues further that sequential trials reduce the probability of settlement because they narrow the range of acceptable settlements.

6.2 Juries

Many legal systems divide the law-finding (or law-applying) and fact-finding functions of trial courts. These systems delegate fact-finding to a *jury*, generally a group of lay individuals chosen more or less randomly to decide one case. This procedure raises several questions.

6.2.1 Jury selection Bowles (1980) compares the cost of jury trials in Britain to the cost of a system of fact-finding by a three-judge court. The cost of a jury trial consists primarily of the production foregone by persons serving on the jury. Bowles notes that high wage earners will attempt to avoid jury service more vigorously than low wage earners. He concludes that a jury trial will be less expensive if the cost of a judge is more than three times the cost of a juror. He does not, however, correct for the speed of the trial.

Martin (1972) also estimates the social cost of the jury system in the United States. He first estimates the occupational distribution of jurors on the assumption that juror days of service are distributed identically to jurors. He then multiplied by the median daily wage rate for each occupation and estimated the social cost at $233 million in 1958 dollars. He then compares the cost of two systems of jury selection: random selection and a "keyman" procedure in which lists are constructed through consultation with community leaders. He finds that random selection is significantly less expensive because community leaders are more likely to draw jurors from high wage occupations than random selection. Finally Martin argues that voluntary service would reduce costs even further.

6.2.2 Jury size and jury voting rules Models of jury size and the effects of jury voting rules must specify how juries deliberate and vote. Many models assume no deliberation. Moreover, until recently, the literature assumed that each juror voted conscientiously; her vote expressed her view of the guilt or innocence of the defendant. When one assumes in addition that each juror is more likely than not to decide correctly and that jurors' judgments are independent of each other, the Condorcet jury theorem applies and one can easily show first, that a unanimity rule minimizes the probability of wrongful convictions; second, that majority rule maximizes the probability of a correct decision; and third, that, as the number of jurors increases, the probability of wrongful conviction under a unanimity rule decreases towards zero and the probability of a correct decision under majority rule increases towards one. Recently, however, analysts have introduced models of strategic voting by jurors and these models yield dramatically different results.

Austen-Smith and Banks (1996) and Feddersen and Pesendorfer (1996) show how radically the assumption of strategic behavior by jurors undermines the Condorcet jury theorem. When a juror acts strategically, the information aggregation feature of the Condorcet jury theorem disappears because each juror now decides how to cast her vote in light only of those instances in which her vote will be pivotal. As a consequence, as Austen-Smith and Banks show clearly, a juror's vote may not reveal her actual view concerning the case. Feddersen and Pesendorfer show, more dramatically, that the probability of wrongful conviction may be higher under a unanimity rule than under a different voting rule. In their model, moreover, non-strategic voting is not an equilibrium. Guarnaschelli, McKelvey and Palfrey (2000) offer some experimental support for the conclusion that jurors vote strategically, but they find unanimity leads to more correct decisions.

These results, however, are sensitive to the specification. Coughlan (2000), for example, analyzes two variants of the Feddersen and Pesendorfer model; in one, there is a possibility of a hung jury and, in the second, the jurors may deliberate. In these environments, unanimity does minimize the probability of wrongful conviction and non-strategic voting is an equilibrium.

These models raise important questions about the appropriate way in which to model juries. These questions parallel those presented in the study of collegial courts, discussed in Chapter 2, where team models in which judges act in a fashion somewhat analogous to the assumption underlying the naive Condorcet jury theorem models contend with political models in which judges act strategically.

In the United States, until the 1970s, juries typically consisted of twelve individuals and required unanimity to render a verdict. Then, the United States Supreme Court ruled that neither the number twelve nor unanimity were constitutionally required in state criminal proceedings. These decisions spurred research into the importance of these requirements.

Klevorick and Rothschild (1979) provide a model of jury deliberation in order to determine whether non-unanimous juries or unanimous juries of fewer than twelve jurors would yield different verdicts than the "standard" twelve-person unanimous jury. Their analysis uses a stationary Markov model to provide a dynamic model of the majority persuasion hypothesis, derived from Kalven and Zeisal (1966), that the final verdict is the same as the majority position on the first ballot. They offer both a discrete and continuous model of jury deliberation. The cores of the models are identical. The jurors enter the jury room with a view on the merits and cast an initial ballot. The vote then changes incrementally as time passes, with one person changing her vote at each instant until unanimity is reached. The transition probabilities are given by the current vote: the probability of one more vote for the plaintiff equals the percentage of jurors who favor plaintiff's case. In this model, one can calculate both the expected number of jury ballots until unanimity is reached (conditional on the initial vote) and the probability that a non-unanimous jury will agree with a unanimous one. Klevorick and Rothschild show that a move to a requirement of ten votes for judgment rather twelve always alters the probability of conviction by less than

0.0055. Their result, of course, depends critically on the manner in which majority pressure operates in the jury room. When they adopt a different assumption concerning transition probabilities, they calculate that the move to ten for judgment may lead to as many one in six of the cases being decided differently. Klevorick and Rothschild also show that this shift substantially reduces the expected number of ballots prior to judgment.

Schwartz and Schwartz (1992, 1995, 1996a) offer a somewhat different approach to jury decision making. The earliest paper addresses three questions concerning the decision rules of juries. First, why do juries fail to reach a verdict? Second, what verdict will a jury reach when it may convict for lesser included offenses or when multiple offenses are litigated simultaneously? Third, how, if at all, will the jury decision rule alter the charges filed by prosecutors? To this end, they assume that a defendant might be charged with any number of counts within some interval. They consider two regimes. In one, the prosecutor chooses one count in the interval, and the jury must choose among three outcomes, conviction on that count, acquittal, or no decision. In the second regime, the prosecutor chooses two counts, one entailing a lesser punishment than the other, and the jury chooses among four outcomes, acquittal on both counts, conviction on the lesser count, conviction on the more severe count, or no decision. In the event of no decision, a retrial before a different jury occurs. Each jury consists of four people, chosen randomly from a population. Each potential juror is an expected utility maximizer, characterized by spatial "preferences" for punishment of the defendant; that is, each juror has an ideal outcome that represents the crime for which she believes the defendant should be convicted. The simple model implies that a defendant always prefers a non-unanimous, super-majority rule to unanimity because his expected verdict is lower under the non-unanimous rule. This result occurs because, though the probability of conviction is greater under non-unanimity, the probability of acquittal rises more rapidly. When jury may convict on a lesser included offense, the analysis is more complex and less clear-cut.

Schwartz and Schwartz (1995) extend the analysis of their prior article in the context of the liability and punishment phases of capital offenses in the United States. They argue that the decision process for fact-finding has three elements: the voting rule, the jury selection process, and the characterization of the set of outcomes among which the jury may choose. They argue that, in a multi-stage fact-finding process, the voting rule must be the same in each stage in order to avoid the jury at one stage nullifying the law governing the jury at a different stage. In addition, only *reciprocal* voting rules will avoid hung juries (where a rule is reciprocal if "conviction" requires c of n votes, then "acquittal" requires $n - c$ of n votes).

Schwartz and Schwartz (1996a) carry the argument of the prior two papers further. They argue that any voting rule should satisfy at least two properties: (1) it should be decisive; and (2) it should satisfy the "one person/ one vote" criterion. This second property does not eliminate any anonymous voting rule, whether majority, supermajority, or submajority. (Super and submajority rules would violate neutrality.) The first criterion identifies majority rule as the unique decisive voting rule when there are only two possible outcomes. To satisfy the desire to minimize wrongful convictions that the unanimity rule is said to promote, Schwartz and Schwartz argue that the size of the jury should be increased perhaps to fifteen.

7. Concluding Remarks

Economic analysis of judicial organization and administration, though it has greatly increased understanding, is only in its infancy. No question has received an exhaustive treatment and many have not been examined at all.

This area suggests a multitude of comparative questions, most of which have not received any attention at all. They are ripe for analysis.

Bibliography

Acemoglu, Daron, Johnson, Simon and Robinson, James A. (2001), "The Colonial Origins of Comparative Development: An Empirical Investigation", *American Economic Review*, 91, 1369–401.
Aranson, Peter H. (1990), "Models of Judicial Choice as Allocation and Distribution in Constitutional Law", *Brigham Young University Law Review*, 794–826.
Ashenfelter, Orley, Eisenberg, Theodore and Schwab, Stewart J. (1995), "Politics and the Judiciary: The Influence of Judicial Background on Case Outcomes", *Journal of Legal Studies*, 24, 257–82.
Austen-Smith, David and Banks, Jeffrey S. (1996), "Information Aggregation, Rationality and the Condorcet Jury Theorem", *American Political Science Review*, 90(1), 34–45.
Backhaus, Jurgen (1992), "General Legislation and the Budget: Commentary", *International Review of Law and Economics*, 12(2), 209–10.
Bafumi, Joseph, Gelman, Andrew, Park, David and Kaplan, Noah (2005), "Issues in Ideal Point Estimation", *Political Analysis*, 13, 171–87.
Bailey, Michael and Chang, Kelley H. (2001)",Comparing Presidents, Senators and Justices: Interinstitutional Preference Estimation", *Journal of Law, Economics and Organization*, 17, 477–507.
Barnard, David (1977), *The Civil Court in Action*, London: Butterworths.
Baum, Lawrence (2006), *Judges and their Audiences: A Perspective on Judicial Behavior*, Princeton, NJ: Princeton University Press.
Berkowitz, Daniel, Pistor, Katjarina, and Richard, Jean-François (2002), "Economic Development, Legality, and the Transplant Effect", *European Economic Review*, 47, 165–95.
Bowles, Roger A. (1980), "Juries, Incentives and Self-Selection", *British Journal of Criminology*, 20, 368–76.
Brace, Paul, Langer, Laura and Hall, Melinda G. (2000), "Measuring the Preferences of State Supreme Court Judges", *Journal of Politics*, 62, 387–413.
Brunet, Edward (1985), "Measuring the Costs of Civil Justice", *Michigan Law Review*, 83, 916–38.
Burbank, Stephen B. and Friedman, Barry (eds.) (2002), *Judicial Independence at the Crossroads: An Interdisciplinary Approach*, Thousand Oaks, CA: Russell Sage.

Cameron, Charles, M. and Clark, Tom S. (2007), "Is the Median Justice Really King?", paper presented at the annual meeting of the American Political Science Association, September.
Cann, Damon (2007), "Beyond Accountability and Independence: Judical Selection and State Court Performance", *Judicature*, 90, 226–32.
Casper, Gerhard and Posner, Richard A. (1974), "A Study of the Supreme Court's Caseload", *Journal of Legal Studies*, 3, 339–75.
Casper, Gerhard and Posner, Richard A. (1976), *The Workload of the Supreme Court*, Chicago IL: American Bar Foundation.
Casper, Gerhard and Zeisel, Hans (1972), "Lay Judges in the German Criminal Court", *Journal of Legal Studies*, 1, 135–91.
Choi, Stephen J., Gulati, G. Mita and Posner, Eric A. (2007), "Professionals or Politicians: The Uncertain Empirical Case for Elected rather than Appointed Judges", Working paper.
Clark, Tom S. and Lauderdale, Benjamin E. (2010), "Locating Supreme Court Opinions in Doctrine Space", *American Journal of Political Science*, 54, 871–90.
Cohen, Mark A. (1991), "Explaining Judicial Behavior or What's 'Unconstitutional' about the Sentencing Commission?", *Journal of Law, Economics, and Organization*, 7, 183–99.
Cohen, Mark A. (1992), "The Motives of Judges: Empirical Evidence from Antitrust Sentencing", *International Review of Law and Economics*, 12(1), 13–30.
Cooter, Robert (1983), "The Objectives of Private and Public Judges", *Public Choice*, 41, 107–32.
Cooter, Robert and Ginsburg, Tom (1966), "Comparative Judicial Discretion: An Empirical Test of Economic Models", *International Review of Law and Economics*, 16, 295–313.
Coughlan, Peter J. (2000), "In Defense of Unanimous Jury Verdicts: Mistrials, Communication and Strategic Voting", *American Political Science Review*, 94, 375–93.
Djankov, Simeon, La Porta, Rafael, Lopez-de-Silvano, Florencio, and Shleifer, Andrei (2003), "Courts", *Quarterly Journal of Economics*, 118, 453–517.
Ebner, P. (1982), *Reducing Pretrial Delay. . . A Look at What State and Local Courts are Doing to Break the Logjam*, Santa Monica, CA: Rand Institute of Civil Justice.
Eisenberg, Theodore and Johnson, Sheila Lynn (1991) "The Effects of Intent: Do We Know How Legal Standards Work?", *Cornell Law Review*, 76, 1151–91.
Elder, Harold W. (1987), "Property Rights Structures and Criminal Courts: An Analysis of State Criminal Courts", *International Review of Law and Economics*, 7, 21–32.
Epstein, Lee, Martin, Andrew, Segal, Jeffrey A. and Westerland, Chad (2007), "The Judicial Common Space", *Journal of Law, Economics and Organization*, 23, 303–25.
Epstein, Lee and Mershon, Carol (1996), "Measuring Poltical Preferences", *American Journal of Political Science*, 40, 261–94.
Farnsworth, Ward (2007). "The Use and Limits of Martin-Quinn scores to Assess Supreme Court Justices with Special Attention to the Problem of Ideological Drift", *Northwestern University Law Review*, 101, 143–55.
Feddersen, Timothy J. and Pesendorfer, Wolfgang (1998), "Convicting the Innocent: The Inferiority of Unanimous Jury Verdicts", *American Political Science Review*, 92, 23–35.
Feeley, Malcolm (1983), *Court Reform on Trial: Why Simple Solutions Fail*, New York: Basic Books.
Feld, Lars and Voigt, Stefan (2003), "Economic Growth and Judicial Independence: Cross-Country Evidence Using a New Set of Indicators", *European Journal of Political Economy* 19, 497–527.
Feld, Lars and Voigt, Stefan (2004), "Making Judges Independent: Some Proposals Regarding the Judiciary", available on SSRN.
Flanagan, Robert J. (1987), *Labor Relations and the Litigation Explosion*, Washington, DC: Brookings Institution.
Friedman, David (1979), "Private Creation and Enforcement of Law: A Historical Case", *Journal of Legal Studies*, 8, 399–415.
Galanter, Marc (1986), "The Day after the Litigation Explosion", *Maryland Law Review*, 46, 3–39.

Gely, Rafael and Spiller, Pablo T. (1990), "A Rational Choice Theory of Supreme Court Statutory Decisions with Applications to the *State Farm* and *Grove City* Cases", *Journal of Law, Economics, and Organization*, 6, 263–300.

Gillespie, Robert W. (1976), "The Production of Court Services: An Analysis of Scale Effects and Other Factors", *Journal of Legal Studies*, 5, 243–65.

Ginsburg, Tom (2003), *Judicial Review in New Democracies: Constitutional Courts in Asian Cases*, New York: Cambridge University Press.

Glaeser, Edward L. and Shleifer, Andrei (2002), "Legal Origins", *Quarterly Journal of Economics*, 117, 1193–229.

Goldman, Jerry, Hooper, Richard L. and Mahaffey, Judy (1976), "Caseload Forecasting Models for Federal District Courts", *Journal of Legal Studies*, 5, 201–42.

Goldman, Jerry and Marks, Kenneth S. (1980), "Diversity Jurisdiction and Local Bias: A Preliminary Empirical Inquiry", *Journal of Legal Studies*, 9, 93–104.

Gravelle, Hugh S.E. (1983), "Judicial Review and Public Firms", *International Review of Law and Economics*, 3, 187–205.

Greenberg, Paul E. and Haley, James A. (1986), "The Role of the Compensation Structure in Enhancing Judicial Quality", *Journal of Legal Studies*, 15, 417–26.

Griffiths, J. (1991), "De Rechtbank als Fietsenfabriek" (The Court as Bicycle Manufacturer), *Nederlands Juristenblad*, 66, 129–30.

Guarnaschelli, Serena, McKelvey, Richard D. and Palfrey, Thomas R. (2000), "An Experimental Study of Jury Decision Rules", *American Political Science Review*, 94, 407–23.

Guarnieri, Carlo (2004), "The Appointment and Career of Judges in Continental Europe", *Legal Studies*, 24, 169–87.

Haley, John O. (2007), "The Japanese Judiciary: Maintaining Integrity, Autonomy, and the Public Trust", in Daniel Foote (ed.), *Law in Japan: A Turning Point?* Seattle: University of Washington Press.

Hanssen, F. Andrews (2002), "On the Politics of Judicial Selection: Lawyers and State Campaigns for the Merit Plane", *Public Choice*, 110, 79–97.

Hanssen, F. Andrews (2004a), "Is there a Politically Optimal Level of Deterrence?", *American Economic Review*, 94, 712–29.

Hanssen, F. Andrews (2004b), "Learning about Judicial Independence: Institutional Change in State Courts", *Journal of Legal Studies*, 33, 431–62.

Harvey, Anna (2006), "What Makes a Judgment Liberal? Measurement Error in the United States Supreme Court Judicial Database", NYU Department of Politics Working Paper, November.

Hazard, Geoffrey C., Jr. (1965), "Rationing Justice", *Journal of Law and Economics*, 8, 1–10.

Helland, Eric and Tabarrok, Alexander (2002), "The Effects of Electoral Institutions on Tort Awards", *American Law and Economics Review*, 341–70.

Helmke, Gretchen (2005), *Courts under Constraints: Judges, Generals and Presidents in Argentina*, New York: Cambridge University Press.

Higgins, Richard A. and Rubin, Paul H. (1980), "Judicial Discretion", *Journal of Legal Studies*, 9, 129–38.

Iaryczower, Matias, Spiller, Pablo and Tomassi Mariano (2002), "Judicial Decision Making in Unstable Environments: Argentina 1935–1998", *American Journal of Political Science*, 46, 699–716.

Jensen, Michael, Meckling, William H. and Holderness, Clifford (1986), "Analysis of Alternative Standing Doctrines", *International Review of Law and Economics*, 6, 205–16.

Kalven, James and Zeisal, Hans (1966), *The American Jury*, Boston, MA and Toronto: Little Brown and Co.

Kaplow, Louis and Shavell, Steven (1992), "Private vs Socially Optimal Provision of Ex Ante Legal Advice", *Journal of Law, Economics and Organization*, 8, 306–20.

Karotkin, Drora (1994), "Effect of the Size of the Bench on the Correctness of Court Judgments: The Case of Israel", *International Review of Law and Economics*, 14(3), 371–5.

Katz, Avery (1988), "Judicial Decision Making and Litigation Expenditures", *International Review of Law and Economics*, 8, 127–43.

Klerman, Daniel S. and Mahoney, Paul G. (2005), "The Value of Judicial Independence: Evidence from Eighteenth Century England", *American Law and Economics Review*, 7, 1–27.

Klerman, Daniel S. and Mahoney Paul G. (2007), "Legal Origin?", *Journal of Comparative Economics*, 35, 278–93.

Klevorick, Alvin K. (1977), "Jury Composition: An Economic Approach", in Siegan, Bernard H. (ed.), *The Interactions of Economics and the Law*, Lexington, MA: Lexington Books.

Klevorick, Alvin K. and Rothschild, Michael (1979) "A Model of the Jury Decision Process", *Journal of Legal Studies*, 8, 141–64.

Kornhauser, Lewis A. and Sager, Lawrence G. (1986), "Unpacking the Court", *Yale Law Journal*, 96, 82–117.

Landes, William M. (1971), "An Economic Analysis of the Courts", *Journal of Law and Economics*, 14, 61–107.

Landes, William M. (1993), "Sequential versus Unitary Trials: An Economic Analysis", *Journal of Legal Studies*, 22(1), 99–134.

Landes, William M. and Posner, Richard A. (1975), "The Independent Judiciary in an Interest Group Perspective", *Journal of Law and Economics*, 18, 875–901.

Landes, William M. and Posner, Richard A. (1979), "Adjudication as a Private Good", *Journal of Legal Studies,* 8, 235–84.

Landes, William M. and Posner, Richard A. (1980), "Legal Change, Judicial Behavior and the Diversity Jurisdiction", *Journal of Legal Studies*, 9, 367–86.

Landes, William M. and Posner, Richard A. (1994), "The Economics of Anticipatory Adjudication", *Journal of Legal Studies,* 23, 683–720.

La Porta, Rafael, Lopez-de-Silanes, Florencio, Pop-Eleches, Cristian and Shleifer, Andrei (2004), "Judicial Checks and Balances", *Journal of Political Economy*, 112, 445–70.

La Porta, Rafael, Lopez-de-Silanes, Florencio, Shleifer, Andrei, and Vishny, Robert W. (1997), "Legal Determinants of External Finance", *Journal of Finance*, 52, 1131–50.

La Porta, Rafael, Lopez-de-Silanes, Florencio, Shleifer, Andrei and Vishny, Robert (1998), "Law and Finance", *Journal of Political Economy*, 106, 1113–55.

Lee, Injae (2003), "Essays on Legal Sytem and Economic Performance", Ph.D. Dissertation in the NYU Department of Economics, January.

Levin, Martin A. (1975), "Delay in Five Criminal Courts", *Journal of Legal Studies*, 4, 83–131.

Levine, Ross (2005), "Law, Endowments, and Property Rights", *Journal of Economic Perspectives*, 19, 61–88.

Lindquist, Stefanie A. and Klein, Daniel E. (2006), "The Influence of Jurisprudential Considerations on Supreme Court Decisionmaking: A Study of Conflict Cases", *Law and Society Review*, 40, 135–62.

Mahoney, Paul G. (2001), "The Common Law and Economic Growth: Hayek Might be Right", *Journal of Legal Studies*, 30, 1–31.

Martin, Andrew D. (2007), "Assessing Preference Change on the US Supreme Court", *Journal of Law, Economics, and Organization*, 23, 365–85.

Martin, Andrew and Quinn, Kevin M. (2002), "Dynamic Ideal Point Estimation via Markov Chain Monte Carlo for U.S. Supreme Court 1953–1999", *Political Analysis*, 10, 134–53.

Martin, Andrew and Quinn, Kevin M. (2005)",Can Ideal Point Estimates be Used as Explanatory Variables?", Washington University at St. Louis Department of Political Science Working Paper.

Martin, Donald L. (1972), "The Economics of Jury Conscription", *Journal of Political Economy*, 80, 680–702.

Maskin, Eric and Tirole, Jean (2004), "The Politician and the Judge: Accountability in Government", *American Economic Review*, 94, 1034–54.

Melumad, Nahum D. and Thoman, Lynda (1990), "On Auditors and the Courts in an Adverse Selection Setting", *Journal of Accounting Research*, 28, 77–120.

Miller, Arthur R. (1984), "The Adversary System: Dinosaur or Phoenix", *Minnesota Law Review*, 69, 1–37.
Miller, Geoffrey P. (1989), "Comment: Some Thoughts on the Equilibrium Hypothesis", *Boston University Law Review*, 69, 561–8.
Noam, Eli M. (1981), "A Cost-benefit Model of Criminal Courts", *Research in Law and Economics*, 3, 173–83.
Noll, Roger G. (1992), "Judicial Review and the Power of the Purse: Comment", *International Review of Law and Economics*, 12(2), 211–13.
Pacelle, Richard L., Marshall, Bryan W., and Curry, Brett W. (2007), "Keepers of the Covenant or Platonic Guardians? Decision Making on the US Supreme Court", *American Politics Research*, 35, 694–725.
Pastor, Santos (1989), "Economìa de la Justicia (I)" (Economics of Litigation I), *Revista de Economìa Pública*, 5, 131–69.
Pastor, Santos (1990a), "Economìa de la Justicia (II)" (Economics of Litigation II), *Revista de Economìa Pública*, 6, 69–86.
Pastor, Santos (1990b), "Economìa de la Justicia" (The Spanish Courts and the Economic Analysis), *Revista de Economìa*, 4, 65–9.
Pastor, Santos (1991), "Informe sobre la litigación, recursos y acceso de los cuidadanos a la Justicie" (Report on Litigation, Courts Inputs and Access to Justice), in Ministerio de Justicia, *Materiales para una reforma Procesal*, Madrid.
Perez-Linan, Anibal, Ames, Barry and Seligson, Mitchell A. (2006), "Strategy Careers and Judicial Decisions: Lessons from the Bolivian Courts", *Journal of Politics*, 68, 284–95.
Pinello, Daniel R. (1999), "Linking Party to Judicial Ideology in American Courts: A Meta-Analysis", *The Justice System Journal*, 20, 219–54.
Posner, Richard A. (1973), "An Economic Approach to Legal Procedure and Judicial Administration", *Journal of Legal Studies*, 2, 399–458.
Posner, Richard A. (1983), "Will the Federal Courts of Appeals Survive until 1984? An Essay on Delegation and Specialization of the Judicial Function", *Southern California Law Review*, 56, 761–91.
Posner, Richard A. (1984), "The Meaning of Judicial Self-Restraint", *Indiana Law Journal*, 59, 1–24.
Posner, Richard A. (1985), *The Federal Courts: Crisis and Reform*, Cambridge, MA: Harvard University Press.
Posner, Richard A. (1986), "The Summary Jury Trial and Other Methods of Alternative Dispute Resolution: Some Cautionary Observations", *University of Chicago Law Review*, 53, 366–93.
Posner, Richard A. (1989), "Coping with the Caseload: A Comment on Magistrates and Masters", *University of Pennsylvania Law Review*, 137, 2215–18.
Posner, Richard A. (2008), *How Judges Think*, Cambridge, MA: Harvard University Press.
Priest, George L. (1989), "Private Litigants and the Court Congestion Problem", *Boston University Law Review*, 69, 527–59.
Ramseyer, J. Mark (1994), "The Puzzling (In)dependence of Courts: A Comparative Approach", *Journal of Legal Studies*, 23(2), 721–47.
Ramseyer, J. Mark and Rasmusen, Eric B. (2003), *Measuring Judicial Independence: The Political Economy of Judging in Japan*, Chicago, IL: Chicago University Press.
Ramseyer, J. Mark and Rasmusen, Eric B. (2006), "The Case for Managed Judges: Learning from Japan after the Political Upheaval of 1993", *University of Pennsylvania Law Review* 154, 1879–930.
Revesz, Richard L. (1990), "Specialized Courts and the Administrative Lawmaking System", *University of Pennsylvania Law Review*, 138, 1111–76.
Revesz, Richard L. (1997)",Environmental Regulation, Ideology, and the D.C. Circuit", *Virginia Law Review*, 83, 1717–92.
Roe, Mark J. (2007), "Juries and the Political Economy of Legal Origin", *Journal of Comparative Economics*, 35, 294–308.

Salzberger, Eli and Fenn, Paul (1999), "Judicial Independence: Some Evidence from the English Court of Appeal", *Journal of Law and Economics*, 42, 831–47.
Savchak, Elisha Carol, Hansford, Thomas G., Songer, Donald R., Manning, Kenneth L. and Carp, Robert A. (2006) "Taking it to the Next Level: The Elevation of District Court Judges to the US Courts of Appeals", *American Journal of Political Science*, 50, 478–93.
Scheiner, Alan Howard (1991), "Judicial Assessment of Punitive Damages, the Seventh Amendment, and the Politics of Jury Power", *Columbia Law Review*, 91, 142–226.
Schwartz, Edward P. and Schwartz, Warren F. (1992), "Decision Making by Juries under Unanimity and Supermajority Voting Rules", *Georgetown Law Journal*, 80, 775–907.
Schwartz, Edward P. and Schwartz, Warren F. (1995), "Deciding Who Decides Who Dies: Capital Punishment as a Social Choice Problem", *Legal Theory*, 1, 113–48.
Schwartz, Edward P. and Schwartz, Warren F. (1996a), "Simple Majority Rule for Criminal Jury Trials: The Verdict is Now In", Manuscript.
Schwartz, Edward P. and Schwartz, Warren F. (1996b), "The Challenge of Peremptory Challenges", *Journal of Law, Economics and Organization*, 12, 325–94.
Segal, Jeffrey A. (2007), "Measuring Political Preferences", *Law and Courts*, 17, 1–5.
Segal, Jeffrey A. and Cover, Albert D. (1989), "Ideological Values and the Votes of U.S. Supreme Court Justices", *American Political Science Review*, 83, 557–65.
Segal, Jeffrey A. and Spaeth, Harold J. (2002), *The Supreme Court and the Attitudinal Model Revisited*, New York: Cambridge University Press.
Shanley, Michael G. (1991), "The Distribution of Posttrial Adjustments to Jury Awards", *Journal of Legal Studies*, 20, 463–81.
Shavell, Steven (1988), "Legal Advice about Contemplated Acts: The Decision to Obtain Advice, its Social Desirability, and Protection of Confidentiality", *Journal of Legal Studies*, 17, 123–50.
Shavell, Steven (1992), "Liability and the Incentive to Obtain Information about Risk", *Journal of Legal Studies*, 21, 259–70.
Shavell, Steven (1995), "Alternative Dispute Resolution: An Economic Analysis", *Journal of Legal Studies*, 24, 1–28.
Shepherd, Joanna (2007). "The Influence of Retention Politics on Judges' Voting", Emory Public Law Research Paper, available at ssrn.com/abstract=997491.
Sisk, Gregory C. and Heise, Michael (2005), "Judges and Ideology: Public and Academic Debates about Statistical Measures", *Northwestern Law Review*, 99, 743–803.
Sociaal Cultureel Planbureau (1990), *Doelmatig Rechtspreken* (Efficient Administration of Justice), SCP Cahier no. 88, 's-Gravenhage: Staatsdrukkerij.
Songer, Donald R., Sheehan, Reginald S., and Haire, Susan B. (2000), *Continuity and Change on the United States Courts of Appeal*, Ann Arbor, MI: University of Michigan Press.
Spaeth, Harold (2006), "The U.S. Supreme Court Judicial Data Base", www.as.uky.edu/polisci/ulmerproject/sctdata.html.
Stearns, Maxwell (1995), "Standing Back from the Forest: Justiciability and Social Choice", *California Law Review*, 83, 1309–413.
Stearns, Maxwell (1996), "How Outcome Voting Promotes Principled Issued Identification: A Reply to Professor John Rogers and Others", *Vanderbilt Law Review*, 49, 1045–67.
Stephenson, Matthew C. (2003), "'When the Devil turns . . .': The Political Foundations of Independent Judicial Review", *Journal of Legal Studies*, 32, 59–89.
Stratmann, Thomas and Garner, Jared (2004), "Judicial Selection: Politics, Biases and Constituency Demands", *Public Choice*, 118, 251–70.
Straussman, Jeffrey D. (1986), "Courts and Public Purse Strings: Have Portraits of Budgeting Missed Something?", *Public Administration Review*, 4, 315–51.
Toharia, Jose (1975), "Judicial Independence in an Authoritarian Regime: The Case of Contemporary Spain". *Law and Society Review*, 9, 475–96.
Yoon, Albert (2006), "Pensions, Politics and Judicial Tenure: An Empirical Study of Federal Judges, 1869–2002", *American Law and Economics Review*, 8, 143–80.

12 Negative-expected-value suits
Lucian A. Bebchuk and Alon Klement

This chapter reviews the state of knowledge about why (and when) plaintiffs with negative-expected-value (NEV) suits can extract a positive settlement amount from the defendant. The literature on the subject has continued to grow since the publication of the earlier review by Bebchuk (1998), and we attempt to reflect in this chapter all the advances made since that time.

1. Definition of NEV suits
A negative-expected-value (NEV) suit is one in which the plaintiff would obtain a negative expected return from pursuing the suit all the way to judgment – that is, one in which the plaintiff's expected total litigation costs would exceed the expected judgment. Thus, denoting by C_p and C_d the total litigation costs of the plaintiff and the defendant respectively and by W the expected judgment, a suit is an NEV suit if $C_p > W$.

It should be emphasized that an NEV suit need not be a frivolous suit – that is, a suit in which the plaintiff is unlikely to win. The expected judgment is a product of the likelihood of a plaintiff's victory and the amount at stake. Therefore, a meritorious suit – one in which the likelihood of a plaintiff victory is quite high – might be NEV if the litigation costs involved are sufficiently large relative to the amount at stake.

2. The Puzzle of NEV suits
It is generally believed that cases with NEV suits are abundant, and that plaintiffs with NEV suits are frequently able to extract a positive amount from the defendant to settle the case. But why would a rational defendant agree to pay any settlement amount to a plaintiff with an NEV suit? This is the question that the literature has sought to answer.

The early literature on litigation has largely abstracted from the question of NEV suits (see Gould 1973; Landes 1971; and Posner 1973). And the first papers on litigation decisions under asymmetric information (see Bebchuk 1984; P'ng 1983; and Reinganum and Wilde 1986) have explicitly limited their analysis to cases in which the plaintiff's suit is known to have a positive expected value (a PEV suit). But work done since the mid-1980s has put forward a number of explanations for the potential success of plaintiffs with NEV suits to extract a settlement. This literature has shown that a plaintiff with an NEV suit will not be able to extract a settlement offer if the following assumptions are satisfied:

(1) there is no asymmetry of information between the parties;
(2) the plaintiff's litigation costs are not divisible;
(3) the defendant does not have to incur some upfront costs before the plaintiff incurs any costs;
(4) the expected value of the judgment is expected to remain below total litigation costs throughout the litigation;
(5) the plaintiff does not have a reputation that enables it to bind itself to going to trial if the defendant refuses to settle; and
(6) the plaintiff does not employ some special contractual arrangements with the plaintiff's lawyer.

The following discussion demonstrates how relaxing each of these assumptions allows the NEV plaintiff to extract a settlement.

2.1. Asymmetric Information

Since the early 1980s much of the literature on litigation has focused on the consequences of asymmetric information, using a model of litigation decisions under asymmetric information put forward in Bebchuk (1984). As it turns out, the presence of an informational asymmetry is also relevant to NEV suits. Bebchuk (1988) extended the model of litigation decisions under asymmetric information of Bebchuk (1984) to NEV suits and demonstrated that the presence of an informational asymmetry can explain the success of some NEV suits. The asymmetric information explanation was also subsequently examined by Katz (1990).

To see the role that asymmetric information can play in this context, consider the situation of a defendant who does not know whether the expected value to the plaintiff from going to trial is positive or negative. This uncertainty might result from private information that the plaintiff has either about her litigation costs, C_p or about the expected judgment W. In this case, in deciding whether to make a positive settlement offer to the plaintiff, the defendant will consider two possibilities. On the one hand, the plaintiff might have an NEV suit, in which case offering to settle would be wasteful since the plaintiff would not go to trial anyway. On the other hand, the plaintiff might have a PEV suit, in which case making a settlement offer would possibly prevent litigation and produce a beneficial settlement. Balancing these two considerations, the defendant might elect to make a settlement offer, which the plaintiff will of course take if the plaintiff's suit is in fact an NEV suit.

It is possible to derive the conditions under which a plaintiff with an

NEV suit can extract a settlement offer due to the presence of informational asymmetry (see Bebchuk (1988, pp. 445-6). For example, the greater the defendant's expected litigation costs and the lower the probability attached by the defendant to the suit being an NEV suit, the more likely the possibility that the defendant will make a settlement offer.

Finally, the plaintiff's private information may be revealed through pre-trial discovery and disclosure. As Schwartz (2003) and Schwartz and Wickelgren (2009) suggest, if defendants' costs of pre-trial discovery are sufficiently low, it may allow them to separate between NEV and PEV plaintiffs and render the litigation threat of NEV plaintiffs non-credible.

2.2. Divisibility of Litigation Costs

Bebchuk (1996, 1997) has shown that the divisibility of the litigation process can provide a plaintiff with a credible threat, and enable it to extract a settlement, even if the plaintiff is known by the defendant to have an NEV suit. What underlies the considered explanation is the recognition that litigation costs are generally not incurred all at once in a lump-sum fashion – but rather are spread over a period of time, with bargaining possibly taking place on numerous occasions throughout this period. This divisibility turns out to play an important strategic role.

To see the strategic implications of divisibility, consider a case in which W is 100 and C_p and C_d are both 120. Initially, suppose that there is only one litigation stage in which all of the parties' litigation costs must be incurred in a lump-sum, indivisible fashion. In this case, in the negotiations preceding this indivisible stage, the plaintiff will not have a credible threat; for, if the defendant refuses to settle, the plaintiff can be expected to drop its case. Anticipating this, the defendant will refuse to settle for any positive amount.

Suppose, however, that the litigation costs in the case under consideration are expected be incurred in two equal-cost stages and that the parties can engage in settlement negotiations not only before the first stage but also between the two stages. Analyzing this case by backward induction, let us start by considering the bargaining round between the two stages. Assuming that the parties reach this round, the plaintiff will have a credible threat to proceed to judgment. At this stage, the cost of the first stage of litigation is already sunk, and going all the way to judgment would provide an expected judgment of 100 and involve an additional cost of only 60.

Thus, if the parties somehow reach the bargaining round between the two stages, the plaintiff will have a credible threat and will be able to extract a settlement. Since the expected judgment is 100, and each party faces an additional cost of 60, the parties can be expected to settle at some point in the range between 40 and 160, with the location of the point depending on the parties' relative bargaining power.

Now suppose that should the parties reach the bargaining round between the two litigation stages, the plaintiff can be expected to obtain a settlement amount that exceeds 60. Let us proceed in the process of backward induction one stage back in time. In the bargaining round before the first litigation stage, it is now the case that the plaintiff will have a credible threat to proceed through this litigation stage. For proceeding through the first stage will cost the plaintiff 60 but can be expected to provide the plaintiff with a settlement amount exceeding 60. The presence of this credible threat to proceed will enable the plaintiff to extract a settlement offer in the bargaining round preceding the first stage of litigation.

The above example shows that a two-stage division can provide an NEV plaintiff with a credible threat to proceed with litigation, and enable her to extract a settlement from the defendant. A division into more than two stages can further expand the set of situations in which the plaintiff has a credible threat. To see this, suppose that C_p and C_d are 120 each as before but that W is only 50. In this case, with a division of the litigation process into two equal-cost stages, the plaintiff will not have a credible threat and will fail to obtain a positive settlement amount. In contrast, with a division into three equal-cost stages, and assuming that the parties have equal bargaining power (or at least that the bargaining power is not too skewed in favor of the defendant), the plaintiff will have a credible threat and succeed in extracting a positive settlement amount. Indeed, Bebchuk (1997) provides a proof that a finer division of the litigation process might sometimes improve – and can never worsen – the strategic position of the plaintiff and its ability to extract a settlement.

While divisibility can expand the set of circumstances in which an NEV plaintiff can obtain a settlement, divisibility cannot always provide an NEV plaintiff with a credible threat. There are cases of NEV suits in which, no matter how finely the litigation process is divided, the plaintiff will not have a credible threat. An analysis of the factors that determine when divisibility can and cannot provide a credible threat can be found in Bebchuk (1996) and, more fully, in Bebchuk (1997). Moreover, as Klement (2003) shows, defendants who hold private information may stonewall and sometimes deter plaintiffs from bringing NEV suits, notwithstanding divisibility of their litigation costs. Schwartz and Wickelgren (2009) examine the robustness of the analysis in Bebchuk (1996) to bargaining structures with outside options, and argue that divisibility cannot restore credibility when parties have an option to postpone a court decision indefinitely.

2.3. Upfront Costs by the Defendant

Another explanation for the success of NEV plaintiffs, which was put forward by Rosenberg and Shavell (1985), can apply even if the plaintiff's litigation costs are not at all divisible. Rosenberg and Shavell focused on those situations in which, after the plaintiff files a suit at no or little cost, the defendant must incur some significant costs of responding (because failure to respond would lead to default or summary judgment against the defendant) before the plaintiff has to incur any costs. Because only the defendant must incur costs during the initial stage of litigation (the first stage is a "cost-free" stage for the plaintiff), the plaintiff can credibly threaten to proceed through the first stage and thus impose the upfront costs on the defendant. In this situation, even if the defendant knows that the plaintiff will drop the case once the defendant responds and incurs its upfront costs, the defendant will be willing to pay a settlement (which might be up to the costs of responding) to avoid incurring these upfront costs. As Rosenberg and Shavell (2006) demonstrate, if defendants can ask the court to prevent early settlements by refusing to enforce them, they can deter plaintiffs from bringing NEV suits.

Bebchuk (1996) generalizes the Rosenberg-Shavell point by combining cost-free stages with divisibility of the litigation process. Suppose that the plaintiff is expected to have a cost-free stage at some point during the litigation process. Then, it can be shown that, if the defendant's cumulative expenses up to the cost-free stage are expected to be sufficiently large compared with the plaintiff's cumulative expenses up to that stage, the plaintiff will have a credible threat to begin with and will be able to extract a settlement.

2.4. New Information at Intermediate Points

During the litigation process, the parties might get some additional information which might lead them to revise their estimate of the expected value of the judgment. Thus far, we have assumed that the parties' estimate of the expected value of the judgment is expected to remain below total litigation costs throughout the litigation. Under this assumption, getting a settlement is the only way in which the plaintiff might end up with a positive return from the litigation. Cornell (1990) and Landes (1993) extend the analysis to cases in which the plaintiff might get favorable information at some intermediate point which may turn the plaintiff's suit into a positive-expected-value suit. If the plaintiff does not get such favorable information, he will drop the suit at that point and save his remaining litigation costs. The plaintiff thus has an option whether to progress with litigation or not. If she does not exercise this option then she does not incur the remaining costs.

To give a simple example, suppose that the judgment can be either 0 or 200 with equal probabilities, so the expected judgment, W, is 100, and C_p is 120. Since litigation costs are higher than the expected judgment, this is an NEV suit. Suppose, however, that litigation is divided into two equal-costs stages, and that the plaintiff learns the value of the judgment between the two stages. Unlike Bebchuk (1996), suppose also that the parties do not expect to bargain between the two stages (Grundfest and Huang (2006) combine the two models and allow bargaining between stages, when costs are divisible and information can be revealed throughout the litigation).

In this case, the plaintiff will pursue litigation only if she learns that the judgment is 200, leaving her with a net 140. Since the probability that the judgment would be 200 is 0.5, this implies that the plaintiff's expected value from litigation, before incurring her first-stage litigation costs, is 70, and since it is higher than her initial costs, 60, her litigation threat is credible and she might extract a settlement offer.

2.5. Repeat Playing and Reputation

Thus far the analysis has focused on one-shot litigation. But if any one of the parties is a repeat player, this party might develop a reputation which might enable it to bind itself to take a different course of action than the one that it would be expected to take in the case of one-shot litigation.

To begin, even if none of the factors that have been thus far considered is present, a plaintiff with an NEV suit might nonetheless succeed in extracting a settlement if the plaintiff or his lawyer is a repeat player with reputation of going to trial if a settlement is refused in cases of this sort. This reputation would provide the plaintiff with a credible threat to go to trial, and the credibility of this threat might induce the defendant to settle (see Farmer and Pecorino 1996). On the other hand, even if some of the factors discussed above are present to an extent that would enable an NEV plaintiff to extract a settlement offer in a one-shot litigation, the plaintiff might not succeed in extracting an offer if the defendant is a repeat player with reputation of not settling cases of this sort (see Miceli 1993).

2.6. Contingent Fees and Retainer Arrangements

Thus far, we have abstracted from the nature of the contract between the plaintiff and the plaintiff's lawyer. But, as Croson and Mnookin (1996), Bebchuk and Guzman (2000) and Chen (2006) point out, the plaintiff might be able to create a credible threat to go to trial by using a contingency fee or a retainer arrangement.

To see how lawyer-client arrangements might affect the plaintiff's credibility, consider a case in which W is 100. Suppose that the litigation costs to the plaintiff consist only of attorney fees, and let us further suppose that, if the plaintiff were to pay its lawyer on an hourly fee basis, C_p would be 125 – made up of 20 for hours spent on the preparatory stage before settlement negotiations take place and 105 for hours spent on the trial that would take place in the event of no settlement. Under an hourly fee arrangement, the plaintiff's suit is of course an NEV one.

Now consider what would happen if the plaintiff were to hire its lawyer on a contingency fee, with the lawyer promised 20% of the plaintiff's recovery (whether in settlement or in judgment). In this case, when the parties reach the stage of settlement negotiations, the plaintiff will have a credible threat to go to trial if the defendant refuses to settle for at least 100. Thus, with such a contingency fee arrangement, the parties can be expected to settle after the initial preparatory stage for an amount of 100 or more. It remains to consider why the lawyer would agree to such a contingency fee arrangement. But if the parties can indeed be expected to settle for at least 100 after the initial stage of preparations, being promised 20% of the expected settlement would be sufficient to compensate the lawyer for the actual work that the lawyer would be expected to do during the preparatory stage.

3. Normative Implications

In closing, we wish to highlight the fact that the literature that this chapter surveys has largely focused on positive analysis – on understanding the conditions under which NEV suits will be brought and succeed. The conclusion that the literature has reached – that NEV plaintiffs can in many cases succeed in extracting a settlement – suggests that the threat of using legal sanctions can provide plaintiffs with recovery in a larger set of circumstances than had been recognized by the preceding literature. This feature of the legal system might sometimes have beneficial consequences and sometimes undesirable ones.

With respect to NEV suits that are meritorious (and are NEV simply because the required litigation costs would be large relative to the amount at stake), an NEV plaintiff's ability to extract a settlement offer might well be socially beneficial. In contrast, with respect to NEV suits that are frivolous, an NEV plaintiff's ability to extract a settlement offer might well have undesirable consequences.

The literature surveyed here shows that the partition of all lawsuits to those that can extract a positive settlement and those that cannot does not necessarily overlap with the partition between NEV suits and PEV suits. As Shavell (1997) aptly demonstrates, neither partition overlaps with that between socially desirable and socially undesirable lawsuits.

Now that we have obtained some substantial understanding concerning when NEV suits can succeed, the challenge for future work in this area is to design rules and policies that would produce as close a correlation as possible between the success and merits of NEV suits.

References

Bebchuk, L.A. (1984), "Litigation and Settlement under Imperfect Information", *Rand Journal of Economics*, 15, 404–15.
Bebchuk, L.A. (1988), "Suing Solely to Extract a Settlement Offer", *Journal of Legal Studies*, 17, 437–49.
Bebchuk, L.A. (1996), "A New Theory concerning the Credibility and Success of Threats to Sue", *Journal of Legal Studies*, 25, 1–25.
Bebchuk, L.A. (1997), "On Divisibility and Credibility: The Effects of the Distribution of Litigation Costs over Time on the Credibility of Threats to Sue", Working paper, Harvard Law School, Cambridge, MA.
Bebchuk, L.A. (1998), "Suits with Negative Expected Value", in Peter Newman (ed.), *The New Palgrave Dictionary of Economics and the Law*, vol. 3, London: Macmillan, 551–4.
Bebchuk, L.A. and Guzman, A. (2000), "The Impact of Fee Arrangements on the Credibility of Threats to Sue", Unpublished manuscript, Harvard Law School, Cambridge, MA.
Chen, Zhiqi (2006), "Nuisance Suits and Contingent Attorney Fees", *Review of Law and Economics*, 2, 363–70.
Cornell, B. (1990), "The Incentive to Sue: An Option Pricing Approach", *Journal of Legal Studies*, 19, 173–87.
Croson, D. and Mnookin, R. (1996), "Scaling the Stonewall: Retaining Lawyers to Bolster Credibility", *Harvard Negotiation Law Review*, 1, 65–83.
Farmer, A. and Pecorino, P. (1998), "A Reputation for Being a Nuisance: Frivolous Lawsuits and Fee Shifting in a Repeated Play Game", *International Review of Law and Economics*, 18, 147–57.
Gould, J.P (1973), "The Economics of Legal Conflicts", *Journal of Legal Studies*, 2, 279–300.
Grundfest, J.A. and Huang, P.H. (2006), "The Unexpected Value of Litigation: A Real Options Perspective", *Stanford Law Review*, 58, 1267–336.
Katz, A. (1990), "The Effect of Frivolous Lawsuits on the Settlement of Litigation", *International Review of Law and Economics*, 10, 3–27.
Klement, A. (2003), "Threats to Sue and Cost Divisibility under Asymmetric Information", *International Review of Law and Economics*, 23, 261–72.
Landes, W.M. (1971), "An Economic Analysis of the Courts", *Journal of Law and Economics*, 14, 61–107.
Landes, W.M. (1993), "Sequential versus Unitary Trials: An Economic Analysis", *Journal of Legal Studies*, 22, 99–134.
Miceli, T.J. (1993), "Optimal Deterrence of Nuisance Suits by Repeat Defendants", *International Review of Law and Economics*, 13, 135–44.
P'ng, I. (1983), "Strategic Behavior in Suit, Settlement, and Trial", *Bell Journal of Economics*, 14, 539–50.
Posner, R.A. (1973), "An Economic Approach to Legal Procedure and Judicial Administration", *Journal of Legal Studies*, 2, 399–458.
Reinganum, J.F. and Wilde, L.F. (1986), "Settlement, Litigation, and the Allocation of Litigation Costs", *RAND Journal of Economics*, 17, 557–66.
Rosenberg, D. and Shavell, S. (1985), "A Model in which Suits are Brought for their Nuisance Value", *International Review of Law and Economics*, 5, 3–13.
Rosenberg, D. and Shavell, S. (2006), "A Solution to the Problem of Nuisance Suits: The Option to Have the Court Bar Settlement", *International Review of Law and Economics*, 26, 42–51.
Schwartz, W.F. (2003), "Can Suits with Negative Expected Value Really be Profitable", *Legal Theory*, 9, 83–97.
Schwartz, W.F. and Wickelgren, A.L. (2009), "Advantage Defendant: Why Sinking

Litigation Costs Makes Negative-expected-value Defenses but Not Negative-Expected-Value Suits Credible", *Journal of Legal Studies*, 38, 235–53.

Shavell, S. (1997), "The Fundamental Divergence between the Private and the Social Motive to Use the Legal System", *Journal of Legal Studies*, 26, 575–613.

13 Preclusion
Robert G. Bone

1. Introduction[1]

The law of preclusion deals with the effect of a lawsuit on future litigation. There are two types of preclusion: claim preclusion (also called "res judicata" or "rules of merger and bar") and issue preclusion (also called "collateral estoppel"). Claim preclusion bars a plaintiff from bringing a second suit seeking relief for essentially the same dispute against the same defendant. Issue preclusion prevents a party from relitigating an issue that has already been fully and fairly litigated and determined in a previous lawsuit.

Preclusion rules are said to promote judicial economy, repose, and decisional consistency. Claim preclusion and issue preclusion achieve these goals in different ways. The purpose of claim preclusion is to prevent a plaintiff from splitting up a single lawsuit into separate suits. The purpose of issue preclusion is to prevent wasteful relitigation of factual and legal issues that have already been litigated and decided in a previous suit.

To illustrate, suppose a patient P believes she was injured by the negligence of her doctor D. P sues D for negligence, and loses. Claim preclusion bars P from suing D a second time for breach of contract (or negligence) dealing with the same treatment. This result also holds if P wins her first suit and wants to sue again, perhaps to obtain more damages.

Now suppose that the jury in P's first suit actually determines that D negligently practiced medicine without adequate training, and suppose that D treated P for another illness. P now sues D for negligence in the course of that treatment. Claim preclusion does not apply to bar P from bringing this second suit since it deals with a different matter than the first. Issue preclusion might apply, however, and bind D to the determination of negligence in the first suit, assuming that the issue of inadequate training is common to both.

In brief, there are four requirements for claim preclusion. First, the initial lawsuit must have ended in a final judgment on the merits. Second, it must be the case that the plaintiff *could* have included in the first lawsuit the new matter (for example, new causes of action, new theories, new

---

[1] This entry is based on the treatment of preclusion in Bone (2003), at 232–58.

remedies, and so on) that she raises for the first time in a second suit. Third, the new matter must be closely enough related to the subject matter of the first suit that it *should* have been raised in that suit. How close the relationship need be is a subject of some disagreement and it is discussed briefly below. Fourth, claim preclusion, unlike issue preclusion, almost always requires that the parties be the same in the second suit as in the first.

There are three legal requirements for issue preclusion. First, issue preclusion normally requires a final judgment in the first suit, although it sometimes applies when the first suit ends in a settlement. Second, the issue in the second suit to which preclusion applies must be identical to an issue actually raised in the first suit. Third, the identical issue in the first suit must have been actually litigated, actually decided, and essential to the judgment in that suit.

It is important to note that issue preclusion, unlike claim preclusion, can apply even if there is a different party in the second suit. This is known as nonmutual issue preclusion and it is the focus of much of the economic literature, as described below. The following discussion first explores the economics of claim preclusion and then discusses some aspects of issue preclusion.

2. Claim Preclusion

2.1 Claim Preclusion by Agreement

The policies underlying claim preclusion – judicial economy, repose, and decisional consistency – assume that parties would litigate a dispute repeatedly if preclusion rules did not stop them. Hay (1993) questions this assumption. He argues that the prospect of costly relitigation will cause rational parties to settle the first suit and, as part of their settlement, to agree not to relitigate.[2] If parties do this, however, there will be only one round of litigation and thus no reason to be concerned

---

[2] To illustrate, suppose that P sues D for medical malpractice in the first suit. Suppose as well that P and D agree on P's likelihood of success, p, and the expected trial award, w. Also, suppose that P expects to spend c_π and D expects to spend c_Δ litigating the suit all the way through trial. Finally, for simplicity, assume that all the rounds of litigation are mutually independent and that the costs of litigation for each round are the same; in other words, p, c_π, and c_Δ remain constant. For P to be willing to sue initially, it must be the case that $pw - c_\pi > 0$. Since first-round litigation costs are sunk, P should be willing to file again if she loses the first lawsuit because $pw - c_\pi > 0$ holds for the second round too. Now suppose that P wins the first lawsuit and receives a judgment of w. D should be willing to file a second lawsuit to set aside the judgment if the expected loss from the second lawsuit is less than the judgment; in other words, if $pw + c_\Delta < w$. Combining these two

about multiple suits. It follows that claim preclusion rules must be justified on grounds other than judicial economy, repose, and decisional consistency.

Hay discusses two justifications. The first has to do with reducing error costs. In the absence of a claim preclusion rule, the settlement in the first round will be affected by the prospect of relitigation in multiple future rounds. The bargaining power conferred by the threat of future relitigation is not always symmetrically distributed, and when it is not, the first round settlement is likely to be skewed in favor of the party with the advantage.[3] Formal claim preclusion rules remove this distortion.

The second reason for claim preclusion rules has to do with reducing the transaction costs of negotiating a private preclusion agreement. These transaction costs can be substantial because parties must devise some way to bind themselves to their promises. A breach of contract claim will not do because it simply replicates the relitigation problem that the parties seek to avoid. There are ways to handle this problem informally, but they can be complicated to design. For example, the parties might give penalty bonds in escrow and instruct the escrow agent to forfeit the bond if a party seeks to relitigate. Agreeing on the amount of the bond and the precise structure of the escrow arrangement can be costly and a formal preclusion rule avoids those costs.

This transaction cost argument calls for formal claim preclusion rules that mimic what most parties would agree to without them. Otherwise, parties would simply contract around the formal rules and recreate the transaction costs that the rules were meant to avoid. It seems reasonable to assume that most parties would agree to only one round of litigation and therefore current claim preclusion rules that limit parties to one round probably make sense on this ground.

2.2 Scope of Claim Preclusion

Claim preclusion rules preclude a second lawsuit only when the subject matter of the second suit is closely enough related to the subject matter of the first suit to warrant a normative conclusion that the plaintiff should have brought all matters together in the first suit. Current law recognizes two different approaches to defining the requisite relational proximity.

---

constraints, we have that litigation will continue repeatedly no matter what the result in the previous round if p satisfies: $1 - c_\Delta/w > p > c_\pi/w$.

[3] Bone (2003) suggests, without rigorous proof, that the equilibrium of this multi-round litigation game is a first-round settlement that depends on each party's evaluation of his opponent's "staying power;" that is, the number of rounds his opponent would be willing to litigate assessed from the perspective of the first round. The party with greater "staying power" will get a more favorable settlement.

The narrow approach, still used in some states, is called the "legal right" test. This test holds that a plaintiff must bring in one lawsuit those elements that make up a single legal right. For example, a plaintiff could sue first for breach of a copyright license and then for copyright infringement in a second suit involving the same underlying events if the law recognized breach of contract as a different "legal right" than infringement of copyright.

The broad approach, used in the federal courts and in several states, is called the "transaction test." This test holds that a plaintiff must bring in one lawsuit all those elements that are transactionally related. Roughly speaking, this includes all causes of action, remedies, and factual and legal theories that arise from the same transaction or series of related transactions. In the copyright example, a court applying the transaction test would likely preclude the second lawsuit (for copyright infringement) after final judgment in the first lawsuit (for breach of contract) if the two causes of action arise from the same real world factual dispute.

Bone (2003) informally analyzes how broad the claim preclusion rules should be. If the first suit settles, the parties are likely to include all the transactionally related aspects of their dispute in that single settlement. Therefore, it makes sense to adopt the transaction test in this case, since it is the rule to which the parties are likely to agree on their own if they bargained for a claim preclusion rule as part of their settlement.

If the suit goes to trial, however, the matter is more complicated. A broader rule encourages plaintiffs to combine more related elements in one lawsuit and thus creates incentives to construct more complicated suits. In general, the more complicated the suit, the higher the costs of litigating it. A broad rule therefore saves costs by preventing a second suit, but increases costs by encouraging a more complicated first suit. A narrow rule has the opposite effect. If the plaintiff wins her first suit and obtains all the relief she seeks, there will be no further litigation and the narrow rule will have saved the cost of litigating a complicated suit in the first round. On the other hand, if the plaintiff loses her first suit and brings a second suit, as permitted by the narrow rule, there will be a second round of litigation and additional litigation cost. Thus, the relative advantage of a broad rule over a narrow rule depends on the relative cost of litigating a complicated versus a simple first suit, the cost of litigating a second suit if the plaintiff loses the first, and the probability the plaintiff wins a simple first suit (and thus does not proceed with a second suit).[4]

---

[4] One can formalize this result very roughly as follows. Suppose that the plaintiff can bring either of two lawsuits – a small suit that satisfies the legal right test but leaves transactionally related material out (call that LS_{min}) and a larger suit that

3 Issue Preclusion

The argument that private agreement might make formal rules unnecessary is much weaker for issue preclusion than for claim preclusion. Parties are likely to have difficulty agreeing on issue preclusion rules as part of a settlement. Unlike claim preclusion, issue preclusion applies to lawsuits that deal with entirely different disputes but happen to involve the same issue. This broad reach makes the prediction of future suits more difficult and thus the valuation of an issue preclusion clause more uncertain. The resulting uncertainty increases the risk that the parties' valuations will diverge sufficiently to scuttle agreement. Furthermore, the parties themselves cannot bind nonparties to issue preclusion rules by contract, so nonmutual preclusion rules must be imposed by law.

The following discussion focuses on issue preclusion rules when at least one party differs between the first and second suits, and reviews the economic literature on nonmutual issue preclusion and nonparty preclusion.[5]

---

satisfies the transaction test and includes all transactionally related causes of action, legal and factual theories, and so on (call that LS_{max}). Let p be the plaintiff's probability of success for LS_{min}. To simplify, suppose that the plaintiff would file LS_{min} if the legal right test were in effect and LS_{max} if the transaction test were in effect. (It is not too difficult to endogenize this choice, but it would complicate the analysis.) Also, assume the plaintiff can get all the relief she seeks through either LS_{min} or LS_{max}. Let c be the total cost to litigate LS_{min} through trial and $c + k$ the total cost to litigate LS_{max} through trial and let d be the total cost of a second suit that the plaintiff would bring if the legal right test were in effect and the plaintiff lost LS_{min}.

Assuming the plaintiff tries all these lawsuits, the expected cost of the legal right test is $pc + (1 - p)(c + d)$, and the expected cost of the transaction test is $c + k$. Therefore, the legal right test is superior to the transaction test if: $c + k > pc + (1 - p)(c + d)$. Reducing this expression, the condition is:

$$p > (d - k)/d.$$

[5] Issue preclusion differs from *stare decisis*. *Stare decisis* refers to a judicial obligation to give weight to previous decisions of the same issue in analogous situations. Unlike issue preclusion, *stare decisis* allows the judge to depart from the previous decision if she believes that the issue should be decided differently after giving the earlier decision appropriate weight. Issue preclusion affords the judge no such freedom: if issue preclusion applies, the judge *must* follow the decision in the previous suit whether or not she thinks it is correct. There is some discussion of *stare decisis* in the economic literature (Kornhauser 1989; Macey 1989). Rasmusen (1994), for example, shows that judges with an interest in maximizing their own influence over legal policy could settle into an equilibrium in which they all give weight to past decisions, expecting their own decisions to be given similar weight in the future. While each judge has an incentive to defect in Rasmusen's model, they all end up cooperating in equilibrium, a common result for an indefinitely repeated game. Rasmusen's model of *stare decisis*, however, does not transfer neatly to

3.1 Nonmutual Issue Preclusion

Traditionally, issue preclusion was limited by the doctrine of mutuality of estoppel, and the mutuality doctrine is still the law in some states. The mutuality doctrine limits the availability of issue preclusion to those parties who would have been precluded themselves had the issue been determined the other way. In effect, it enforces a kind of symmetry or equality principle: both parties to the second suit must have been at risk of preclusion from the first suit (depending on how the first decision came out).

The problem with the mutuality doctrine is that it drastically limits the availability of preclusion when the precluding party was not a party to the first suit. The reason is that a nonparty to the first suit is rarely subject to preclusion herself. As discussed in Section 3.2 below, a nonparty can be precluded only if she was in "privity" with a party to the first suit. Each person is said to have a right to her own personal "day in court," so privity seldom exists.

To illustrate, suppose P-1 sues D for negligent design of an automobile and the jury finds that D failed to use reasonable care. Suppose now that P-2 sues D for negligent design of the same type of automobile. Under the mutuality doctrine, P-2 can use issue preclusion against D only if P-2 would have been precluded herself had the issue been decided the other way. But P-2 would not have been precluded because she is not in privity with P-1, the party to the first suit. Privity requires actual control over P-1's litigation choices or a close representational relationship with P-1. Assuming P-2 is a stranger to P-1, neither of these requirements is satisfied. Therefore, since P-2 would not have been precluded had the issue of reasonable care come out the other way, the mutuality doctrine prevents P-2 from using preclusion against D.

The federal courts (and the courts of many states) have abolished the mutuality doctrine. In these jurisdictions, it is possible for P-2 to preclude D in our example even though P-2 would not have been precluded by D had the issue been decided the other way. This use of issue preclusion by a nonparty to the first suit is called "nonmutual issue preclusion." There are two types of nonmutual issue preclusion: defensive and offensive. The defensive type involves use of nonmutual issue preclusion by a defendant in the second suit (who was not a party to the first suit). The offensive type involves use of nonmutual issue preclusion by a plaintiff in the second suit

---

preclusion. Preclusion ties the judge's hands more strongly than *stare decisis*, so the private cost of a preclusion rule to the judge is considerably higher. To be sure, a judge has more influence in the future, but at the price of having less influence in the present.

356 *Procedural law and economics*

(who was not a party to the first suit). The negligent design hypothetical above is an example of offensive nonmutual issue preclusion.

When analyzing nonmutual issue preclusion, it is useful to consider trial effects separately from settlement effects.

3.1.1 Trial effects If all lawsuits had to be tried and none could settle, the benefits of nonmutual preclusion would be clear. Nonmutual preclusion saves the litigation costs of adjudicating the same issue repeatedly and avoids inconsistent decisions. The United States Supreme Court focused on these benefits when it abolished the mutuality doctrine and permitted defensive use of nonmutual preclusion in *Blonder-Tongue Laboratories, Inc. v. University of Illinois Foundation*, 402 US 313 (1971), and the Court emphasized the benefits again when it extended its *Blonder-Tongue* holding to permit offensive use of nonmutual preclusion in *Parklane Hosiery v. Shore*, 439 US 322 (1979).

Still, the case for switching to nonmutual preclusion is far from obvious because nonmutual preclusion also creates costs. Commentators have recognized the problems for some time (Currie 1957; Ratliff 1988, analyzing what he calls the "option effect"). Three types of cost are analyzed in the literature. First, the availability of nonmutual preclusion inflates the likelihood of success in later suits, thereby skewing the results in those suits toward the plaintiff (Currie 1957, at 285–9; Note 1978). Second, it creates incentives for plaintiffs to wait before suing to take advantage of possibly favorable decisions in earlier suits, and this strategy discourages efficient joinder (Currie 1957, at 285–9; Hay 1993, at 49). Third, offensive nonmutual issue preclusion creates asymmetric litigation investment in early suits, which skews the results in the defendant's favor (Spurr 1991).

The first type of cost can be illustrated with the negligent automobile design hypothetical above. Assume there are 100 injured automobile owners, P-1 through P-100, and they sue D *seriatim*. Assume that in the absence of preclusion, each plaintiff's chance of success is p. Finally, to simplify the analysis, assume that all the lawsuits turn exclusively on the issue of reasonable care, so each plaintiff is sure to recover if she proves a lack of reasonable care. Under these circumstances, P-1's probability of success is p. If the mutuality doctrine applies (and ignoring possible *stare decisis* effects), all the lawsuits are independent of one another, so each plaintiff's likelihood of success is p, as it should be.

However, if offensive nonmutual issue preclusion applies, P-2 wins if P-1 wins and also if P-2 wins on her own (which becomes relevant only if P-1 loses). Thus, P-2's probability of success is $1 - (1 - p)^2$. By the same reasoning, P-3 has three ways to win: if P-1 wins, if P-2 wins, and if P-3 wins on her own. Therefore, P-3's chance of success is $1 - (1 - p)^3$. More generally, P-k's chance of success is $1 - (1 - p)^k$, which is greater than p for $p > 0$ and $k \geq 2$. Thus, nonmutual preclusion benefits plaintiffs later in the litigation queue.[6]

The second type of cost is related to the first. Given that later suits have a higher probability of success *ex ante*, plaintiffs have incentives to wait and see what happens in the early suits, even when intervention or joinder in those early suits would be efficient from a social point of view. To see why, consider our design negligence situation. When deciding whether to join with P-1 in the first suit, P-2 will compare the benefit of sharing litigation expenses with P-1 by joining with the benefit of a second chance to win by staying out. Suppose the expected trial award for P-1 and for P-2 is w and the probability of success for each is p without preclusion. Suppose that P-1 and P-2 each have litigation costs of c and that D has litigation costs of d when they sue separately, and those litigation costs increase to $c + \varepsilon$ and $d + \varepsilon$ if P-1 and P-2 sue jointly. Finally, assume that P-1 and P-2 split the costs of their joint lawsuit equally, so each pays $(c + \varepsilon)/2$.

On these assumptions, if P-2 joins P-1 in the first suit, P-2's expected gain is: $pw - (c + \varepsilon)/2$. If P-2 stays out and waits to see what happens in P-1's suit, P-2's expected gain is: $[1 - (1 - p^2)]w - (1 - p)c$. Therefore, P-2 waits if and only if: $[1 - (1 - p^2)]w - (1 - p)c > pw - (c + \varepsilon)/2$. This expression reduces to $w > [(1 - 2p)c - \varepsilon]/2(p - p^2)$; in other words, P-2 waits only if the stakes (w) are large enough. And if P-2 waits instead of joining, total litigation costs increase by $(1 - p)(c + d) - 2\varepsilon$. To give a numerical example, suppose $p = 0.5$, $c = d = \$10{,}000$ and $\varepsilon = \$2000$. P-2 will wait out P-1's suit for all w, and P-2's waiting adds litigation costs of $\$6000$.[7]

As for the third type of cost, nonmutual issue preclusion creates asymmetric stakes, which can lead to greater litigation investment by whichever party to the first suit has the larger amount at stake. Since a party who invests more than her opponent is more likely to win, a difference in litigation investment will produce an error risk skewed in favor of the party who invests more. The mutuality doctrine, by eliminating preclusive effects, reduces the litigation investment differential and thus the skewed error risk.

Spurr (1991) confirms this result formally. He uses a simple model in

---

[6] In response to this concern, the United States Supreme Court in *Parklane Hosiery v. Shore*, 439 US 322 (1979), counseled against allowing offensive nonmutual preclusion when there are prior inconsistent decisions.

[7] The *Parklane Hosiery* Court tried to deal with this problem by denying preclusion to a plaintiff who adopts a wait-and-see strategy.

which the plaintiff's likelihood of success is a function of the ratio of plaintiff's to defendant's litigation expenditures, $F(c_\pi/c_\Delta)$, and solves for a Nash equilibrium. Spurr shows that a defendant in the first suit will spend more than the plaintiff when the defendant is at risk of being precluded in future suits (under a nonmutual issue preclusion rule), and that the defendant will do so whether or not it can also preclude subsequent plaintiffs if it wins (under a nonparty preclusion rule).

Even so, the fact that the defendant invests more than the plaintiff and thus stands a better chance of winning is not necessarily a problem for deterrence. This is so because defendant's additional litigation costs can offset to some extent the deterrence-reducing effect of skewed error. Deterrence is a function of defendant's total expected loss ($pw + c_\Delta$), and expected loss depends not only on the expected trial award (pw), but also on litigation costs (c_Δ). Even if skewed error in defendant's favor reduces the expected trial award by reducing plaintiff's likelihood of success (p), the asymmetric stakes increase litigation costs (c_Δ) and thus offset this adverse effect to some extent.

Spurr (1991) analyzes the impact of different combinations of preclusion rules on defendant's aggregate expected loss over multiple suits. He shows, for example, that adding nonparty preclusion to a system that already has nonmutual preclusion might reduce expected loss. His discussion, however, has limited usefulness for evaluating the effect of nonmutual issue preclusion on deterrence, since he does not examine the most relevant scenario, in which the rule that bars nonparty preclusion remains constant while mutuality is abolished and nonmutual preclusion allowed.[8]

3.1.2 Settlement effects Issue preclusion does not apply when the first lawsuit settles before an issue is decided, since then there is no decision that can have preclusive effects. This means that one must evaluate nonmutual preclusion in a world of settlement by how the threat of preclusion in future suits affects the parties' incentives to settle earlier suits.

Che and Yi (1993), Hay (1993), and Note (1992) explore these incentives and settlement effects. Che and Yi use a two-stage model in which a single defendant is sued sequentially by two separate plaintiffs in two different lawsuits. Each plaintiff has private information about damages and the defendant makes a take-it-or-leave-it offer. The authors analyze

---

[8] Spurr does find that the defendant has a lower aggregate expected loss in a system with both nonmutual issue preclusion and nonparty preclusion than in a system with no preclusive effects at all (i.e., with the mutuality doctrine and no nonparty preclusion) (Spurr 1991, at 56–7).

the results for both correlated decisions and correlated damages. For one-way correlation against the defendant, which is produced by allowing offensive nonmutual preclusion but denying nonparty preclusion, the defendant's settlement offer and the settlement rate are always greater in the first period compared to a system with no preclusion at all. This result is intuitive. The defendant can only lose and never gain from correlated decisions and therefore always increases its first-stage offer relative to the situation with no preclusion, and this increases the settlement rate. (This result ignores the additional effect of *stare decisis*, which can favor the defendant.)[9]

In the Che-Yi model, litigation costs and probability of success are exogenously specified. Hay (1993) treats these variables as endogenous. Like Spurr (1991), Hay reasons that the risk of being precluded in future rounds will pressure the defendant to invest much more than the plaintiff in the first round, and the resulting asymmetry will reduce the plaintiff's probability of success. He then argues that a lower probability of success is likely to produce a lower settlement, especially if the defendant bargains hard for settlement at the low end of the range[10] (Hay 1993, at 45–8).

---

[9] Che and Yi also find that symmetric two-way correlation, which is produced by nonmutual preclusion combined with nonparty preclusion, increases both the defendant's settlement offer and the settlement rate in the first period if and only if the plaintiff's winning probability in the first period exceeds a threshold level (Che and Yi 1993, at 406–7). Che and Yi draw two conclusions from these findings. First, they argue that defendants have incentives to invest heavily in the first period when they expect a lawsuit to set an important precedent (and plaintiffs do as well if they can organize) (Che and Yi 1993, at 408–10). Second, they argue that nonmutual offensive issue preclusion without nonparty preclusion encourages nuisance suits by increasing defendant's settlement offer in the first period, thereby making suit more attractive for plaintiffs with weak cases (Che and Yi 1993, at 410–13). However, nonmutual preclusion with nonparty preclusion or defensive nonmutual preclusion without nonparty preclusion deters nuisance suits by reducing defendant's first period offer in a weak case.

[10] Moreover, Hay argues that the defendant has an incentive to bargain hard in order to cultivate a reputation for hard bargaining, which can pay off for settlements in other suits. By contrast, the plaintiff, as a one-shot litigant, has nothing to gain from bargaining hard. The combination of hard bargaining by the defendant and normal bargaining by the plaintiff is likely to yield a settlement in the lower half of the settlement range. This point is important to Hay's result. To see why, consider the following example. Suppose that P-1's probability of success is p without preclusion and q with preclusion ($p > q$). Assume that the expected trial award conditional on success is w. Suppose P-1 invests c and D invests d in the absence of preclusion and suppose that D invests $d + k$ with preclusion. (This is a simplification and ignores strategic interaction effects.) The settlement range in the absence of preclusion is: $[pw - c, pw + d]$. Assuming equal bargaining power, the

Since settlement generates no preclusive effect, Hay argues, the second plaintiff is in roughly the same position as the first and therefore at a similar disadvantage. This repeats for each plaintiff, although the asymmetry of litigation investment diminishes with each round (since fewer suits remain to be litigated). As a result, the aggregate settlement amount the defendant pays to all plaintiffs can be less than what the defendant would pay in the absence of preclusion. Thus, in Hay's model, the defendant benefits from offensive nonmutual issue preclusion, even though the plaintiffs would benefit if all the cases went to trial.[11]

Note (1992) reaches the opposite result. It argues that offensive nonmutual issue preclusion advantages plaintiffs in settlement by giving them a way to "extort" more from the defendant than they could without preclusion. To illustrate, consider the above example involving 100 plaintiffs each with a negligence claim against D, an automobile manufacturer. D knows that if it loses P-1's suit, it loses all 99 subsequent suits (assuming, as the example did, that all lawsuits turn exclusively on the issue of reasonable care). Therefore, D should be willing to pay a premium to settle the first suit and avoid the preclusive effect in 99 future suits. The same is true for P-2's suit. D should be willing to pay a premium to settle this suit, again in order to avoid the preclusive effect in 98 subsequent suits. And so on. The result is that the defendant faces an expected liability in the aggregate greater than what it would have faced in the absence of preclusion. The Note author concludes that although offensive nonmutual issue preclusion benefits later plaintiffs in the queue when all cases go to trial, it benefits earlier plaintiffs when the cases settle instead (Note 1992, at 1943–4).

One way to reconcile Note (1992) with Hay (1993) is to recognize that the Note author makes litigation investment and probability of success

---

Nash bargaining solution is: $pw + (d - c)/2$. The settlement range in the presence of preclusion is: $[qw - c, qw + d + k]$. Assuming equal bargaining power, the Nash bargaining solution is: $qw + (d - c + k)/2 = pw + (d - c)/2 - [(p - q)w - k/2]$. Thus, preclusion reduces the settlement amount only when $p - q > k/2w$. However, if one adds hard bargaining and assumes that it does not scuttle settlement, then P-1 will settle for close to $qw - c$, which is less than $pw - c$.

[11] Hay's results are sensitive to a number of factors that can vary. For example, they depend on settlement negotiations succeeding in the individual suits, but D's hard bargaining strategy can be an obstacle to successful settlement if it angers the plaintiff. Hay also assumes that all the plaintiffs are one-shot litigants, but each of the plaintiff's attorneys is a repeat player and might benefit from developing a hard bargaining reputation. Also, plaintiffs might cooperate, but as Hay points out, offensive nonmutual issue preclusion creates incentives to free ride, which discourages cooperation (Hay 1993, at 48–50).

exogenous variables and ignores outcome effects due to asymmetric litigation investment. A more complete analysis would model both effects – the extortion effect discussed in the Note, and the investment effect discussed in Hay (1993). Although the net result is not entirely clear, it is possible that for a large enough number of lawsuits the extortion effect will dominate, assuming that the function relating differential investment to probability of success is concave. If this prediction is correct, the most significant cost of offensive nonmutual issue preclusion could be settlements improperly skewed against the defendant.

3.2 Nonparty Preclusion

3.2.1 Overview The American law of preclusion rarely binds persons who were not parties. The nonparty must be in "privity" with a party to the first suit. Generally speaking, privity exists when the nonparty controls the party's litigation choices in the first suit, when the nonparty actually agrees to have the party represent her interests, or when the nonparty is "virtually represented" by the party to the first suit.[12] The control needed for preclusion must be almost total, and virtual representation is very difficult to establish. The United States Supreme Court has held that each person has a due process right to her own personal day in court, and this principle severely restricts the occasions in which a nonparty can be precluded. And in a recent case, the Court dealt a severe blow to virtual representation as a doctrine of federal preclusion law.[13]

3.2.2 Trial effects Assume first that all cases go to trial. The benefits of a broad nonparty preclusion rule are obvious: it saves the costs of repeatedly litigating the same issue and provides greater decisional consistency.

To illustrate, suppose that D, a drug company, mass markets a drug that turns out to cause serious injury, and suppose that 1000 users of the drug (P-1 through P-1000), all of whom suffer from the same type of injury and are strangers to one another, sue D separately, each alleging a products liability claim. Suppose in P-1's suit, D proves that the drug could not possibly cause the type of injury. Because of the very narrow nonparty preclusion rules, P-2 can litigate the identical causation issue again, and so

---

[12] There are two other situations not relevant to our discussion here. A nonparty can be precluded when the court properly certifies a class action in the first suit and the "nonparty" is a member of the class, and also when the nonparty is a successor in interest to property that was the subject of the decision in the first suit.
[13] See *Taylor v. Sturgell*, 553 US 880 (2008) (holding that claim preclusion was not permissible on a virtual representation theory).

can P-3 and all the other 997 plaintiffs. A rule that allows nonparty preclusion saves these relitigation costs and also prevents inconsistent decisions of the issue.

However, these benefits must be compared to the costs. Bone (1993) analyzes the costs of a nonparty preclusion rule when all cases go to trial. Two types of cost must be considered. First, a nonparty preclusion rule increases risk-bearing costs by making defendant's total expected liability more uncertain. Second, nonparty preclusion can create asymmetric stakes that benefit the plaintiff.

Consider the effect on risk-bearing costs. To simplify the analysis, assume that causation is the only difficult issue in the 1000 lawsuits and that it is decisive both ways. In other words, assume that the defendant loses all the lawsuits if P-1 wins on causation and that defendant wins all the lawsuits if P-1 loses. Consider a "complete relitigation system," one that denies nonparty preclusion *and* nonmutual preclusion (i.e., applies the mutuality doctrine). In a complete relitigation system, the causation issue is guaranteed to be tried 1000 times (assuming, as we do here, that all cases go to trial). The defendant will lose sometimes and win sometimes. More precisely, if the probability of success on the issue is p, the number of lawsuits is n ($n = 1000$ in the example above), and all suits are mutually independent, the defendant will expect to lose np and win $(1-p)n$. If the expected trial award for each plaintiff is w, defendant's aggregate expected liability (ignoring litigation costs) is npw and the average liability per suit is $npw/n = pw$.

Compare what happens in a "complete preclusion system," one that allows both nonparty preclusion and nonmutual preclusion. In a complete preclusion system, the decision of the causation issue in the first suit is determinative of all the rest. Since the probability of a defendant loss is p, the defendant's aggregate expected liability over n lawsuits is npw and the average liability per suit is pw, exactly the same as it was for the complete relitigation system. Thus, switching from a complete relitigation system to a complete preclusion system does not alter the defendant's expected liability.

However, it does alter the risk of litigation. In a complete relitigation system, all possible combinations of wins and losses occur with some probability. The result is a binomial distribution, in which the probability of x wins and $n - x$ losses is given by: $\{n!/[x!(n - x)!]\}p^x(1 - p)^{n-x}$. The mean of this distribution is np, and the variance is $np(1 - p)$. By contrast, in a complete preclusion system, only two possible outcomes can occur: either the defendant loses all n lawsuits, or the defendant wins all n lawsuits. The former happens with probability p, and the latter with probability $1 - p$. The mean of this two-point distribution is np, the same as for a relitigation system (which is why expected liability is the same). However, the variance is $p(n - np)^2 + (1 - p)(np - 0)^2 = n^2p(1 - p)$. Thus, the variance is much greater for a complete preclusion system than for a complete relitigation system; in this simple model, it is n times greater. And higher variance creates risk-bearing costs for risk-averse actors.

Posner (1992) discusses the second type of cost, skewed error from asymmetric litigation investment. He argues that nonparty preclusion, like nonmutual preclusion, generates asymmetric stakes in the first lawsuit. With nonparty preclusion, D in our drug example wins all 1000 suits if it wins the causation issue in the first suit. Therefore, D has 1000w at stake in the first suit. P-1, by contrast, has nothing to lose or gain from future suits, so her stake is only w. With more at stake, D will invest more and be more likely to win[14] (Posner 1992, at § 21.11).

Thus, a nonparty preclusion rule saves litigation costs, but also creates risk-bearing costs and error costs due to skewed outcomes. It is reasonable to suppose, however, that the cost-saving benefits will exceed the additional risk-bearing and error costs for a large enough number of lawsuits.[15] For one thing, marginal risk-bearing costs probably diminish with the number of lawsuits, whereas marginal litigation costs are likely to remain roughly constant. Moreover, in actual litigation, the common issue is likely not to be dispositive in the way we assumed for our simple example. When the common issue is not dispositive, additional risk-bearing costs from a nonparty preclusion rule will be less because other issues already generate risk.

As for Posner's argument about skewed error, several factors are likely to mitigate the adverse effect (Bone 1993, at 251–6). First, nonparty preclusion gives P-2 through P-1000 a stake in P-1's suit and thus mitigates the free-rider effect and encourages cooperation among plaintiffs. With cooperation, the amount at stake on plaintiff's side increases. Second, attorneys in mass tort cases tend to collect many clients on a contingency fee basis. As a result, the

---

[14] Posner also notes that D might be able to control which P goes to trial first (by delaying some suits and speeding up others). If so, D will have an incentive to go to trial first against a P-1 with the weakest causation evidence or the poorest attorney, thereby adding to its likelihood of success and compounding the expected error cost.

[15] This analysis assumes individual lawsuits and all-or-nothing preclusion rules. It is worth noting some other possibilities that might strike a superior balance between benefit and cost. For example, one might require the trial of a number of individual suits and then bind future parties to the most commonly recurring decision of the issue. Although this increases litigation costs, it reduces risk-bearing costs. Also, one might aggregate a number of individual suits together in a single litigation and then bind future parties to the decision of the issue in that aggregated suit. This increases litigation costs but it also reduces error costs by increasing the plaintiffs' stakes in the first suit.

attorney for P-1 is likely to have hundreds of other plaintiffs as clients and thus will litigate P-1's suit with an eye to potential benefits in future suits. Third, the effect of litigation investment on likelihood of success is subject to declining marginal returns. If w is already large, as one might expect in a personal injury drug case, P-1 is likely to invest a great deal in the litigation, and any additional investment by D due to fear of nonparty preclusion is not likely to make a huge difference to the outcome.

3.2.3 Settlement effects The foregoing analysis assumed trials. If the suits settle instead, nonparty preclusion must be evaluated by how it affects the quantity and quality of settlements. There is not much economic literature on this subject, perhaps because nonparty preclusion is not a significant feature of American preclusion law. The following is a very rough analysis of what might happen if nonparty preclusion were added to a system that already allowed nonmutual preclusion.

As was discussed in Section 3.1.2 above, nonmutual preclusion has two countervailing effects on the defendant's maximum settlement offer: a preclusion effect that raises expected costs and thus increases the offer, and an asymmetric-investment effect that depresses plaintiff's likelihood of success and thus reduces the offer. Adding nonparty preclusion to this system has at least two additional effects. First, it encourages cooperation on the plaintiff's side, which can reduce the investment asymmetry and thus increase the defendant's maximum offer. Second, nonparty preclusion gives the defendant an added benefit from litigating the issue, which should cause the defendant to reduce its maximum offer.

It is unclear how these effects net out. If the investment asymmetry distortion is already small because of the declining marginal utility of litigation investment, the second effect might dominate. In that case, defendant's maximum offer would decrease and the settlement range narrow, which probably makes settlement less likely. As for settlement amount, empowering cooperation among plaintiffs should make it more difficult for the defendant to use a hard bargaining strategy successfully (see Section 3.1.2 above), which might increase the settlement amount. However, defendant's maximum offer decreases more than plaintiff's minimum demand increases when the second effect dominates. And this should reduce the midpoint of the settlement range and thus the settlement amount, assuming equal bargaining power.[16]

---

[16] See Rosenberg (2002) for additional discussion of the trial and settlement effects of preclusion in large-scale litigation, especially the strategic effects of a complete preclusion system.

One thing is clear. There is a pressing need for more work on nonparty preclusion, especially its settlement effects. It seems, however, that the economic arguments for some form of nonparty preclusion in large-scale litigation are strong.[17]

Bibliography

Bone, Robert G., *Rethinking the Day in Court: Ideal and Nonparty Preclusion*, 67 N.Y.U. L. REV. 193 (1993).
Bone, Robert G., ECONOMICS OF CIVIL PROCEDURE 232–58 (2003).
Che, Yeon-Koo and Jong Goo Yi, *The Role of Precedents in Repeated Litigation*, 12 J.L. ECON. & ORG. 399 (1993).
Currie, Brainerd, *Mutuality of Collateral Estoppel: Limits of the Bernhard Doctrine*, 9 STAN. L. REV. 281 (1957).
Hay, Bruce, *Some Settlement Effects of Preclusion*, 1993 U. ILL. L. REV. 21 (1993).
Kornhauser, Lewis A., *An Economic Perspective on Stare Decisis*, 65 CHI.-KENT L. REV. 63 (1989).
Macey, Jonathan R., *Internal and External Costs and Benefits of Stare Decisis*, 65 CHI.-KENT L. REV. 93 (1989).
Note, *A Probabilistic Analysis of the Doctrine of Mutuality of Collateral Estoppel*, 76 MICH. L. REV. 612 (1978).
Note, *Exposing the Extortion Gap: An Economic Analysis of the Rules of Collateral Estoppel*, 105 HARV. L. REV. 1940 (1992).
Posner, Richard A., ECONOMIC ANALYSIS OF LAW (1992).
Rasmusen, Eric, *Judicial Legitimacy as a Repeated Game*, 10 J.L. ECON. & ORG. 63 (1994).
Ratliff, Jack, *Offensive Collateral Estoppel and the Option Effect*, 67 TEX. L. REV. 63 (1988).
Rosenberg, David, Avoiding Duplicative Litigation of Similar Claims: The Superiority of Class Action vs. Collateral Estoppel vs Standard Claims Market, Harvard Law School, Public Research Paper No. 44, Harvard Law and Economics Discussion Paper No. 394, 2002.
Spurr, Stephen, *An Economic Analysis of Collateral Estoppel*, 11 INT'L REV. L. & ECON. 47 (1991).

---

[17] It is important to note, however, that the restrictive approach to nonparty preclusion in American law is probably anchored to a rights-based theory of participation rather than to a utilitarian theory. For a description and critique of the rights-based approach, see Bone (1993).

14 Self-incrimination
Alex Stein

1. Introduction

The Fifth Amendment to the United States Constitution provides that "nor shall [a person] be compelled in any criminal case to be a witness against himself."

This provision is widely known as the privilege against self-incrimination or the right to silence. The right to silence incorporates four basic rules. As a general matter, a person who receives a subpoena or other lawful request to provide information to an authorized tribunal or agency, such as a court or the police, but refuses to do so, is guilty of contempt or a similar crime punishable by fine or imprisonment. The person, however, is exempted from the duty to comply with such a request when his compliance might reveal information exposing him to a prospect of criminal prosecution and conviction. Second, factfinders may not draw any adverse inferences from a criminal defendant's refusal to testify in his defense or answer questions during police interrogation. Third, when the police or other law-enforcement agency elicits an involuntary confession from a suspect, the confession cannot be admitted into evidence and the trial judge must suppress it. Coercive interrogation of a suspect renders the ensuing confession involuntary and inadmissible.[1] Furthermore, a suspect's confession will be deemed involuntary as a matter of law – and, consequently, inadmissible – when the police deprive him of his *Miranda* rights at custodial interrogation. Under *Miranda*, the police must tell the suspect at the beginning of his interrogation that he is entitled to remain silent; that anything he will say might be used as evidence against him at his criminal trial; and that he is entitled to consult an attorney (at his own expense or at the government's expense, if the suspect is poor) and have that attorney present at the interrogation.[2] Finally, criminal defendants and suspects can waive each of the above entitlements. If the waiver is a product of a voluntary and informed decision, the court will recognize it as effective.

---

[1] Suppression of such confessions is dictated not only by the Fifth Amendment's privilege against self-incrimination, but also by common law, as well as by the defendant's constitutional entitlement to due process. See *Withrow v. Williams*, 507 US 680, 693 (1993).

[2] See *Miranda v. Arizona*, 384 US 436 (1966).

In what follows, I survey these rules and their underlying economic justifications.

2. The Utility of the Right to Silence

2.1 The Right to Silence as an Anti-pooling Device

Economic analysis of the right to silence focuses on the right's social costs and benefits. If those benefits exceed the costs, the right will be justified. The right's costs and benefits crucially depend on how it affects the outcomes of criminal investigations and trials. Specifically, those costs and benefits depend on how the right affects the incidence of false positives (erroneous convictions of factually innocent defendants) and false negatives (erroneous exonerations of factually guilty defendants). The right to silence will be justified if it reduces the total social cost of false positives and false negatives in comparison with an alternative legal regime that does not recognize the right.[3]

False positives and false negatives are the consequences of asymmetrical information. A criminal defendant normally knows for certain whether he "did it" or not. The police, prosecution, and courts have no such knowledge. False positives and false negatives are brought about by defendants' choices between staying silent, confessing to the crime and denying the accusations, and by the actions of other participants in the criminal process – the police, prosecution, and courts – that respond to those choices (Seidmann and Stein 2000). These strategic interactions merit detailed analysis.

The first thing to know about the right to silence is that it plays no significant role in cases in which the outcome of the defendant's criminal trial is virtually certain. The right has no effect on a case in which inculpatory evidence is overwhelmingly strong. By the same token, it has virtually no effect on a case featuring weak inculpatory evidence. In the former category of cases, both guilty and innocent defendants face a serious prospect of conviction. The right to silence cannot change this prospect in either direction. For a defendant who faces overwhelming inculpatory evidence, making a confession followed by a guilty plea would normally be the best strategy. This strategy might secure a sentence reduction, and it also would allow the defendant not to expend money and effort on litigating a hopeless case.

---

[3] Both false positives and false negatives dilute deterrence by lowering the expected penalty for potential offenders. False negatives do so by reducing the offender's probability of conviction. False positives do so by eroding the difference between the penalties expected from violating and not violating the law. See Polinsky and Shavell (2000), 60–62.

Defendants facing weak inculpatory evidence will likely be exonerated, regardless of their factual guilt. As in all other cases, an innocent defendant's best strategy in a weak-evidence case is testifying and telling the truth. The prosecution's weak evidence would fail to refute his true exculpatory testimony. The factfinders consequently would have to acquit the defendant. A guilty defendant, in contrast, must always choose between giving a perjured self-exonerating account of the events, staying silent, and confessing. Making a confession followed by a guilty plea is only attractive when the prosecution offers the defendant a favorable plea bargain. Absent such an offer, a guilty defendant must choose between lying and remaining silent. The lying strategy is risky: an uncovered lie would reveal the defendant's "guilty conscience," which would practically guarantee his conviction.

Whether a guilty defendant should remain silent depends on the legal regime. When the legal regime does not allow factfinders to draw adverse inferences from the defendant's silence at interrogation and trial, the defendant's best call is to remain silent. When adverse inferences are allowed, the defendant's choice between silence and lies would depend on how strong those inferences are. If those inferences merely indicate the defendant's possible involvement in the crime – and thus function merely as corroborative evidence – the defendant should stay silent. The prosecution would then fail to prove his guilt beyond a reasonable doubt, and the factfinders would have to acquit him. However, if factfinders always (or predominantly) associate silence with guilt, the defendant would be better off lying. The right to silence therefore has no effect on defendants with exceedingly high payoffs for lying or confessing. For those defendants, the right is essentially irrelevant (Stein 2008).

The right to silence, however, plays a significant role in factually complex ("intermediate") cases, in which the inculpatory evidence is fairly (but not overwhelmingly) strong. These cases present the most acute problem of asymmetrical information. Factfinders know that some defendants are guilty and some innocent, but cannot tell who is guilty and who is innocent. Virtually every defendant knows whether he committed the crime that the prosecution accuses him of. His private knowledge, however, does not turn into public information that factfinders can verify and trust. In the absence of a special incentive to plead guilty (a particularly attractive plea-bargain offer), a guilty defendant will deny the accusations and plead not guilty. Under the regime that allows factfinders to draw adverse inferences from the defendant's silence, guilty defendants will falsely testify about their innocence. Innocent defendants will do the same, but without lying. Factfinders consequently will proceed on the assumption that some self-exonerating accounts are true and some false.

This assumption necessarily reduces the probability of all self-exonerating accounts. As a result, an innocent defendant who cannot corroborate his exculpatory testimony by credible evidence suffers a credibility reduction. This reduction increases the probability of the prosecution's case – an increase that helps the prosecution prove the defendant's guilt "beyond a reasonable" doubt. When that happens, factfinders convict an innocent defendant, which means that, by lying, a guilty defendant imposes a harmful externality on innocent defendants (and society at large) (Seidmann and Stein 2000). Bentham's famous utilitarian analysis of the right to silence, maintaining that the right only helps guilty criminals to escape conviction, failed to notice this externality. This analysis, therefore, is seriously flawed. The present-day supporters of "crime control" – who claim, similarly to Bentham, that the right only helps guilty criminals to escape conviction – have also overlooked it. Contrary to the crime-control view, abolition of the right to silence would not induce guilty criminals to switch from silence to confessions.[4] Rather, it would

---

[4] According to a well-known empirical study, Cassell and Fowles (1998), the right to silence reduces the conviction rate. This study examined the FBI's case-clearance data that correlate with suspects' confessions. Based on these data, the study estimated regression models for a variety of crime categories, using the clearance rate as the dependent variable. To capture the right's effect on the clearance rate, the study created a dummy variable which equals 0 before 1966 (the year in which the Supreme Court decided *Miranda v. Arizona*, 384 US 436 (1966)) and 1 thereafter. This dummy variable was significant at the 0.01 level for serious crimes and was negatively signed, which means that the right to silence had significantly reduced the clearance rate. See id., at 1082–4. For methodological reservations about this study, see Donohue (1998), 1152–6 (casting doubts on whether clearance rates are dependable and methodologically adequate data for measuring the effects of *Miranda* on law enforcement). Also: federal law recognizes the right to silence and a silent defendant's privilege against adverse inferences since 1943; see *Johnson v. United States*, 318 US 189, 198–9 (1943) (holding that, independent of the Fifth Amendment, a prosecutor cannot comment on the defendant's invocation of the right to silence, and asserting that the Supreme Court's supervisory power under Article III, § 1 of the United States Constitution makes it mandatory for federal courts to follow this holding), if not before; see *Twining v. New Jersey*, 211 US 78 (1908) (holding that the right to silence and a silent defendant's privilege against adverse inferences belong to federal law, but are neither "privileges or immunities" nor "due process" within the meaning of the Fourteenth Amendment's restrictions upon states). The *Miranda* Justices expressly modeled their warning requirements on the already established FBI practice of warning suspects: see *Miranda*, 384 US at 483–4 (attesting that "*Over the years* the Federal Bureau of Investigation has compiled an exemplary record of effective law enforcement while advising any suspect or arrested person, at the outset of an interview, that he is not required to make a statement, that any statement may be used against him in court, that the individual may obtain the services of an attorney of his own choice and, more

induce them to switch from silence to self-exonerating lies (Seidmann and Stein 2000, at 499–502).

The right to silence gives guilty criminals an attractive alternative to lying. Because a lie can be discovered and because its discovery will likely lead to the liar's conviction, for at least some criminals silence constitutes a better option. Those criminals would consequently prefer silence to lying. The externality that they otherwise would impose upon innocents (the pernicious pooling effect) will thus be eliminated. As a result, fewer innocent defendants will be convicted than under a regime in which the right to silence does not exist. This outcome, however, will be achieved at a price: some criminals, who otherwise would implicate themselves by lies that could be uncovered, will escape conviction by exercising the right to silence (Seidmann and Stein 2000; Stein 2008).

2.2 The Doctrinal Fit

This anti-pooling rationale is particularly useful as an explanatory tool. It explains and justifies the entire set of rules that derive from the right to silence. These rules hold that:

- The right to silence protects defendants throughout the entire criminal process, which includes interrogation, trial and sentencing hearings.
- The right to silence protects defendants only against compelled disclosure of "testimonial," but not "physical," evidence.
- The right to silence (in the form of the privilege against adverse inferences from silence) does not apply in civil trials.
- Nor does it extend to testimony that may lead to the witness's conviction overseas.

---

recently, that he has a right to free counsel if he is unable to pay. A letter received from the Solicitor General in response to a question from the Bench makes it clear that the present pattern of warnings and respect for the rights of the individual followed as a practice by the FBI is consistent with the procedure which we delineate today." (emphasis added)). As early as in 1952, the FBI's director, J. Edgar Hoover, made an unequivocal statement (quoted in *Miranda*, 384 US at 483, n. 54) that "Special Agents are taught that any suspect or arrested person, at the outset of an interview, must be advised that he is not required to make a statement and that any statement given can be used against him in court. Moreover, the individual must be informed that, if he desires, he may obtain the services of an attorney of his own choice." See Hoover (1952), 182. The 1966 baseline, chosen by Cassell and Fowles, therefore cannot be suitable for analyzing *Miranda*'s effects on the law-enforcement agencies in the states that followed the federal rules (and, of course, on the FBI).

- The right to silence can be set aside when the police attend an ongoing emergency.
- The right's protection against compelled self-incrimination is given only to people, but not to corporate entities.[5]

The remainder of this section will explain and justify each of the above rules in the order presented.

2.2.1 The right to silence as applying to every phase of the criminal process By allowing non-confessing criminals to substitute silence for false self-exonerating statements, the right to silence protects innocent defendants from being pooled with criminals. At the same time, it allows criminals not to implicate themselves by potentially incriminating lies. The right to silence therefore increases the rate of erroneous exonerations in factually complex cases. It does not merely help innocents to achieve deserved acquittals. It also helps criminals to escape conviction. The exoneration prospect, indeed, is the prize that a criminal receives for helping the legal system to cleanse the pool of self-exonerating statements. The resulting exonerations of the guilty consequently determine the right's social cost. For obvious reasons, the legal system is interested in reducing this cost without sacrificing the right's anti-pooling benefit. This desire explains the right's limits discussed below in subsections 2.2.2, 2.2.3, 2.2.4, 2.2.5 and 2.2.6. The right's cost, however, is also a reason for questioning its broad application throughout all phases of the criminal process. Presently, the right to silence applies with full force at interrogations, trials, and sentencing hearings. Is there a good reason for that? Would the right's removal from any of those phases be socially beneficial?

The right to silence cannot be removed from suspects interrogated by the police: its removal will be too costly. If factfinders draw adverse inferences from the defendant's silence at interrogation, guilty suspects would have an incentive to lie to the police. Subsequently, those suspects would have to repeat their lies while testifying in court (if they do not do so, the prosecution would often be able to use their false statements to the police as evidence of guilt).

These suspects' false statements will consequently pool with the uncorroborated true testimonies given by innocent defendants. Facing this pooling, factfinders will have to reduce the probability of truthfulness that attaches to all such self-exonerating testimonies.

The right to silence also cannot easily be removed from the criminal trial.

---

[5] See Bierschbach and Stein (2005), 1775–6.

For reasons already given, this removal would motivate guilty defendants to pool with innocents by falsely testifying in their defense – a pooling that would cause factfinders to discount the credibility of every defendant's testimony. Apart from creating this pernicious effect, the right's unavailability at the trial stage would motivate guilty suspects to lie to the police as well. Those lies would often be a guilty defendant's strategic necessity.

Anticipating the prosecution's attempt to rebut his testimony at a forthcoming trial, a guilty suspect would often need to give a prior consistent statement that will bolster his credibility as a witness (Seidmann and Stein 2000, at 489–95).

After pleading guilty, a defendant retains the right to silence at his sentencing hearing. In determining sentencing facts, the judge cannot draw adverse inferences from the defendant's failure to testify at the hearing. This rule, too, has a compelling anti-pooling rationale. Removal of the right to silence from sentencing hearings would induce guilty defendants to plead not guilty. Some of those defendants would remain silent at their trials and enjoy the pre-conviction protection against adverse inferences. Others would falsely testify to their innocence and adversely affect innocent defendants by impugning the credibility of their truthful self-exonerating accounts. Neither of those scenarios is beneficial to society (Seidmann and Stein 2000, at 495–8).

2.2.2 The right to silence as restricted to "testimonial" evidence The right to silence only protects defendants from compelled production of "testimonial" evidence. The right does not extend to "physical" evidence, which includes writings that already exist (as opposed to writings that a suspect or a criminal defendant might be asked to generate).

This limitation squarely aligns with the anti-pooling rationale. Under this rationale, the right to silence should only be recognized when guilty defendants need inducement for avoiding pooling with the innocent. The right should only extend to evidence that can create this pooling effect. Such externality-laden evidence reduces the credibility of self-exonerating evidence tendered by the innocent. Any such evidence therefore should be considered "testimonial" for purposes of the right to silence, and defendants should not be required to produce it. All other evidence should be categorized as "physical"; the right to silence should not protect defendants against compelled disclosure of such evidence. Factfinders, consequently, should be authorized to draw adverse inferences against a defendant who refuses to provide "non-testimonial" or "physical" evidence (Seidmann and Stein 2000, at 475–81).

Utterances and their non-verbal equivalents – for example, sign language and a person's nodding of her head for a "yes" – clearly fall into the "testimonial" category. But evidence would also classify as "testimonial" in any case in which its producer can shape its content and meaning. This evidence-shaping ability makes the evidence externality-laden. For example, a handwriting sample that a suspect produces at the police station is "testimonial" because a guilty suspect might replicate an innocent person's handwriting.[6] By contrast, handwritings that already exist fall into the "physical" evidence category because their contents and meanings do not depend on the defendant's thought processes; a qualified expert (and sometimes a nonexpert witness as well) can authenticate such samples.

By the same token, the right to silence protects the defendant against compelled production of a document that involves an implicit acknowledgment of his possession of the document and of the document's authenticity and relevancy to the trial. To obtain a potentially inculpatory document ("physical" evidence for purposes of the Fifth Amendment), the government must lawfully seize it from the defendant. To compel the defendant to produce the document, it must first guarantee that the defendant's act of production – an implicit testimonial activity – will not be used as evidence against him. Absent this "use immunity," the defendant will be free not to produce the document. Furthermore, the government cannot compel a defendant to assemble documents for its criminal investigations even when it guarantees use immunity. Assembling documents is identical to testifying about the documents' nature and contents.[7]

Both production and assembly of documents are externality-laden because their results depend on the producer's or assembler's choice and opportunity to manipulate. A guilty defendant will produce only those documents that can help him establish his innocence. Aware of this self-serving motivation, factfinders will reduce the credibility of any assembly and production of documents by a criminal defendant and of any claim that defendants can make about documents' existence, authenticity, and custody. As a result of this undeserved credibility-reduction, some innocents might be found guilty (Seidmann and Stein 2000).

2.2.3 The right to silence as confined to criminal trials The rule against adverse inference from the defendant's silence only applies in criminal

---

[6] The Supreme Court, however, has refused to recognize that the right to silence protects defendants against compelled production of handwriting samples. See *Gilbert v. California*, 388 US 263, 266–7 (1967). This refusal is the only part of the Fifth Amendment jurisprudence that does not align with the anti-pooling rationale: see Seidmann and Stein (2000), 477.

[7] See *United States v. Hubbell*, 530 US 27 (2000).

trials. In civil cases and other non-criminal proceedings, such inferences are generally allowed.

The anti-pooling rationale fully justifies this limitation of the right to silence. The pooling problem that the right attenuates does not exist in civil and other non-criminal proceedings because those proceedings do not involve innocents who face the possibility of wrongful conviction and punishment. To be sure, the unavailability of the right motivates liars to pool with truth-tellers in those proceedings as well, but this pooling occurs outside the machinery of criminal justice. The legal system consequently need not sacrifice probative evidence in order to prevent or mitigate this pooling effect. There is no good reason for doing so in civil cases, where the cost of false positives and false negatives is roughly the same.[8]

2.2.4 The right to silence as confined to same-sovereign prosecutions A witness in a state proceeding can invoke the privilege against self-incrimination out of concern regarding a federal prosecution, and vice versa. By the same token, a witness in a state proceeding can successfully claim the privilege by referring to a prosecution in another state. The privilege, however, will not apply when the witness's testimony (or disclosure of other protected information) exposes him to the prospect of conviction outside the United States.

The anti-pooling rationale justifies this same-sovereign limitation as well. The limitation generates no pernicious pooling inside the American criminal justice system. When a criminal tried in another country chooses to lie, his lies do not increase the risk of wrongful conviction for innocent defendants in the United States. The externality that his lies generate occurs overseas. Consequently, there is no need to eliminate this externality by upholding the right to silence that taxes the American system. The same-sovereign limitation helps generate probative evidence for American courts and law-enforcement agencies, and there is no good economic reason to forego this benefit in order to protect foreign innocents. Those innocents ought to be taken care of by their own legal systems.[9]

2.2.5 The emergency exception to the right to silence Under the emergency exception to the right to silence, a self-incriminating statement that the police obtain from a suspect while attending an ongoing crime-related

---

[8] See Stein (2005), 143–8.
[9] An international treaty setting up cooperative law-enforcement between the United States and the foreign country might alter this analysis. See Seidmann and Stein (2000), at 483.

Self-incrimination 375

emergency is admissible as evidence at the suspect's subsequent trial regardless of whether the suspect received the *Miranda* warnings.[10]

The right's functioning as an anti-pooling device justifies this exception. Statements that this exception makes admissible are invariably inculpatory. As such, they never pool with self-exonerating accounts of innocent defendants.

2.2.6 The right to silence as belonging to persons, not corporations The right to silence protects only natural persons, as opposed to corporations. Nor does it extend to a corporate agent or employee who is required under the color of law to provide documents or other information tending to incriminate the corporation. A corporate agent or employee can only claim the right in his personal capacity; and even this personal entitlement is qualified by the "collective entity" rule. Under this rule, a person's assumption of a corporate job entails a duty to produce corporate documents regardless of the self-incriminating consequences to the person. This special rule intensifies deterrence against corporate crime (Bierschbach and Stein 2005).

Forcing a corporate insider to testify against her corporation induces the insider to lie. This perjured testimony pools with true testimonies of insiders of other corporations that face criminal accusations. This pooling increases the risk of undeserved conviction for innocent corporations. But the repercussions of such convictions for a natural person – a stockholder, a director or an employee – are strictly pecuniary, as in civil cases in which false negatives are as harmful as false positives. Consequently the right to silence does not apply.

The "collective entity" rule, therefore, is the only serious departure from the right to silence. A corporate insider must comply with a legal requirement to produce documents even when the act of production implicitly acknowledges some fact that might incriminate the insider. Unlike regular defendants, the insider will not be entitled to "use immunity" under such circumstances. As a result, a guilty insider's production of innocent-looking documents will pool with an innocent insider's production of innocent documents. This pooling will cause factfinders to reduce the credibility of innocent insiders to the detriment of those insiders.

This credibility reduction and the consequent increase in the rate of erroneous convictions are socially undesirable. The "collective entity" rule, however, can still be justified as a means of increasing the law-enforcers' access to corporate documents. This access facilitates the

---

[10] See *New York v. Quarles*, 467 US 649 (1984).

2.3 Variations

The anti-pooling rationale of the right to silence has four important variations. An attempt has been made to estimate the right's effect on social welfare (Seidmann 2005). This attempt produced a formal model in which factfinders receive negative payoffs for each erroneous conviction and acquittal. To align the factfinders' preferences with society's welfare, the payoffs are set to represent the socially accepted tradeoff between erroneous acquittals and erroneous convictions. Correspondingly, factfinders receive $-D$ when they convict an innocent defendant and $-(1-D)$ when they acquit a guilty defendant. D is the probability threshold for convictions: when the probability of a defendant's guilt equals D, the factfinders are indifferent between acquitting and convicting him. Under this model, the right to silence reduces the rate of erroneous convictions as a by-product of raising the incidence of erroneous acquittals. The right consequently reduces social welfare by systematically suppressing probative inculpatory evidence: the defendant's unwillingness to speak to the police or to testify in his defense. This suppression causes factfinders to acquit defendants whose real probability of guilt is greater than D and who, in all likelihood, are guilty as charged.

The big question, however, is whether the avoided convictions of innocent defendants *can* improve social welfare substantially enough to offset the harm caused by the acquittals of the guilty. Consider a setup in which the right to silence is not available and the pooling problem is particularly acute. As a result, factfinders discount the credibility of all uncorroborated self-exonerating testimonies. This discounting makes the conviction of an innocent defendant f times more likely than under the previous regime. To tackle this problem, the system's designer modifies the payoffs for factfinders. From now on, factfinders will pay fD, instead of D, for every conviction of the innocent, and $(1 - fD)$, instead of $(1 - D)$, for every acquittal of the guilty. Will those factfinders agree to switch to a legal regime in which their payoffs are set as before, but the right to silence is available? The answer to this question crucially depends on f. This figure may heighten the level of proof for convictions to a degree that would hardly allow the factfinders to convict any criminal. The right to silence, therefore, might bring along an important sorting benefit that will legitimize a socially beneficial reduction of the criminal standard of proof. This insight verifies an observation that the right to silence and the criminal proof standard are complementary policy tools (Seidmann and Stein 2000).

Second, in some settings, the right to silence can benefit innocent defendants directly. Because inculpatory evidence may be inaccurate, it may indicate that the defendant is guilty even when he is innocent. The defendant's true self-exonerating story consequently may appear false, thus further increasing the probability of his guilt in the factfinders' eyes. For example, the defendant may have a completely true alibi contradicted by a number of perjurous or mistaken witnesses that have credible appearance. For such defendants, the best trial strategy is silence. A rule that prohibits adverse inferences from silence therefore can help innocent defendants by preventing factfinders' error (Leshem 2010).

Third, the right to silence may be combined with stringent disclosure requirements from the prosecution. These requirements will further motivate innocent defendants to disclose exculpatory evidence, while their guilty counterparts still prefer silence or lies. This dynamic will increase social welfare by bolstering the separation between guilty and innocent defendants (Mialon 2005).

Finally, there is a good economic reason for extending the privilege against adverse inferences to *some* civil cases. The unavailability of this privilege under extant law motivates civil defendants to avoid adverse inferences by searching for exonerating evidence. If the evidence that a defendant finds is likely to exonerate him, the defendant would happily adduce it. This evidence would forestall the adverse inference and help the defendant defeat the lawsuit. On the other hand, if the evidence identifies the defendant as potentially (or actually) liable, the defendant would simply suppress it. Theoretically, he must comply with the discovery rules and let the plaintiff have this evidence. But the actual enforcement of those rules is far from perfect, and the defendant would exploit this shortcoming. He would take advantage of the plaintiff's unawareness of his discovery and possession of the evidence unfavorable to his case.

The defendant will search for favorable evidence whenever its expected value is greater than the cost of the search. As I already indicated, the imperfect discovery regime allows the defendant to ignore the prospect of finding unfavorable evidence. Because the defendant can hide such evidence, his expected loss from finding it equals (roughly) zero. The defendant's search for evidence consequently has little or no effect on his primary activity and its risks of harming another person. Evidence that the defendant finds and subsequently hides or adduces may affect the outcome of the litigation, but this effect is merely a transfer of wealth from one party to another, which is of no social value. Hence, the defendant's expenditure on the search is privately beneficial, but socially wasteful. The defendant's incentive to carry out a socially inefficient search for evidence thus needs to be reduced. To this end, the lawmaker can interpose a rule blocking adverse inferences from a defendant's failure to adduce exonerating evidence (Wickelgren 2010).[11]

3. The Economics of Confessions

3.1 The Meaning of "Voluntariness"

Defendants confessing to a crime substantially increase their probability of being convicted and punished. With all other things being equal, confession reduces the confessor's welfare. The magnitude of this reduction – the expected harm from confessing – equals the increase in the confessor's probability of being convicted multiplied by the punishment for the underlying crime.

But for most defendants, "all other things" are virtually never equal. First, some defendants – guilty and innocent – may be facing strong inculpatory evidence and a correspondingly high probability of conviction. For them, confessing to the crime and subsequently entering a guilty plea would often be a better call than spending money and effort on a hopeless trial.

Second, the punishment for convicted defendants who did not confess and plead guilty may be set much higher than the punishment for confessors. The increase in the expected punishment may induce some defendants – guilty and innocent alike – to confess and plead guilty even when the inculpatory evidence is not strong.

Third, the law may separately punish defendants for staying silent and for lying during police interrogation or in court. For defendants whose self-exonerating stories may be found false – rightly or wrongly – this special penalty would have the same effect as an increased punishment for non-confessors. For guilty defendants who consider remaining silent, the effect of the penalty for silence would be different. Facing this penalty, some guilty defendants might decide to lie in their defense. By doing so, they would pool their false exculpatory statements with true self-exonerating accounts tendered by innocent defendants. Factfinders consequently would discount the probability of true exculpatory statements that have no corroboration. This socially deleterious dynamic was explained in Section 2.

Finally, confessing to a crime may remove physical and psychic pressures that the police may exert upon suspects, both guilty and innocent. Those pressures may be strong enough to elicit a confession from both types of defendant.

---

[11] Adverse inferences, presumptions, and similar evidentiary devices are therefore no substitute for an aggressive discovery regime: see Stein (1996), 337–8.

The upshot is that confessions are never given for free.[12] They are triggered by fear and favor. Fears instilled and favors promised define the defendant's benefit from confessing. A rational defendant confesses to a crime only in exchange for a benefit: a sentence reduction, a saving of trial expenses, and sometimes removal of a threat that comes from the underworld or a state agent. Some of those benefits motivate guilty defendants to confess and plead guilty. Other benefits extract false confessions from innocent defendants. Neither benefit elicits a confession that can be considered factually "voluntary."

Factual voluntariness, indeed, makes no sense at all because criminal suspects and defendants are not free from interrogations, trials, custody, and bail restrictions. These mechanisms of criminal justice situate every defendant under fears and favors that elicit confessions. Those fears and favors make virtually any confession factually involuntary.[13] Courts in the United States therefore did not adopt factual voluntariness as a criterion for the admissibility of confessions. The prevalent voluntariness criterion for confessions' admissibility is normative, rather than factual.

The courts' voluntariness jurisprudence tackles two fundamental problems. The first problem is pooling of the guilty and the innocent. To resolve this problem, the voluntariness criterion needs to separate true confessions from false confessions to the extent feasible. The second problem is law-enforcers' position as self-seeking agents. There is no alignment between society's interest in the conviction of the guilty and the exoneration of the innocent and the law-enforcers' personal interests. The law-enforcers – police, prosecutors, and judges – have an incentive to boost their careers, prestige, and salaries while economizing their efforts. Confessions, guilty pleas, and asymmetrical information help them realize this goal. By eliciting a confession from a suspect, police officers can expedite the closing of the investigation. By obtaining a guilty plea from the defendant, the prosecutor can avoid an effort-consuming and unpredictable trial and successfully close the case. Confessions and guilty pleas also enable judges to streamline criminal proceedings and clear dockets.

Law-enforcers typically prefer true confessions and guilty pleas over false confessions and guilty pleas. This preference aligns with social good. But law-enforcers might also prefer false confessions and guilty pleas to

---

[12] For a good, but fictional, counterexample, see Fyodor N. Dostoyevsky, *Crime and Punishment* (1866) (Wordsworth, 2000).

[13] The legal system can eliminate those fears and favors by making all confessions inadmissible as evidence and by abolishing guilty pleas. This extreme measure will dramatically increase the cost of criminal law-enforcement and intensify the pooling of guilty and innocent defendants.

effort-intensive and time-consuming investigations and trials. This preference does not align with social good. The law-enforcers may nonetheless pursue it. By doing so, they would impose serious agency costs on society.

Under asymmetrical information, no confession and guilty plea is demonstrably false or true. Any confession and guilty plea consequently can be claimed to be both true and false. The probabilities of those claims vary from case to case, with some claims being more persuasive than others. Yet, the vast majority of those claims are easy to make but difficult to refute. Defendants have an incentive to claim that they are innocent even when they are guilty. Their self-serving stories about making a false confession under pressure therefore will always be questioned. By the same token, police and prosecutors have an incentive to claim – both rightly and wrongly – that defendants' confessions are true.

More often than not, judges will act upon a similar self-legitimizing motivation. A career-driven judge does not openly acknowledge that she admits confessions into evidence and accepts guilty pleas in order to streamline the proceedings and lock criminals in.

The credibility contest between the defendants' and the law-enforcers' self-serving claims is far from being equal. Law-enforcers will virtually always have an upper hand in this contest. As an initial matter, society gives criminal defendants very little credibility relative to that of law-enforcers (who protect it from crime). Police and prosecutors also have enormous resources and a far greater ability than defendants to gather evidence. Furthermore, police and prosecutors can allocate their resources as they deem appropriate. Consequently, they can threaten to use those superior resources against any recalcitrant defendant who refuses to confess and plead guilty. This strategy of extracting confessions and guilty pleas will be analogous to predatory pricing that exploits inequality in firms' access to capital markets (Posner 1999, at 1505 and n. 59).

Credibility contests between defendants, on the one hand, and police and prosecution, on the other hand, are settled primarily by courts. Courts, however, have a strong incentive to streamline the adjudicative process by relying on confessions and guilty pleas. Doing so will economize the judge's effort and help her establish a popular reputation for being "tough on crime." As already indicated, these incentives make courts biased in favor of the police and the prosecution. This systemic bias can easily influence the jury as well. The judge's decision to admit the defendant's confession into evidence has a potential for over-influencing the jurors' verdict. An average juror will treat any confession cleared by the judge as "admissible" as creditworthy. The confession consequently becomes indicative of the defendant's guilt and gives the juror a good reason to return a guilty verdict.

To tackle these problems, the voluntariness requirement for confessions encompasses two sets of rules. The first set aims at separating the guilty from the innocent. To this end, it renders illegitimate any threat and favor capable of eliciting false confessions and guilty pleas. Any such threat and favor renders the confession "involuntary" and inadmissible. The second set of rules motivates law-enforcers to act as faithful agents for society. To achieve this outcome, the rules lay down a checklist by which courts must monitor police and prosecutorial misconduct. This compulsory monitoring motivates prosecutors to monitor police interrogations – a motivation that weakens the police's ability to count on the prosecutor's help in covering up misconduct.

3.2 Separating between True and False Confessions
The law separates between true and false confessions by setting up rules of admissibility and sufficiency. The admissibility rules specify and ban methods of interrogation capable of eliciting false confessions from innocent suspects. Those unlawful methods include violence, torture, and threats thereof, otherwise degrading and inhuman treatments, and severe psychological pressures. An average suspect experiencing any of those interrogation methods becomes willing to confess to the crime in order to avoid the suffering. This suspect may be either guilty or innocent: a guilty suspect will confess to the crime he actually committed; an innocent suspect will tell the interrogators anything they want him to say. The suspect's confession consequently becomes unreliable. Instead of separating the guilty from the innocent, it pools them together. Any such confession therefore is inadmissible and can never be used as evidence against the defendant.

To be admissible, a defendant's confession to the police must be free of such coercive interrogation methods. Many states require the prosecution to prove this fact to the trial judge beyond a reasonable doubt. Other jurisdictions, including federal courts, are satisfied by a preponderance of the evidence – the minimal constitutional proof requirement.[14] Under both regimes, the trial judge must conduct a special hearing to examine the propriety of the defendant's interrogation by the police. The judge will proceed on the assumption that a rational suspect, guilty or innocent, does not confess to the crime absent overwhelming reasons for making a confession. Based on this assumption, the judge will try to ascertain the reasons that prompted the defendant to speak against his own interest.

---

[14] See *Lego v. Twomey*, 404 US 477 (1972).

Judges will normally apply the voluntariness standard in a way most favorable to the defendant. The main reason for that is the rule against double jeopardy. Under this rule, acquittals are not appealable but convictions are. This asymmetric system of appeals skews errors in the application of the voluntariness standard (and some other legal requirements) against the prosecution. The trial judge is well aware of the fact that an error in admitting an involuntary confession into evidence will likely lead to a reversal of the defendant's conviction by the appellate court. Following such reversal, the defendant cannot face another trial for the same crime: the rule against double jeopardy will prevent it (jeopardy attaches to a trial when the jury is empanelled and sworn, or, in bench trials, after the first witness has taken oath). On the other hand, the judge's erroneous suppression of the defendant's confession brings about no prospect of reversal because the prosecution cannot appeal. The asymmetrical appeal system interacts with judges' fear of reversal. As such, it creates a strong pro-defendant pressure on the judges' determinations of "voluntariness." Facing this one-sided pressure, both trial and appellate courts tend to decide borderline cases in the defendant's favor and rule his confession involuntary and inadmissible (Stith 1990).

To convince the judge that the defendant's interrogation was not coercive, the prosecution normally would have to explain the confession's rationality. Typically, the prosecution would have to show that the defendant confessed to the crime after being confronted with inculpatory evidence that persuaded him that denying the accusations is pointless. The prosecution therefore would need to adduce inculpatory evidence besides the confession. Another reason for having such independent evidence is the formal corroboration requirement, which is well-nigh universal. This requirement does not allow factfinders to find the defendant guilty on the basis of his confession alone. Evidence other than the defendant's own words must verify the confession. Absent such evidence, the defendant would be entitled to a directed acquittal.

Accordingly, the prosecution and the police have a strong incentive to search for evidence credibly separating the guilty from the innocent. Arguably, this incentive is not strong enough to induce the desired separation. Many scholars believe that police and prosecutors need to have a more robust incentive for conscientiously working to eliminate erroneous convictions (Garrett 2010). To this end, some scholars have proposed a sentence reduction for every defendant whose conviction rests primarily on his confession to the police (Fisher and Rosen-Zvi 2008).

3.3 Monitoring Law-Enforcers

The historic *Miranda* decision[15] laid down the currently prevalent four warnings requirement and the exclusionary rule. *Miranda* requires that, at the outset of a suspect's custodial interrogation, the police advise the suspect of his right to remain silent; of the prospect that any part of his statement will be used as evidence against him in a criminal trial; of his right to consult an attorney and to have an attorney present at his questioning; and, finally, of the right to be represented by an attorney at the government's expense when the suspect cannot afford to hire his own attorney. The suspect may remain silent indefinitely, or until he has consulted with an attorney and secured the attorney's presence at the interrogation. Alternatively, the suspect can make a knowing, intelligent, and voluntary waiver of the *Miranda* rights and speak to the police. The police's failure to follow *Miranda* leads to an automatic suppression of the suspect's confession. A confession obtained in violation of *Miranda* is deemed involuntary and is consequently inadmissible. The *Miranda* exclusionary rule, however, does not extend to physical evidence that the police obtain with the help of the suspect's unwarned – but not physically coerced – confession.[16]

This exclusionary rule performs an important prophylactic role: the police's need to align their interrogations with *Miranda* minimizes the suspect's prospect of being coerced into making a confession. Suppression of a suspect's confession deters police misconduct better than do criminal punishment, disciplinary sanctions, and tort remedies. These alternative sanctions do not efficaciously detect and deter police misconduct. All of them require a separate proceeding – criminal, civil, or disciplinary – which makes them more expensive to administer than *Miranda*'s exclusionary rule. To secure those sanctions' application, the defendant needs to convince the court (or a disciplinary tribunal) that he was a victim of coercive interrogation. Relative to a *Miranda* violation, those allegations are difficult to prove. Moreover, the victim's remedies under *Miranda*'s

---

[15] *Miranda v. Arizona*, 384 US 436 (1966).
[16] *United States v. Patane*, 542 US 630 (2004). The *Miranda* exclusionary rule has another important limitation: the impeachment exception. Under this exception, if the defendant testifies contrary to his *Miranda*-barred confession, the prosecution can use that confession to impeach the defendant's testimony in court: see *Harris v. New York*, 401 US 222 (1971). Note that this exception does not extend to unreliable confessions elicited by coercive interrogation methods: see *Mincey v. Arizona*, 437 US 385 (1978). The impeachment exception has a solid economic explanation: it curbs the defendants' perverse motivation to use the exclusionary rule as a shield for perjury.

alternatives can only be compensation for the damage suffered and moral vindication, as opposed to an acquittal or non-prosecution. Those remedies will often fail to provide a sufficiently strong incentive for the victim and his attorney to press charges against the police. To fix this incentive and to threaten the police with a high expected penalty for misconduct, the law needs to heighten the victim's compensation and intensify the criminal and disciplinary punishments for defaulting police officers. But if those sanctions become an effective deterrent, there would be no evidentiary gains relative to the *Miranda* regime because the police would not have the evidence that *Miranda* presently suppresses.[17]

4. Waiver of the Self-Incrimination Privilege

As a general rule, defendants and suspects can waive any of their rights under the privilege against self-incrimination. The waiver, however, must be voluntary and informed in order to be considered effective. The same requirement applies to a plea of guilty or *nolo contendere* before the court. Before accepting any such plea, the court ought to make sure that the defendant fully understands the plea's nature, is informed of his rights and is not acting under compulsion.[18]

Moreover, a defendant can waive his self-incrimination privilege together with the right (under Federal Rule of Evidence 410 and its state equivalents) to suppress any statement he made during plea negotiations and proffer sessions.[19] Under the *Mezzanatto* rule, this waiver is effective (provided, again, that the defendant made it knowingly and voluntarily). Based on this waiver, the prosecution can use the defendant's admissions to discredit his testimony and other evidence contradicting those admissions.

The *Mezzanatto* rule has a sound economic justification. In negotiating a plea bargain, the prosecution often needs to rely on the defendant's representations, for example, on those that describe his part in the crime relative to other participants. The defendant's entitlement to suppress anything he says makes his representations "cheap talk" upon which the prosecution cannot rationally rely. The prosecution consequently cannot engage in a meaningful negotiation with the defendant. Many defendants, however, find it in their interest to participate in proffer sessions and negotiate pleas with the prosecution. Society, too, has an obvious interest in substituting costly trials by plea bargains that streamline convictions.

---

[17] See Posner (1999), 1533.
[18] See Federal Rule of Criminal Procedure 11(b).
[19] *United States v. Mezzanatto*, 513 US 196 (1995).

Defendants therefore need to be able to communicate with the prosecution credibly. To have credibility, they need to be able to make representations qualifying as "costly signals": in order to be believed, the defendant must commit himself to a real and painful penalty for cheating. This is what the *Mezzanatto* rule does: it facilitates deals between criminal defendants and prosecution (Rasmusen 1998).

Bibliography

Bierschbach, Richard A. and Stein, Alex (2005), "Overenforcement," 93 *Georgetown Law Journal* 1743–81.
Cassell, Paul G. and Fowles, Richard (1998),"Handcuffing the Cops? A Thirty-Year Perspective on Miranda's Harmful Effects on Law Enforcement," 50 *Stanford Law Review* 1055–145.
Donohue, John J., III (1998), "Did Miranda Diminish Police Effectiveness?," 50 *Stanford Law Review* 1147–80.
Fisher, Talia and Rosen-Zvi, Issachar (2008), "The Confessional Penalty," 30 *Cardozo Law Review* 871–916.
Garrett, Brandon L. (2010), "The Substance of False Confessions," 62 *Stanford Law Review* 1051–119.
Hoover, J. Edgar (1952), "Civil Liberties and Law Enforcement: The Role of the FBI," 37 *Iowa Law Review* 175.
Leshem, Shmuel (2010), "The Benefits of a Right to Silence for the Innocent," 41 *RAND Journal of Economics* 398–416.
Mialon, Hugo M. (2005), "An Economic Theory of the Fifth Amendment," 36 *RAND Journal of Economics* 833–48.
Polinsky, A. Mitchell and Shavell, Steven (2000), "The Economic Theory of Public Enforcement of Law," 38 *Journal of Economic Literature* 45–76.
Posner, Richard A. (1999), "An Economic Approach to the Law of Evidence," 51 *Stanford Law Review* 1477–546.
Rasmusen, Eric (1998), "*Mezzanatto* and the Economics of Self-Incrimination," 19 *Cardozo Law Review* 1541–84.
Seidmann, Daniel J. (2005), "The Effects of a Right to Silence," 72 *Review of Economic Studies* 593–614.
Seidmann, Daniel J. and Stein, Alex (2000), "The Right to Silence Helps the Innocent: A Game-Theoretic Analysis of the Fifth Amendment Privilege," 114 *Harvard Law Review* 430–510.
Stein, Alex (1996), "Allocating the Burden of Proof in Sales Litigation: The Law, its Rationale, a New Theory, and its Failure," 50 *University of Miami Law Review* 335–44.
Stein, Alex (2005), *Foundations of Evidence Law*, Oxford: Oxford University Press.
Stein, Alex (2008), "The Right to Silence Helps the Innocent: A Response to Critics," 30 *Cardozo Law Review* 1115–40.
Stith, Kate (1990), "The Risk of Legal Error in Criminal Cases: Some Consequences of the Asymmetry in the Right to Appeal," 57 *University of Chicago Law Review* 1–61.
Wickelgren, Abraham (2010), "A Right to Silence for Civil Defendants?" 26 *Journal of Law, Economics and Organization* 92–114.

15 Settlement
Andrew F. Daughety and Jennifer F. Reinganum*

1. Introduction

This survey, which updates and expands upon an earlier *Encyclopedia* entry[1] on the modeling of pretrial settlement bargaining, organizes current main themes and recent developments.[2] The basic concepts used are outlined as core models and then several variations on these core models are discussed. As with much of law and economics, a catalog of even relatively recent research would rapidly be out of date. The focus here is on articles that emphasize formal models of settlement negotiation and the presentation is organized in game-theoretic terms, this now being the principal tool employed by analyses in this area. The discussion is aimed at the not-terribly-technical nonspecialist. In this survey some of the basic notions and assumptions of game theory are presented and applied, but some of the more recent models of settlement negotiation rely on relatively advanced techniques; in those cases, technical presentation will be minimal and intuition will be emphasized.[3]

---

* We thank the Division of Humanities and Social Sciences, Caltech; the Berkeley Center for Law, Business and the Economy, Boalt Law School, the University of California, Berkeley; and NYU Law School for providing a supportive research environment. We also thank Jeremy Atack, A. Mitchell Polinsky, Richard Posner, Robert Rasmussen, David Sappington, Steven Shavell, John Siegfried and Kathryn Spier for helpful comments and suggestions on the previous version of this chapter.

[1] Daughety (2000).

[2] There has now been a sequence of surveys in this area. An early review, in the context of a broader consideration of the economics of dispute resolution and the law, is Cooter and Rubinfeld (1989). Miller (1996) provides a non-technical review addressing policies that encourage settlement. Hay and Spier (1998) focus on settlement, while Spier (2007) addresses the broader area of litigation in general (for example, including models of courts). Finally, Daughety and Reinganum (2005) especially address multi-litigant settlement issues.

[3] For the interested reader, a useful source on game theory applications in law and economics is Baird, Gertner and Picker (1994). Two quite readable books on game theory, modeling, and a number of related philosophical issues are Binmore (1992) and Kreps (1990). Finally, Chapters 7 through 9 of Mas-Colell, Whinston and Green (1995) provide the technically sophisticated reader with a convenient,

What is the basic image that emerges from the settlement bargaining literature? It is that settlement processes act as a type of screen, sorting amongst the cases, presumably causing the less severe (for example, those with lower true damages) to bargain to a resolution (or to do this very frequently), while the more severe (for example, those with higher damages) may proceed to be resolved in court. Furthermore, we now see that under some conditions the presence of multiple parties can readily cause bargaining to collapse, while under other conditions multiplicity can lead to increased incentives for cases to settle.

The fact that some cases go to trial is often viewed in much of this literature as an inefficiency. While this survey adopts this language, one might also view the real possibility of trial as necessary to the development of case law and as a useful demonstration of the potential costs associated with decisions made earlier about levels of care. In other words, the possibility of trials may lead to greater care and to more efficient choices overall. Moreover, the bargaining and settlement literatures have evolved in trying to explain the sources of negotiation breakdown: the literature has moved from explanations based fully on intransigence to explanations focused around information. This is not to assert that trials don't occur because of motives outside of game-theoretically-based economic analysis, just that economic attributes contribute to explaining an increasing share of observed behavior.

In the next few sections (comprising Part A), significant features of settlement models are discussed and some necessary notation is introduced; this part ends with a simplified example indicating how the pieces come together. Part B examines the basic models in use, varying the level of information that litigants have and the type of underlying bargaining stories that are being told. Part C considers a range of "variations" on the Part B models, again using the game-theoretic organization introduced in Part A.

A. BASIC ISSUES, NOTIONS AND NOTATION

2. Overview

In this part the important features of the various approaches are discussed and notation that is used throughout is introduced. Paralleling the presentation of the models to come, the current discussion is organized to

---

efficient and careful presentation of the basic techniques of modern (noncooperative) game theory, while Chapters 13 and 14 provide a careful review of the basics of information economics.

address: (1) players; (2) actions and strategies; (3) outcomes and payoffs; (4) timing; (5) information; and (6) prediction. A last section provides a brief example. Words or phrases in italics are terms of special interest.

3. Players

The primary participants (usually called *litigants* or *players*) are the plaintiff (P) and the defendant (D); a few models have allowed for multiple Ps or multiple Ds (see Section 15.3), but for now assume one of each. Secondary participants include attorneys for the two litigants (A_P and A_D, respectively), experts for the two participants (X_P and X_D, respectively) and the court (should the case go to trial), which is usually taken to be a judge or a jury (J). Most models restrict attention to P and D, either ignoring the others or relegating them to the background. As an example, a standard assumption when there is some uncertainty in the model (possibly about damages or liability, or both) is that, at court, J will learn the truth and make an award at the true value (that is, the award will be the actual damage and liability will be correctly established). Moreover, J is usually assumed to have no strategic interests at heart (unlike P, D, the As, and the Xs). Section 15.2 considers some efforts to incorporate J's decision process in a substantive way.

Finally, uncertainty enters the analysis whenever something relevant is not known by at least one player. Uncertainty also arises if one player knows something that another does not know, or if the players move simultaneously (for example, they simultaneously make proposals to each other). These issues will be dealt with in the sections on timing (6) and information (7), but sometimes such possibilities are incorporated by adding another "player" to the analysis, namely nature (N), a disinterested player whose actions influence the other players in the game via some probability rule.

4. Actions and Strategies

An *action* is something a player can choose to do when it is their turn to make a choice. For example, the most commonly modeled action for P or D involves making a *proposal*. This generally takes the form of a demand from P of D or an offer from D to P. This then leads to an opportunity for another action which is a *response* to the proposal, which usually takes the form of an acceptance or a rejection of a proposal, possibly followed by yet another action such as a *counterproposal*. Some models allow for multiple periods of proposal/response sequences of actions.

When a player has an opportunity to take an action, the rules of the game specify the allowable actions at each decision opportunity. Thus, in the previous example, the specification of allowed response actions did not include delay (delay will be discussed in Section 18). Actions chosen at one point may also limit future actions: if "good faith" bargaining is modeled as requiring that demands never increase over time,[4] then the set of actions possible when P makes a counterproposal to D's counterproposal may be limited by P's original proposal.

Other possible actions include choosing to employ attorneys or experts, initially choosing to file a suit or finally choosing to take the case to court should negotiations fail. Most analyses ignore these either by not allowing such choices or by assuming values for parameters that would make particular choices "obvious." For example, many analyses assume that the net expected value of pursuing a case to trial is positive, thereby making credible such a threat by P during the negotiation with D; this topic will be explored more fully in Section 16.1.

In general, a *strategy* for a player provides a complete listing of actions to be taken at each of the player's decision opportunities and is contingent on: (1) the observable actions taken by the other player(s) in the past; (2) actions taken by the player himself in the past; and (3) the information the player currently possesses. Thus, as an example, consider an analysis with no uncertainty about damages, liability, or what J will do, wherein P proposes, D responds with acceptance or a counterproposal, followed by P accepting the counterproposal or choosing to break off negotiations and go to court. A strategy for P would be of the form "propose an amount x; if D accepts, make the transfer and end, while if D counterproposes y, choose to accept this if y is at least z, otherwise proceed to court." P would then have a strategy for each possible x, y and z combination.

An analogy may be helpful here. One might think of a strategy as a book, with pages of the book corresponding to opportunities in the game for the book's owner to make a choice. Thus, a typical page says "if you are at this point in the book, take this action." This is not a book to be read from cover-to-cover, one page after the previous one; rather, actions taken by players lead other players to go to the appropriate page in their book to see what they do next. All the possible books (strategies) that a player might use form the player's personal library (the player's strategy set).

There are times when being predictable as to which book you will use is useful, but there can also be times when unpredictability is useful. A sports analogy from soccer would be to imagine yourself to be a goalie on the A team, and a member of the B team has been awarded the chance to make a shot on your goal. Assume that there is insufficient time for you to react fully to the kick, so you are going to have to move to the left or to the right as the kicker takes his shot. If it is known that, in such circumstances, you

---

[4] See, for example, Ståhl (1972) and Schwartz and Wen (2007).

390 *Procedural law and economics*

always go to your left, the kicker can take advantage of this predictability and improve his chance of making a successful shot. This is also sometimes true in settlement negotiations: if P knows the actual damages for which D is liable, but D only knows a possible range of damages, then D following a predictable policy of never going to court encourages P to make high claims. Alternatively, D following a predictable policy of always going to court no matter what P is willing to settle for may be overly costly to D. *Mixed strategies* try to address this problem of incorporating just the right amount of unpredictability and are used in some settlement models. Think of the individual books in a player's library as *pure* strategies (pure in the sense of being predictable) and think of choosing a book at random from the library, where by "at random" we mean that you have chosen a particular set of probability weights on the books in your library. In this sense, your chosen set of weights is now your strategy (choosing one book with probability one and everything else with probability zero gets us back to pure strategies). A list of strategies, with one for each player (that is, a selection of books from all the players' libraries), is called a *strategy profile*.

5. Outcomes and Payoffs

An *outcome* for a game is the result of a strategy profile being played. Thus, an outcome may involve a transfer from D to P reflecting a settlement or it might be a transfer ordered by a court or it might involve no transfer as P chooses not to pursue a case to trial. If the reputations of the parties are of interest, the outcome should also specify the status of that reputation. In plea bargaining models, which will be discussed in Section 17.4, the outcome might be a sentence to be served. In general, an outcome is a list (or vector) of relevant final attributes for each player in the game.

For each player, each outcome has an associated numerical value called the *payoff*, usually a monetary value. For example, a settlement is a transfer of money from D to P; for an A or an X the payoff might be a fee. For models that are concerned with risk preferences, the payoffs would be in terms of the utility of net wealth rather than in monetary terms. Payoffs that are strictly monetary (for example, the transfer itself) are viewed as reflecting risk-neutral behavior on the part of the player.

Payoffs need not equal expected awards, since parties to a litigation also incur various types of costs. The cost most often considered in settlement analyses is called a *court cost* (denoted here as k_P and k_D, respectively). An extensive literature has developed surrounding rules for allocating such costs to the litigants and the effect of various rules on the incentives to bring suit and the outcome of the settlement process; this is addressed in Section 17.2. Court costs are expenditures which will be incurred should the case go to trial and are associated with preparing for and conducting a trial; as such they are avoidable costs (in contrast with sunk costs) and therefore influence the decisions that the players (in particular P and D) make. Generally, costs incurred in negotiating are ignored, though some papers reviewed in Sections 11.2 and 18 emphasize the effect of negotiation costs on settlement offers and the length of the bargaining horizon. Unless specifically indicated, we assume that negotiation costs are zero. Finally, in Section 16.2, filing costs (that is, a cost incurred before negotiation begins) are considered.

The total payoff for a player labeled i (that is, i = P, D, . . .) is denoted π_i. Note that this payoff can reflect long-term considerations (such as the value of a reputation or other anticipated future benefits) and multiple periods of negotiation. Generally, players in a game maximize their payoffs and thus, for example, P makes choices so as to maximize π_P. For convenience, D's payoff is written as an expenditure (if D countersues, then D takes the role of a plaintiff in the countersuit) and thus D is taken to minimize π_D (rather than to maximize $-\pi_D$). While an alternative linguistic approach would be to refer to the numerical evaluation of D's outcome as a "cost" (which is then minimized, and thereby not use the word payoff with respect to D), the use of the term payoff for D's aggregate expenditure is employed so as to reserve the word cost for individual expenditures that each party must make.

Finally, since strategy profiles lead to outcomes which yield payoffs, this means that payoffs are determined by strategy profiles. Thus, if player i uses strategy s_i, and the strategy profile is denoted s (that is, s is the vector, or list $(s_1, s_2, \ldots, s_n)$, where there are n players), then we could write this dependence for player i as $\pi_i(s)$.

6. Timing

The sequence of play and the horizon over which negotiations occur are issues of timing and of time. For example: do P and D make simultaneous proposals or do they take turns? Does who goes first (or who goes when) influence the outcome? Do both make proposals or does only one? Can players choose to delay or accelerate negotiations? Are there multiple rounds of proposal/response behavior? Does any of this sort of detail matter in any substantive sense?

Early settlement models abstracted from any dynamic detail concerning the negotiation process. Such models were based on very general theoretical models of bargaining (which ignored bargaining detail and used desirable properties of any resulting bargain to characterize what it must be) initially developed by Nash (1950). More recent work on settlement negotiations, which usually provides a detailed specification of how bargaining is assumed to proceed (the strategies employed and the sequencing of bargaining play are specified), can be traced to results in the theoretical bargaining literature by Nash (1953), Ståhl (1972), and Rubinstein (1982). Nash's 1950 approach is called *axiomatic*, while the Ståhl/Rubinstein improvement on Nash's 1953 approach is called *strategic*; the two approaches are intimately related. Both approaches have generated vast literatures which have considered issues of interest to analyses of settlement bargaining; a brief discussion of the two approaches is provided in Sections 10 and 11 so as to place the settlement applications in a unified context. The discussion below also addresses the institutional features that make settlement modeling more than simply a direct application of bargaining theory.

When considered, time enters settlement analyses in two basic ways. First, do participants move simultaneously or sequentially? This is not limited to the question of whether or not P and D make choices at different points on the clock. More significant is whether or not moving second involves having observed what the first-mover did. Two players who make choices at different points in time, but who do not directly influence each other's choices (perhaps because the second-mover cannot observe or react to what the first-mover has done) are viewed as moving simultaneously: that my choice and your choice together influence what each of us receives as a payoff (symbolized in the payoff notation as $\pi_i(s)$ for player i) does not make moving at different points in time significant in and of itself. The real point here is whether all relevant decision-makers must conjecture what the others are likely to do, or whether some can observe what others actually *did*. This is because the second-mover is influenced by the first-mover's choice and because they *both* know this, the first-mover's choice is affected by his ability to influence the second-mover. Asymmetry in what choices depend upon (in this sense) is modeled as choices being made in a sequence; symmetry is modeled as choices being made simultaneously. As will be seen in the example to be discussed in Section 9, who moves when can make a very significant difference in what is predicted. Note that a sequence of simultaneous decisions is possible (for example, P and D both simultaneously make proposals and then both simultaneously respond to the proposals).

A second way that time enters is in terms of the length of the horizon over which decisions are made. The main stream of research in the strategic bargaining literature views the horizon as infinite in length; this is done to eliminate the effect of arbitrary end-of-horizon strategic behavior. Settlement models, on the other hand, typically take the negotiation horizon as finite in length (and often very short, say, two periods). This is done for two reasons. First, while some cases may seem to go on forever, some form of termination actually occurs (cases are dropped, or resolved through negotiation or meet a court date). While setting a court date is not an iron-clad commitment, few would argue that an infinite number of continuances is realistic. Second, in the more informationally complex models, this finite horizon restriction helps provide more precise predictions to be made than would otherwise be possible. Thus, in most settlement models there is a last opportunity to negotiate, after which either the case proceeds to trial or terminates (either because the last settlement proposal is accepted or the case is dropped). This is important because court costs are incurred only if the case actually proceeds to trial; that is, after the last possible point of negotiations. If negotiations were to continue during the trial, the ability to use the avoidance of these costs to achieve a settlement obviously is vitiated: as the trial proceeds, the portion of costs that is sunk becomes larger and the portion that is avoidable shrinks. This problem has not been addressed generally, though papers by Spier (1992), Bebchuk (1996), and Schwartz and Wicklegren (2009) consider significant parts of this issue; Spier is discussed in more detail in Section 18, while the other two articles are discussed in Section 16.2.

7. Information

In Shavell (1982), the range over which litigants might bargain when assessments about outcomes may be different is analyzed as a problem in decision theory (a game against nature, N); this raises the issue of who knows what, when, why and how. Shavell's paper indicated that differences in assessments by P and D as to the likelihood of success at trial, and the likely award, can lead to trial as an outcome. While Shavell's paper did not consider strategic interaction among the players (for the first paper to incorporate strategic behavior, see P'ng (1983)), the role of information has become a central theme in the literature that has developed since, with special emphasis on accounting for informational differences and consistent, rational behavior. Moving momentarily from theory to empirical analysis, Farber and White (1991) use data from a hospital to investigate whether seemingly asymmetrically distributed information influenced settlement rates and the speed with which cases settled; they find that it did.

Informational considerations involve what players individually know and what they must guess about (where such guessing presumably involves some form of organized approach). Many of the analyses in the literature use different informational structures (who knows what when) and in this survey a variety of such structures will be presented. As a starting example, consider Pat, who developed an improved framitz (a tool for making widgets). Pat took the tool to the Delta Company (D), with the notion that Delta would manufacture the tool and Pat would become rich from her share of the profits. Delta indicated that the tool was not likely to be financially viable and Pat went back to work on other inventions. Some years later Pat noticed that many people who made widgets were using a slightly modified version of her tool made by Delta. Pat (P) decided to sue Delta (D) for misappropriation of intellectual property, and for convenience assume that while D's liability is clear, the assessment of a level of compensation to P is less clear. D's familiarity with the profits made (and experience with creative accounting procedures) means that D has a better idea of what level of total profits might be proved in court. Both P's attorney and D's attorney have (potentially similar) estimates of what the court is likely to do with any particular evidence on the level of profits of the tool (how the court, J, might choose to allocate the costs and revenues of the tool to P and D). Simplifying, there are two sources of uncertainty operating here: uncertainty by P and D about J and uncertainty by P about what D knows.

First, both P and D cannot predict perfectly what J will choose as an award: here each faces an essentially similar level of uncertainty (there is no obvious reason to assert the presence of an asymmetry in what is knowable). Moreover, we will assume that this assessment of J's likely actions, while probabilistic, is *common knowledge*. Common knowledge connotes the notion that were P and D to honestly compare their assessments of J's likely actions for each possible set of details about the profits made by D, their assessments would be exactly the same, and P and D know that the other knows this, and P and D know that the other knows that the other knows this, and so on (see Aumann, 1976; Geanakoplos and Polemarchakis, 1982; and Binmore, 1992, for two early technical papers and a game theory text with an extensive prose discussion of common knowledge).

Thus, P and D have the same information with regard to J; we might call this *imperfect* or *symmetrically uncertain* information to contrast it with the clear asymmetry that exists between P and D with respect to the information about revenues and costs that D knows. This latter notion of uncertainty is referred to as *asymmetric* information, and it is a main attribute of much of the recent work on settlement. Finally, if actual damage was common knowledge and if P and D truly knew exactly what J would choose as an award and if that were common knowledge, the resulting information condition is called *perfect information*.

A nice story which makes the differences in informational settings clear is due to John Roberts of Stanford University. Consider a card game played by at least two people, such as poker. If all hands were dealt face up and no more cards were to be dealt, this would be a situation of perfect information. If, instead, hands are dealt with (say) three cards face up and two cards face down, but no one can look at their "down" cards, this is a setting of imperfect information. Finally, asymmetric information (also called *incomplete* information) would involve each player being able to look at their down cards privately before taking further actions (asking for alternative cards, betting, etc.). Note that in this last case we see the real essence of asymmetric information: it is not that one party is informationally disadvantaged when compared with the other (as in the case of Pat and Delta) as much as that the players have *different* information from each other.

One caution about the foregoing example. The perfect information case seems to be rather pointless: players without the best hand at the table would choose not to bet at all. Perfect information models are really not as trivial as this example might seem to suggest, since they clarify significantly what the essential elements of an analysis are and they provide a comparison point to evaluate how different informational uncertainties affect the efficiency of the predicted outcome.

Timing in the play of the game is also a potential source of imperfect information. If P and D make simultaneous proposals (which might be resolved by, say, averaging), then when they are each considering what proposal to make they must conjecture what the other might choose to propose: what each will do is not common knowledge. Even if all other information in the analysis were perfect, this timing of moves is a source of imperfect information.

The incorporation of informational considerations (especially asymmetric information) has considerably raised the ante in settlement modeling. Why? Is this simply a fad or an excuse for more technique? The answer is revealed in the discussion of the basic models and their variations. As indicated earlier, the problem with analyses that assumed perfect or imperfect information was that many interesting and significant phenomena were either attributed to irrational behavior or not addressed at all. For example, in some cases negotiations fail and a trial ensues, even though both parties may recognize that going to court is very costly; sometimes cases fail to settle quickly, or only settle when a deadline approaches. Moreover, agency problems between lawyers and clients, discovery, disclosure, various rules for allocating court costs or for admitting evidence have all been the subject of models using asymmetric information.

7.1 Modeling Uncertainty

Models with perfect information specify parameters of the problem with no uncertainty attached: liability is known, damages are known, what J will do is known, costs are known, and so on. Imperfect information models involve probability distributions associated with one or more elements of the analysis, but the probability distributions are common knowledge, and thus the occurrence of uncertainty in the model is symmetric. For example, damages are "unknown" means that all parties to the negotiation itself (all the players) use the same probability model to describe the likelihood of damage being found to actually have been a particular value. Thus, for example, if damage is assumed to take on the value d_L (L for low) with probability p and d_H (H for high) with probability (1 − p), then the expected damage, $E(d) = pd_L + (1 - p)d_H$ is P's estimate ($E_P(d)$) as well as D's estimate ($E_D(d)$) of the damages that will be awarded in court. Usually, the court (J) is assumed to learn the "truth" should the case go to trial, so that the probability assessment by the players may be interpreted as a common assessment as to what the court will assert to be the damage level, possibly reflecting the availability and admissibility of evidence as well as the true level of damage incurred. Note that such models are not limited to accounting only for two possible events (for example, perhaps the damage could be any number between d_L and d_H); this is simply a straightforward extension of the probability model. On the other hand, since P and D agree about the returns and costs to trial, there is no rational basis for actually incurring them and the surplus generated by not going to trial can be allocated between the players as part of the bargain struck.

With asymmetric information, players have different information and thus have different probability assessments over relevant uncertain aspects of the game. Perhaps each player's court costs are unknown to the other player, perhaps damages are known to P but not to D, or the likelihood of being found liable is better known by D than by P. Possibly P and D have different estimates, for a variety of reasons, as to what J will do. All of these differences in information may influence model predictions, but the nature of the differences is itself something that must be common knowledge.

Consider yourself as one of the players in the version of the earlier card game where you can privately learn your down cards. Say you observe that you have an Ace of Spades and a King of Hearts as your two down cards. What can you do with this information? The answer is quite a bit. You know how many players there are and you can observe all the up cards. You can't observe the cards that have not been dealt, but you know how many of them there are. You also know the characteristics of the deck: four suits, 13 cards each, and no repeats. This means that given your down cards you could (at least theoretically) construct probability estimates of what the other players have and know what estimates they are constructing about what you have. This last point is extremely important, since for player A to predict what player B will do (so that A can compute

Table 15.1   Hands of cards for A and B

	UP	DOWN
A	4♠, K♦	K♥
B	Q♥, A♣	2♣

Note: Entries provide face value of card and suit.

what to do), A also needs to think from B's viewpoint, which includes predicting what B will predict about what A would do.

To understand this, let's continue with the card game and consider a simple, specific example (we will then return to the settlement model to indicate the use of asymmetric information in that setting). Assume that there are two players (A and B), a standard deck with 52 cards (jokers are excluded) and the game involves two cards dealt face up and one card dealt face down to each of A and B; only one down card is considered to simplify the presentation. Table 15.1 shows the cards that have been dealt face up (available for all to see) and face down (available only for the receiver of the cards, and us, to see).

By a player's *type* we mean their down cards (their private information), so A is a K♥-type while B is a 2♣-type, and only they know their own type. A knows that B is one of 47 possible types (A knows B can't be a K♥ or any of the up cards) and, for similar reasons, B knows that A is one of 47 possible types. Moreover, A's model of what type B can be (denoted $p_A(t_B \mid t_A)$) provides A with the probability of each possibility of B's type (denoted t_B) conditional (which is the meaning of the vertical line) on A's type (denoted t_A). The corresponding model for B that gives a probability of each possibility of A's type is denoted $p_B(t_A \mid t_B)$.[5]

In the particular case at hand t_A = K♥, so once A knows his type (sees his down card) he can use $p_A(t_B \mid K♥)$ to compute the possibilities about B's down card (type). But A actually could have worked out his strategy for each possible down card he might be dealt (and the possible up cards) *before* the game; his strategy would then be a function that would tell him what to do for each possible down-card/up-card combination he might be dealt in the game. Moreover, since he must also think about what B will do

---

[5]   Note that all the probability models are formally also conditioned on all the up cards. For example, if we are especially careful we should write $p_A(t_B \mid t_A, 4♠, K♦, Q♥, A♣)$ and $p_B(t_A \mid t_B, 4♠, K♦, Q♥, A♣)$, which we suppress in the notation employed.

and B will not know A's down card (and thus must use $p_A(t_B | t_A)$, where t_A takes on a number of possible values, as his probability model for what A will use about B's possible down cards), then this seemingly extra effort (that is, A working out a strategy for each possible type) isn't wasted, since A needs to do it anyway to model B modeling A's choices. What we just went through is what someone analyzing an asymmetric information game must do for every player.

Finally, for later use, observe that these two probability models are *consistent* in the sense that they come from the *same* overall model $p(t_A, t_B)$ which reflects common knowledge of the deck that was used. In other words, the foregoing conditional probabilities in the previous paragraph both come from the overall joint probability model $p(t_A, t_B)$, using the usual rules of probability for finding conditional probabilities.

So what does this mean for analyzing asymmetric information models of settlement? It means, for example, that if there is an element (or there are elements) about which there is incomplete information, then we think of that element as taking on different possible values (which are the types) and the players as having probability models about which possible value of the element is the true one. For example, if P knows the actual level of damages, then P has a probability model placing all the probability weight on that realized value. If D only knows that the level of damages is between d_L and d_H, then D's model covers all the possible levels of damage in that interval. The foregoing is an example of a *one-sided* asymmetric information model, wherein one player is privately informed about some element of the game and the other must use a probability model about the element's true value; who is informed and the probability assessment for the uninformed player is common knowledge. *Two-sided* asymmetric information models involve both players having private information about either the same element or about different elements. Thus, P and D may, individually, have private information about what an independent friend-of-the-court brief (still in preparation for submission at trial) may say, or P may know the level of damage and D may know whether the evidence indicates liability or not (two-sided asymmetric information analyses will be discussed further in Section 12.4).

7.2 Consistent versus Inconsistent Priors
The card game examples above, in common with much of the literature on asymmetric information settlement models, involve games with consistent priors. Some papers on settlement bargaining use "divergent expectations" to explain bargaining failure, and this may reflect "inconsistent" priors. In this section, we discuss what this means and how it can affect the analysis.

Settlement 399

A game has *consistent priors* if each player's conditional probability distribution over the other player's type (or other players' types) comes from the same overall probability model. In the card game example with A and B, we observed that there was an overall model $p(t_A, t_B)$ which was common knowledge, and the individual conditional probability models $p_A(t_B \mid t_A)$ and $p_B(t_A \mid t_B)$ could have been found by using $p(t_A, t_B)$.[6] This was true because the makeup of the deck and the nature of the card-dealing process were common knowledge. What if, instead, the dealer (a stranger to both A and B) first looked at the cards before they were dealt and chose which ones to give to each player? Now the probability assessments are about the dealer, not the deck, and it is not obvious that A and B should agree about how to model the dealer. Perhaps if A and B had been brought up together, or if they have talked about how to model the dealer, we might conclude that the game would have consistent priors (though long-held rivalries or even simple conversations themselves can be opportunities for strategic behavior). However, if there is no underlying $p(t_A, t_B)$ that would yield $p_A(t_B \mid t_A)$ and $p_B(t_A \mid t_B)$ through the standard rules of probability, then this is a model employing *inconsistent priors*.

For example, if P and D each honestly believe they will win for sure, they must have inconsistent priors, because the joint probability of both winning is zero. While such beliefs might be held, they present a fundamental difficulty for using models which assert rational behavior: how can both players be rational, both be aware of each other's assessment, aware that the assessments fundamentally conflict, and not use this information to revise and refine their own estimates? The data of the game must be common knowledge, as is rationality (and more, as will be discussed in the next section), but entertaining conflicting assessments themselves is in conflict with rationality. Alternatively put, for the consistent application of rational choice, differences in assessments must reflect differences in private information, not differences in world views. Presented with the same information, conflicts in assessments would disappear.

To understand the problem, consider the following example taken from Binmore (1992, p. 477). Let A and B hold prior assessments about an uncertain event (an election). A believes that the Republican will win the election with probability 5/8 and the Democrat will win it with probability 3/8. B believes that the Democrat will win with probability 3/4 and the

---

[6] To be more precise, let $p(t_A)$ be the sum of the $p(t_A, t_B)$ values over all possible values of t_B and, similarly, let $p(t_B)$ be the sum of the $p(t_A, t_B)$ values over all possible values of t_A. Then $p_A(t_B \mid t_A) = p(t_A, t_B)/p(t_A)$ and $p_B(t_A \mid t_B) = p(t_A, t_B)/p(t_B)$.

Republican with probability 1/4. Now if player C enters the picture, he can offer A the following bet: A wins $3 if the Republican wins and pays C $5 if the Democrat wins. C offers B the following bet: B wins $2 if the Democrat wins and pays C $6 if the Republican wins. Assume that A and B are risk-neutral, are well aware of each other's assessments, and stick to the foregoing probabilities and that C pays each of them a penny if they take the bets. Then both A and B will take the bets and for *any* probability of the actual outcome, C's expected profits are $2.98 ($3 less the two pennies). This is derisively called a "money pump" and works because of the inconsistent priors; that is, neither A nor B updates his assessment in response to the assessments that the other is using. In an analysis employing incentives and rational choice, introducing something inconsistent with rational behavior creates a problem in terms of the analysis of the model and the comparison of any results with those of other analyses.

How important consistent priors are to the analysis has been made especially clear in work on analyzing asymmetric information games. Starting from basic principles of rational decision-making, anyone making a choice about something unknown must make some assumptions about what characterizes the unknown thing (usually in the form of a probability distribution). To have two players playing an asymmetric information game means, essentially, that they are playing a family of games, one for each possible pair of types (that is, one game for each pair of possible players). But which one are they playing? This is solved by superimposing a probabilistic choice by Nature (N), where each game is played with the probability specified by the overall distribution over types (denoted earlier in the card examples as $p(t_A, t_B)$). If this distribution doesn't exist (that is, if priors are inconsistent), we can't do this and players are left not properly anticipating which game might be played. This transformation of something that is difficult to analyze (an asymmetric information game) into something that we know how to analyze (a game with imperfect information) won John Harsanyi a share (along with John Nash and Reinhard Selten) of the 1994 Nobel Prize (the original papers are Harsanyi, 1967, 1968a, and 1968b).

Thus, while players may hold different assessments over uncertain events, the notion of consistent priors limits the causes of the disagreement to differences in things like private information, and not to alternative modes of analysis; thus, players cannot paper over differences by "agreeing to disagree." It is through this door that a literature, initially spawned by dissatisfaction with the perfect (and imperfect) information prediction that cases always settle, has proceeded to explain a variety of observed behavior with asymmetric information models of settlement bargaining.

Inconsistent priors may occur because one or both players thinks that the other player is irrational, and such beliefs need not be irrational. Laboratory experiments (see Babcock et. al., 1995) have found seemingly inconsistent priors that arise from a "self-serving" bias reflecting anticipated opportunities by players in a settlement activity. Bar-Gill (2006) develops a model employing evolutionary game theory to explain why a bias towards optimism on the part of lawyers and their clients might persist: optimism acts as a credible commitment device that leads to more favorable settlement (in this case, by shifting the "settlement range" – that is, the range of feasible bargained outcomes). However, as with other inconsistent-priors models, while each litigant knows the other's assessment of winning at trial (and even knows the degree to which both assessments are incorrect relative to a "true" assessment), each litigant is incapable of using such information to adjust his own assessment.[7]

One last point before passing on to prediction. Shavell (1993) has observed that when parties seek nonmonetary relief and the bargaining involves an indivisible item, settlement negotiations may break down, even if probability assessments are the same. An example of such a case would be child custody in a state with sole custody laws. This survey restricts consideration to cases involving non-lumpy allocations.

8. Prediction

The main purpose of all of the settlement models is to make a prediction about the outcome of bargaining, and the general rule is the more precise the prediction the better. The main tool used to make predictions in the recent literature is the notion of *equilibrium*. This is because most of the recent work has relied upon the notion of *noncooperative* game theory, whereas earlier work implicitly or explicitly employed notions from *cooperative* game theory. The difference is that in a cooperative game, players (implicitly or explicitly) bind themselves *ex ante* to require that the solution to the game be efficient ("no money is left on the table"), while the equilibrium of a noncooperative game does not assume any exogenously enforced contractual agreement to be efficient, and may end up not being efficient. We consider these notions in turn (for a review of laboratory-based tests of bargaining models, see Roth, 1995).

8.1 Nash Equilibrium in Noncooperative Games

A strategy profile provides an equilibrium if no individual player can unilaterally change his part of the strategy profile and make himself better

---

[7] We rejoin this topic when we consider "divergent expectations" as an alternative to asymmetric information in Section 13.2.

off; this notion of equilibrium is often called *Nash equilibrium* (after Nash, 1951), but its antecedents go far back in history. Using the notation introduced earlier, let s* be an *equilibrium profile*; for convenience, assume the game has two players, named 1 and 2, so s* = (s_1^*, s_2^*) and s_1 and s_2 are any other strategies that Players 1 and 2, respectively, could use. Then Player 1 is prepared to stay with s_1^* if:

$$\pi_1(s_1^*, s_2^*) \geq \pi_1(s_1, s_2^*)$$

for every possible s_1 Player 1 could choose; that is, if Player 1 expects Player 2 to use strategy s_2^*, then Player 1 can do no better than to choose strategy s_1^*. Similarly, Player 2 is prepared to stay with s_2^* if:

$$\pi_2(s_1^*, s_2^*) \geq \pi_2(s_1^*, s_2)$$

for every possible s_2 Player 2 could choose. As stated earlier, in an equilibrium no player can unilaterally improve his payoff by changing his part of the equilibrium strategy profile.

Without generating more notation, the above conditions for a Nash equilibrium in a perfect information setting can be extended directly to the imperfect information setting. Here, the payoffs shown in the above inequalities are replaced by expected payoffs (the expectation reflecting the presence of uncertainty in one or more elements in the payoff function). Finally, in the case of asymmetric information, strategies and expectations are dependent upon type (and, if action takes place over time, on previous actions by other players which might provide some insight about those other players' types), and thus the equations must now hold for every player type and must reflect the individual player's conditional assessment about the other player(s). This last version is sometimes called a Bayesian Nash equilibrium to emphasize the role that the conditional probability distributions have in influencing the strategies that players use (for more detail, see Mas-Colell, Whinston and Green, 1995, Chapter 8 when agents move simultaneously and Chapter 9 for a discussion of equilibrium notions when agents move sequentially).

Note that in all the variations on the definition of Nash equilibrium, there is a reference to no individual choosing to "defect" from the strategy profile of interest. What about coalitions of players? Class action suits involve forming coalitions of plaintiffs, joint and several liability impacts coalitions of defendants and successful ("real world") bargaining strategy sometimes requires building or breaking coalitions (see Lax and Sebenius, 1986). Issues of coalitions have been of great interest to game theorists and equilibrium notions have been developed to account for coalition defection from a putative equilibrium strategy profile (see Binmore, 1985; Bernheim, Peleg and Whinston, 1987; Binmore, 1992; Greenberg, 1994; and Okada, 1996, for a small sample of work on this topic), but this is still an area of interest. We return to discuss coalition formation in class action suits in Section 15.3.

8.2 Cooperative Solutions

If two people are to divide a dollar between them (and both get nothing if they do not come to an agreement), then *any* allocation of the dollar such that each player gets more than zero is a Nash equilibrium, meaning that there is no predictive "bite" to our definition of equilibrium in this bargaining context (prediction improvements, called refinements, exist and often have considerable bite; more on this later). In yet another seminal contribution, Nash (1950) provided a remarkable result that still provides context, and a reference point, for many analyses (cooperative and non-cooperative) of bargaining. His approach was to focus on the outcome of the bargaining game and to ignore the details of the bargaining process entirely, thereby also skipping the notion of requiring an equilibrium as the prediction mechanism. He posed the question: what desirable properties (called axioms) should a bargaining solution possess in order that a problem have a *unique* prediction? As mentioned earlier, by *solution* we mean that, *ex ante*, the two players would be prepared to bind themselves to the outcome which the solution provides. This approach is presented in more detail in Section 10 and is called the *axiomatic approach*, while bargaining models based on the analysis in Section 8.1 are called the *strategic approach*.

Nash's axioms can be summarized as follows (see Binmore, 1992). First, the solution should not depend on how the players' utility scales are calibrated. This means that standard models of utility from decision theory may be employed (see, for example, Baird, Gertner and Picker, 1994). If payoffs are in monetary terms, this also means that players using different currencies could simply use an exchange rate to convert everything to one currency. Second, the solution should always be efficient. Third, if the players agree to one outcome when a second one is also feasible, then they never agree to the second one when the first one is feasible. Fourth, in a bargaining game with two identical players, both players get the same payoffs. The remarkable result is that whether the game is in utilities or money terms, the four axioms result in a *unique* solution (called the *Nash Bargaining Solution* or *NBS*) to the bargaining game. We return to this in Section 10.

There is a very important linkage between predictions using refinements of Nash equilibrium and predictions using a cooperative solution. One of the most remarkable and far-reaching results of game theory which emerged during the 1970s and 1980s has been the delineation of conditions under which the equilibria for properly structured noncooperative games would be (in the lingo, would *support*) solutions to properly related cooperative games. In our particular case, there are conditions on the data for the strategic approach which guarantee that the equilibrium predicted for that model is the NBS of the associated bargaining problem. In other words, under certain conditions, the noncooperative equilibrium is an efficient outcome and under further conditions it is a particular efficient outcome.

Since we've not explored the axiomatic or strategic approaches in detail yet, let us consider an example likely to be familiar to most readers: the classic model of the conflict between group and individual incentives captured in the "Prisoner's Dilemma" (see Baird, Gertner, and Picker, 1994). While the one-shot version of the Prisoner's Dilemma leads to inefficiency, a variety of noncooperative formulations (for example, involving repetition of the Prisoner's Dilemma) have been developed wherein individual choices of strategies lead to the socially optimal outcome (that is, efficiency). The same techniques have been applied in a variety of settings, including bargaining. Thus, we now have a better understanding of how institutions, incentives, and behavior may or may not substitute for artificially imposed binding agreements in achieving an efficient outcome. This also means that sources of inefficiencies ("money left on the table," and thus wasted), brought about by institutional constraints, incentives, and noncooperative behavior, can be better understood.

9. An Example of a Model of Settlement Negotiation

Before venturing into the section describing the range of settlement models, a brief example will help clarify the concepts raised above. Reconsider Pat and Delta's negotiation with the following further simplifications and some numerical values. First, assume that the only source of uncertainty is Delta's liability (that is, whether Delta will be held liable) and that Pat and Delta are symmetrically uninformed about this and adopt the same estimate of Delta's likelihood of being found liable. Damages are known by all, as are court costs. Moreover, there are no attorneys or experts and J will simply award the actual damages if Delta is found to be liable. Second, we will consider two simple bargaining stories.

(1) P makes a demand of D, followed by D accepting or rejecting the demand. Acceptance means a transfer from D to P; rejection means that J orders a transfer from D to P (the two transfers need not be the same) and both parties pay their court costs. Third, it is also common

knowledge that if D is indifferent between accepting the proposal and rejecting it, D will accept it.

(2) D makes an offer to P, followed by P accepting or rejecting the offer. Acceptance means a transfer from D to P; rejection means that J orders a transfer from D to P (again, the two transfers need not be the same) and both parties pay their court costs. Third, it is also common knowledge that if P is indifferent between accepting the proposal and rejecting it, P will accept it.

Let $d = 100$ be the level of damages and $\ell = 0.5$ be the likelihood of D being found liable by J for the damage d. Let court costs be the same for both players with $k_P = k_D = 10$. Note that the expected compensation ℓd exceeds the plaintiff's court cost k_P, so that should D reject P's demand in case (1), or offer too little in (2), it is still worth P's effort to go to trial. Note also that this ignores the possibility of bankruptcy of D. All of the above, that both players are rational (that is, P maximizes, and D minimizes, their respective payoffs) and the bargaining story being analyzed are common knowledge. One final bit of notation: let s be a settlement proposal.

9.1 Analyzing the Case Wherein P Makes a Demand

The first task is to find out if settlement is possible (the *admissible* settlements). We start with D, as P must anticipate D's choice when faced with P's demand. D and P know that if the case goes to trial, D will expend either $d + k_D$ or k_D (110 or 10), the first with probability ℓ and the second with probability $(1 - \ell)$; thus D's expected expenditure at trial (payoff from the outcome go to trial) is $\ell d + k_D$ (that is, 60). Note that in this circumstance, P's payoff from the outcome labeled trial is $\ell d - k_P$ (that is, 40). Thus, D will accept any settlement demand not exceeding this expected expenditure at trial if the following inequality holds:

$$s \leq \ell d + k_D. \tag{15.1}$$

P wishes to maximize her payoff which depends upon P's demand and the choice made by D: $\pi_P = s_P$ if D accepts the demand s_P or $\pi_P = \ell d - k_P$ if D rejects the demand.

More carefully, using our earlier notation that the indicated payoff depends upon the strategy profile, we would have $\pi_P(s_P, \text{accept}) = s_P$; that is, the payoff to P from her using the strategy "make the settlement demand s_P" and D using the strategy "accept" is the transfer s_P. Similarly, we would have $\pi_P(s_P, \text{reject}) = \ell d - k_P$. In the rest of this example, we will suppress this notation when convenient, but understanding it will be of value later.

Observe that the maximum settlement demand that P can make ($s_P = \ell d + k_D$, as shown in inequality (15.1)) exceeds P's payoff from court. Thus, P maximizes the payoff *from the game* by choosing $\ell d + k_D$ as her settlement demand, which D accepts since D cannot do better by rejecting the proposal and facing trial. Thus, to summarize: (1) the players are P and D; (2) the action for P is the demand s_P (this is also P's strategy), while the action for D is to accept or reject and D's optimal strategy is to accept if s_P satisfies inequality (15.1) and to reject otherwise; (3) the outcomes are settlement and transfer with associated payoffs $\pi_P = s_P$ and $\pi_D = s_P$, or proceed to trial and transfer with associated payoffs $\pi_P = \ell d - k_P$ and $\pi_D = \ell d + k_D$; (4) the timing is that P makes a demand and D chooses accept or reject; (5) information is imperfect in a very simple way in that P and D share the same assessment about the trial outcome with respect to liability. Note that it is unnecessary to model a choice for P about going to court if her demand were rejected because of the assumption that the expected compensation exceeds plaintiff trial costs. Moreover, since nothing in the settlement phase will influence the trial outcome itself should trial occur, J is not a player in a meaningful sense. The prediction (the equilibrium) of this game is that the case settles, the resulting transfer from D to P is $\ell d + k_D$ (in the numerical example, 60) and the game payoffs are $\pi_P = \pi_D = \ell d + k_D$ (60).

9.2 Analyzing the Case Wherein D Makes an Offer
We now start with P in order to find the admissible settlements. Given the foregoing, P will accept any settlement offer that yields at least what she would get in court:

$$s \geq \ell d - k_P. \tag{15.2}$$

D wishes to minimize his payoff, which depends upon the offer he makes and the choice made by P: $\pi_D = s_D$ if P accepts the offer s_D or $\pi_D = \ell d + k_D$ if P rejects the offer. Thus D minimizes his payoff from the game by choosing $\ell d - k_P$ as his settlement offer, which P accepts since P cannot do better by rejecting the proposal and going to trial. Thus, to summarize: (1) the players are P and D; (2) the action for D is the offer s_D (this is also D's strategy), while the action for P is accept or reject and P's optimal strategy is to accept if s_D satisfies inequality (15.2) and to reject otherwise; (3) the outcomes are settlement and transfer with associated payoffs $\pi_D = s_D$ and $\pi_P = s_D$, or proceed to trial and transfer with associated payoffs $\pi_D = \ell d + k_D$ and $\pi_P = \ell d - k_P$; (4) the timing is that D makes an offer and P chooses to accept or reject; (5) information is imperfect in the same way as in the first case. The prediction (the equilibrium) of this game is that the case settles, the resulting transfer from D to P is $\ell d - k_P$ (40) and the game payoffs are $\pi_P = \pi_D = \ell d - k_P$ (40).

9.3 Bargaining Range and Bargaining Efficiency

A clear implication of the foregoing analysis is that who moves last has a significant impact on the allocation of the surplus generated by not going to court. One could think of the process in the following way. D pays ℓd to P no matter what procedure is used. P and D then contribute their court costs to a fund (called surplus) which they then split in some fashion. If the bargaining process involves P making a demand and D choosing only to accept or reject, then P gets all the surplus. If the roles are reversed, so are the fortunes. This might suggest that the two cases studied provide the extremes (the *bargaining range* or *settlement range*) and that actual bargaining will yield something inside this range. The answer, we shall see, is maybe yes and maybe no. In the preceding analysis, bargaining was efficient (no cases went to trial; again the reader is cautioned to recall the earlier discussion of the use of the word "efficiency") since all information was symmetric and the first mover could make a take-it-or-leave-it proposal (cognizant of the second-mover's ability to go to trial). Efficiency will fail to hold when we allow for asymmetric information. This will occur not because of mistakes by players, but because of the recognition by both players that information which is distributed asymmetrically will impose a cost on the bargaining process, a cost that often falls on the better-informed party.

B. BASIC MODELS OF SETTLEMENT BARGAINING

10. Perfect and Imperfect Information Models: Axiomatic Models for the Cooperative Case

The perfect-information model (and its first cousin, the imperfect-information model), versions of which appear in Landes (1971), Gould (1973), and Posner (1973), is an important starting place as it focuses attention on efficient bargaining outcomes. Many of the earlier models employed risk aversion, which will be addressed in Section 17.1. For now, and so as to make the presentations consistent with much of the more recent literature, payoffs will be assumed to be in dollar terms with risk-neutral players.

10.1 Perfect Information

We start with the perfect-information version. In keeping with the earlier discussion, the following model emphasizes final outcomes and suppresses bargaining detail. While the analysis below may seem like analytical overkill, it will allow us to structure the problem for later, more complex, discussions in this part and in Part C.

The players are P and D; further, assume that the level of damages, d, is commonly known and that D is fully liable for these damages. Court costs are k_P and k_D, and each player is responsible for his own court costs. Each player has an individual action he can take that assures him a particular payoff. P can stop negotiating and go to court; thus the payoff to P from trial is $\pi_P^t = d - k_P$ (note the superscript t for trial) and the payoff to D from trial is $\pi_D^t = d + k_D$. Under the assumption that $d - k_P > 0$, P has a *credible threat* to go to trial if negotiations fail. For the purposes of most of this chapter (and most of the literature), we assume this condition to hold (the issue of it failing will be discussed in Section 16.1). By default, D can "assure" himself of the same payoff by stopping negotiations, since P will then presumably proceed to trial; no other payoff for D is guaranteed via his individual action. The pair (π_D^t, π_P^t) is called the *threat* or *disagreement point* for the bargaining game (recall that D's payoff is an expenditure).

What might they agree on? One way to capture the essence of the negotiation is to imagine both players on either side of a table, and that they actually place money on the table (abusing the card-game story from earlier, this is an "ante") in anticipation of finding a way of allocating it. This means that D places $d + k_D$ on the table and P places k_P on the table. The maximum at stake is the sum of the available resources, $d + k_P + k_D$, and therefore any outcome (which here is an allocation of the available resources) that does not exceed this amount is a possible settlement.

P's payoff, π_P, is his bargaining outcome allocation (b_P) minus his ante (that is, $\pi_P = b_P - k_P$). D's payoff, π_D, is his ante minus his bargaining outcome allocation (b_D); thus D's *cost* (loss) is $\pi_D = d + k_D - b_D$. Since the joint bargaining outcome ($b_P + b_D$) cannot exceed the total resources to be allocated (the money on the table), $b_P + b_D \leq d + k_D + k_P$, or equivalently, P's gain cannot exceed D's loss: $\pi_P = b_P - k_P \leq d + k_D - b_D = \pi_D$. Thus, in payoff terms, the outcome of the overall bargaining game must satisfy: (1) $\pi_P \leq \pi_D$; (2) $\pi_P \geq \pi_P^t$ and (3) $\pi_D \leq \pi_D^t$. That is, whatever is the outcome of bargaining, it must be feasible and individually rational. In bargaining outcome terms, this can be written as: (1′) $b_P + b_D \leq d + k_D + k_P$; (2′) $b_P \geq d$ and (3′) $b_D \geq 0$. For the figures that follow, we restate (2′) as $b_P - d \geq 0$.

Figure 15.1(a) illustrates the settlement possibilities. The horizontal axis indicates the net gain ($-\pi_D$) or net loss (that is, total expenditure, π_D) to D. The vertical axis indicates the net gain (π_P) or net loss ($-\pi_P$) to P. The sloping line graphs points satisfying $\pi_P = \pi_D$ while the region to the left of it involves allocations such that $\pi_P < \pi_D$. The best that D could possibly

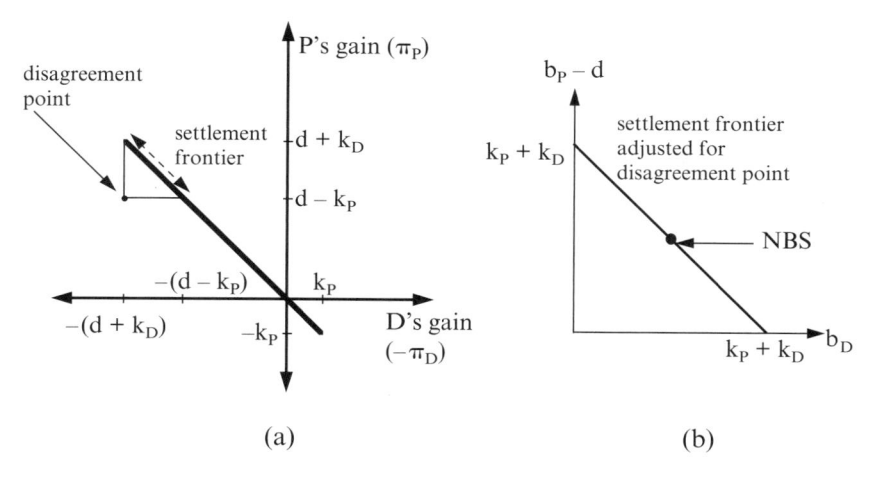

Figure 15.1 Settlement under perfect information

achieve is to recover his ante $d + k_D$ and get k_P, too; this is indicated at the right-hand lower-end of the line at the point $(k_P, -k_P)$, meaning D has a net gain of k_P and P has a net loss of k_P. At the other extreme (the upper-left end point) is the outcome wherein P gets all of $d + k_P + k_D$, meaning P has a net gain of $d + k_D$, which is D's net loss.

Note also that points below the line represent inefficient allocations: this is what is meant by "money left on the table." The disagreement point $(-(d + k_D), d - k_P)$ draws attention (observe the thin lines) to a portion of the feasible set that contains allocations that satisfy inequalities (2) and (3) above: every allocation in this little triangle is individually rational for both players. The placement of the disagreement point reflects the assertion that there is something to bargain over; if the disagreement point were above the line $\pi_P = \pi_D$ then trial is unavoidable, since there would be no settlements that jointly satisfy (2) and (3) above. This triangular region, satisfying inequalities (1), (2) and (3), is the *settlement set* (or *bargaining set*) and the endpoints of the portion of the line $\pi_P = \pi_D$ that is in the settlement set are called the *concession limits*; between the concession limits (and including them) are all the efficient bargaining outcomes under settlement, called the *settlement frontier*. Another way that this frontier is referred to is that if there is something to bargain over (that is, the disagreement point is to the left of the line), then the portion of the line between the concession limits provides the *bargaining range* or the *settlement range*, which means that a range of offers by one party to the other can be deduced that will make at least one party better off, and no party worse off, than the disagreement point.

Figure 15.1(b) illustrates the settlement set as bargaining outcomes, found by subtracting the disagreement point from everything in the settlement set, so now the disagreement point is the origin. Doing this helps adjust the region of interest for asymmetries in the threats that P and D can employ. This leaves any remaining asymmetries in power or information in the resulting diagram. In the case at hand, the only power difference might appear in the difference between the costs of going to trial; other power differences such as differences in risk preferences or patience will be discussed in Section 17.1, while informational differences will be discussed in the sections on asymmetric information in Parts B and C.

Notice that, in view of (2′) and (3′), the vertical (non-negative) axis is labeled $b_P - d$, while the horizontal (non-negative) axis is labeled b_D. Moreover, since aggregate trial costs determine the frontier in Figure 15.1(b), the bargaining problem here is symmetric. The Nash Bargaining Solution (NBS) applies in either picture, but its prediction is particularly obvious in Figure 15.1(b): recalling the discussion in Section 8.2, requiring the solution to be efficient (axiom 2) and that, when the problem is symmetric the solution is, too (axiom 4), means that splitting the saved court costs is the NBS in Figure 15.1(b). Thus, to find the NBS in Figure 15.1(a), we add the disagreement point *back into the solution from* Figure 15.1(b). Therefore, under the NBS, P's payoff is $\pi_P = d - k_P + (k_P + k_D)/2 = d + (k_D - k_P)/2$. D's net position is $-(d + k_D) + (k_P + k_D)/2$. In other words, D's payoff (his expenditure, π_D) is $\pi_D = d + (k_D - k_P)/2$. The result that players should "split the difference" *relative to the disagreement point* is always the NBS solution for any bargaining game with payoffs in monetary terms.

Observe that if court costs are the same, then at the NBS, P and D simply transfer the liability d (that is, $\pi_P = \pi_D = d + 0/2 = d$). If D's court costs exceed P's, P receives more from the settlement than the actual damages, reflecting his somewhat stronger relative bargaining position embodied in his threat with respect to the surplus that P and D can jointly generate by not going to court. A similar argument holds for P in the weaker position, with higher costs of going to court: he settles for less than d, since $k_D - k_P < 0$.

10.2 Imperfect Information

This is essentially the same model, so only the variations will be remarked upon. Assume that P and D have the same probability assessments for the two court costs and assume that they also have the same probability assessments over expected damages. This latter possibility could reflect that the level of damages is unknown (for example, as discussed in Section 7.1), but that liability is taken to be assured. Then they both see expected damages as E(d). Alternatively, perhaps damages are known to be d but liability is less clear but commonly assessed to be ℓ; that is, ℓ is the common assessment that D will be held liable for damages d and $(1 - \ell)$ is the common assessment that D will not be held liable at all. Then $E(d) = d\ell$ (an admitted but useful abuse of notation). Finally, if there are common elements influencing the values that d might take on and the likelihood of D being held liable, and if the assessments of the possible values and their joint likelihood is common knowledge, then again we will write the expected damages from trial as E(d). Again, this is abusing the notation, but avoids needless technical distinctions. The point is that in an imperfect information setting, we simply take the preceding analysis and replace all known parameters with their suitably constructed expectations, yielding the same qualitative results: no trials occur in equilibrium, strong plaintiffs (that is, those with lower trial costs than D) settle for somewhat more than their expected damages, and so forth.

10.3 Other Axiomatic Solutions, with an Example Drawn from Bankruptcy

Nash's solution to the bargaining problem inspired an enormous scholarly literature (actually, a veritable cottage industry of variations, alterations, and modifications) that continues to this day. In this section, we will discuss one of the alternative bargaining solutions and why it may be particularly relevant for some problems in law and economics research. To do this observe that in the foregoing material, once we adjusted for the disagreement point, the litigants appeared to be otherwise symmetric (see Figure 15.1(b)).

Now consider the following bargaining scenario. Two investors, A and B, have invested (respectively) I_A and I_B in a firm that has now gone bankrupt; that is, the (liquidated) value of the firm, V, is less than $I_A + I_B$, so the only issue is what shares of V should be allocated to A and to B. For the case at hand, also assume that V is larger than either stand-alone investment (that is, $V > \max[I_A, I_B]$) so that we can readily locate the settlement set in a diagram. Also, let the disagreement point be that both investors walk away with nothing if there is no agreement, and there are no costs of bargaining. Figure 15.2(a) illustrates the NBS when we ignore the size of the investments; here the problem is simply to allocate V between the two bargainers, so the NBS is where the 45° line from the origin crosses the frontier. Figure 15.2(b) now illustrates the incorporation of the original investments into the diagram, and reflects the intuitive constraint that no agent recovers more than what he invested when the value of the firm is less than the aggregate initial investment (or otherwise there may be moral hazard problems if an investor can influence the likelihood

412 *Procedural law and economics*

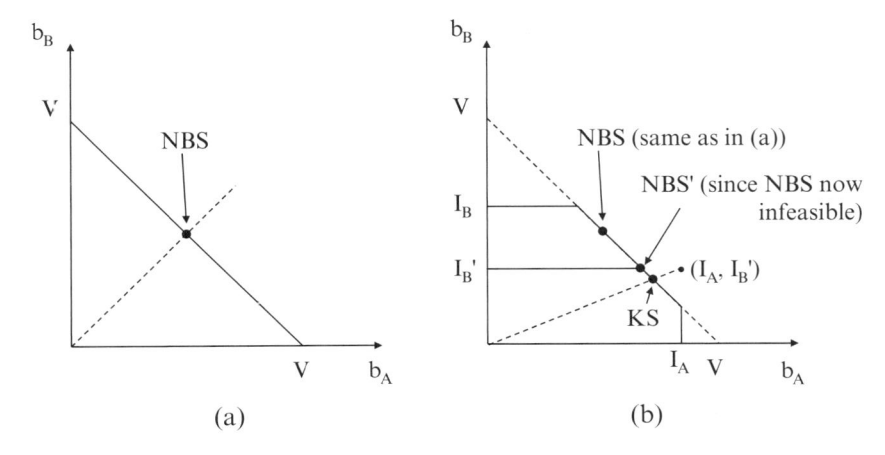

Figure 15.2   Alternative bargaining solutions under bankruptcy

of a bankruptcy). The bargaining set is more rectangular than in Figure 15.2(a), except that the downward-sloping line cuts off the upper corner of the set of possible bargains; this occurs because $V < I_A + I_B$. Alternatively, this settlement set is the same as Figure 15.2(a) except that two triangular sections have been cut off, one above I_B and one to the right of I_A.

From our earlier discussion of the NBS in Section 8.2 we know from Nash's third axiom ("Third, if the players agree to one outcome when a second one is also feasible, then they never agree to the second one when the first one is feasible.") that since the "chopping-off" of the two triangular regions did not cut away the original solution, it is still the solution to the bargaining problem. Notice this solution might be objectionable to A: as drawn, A has invested more than B, but B continues to get the same amount as in Figure 15.2(a). Let us take this one step further: if B's original investment is at I'_B, we see in Figure 15.2(b) that now the original NBS is no longer feasible. It can be shown that the new solution is at the point indicated as NBS'.[8] This outcome seems even more unsatisfactory: B's recovery is now equal to his initial investment and A gets the residual ($b_A = V - I'_B$), even though A invested considerably more than B did. This is problematical because, when A and B are initially considering making investments in the firm, if the agreement made then is to use the NBS to resolve liquidation of the enterprise should that ever become

---

[8] The NBS is found by solving max $b_A b_B$ subject to $b_A + b_B \leq V$, $0 \leq b_A \leq I_A$, $0 \leq b_B \leq I_B$.

necessary, both investors now may choose to reduce the initial investments each makes, since using the NBS appears to be biased towards repaying the smaller investor and leaving the larger investor to simply pick up the residual.

The problem here is that both concession limits do not directly affect the bargaining solution, but one might think that they should.[9] In our earlier analysis (where the settlement set was a triangle, such as in Figure 15.1), this did not matter, but in the bankruptcy problem it clearly does. Kalai and Smorodinsky (1975) proposed a bargaining solution which employed an alternative to the third axiom, replacing it with one that makes both concession limits matter. Their axiom, which argues that a monotonic improvement in one bargainer's possible options without reducing the second bargainer's options should never work against the first bargainer, means that the "KS" solution is found by constructing the smallest rectangle that contains the settlement set (this smallest rectangle is obviously driven by the concession limits) and then finding the outcome where the upward-sloping diagonal of the rectangle (in Figure 15.2(b), this is the line joining the origin and the point (I_A, I'_B)) crosses the downward-sloping frontier. When the settlement set resembles a triangle, as in Figure 15.1, then the KS solution and the NBS are the same. In the case of our bankruptcy example with the "trimmed brick," however, the KS solution will always end up in the interior of the downward-sloping frontier (that is, on the face of the trimmed side of the brick), so that each party is treated (qualitatively) similarly in that each receives a fractional share of their investment back, and not all of it.

The KS solution is but one of an enormous number of alternative bargaining solutions that have been proposed as scholars have examined different axioms, or modifications of different axioms.[10] Thus, the "bottom line" here is that some caution is needed before simply proceeding with any particular model of settlement bargaining; other solutions besides the NBS may be more appropriate. We'll see another caution about the use of the NBS in Section 12.

---

[9] It is worth noting that this is not the only objection some scholars have raised to this axiom, but discussion of the other objections is likely to lead us too far afield.

[10] For example, relaxing the symmetry axiom (the fourth axiom above) wherein identical players should be treated identically, gives a generalized NBS that allows for other differences in bargaining power besides those we have considered. An example of such a difference that might otherwise be difficult to include in the analysis is if one bargainer is more patient than the other bargainer.

11. Perfect and Imperfect Information Models: Strategic Models for the Noncooperative Case

Again, we start with the perfect information case. Furthermore, since the actual bargaining procedure is to be specified, the length of the bargaining horizon now enters into the analysis. The generic style of the models to be considered is that one player makes a proposal followed by the other player choosing to accept or reject the proposal. Concatenating as many of these simple proposal/response sequences as we choose provides the basic story.

Some questions, however, remain. First, is the proposer the same player each time? In general, we will assume that if there is more than one round of proposal/response, then proposers alternate (an important exception is Spier, 1992, where the plaintiff always proposes; this will be discussed in Section 18). If there is more than one round, the next proposal is often thought of as a counterproposal to the one before it.

Second, how many periods of proposal/response will there be? This turns out to be a very significant question. Recall that in the cooperative model P and D were committed to finding an efficient bargaining outcome. Here, no such commitment is made; instead, we want to know when noncooperative bargaining will be efficient. However, certain types of commitments in strategic models still may occur. The reason this is of interest is that commitment generally provides some power to the player who can make a commitment. For example, if there is one round of proposal/response, then the proposer has the ability to make an all-or-nothing proposal (more carefully put, all-or-court proposal). As was seen in the examples in Section 9, this led to a settlement that was efficient but rather one-sided. In particular, the proposer was able to achieve the point on the settlement frontier that is the responder's concession limit. This is a reflection of the commitment power that the proposer enjoys of *not* responding to any counterproposals that the responder might desire to make: these are ruled out by the structure of the game analyzed when there is only one round of play. This is why this game is often referred to as an *ultimatum game*. A *random proposer game* is simply a random choice as to which ultimatum game is played. Ultimatum games form the basis for many of the asymmetric information settlement analyses we shall examine, and some papers proceed to then consider a random proposer game as a means of suggesting whether the overall analysis is likely to be robust to choice of proposer.

Almost at the other end of the spectrum of theoretical bargaining analyses is the Rubinstein infinite-horizon model (Rubinstein, 1982). In this model, an infinite number of rounds of proposal/response occur wherein the proposer's identity alternates. In the settlement setting, each round allows P to choose to break off negotiations and go to trial. Here there are two somewhat more subtle forms of commitment in place of the power to make all-or-nothing proposals. First, if there is a positive interval of time between one round and the next, and if "time is money," meaning (for example) that costs are accruing (perhaps experts are being kept available, or lawyers are accruing time), then the fact that during a round only one proposal is being considered (the proposer's) provides some power to the proposer.

Second, who goes first is still significant. Rubinstein considers a simple "shrinking pie" example wherein each player discounts money received in the future relative to money received now. This encourages both players to want to settle sooner rather than later (all else equal). Thus, delay here yields inefficiency. Rubinstein uses a notion of Nash equilibrium that incorporates the dynamics of the bargaining process (this extra property of equilibrium is called *sequential rationality*, which will be discussed in more detail in Section 11.1) which results in a unique prediction for the bargaining game. In particular, in equilibrium there is no delay and (if both players are identical) the player who goes first gets more than half of the amount at stake.

Models that shrink the time interval associated with each round find that both sources of power go away as the time interval between proposals becomes vanishingly small. Note that, even with positive intervals, the effect of commitment (in this case, a short-run commitment to a proposal) is not as strong as in the ultimatum game, since counterproposals can occur and players generally cannot bind themselves to previous proposals they've made. In other words, such infinite horizon models can generate efficient settlement at points on the frontier other than the concession limits. In fact, under certain conditions these analyses predict the NBS (or some variant) as the unique equilibrium of the strategic bargaining game. Note that the fact that a strategic model employs perfect information does not guarantee that the predicted outcome is efficient. A particularly striking example of this is contained in Fernandez and Glazer (1991), who consider wage negotiations between a union and a firm under perfect information and yet obtain inefficient equilibria. The source of the inefficiency is a pre-existing wage contract. In Section 15.3, we will see that settlement bargaining with multiple litigants can also give rise to inefficient equilibria, even though information is complete.

Another difference between settlement applications and the general literature on bargaining concerns the incentive to settle as soon as possible, all else equal. Generally, in the settlement context, P wants to settle sooner but D wants to settle later. While countervailing pressures, such as costs that increase with time, may encourage D to settle as early as possible, the fact that payment delayed is generally preferred by the payer (due to the time value of money) means that D's overall incentives to settle soon can be mixed and delay may be optimal. Moreover, as observed in Spier (1992), unlike the Rubinstein model, if both P and D have the same discount rate, then the pie itself is *not* shrinking (assuming no other costs of bargaining). This is because the effect of the opposed interests and the same discount rates is to cancel out. Therefore, in a multiperiod settlement model, delay due to the time value of money does not, in and of itself, imply inefficiency. We will return to this shortly.

Finally, a yet further difference between settlement bargaining and many traditional models of bargaining between participants in a market is called the "common value" or "interdependent value" attribute of settlement bargaining.[11] In a traditional market-transaction model involving bargaining between a buyer and a seller, if bargaining fails for one reason or another, usually the buyer and the seller part ways, so that the only term of interest in the model of bargaining is the expected value of the transaction. In settlement bargaining, this term appears as the expected settlement value, but there is generally a second term which is what happens when settlement negotiations fail, namely trial. Thus, unlike the traditional market transaction model, in a settlement model there is a term that links the expected payoffs of the litigants (the expected transfer via trial). This plays a central role, as well, in the discussion of multiple litigants in Section 15.3.

11.1 Sequential Rationality

Note that in much of the preceding discussion an implicit notion was that a player's strategy anticipates future play in the game. A strategy is *sequentially rational* if it is constructed so that the player takes an *optimal* action at each possible decision opportunity that the player has in the future. Earlier, in the discussion of the disagreement point, sequential rationality was used by P. The threat to go to trial if bargaining failed to provide a payoff at least as great as what could be obtained at trial was sequentially rational: it was a credible threat because if P got to that point, he would choose to fulfill the threat he had made. Applying sequential rationality to the strategies players use, and to the analysis players make of what strategies *other* players might use, means that strategies based on threats that a rational player would not carry out (incredible threats) are

---

[11] For discussions of interdependent values of bargainers in a market transactions setting, see Vincent (1989) and, more recently, Deneckere and Liang (2006).

ruled out. Many of the improvements in making predictions for asymmetric information models that have occurred over the last 25 years have involved employing sequential rationality, generally in conjunction with further amplifications of what rational behavior implies. Rubinstein finds a unique prediction in the infinite-horizon alternating offers game (for short, the Rubinstein game) because he predicts Nash equilibria which enforce sequential rationality (called *subgame perfect equilibrium*; for a discussion of some applications of subgame perfection in law and economics, see Baird, Gertner and Picker, 1994). In the Rubinstein game, even though the horizon is infinite, the (sequentially rational) Nash equilibrium is a unique, specific, efficient bargaining allocation which is proposed and accepted in the first round. Thus, efficiency (both in terms of fully allocating what is available to bargain over as well as doing it without delay) is a *result*, not an assumption.

11.2 Settlement Using Strategic Bargaining Models in the Perfect Information Case

The discussion in Section 9 provides the details of the ultimatum game version of settlement. Since that application technically involved imperfect information (the assessment about liability), a careful treatment means that we would take $\ell = 1$, yielding the payoffs for the ultimatum model with P as proposer (the P-proposer ultimatum model) to be $\pi_P = \pi_D = d + k_D$, while the D-proposer ultimatum model's payoffs would be $\pi_P = \pi_D = d - k_P$. The rest of this section is therefore devoted to the analysis in the infinite horizon case.

The tradeoff between D's natural interest to delay payment and any incentives to settle early (in particular, P's credible threat to go to court and any negotiation costs borne by D) is explored in the settlement context in Wang, Kim and Yi (1994); they also consider an asymmetric information case which will be discussed in Section 12.4. In the perfect information analysis, D proposes in the first round, but is subject in each round to an additional cost, c, which reflects per period negotiating costs but is charged *only* if the negotiations proceed to the next period. One could include a cost of this sort for P, too, but it is the difference between P's and D's negotiating costs that matters, so letting P's cost be zero is not a meaningful limitation.

Let δ (a fraction between zero and one) be the common discount rate used by the players for evaluating and comparing money flows at different points in time; that is, a player is indifferent between receiving $1 next period and $$\delta$ this period. Note that this effect could be undone if, at trial, damages were awarded with interest from the date of filing the suit; this does not occur in their model. Wang, Kim and Yi show that if $\delta c/(1 - \delta^2)$

$> d - k_P$, then the unique subgame perfect equilibrium is for D to offer $\delta^2 c/(1 - \delta^2)$ to P; if instead $\delta c/(1 - \delta^2) < d - k_P$, then the unique subgame perfect equilibrium involves D offering $\delta(d - k_P)$ to P. For a careful proof of this, see Wang, Kim and Yi (1994); for our purposes, let us use some crude intuition (sweeping all sorts of technical details under the rug) to understand this result.

To see what is going on, consider D's viewpoint and think about three time periods. If s is what D would offer at time period three, then P knows that he can demand $\delta s + \delta c$ at period two ($\delta s + \delta c$ is what it will cost D to wait and make the offer s in period three). P will prefer this to going to trial if $\delta s + \delta c > d - k_P$. Thus, in period one, the maximum D must offer is $\delta(\delta s + \delta c)$. Since periods one and three look the same (that is, the three-period sequence repeats out to infinity in this model), s is the solution to $\delta(\delta s + \delta c) = s$; solving for s yields $s = \delta^2 c/(1 - \delta^2)$. In this sense, $\delta c/(1 - \delta^2) > d - k_P$ really is a statement that the cost of delay is high from D's viewpoint, which is why D must offer something higher than the discounted value of going to trial, that is, $\delta(d - k_P)$.

Even if costs are low (that is, $\delta c/(1 - \delta^2) < d - k_P$), D must still worry about P's choice of going to court, but P can no longer exploit D's cost weakness to further improve the bargain in his favor. Thus, D can offer the discounted value of P's concession limit, namely $\delta(d - k_P)$, since P cannot choose to go to court until next period and therefore might as well accept $\delta(d - k_P)$ now.

To summarize, the players are P and D, actions in each period involve proposals followed by accept/reject from the other player, with P able to choose to go to court when it is his turn to propose. Payoffs are as usual with the added provisos concerning the discount rate δ reflecting the time value of money, and the per period cost c, for the defendant, which is incurred each time negotiators fail to agree. The bargaining horizon is infinite and information is perfect. The result is that: (1) P and D settle in the first period; (2) the prediction is unique and efficient; (3) if negotiation costs are sufficiently high, then the prediction is on the settlement frontier, between the discounted values of the concession limits and (4) otherwise it is at the discounted value of P's concession limit, reflecting the fact that D moved first.

11.3 The Imperfect Information Case

The extension of the ultimatum game results of Section 9 to the imperfect information case parallels the discussion in Section 10.2. This is similarly true for the multiperiod case, which is why this issue has not received much attention.

12. Analyses Allowing for Differences in Player Assessments due to Private Information

In this section, we consider models that account for differences in the players' assessments about items such as damages and liability based on the private information players possess when they bargain. We focus especially on two models: one developed by Bebchuk (1984) and one developed by Reinganum and Wilde (1986). Most of the analyses in the current literature are based on one of these two primary settlement models, both of which analyze ultimatum games and both of which assume one-sided asymmetric information; that is, there is an aspect of the game (typically a variable such as damages or liability, though it could also be the product of damages and the likelihood of being found liable) about which P and D have different information, and only one of the players knows the true value of the variable during bargaining. Since the model structure is so specific (the ultimatum game) and the distribution of information is so one-sided, we also consider what models with somewhat greater generality suggest about the reasonableness of the two prime workhorses of the current settlement literature. For a survey of asymmetric information bargaining theory, see Kennan and Wilson (1993).[12]

Before proceeding, however, one might wonder why we do not seem to consider the Nash Bargaining Solution as a means for solving the asymmetric information settlement games of interest. The most direct answer is to think back to the second of the four axioms (see Section 8.2): the bargaining solution should be efficient. When information is incomplete, efficiency is not possible to guarantee without the intervention of an all-knowing third party. Perhaps a court could fulfill this role, but the whole point of settlement negotiation is to reduce the likelihood of going to court. Perhaps we could expect the two litigants to exchange information, but if one of them relies on the honesty of the exchange, it does not strain credulity to believe that the other might take strategic advantage of this. Thus, while information can be exchanged, this is usually a costly discovery process, and discovery itself is likely to be an incomplete, or at least strategically manipulable, process that is costly to employ. In other words, even if an informed party would like to communicate some information to the other party, he can't in general do this costlessly and the presence of a disclosure cost means that some information will not be disclosed. Lack of complete disclosure, in turn, means that efficiency cannot be assured; money may be left on the table. In the context of labor-management relations, this means a

---

[12] For a discussion of the settlement frontier under inconsistent priors, see Chung (1996).

strike may occur even though it turns out that it would have been advantageous to all involved to achieve an agreement rather than weather a strike. Similarly in settlement bargaining, it may be necessary to engage in costly actions (intense discovery and deposition of experts, and possibly trial) due to the incompleteness of information and the inability of the parties involved to costlessly and credibly exchange the information that would be needed to be efficient. Thus, our analysis must allow for an inefficient outcome, so the approach used is via strategic, rather than axiomatic, analysis. Therefore, cooperative solutions, such as the NBS or KS solutions, will not address a primary problem associated with asymmetric information bargaining, namely inefficient outcomes wherein bargaining fails even though a surplus might exist to share. While the cooperative solutions have an appealing attribute, sharing the surplus, the strategic approach will focus on analyzing ultimatum games with take-it-or-leave-it offers. In view of this, some papers have tried to address this extreme analysis via the use of random proposer models that incorporate the polar-opposite ultimatum games, with the intuitive argument that if the two ultimatum games share similar qualitative results, then whatever bargaining process would actually occur is likely to also share those qualitative aspects.

12.1 Yet More Needed Language and Concepts: Screening, Signaling, Revealing and Pooling

Reaching back to Section 7, a one-sided information model is like a card game where only one player has a down card and knows the value of that card. That player is privately informed and, because of consistent priors, both players know that the probability model being used by the uninformed player is common knowledge.

Since the basic bargaining process (an ultimatum game) involves one round of proposal and response, the fact that only one of the players possesses private information about something that is important to both means that *when* the informed player acts is, itself, important. A *screening* model (also sometimes called a *sorting* model) involves the uninformed player making the proposal and the informed player choosing to accept or reject the proposal. A *signaling* model involves the reverse: the informed player makes the proposal and the uninformed player chooses to accept or reject it. Note that the word "signaling" only means that the proposal is made by the informed player, not that the proposal itself is necessarily informative about the private information possessed by the proposer. Bebchuk's model is a screening model and Reinganum and Wilde's model is a signaling model.

These are noncooperative models of bargaining, so our method of prediction is finding an equilibrium (rather than a cooperative solution).

In both cases, sequential rationality is also employed. Generally, in the case of a screening model, this yields a unique prediction. In the case of a signaling model, sequential rationality is generally insufficient to produce a unique prediction. The reason is that since the uninformed player is observing the informed player's action in this case, the action itself may reveal something about the private information of the proposer. When this happens, further "refinement" of the set of predictions (set of equilibria) is used to hone in on a unique prediction.[13]

To understand this, consider a modification of the card game story from Section 7.1. Table 15.2 shows the hands for players A and B and, as before, only A knows his down card:

Table 15.2   Hands of cards for A and B

	UP	DOWN
A	A♦, Q♦, J♦, 10♦	2♥
B	10♣, 10♠, 9♠, 5♦, 2♣	

Note: Entries provide face value of card and suit.

To fill out the story, all the above cards have just been dealt, after players put some money on the table, from a standard 52-card deck. The rules are that player A may now discard one card (if it is the down card, this is done without revealing it) and a new card is provided that is drawn from the undealt portion of the deck. A can also choose not to discard a card. If he does discard one, the new card is dealt face up if the discard was an up card and is dealt face down otherwise. After this, A and B can add money to that already on the table or they can surrender their share of the money currently on the table ("fold"); for convenience, assume that a player must fold or add money (a player can't stay in the game without adding money to that already on the table). The cards are then compared, privately, by an honest dealer, and any winner gets all the money while a tie splits the money evenly amongst those who have not folded. The comparison process in this case means that, for player A, a new down card that matches his Ace, Queen or Jack card with the same face value (that is, A ends up with two Aces or two Queens or two Jacks) will beat B's hand, as will any diamond in conjunction with A's up cards currently showing. Other draws mean that A will either tie (a 10♥) or lose.

---

[13]   See, for example, Chapters 9 and 13 of Mas-Colell, Whinston and Green (1995).

Before A chooses whether and what to discard, B knows that the down card could be any of 43 cards with equal likelihood. Now if A discards his down card, based on sequential rationality, B knows that it was not an Ace, a Queen, a Jack or a Diamond. This information can be used by B *before* he must take any action. He may choose to fold, or he may choose to add money, but this decision is now influenced by what he believes to be A's private information, A's new down card. These beliefs take the form of an improved probability estimate over A's type (adjusting for what has been observed). These assessments are called *beliefs*, and in an asymmetric information model, players form beliefs based upon the prior assessments and everything that they have observed before each and every decision they make. The addition of the need to account for what beliefs players can reasonably expect to hold makes the signaling game more complex to analyze than the screening game.

A few more observations about the card game are in order. First, even though this was a signaling game, the signal of discarding did not completely inform the uninformed player of the content of the private information. A strategy for the informed player is *revealing* if, upon the uninformed player observing the action(s) of the informed player, the uninformed player can correctly infer the informed player's type. In this sense, each type of player has an action that distinguishes it from all the other types. For example, in the settlement context, where P is privately informed about the true level of damages but D only knows the prior distribution, a revealing strategy would involve each possible type of P (each possible level of damages) making a different settlement demand, such as P demands his true damages plus D's court costs. If instead P always asked for the average level of damages, independent of the true level, plus court costs, then P would be using a *pooling* strategy: different types of P take the same action and therefore are observationally indistinguishable.

In the card game above, A choosing to discard his down card has some elements of a revealing strategy (not all types would choose this action) and some elements of a pooling strategy (there are a number of types who would take the same action). This is an example of a *semi-pooling* or *partial pooling* strategy. Notice that if the deck had originally consisted of *only* the eleven cards A♦, K♦, Q♦, J♦, 10♦, 10♣, 10♠, 9♠, 5♦, 2♣, 2♥, then B could use the action "discard" to distinguish between the private information "initial down-card = K♦" and "initial down-card = 2♥" because discarding the down-card is only rational for the player holding a 2♥. Thus, discarding or not discarding in this special case is a fully revealing action. In this particular example, we got this by changing the size of the deck (thereby changing the number of types), but this is not always necessary. In many signaling models, extra effort placed on making predictions, even in the presence of a continuum of types, leads to fully revealing behavior; we will see this in the signaling analysis below.

Finally, a *revealing equilibrium* means that the equilibrium involves the complete transmission of all private information. In a revealing equilibrium, the privately informed player is employing a revealing strategy. In a *pooling equilibrium*, no private information is transmitted: at the end of the game, no more is necessarily known by the uninformed player than was known before play began. More generally, in a *partial pooling equilibrium*, some of the types have been revealed through their actions and some of the types took actions which do not allow us to distinguish them from one another.

12.2 Where You Start and Where You End

As will be seen below, a typical screening model produces partial pooling equilibria as its prediction; in fact, the equilibrium is often composed of two big pools (a bunch of types do this and the rest do that) and is only fully revealing if each pool consists of one type.[14] In other words, if the private information in the model takes on more than two values, some pooling will typically occur in the equilibrium prediction of a screening model. On the other hand, a typical signaling model has all three types of equilibria (revealing, fully pooling, partial pooling) as predictions, but with some extra effort concerning rational inference (called *refinements* of equilibrium), this often reduces to a unique prediction of a revealing equilibrium.

12.3 One-Sided Asymmetric Information Settlement Process Models: Examples of Analyses

In the subsections to follow, we will start with the same basic setting and find the results of applying screening and signaling models. Bebchuk's 1984 paper considered an informed defendant (concerning liability) responding to an offer from an uninformed plaintiff; Reinganum and Wilde's 1986 paper considered a plaintiff with private information about damages making a demand of an uninformed defendant. Initially, information will be modeled as taking on two levels (that is, a two-type model is employed) and a basic analysis using each approach will be presented and solved. The result of allowing for more than two types (in particular, a continuum of types) will then be discussed in the context of the alternative approaches.

Since most of the discussion earlier in this survey revolved around

---

[14] Of course, if one of the pools involves types who go to court, and the court is perfectly informed, then any type in that pool is thereby "revealed" at trial.

damages, both approaches will be applied to private information on damages, suggesting a natural setting of an informed P and an uninformed D (note, however, that the earlier example of Pat and Delta was purposely posed with Delta as the informed party to emphasize that the analysis is applicable in a variety of settings). More precisely, the level of damages is assumed to take on the value d_L (L for low) or d_H (H for high), meaning that P suffers a loss and it takes on one of these two levels, which is private information for P. Moreover, $d_H > d_L > 0$. The levels are common knowledge as is D's assessment that p is the probability of the low value being the true level of damages. If the case were to go to trial, then J will find out the true level of damages (whether the damages were equal to d_L or equal to d_H) and award the true damages to P.[15] Thus $E_D(d) = pd_L + (1 - p)d_H$ is D's prior (that is, before bargaining or trial) estimate of the expected damages that he will pay if he goes to trial; P knows whether the damages paid will be d_L or d_H. Should the case go to trial, each player pays his own court costs (k_P and k_D, respectively) and, for simplicity again, assume that $d_L > k_P$; relaxing this assumption is discussed in Section 16.1. Finally, in each case, the structure of the bargaining process is represented by an ultimatum game. In particular, the player who responds will choose to accept the proposal if he is indifferent between the payoff resulting from accepting the proposal and the payoff resulting from trial. *Without any more information*, D's *ex ante* (that is, before bargaining) expected payoff from trial is $E_D(d) + k_D$; P's payoff from trial is $d_L - k_P$ if true damages are d_L, and $d_H - k_P$ if true damages are d_H.

12.3.1 Screening: a two-type analysis In this model D offers a settlement transfer to P of s_D and P responds with acceptance or rejection. For the analysis to be sequentially rational (that is, we are looking for a subgame perfect equilibrium), we start by thinking about what P's strategy should be for *any* possible offer made by D in order for him to maximize his overall payoff from the game. If $s_D \geq d_H - k_P$, then no matter whether damages are high or low, P should accept and settle at s_D. If $s_D < d_L - k_P$, then no matter whether damages are high or low, P should reject the offer and go to trial. If s_D is set so that it lies between these two possibilities, that is, $d_H - k_P > s_D \geq d_L - k_P$, then a P with high damages should reject the offer, but a P with low damages should accept the offer. This last offer is

---

[15] Note that this discussion is as if D's liability is assured ($\ell = 1$). Alternatively, D and P have a common assessment of D's liability and this has already been incorporated into the damage levels d_L and d_H. We factor out liability in this discussion so as to minimize unneeded notation.

said to *screen* the types; note that the offer results in the revelation of the private information. Thus P's optimal action is contingent upon the offer made; we have found P's strategy and it involves rational choice. D can do this computation, too, for each possible type of P that could occur, so from D's viewpoint, he models P as having a strategy that depends both on P's type and upon D's offer.

As always, D's objective is to minimize expected expenditure and he must make an offer before observing any further information about P; thus, D cannot improve his assessments as occurred in the card game. D knows, however, that some offers are better than others. For example, the lowest offer in the range $d_H - k_P > s_D \geq d_L - k_P$, namely $s_D = d_L - k_P$, is better than any other offer in that range, since it doesn't change the result that H-type Ps will reject and L-type Ps will accept, and its cost to D is least when compared to other possible offers in this range. The expected cost of screening the types is $p(d_L - k_P) + (1 - p)(d_H + k_D) = E_D(d) + k_D - p(k_P + k_D)$, since the offer elicits acceptance with probability p (the probability of L-types) and generates a trial and attendant costs with probability $(1 - p)$. The payoff from making offers that both types reject is $E_D(d) + k_D$. Finally, the expected cost from making an offer that both types will accept is simply the cost of the offer that the H-type will accept, namely $d_H - k_P$.

A comparison of the payoffs from the different possible offers that D could make indicates that it is always better for D to make an offer of at least the L-type's concession limit (that is, the value of s_D specified above, $d_L - k_P$). This is because the expected cost to D of screening the types, $E_D(d) + k_D - p(k_P + k_D)$, is less than the expected cost from making any offer less than s_D, since such an offer guarantees trial and has an expected cost of $E_D(d) + k_D$.

It may be optimal to pool the types; that is, to make an offer at the H-type's concession limit $(d_H - k_P)$, which will therefore be accepted by P independent of his actual damages incurred. To see if it is, compare the expected cost to D of the screening offer, $E_D(d) + k_D - p(k_P + k_D)$, with the expected cost to D of the pooling offer, $d_H - k_P$; it is optimal to screen (rather than pool) the types if $E_D(d) + k_D - p(k_P + k_D) < d_H - k_P$; that is, if:

$$p > (k_P + k_D)/(d_H - d_L + k_P + k_D). \qquad \text{(SSC)}$$

Inequality above is the *simple screening condition* (SSC) (simple because it considers two types only); it indicates that the relevant comparison between screening the types or pooling them involves total court costs ($k_P + k_D$), the difference between potential levels of damages ($d_H - d_L$) and the relative likelihood of H- and L-types. Given court costs and the gap between high and low damages, the more likely it is that P has suffered low damages rather than high damages, the more likely D should be to screen the types and thereby only rarely go to trial (and then, always against an H-type). If the likelihood of facing an H-type P is sufficiently high (that is, p is low), then it is better to make an offer that is high enough to settle with both possible types of plaintiff. Therefore, with pooling there are no trials, but with screening trials occur with probability $(1 - p)$. Condition (SSC) also suggests that, for a given probability of low-damage Ps and a given gap between the levels of damages, sizable trial costs auger for pooling (that is, settling with both types of P).

Finally, the model allows us to compute the efficiency loss and to recognize its source. To see this, imagine the above analysis in the imperfect information setting; in particular, for this setting both P and D do not know P's type, and they agree on the estimate of damages, $E_D(d)$, and that liability of D for the true damages is certain. In the imperfect information version of the D-proposer ultimatum game, D's optimal offer is $E_D(d) - k_P$, P's concession limit under imperfect information. Since in that setting P doesn't know his type, he would settle at $E_D(d) - k_P$ rather than require $d_H - k_P$ (which is greater than $E_D(d) - k_P$) to avoid trial if he is an H-type. Thus, the difference in D's payoff under imperfect information ($E_D(d) - k_P$) and that under the asymmetric information analyzed above ($E_D(d) + k_D - p(k_P + k_D)$) is $(1 - p)(k_P + k_D)$. This extra cost to D comes from the fact that D recognizes that P knows his own type and will act accordingly. Note that this is not a transfer to P; it is an efficiency loss. This loss is a share of the surplus that, under perfect or imperfect information, would have been avoided by settling rather than going to trial, and is a loss that is due to the presence of an asymmetry in the players' information.

12.3.2 Screening with many types The principle used above extends to settings involving finer distinctions among levels of private information. In particular, this subsection will outline the nature of the model when applied to a continuum of types, such as a plaintiff whose level of damages could take on any value between two given levels of damages (that is, d may take on values between, and including, d_L and d_H; $d_L \leq d \leq d_H$). This is formally equivalent to Bebchuk's original model (Bebchuk, 1984), even though his analysis presented a D who was privately informed about liability in a P-proposer setting with known damages. Thus, differences in the presentations between this discussion and Bebchuk's are due to the shift of the proposer and the source of private information; there are no substantive differences between the analyses.

As always, D's probability assessment of the likelihood of the different

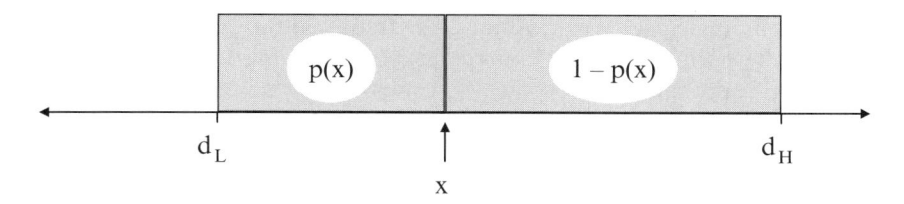

Figure 15.3 Screening with a continuum of types

possible levels of damages is common knowledge and is denoted p(d), which provides the probability that damages are no more than any chosen value of d. Figure 15.3 illustrates the intuition behind the analysis. The distribution of possible levels of damages as drawn implies equal likelihood, but this is for illustrative purposes only; many (though not all) probability assessment models would yield similar qualitative predictions. Figure 15.3 illustrates a level of damages, x, intermediate to the two extremes, d_L and d_H, and that the fraction of possible damage levels at or below x is given by p(x). Alternatively put, if D offers $s = x - k_P$, a P who has suffered the level of damages x would be indifferent between the offer and the payoff from going to trial. Moreover, this offer would also be accepted by any P with damages less than x, while any P with damages greater than x would reject the offer and go to trial. The expected expenditure associated with offers that are accepted is sp(x). Note that the particular value x that made the associated P indifferent between settling and going to trial depends upon the offer: $x(s) = s + k_P$. This is accounted for by explicitly recognizing this dependence: if D makes an offer s_D, then the expected expenditure associated with accepted offers is $s_D p(x(s_D))$.

Two observations are in order. First, as s_D increases, the "marginal" type $x(s_D)$ (also known as the "borderline" type; see Bebchuk, 1984) moves to the right and this would increase $p(x(s_D))$. Thus, this expected expenditure is increasing in the offer both because the offer itself goes up and as it increases, so does the likelihood of it being accepted. Second, while the types of P that reject the offer and go to trial are "revealed" by the award made by J (who learns the true d and awards it), as long as $x \neq d_L$ there is residual uncertainty in every possible outcome of the game: the offer pools those who accept, and their private information is not revealed (other than the implications to be drawn from the fact that they must have damages that lie to the left of x in Figure 15.3). The fact that the equilibrium will therefore involve only partial revelation is the main difference between the two-type model (where screening reveals types) and the model with a continuum of types.

428 *Procedural law and economics*

To minimize expected expenditure,[16] D trades off the expected expenditure from settling with the expected expenditure for trial, where trial occurs with probability $1 - p(x(s_D))$. Under appropriate assumptions on $p(x)$, this latter expenditure is declining in s_D, yielding an optimal offer (s_D^*) for D that makes the type of P represented by the level of damages $x(s_D^*)$ the marginal type.

As an example, if all levels of damages are equally likely, as illustrated in Figure 15.3 above, then as long as the gap between the extreme levels of damages exceeds the total court costs (that is, $d_H - d_L \geq k_P + k_D$), the equilibrium screening offer is $s_D^* = d_L + k_D$ and the marginal type is a P with level of damages $d_L + k_D + k_P$; Ps with damages at or below this level accept the offer, while those with damages in excess of this level reject the offer. Thus, "P has been screened." Note that should the gap in levels of damages be less than aggregate trial costs ($d_H - d_L < k_P + k_D$), then D simply pools all the types with the offer $d_H - k_P$.

12.3.3 Signaling: a two-type analysis This approach employs a P-proposer model in which P makes a settlement demand followed by D choosing to accept or reject the proposal. Given the assumptions made in the discussion before subsection 12.3.1, a rejection leads to P going to trial, at which J learns the true level of damages and awards P their value.

As discussed in Section 4, in the circumstances of this ultimatum game, D should use a mixed strategy: if demands at or below some level were always accepted, while those above this level were always rejected, some types of P would be compensated more than might be necessary and D would go to court more often than necessary. Here a mixed strategy should respond to the demand made: low demands should be rejected less often than high demands, if only because a high demand is more advantageous to a greater percentage of possible types of Ps, and therefore requires D to be more vigilant.

The notion that lower types (those with lesser damages) of P have an incentive to try to be mistaken for higher types (those with greater damages) – called *mimicry* – plays a central role in the analysis. D's use of a mixed strategy, dependent upon the demand made, provides a counter-incentive which can make mimicry unprofitable: a greedy demand at the settlement bargaining stage, triggering a greater chance of rejection, may

---

[16] For those desiring a precise mathematical statement of what follows, D picks the value x that minimizes $p(x)(x - k_P) + \int_I (t + k_D) dp(t)$, where $I = [x, d_H]$ is the interval of types who would reject the offer and go to trial. If x^* is the optimum, then D's equilibrium offer is $s_D^* = x^* - k_P$. As long as $p'(x)/p(x)$ is monotonically decreasing, this optimization problem has a unique minimum.

therefore more readily lead to much lower payoffs at trial (where the true level of damages is revealed with certainty and P then must pay his court costs from the award) than would have occurred at a somewhat lower demand.

P's demand is s_P, which D responds to by rejecting it with probability $r_D(s_P)$ or accepting it, which occurs with probability $1 - r_D(s_P)$. Clearly, if the demand is $d_L + k_D$, then D should accept this demand as D can do no better by rejecting it. For convenience, we will define s_L to be this lowest-type demand, and thus, $r_D(s_L) = 0$. On the other hand, if P were to make a demand higher than what would be D's expenditure at trial associated with the highest type, namely $d_H + k_D$, then D should reject any such demand for sure. It is somewhat less clear what D should do with $d_H + k_D$, which for convenience we denote as s_H. As will be shown below (in both the two-type and the continuum of types models), D's equilibrium strategy will set $r_D(s_H)$ to be less than one. This will provide an incentive for greedy Ps to demand at most s_H (technically, this is for the benefit of specifying an equilibrium, and it turns out not to hurt D). Since P knows what D knows, P can also construct the $r_D(s_P)$ function that D will use to respond to any demand s_P that P makes. P uses this function to decide what demand will maximize his payoff.

While there are demand/rejection probability combinations that can generate all three types of equilibria (revealing, pooling and partial pooling), the focus here is on characterizing a revealing equilibrium. To do this, we take our cue from the appropriate perfect-information ultimatum game. In those analyses, if it was common knowledge that P was a high type, he could demand and get s_H, while if it was common knowledge that P was a low type, he could demand and get s_L. Making such demands clearly provides an action that could allow D to infer that, should he observe s_L, it must have come from a low type, while if he observed s_H, it must have come from a high type. While wishing doesn't make this true, incentives in terms of payoffs can, so that a low-damage P's best choice between s_L and s_H is s_L and a high-damage P's best choice between s_L and s_H is s_H. In particular, consider the following two inequalities (since $r_D(s_L) = 0$, the following inequalities employ the notation r for the rejection probability; we will then pick a particular value of r to be the value of D's rejection strategy, $r_D(s_H)$):

$$s_L \geq (1 - r)s_H + r(d_L - k_P) \tag{ICL}$$

and

$$s_L \leq (1 - r)s_H + r(d_H - k_P). \tag{ICH}$$

430 *Procedural law and economics*

Inequality (ICL) (*incentive compatibility condition for the low type*), states that D's choice of r is such that when P has the low level of damages, his payoff is at least as good when he demands s_L as what his payoff would be by mimicking the high-damages P's demand s_H, which is accepted with probability $(1 - r)$, but is rejected with probability r (resulting in the P of either type going to court). Note that, since J would learn the true type at court, a low-type P gets $d_L - k_P$ if his demand is rejected. In other words, on the right is the expected payoff to a P with the low level of damages from misrepresenting himself as having suffered high damages. Inequality (ICH) (*the incentive compatibility condition for the high type*) has a similar interpretation, but now it is for the high types: they are also no worse off by making the settlement demand that reflects their true type (the expected cost on the right side of the inequality) than they would be if they misrepresented themselves. When r, s_L and s_H satisfy *both* (ICL) and (ICH), then these strategies for D and the two types of P yield a revealing equilibrium.

Substituting the values for s_L and s_H and solving the two inequalities yields the following requirement for r:

$$(d_H - d_L)/[(d_H - d_L) + (k_P + k_D)] \leq r \leq (d_H - d_L)/(k_P + k_D).$$

While the term on the far right is, by an earlier assumption, greater than one, the term on the far left is strictly less than one. In fact, for *each* value of r (pick one arbitrarily and call it r' for now) between the value on the left and one, there is a revealing equilibrium involving the low-damages P demanding s_L, the high-damages P demanding s_H and D responding via the rejection function with $r_D(s_L) = 0$ and $r_D(s_H) = r'$. In the equilibrium just posited, a low-damage P reveals himself and always settles with D at $d_L + k_D$ and a high-damage P always reveals himself, possibly (that is, with probability $(1 - r')$) settling with D at $d_H + k_D$ and possibly (with probability r') going to court and achieving the payoff $d_H - k_P$. Note that the strategies for the players are very simple: P's demand is his damages plus D's court costs; D's strategy is to always accept a low demand and to reject a high demand with a given positive, but fractional, probability.

For what follows we will pick a particular value of r in the interval, namely, let $r_D(s_H) = (d_H - d_L)/[(d_H - d_L) + (k_P + k_D)]$, the smallest value. There are technical reasons (refinements) that have been alluded to earlier, concerning extensions of notions of rationality, to support this choice, but another motivation is that the smallest admissible r, $r_D(s_H)$, is the most efficient of the possible choices. All the r values that satisfy the incentive conditions (ICL) and (ICH) provide the same expected payoff to

D, namely $E_D(d) + k_D$. P's expected payoff (that is, computed before he knows his type) is $E_D(d) + k_D - (1 - p)(k_P + k_D)r$, for *any* r that satisfies both incentive compatibility conditions, so using $r_D(s_H)$ minimizes the efficiency loss $(1 - p)(k_P + k_D)r$. Note also that using the specified $r_D(s_H)$ as the rejection probability for a high demand means that the likelihood of rejection is inversely related to total court costs, but positively related to the difference between possible levels of damages. This is because, while increased court costs minimize the threat of going to court, an increased gap between d_H and d_L increases the incentive for low-damage Ps to claim to be high-damage Ps, thereby requiring more vigilance on the part of D. D accomplishes this by increasing $r_D(s_H)$.

12.3.4 Signaling with many types While the principle used above extends to the case of a continuum of values of the private information, the extension itself involves considerably greater technical detail.[17] The presentation here will summarize results in much the same manner as used in Section 12.3.2 to summarize screening with a continuum of types. This presentation is based on the analysis employed in Reinganum and Wilde (1986), though that model allows for non-strategic errors (that is, exogenously specified errors) by J and awards that are proportional to (rather than equal to) damages.

The basic results developed in the two-type model remain: (1) a revealing equilibrium is predicted; (2) P makes a settlement demand equal to damages plus D's court cost and (3) D uses a mixed strategy to choose acceptance or rejection. The likelihood of rejection is increasing in the demand made, and therefore in the damages incurred, and is decreasing in court costs. This means that the distribution of levels of damages that go to trial involves, essentially, the entire spectrum of damages, though it consists of preponderantly higher rather than lower damages (relative to the initial distribution).

Figure 15.4 shows an example which starts with the same assessment over damages as envisioned in the continuum screening model in Section 12.3.2. As is shown in the graph displayed in the upper left of Figure 15.4, again assume that each possible level of damages is equally likely. Following the gray arrow, the graph in the upper right shows the equilibrium settlement demand function for P: it is parallel to the 45° line (the

---

[17] For those desiring mathematical detail, P's maximization (in a revealing equilibrium) yields a first-order condition which characterizes D's rejection function via the differential equation $1 - r(x) - (k_P + k_D)r'(x) = 0$. The boundary condition is that $r(d_L) = 0$: the demand associated with the lowest type should not be rejected. P's equilibrium demand (for any damages x) is $s_P^* = x + k_D$.

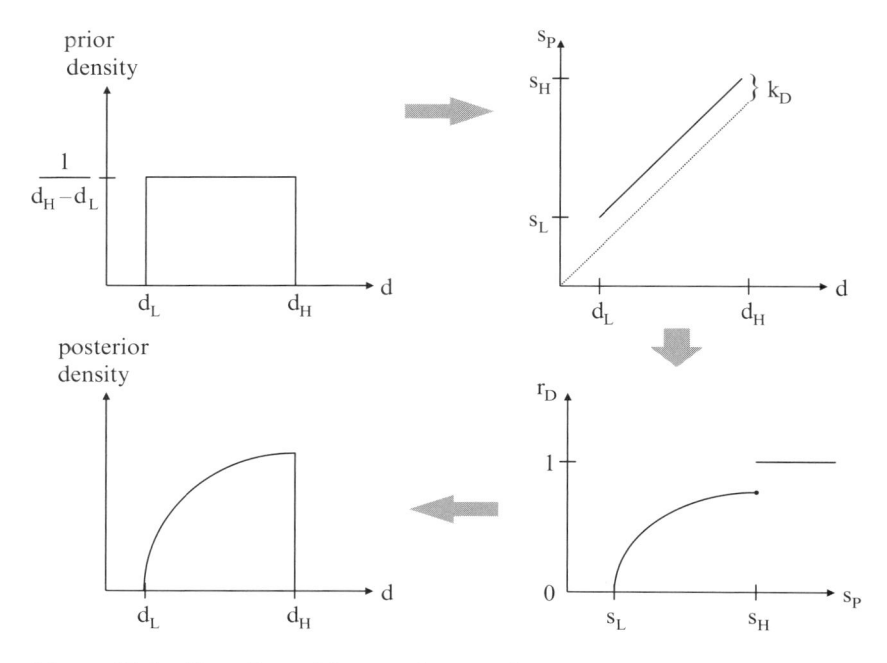

Figure 15.4   Signaling with a continuum of types

dotted line) and shifted up by the amount k_D. Thus, P's settlement demand function $s_P(d) = d + k_D$, where d is P's type (level of damages actually incurred). Thus, for example, $s_P(d_L) = d_L + k_D$ (this is s_L on the vertical axis). The graph below the settlement demand function (follow the fat gray arrow) displays D's rejection function. Demands at or below s_L are accepted and demands above s_L are rejected with an increasing likelihood up to the demand $s_H = d_H + k_D$. This is rejected with a positive but fractional likelihood (the dot is to show the endpoint of the curve); anything higher yet is rejected with certainty. Finally, following the gray arrow to the lower left of Figure 15.4, the posterior assessment of damages for cases going to trial is shown. The word posterior is used to contrast it with the assessment D used before bargaining commenced (the prior assessment). The effect of settlement bargaining is to create an assessment model at the start of the next stage of the legal process which is shifted upwards; that is, which emphasizes the higher-damage cases. This contrasts with the resulting distribution of cases that emerge from a screening process. The result of the screening model applied to the "box-shaped" prior assessment shown in Figures 15.3 and 15.4 would be a box-shaped posterior assessment model over the types that rejected the screening offer.

12.4 How Robust are One-Sided Asymmetric Information Ultimatum Game Analyses?

As the earlier discussion of the various approaches used in perfect information suggests, model structure and assumptions play an important role in the predictions of the analysis. Is this a problem of "tune the dial and get another station?" In some sense it seems to be. Such models seem to provide conflicting predictions which: involve proposing one or the other player's concession limit (not in between, as the Nash Bargaining Solution provided); sometimes fully reveal private information, other times do not; and strongly restrict when and if players can make proposals at all.

However, some consistent threads emerge. Asymmetric information will generally result in some degree of inefficiency in the bargaining process due to some use of trial by the players. The extent of inefficiency is related to the nature of the distribution of the information, the range of the possible values that the private information can take on and the level of court costs. Higher court costs encourage settlement and influence the transfer between P and D. Asymmetric information means that the relatively less informed player needs to guard against misrepresentation by the more informed player, and must be willing to employ the threat of court. The signaling model indicated another aspect of this: even though P was informed and made the proposals, it was P who bore an inefficiency cost (D's expected payoff was what it would have been under imperfect information). This is because the private information that P possesses cannot be credibly communicated to D without a cost being incurred by P via the signaling of the information.

Clearly, both models use a highly stylized representation of bargaining. How restrictive is this? While this question is difficult to address very generally, some tests of the robustness of the model structure and the predictions exist. These analyses are of two types. (1) Would changes in sequence matter (who moves when, whether moves must be sequential, what if there were many opportunities to make proposals)? (2) Is the one-sided nature of information important; would each player having information on a relevant attribute of the game affect the outcome in a material way?

Papers by Daughety and Reinganum (1993), Wang, Kim and Yi (1994) and Spier (1992) address aspects of the first question above. Daughety and Reinganum provide a two-period model that allows players to move simultaneously or sequentially. Here, P and D can individually make (or individually not make) proposals in the first period and then choose to accept or reject whatever comes out of the first period during a second period; a rejection by either individual of the outcome of the first period means going to court. What comes out of the first period is: (1) no proposal, which guarantees court; (2) one proposal, provided by whomever made it; or (3) an intermediate version of two proposals if both players make one; the intermediate proposal is a general, commonly known function of the two individual proposals. An example of such a "compromise" function would be one that averaged the proposals, but the analysis is not restricted to that particular assumption. Note that this means that if both players make proposals, then intermediate outcomes are possible candidates as equilibria of the overall game. The model allows one-sided asymmetric information, but examines both possible cases in which a player is informed. The general result is that players do not choose to wait: they both make proposals in the first period. Thus, formally, the ultimatum structure wherein only one player makes a proposal is rejected as inconsistent with endogenously generated timing. However, the unique equilibrium of the game has the same payoffs as either that of the ultimatum signaling game or the ultimatum screening game; which one depends only on the compromise function used and which player is informed. Thus, in this sense, the ultimatum game provides a valuable tool of prediction.

The Wang, Kim and Yi (1994) paper discussed earlier in Section 3.2.2 also contains a continuum-type, one-sided asymmetric information model based on Rubinstein (1985). Wang, Kim and Yi consider the case of an informed P and an uninformed D, with D as first proposer. In subsequent periods proposers alternate. They show that the settlement outcome is consistent with a one-period D-proposer screening ultimatum game as discussed above. Finally, Spier (1992) (discussed in more detail in Section 18 below) also employs a dynamic model (in this case, a finite horizon model) with negotiating and trial costs. In her model, if negotiating costs are zero, then all bargaining takes place in the last period. Together, the three papers provide some limited theoretical support for using the ultimatum game approach to represent one-sided asymmetric information settlement problems.

The second issue, concerning one-sided versus two-sided information, is addressed in papers by Schweizer (1989), Daughety and Reinganum (1994), and Friedman and Wittman (2006).[18] Both Schweizer and Daughety and Reinganum consider ultimatum games where P is privately informed about damages and D is privately informed about liability. Schweizer considers a P-proposer model with two types on both sides while Daughety and Reinganum consider both P- and D-proposer models with a continuum of types on both sides. The results are fundamentally the same: the proposer signals and uses the signal to screen the responder. Thus, proposer types

---

[18] Sobel (1989) also considers a two-sided model, but his interest is discovery; this paper will be discussed in Section 19.

are revealed fully and responders are partially pooled. Friedman and Wittman consider a simultaneous-move game wherein each side receives a private signal and makes a proposed settlement offer. Offers are averaged and if the transfer is feasible (D offers no less than P demands), then a transfer is effected, otherwise trial ensues, at which point the court learns the private signals, averages them and makes a transfer. Thus, a specific protocol is employed.[19] Again, trial can occur in equilibrium, increases in trial costs reduce the likelihood of trial, and the distribution of cases that proceed to trial is altered by the presence of settlement bargaining.

In sum, it would appear that the screening and signaling models have reasonably robust qualitative properties (especially when viewed as alternatives, with the likely model a composite such as might arise via a random-proposer analysis) that survive relaxation of some of the underlying structure and that the intuition derived from the separate analyses survives the integration of both types of models in a more comprehensive analysis.

13. Summing Up the Theory

13.1 Comparing the Two-Type Models: Imperfect and Asymmetric Information

This section provides two means of comparison. First, employing specific numerical values, Table 15.3 below presents computations for the same data from imperfect, screening and signaling analyses; it also acts as a convenient summary of the strategies and payoffs for the different models. While the results do not purport to indicate magnitudes of differences in the predictions made, it will suggest directional differences. The directional differences will be amplified, based on the two-type analyses provided earlier, as the second means of comparison.

Table 15.3 considers a two-type model wherein P is informed of the true level of damages and D is not. D's prior assessment on the two levels of damages is that they are equally likely (this is to make comparisons easier). Court costs are the same for the two players and liability by D for damages is certain. Specific values of the data are provided at the top of Table 15.3. Note that (SSC) holds as shown. D's expectation of damages ($E_D(d)$) is the common expectation under imperfect information.

Table 15.3 concentrates on the ultimatum game predictions, but the

---

[19] This model also uses a special version of the notion of common value settlement bargaining since, rather than discover the "true" value of the parameter of interest (such as d), the court only learns the litigants' private signals, which it then averages. If these signals are unbiased, then the court's decision, in expectation, is the same as what normally occurs in the rest of the settlement bargaining literature.

Table 15.3 Ultimatum game results under imperfect and asymmetric information

Data: $d_H = 75$, $d_L = 25$, $\ell = 1$, $k_P = k_D = 10$, $p = 0.5$.
Thus, $E_D(d) = 50$ and (SSC) is met: $p = 0.5 > (k_p + k_D)/(d_H - d_L + k_P + k_n) = 0.29$

Model	D-proposer	NBS	P-proposer
Imp. Information	$s_D = E_D(d) - k_P = 40$	$s_D = s_P = 50$	$s_P = E_D(d) + k_D = 60$
	$\pi_D = 40$	$\pi_D = 50$	$\pi_D = 60$
	$\pi_P = 40$	$\pi_P = 50$	$\pi_P = 60$
	efficient	efficient	efficient
	no trials	no trials	no trials
Asy. Information: Screening	$s_D = d_L - k_P = 15$		
	$\pi_D = ps_D + (1-p)(d_H + k_P) = 50$		
	$\pi_L = d_L - k_P = 15$		
	$\pi_H = d_H - k_P = 65$		
	inefficient:		
	loss $= (1 - p)(k_P + k_D) = 10$		
	$\pi_D = E_D(d) + k_D - (1 - p)(k_P + k_D)$		
	$\quad = 50$		
	$\pi_P = p\pi_L + (1 - p)\pi_H = 40$		
	probability of trial $= (1 - p) = 0.5$		

Asy. Information: Signaling

$s_L = d_L + k_D = 35$
$s_H = d_H + k_D = 85$
$r_D(s_L) = 0$
$r_D(s_H) = (d_H - d_L)/(d_H - d_L + k_P + k_D)$
$\quad = 0.71$
$\pi_D = ps_L + (1-p)[(1 - r_D(s_H))s_H + r_D(s_H)s_H]$
$\quad = 60$
$\pi_L = s_L = 35$
$\pi_H = (1 - r_D(s_H))s_H + (r_D(s_H))(d_H - k_P)$
$\quad = 70.71$
inefficient:
loss $= (1-p)(k_P + k_D)r_D(s_H) = 7.14$
$\pi_D = E_D(d) + k_D$
$\quad = 60$
$\pi_P = p\pi_L + (1-p)\pi_H$
$\quad = 52.86$
probability of trial $= (1-p)r_D(s_H) = 0.36$

relevant imperfect information NBS is also provided, as shown near the top. Given the information endowments, the only asymmetric information D-proposer model is a screening model and the only P-proposer asymmetric information model is a signaling model. The table provides the proposer's proposal, the responder's strategy in the signaling case and the payoffs to the players. Note that π_L provides the payoff to a P with low damages, while π_H provides the payoff to a P with high damages. Finally, in the asymmetric information case, π_P provides the expected payoffs to a P before damages are observed so that *ex ante* efficiency can be evaluated. The statement "efficient" means that the outcome is on the settlement frontier, while "inefficient" means that the solution lies below the frontier, with the efficiency loss calculated as shown. Finally, the source of inefficiency, that some cases go to trial, is indicated by providing the probability of trial derived from the model used.

The example and the formulas in the table indicate that the efficiency losses predicted by the screening and signaling models, as compared with the efficient solutions in the imperfect information model, differ from one another. More generally, as long as p meets the simple screening condition (SSC) of Section 12.3.1, the signaling model predicts less of an efficiency loss than the screening model. This is because while a low-damages P settles out of court in both models, a high-damages P always goes to court under a screening model, while he only goes to court with a fractional likelihood under the signaling model. Note also, however, that when p does not satisfy (SSC), then the screening model's prediction is fully efficient (since all cases settle) while the signaling model still predicts an inefficient outcome.

A similar type of comparison could be performed for the ultimatum games involving asymmetric information about the likelihood of liability (with damages commonly known) or about the expected payoff from trial (that is, the product of damages and the likelihood that D is found liable). Typically, such analyses assume that D has private information about the true likelihood of being found liable. In the screening model, the higher-likelihood Ds settle and the lower-likelihood Ds reject P's offer and proceed to trial. In the signaling model, the higher-likelihood D makes an offer that P accepts, while the lower-likelihood D makes a lower offer that P rejects with an equilibrium rejection probability. Most notably, in the case wherein there is a continuum of types, the distribution of cases that go to trial include essentially all the D-types (with the preponderance of types being less likely to be held liable).

13.2 Asymmetric Information versus Other Models of Settlement Bargaining

It is worthwhile to take a moment to contrast the settlement bargaining literature using asymmetric information with the vast literature which has grown out of a paper by Priest and Klein (1984). Thoroughly reviewing the literature in this area (mainly empirical studies with a variety of predictions) would take us too far from our main purpose, but a few words are appropriate. The Priest-Klein model employs an inconsistent priors approach to examine the selection of cases that proceed to trial; the approach is often referred to as "divergent expectations" and generally assumes that the two litigants have inconsistent priors such that if both litigants' priors are "optimistic," then settlement can fail (the plaintiff's reservation value based on the expected payoff from trial will exceed the defendant's reservation value based on the expected cost of trial). The Priest-Klein model implies that the selection of cases that go to trial involves cases wherein the likelihood of either side winning approaches 50%. Waldfogel (1998) uses data from federal civil cases filed between 1979 and 1986 in the Southern District of New York, and compares a divergent expectations model with a one-sided asymmetric information screening model. Since a screening (or signaling) model with one-sided asymmetric information predicts that only the "strong" cases go to trial, then this model tends to shift the distribution of cases away from the 50% point, towards the extremes, a contrast with the Priest-Klein model.[20] Waldfogel reports that the divergent expectations model is generally consistent with the data, while the asymmetric information model is not. He also reports that asymmetric information modeling appears to be consistent with cases that terminated "early" (that is, where adjudication occurred before the complaint by the plaintiff was responded to via discovery and trial).

Note, however, that this "horse race" is not on a level playing field in the sense that the divergent expectations model is a two-sided model, while the asymmetric information model that is used for comparison purposes is one-sided. As Gertner and Miller (1995) argue, since it is difficult to understand how divergent opinions about each litigant's likelihood of success are likely to be communicated (as a standard divergent expectations model implicitly assumes), then such divergent opinions may be best thought of as private information, making the divergent expectations model more of

---

[20] As Shavell (1996) shows for the two-type screening case (and as is clearly also true for the signaling case and the continuum screening case), by varying parameters one can get essentially any prediction about the plaintiff win rate that is desired.

a special version of an asymmetric information model![21] Thus, the "horse race" should presumably reflect the differences that might come about between a two-sided inconsistent priors asymmetric information model and a two-sided consistent priors asymmetric information model.

Two papers discussed earlier (see Section 12.4) as part of the asymmetric information settlement bargaining literature that assume two-sided asymmetric information are Friedman and Wittman (2006) and Daughety and Reinganum (1994). As Friedman and Wittman note (see pp. 109–10), their predictions from a model of simultaneous offers are not distinguishable from those arising from a Priest-Klein model. In the Daughety and Reinganum analysis, each litigant has private information, but an ultimatum game model is analyzed. In that paper, the first-mover signals and the second-mover is screened. So if the private information for P (respectively, D) is about liability, and P's (respectively, D's) private information is ℓ_P (respectively, ℓ_D), then weak Ps (those with low values of ℓ_P) and weak Ds (those with high values of ℓ_D) will be more likely to settle, trimming the distribution from both ends – again, resembling the primary characteristic of the Priest-Klein approach.

Summing up, we are left with two essential points to consider. First, a divergent expectations model is probably best treated as an (inconsistent priors) asymmetric information model, as argued by Gertner and Miller, so that the issue is not so much asymmetric information as it is how priors arise. Second, (consistent priors) asymmetric information models with two-sided information exist; they are not intensively employed in theoretical analyses because they are considerably more complex than the one-sided models *and* because a random-proposer model, consisting of randomized selection between the two single-sided models, appears to cover the range of possible bargaining payoffs (though there is no theorem to this extent). Therefore, an empirical "horse race" on a level playing field may be difficult to achieve, since it will be a test of which information is taken as private and whether priors over that information are consistent or inconsistent.

Again, all this is not to say that inconsistent priors models are unworthy of exploration, just that the nature of the inconsistency needs to be developed very precisely. A nice example of such an analysis occurs in two recent papers by Yildiz (2003, 2004). In Yildiz (2003), bargainers play a modified version of the Rubinstein game: at each stage, Nature picks who will make an offer in each period, so that strict alternation of moves need not occur. The bargainers hold assessments over the likelihood that they will be picked ("recognized" by Nature) to make an offer in a period,

---

[21] In Section 19.3, we provide more detail on Gertner and Miller (1995).

and such assessments can reflect optimism in the sense that the sum of the players' assessments as to being recognized by Nature and being allowed to make the offer next period could exceed one. Making an offer entails the ability to exploit a rent by forcing the other bargainer to accept or face a diminished pie in the next period. While delay is a possible outcome, Yildiz shows that (if the degrees of optimism are common knowledge) if both litigants are sufficiently optimistic, delay will *not* occur. This is because optimism about large rents to be extracted in the future leads to less room to bargain and therefore lower rents to be extracted in the current time period, so that it is better to settle than wait. Thus, excessive optimism does not, in and of itself, lead to inefficiency. However, as Yildiz (2004) shows, learning over time about the likelihood of being the next one to make an offer can lead to delay.

C. VARIATIONS ON THE BASIC MODELS

14. Overview

This part locates and briefly reviews a number of recent contributions to the settlement literature. Two cautions should be observed. First, no effort will be made to discuss unpublished work. This is motivated primarily by the fact that such work is, generally, not as accessible to most readers as are the journals in which published work has appeared. There are some classic unpublished papers (some of which have significantly influenced the existing published papers) that are thereby slighted, and our apologies to their authors. Potentially, such a policy also hastens the date of the succeeding survey.

Second, the selection to be discussed is a subset of the existing published papers: it is not meant to be comprehensive. Instead, the selection is meant to show ideas that have been raised, or how approaches have been revised. A limited number of papers that address relevant issues, but which are not focused on settlement itself, are also mentioned.

Following the outline of Part A, papers will be grouped as follows: (1) players; (2) actions and strategies; (3) outcomes and payoffs; (4) timing and (5) information. Not surprisingly, many papers could conceivably fit in a number of categories, and a few cross-references will be made.

15. Players

15.1 Attorneys

Watts (1994) adds an attorney for P (denoted A_P) to the set of players in a screening analysis of a P-proposer ultimatum game; D is privately informed about expected damages at trial (for a discussion of agency problems in contingent fee arrangements, see Miller, 1987). The main role of A_P is expertise: A_P can engage, at a cost, in discovery efforts which release some predetermined portion of D's information. The cost to A_P is lower than the cost of obtaining the same information would be to P. Moreover, more precise information about D's likely type costs more to obtain (for either P or A_P) than less precise information (precision is determined exogenously in this model). Before bargaining with D, P can choose whether or not to hire A_P, and attorneys are paid on a contingency basis. If hired, A_P obtains information about D's type and then makes a settlement proposal to D. Given the precision of obtainable information and the expertise of A_P (that is, A_P's cost of obtaining information as a fraction of P's cost of obtaining the same information), Watts finds a range of contingency fees that P and A_P could agree upon (a settlement frontier for *P and A_P* to bargain over); she also finds that their concession limits decrease as the expected court award in the settlement problem with D increases.

Kahan and Tuckman (1995), Polinsky and Rubinfeld (2002), and Chen and Wang (2006) also provide models in which, once hired under a contingent-fee contract, A_P chooses the settlement demand, whether to proceed to trial, and how much to spend at trial, if negotiations fail. Kahan and Tuckman examine the impact of split-award statutes (this paper is discussed further in Section 17.3 below). Polinsky and Rubinfeld examine the impact of contingent fees; they find that the common intuition that A_P will settle too often and for too little may be overturned when litigation costs are endogenous. Since A_P will choose lower effort at trial, litigation costs may actually be lower under contingent fees, which tends to make A_P a tougher pretrial bargainer.[22] Chen and Wang examine the impact of fee-shifting based on the trial outcome; they find that A_P will bargain more aggressively under the "loser pays" rule than under the "pay your own" rule.

In all of these papers, there is an "agency" problem in the sense that A_P's choices would not coincide with those that maximize the plaintiff's side's payoff (call these the "benchmark outcome" choices), due to the fact that under a contingency fee, A_P receives a fraction of the award or settlement but pays all of the costs in the event of trial. Polinsky and Rubinfeld (2003) propose a compensation scheme for plaintiffs' lawyers that would align the incentives of lawyers with those of their clients. In order to achieve

---

[22] See also Rickman (1999) for a somewhat different model wherein an attorney can be a tougher bargainer when compensated via a contingent fee.

this alignment, it is necessary for A_P to bear the same share of the costs as he receives of the award (or settlement); let this share be denoted α. By hypothesis, the client cannot pay a share of the costs (which is the main rationale for using a contingent fee) so this must be paid by a "third-party administrator." Essentially, the attorney contracts with a third-party administrator under the following terms: the third-party administrator will pay the attorney the share $1 - \alpha$ of the attorney's expected litigation costs based on his actual choices (leaving the attorney to bear the share α of these costs). In exchange, the attorney makes a lump-sum up-front payment to the third-party administrator that is equal to the amount $(1 - \alpha)$ times the attorney's expected litigation costs in the *benchmark* outcome. Since this contract induces the attorney to make the benchmark outcome choices, the attorney's and client's interests are aligned and the third-party administrator breaks even.

15.2 Judges and Juries

As mentioned earlier, J is generally modeled in this literature as learning the truth and making awards equal to the true damages. Some models have allowed for unsystematic error on the part of J. For instance, Hylton (2002) and Landeo, Nikitin and Baker (2006) model the life-cycle of a tort (from the choice of precaution through the occurrence of harm, filing suit, settlement negotiations and trial) under the assumption that the court makes random errors. Hylton's court errs with respect to the defendant's liability, and this has an ambiguous effect on the settlement rate, while Landeo, Nikitin and Baker's court errs with respect to the level of the award, which turns out to promote settlement.

In the basic asymmetric information models described earlier, the informed player usually computes payoffs at trial on the basis that their true type will be fully revealed in court. Thus, a useful extension of the basic model would indicate how J learns the true type or, if J doesn't learn the true type, what J does in that event. In general, what the parties anticipate that J will know (and how J might learn it) could influence the settlement strategies and outcomes.

Daughety and Reinganum (1995) consider a J whose omniscience is parametric (that is, with an exogenously specified probability, J learns the truth; if not, J must infer it based upon P and D's observable actions) in a continuum-type ultimatum game signaling model, wherein P is informed about damages and D is not. J is a second "receiver" of a signal. If all that is observable to J is the failure of settlement negotiations (for example, because the content of failed settlement negotiations is inadmissible as evidence at trial), then when J observes that a case comes to trial, he can infer the distribution of such cases (using the posterior model shown in

Figure 15.4) and pick a best award (note that this means that all the elements of the settlement game are common knowledge to J, as is this fact to P, D and J). If J can also observe P's settlement demand, then he uses that information, too. The result is that this feeds back into the settlement process, resulting in P making demands to influence J.[23] As J's dependence on such information increases (omniscience decreases), revelation via the settlement demand disappears as more and more types of P pool by making a high demand (P "plays to the judge"). The result can be that, for sufficiently high reliance on observation instead of omniscience, J has even less information than if he couldn't observe P's settlement demand at all (and must rely on the posterior distribution of unsettled cases).

Influencing J is also the topic of Rubinfeld and Sappington (1987) which, while not focused on settlement *per se*, does model how effort by players can inform J. The setting is nominally a criminal trial, but the point potentially applies to civil cases, too: if innocent Ds should be able (more readily than guilty Ds) to obtain evidence supporting their innocence, then the amount of effort so placed can act as a signal to J of D's innocence or guilt. This is not a perfect signal, in the sense that the types of D are not fully revealed. As in much of the literature dealing with criminal defendants (this is discussed in more detail in Section 17.4 below), J here maximizes a notion of justice that trades off the social losses from punishing the innocent versus freeing the guilty and accounts for the costs incurred by D in the judicial process.

One final note on this topic. There is an enormous literature on jury and judicial decision-making spread across the psychology, political science, sociology and law literatures that has yet to have the impact it deserves on formal models of settlement bargaining.

15.3 Multiple Litigants
Many settings involve multiple litigants (for example, airline crashes, drug side-effects, etc.).[24] Che and Yi (1993) consider a game in which D faces two Ps sequentially. The model is a sequence of two D-proposer ultimatum games, where D faces informed Ps in the two games. The outcome

---

[23] Kim and Ryu (2000) reconsider the admissibility issue under somewhat different assumptions; they use a screening model (so the uninformed defendant now makes the offer) and the judge is assumed to receive a noisy signal about damages. They find that when the judge observes D's offer and P's rejection, then P will reject a larger set of offers in order to influence to her advantage the judge's subsequent beliefs about the level of damages.

[24] See Daughety and Reinganum (2005) and Spier (2007) for a more in-depth discussion of multi-litigant models.

in the first trial may be precedential for the second trial in the following sense: if the first plaintiff (P_1) wins (respectively, loses) her case, then the second plaintiff (P_2) has a higher likelihood of winning (respectively, losing) her case. D can avoid setting a precedent by settling with P_1. They find that there is a critical value of D's likelihood of winning the first case such that, if D's likelihood of winning exceeds this critical level, then he is less willing to settle with P_1 (because he anticipates setting a favorable precedent for the second case), while if D's likelihood of winning is less than this critical level, then he is more willing to settle with P_1 (because he anticipates setting an unfavorable precedent for the second case).[25]

Yang (1996) also uses a sequence of two D-proposer ultimatum games where D faces informed Ps, but now the damages are correlated. Note that when D plays the second ultimatum game, the correlation of levels of damages over plaintiffs means that learning in game one affects D's strategy in game two, thereby feeding back into D's game one strategy choice. Yang includes the decision by both informed Ps to initially file their respective cases. Thus, D's actions with respect to P_1, and the likely outcome from going to trial, may deter P_2 from filing. Yang finds conditions under which this causes D, in dealing with P_1, to be more or less aggressive than the one-p model would find. While more aggressive play (being "tough") against P_1 may seem intuitive, less aggressive play is also reasonable if going to trial will reveal information that would encourage P_2 to file (such as, that P_1 had high damages). Why would this encourage P_2, who knows his own damages? Assume that P_2 is a low-level-of-damages plaintiff. By making a pooling offer to P_1, D does not learn P_1's type, and P_2 would be aware of this ignorance. Thus, P_2 knows that D is still uninformed, and cannot capitalize on D having received "bad news" that P_1 is a high-level-of-damages plaintiff, shifting upward D's prior assessment about P_2 (recall that D takes damages as correlated). There is a strategic advantage to not being informed if the knowledge of the information places you at a disadvantage. If D remains uninformed, then if P_2 is low she can't expect D to overestimate her as high and make a second pooling offer.

Several other issues become salient when there are multiple litigants on one (or both) sides of a case. For instance, suppose that a single plaintiff is suing multiple defendants who are subject to "joint and several liability;" that is, each defendant may (in principle) be held liable for the full

---

[25] Briggs et al. (1996) consider a government antitrust suit, which may be followed by a private suit for damages. They show that the government suit will settle less often when there is the potential for a follow-on suit. This is because settlement is taken as an admission of liability in their model (which invites the follow-on suit), while there is a chance of winning at trial (which deters the follow-on suit).

amount of the plaintiff's harm, even though each defendant may have contributed fractionally to the occurrence of that harm.[26] Kornhauser and Revesz (1994a, 1994b) provide a complete-information model in which two defendants (D_1 and D_2) have contributed equally to a plaintiff's harm. P has a probability of prevailing against each defendant separately, as well as a probability of prevailing against both defendants in a single trial; the latter probability may exhibit some degree of correlation. Specifically, suppose that p is the probability that P will prevail against D_1 alone and that δp is the probability that P will prevail against D_2, having prevailed against D_1, in a trial against both defendants. If $\delta = 1$, then the cases are uncorrelated (two coins are flipped, each with probability p of coming up Heads), while if $\delta = 1/p$, then the cases are perfectly correlated (a single coin flip, with probability p of coming up Heads, applies to both cases). The plaintiff makes simultaneous settlement offers to D_1 and D_2, who decide noncooperatively whether to accept or reject their respective offers (if only one defendant settles, then the amount of the settlement is deducted from the total damages, and the second defendant is only responsible for the residual). Although one might expect all cases to settle under conditions of common knowledge, Kornhauser and Revesz show that both cases go to trial when the correlation is sufficiently low, and both cases settle when the correlation is sufficiently high.

Spier (2002) uses a related model to analyze the problem of two plaintiffs (P_1 and P_2) facing a single potentially insolvent defendant. In this model, D makes simultaneous offers to the two plaintiffs, who decide noncooperatively whether to accept or reject their respective offers. If only one plaintiff accepts, then the amount of her settlement is deducted from D's available wealth. Again, each plaintiff has a probability of prevailing against D separately, and a probability of prevailing against him when they both go to trial; again, this latter probability may involve some correlation. In this model, it turns out that both cases go to trial when the correlation is sufficiently high, while both cases settle when the correlation is sufficiently low. Again, it is worth noting that both the Kornhauser and Revesz papers, and the Spier paper, show that the presence of multiple litigants alone can cause bargaining failure; both papers involve complete information (though information is imperfect in the sense that simultaneous moves occur).

Class action lawsuits involve situations wherein the plaintiff's side (or the defendant's side, or both sides) consists of several litigants whose cases

---

[26] A recent review of the current status of joint and several liability is contained in Marcus (2007).

are consolidated through class certification because the issues in dispute are sufficiently similar (for example, the defendant's liability, the extent of damages, or both). Individual litigants may opt out of the class and pursue their own suits separately. One reason for opting out is to avoid "damages averaging;" if each member of a plaintiff class will be awarded the average damages associated with the class membership, then a plaintiff with high damages may prefer to pursue an individual suit. Che (1996) provides a model of class formation in which plaintiffs may have high or low damages, and any settlement or award obtained by the class is divided equally among the class members. Although each plaintiff's harm is known within the class, D is unable to observe the plaintiffs' types (that is, their damages levels). Che finds that the class must include both high- and low-damaged plaintiffs; moreover, some high-damaged plaintiffs and some low-damaged plaintiffs must opt out of the class. This is because if only plaintiffs of one type chose the same action (whether that action is to join the class or to opt out of it), then that action would serve as a perfect signal of the plaintiff's type, and others (of both types) would be induced to send the same signal, or avoid sending it, depending on the inference drawn. For example, if only high-damaged plaintiffs opt out of the class, then D would be willing to make a high settlement offer to opt-outs; but then a low-damaged plaintiff could opt out and receive a high settlement offer, upsetting the hypothesized equilibrium. Che (2002) reconsiders this model under the assumption that the plaintiffs' damages are their individual private information even within the class, so the class must use an internal allocation mechanism to induce its members to reveal their types truthfully. In this case, the class will require a higher settlement offer (than if it did not have this internal information problem) because the settlement will also have to cover the information rents that are necessary to induce truthful revelation.

Che and Spier (2008) examine a dynamic model of settlement bargaining between a defendant and the members of a plaintiff class. There are scale economies in litigation, so that more plaintiffs reduce the cost per plaintiff of trial. If no single plaintiff would proceed to trial on her own, then Che and Spier demonstrate how a defendant can use sequential bargaining with different offers to different plaintiffs to undermine the credibility of suit by the plaintiff class. Essentially, when D settles with a given plaintiff, she drops out of the suit, thus raising the cost per plaintiff for those who remain in the class. Eventually, continuing on to trial becomes too expensive for the remaining class members, who then drop their suit. This result is robust to changing the timing of moves, as now plaintiffs "compete" for settlement offers, and (at least to some extent) to private information on the part of the plaintiffs. However, some collective strategies on the part of the class members can be effective at preventing the class from unraveling; these include considering only non-discriminatory offers, requiring a unanimous vote to accept an offer, or making side payments within the class.

Some lawsuits need not involve multiple litigants, but end up doing so because of litigant-generated externalities. Two prominent examples are the use of confidentiality agreements and most-favored-nation clauses in settlements. If a single defendant (with private information about his likelihood of being found liable) has harmed multiple plaintiffs, then the existence and outcome of an early plaintiff's case can be informative to a later plaintiff. If suppressing this information is of value to D, then the early plaintiff can charge D (in terms of a higher settlement demand) for providing confidentiality. Daughety and Reinganum (1999, 2002) provide models in which the parties in an instant case may engage in confidential settlement; this is to the detriment of future plaintiffs, but confidentiality reduces litigation costs overall by increasing the likelihood that the early suit settles and by reducing the likelihood that the later suit is filed. These models differ in the degree to which D's liability is correlated across cases; when it is weakly correlated, then the early plaintiff is able to extract the full value of confidentiality to D, leaving his incentives for care intact, but when it is strongly correlated, then D retains some of the value of confidentiality (that is, he receives an information rent) and his incentives for care are undermined.

A "most-favored-nation" (MFN) clause in a settlement agreement between a defendant and one or more early-settling plaintiffs specifies that, should the defendant subsequently settle with another plaintiff on more favorable terms, then the early-settling plaintiffs are retroactively entitled to the same (more favorable) terms. Spier (2003a, 2003b) considers a defendant facing many plaintiffs, each of whom has private information about her harm. D has the opportunity to make an offer in each of two periods (thus, this is a screening model since the uninformed player moves first). A plaintiff can accept the first offer or wait for the second offer; then she can accept the second offer or choose trial. When bargaining without an MFN, Spier shows that D will make an increasing sequence of offers. Anticipating this, some plaintiffs who prefer the first offer to trial will nevertheless wait for the higher second offer, and D will incur bargaining and delay costs for two periods. However, if the first offer includes an MFN, then in equilibrium D's second offer will never be higher than the first (for then D would have to retroactively compensate those plaintiffs who settled in the first period, and this serves as a deterrent to raising his second-period offer). Thus, D can use an MFN to commit himself to a first-and-final settlement offer; knowing this, plaintiffs have no strategic reason to delay settlement, and D's bargaining and delay costs are confined to one period. Depending on the distribution of damages, the use of an MFN may result in a higher or lower frequency of trial; that is, there are some distributions for which the use of an MFN reduces expected litigation costs.

Daughety and Reinganum (2004) examine the use of an MFN by an early-bargaining plaintiff who anticipates the subsequent arrival of another plaintiff. Again, the plaintiffs have private information about their harms, but now the plaintiffs make the settlement demands (thus, this is a signaling model since the informed player moves first). Recall that in the signaling model, the privately-informed plaintiff has an incentive to inflate her demand, so the defendant must reject higher demands with a higher probability in order to deter this behavior. Daughety and Reinganum find that an early-settling plaintiff will find it optimal to include an MFN with her settlement demand for two reasons. First, if D accepts the demand, then the early plaintiff has the opportunity to receive a retroactive payment should D settle with the later plaintiff on better terms (and this will occur in equilibrium with positive probability). Second, because the early plaintiff puts this extra payment at risk if she makes a higher demand, D need not reject the early plaintiff's demand as often in order to deter her from inflating it. This use of an MFN by the early-settling plaintiff leaves D's equilibrium payoff unchanged, while the early plaintiff benefits at the expense of the later plaintiff. Overall, expected litigation costs are lower when an MFN is used, again for two reasons. First, as mentioned above, D rejects the early plaintiff's demand less often. Second, with an MFN in place, the later plaintiff moderates her demand when it would trigger the MFN, and lower demands are rejected less often by D.

16. Actions and Strategies

16.1 Credibility of Proceeding to Trial should Negotiations Fail
In the screening examples in Section 12.3 above, an uninformed D made an offer to an informed P, with liability commonly known but the level of damages the source of the informational asymmetry. For convenience of exposition, consider the reversed setting, with D informed about the likelihood of being found liable at trial, P uninformed, but both commonly knowledgeable about the level of damages (this is the original Bebchuk example). Thus, a screening analysis means a P-proposer ultimatum model. In this context, Nalebuff (1987) examines the assumption that P is committed to proceeding to trial after bargaining fails (alternatively put, he relaxes the assumption that there is a minimum positive

likelihood of liability that, multiplied by the level of damages, would exceed P's court costs: this is the analogy to our earlier assumption that $d_L > k_P$ holds).[27]

Nalebuff considers cases that, initially, have "merit": $E_P(d) > k_P$. He appends a second decision by P (concerning whether or not to take the case to trial) to the P-proposer ultimatum game screening model. After observing the response by D to the screening demand made by P, P recomputes $E_P(d)$ using his posterior assessment; denote this as $E_P(d|$ D's response), meaning P's expectation of the level of damages which will be awarded in court given D's choice to accept or reject the offer. Since all types whose true likelihood of liability implied levels of expected damages in excess of that associated with the demand (that is, the more likely-to-be-liable types of D) have accepted the demand, the collection of types of D who would reject the demand by P are those with stronger cases (that is, those that are less likely to be held liable). Thus, P's new expected payoff from proceeding to trial, $E_P(d|$ D's response) $- k_P$, is lower than before the bargaining began ($E_P(d) - k_P$). The decision by P as to whether or not to actually litigate *after* seeing the outcome of the screening offer results in a reversal of some of the predictions made by the original screening model about the impact that changes in the levels of damages and court costs will have on settlement demands and the likelihood of trial.

For example, Nalebuff shows that the settlement demand in the relaxed model is *higher* than that in the model with commitment. Why would this happen? To see why, consider what happens in stages. When P is making his settlement demand, he is also considering the downstream decision he will be making about going to trial and must choose a settlement demand that makes his later choice of trial credible. If P can no longer be committed to going to trial with any D who rejects his screening demand, this means that he will use $E_P(d|$ D's response) to decide about going to trial, and this is now heavily influenced by the presence of "tough" types; those types that are "weak," that is, who have high likelihoods of liability, have accepted P's offers. Thus, if P raises his settlement demand, some of the intermediate types will pool with the tough types, resulting in $E_P(d|$ D's response) $- k_P > 0$, making the threat of trial credible. Thus, the effect of relaxing the assumption that P necessarily litigates any case that rejects his settlement demand actually results in an increased demand being made.

---

[27] Several papers discussed below have integrated a Nalebuff-inspired credibility constraint into their analyses of related issues.

16.2 Filing and Pursuing a Claim

One potential effect of a cost associated with filing a suit is to provide a disincentive for a P pursuing what is known as a "nuisance" suit. The definition of what a nuisance is varies somewhat, but generally, such a suit has a negative expected value (NEV) to P; that is, $E_P(d) < k_P$; such a suit is not one that P would actually pursue to trial should negotiations fail (note that this ignores any psychic benefits that P may derive from "having his day in court" which might make such a suit have a positive expected utility). Clearly, the reason for consideration of NEV suits is the perception that plaintiffs can pursue NEV suits and obtain settlements: the asymmetry of information between an informed P and an uninformed D allows plaintiffs with NEV suits to mimic PEV suits (positive expected value suits) and extract a settlement. Two questions have arisen in this context: what contributes to the incentive for plaintiffs to pursue NEV suits and what attributes of the process might reduce or eliminate it?

An example may be of use at this point. Consider a D facing three possible types of P, with possible damages $d_N = 0$, $d_L = \$10,000$ and $d_H = \$50,000$, respectively and with associated likelihoods $p_N = 0.1$, $p_L = 0.3$ and $p_H = 0.6$ (N here stands for "nuisance"). Further assume both P and D have court costs of $2,000. The screening equilibrium involves the firm offering $8,000 and settling with the nuisance and the low-damages type and going to court against the high-damages type: the nuisance-type benefitted from the presence of the low-damage type and the expected costs to the firm are higher (an average expected cost of $34,400 per case) than would obtain if the nuisance type had not been present (an average expected cost of $33,600 per case).

P'ng (1983), in one of the earliest papers to consider strategic aspects of settlement bargaining, endogenizes both the choice by P to file a case and the choice to later drop the case should bargaining fail; NEV suits are considered, but the level of settlement is exogenously determined in this model. Rosenberg and Shavell (1985) found NEV suits can occur if filing costs for P are sufficiently low when compared with D's defense costs and if D must incur these costs before P must incur any settlement or trial costs. Bebchuk (1988) provides an asymmetric information (P is informed), D-proposer ultimatum game that specifically admits NEV suits (that is, no assumption is made that all suits are PEV). Filing costs are zero. Bebchuk shows how court costs and the probability assessment of the possible levels of damages influences settlement offers and rates. He finds that when NEV suits are possible, a reduction in settlement offers in PEV cases and an increase in the fraction of PEV cases that go to trial, when compared with an analysis assuming only PEV suits, is predicted.

Katz (1990) considers how filing and settlement bargaining affects incentives for frivolous lawsuits. By a frivolous suit, Katz means one with zero damages and positive court costs; the numerical example above involved a frivolous suit. Katz appends a filing decision made by an informed P to a D-proposer ultimatum game. This is a two-type model (the paper also includes a continuum-type extension) with $d_L = 0$. The modification of the D-proposer model is that the offer is either the high-damage P's concession limit or zero, so the strategy for D becomes the probability of making the high-damage concession limit offer. P's filing strategy is whether or not to file; if he files, P incurs a cost f_P. Of course, once incurred, this cost is sunk. Under the assumption that $d_H - k_P - f_P > 0$, and if a condition similar in notion to (SSC) is violated, then in equilibrium both types of Ps file cases, D pools the Ps by offering the high-damage P's concession limit, $d_H - k_P$, to all Ps and all Ps accept. Katz also addresses a case selection issue: such a policy by D will attract frivolous cases, changing the likelihood that a randomly selected case is frivolous. Thus, the profits from filing a frivolous case will be driven to zero. In this "competitive" equilibrium, Katz shows that the likelihood of trial is not a function of p or k_D, but it is increasing in f_P and decreasing in $E_D(d)$.

Rosenberg and Shavell (2006) suggest that, once P files suit, D should have the option to petition the court not to enforce any settlement agreement that D might conclude with the instant P. D would exercise this option when he expects that P's suit has negative expected value; anticipating this, such a P would be deterred from filing suit. Absent this commitment, D would be unable to prevent himself from settling with P. Of course, this procedure would facilitate the deterrence of even valid NEV suits (not just frivolous suits). Moreover, if D is uncertain about whether the suit is NEV or PEV and he exercises this option, then he would not be able to settle the case upon learning subsequently that it is PEV.

A recent line of research reconsiders whether an NEV suit can be pursued credibly, even when it is common knowledge that it is an NEV suit. Bebchuk (1996) argues that some NEV suits can be made credible if litigation costs are divisible and can be sunk strategically during the pretrial time period.[28] The key is to ensure that, at every pretrial stage, the next installment of litigation costs is sufficiently small as to render credible the plaintiff's threat to proceed to the next stage (and, ultimately, to trial).

---

[28] Klement (2003) argues that Bebchuk's result is not robust to the inclusion of private information on the part of D about his expected liability. The uninformed party P is assumed to make a series of settlement demands, each of which entails sinking more of the total litigation costs; by rejecting P's demands, D signals that his expected liability is low. It is shown that this "stonewalling" by D can deter many NEV suits regardless of the extent of cost divisibility.

At the last pretrial stage, if P has already sunk enough of the litigation costs, then she will have a credible threat to go to trial, and the parties will settle; Bebchuk uses a random-proposer model to determine the amount of the settlement. Anticipating that settlement will occur should the parties reach the last pretrial stage, if the next installment of litigation costs is less than the expected settlement, then the parties will settle in the penultimate pretrial stage. This backward induction continues with the result that, if each installment of litigation costs is not too large, then settlement will occur in the first pretrial stage, despite the fact that it is common knowledge that the expected value of P's suit is less than P's total litigation costs.

Schwartz and Wickelgren (2009) argue that plaintiffs cannot use this "cost-sinking" strategy in order to render NEV suits credible. The crux of their argument is that Bebchuk has assumed a random-proposer model in which one litigant makes the offer, while the other can only accept or reject; that is, there is no opportunity to make a counteroffer. In the random-proposer model, P will receive none of the surplus when D is the proposer and P will receive all of the surplus when she is the proposer. Schwartz and Wickelgren argue that bargaining is better-modeled as a sequence of alternating offers in which P has the outside option of going to trial; moreover, in their model, the parties can make as many offers and counteroffers as they like within each pretrial stage. They then assert that, at *every* stage, D only needs to offer P an amount that is just sufficient to make her prefer settlement to her outside option, giving P essentially none of the surplus from settlement. Schwartz and Wickelgren argue that, whatever P demands, D should simply counteroffer with this "just sufficient" offer (and keep on doing so indefinitely). It is credible for D to do this since he does not lose from delay (while the plaintiff does). Although both parties have equal formal bargaining power in the sense that each party can always make a counteroffer, their asymmetric time preferences allow D to push P to her concession limit (the value of her outside option). Thus, under this bargaining protocol, it is not possible for the plaintiff to extract a settlement when it is common knowledge that her suit is NEV.

A crucial difference between the Bebchuk model and that of Schwartz and Wickelgren is that Bebchuk assumes a fixed finite number of offers; for example, if making and responding to offers is costly and there is a deadline, then there is a "last" offer and there is a positive probability that P will make the last offer. Schwartz and Wickelgren assume an indefinite number of offers; for example, if it is possible to make offers and respond to them arbitrarily quickly, then there is no "last" offer. In this case, D's ability always to make a counteroffer results in P receiving simply the value of her outside option, which is negative by hypothesis. Clearly, both of these underlying "stories" about bargaining are abstractions to some extent; the careful analysis provided by these two articles indicates that whether one believes that cost-sinking can be used to render an NEV suit credible will depend on which of these stories one deems more representative of "real" settlement bargaining. This also suggests that a game wherein the proposal/response-period length and frequency are determined endogenously would be of interest. For instance, suppose that every proposal requires careful evaluation by an attorney, which is a costly and time-consuming activity. Would it be optimal for a party to hire a busy lawyer (that is, one with other clients in the queue with equally pressing issues) in order to make credible a certain amount of delay (and perhaps thereby generate a "last" period)?

16.3 Counterclaims
Using an imperfect information model, Landes (1994) shows that counterclaims (suits filed by D against P as part of the existing action by P against D, rather than filed as a separate lawsuit) do not always reduce P's incentive to sue, and may (by raising the stakes in the game) actually increase the likelihood of the case going to trial. This is based on mutual optimism about each player's own claim (mutual optimism involves each player expecting to win the action that they initiated; this need not involve inconsistent priors, as discussed in Section 6). Under these conditions, the counterclaim reduces the size of the settlement frontier (and possibly eliminates it).

17. Outcomes and Payoffs

17.1 Risk Aversion
Most of the earliest analyses allowed for risk aversion by assuming that payoffs were in utility rather than monetary terms. The Nash Bargaining Solution can be applied to such problems (now all four axioms come into play), again yielding a unique solution, though not necessarily where the 45° line crosses the frontier. The solution is efficient (due to axiom 2; see Section 8.2) in perfect and imperfect information cases. The divergence of the solution from the 45° line reflects the relative risk aversion of the two players, with the more risk-averse player receiving a smaller share of the pie (see, for example, Binmore, 1992, pp. 193–4).

There is a similar analysis in the perfect information strategic bargaining literature, where risk is introduced into an infinite horizon game by ignoring the time value of money but incorporating a probability of negotiations breaking down. Once again, for players whose preferences over outcomes reflect aversion to risk, the less risk-averse player gets the greater share of the pie (see Binmore, Rubinstein and Wolinsky, 1986).

In the settlement context, Farmer and Pecorino (1994) view a player's risk preferences as private information. While trial outcomes are uncertain, the likelihood of the outcomes themselves is common knowledge. P is taken to be risk averse (that is, privately informed of his risk preferences) and D is risk neutral and uninformed; the model allows for two types of P (extension to three types is also considered). This is a D-proposer ultimatum model; if the roles of proposer were reversed, then P's risk aversion would not interfere with an efficient settlement solution, so the order here is crucial to obtaining the possibility of trial. A standard screening condition is found (not unlike (SSC)), but more interesting is the result that increases in the uncertainty of the trial outcome result in the screening condition being more readily met, thereby increasing the likelihood of trial (a result consistent with the earlier analysis involving risk aversion). This occurs because it is the most risk-averse Ps that settle, and the greater the uncertainty, the more they are prepared to accept a settlement in lieu of court, which encourages D to make tougher offers.

17.2 Offer-Based Fee-Shifting Rules

Many settlement papers consider the allocation of court costs (fee-shifting) as part of their overall analysis. Typically, comparisons are made between the "American" system (each player pays their own costs) and the "British" system (the loser pays all costs). The very common association in the literature of loser pays with Britain potentially understates the contrast; see Posner (1992), who uses the term "English and Continental" to emphasize that a significant portion of the world uses loser pays. All the discussions in this survey have employed the pay-your-own system. The allocation of court costs is an extensive topic, with a typical result being that the loser-pays system discourages low-probability-of-prevailing plaintiffs more than the pay-your-own system (see Shavell, 1982), but other observations are that it may (or may not) adversely affect the likelihood of settlement (see Bebchuk, 1984, and Reinganum and Wilde, 1986). A more recent extension of the basic fee-shifting discussion to making fee-shifting dependent upon the magnitude of the outcome is discussed in Bebchuk and Chang (1996). Finally, Klement and Neeman (2005) ask what settlement procedure and litigation cost allocation system minimizes expected litigation cost subject to maintaining a constant level of deterrence. They find that the optimal procedure involves an upper bound on the allowable rate of settlement (excessive settlement undermines deterrence). Moreover, any procedure that achieves this upper bound must involve the "loser pays" cost-shifting arrangement. Since the general area of fee-shifting is a separate topic in its own right (which is likely to be addressed in a number of other surveys in these volumes), this survey will not attempt to cover it.

A related issue is recent work on Rule 68 of the US Federal Rules of Civil Procedure, as an example of a variety of *offer-based* fee-shifting rules which directly address settlement offers made by defendants and rejected by plaintiffs. First, it should be noted that, under long-standing practice, and also under many state rules of evidence and US Federal Rule of Evidence 408, information on settlement proposals and responses is not generally admissible as evidence at trial; a similar type of restriction usually applies in criminal cases to information about plea bargaining. Rule 68 includes restrictions on the use of settlement proposals at trial.

Thus, in the case of offer-based fee-shifting, offers are not used in court to infer true damages or actual liability; rather they influence the final payoffs from the game *after* an award has been made at trial. Rule 68, for example, links settlement choices to post-trial outcomes by penalizing a plaintiff for certain costs (court costs and, sometimes, attorney fees) when the trial award is less favorable than the defendant's "final" proposal (properly documented). As Spier (1994a) points out, the stated purpose of such a rule is to encourage settlement (Spier also provides other examples of offer-based rules similar in nature to Rule 68). Spier employs screening in a D-proposer ultimatum game. In comparison to the likelihood of settlement without Rule 68, she finds that under Rule 68: (1) disputes by P and D over damages are more likely to settle; and (2) disputes over liability or the likelihood of winning are less likely to settle. Spier also finds that the design of a bargaining procedure and fee-shifting rule that maximizes the probability of settlement yields a rule that penalizes either player for rejecting proposals that were better than the actual outcome of trial, providing some theoretical support for offer-based fee-shifting rules such as Rule 68.

17.3 Damage Awards
In previous sections of this summary, the award at trial has been the level of damages associated with the plaintiff who goes to court. This, minus court costs, becomes P's threat. This is based on J choosing an award that best approximates P's damages. Other criteria for choosing awards are also reasonable. For example, J might choose awards that maximize overall social efficiency or that minimize the probability of trial.

Polinsky and Che (1991) study decoupled liability: what D pays need not be what P receives. By decoupling, incentives for plaintiffs to sue can be optimized, while incentives for potential defendants to improve the level of care can be increased; that is, both goals can be pursued without necessarily conflicting. In particular, they show that the optimal payment by D will equal his wealth and the optimal award to P will be somewhat lower, as long as D is not too wealth-constrained (when D's wealth is too small, then the optimal award to P may exceed D's wealth). Choi and Sanchirico (2004) show that when effort at trial is also endogenous, then the optimal payment by D may well be less than his wealth, since raising the payment by D induces a more vigorous (and expensive) defense. Moreover, the optimal recovery by P may well exceed the optimal payment by D. Finally, Chu and Chien (2007) use a screening model to argue that, if settlement negotiations take place under asymmetric information, then the optimal award to P cannot be lowered beyond a certain threshold (which depends on the specified payment by D) without undermining P's ultimate threat to take the case to trial. As in Nalebuff (1987), when the credibility of P's threat is in doubt, P must make a higher demand and induce more defendant types to reject it, so as to retain a sufficiently rich defendant pool to justify taking the case to trial. Thus, lowering P's award beyond this threshold does not have the intended effect of reducing trials; indeed, it has the opposite effect. The optimal decoupled liability rule in this context involves setting P's award at the threshold level (which establishes a specific relationship between P's award and D's payment) and then choosing D's payment optimally; the authors provide conditions under which the optimal payment by D is greater than, but approximately proportional to, P's harm.

Kahan and Tuckman (1995), Daughety and Reinganum (2003) and Landeo and Nikitin (2006) consider the effect of a split-award statute (whereby a state takes a fraction of any punitive damages award) on incentives to file suit and settle. Kahan and Tuckman employ a complete-information model wherein trial effort is endogenous and P's lawyer receives a contingent fee. They find the effect of a split-award statute on settlement to be mixed. Although P's side receives only a fraction of the award at trial, this reduction in the stakes reduces equilibrium trial effort, thus making trial less expensive to pursue. Daughety and Reinganum provide an incomplete-information model of settlement with exogenous trial costs; again P's lawyer receives a contingent fee. Both a screening and a signaling version of the model are considered; in both versions, they find that a split-award statute results in a higher likelihood of settlement and a lower expected settlement amount for a given case. However, the fact that P is more willing to settle can make a plaintiff's lawyer more willing to take the case, with the result that some weaker cases may be filed under a split-award statute. Landeo and Nikitin add a further prior stage in which the (potential) D chooses care; they find that a split-award statute reduces care and they provide conditions under which a split-award statute will reduce the equilibrium probability of trial (including its effects on both filing and settlement).

Spier (1994b) considers coupled awards in an asymmetric information setting, and finds that the level of settlement costs influences the nature of the award that minimizes social cost (precaution costs plus litigation costs plus harm). Note that, here, precaution is one-sided: precaution on the part of a potential P is not included. Spier considers a two-type screening D-proposer ultimatum game and allows for two awards, a_H and a_L, for circumstances where the level of damages is High or Low, respectively, and thus the payoff from trial is the award minus court costs. Spier uses a condition such as (SSC) and shows that, if total court costs are low enough, the socially optimal award is equal to the level of damages *plus* P's court costs (as D will make a screening offer in those circumstances), while if total court costs are sufficiently high, the optimal award is the *expected* damages plus P's court costs (as D will be making a pooling offer). Therefore, simply compensating for actual damages is not socially optimal (recall also that court costs are fixed). Moreover, "fine tuning" the award to reflect P's actual level of damages is socially optimal only if total court costs are not too high.

17.4   Other Payoffs: Plea Bargaining
As an example of a significantly different payoff measure, consider negotiations between a defendant (D) in a criminal action and a prosecutor (P). This type of settlement bargaining, called plea bargaining, has been addressed in a number of papers. Early papers in this area are Landes (1971), Grossman and Katz (1983), and Reinganum (1988). In Landes' model, the payoffs are expected sentence length for P versus expected wealth (wealth in two states: under conviction and under no conviction) for D, who is guilty. In Grossman and Katz' model, D may be innocent, and he knows (privately) whether he is guilty or innocent (a two-type model). D seeks to minimize the disutility of punishment (he is risk averse), while the uninformed prosecutor maximizes a notion of justice that trades off the social losses from punishing the innocent versus freeing the guilty; the Grossman and Katz analysis is a screening model, with innocent defendants choosing trial.

Reinganum's model involves two-sided asymmetric information: D knows (privately) whether he is guilty or innocent (two types), while P knows (privately) the strength of the case; that is, the probability that the case will yield a conviction at trial (a continuum of types). Guilt and evidence are correlated, so there is a relationship between the two sets of types. A special case of this relationship appears in Grossman and Katz and was also employed in Rubinfeld and Sappington (1987), discussed in Section 15.2: innocent defendants can more readily obtain supporting evidence than can guilty ones. P's payoff is social justice minus resource costs, while D's payoff to be minimized is the expected sentence plus the disutility of trial. Reinganum finds that P's plea offer (which signals the strength of his case) is accepted by a mixture of innocent and guilty defendants; thus, defendant types are not screened perfectly in equilibrium.

Baker and Mezzetti (2001) extend the Grossman and Katz plea bargaining model to include P's costly evidence generation following failed plea negotiations; evidence can help filter out innocent defendants and increase the likelihood that a guilty defendant will be convicted. This modification results in an equilibrium in which all innocent defendants and some guilty defendants reject the plea bargain. Since the defendant types are not screened perfectly, it is optimal for P to try a fraction of the cases in which plea bargaining failed.

Bjerk (2007) also envisions a role for evidence generation following plea bargaining, but this evidence is not observed by P prior to trial, but rather by the jury during trial. The prosecutor has an initial observation on evidence, and this initial strength of P's case against D is common knowledge to P and D. Furthermore, it is common knowledge that the evidence observed by the jury at trial will be even stronger (respectively, weaker) if D is guilty (respectively, innocent). The jury observes neither the initial evidence nor the offer made by P to D. If the initial evidence against D is sufficiently strong, then in equilibrium P makes a plea offer that is rejected by all Ds. On the other hand, if the initial evidence against D is weaker, then in equilibrium P makes an offer that is accepted only by guilty Ds. When a case comes before them, jurors cannot know whether it involves an innocent defendant (who rejected a screening offer) or a defendant of either type (who rejected a harsh pooling offer); thus, jurors will convict (respectively, acquit) those Ds against whom the evidence realized at trial is sufficiently strong (respectively, weak).

Kobayashi (1992), Reinganum (1993), Miceli (1996), and Franzoni (1999) examine the effect of plea bargaining on the decision to commit a crime. Kobayashi considers conspiracies: there are two defendants (for example, a price-fixing case) who face different (exogenously determined) initial probabilities of conviction based on the existing evidence. Each D can, however, provide information on the other D which increases that second D's likelihood of conviction. Kobayashi assumes that the D with the higher initial conviction probability (the "ringleader") also has more information on the other D (the "subordinate"). Here P makes simultaneous offers to each D so as to maximize the sum of the expected penalties from the two Ds. Litigation costs are taken to be zero so as to focus on plea bargaining as information gathering. He finds that "unfair" plea bargains, wherein the ringleader receives a smaller penalty than the subordinate, can improve deterrence. Reinganum's model takes all Ds as guilty and therefore takes P's payoff as expected sentence length minus resource costs. In this model, the level of enforcement activities (as chosen by the police) and the expected sentence (as determined by plea bargaining) both influence D's initial choice to engage in criminal behavior. Miceli considers two possible objectives for a prosecutor; he finds that a P who maximizes the expected sentence minus resource costs effectively implements a legislature's preferences over sentencing (that is, a low probability of a long sentence), while a P who trades off the social losses from punishing the innocent versus freeing the guilty is unwilling to implement such a policy and instead offers a substantial sentence discount in plea bargaining. Finally, Franzoni assumes that P first bargains with D and then, if D rejects the plea offer, P decides how much to spend on an investigation. The investigation is assumed (always) to verify innocence, and to verify guilt with a probability that increases with the amount spent. Since innocent Ds always reject plea offers, P's offer must induce enough guilty D's to reject in order to make the subsequent pursuit of an investigation credible (recall Nalebuff, 1987, discussed in Section 16.1). This credibility requirement results in less thorough investigations, lower sentences, and more crime than would occur if P was able to commit *ex ante* to the extent of investigation.

18. Timing

Five theoretical papers have focused especially on the implications of changing the timing assumption in the models used: Spier (1992), Daughety and Reinganum (1993), Wang, Kim and Yi (1994), Bebchuk (1996), and Schwartz and Wickelgren (2009). The papers by Daughety and Reinganum and by Wang, Kim and Yi were discussed in Section 12.4 above. These two papers (along with Spier's) analyzed models that contributed some support for the one-sided asymmetric information ultimatum games. The papers by Bebchuk, and Schwartz and Wickelgren examine what happens if the settlement interval is subdivided and litigation costs are sunk over multiple periods; this has important implications for the credibility of lawsuits, and these two papers were discussed in Section 16.2.

Spier (1992) considers a finite-horizon sequence of P-proposer ultimatum games, with D informed about the damages for which he is liable (a continuum-type model). She finds a "deadline effect" in which there is a high likelihood of settlement in the last period. Moreover, the distribution of settlements over time can be U-shaped in the sense that there is a high likelihood of settlement in both the first and the last periods, with a low likelihood of settlement in the intervening periods. P is viewed as incurring two costs: (1) each extra period incurs a negotiating cost (this accounts for the high likelihood of early settlement) and (2) going to trial incurs a court cost (this accounts for the high likelihood of settlement just before trial).

D incurs neither cost, which is not a restrictive assumption in this analysis. Both P and D discount money in future periods at the same discount rate. Thus, the analysis involves subdividing the bargaining period into a sequence of periods and associating a delay cost for each period that settlement is not reached. Since the pie itself is not shrinking, the delay cost provides a clear incentive to P to settle sooner. On the other hand, P is uninformed and may need to use the approach of the end of the horizon to get D to reveal information through his rejection policy. This tradeoff leads to some settlements being made immediately and some being made in the last possible period when D faces the imminent possibility of trial.[29] Fenn and Rickman (1999) extend Spier's model to reflect the English cost allocation system and obtain similar results.

Two empirical papers have documented deadline effects. Fournier and Zuehlke (1996) test the predictions of Spier's finite horizon model with data from a survey of civil lawsuits from 1979–1981 in US federal courts. They find results that are consistent with computer simulation predictions based on Spier's analysis. Deffains and Doriat (1999) examine several different case classifications within two jurisdictions in France, where settlement is relatively rare (overall, about one quarter of cases settle). They find that, for several combinations of case type and jurisdiction, a deadline effect arises, though there are other combinations that do not appear to be subject to a deadline effect.

Kessler (1996) and Fenn and Rickman (2001) do not look for a deadline effect *per se*, but seek to identify causes of settlement delay. Kessler notes that approximately half of the states impose prejudgment interest on the theory that a defendant cannot thereby gain by delaying settlement. However, if the interest rate is equal to the common discount rate of the parties, then both P and D are indifferent about the timing of settlement (and otherwise at least one party may have an incentive to delay, though, under complete information, settlement occurs immediately and the effect of prejudgment interest is simply to shift the settlement amount). If there is private information, then prejudgment interest may actually result in more delay, since it increases the mean and variance of the stakes. Kessler's empirical analysis of US automobile bodily injury claims also incorporates other attributes of the prejudgment interest statutes, which may have independent effects on settlement delay. He finds that prejudgment interest

---

[29] Spier also considers an infinite-horizon extension, where P may choose to go to court in each period; this provides a model that allows for an endogenous date for trial. The model yields a range of equilibria (this is not unusual in strategic bargaining games with outside alternatives); the range runs from efficient to fully inefficient (all cases go to trial in the second period).

statutes do increase delay in settlement (an unintended consequence), as does a measure of the court's backlog (this hints at a deadline effect since a shorter backlog suggests a shorter time-to-trial, that is, an earlier deadline), and the use of comparative negligence (an indicator of the complexity of the case). Fenn and Rickman (2001) use a database of motor vehicle accidents in the UK. They find that delay is longer when the insurance company (defendant) is more convinced that it is not responsible, when the case is of high value and when the bargaining costs are low.

19. Information

19.1 Acquiring Information from the Other Player: Discovery and Disclosure

Shavell (1989) examines the incentives for informed players to voluntarily release private information in a continuum-type, informed-P, D-proposer ultimatum game. Before D makes a proposal, P can costlessly reveal his hidden information to D; he may also choose to stay silent. Shavell shows that silence implies that P's information involves low types (for example, that P's level of damages is low). Shavell considers two possibilities: claims by P are costlessly verifiable by D or some types of P cannot make verifiable claims; for convenience, call the first analysis an *unlimited verifiable claims* (UVC) model and the second a *limited verifiable claims* (LVC) model (in the LVC model, those types of P unable to make verifiable claims is an exogenously specified fraction u). In the UVC model, all Ps whose true type is less than or equal to a given value stay silent, while all those above that value make their claims. Since the claims are verifiable, D settles with those types by offering their concession limit and settles with the silent types by offering a settlement offer designed to reflect this group's types. Thus, there are no trials in equilibrium. Under discovery rights for D that provide mandatory disclosure, all types of P reveal, resulting in a reduced expenditure for D: each type of P settles for their concession limit.

In the LVC model, there will be trials. The reason is that the silent Ps now include those types who cannot make verifiable claims; some of these will have higher levels of damages than the offer made to the group of silent types, and will thus reject the offer and then go to trial (this relies on the assumption that u is independent of the level of damages). The rest of the silent types will settle, as will those whose claim is both greater and verifiable. Discovery now means that D can settle with $(1 - u)$ of the possible types of P at their concession limit and must screen the silent types, all of whom have unverifiable claims and, thus, some of whom will proceed to court (if the continuum-type version of (SSC) holds). Again, total D expenditures will generally be reduced from the original LVC payoff.

Mandatory disclosure in the LVC case raises the screening offer for the silent group, since those lower types with verifiable claims have settled at their concession limit. Thus, the probability of trial will be reduced relative to the original LVC outcome. Moreover, those with verifiable claims would have settled with or without mandatory disclosure.

Sobel (1989) provides a two-sided asymmetric information model that examines the impact of discovery and voluntary disclosure on settlement offers and outcomes; significantly, discovery generates costs and this affects results. He sandwiches one of two possible discovery processes between an initial D-proposer ultimatum game and a final P-proposer ultimatum game. Settlement in the D-proposer model ends the game, while rejection leads to the possibility of either mandatory discovery or no discovery of D's private information by P. This is then followed by the P-proposer ultimatum game. The cost of disclosure to D is denoted c. In a voluntary disclosure setting, D's choice to disclose is costly, and therefore might be used by D to signal that the information was credible. By making P the final proposer, P is able to extract all the surplus from settlement. Thus, D has no reason to voluntarily disclose information if $c > 0$. This contrasts with results, for example, by Milgrom and Roberts (1986), who model costless voluntary disclosure and find that such disclosure can be fully revealing. As Sobel observes, this suggests that such a conclusion is sensitive to the assumption that $c = 0$. Sobel also finds that mandatory disclosure reduces the probability of trial and may bias the selection of cases that go to trial, generating a distribution in which P wins more often.

Cooter and Rubinfeld (1994) use an analysis based on an axiomatic settlement model with prior assessments that may be inconsistent; discovery may or may not eliminate inconsistency. For example, discovery may reveal a player's private information or it may cause a player to adopt an alternative perspective about what may come out of a trial. Either way, an NBS is applied to a settlement frontier adjusted by the difference in expected trial payoffs. One of the main results is the proposal of an allocation of discovery costs so as to provide disincentives for abuse by either player. The proposed allocation assigns discovery costs to each party up to a switching point, at which point incremental costs are shifted to the requesting player.

Farmer and Pecorino (2005) consider both screening and signaling models of settlement in which the plaintiff has private information about her damages. In both cases, the plaintiff has the option to disclose her private information (at a cost) and the defendant has the option to force mandatory disclosure (at a cost) before settlement negotiations. In the screening model, the defendant makes the settlement offer; in this case, the plaintiff will never disclose voluntarily, since the defendant will then offer her only her concession limit, but the defendant may engage in mandatory disclosure. On the other hand, in the signaling model the plaintiff makes the demand and the demand reveals her true damages; in this case, the defendant will never engage in mandatory disclosure, but a plaintiff with high damages may disclose voluntarily, since this allows her to push the defendant to his concession limit.

19.2 Acquiring Information from Experts
As discussed in Section 15.1, Watts (1994) considers a model with an agent that provides expertise in the sense that they can acquire information for a player more cheaply than the player can themselves. She shows how to view the problem as one of bargaining between the player and the agent and provides some comparative statics about their settlement frontier.

In Daughety and Reinganum (1993), a model allowing simultaneous or sequential moves by both players (this is discussed in more detail in Section 12.4) is embedded in a model which allows uninformed players to acquire information from an expert before settlement negotiations begin. The information, which is costly, is what an informed player would know. Thus, a player may start the game already informed (called *naturally informed*) or start uninformed but able to acquire the information at a cost $c > 0$; for convenience, assume that court costs are the same for the two players and denote them as k. If both players are uninformed, then, in equilibrium, neither will choose to buy the information. This is because informational asymmetry results in some possible cases going to trial, while symmetric uncertainty involves no trials. With one of the players naturally informed and one uninformed, then, as discussed earlier, depending on the form of the compromise function, the equilibrium involves either payoffs consistent with an ultimatum screening model or payoffs consistent with an ultimatum signaling model. In those conditions which lead to the screening game payoffs, the uninformed player will choose to buy the information if $c \leq k$. Alternatively, in those conditions which lead to signaling game payoffs, the uninformed player will *not* acquire the information. Thus, uninformed players will not always choose to "re-level the playing field" by purchasing information; signaling will provide it if a revealing equilibrium is anticipated.

19.3 Procedures for Moderating the Effects of Private Information
Gertner and Miller (1995) examine the impact of settlement escrows on the likelihood and timing of settlement. A settlement escrow involves a particular bargaining protocol wherein P submits a demand and D submits an offer to a neutral third party (the escrow agent). If the offer exceeds the demand, then the escrow agent imposes the average of the demand and the

offer as the settlement amount. On the other hand, if the demand exceeds the offer, the third party simply reports back that there was no overlap. The parties can then proceed to bargain further or go to trial. There are two crucial features of this protocol. First, if the offer exceeds the demand, then the settlement is imposed on the parties; thus, if D learns that P's case is weak because P accepted D's offer, it is too late for D to make use of this information, as settlement is imposed. Second, while the failure to settle is informative to each party about the other's private information, it is not fully revealing. Thus, the incentive to distort one's demand or offer is muted and the parties tend to make more "reasonable" demands and offers. The authors predict that more cases will be settled (and settled earlier) when a settlement escrow is used.

Babcock and Landeo (2004) conduct an experimental study of settlement escrows. The experiment involves P having private information about her damages. In the no-escrow treatment, P makes a demand of D; D can accept the offer or reject it and make a counteroffer. Since D can take advantage of any information that P signals through her demand, every type of P will be tempted to make a high pooling demand (or no demand at all), simultaneously reducing the information content of her demand and inducing a higher likelihood of rejection by D. They find that the escrow treatment, which is predicted to mute these incentives and result in more "reasonable" demands, does indeed perform as predicted. When there was asymmetric information about P's damages, a case was more likely to settle, to settle sooner, and to settle for an amount that is closer to true damages, when a settlement escrow protocol was used.

D. CONCLUSIONS

20. Summary

The modeling of settlement bargaining has been influenced primarily by law, economics and game theory. In many ways, it is still developing and expanding, and hopefully deepening. The more recent analyses employ, primarily, a mix of information economics and bargaining theory (both cooperative and noncooperative) to examine, understand and recommend improvements in legal institutions and procedures. Mechanism design, behavioral economics, and considerations of settlement in the context of judicial decision-making have started to add further concepts and context to the research.

There has been a tug-of-war between the desire to address interesting behavior and the current limited ability to relate seemingly irrational acts to rational choice. As the development of technique has progressively allowed this to be accomplished, and as the intuition as to why seeming irrationality may be rational has driven improvement in technique, a broader picture of what elements contribute to, or impede, dispute resolution has evolved.

Issues have led techniques, a good thing. There is an aspect that could use improvement: empirical or laboratory studies of the details of the settlement process are still comparatively rare (though this review has touched on some). In an area where 97% of the outcomes are partially or totally unobservable by researchers, empirical studies are hard to do, and the few that have been done have undoubtedly involved hard work. The development of improved data sources (such as the medical malpractice databases in Florida and Texas) bodes well, as does the development of econometric techniques for carefully analyzing dynamic processes.

Laboratory studies (experimental economics and related efforts in sociology and psychology) are expanding, but the more subtle predictions of some of these models mean that laboratory studies have to walk a fine line between being a test of a particular model's prediction or ending up mainly gauging a subject's IQ. Such studies are still very labor-intensive (on the part of the researcher), though software development and the further entry of researchers into this area bodes well.

The previous version of this survey, in 2000, ended with the following observation:

> Most of the work in this area (covering the last quarter century) has occurred in the last dozen years (and most of that has occurred in the last half-dozen years), indicating an accelerating interest and suggesting that the next survey will have a lot more new, useful theory and detailed empirical and laboratory tests to report, a good thing, too. (Daughety, 2000)

In the intervening years, there has been a progression of surveys of this material (see footnote 2) which reflects the expanding scholarly interest in understanding the forces that affect settlement in both simple and complex litigation settings. The above forecast appears to have been borne out and also appears to be as valid to make about tomorrow as it was to make about today.

Bibliography

Babcock, Linda and Landeo, Claudia M. (2004), "Settlement Escrows: An Experimental Study of a Bilateral Bargaining Game," *Journal of Economic Behavior and Organization*, 53, 401–17.

Baker, Scott and Mezzetti, Claudio (2001), "Prosecutorial Resources, Plea Bargaining, and the Decision to Go to Trial," *Journal of Law, Economics, and Organization*, 17, 149–67.

Bar-Gill, Oren (2006), "The Evolution and Persistence of Optimism in Litigation," *Journal of Law, Economics, and Organization*, 22, 490–507.

Bebchuk, Lucian Arye (1984), "Litigation and Settlement under Imperfect Information," *RAND Journal of Economics*, 15, 404–15.
Bebchuk, Lucian Arye (1988), "Suing Solely to Extract a Settlement Offer," *Journal of Legal Studies*, 17, 437–50.
Bebchuk, Lucian Arye (1996), "A New Theory Concerning the Credibility of Success of Threats to Sue," *Journal of Legal Studies*, 25, 1–26.
Bebchuk, Lucian Ayre and Chang, Howard F. (1996), "An Analysis of Fee Shifting Based on the Margin of Victory: On Frivolous Suits, Meritorious Suits, and the Role of Rule 11," *Journal of Legal Studies*, 25, 371–404.
Bjerk, David (2007), "Guilt Shall Not Escape or Innocence Suffer: The Limits of Plea Bargaining When Defendant Guilt is Uncertain," *American Law and Economics Review*, 9, 305–29.
Briggs, H.C., III, Huryn, K.D. and McBride, M.E. (1996), "Treble Damages and the Incentive to Sue and Settle," *RAND Journal of Economics*, 27, 770–86.
Che, Yeon-Koo (1996), "Equilibrium Formation of Class Action Suits," *Journal of Public Economics*, 62, 339–61.
Che, Yeon-Koo (2002), "The Economics of Collective Negotiation in Pretrial Bargaining," *International Economic Review*, 43, 549–75.
Che, Yeon-Koo (2008), "Exploiting Plaintiffs through Settlement: Divide and Conquer," *Journal of Institutional and Theoretical Economics*, 164, 4–23.
Che, Yeon-Koo and Spier, Kathryn E. (2008), "Exploiting Plaintiffs through Settlement; Divide and Conquer," *Journal of Institutional and Theoretical Economics*, 164, 4–30.
Che, Yeon-Koo and Yi, Jong Goo (1993), "The Role of Precedents in Repeated Litigation," *Journal of Law, Economics and Organization*, 9, 399–424.
Chen, Kong-pin and Wang, Jue-Shyan (2006), "Fee-Shifting Rules in Litigation with Contingency Fees," *Journal of Law, Economics, and Organization*, 23, 519–46.
Choi, Albert and Sanchirico, Chris William (2004), "Should Plaintiffs Win What Defendants Lose? Litigation Stakes, Litigation Effort, and the Benefits of Decoupling," *Journal of Legal Studies*, 33, 323–54.
Chu, C.Y. Cyrus and Chien, Hung-Ken (2007), "Asymmetric Information, Pretrial Negotiation and Optimal Decoupling," *International Review of Law and Economics*, 27, 312–29.
Chung, Tai-Yeong, (1996) "Settlement of Litigation under Rule 68: An Economic Analysis," *Journal of Legal Studies*, 25, 261–86.
Cooter, Robert D. and Rubinfeld, Daniel L. (1989), "Economic Analysis of Legal Disputes and their Resolution," *Journal of Economic Literature*, 27, 1067–97.
Cooter, Robert D. and Rubinfeld, Daniel L. (1994), "An Economic Model of Legal Discovery," *Journal of Legal Studies*, 23, 435–63.
Daughety, Andrew F. (2000), "Settlement," in B. Bouckaert and G. DeGeest (eds.), *Encyclopedia of Law and Economics*, Cheltenham, UK and Northampton, MA, USA: Edward Elgar, vol. 5, 95–158.
Daughety, Andrew F. and Reinganum, Jennifer F. (1993), "Endogenous Sequencing in Models of Settlement and Litigation," *Journal of Law, Economics and Organization*, 9, 314–48.
Daughety, Andrew F. and Reinganum, Jennifer F. (1994), "Settlement Negotiations with Two Sided Asymmetric Information: Model Duality, Information Distribution, and Efficiency," *International Review of Law and Economics*, 14, 283–98.
Daughety, Andrew F. and Reinganum, Jennifer F. (1995), "Keeping Society in the Dark: on the Admissibility of Pretrial Negotiations as Evidence in Court," *RAND Journal of Economics*, 26, 203–21.
Daughety, Andrew F. and Reinganum, Jennifer F. (1999), "Hush Money," *RAND Journal of Economics*, 30, 661–78.
Daughety, Andrew F. and Reinganum, Jennifer F. (2002), "Informational Externalities in Settlement Bargaining: Confidentiality and Correlated Culpability," *RAND Journal of Economics*, 33, 587–604.

Daughety, Andrew F. and Reinganum, Jennifer F. (2003), "Found Money? Split-Award Statutes and Settlement of Punitive Damages Cases," *American Law and Economics Review*, 5, 134–64.

Daughety, Andrew F. and Reinganum, Jennifer F. (2004), "Exploiting Future Settlements: A Signaling Model of Most-Favored-Nation Clauses in Settlement," *RAND Journal of Economics*, 35, 467–85.

Daughety, Andrew F. and Reinganum, Jennifer F. (2005), "Economic Theories of Settlement Bargaining," *Annual Review of Law and Social Sciences*, 1, 35–59.

Deffains, Bruno and Doriat, Myriam (1999), "The Dynamics of Pretrial Negotiation in France: Is there a Deadline Effect in the French Legal System?," *International Review of Law and Economics*, 19, 447–70.

Gertner, Robert H. and Miller, Geoffrey P. (1995), "Settlement Escrows," *Journal of Legal Studies*, 24, 87–122.

Farber, Henry S. and White, Michelle J. (1991), "Medical Malpractice: An Empirical Examination of the Litigation Process," *RAND Journal of Economics*, 22, 199–217.

Farmer, Amy and Pecorino, Paul (1994), "Pretrial Negotiations with Asymmetric Information on Risk Preferences," *International Review of Law and Economics*, 14, 273–81.

Farmer, Amy and Pecorino, Paul (2005), "Civil Litigation with Mandatory Discovery and Voluntary Transmission of Private Information," *Journal of Legal Studies*, 34, 137–59.

Fenn, Paul and Rickman, Neil (1999), "Delay and Settlement in Litigation," *Economic Journal*, 109, 476–91.

Fenn, Paul and Rickman, Neil (2001), "Asymmetric Information and the Settlement of Insurance Claims," *The Journal of Risk and Insurance*, 68, 615–30.

Fournier, Gary M. and Zuehlke, Thomas W. (1996), "The Timing of Out-of-court Settlements", *RAND Journal of Economics*, 27, 310–21.

Franzoni, Luigi Alberto (1999), "Negotiated Enforcement and Credible Deterrence," *Economic Journal*, 109, 509–35.

Friedman, Daniel and Wittman, Donald (2006), "Liitigation with Symmetric Bargaining and Two-Sided Incomplete Information," *Journal of Law, Economics, and Organization*, 23, 98–126.

Gertner, Robert H. and Miller, Geoffrey P. (1995), "Settlement Escrows," *Journal of Legal Studies*, 24, 87–122.

Gould, John P. (1973), "The Economics of Legal Conflicts," *Journal of Legal Studies*, 2, 279–300.

Grossman, Gene M. and Katz, Michael L. (1983), "Plea Bargaining and Social Welfare," *American Economic Review*, 73, 749–57.

Hay, Bruce L. and Spier, Kathryn E. (1998), "Settlement of Litigation," in P. Newman (ed.), *The New Palgrave Dictionary of Law and Economics*, Basingstoke: Macmillan Reference Limited, vol. 3, 442–51.

Hylton, Keith N. (2002), "An Asymmetric-Information Model of Litigation," *International Review of Law and Economics*, 22, 153–75.

Kahan, Marcel and Tuckman, Bruce (1995), "Special Levies on Punitive Damages: Decoupling, Agency Problems, and Litigation Expenditures," *International Review of Law and Economics*, 15, 175–85.

Katz, Avery (1990), "The Effect of Frivolous Lawsuits on the Settlement of Litigation," *International Review of Law and Economics*, 10, 3–27.

Kessler, Daniel (1996), "Institutional Causes of Delay in the Settlement of Legal Disputes," *Journal of Law, Economics, and Organization*, 12, 432–60.

Kim, Jeong-Yoo and Ryu, Keunkwan (2000), "Pretrial Negotiation Behind Open Doors versus Closed Doors: Economic Analysis of Rule 408," *International Review of Law and Economics*, 20, 285–94.

Klement, Alon (2003), "Threats to Sue and Cost Divisibility under Asymmetric Information," *International Review of Law and Economics*, 23, 261–72.

Klement, Alon and Neeman, Zvika (2005), "Against Compromise: A Mechanism Design Approach," *Journal of Law, Economics, and Organization*, 21, 285–314.

Kobayashi, Bruce H. (1992), "Deterrence with Multiple Defendants: An Explanation for 'Unfair' Plea Bargaining," *RAND Journal of Economics*, 23, 507–17.
Kornhauser, Lewis A. and Revesz, Richard L. (1994a), "Multidefendant Settlements: The Impact of Joint and Several Liability," *Journal of Legal Studies*, 23, 41–76.
Kornhauser, Lewis A. and Revesz, Richard L. (1994b), "Multidefendant Settlements under Joint and Several Liability: The Problem of Insolvency," *Journal of Legal Studies*, 23, 517–42.
Landeo, Claudia M. and Nikitin, Maxim (2006), "Split-Award Tort Reform, Firm's Level of Care, and Litigation Outcomes," *Journal of Institutional and Theoretical Economics*, 162, 571–600.
Landeo, Claudia, Nikitin, Maxim and Baker, Scott (2006), "Deterrence, Lawsuits, and Litigation Outcomes under Court Errors," *Journal of Law, Economics, and Organization*, 23, 57–97.
Landes, William M. (1971), "An Economic Analysis of the Courts," *Journal of Law and Economics*, 14, 61–107.
Landes, William M. (1994), "Counterclaims: An Economic Analysis," *International Review of Law and Economics*, 14, 235–44.
Miceli, Thomas J. (1996), "Plea Bargaining and Deterrence: An Institutional Approach," *European Journal of Law and Economics*, 3, 249–64.
Miller, Geoffrey P. (1987), "Some Agency Problems in Settlement," *Journal of Legal Studies*, 16, 189–215.
Miller, Geoffrey P. (1996), "Settlement of Litigation: A Critical Retrospective," in Larry Kramer (ed.), *Reforming the Civil Justice System*, New York: New York University Press.
Nalebuff, Barry (1987), "Credible Pretrial Negotiation," *RAND Journal of Economics*, 18, 198–210.
P'ng, Ivan P.L. (1983), "Strategic Behavior in Suit, Settlement, and Trial," *Bell Journal of Economics*, 14, 539–50.
Polinsky, A. Mitchell and Che, Yeon-Koo (1991), "Decoupling Liability: Optimal Incentives for Care and Litigation," *RAND Journal of Economics*, 22, 562–70.
Polinsky, A. Mitchell and Rubinfeld, Daniel L. (2002), "A Note on Settlements under the Contingent Fee Method of Compensating Lawyers," *International Review of Law and Economics*, 22, 217–25.
Polinsky, A. Mitchell and Rubinfeld, Daniel L. (2003), "Aligning the Interests of Lawyers and Clients," *American Law and Economics Review*, 5, 165–88.
Posner, Richard A. (1973), "An Economic Approach to Legal Procedure and Judicial Administration," *Journal of Legal Studies*, 2, 399–458.
Priest, George L. and Klein, Benjamin (1984), "The Selection of Disputes for Litigation," *Journal of Legal Studies*, 13, 1–56.
Reinganum, Jennifer F. (1988), "Plea Bargaining and Prosecutorial Discretion," *American Economic Review*, 78, 713–28.
Reinganum, Jennifer F. (1993), "The Law Enforcement Process and Criminal Choice," *International Review of Law and Economics*, 13, 115–34.
Reinganum, Jennifer F. and Wilde, Louis L. (1986), "Settlement, Litigation, and the Allocation of Litigation Costs," *RAND Journal of Economics*, 17, 557–66.
Rickman, Neil (1999), "Contingent Fees and Litigation Settlement," *International Review of Law and Economics*, 19, 295–317.
Rosenberg, David and Shavell, Steven (1985), "A Model in which Suits are Brought for their Nuisance Value," *International Review of Law and Economics*, 5, 3–13.
Rosenberg, David and Shavell, Steven (2006), "A Solution to the Problem of Nuisance Suits: The Option to have the Court Bar Settlement," *International Review of Law and Economics*, 26, 42–51.
Schwartz, Warren F. and Wickelgren, Abraham L. (2009), "Advantage Defendant: Why Sinking Litigation Costs Makes Negative Expected Value Defenses, but not Negative Expected Value Suits, Credible," *Journal of Legal Studies*, 38, 235–53.

Schweizer, Urs (1989), "Litigation and Settlement under Two Sided Incomplete Information," *Review of Economic Studies*, 56, 163–77.
Shavell, Steven (1982), "Suit, Settlement and Trial: A Theoretical Analysis under Alternative Methods for the Allocation of Legal Costs," *Journal of Legal Studies*, 11, 55–81.
Shavell, Steven (1989), "Sharing of Information Prior to Settlement or Litigation," *RAND Journal of Economics*, 20, 183–95.
Shavell, Steven (1993), "Suit Versus Settlement When Parties Seek Nonmonetary Judgments," *Journal of Legal Studies*, 22, 1–14.
Shavell, Steven (1996), "Any Probability of Plaintiff Victory at Trial is Possible," *Journal of Legal Studies*, 25, 493–501.
Sobel, Joel (1989), "An Analysis of Discovery Rules," *Law and Contemporary Problems*, 52, 133–60.
Spier, Kathryn E. (1992), "The Dynamics of Pretrial Negotiation," *Review of Economic Studies*, 59, 93–108.
Spier, Kathryn E. (1994a), "Pretrial Bargaining and the Design of Fee-Shifting Rules," *RAND Journal of Economics*, 25, 197–214.
Spier, Kathryn E. (1994b), "Settlement Bargaining and the Design of Damage Awards," *Journal of Law, Economics and Organization*, 10, 84–95.
Spier, Kathryn E. (2002), "Settlement with Multiple Plaintiffs: The Role of Insolvency," *Journal of Law, Economics, and Organization*, 18, 295–323.
Spier, Kathryn E. (2003a), "The Use of Most-Favored-Nation Clauses in Settlement of Litigation," *RAND Journal of Economics*, 34, 78–95.
Spier, Kathryn E. (2003b), "Tied to the Mast: Most-Favored-Nation Clauses in Settlement Contracts," *Journal of Legal Studies*, 32, 91–120.
Spier, Kathryn E. (2007). "Litigation," in A. Mitchell Polinsky and Steven Shavell (eds.) *Handbook of Law and Economics*, Amsterdam: Elsevier B.V., vol. 1, 259–342.
Waldfogel, Joel (1998), "Reconciling Asymmetric Information and Divergence Expectations Theories of Litigation," *Journal of Legal Studies*, 41, 451–76.
Wang, Gyu Ho, Kim, Jeong Yoo and Yi, Jong Goo (1994), "Litigation and Pretrial Negotiation under Incomplete Information," *Journal of Law, Economics and Organization*, 10, April, 187–200.
Watts, Alison (1994), "Bargaining through an Expert Attorney," *Journal of Law, Economics and Organization*, 10, 168–86.
Yang, Bill (1996), "Litigation, Experimentation and Reputation," *International Review of Law and Economics*, 16, 491–502.

Other References

Aumann, Robert J. (1976), "Agreeing to Disagree," *Annals of Statistics*, 4, 1236–9.
Babcock, Linda, Loewenstein, George, Issacharoff, Samuel and Camerer, Colin (1995), "Biased Judgments of Fairness in Bargaining," *The American Economic Review*, 85, 1337–43.
Baird, Douglas G., Gertner, Robert H. and Picker, Randal C. (1994), *Game Theory and the Law*, Cambridge, MA: Harvard University Press.
Bernheim, B. Douglas, Peleg, Bezalel and Whinston, Michael D. (1987), "Coalition Proof Nash Equilibria, I: Concepts," *Journal of Economic Theory*, 42, 1–12.
Binmore, Ken (1985), "Bargaining and Coalitions," in Alvin E. Roth (ed.), *Game-Theoretic Models of Bargaining*, Cambridge: Cambridge University Press.
Binmore, Ken (1992), *Fun and Games: A Text on Game Theory*, Lexington, MA: D.C. Heath and Company.
Binmore, Ken, Rubinstein, Ariel and Wolinsky, Asher (1986), "The Nash Bargaining Solution in Economic Modelling," *RAND Journal of Economics*, 17, 176–88.
Deneckere, Raymond and Liang, Meng-Yu (2006), "Bargaining with Interdependent Values," *Econometrica*, 74, 1309–64.
Fernandez, Raquel and Glazer, Jacob (1991), "Striking for a Bargain between Two Completely Informed Agents," *American Economic Review*, 81, 240–52.

Geanakoplos, John and Polemarchakis, Heraklis (1982), "We Can't Disagree Forever," *Journal of Economic Theory*, 28, 192–200.
Greenberg, Joseph (1994), "Coalition Structures," in Robert J. Aumann and Sergiu Hart (eds.), *Handbook of Game Theory*, Vol. 2, Amsterdam: North Holland-Elsevier.
Harsanyi, John C. (1967, 1968a, 1968b), "Games with Incomplete Information Played with 'Bayesian Players'," *Management Science*, 14, 159–82, 320–34 and 486–502.
Huang, Peter H. (1995), "Strategic Behavior and the Law: A Guide for Legal Scholars to *Game Theory and the Law* by Douglass Baird, et al. and Other Game Theory Texts," *Jurimetrics Journal of Law, Science and Technology*, 36, 99–114.
Kalai, Ehud and Smorodinsky, Meir (1975), "Other Solutions to the Nash's Bargaining Problem," *Econometrica*, 43, 513–18.
Kennan, John and Wilson, Robert (1993), "Bargaining with Private Information," *Journal of Economic Literature*, 31, 45–104.
Kreps, David M. (1990), *Game Theory and Economic Modelling*, Oxford: Oxford University Press.
Lax, David A. and Sebenius, James K. (1986), *The Manager as Negotiator*, New York: The Free Press.
Marcus, Nancy C. (2007), "Phantom Parties and Other Practical Problems with the Attempted Abolition of Joint and Several Liability," *Arkansas Law Review*, 60, 437–505.
Mas-Colell, Andreu, Whinston, Michael D. and Green, Jerry R. (1995), *Microeconomic Theory*, New York: Oxford University Press.
Milgrom, Paul and Roberts, John (1986), "Relying on the Information of Interested Parties," *RAND Journal of Economics*, 17, 18–32.
Nash, John F. (1950), "The Bargaining Problem," *Econometrica*, 18, 155–62.
Nash, John F. (1951), "Non-Cooperative Games," *Annals of Mathematics*, 54, 286–95.
Nash, John F. (1953), "Two-person Cooperative Games," *Econometrica*, 21, 128–40.
Okada, Akira (1996), "A Noncooperative Coalitional Bargaining Game with Random Proposers," *Games and Economic Behavior*, 16, 97–108.
Posner, Richard A. (1992), *Economic Analysis of Law*, Fourth Edition, Boston, MA: Little, Brown and Company.
Roth, Alvin E. (1995), "Bargaining Experiments," in John H. Kagel and Alvin E. Roth (eds.), *The Handbook of Experimental Economics*, Princeton, NJ: Princeton University Press, 253–348.
Rubinfeld, Daniel L. and Sappington, David E.M. (1987), "Efficient Awards and Standards of Proof in Judicial Proceedings," *RAND Journal of Economics*, 18, 308–15.
Rubinstein, Ariel (1982), "Perfect Equilibrium in a Bargaining Model," *Econometrica*, 50, 97–110.
Rubinstein, Ariel (1985), "A Bargaining Model with Incomplete Information about Time Preferences," *Econometrica*, 53, 1151–72.
Schwartz, Jesse A. and Wen, Quan (2007), "Wage Negotiation under Good Faith Bargaining," *International Game Theory Review*, 9, 551–64.
Ståhl, Ingolf (1972), *Bargaining Theory*, Stockholm: Economics Research Institute.
Vincent, Daniel R. (1989), "Bargaining with Common Values," *Journal of Economic Theory*, 48, 47–62.
Yildiz, Muhamet (2003), "Bargaining without a Common Prior – An Immediate Agreement Theorem," *Econometrica*, 71, 793–811.
Yildiz, Muhamet (2004), "Waiting to Persuade," *Quarterly Journal of Economics*, 119, 223–48.

16 The social versus private incentive to sue
Thomas J. Miceli

1. Introduction

The economic theory of tort law is based on the idea that the threat of liability provides potential injurers (those engaged in risky activities) with efficient incentives to take care to avoid accidents by forcing them to internalize the risk that their behavior creates.[1] Unlike direct regulation or externality taxes, however, liability is a private remedy that can only be imposed if accident victims are willing to file suit to seek compensation. Early models ignored the cost of litigation and therefore sidestepped the impact of legal costs, both on the private incentive to sue, and on the social value of lawsuits as a means of internalizing harm.

Shavell (1982) was the first to explicitly compare the private and the social value of lawsuits in a costly legal system.[2] He pointed out that, while the private value of a suit depends solely on a plaintiff's comparison of the payment he or she expects to receive at trial with the cost of filing suit, the social value depends on the extent to which lawsuits induce the defendant to undertake socially desirable accident prevention. A key finding of his analysis was that there is no necessary connection between these two values. That is, a suit may be privately valuable but not socially valuable, or the reverse may be true. As a result, in an unrestricted legal system, there may be either too much or too little litigation from a social perspective.

Section 2 of this chapter reviews this basic argument, focusing on the case of a strict liability rule and assuming that all cases go to trial. Sections 3 and 4 then extend the model, first to consider a negligence rule, and then to allow settlements. Both extensions entail some modifications of the foregoing conclusions but do not nullify the basic insights. Section 5 considers several further extensions of the model, including the lawmaking function of trials, the impact of different cost allocation rules, and bilateral care accidents. Finally, Section 6 summarizes the conclusions.

---

[1] The first formal model of accidents was by Brown (1973). For comprehensive surveys of this literature, see Shavell (1987), Landes and Posner (1987), and Shavell (2004, Chapters 8–12).

[2] Also see Menell (1983), Kaplow (1986), Rose-Ackerman and Geistfeld (1987), and Shavell (1997, 1999).

2. The Basic Model

Consider a unilateral care accident model in which potential injurers can invest in care of x dollars to reduce the probability of an accident, $p(x)$, where $p' < 0$, $p'' > 0$. In the event of an accident, the victim suffers a loss of L dollars that is observable to the victim at the time of the accident but not to the injurer. The injurer, however, knows the distribution function of L conditional on an accident, which is given by $F(L)$. The victim (plaintiff) can file suit at cost k, and the cost of a trial is c_p to the plaintiff and c_d to the defendant. In the basic model, we assume that liability is strict and that all cases go to trial; later, we introduce a negligence rule and allow the possibility of settlement prior to trial.

Once an accident occurs, the plaintiff files suit if her expected gain at trial, $L - c_p$, exceeds the filing cost, or if $L \geq k + c_p$. This represents the condition for a suit to be *privately valuable*. The resulting probability of a suit, conditional on an accident, is $1 - F(k + c_p)$.

To examine the social value of suits, we need to examine the incentives they create for defendants to take care to avoid accidents. In the event of an accident, the defendant's expected costs, including liability and litigation costs, are given by

$$A = (1 - F(c_p + k))E(L + c_d | L \geq k + c_p) = \int_{k+c_p}^{\infty} (L + c_d) dF(L). \quad (16.1)$$

Given A, the defendant chooses care to minimize his expected accident plus litigation costs:

$$x + p(x)A. \quad (16.2)$$

The resulting first-order condition

$$1 + p'(x)A = 0 \quad (16.3)$$

determines the injurer's optimal care, denoted $\hat{x}$. Totally differentiating (16.3) and using (16.1) implies that

$$\frac{\partial \hat{x}}{\partial k} < 0, \quad \frac{\partial \hat{x}}{\partial c_p} < 0, \quad \frac{\partial \hat{x}}{\partial c_d} > 0. \quad (16.4)$$

Thus, an increase in the plaintiff's filing or trial costs reduces the defendant's care by lowering the probability of a suit, conditional on an accident. Conversely, an increase in the defendant's trial costs increases his care by raising the expected cost of an accident.

The social desirability of lawsuits depends on how they affect overall social costs, including the plaintiff's damages plus total litigation costs. Expected social costs conditional on an accident are given by

$$H = E(L) + (1 - F(k + c_p))(k + c_p + c_d), \quad (16.5)$$

where $E(L)$ is the plaintiff's expected loss in the event of an accident. Comparing (16.5) and (16.1) shows that $A < H$; that is, defendants do not face the full social costs of an accident. This is true for two reasons: first, defendants ignore the damages suffered by victims who do not file suit, and second, they ignore the filing and trial costs of victims who do file. As a result, the threat of lawsuits *underdeters* injurers.

Given this underdeterrence, we now ask whether lawsuits are socially desirable. First, we compute expected social costs, evaluated at the defendant's privately optimal care choice. The resulting cost expression is

$$\hat{x} + p(\hat{x})H. \quad (16.6)$$

In contrast, if lawsuits are prohibited (or, equivalently, if the liability rule is switched to no liability), then injurers will take no care and no victims will file suit. Expected social costs in that case are

$$p(0)E(L). \quad (16.7)$$

Lawsuits are *socially valuable* if (16.6) is less than (16.7), or, using (16.5), if

$$p(\hat{x})[1 - F(k + c_p)](k + c_p + c_d) < p(0)E(L) - [\hat{x} + p(\hat{x})E(L)]. \quad (16.8)$$

The left-hand side of this condition represents the expected litigation costs of allowing lawsuits, while the right-hand side represents the deterrence benefits of lawsuits. Generally, this condition may or may not hold, implying that lawsuits may or may not be socially desirable. While the threat of suits is necessary to induce injurers to take care under a strict liability rule, the cost of using the legal system may outweigh the resulting deterrence benefits.

Further, there is no necessary relationship between the private and social value of lawsuits. As noted, the private value of a suit is solely determined by comparing an individual plaintiff's loss to her cost of bringing suit. Thus, when plaintiffs vary in their individual losses, some will find a suit privately valuable and others will not, regardless of the social value of suits. In contrast, the social value of lawsuits is based on aggregate costs across all plaintiffs since that is what determines the expected costs faced by injurers at the time they make their care choices. Thus, there will be too many suits when they are not socially valuable (i.e., when (16.8) does not hold), and there may be too many or too few when they are socially valuable (i.e., when (16.8) holds).[3]

2.1 An Example

A numerical example helps to illustrate the preceding points. Let the accident technology be given by $p(x) = 0.005e^{-\theta x}$, where $\theta > 0$ is a parameter reflecting the productivity of injurer care. Note that $p' = -0.005\theta e^{-\theta x} < 0$ and $p'' = 0.005\theta^2 e^{-\theta x} > 0$, as required, and $p(0) = 0.005$. Also let $k=\$50$, $c_p = c_d = \$300$, and suppose that L is distributed uniformly on $[0, \$1,000]$. Thus, $E(L) = \$500$, and, from (16.1), $A = \$633.75$.

Now suppose that $\theta = 1$. Then, from (16.3), the injurer's optimal care when lawsuits are allowed is $\hat{x} = \$1.153$. Substituting this value into $p(x)$ yields the risk of an accident: $p(\hat{x}) = 0.00158$.[4] The left-hand side of condition (16.8), the expected litigation costs of allowing lawsuits, therefore equals $\$0.668$, while the right-hand side, the expected deterrence benefits of lawsuits, equals $\$0.557$. Since the left-hand side is larger, lawsuits are not socially valuable in this example.

To find a counterexample where lawsuits are socially valuable, let $\theta = 2$, implying that injurer care is more productive than in the previous example. Proceeding as above, we find that the injurer's optimal care is now $\hat{x} = \$0.923$, while the resulting risk of an accident is $p(\hat{x}) = 0.00079$. The left-hand side of (16.8) in this case is $\$0.334$, and the right-hand side is $\$1.182$. Thus, lawsuits are now socially valuable. Finally, note that in both examples, the cost of a suit to plaintiffs is $k + c_p = \$350$, meaning that those plaintiffs with $L \geq \$350$ file suit, while those with $L < \$350$ do not. Thus, in both examples, 65% of victims find suits privately valuable.

2.2 Corrective Policies

To what extent can the government enact corrective policies to achieve the socially optimal outcome? Observe first that if (16.8) does not hold, lawsuits are not socially desirable and therefore should be banned (or a rule of no liability should be instituted).

The problem is more complicated if (16.8) holds. Although suits are

---

[3] It is not possible to say in general whether there are too many or too few suits when (16.8) holds because, although not all victims file in this case, it is not necessarily true that adding more suits will be socially desirable. It depends on whether the extra cost is outweighed by the increased deterrence gains.

[4] It is easy to verify that $\hat{x} = -(1/\theta) \ln [1/(0.005 A\theta)]$ and $p(\hat{x}) = 1/(\theta A)$.

socially desirable in this case, and a fraction $1 - F(k + c_p)$ of victims find them privately desirable, we have seen that injurers will take too little care because they ignore the losses of those victims who do not file suit, as well as the litigation cost of those victims who do. In principle, this can be remedied either by directly subsidizing suits so that more victims file, or by charging defendants damages in excess of the losses suffered by victims.[5] Both of these policies, however, would have the undesirable effect of increasing the number of lawsuits, thereby raising litigation costs. Thus, overall social costs are not necessarily reduced. A better approach would therefore be to impose a tax on defendants to be paid to the government rather than to plaintiffs, thus increasing incentives for care without incurring the higher litigation costs.[6] In any event, enacting the optimal corrective policy, while possible in theory, would be difficult in practice and would require information that is not easily obtained by policymakers.

3. The Model under a Negligence Rule

This section extends the model to the case of a negligence rule. Under a perfectly functioning negligence rule,[7] an accident victim will file suit if $L \geq k + c_p$ *and* if the injurer was negligent. An injurer is judged negligent if he failed to comply with the due standard of care, z, in which case he is fully liable for the plaintiff's losses. Alternatively, the injurer can meet the due standard and avoid all liability. This is an important advantage of negligence over strict liability because it means that injurers can be induced to take care by the *threat* of a lawsuit rather than by the actual filing of suits.[8]

The injurer's problem under negligence is to choose x to minimize

---

[5] A similar rationale underlies the economic theory of punitive damages (Shavell, 2004, pp. 243–7).

[6] The logical limit of this proposal would be to raise the cost imposed on defendants while simultaneously lowering the award to plaintiffs so as to improve incentives while *reducing* the number of suits. Such a policy is referred to as "decoupled liability" (Polinsky and Che, 1991). As a practical matter, however, the state is limited to policies that award plaintiffs *no less* than their actual losses, in which case the number of lawsuits cannot be reduced below $1 - F(k + c_p)$.

[7] In reality, the negligence rule may function imperfectly for a number of reasons. For example, injurers may be uncertain about the due standard (Craswell and Calfee, 1986), or courts may apply the due standard with error (P'ng, 1986; Polinsky and Shavell, 1989; Hylton, 1990).

[8] An offsetting cost of negligence is that if a case does go to trial, it will likely be costlier compared to strict liability because, in addition to causation, the plaintiff must prove fault.

$$\begin{cases} x, & \text{if } x \geq z \\ x + p(x)A, & \text{if } x < z, \end{cases} \quad (16.9)$$

where A is defined by (16.1). The solution to this problem depends on the due standard, z. An obvious candidate is first-best care, x^*, which is defined to be the level of care that minimizes expected accident costs in the absence of litigation costs, or $x + p(x)E(L)$. From (16.1) it should be apparent that A may be larger or smaller than $E(L)$. It may be larger because it includes the defendant's trial costs in addition to liability, but it may be smaller because it does not include the losses suffered by victims who do not find it worthwhile to file suit. Thus, the level of care that minimizes the second line of (16.9), which we defined above to be $\hat{x}$, may be larger or smaller than $x^* = z$. If $\hat{x} > x^*$, the injurer will clearly comply with the due standard and, unlike the case under strict liability, the first-best outcome can be achieved. Specifically, the injurer will take the efficient level of care and no victims will file suit, so no litigation costs are incurred. In this case, there is no possibility of an excessive private incentive to sue.

Alternatively, if $\hat{x} < x^*$, the injurer may or may not comply with the due care standard. If $\hat{x}$ is not too far below x^*, he will comply, and the first-best outcome will still be achieved.[9] However, if $\hat{x}$ is significantly below x^*, the injurer will find it cheaper not to comply but will instead choose $\hat{x}$ and be found negligent. In that case, the outcome is identical to that under strict liability, and the conclusions regarding the social versus private desirability of suit from that case carry over.

In the example from above, when $\theta = 1$, $x^* = z = \$0.916$. Thus, since $\hat{x} = \$1.153$, the injurer will comply with the due standard, and the first-best outcome is achieved. (The same result occurs when $\theta = 2$.)

4. The Model when Settlement is Possible

We now amend the above model to allow the settlement of lawsuits before trial (Shavell, 1999).[10] For simplicity, we assume that settlement involves no costs to either party, though trials continue to cost c_p and c_d to plaintiffs and defendants, respectively. However, plaintiffs must incur the filing cost k whether they settle or go to trial.

Consider first the settlement-trial decision, given that an accident has occurred and a plaintiff has filed suit. Since the defendant cannot observe an individual plaintiff's loss, he must make a single settlement offer S to

---

[9] In particular, the injurer will comply if $x^* \leq \hat{x} + p(\hat{x})A$.
[10] We focus only on strict liability as the qualitative conclusions reached concerning a negligence rule in the model without settlement continue to apply.

478   *Procedural law and economics*

minimize his expected costs (an amount to be derived shortly). A plaintiff of type L will accept the offer if

$$S \geq L - c_p \qquad (16.10)$$

and refuse otherwise. Thus, plaintiffs with $L \leq S + c_p$ will settle, while those with $L > S + c_p$ will go to trial.[11] The resulting probability of a trial, conditional on an accident occurring and a suit being filed, is $1 - F(S + c_p)$.

In this case, the expected cost facing the defendant, conditional on an accident, is

$$R(S) = F(S + c_p)S + \int_{S+c_p}^{\infty} (L + c_d) dF(L). \qquad (16.11)$$

The defendant chooses the settlement offer, S, to minimize this expression. The resulting first-order condition (assuming an interior solution) is

$$F(S + c_p) - (c_p + c_d)f(S + c_p) = 0, \qquad (16.12)$$

where $f(\cdot)$ is the density function associated with $F(\cdot)$. Let S^* represent the optimal settlement amount implied by (16.12).

We can now determine the private value of suit in this case. We will assume throughout that $S^* > k$, in which case a suit is privately valuable for all plaintiffs, regardless of their particular loss. Those with $L \leq S^* + c_p$ will therefore file and settle, yielding them a net return of $S^* - k$, while those with $L > S^* + c_p$ will file and go to trial, yielding them a net return of $L - c_p - k$ (which is positive given $S^* > k$).[12] Compared to the model

---

[11] Note that the plaintiff's filing cost does not matter for the plaintiff's acceptance decision because it is sunk.

[12] Another possible solution to the defendant's settlement problem is to offer $S = 0$ (actually, any $S < k$) rather than S^*, in which case victims whose losses are less than the filing plus trial costs (i.e., those with $L < k + c_p$) would not rationally file suit. (Such cases are sometimes referred to as negative expected value cases.) The gain from this strategy is that the defendant avoids paying a positive settlement to these victims, but the cost is that he must incur trial costs with those victims who do file suit (those with $L \geq k + c_p$). The strategy of offering a zero settlement amount will be optimal if the gain exceeds the cost, which is more likely to be true the larger is the fraction of plaintiffs with $L < k + c_p$ in the population of plaintiffs. (See Bebchuk (1988) and Katz (1990).) In that case, the outcome is the same as when settlements are not possible.

without settlement, more suits will be filed in this case because the possibility of settlement induces plaintiffs with $L < k + c_p$ to file, whereas they did not find it worthwhile to file in the above model.

As above, the social value of suit depends on its ability to induce injurers to take care. The injurer's minimized cost when settlement is possible is the minimized value of (16.11), or $R(S^*)$. His optimal care choice therefore minimizes

$$x + p(x)R(S^*). \tag{16.13}$$

The resulting first-order condition

$$1 + p'(x)R(S^*) = 0, \tag{16.14}$$

defines the optimal level of care $\tilde{x}$. It is interesting to compare the defendant's care in this case with the model in which settlement was not possible. Since the defendant always has the option in the current model to take all cases to trial by offering $S = 0$,[13] it must be the case that his costs are lower (or at least no higher) when he has the option to settle. Thus, $R(S^*) \leq A$, implying that $\tilde{x} \leq \hat{x}$. Thus, the possibility of settlement will tend to reduce the defendant's incentive to take care (Polinsky and Rubinfeld, 1988).

Consider next expected social costs when settlement is possible. Conditional on an accident having occurred, these costs are

$$H_S = E(L) + k + (1 - F(S^* + c_p))(c_p + c_d). \tag{16.15}$$

Subtracting the injurer's minimized costs from this quantity yields

$$H_S - R(S^*) = \int_0^{S^* + c_p} (L + k - S^*)dF(L) + [1 - F(S^* + c_p)](k + c_p). \tag{16.16}$$

In contrast to the case where settlement was not possible, this comparison is ambiguous. As before, social costs tend to be higher than private costs because the defendant ignores the plaintiff's filing and trial costs for those cases that go to trial. This is captured by the second term in (16.16). The first term, however, is ambiguous in sign, given our assumption that $S^* > k$. This reflects the fact that for cases that settle, the defendant overcompensates those plaintiffs whose damages plus filing costs are

---

[13] See footnote 12.

less than the amount the defendant ends up paying them. Thus, although the defendant will not generally take the efficient level of care, we cannot determine whether he is over- or underdeterred (though underdeterrence seems to be the more plausible outcome).[14]

As before, the condition for lawsuits to be socially desirable in this case is

$$\tilde{x} + p(\tilde{x})H_S < p(0)E(L), \qquad (16.17)$$

which is ambiguous in sign, based on the same factors discussed in connection with condition (16.8).

Continuing with the above example, we find that when settlement is possible, $S^* = \$300$ and $R(S^*) = \$620$.[15] Thus, $S^* > k$ and $R(S^*) < A$ ($= \$633.75$) as required. In the case where $\theta=1$, the injurer's optimal care choice is $\tilde{x} = \$1.131$, and the resulting risk of an accident is $p(\tilde{x}) = 0.00161$. Thus, compared to the case where settlement was not allowed, the injurer takes less care ($\$1.131 < \$1.153$), and the probability of an accident is correspondingly higher ($0.00161 > 0.00158$). Finally, condition (16.17) holds in this case ($\$2.403 < \$2.5$), implying that suits are socially desirable. Recall that this was not true in the above example without settlements for the case of $\theta = 1$. The opposite conclusion is obtained here because the possibility of settlement lowers the social cost of lawsuits more than it reduces incentives for care.

5. Extensions
This section discusses several extensions of the basic model.

5.1. The Lawmaking Function of Trials
An important social benefit of trials not accounted for in the model to this point is their lawmaking function. Trials potentially perform this function by allowing judges the opportunity to evaluate existing legal rules (precedents) and possibly replace them with more efficient rules (by which we mean rules that lower social costs by creating better incentives for injurers, and possibly victims, to invest in accident avoidance). Settlements cannot perform this function because cases that settle never come before the court

---

[14] A comparison of social costs in the models with and without settlement similarly shows that the possibility of settlement may raise or lower social costs (i.e., $H_S - H$ is ambiguous in sign). On one hand, settlement causes some cases to be filed that otherwise would not have been, thereby raising filing costs, but on the other, settlement allows some trial costs to be saved.

[15] For the case of a uniform distribution for L, it turns out that $S^* = c_d$.

to be evaluated. Thus, to the extent that trials tend to promote the selection of more efficient rules over time, they are socially valuable. The key question, then, is whether or not this favorable selection is likely to occur.

Two possible mechanisms have been proposed.[16] The first, originally advanced by Richard Posner, is that common law judges consciously (or unconsciously) promote efficiency by selecting more efficient rules. (See, for example, Posner, 2003, p. 252.) This view, however, has not attracted much appeal because it relies on the motivation and incentives of judges, neither of which is well-understood.[17] Another line of literature, beginning with Rubin (1977) and Priest (1977), has therefore suggested that the law may evolve toward efficiency without the help of judges. According to this "selective litigation" argument, inefficient laws will tend to be litigated more often than efficient laws because the former impose higher costs on victims. As a result, inefficient laws will come before the court to be evaluated more often. And as long as judges are neither completely bound by precedent nor systematically biased *against* efficiency, then inefficient laws will be overturned at a higher rate, and the law will gradually evolve toward efficiency.

More recent literature has attempted to incorporate the possible bias of judges into this selective litigation model. Extending a framework developed by Gennaioli and Schleifer (2007a, 2007b), Miceli (2009) has shown that the direction of legal change depends on the relative strength of selective litigation and judicial bias. Specifically, the law will tend to evolve toward efficiency provided that the fraction of judges biased against the efficient rule is less than the conditional probability that a case reaching trial involves an inefficient law.

5.2. *Deterministic Damages*

Menell (1983) extended Shavell's (1982) original model by proposing a different formulation of the accident technology in which the victim's damages are a deterministic function of the injurer's care rather than being probabilistic. That is, damages occur with certainty but are decreasing in the injurer's care: $L = L(x)$, where $L' < 0$. Such a model is perhaps more descriptive of breach of contract or nuisance cases rather than accidents. An implication of this alternative specification is that the injurer can determine, by his choice of care, whether or not the victim finds a suit profitable.

---

[16] For a more thorough discussion of this issue, see Cooter and Rubinfeld (1989, pp. 1091–4).

[17] But see Posner (1995, Chapter 3) and Miceli and Cosgel (1994) for some initial efforts in that direction.

Specifically, by choosing x such that $L(x) \leq k + c_p$, he can forestall a suit. Using this model, Menell (1983) showed that the injurer's private choice of care coincides with the socially optimal choice. However, Kaplow (1986) and Rose-Ackerman and Geistfeld (1987) showed that it remains true that the victim's private incentive to sue is not necessarily optimal. Thus, a rule prohibiting suit might still be socially desirable. The details of these results are provided in the Appendix.

5.3. Alternative Cost Rules

To this point, the analysis has concentrated on the American rule for cost allocation, under which plaintiffs and defendants pay their own legal costs. It has often been proposed, however, that switching to the English, or "loser-pays," rule would lower litigation costs by discouraging plaintiffs from filing cases that have no value at trial (so-called frivolous suits). In the context of the model employed here, all cases with $L > 0$ have value in the sense that they would produce a positive judgment at trial.[18] In this case, a loser-pays rule actually encourages more suits to be filed as compared to the American rule because plaintiffs do not expect to incur the cost of a trial. This increase in litigation, however, is inefficient when suits are not socially valuable, and may or may not be efficient when suits are socially valuable. Thus, as a general proposition, there is no reason to believe that the loser-pays rule will systematically improve the efficiency of the legal system (Shavell, 1997; Rose-Ackerman and Geistfeld, 1987). The same conclusion applies to contingent fees, under which plaintiffs only pay their legal fees if they receive a positive settlement amount or win at trial.

5.4. Bilateral Care Accidents.

Finally, we briefly consider how the conclusions from the unilateral care accident model extend to the case of bilateral care, where victims can also take care to avoid accidents.[19] Formally, the probability of an accident in this case becomes $p(x,y)$, where victim care, y, reduces p in the same manner as x. All other elements of the model remain the same.

Note first that the filing decision of victims is unaffected by this change, as victims still decide whether or not to sue based on a comparison of their expected gain at trial to the filing cost. The real difference concerns the deterrent effect of suits. Suppose first that suits are allowed and liability is strict. Then, as before, the injurer will invest in a positive level of care

---

[18] I restrict attention to strict liability, though the basic conclusions apply to negligence as well.
[19] This situation has been studied by Miceli (2008).

because he expects to face lawsuits by some victims. (Specifically, he will choose x to minimize (16.2) with $p(x)$ replaced by $p(x,y)$, taking y as given.) As for victims, they will also choose a positive level of care; specifically, they will choose y to minimize their expected uncompensated losses, which consist of their actual damages multiplied by the probability that they will not sue, plus their litigation costs multiplied by the probability that they will sue. (Remember that victims do not know their actual damage until an accident occurs.) Thus, both injurers and victims take some care under strict liability, though neither takes the efficient level of care.

Now suppose that suits are prohibited (or equivalently that the rule is no liability). In that case, injurers will take *no care* because they face no risk of a suit, but victims will take *efficient care*, given $x = 0$. That is, they will choose y to minimize their full expected costs (care plus expected damages). As in the unilateral care model, the desirability of suits depends on a comparison of social costs in the two cases. The main difference here is that trials may actually result in less overall deterrence, given the incentives for victim care under a rule prohibiting trial. This will tend to make suits less valuable as a means of promoting deterrence in situations where victim care is very productive in reducing accident risk. Finally, as in the unilateral care case, a negligence rule may be able to achieve the first-best outcome in which both injurers and victims take efficient care, and no suits are filed, though this outcome is not assured.

6. Conclusion

The principal conclusions of this chapter can be summarized as follows. First, the private value of a lawsuit depends on the plaintiff's expected gain at trial compared to his or her cost of filing suit, while the social value depends on the incentives lawsuits create for injurers to undertake efficient care to prevent accidents. Second, the social and private value of lawsuits generally differ, but there is no necessary relationship between them – that is, there may be too many or too few suits. Third, while corrective policies could theoretically resolve this disconnect, there is no simple policy, and the requisite information, especially regarding the deterrent effects of lawsuits, is not easily obtained by policymakers. Fourth, a negligence rule potentially leads to the first-best outcome (efficient injurer care and no suits) because victims will be discouraged from filing if the injurer meets the due standard. Several factors, however, make this outcome unlikely in practice. Fifth, the possibility of settlement generally reduces the deterrent effects of lawsuits by lowering the cost of accidents to injurers. However, settlement increases the private value of suits by inducing some plaintiffs to file who would not have done so in the absence of settlement (those at the low end of the damage distribution). Thus, the social value of suits may or may not increase compared to the model without settlement. Sixth, the lawmaking function of trials increases the social value of trials relative to a rule prohibiting trial. Finally, introducing victim care into the model will tend to make a rule prohibiting trial more desirable because of the incentives it creates for victims to take care.

References

Bebchuk, Lucian (1988), 'Suing Solely to Extract a Settlement Offer', **17** *Journal of Legal Studies*, 437–50.
Brown, John (1973), 'Toward an Economic Theory of Liability', **2** *Journal of Legal Studies*, 323–49.
Cooter, Robert, and Daniel Rubinfeld (1989), 'An Economic Analysis of Legal Disputes and their Resolution', **27**, 1067–97.
Craswell, Richard, and John Calfee (1986), 'Deterrence and Uncertain Legal Standards', **2**, 279–303.
Gennaioli, Nicola, and Andrei Schleifer (2007a), 'The Evolution of the Common Law', **115**, 43–68.
Gennaioli, Nicola, and Andrei Schleifer (2007b), 'Overruling and the Instability of Law', **35** *Journal of Comparative Economics*, 309–28.
Hylton, Keith (1990), 'Costly Litigation and Legal Error under Negligence', **6** *Journal of Law, Economics, and Organization*, 433–52.
Kaplow, Louis (1986), 'Private versus Social Costs in Bringing Suits', **15** *Journal of Legal Studies*, 371–85.
Katz, Avery (1990), 'The Effect of Frivolous Litigation on the Settlement of Legal Disputes', **10** *International Review of Law and Economics*, 3–27.
Landes, William, and Richard Posner (1987), *The Economic Structure of Tort Law*, Cambridge, MA: Harvard University Press.
Menell, Peter (1983), 'A Note on Private versus Social Incentives to Sue in a Costly Legal System', **12** *Journal of Legal Studies*, 41–52.
Miceli, Thomas (2008), 'A Note on the Social versus Private Value of Suits when Care is Bilateral', **4** *Research in Law and Economics*, 373–82.
Miceli, Thomas (2009), 'Legal Change: Selective Litigation, Judicial Bias, and Precedent', **38** *Journal of Legal Studies*, 157–68.
Miceli, Thomas, and Metin Cosgel (1994), 'Reputation and Judicial Decision-making', **23** *Journal of Economic Behavior and Organization*, 31–51.
P'ng, I.P.L. (1986), 'Optimal Subsidies and Damages in the Presence of Legal Error', **6** *International Review of Law and Economics*, 101–5.
Polinsky, A. Mitchell, and Y.K. Che (1991), 'Decoupling Liability: Optimal Incentives for Care and Litigation', **22** *Rand Journal of Economics*, 562–70.
Polinsky, A. Mitchell, and Daniel Rubinfeld (1988), 'The Deterrent Effects of Settlements and Trials', **8** *International Review of Law and Economics*, 109–16.
Polinsky, A. Mitchell, and Steven Shavell (1989), 'Legal Error, Litigation, and the Incentive to Obey the Law', **5** *Journal of Law, Economics, and Organization*, 99–108.
Posner, Richard (1995), *Overcoming Law*, Cambridge, MA: Harvard University Press.
Posner, Richard (2003), *Economic Analysis of Law*, 6th edition, New York: Aspen Law & Business.
Priest, George (1977), 'The Common Law Process and the Selection of Efficient Rules', **6**, 65–82.
Rose-Ackerman, Susan, and Mark Geistfeld (1987), 'The Divergence between Social and Private Incentives to Sue: A Comment on Shavell, Menell, and Kaplow', **16** *Journal of Legal Studies*, 483–91.
Rubin, Paul (1977), 'Why is the Common Law Efficient?' **3** *Journal of Legal Studies*, 51–63.

Shavell, Steven (1982), 'The Social versus the Private Incentive to Bring Suit in a Costly Legal System', **11** *Journal of Legal Studies*, 333–9.
Shavell, Steven (1987), *Economic Analysis of Accident Law*, Cambridge, MA: Harvard University Press.
Shavell, Steven (1997), 'The Fundamental Divergence between the Private and the Social Motive to Use the Legal System', **26** *Journal of Legal Studies*, 575–612.
Shavell, Steven (1999), 'The Level of Litigation: Private versus Social Optimality of Suit and of Settlement', **19** *International Review of Law and Economics*, 99–115.
Shavell, Steven (2004), *Foundations of Economic Analysis of Law*, Cambridge, MA: Belknap Press.

Appendix

In Menell's (1983) model, the injurer can forestall suit by choosing care such that $L(x) \leq k + c_p$ (assuming that when indifferent, the victim does not file). Obviously, the injurer will never choose more care than necessary. Thus, define x_n by the equation

$$L(x_n) = k + c_p. \tag{16.A1}$$

If the injurer instead chooses a level of care that results in a suit, he will choose x to minimize $x + L(x) + c_d$. Let x' be the resulting care level. (Thus, x' solves the first-order condition $1 + L' = 0$.) The injurer will choose x_n, and forestall suit, if and only if

$$x_n \leq x' + L(x') + c_d. \tag{16.A2}$$

Now consider social costs. If the injurer chooses x_n, social costs are $x_n + L(x_n)$, whereas if he chooses x', social costs are $x' + L(x') + k + c_p + c_d$. It is therefore socially optimal for the injurer to choose x_n if and only if

$$x_n + L(x_n) \leq x' + L(x') + k + c_p + c_d. \tag{16.A3}$$

Substituting for $L(x_n)$ from (16.A1) and cancelling terms immediately transforms (16.A3) into (16.A2). Thus, the social and private conditions are identical.

The preceding has assumed that suits are always allowed, but now consider the possible optimality of a rule prohibiting suit. Suppose first that suits occur according to the above analysis (i.e., the inequality in (16.A2) is reversed). If in this case suits were prohibited, the injurer would take zero care, yielding social costs of $L(0)$. This is preferred to the outcome with suits if and only if

$$L(0) < x' + L(x') + k + c_p + c_d. \tag{16.A4}$$

Since this condition may or may not hold, a rule prohibiting suits may be optimal.

Alternatively, suppose that (16.A2) holds, so the defendant forestalls suits (though suits are allowed). It is socially desirable for the state to prohibit suits in this case if

$$L(0) < x_n + L(x_n). \tag{16.A5}$$

Again, this condition may or may not hold. (Obviously, it will not hold for $x_n \leq x'$ since, by definition, $x + L(x)$ is decreasing in x up to x'. Thus, it can only hold for x_n substantially greater than x'. But note that this is not ruled out by (16.A2).) If (16.A5) holds, then a rule prohibiting suit would be desirable even though the defendant forestalls suits by his choice of care. (While the prohibition of suits does not save litigation costs in this case, it reduces the defendant's choice of care from x_n to zero which, if (16.A5) holds, lowers social costs.)

17 Trial selection theory and evidence
Keith N. Hylton and Haizhen Lin

1. Introduction

This chapter presents a review of trial selection theory. We use the term "trial selection theory" to refer to models that attempt to explain or predict the characteristics that distinguish cases that are litigated to judgment from those that settle, and the implications of those characteristics for the development of legal doctrine and for important trial outcome parameters, such as the plaintiff win rate. Using this definition, trial selection theory can be said to have started with Priest and Klein (1984).

Trial selection theory is important for many reasons. People often refer to plaintiff win rates in an attempt to assess whether the law works as it should in certain areas of litigation.[1] Low plaintiff win rates are often cited as a sign that the law favors defendants, and conversely. Trial selection theory is useful in any effort to draw reliable inferences from trial outcome statistics.

Another reason trial selection theory is useful is that it helps us understand how litigation influences the path of the law. If, for example, the most uncertain cases are the ones that go to trial, then the law will not exhibit a pro-plaintiff or pro-defendant bias over time. If, on the other hand, the cases that go to trial tend to be those with facts that favor defendants, then we will observe legal rules that exhibit a pro-defendant bias.

On a more confounding level, trial selection theory implies that legal analysts have to read court decisions with care, in order to avoid confusing characteristics of the sample of litigated cases with characteristics of all legal disputes. If the cases that make it all the way to litigation form an unrepresentative sample of legal disputes, then certain features of decided cases may be unreliable signals of the decision-making process of courts. For example, a legal analyst who observes that all of the cases in which defendants are held negligent involve facts in which the reasonable level of precaution is difficult to determine might draw the conclusion that courts find the negligence standard difficult to apply, when in fact the easy-to-determine negligence cases never went all the way to judgment.

---

[1] On the political uses of win rate data see, e.g., Daniels and Martin (1995).

The best-known trial selection theory is the "divergent expectations" model of Priest and Klein. According to the theory of Priest and Klein, only the most uncertain disputes (i.e., coin tosses) make it all the way to a court judgment, and as a result plaintiff win rates tend toward 50 percent unless the parties have asymmetric stakes. The best-known alternative to the divergent expectations theory is the informational asymmetry theory, which holds that plaintiff win rates will tend toward 50 percent only when neither party has the informational advantage, and otherwise the win rate will be greater for the informed party. However, the divergent expectations and asymmetric information theories are by no means the only possible models of trial selection.[2]

Section 2 presents a review of the literature. Section 3 presents a general model that includes Priest-Klein and asymmetric information theories as special cases. Section 4 discusses practical considerations in asymmetric information models of litigation. Section 5 discusses empirical evidence on trial selection theory.

2. Literature Review

The trial selection literature consists of two parts. One consists of studies of the economics of the settlement decision. The other consists of studies of the selection of disputes for litigation and the implications of that process for important parameters such as the rate of plaintiff victory.

2.1. The Settlement Decision

The foundation for much of the literature on the economics of settlement is the Landes-Posner-Gould (LPG) settlement model,[3] which implies that settlement occurs when the difference between the plaintiff's and the defendant's predictions of the judgment (divergence in expectations) is less than the total cost of litigation. The LPG model is based on a rationality (or incentive compatibility) constraint on settlements: a settlement has to be perceived by the plaintiff and by the defendant as improving his position relative to litigation. The LPG condition is assumed to be both a necessary and sufficient condition for settlement. The model ignores questions of strategic behavior and informational asymmetry.

Much of the literature examining the economics of settlement builds on the LPG framework. Shavell (1982), setting out the most complete early formal analysis of the litigation-settlement decision, suggests that

---

[2] See, e.g., Eisenberg and Farber (1997), and discussion within.
[3] See Landes (1971), Gould (1973), and Posner (1973).

litigation results from excessive optimism on the part of plaintiffs and defendants.

The literature on the economics of settlement has been expanded significantly by incorporating asymmetric information and strategic behavior. The first article to introduce strategic behavior and informational asymmetry was P'ng (1983), followed closely by Bebchuk (1984). The informational asymmetry framework introduced in the P'ng and Bebchuk articles assumed that the defendant has an informational advantage in litigation. However, P'ng's is a signaling model in which the informed defendant makes the settlement offer, while Bebchuk's is a screening model in which the uninformed plaintiff makes a settlement demand. The asymmetric information models demonstrate that there are cases litigated under conditions that would not lead to litigation in the LPG model.

The asymmetric information literature of settlement has expanded significantly since the P'ng and Bebchuk articles. Spier (1992) examines the path of settlement negotiations over stages. Daughety and Reinganum (1993) present a model that incorporates different informational advantage assumptions and examine the implications for settlement and trial. Hay (1995) examines the influence of discovery on settlement negotiations.

2.2. Selection Hypothesis or Effect

The second major strand of literature on the economics of trial selection is a set of articles focusing on the selection hypothesis (or selection effect) introduced by Priest and Klein (1984). The selection framework of Priest and Klein assumes that parties in litigation have symmetric information and does not explicitly incorporate strategic behavior. The Priest-Klein selection hypothesis holds that only the most uncertain disputes go all the way to a judgment in litigation. The resulting win rate for plaintiffs is 50 percent, because trials are just as uncertain as coin tosses. If, on the other hand, parties have asymmetric stakes, the plaintiff win rate may exceed or fall below 50 percent under the Priest-Klein model.[4] Priest and Klein introduced empirical evidence to support their hypothesis. Eisenberg (1990) found significant deviations from the 50 percent hypothesis.

The selection hypothesis literature, like the settlement literature generally, has been expanded by the incorporation of strategic behavior and asymmetric information. The first paper to consider the implications of asymmetric information for the selection hypothesis was Hylton (1993).

---

[4] For an early critique of the Priest-Klein model, see Wittman (1985). Wittman found that in a more general model there was no tendency toward a 50 percent win rate.

The second paper was Shavell (1996). Since the analysis in Hylton was largely informal, the Shavell article introduces the first formal model of the selection hypothesis in the context of informational asymmetry.

Hylton (1993) concluded that the Priest-Klein 50 percent hypothesis was correct in the informational symmetry setting, but that plaintiff win rates would deviate from 50 percent in the information asymmetry setting. Specifically, plaintiff win rates should be less than (greater than) 50 percent when defendants (plaintiffs) have the informational advantage in litigation. Hylton argued that the empirical evidence presented in Eisenberg (1990) on plaintiff win rates supports this hypothesis.

Shavell, building on the screening model of Bebchuk (1984), concluded that any win rate percentage could be observed, and that there was no clear tendency for the plaintiff win rate to be less than or greater than 50 percent in the context of informational asymmetry. Shavell found that the differential settlement incentives tended to depress plaintiff win rates when the defendant had the informational advantage, but found no basis for concluding that the win rate in that setting would be less than 50 percent.

Hylton (2002) presents an alternative model of the selection effect within the informational asymmetry context. The alternative model builds on the signaling framework of P'ng (1987) to analyze the trial outcome parameters under informational asymmetry. The signaling framework delivers results that differ from the screening framework employed by Shavell. The results of the signaling model are generally consistent with the informal analysis of Hylton (1993).

More recent literature has attempted to test Priest-Klein and asymmetric information theories of the selection effect, as well as introduce additional theories. Eisenberg and Farber (1996) introduce the litigious-plaintiff hypothesis, which holds that win rates can be understood according to the plaintiff's cost of litigation, which varies more for individuals than for corporations. Kessler, Meites, and Miller (1996) find that the Priest-Klein model tends to be confirmed in settings that are consistent with its assumptions (symmetric information and symmetric stakes), but that win rates deviate from 50 percent under informational asymmetry and in other contexts. Waldfogel (1998) finds that the empirical evidence supports the Priest-Klein model with deviations from 50 percent due to asymmetry in litigation stakes.

2.3. Overview

Many contributions to the trial selection literature do not distinguish the two strands (settlement versus selection effects) identified in the foregoing discussion. Yet it is important to distinguish the general models of litigation and settlement from the models of the selection effect on trial outcomes. Many of the general models of settlement do not yield testable hypotheses concerning trial outcomes. In contrast, the selection effects literature, beginning with Priest and Klein, aims to generate testable predictions on important trial outcome parameters.

In particular, the asymmetric information models of settlement generate substantial variation in their predictions. The signaling approach introduced in P'ng (1983) and explored in P'ng (1987) yields different equilibrium outcomes than the screening model introduced in Bebchuk (1984). There is no single asymmetric information model of settlement that produces a set of standard results. Given this, it seems appropriate to either examine asymmetric information models in the context of their particular assumptions, or to attempt to minimize the importance of the assumptions. In the model below, we attempt the latter strategy by introducing uncertainty in the litigants' predictions. The model below reconciles Priest-Klein and asymmetric information hypotheses.

3. Model

3.1. Assumptions

In this section, we will set up a simple model of trial selection, based on Hylton (2006), that includes the Priest-Klein model as a special case. The first component of this model is the Landes-Posner-Gould (LPG) rationality condition. Under the LPG model, parties choose to litigate rather than settle a dispute if and only if

$$(P_p - P_d) > \gamma, \tag{17.1}$$

where P_p = plaintiff's estimate of the probability of a verdict in his favor, P_d = defendant's estimate of the probability of a verdict in plaintiff's favor; $\gamma = C/J$, where C = the sum of the plaintiff's litigation cost (C_p) and the defendant's litigation cost (C_d), and J = the value of the judgment. We assume that the settlement cost is zero. If the LPG litigation condition (17.1) holds, the set of mutually beneficial settlement agreements is empty, so the parties choose to litigate.[5]

---

[5] For an asymmetric information model in which the LPG condition continues to determine litigation outcomes, see Hylton (2002). By relying on the LPG framework, we are assuming that the nonexistence of a mutually beneficial settlement is the main determinant of litigation.

492 *Procedural law and economics*

The second basic component of this model is the assumption that each party's predictions can be modeled as the sum of a rational estimate and an idiosyncratic error term

$$P_p = P'_p + \varepsilon_p \tag{17.2}$$

$$P_d = P'_d + \varepsilon_d \tag{17.3}$$

If Ω_p represents the information set of the plaintiff, and Ω_d represents the information set of the defendant, then $P'_p = E(P_p|\Omega_p)$, $P'_d = E(P_d|\Omega_d)$, $E(\varepsilon_p|\Omega_p) = 0$, $E(\varepsilon_d|\Omega_d) = 0$.

The third basic component of the model is a specification of the plaintiff's and the defendant's rational estimates of the probability of a verdict in favor of the plaintiff. Let W = the probability that the defendant in a legal dispute violated the legal standard. Let Q_1 = the probability that a defendant who has violated the legal standard will be found innocent (type-1 judicial error). Let Q_2 = the probability that a defendant who has not violated the legal standard will be found guilty (type-2 judicial error). So that courts are at least as accurate as coin tosses, we will assume that $1 - Q_1 > Q_2$. The plaintiff's rational estimate of a verdict in the plaintiff's favor can be expressed as a function of the compliance and judicial-error probabilities:

$$P'_p = W_p(1 - Q_{1p}) + (1 - W_p)Q_{2p}, \tag{17.4}$$

where $W_p = E(W|\Omega_p)$, $Q_{1p} = E(Q_1|\Omega_p)$, $Q_{2p} = E(Q_2|\Omega_p)$. Similarly, $P'_d = W_d(1 - Q_{1d}) + (1 - W_d)Q_{2d}$.

We focus on two types of information set immediately below. One is the case in which the litigant has minimal case-specific information and forms a rational estimate of the likelihood of a verdict on the plaintiff's side using that minimal information. This is the case of the uninformed litigant. The other is the case in which a litigant has private information and knows whether the defendant complied with the legal standard. For example, an uninformed malpractice plaintiff will know that he has been injured, but will not know whether the injury is due to the defendant's negligence. An informed malpractice defendant will know not only that he has injured the patient, but also whether or not he was negligent.

In the case of the uninformed litigant, we will assume that his rational predictions are accurate and equal to the true case-specific probabilities of compliance and of error (given minimal case-specific information). Thus, if the plaintiff is uninformed, his prediction is the objective probability of a verdict in favor of the plaintiff, i.e., $P'_p = W(1 - Q_1) + (1 - W)Q_2$.

Similarly, if the defendant is uninformed, $P'_d = W(1 - Q_1) + (1 - W)Q_2$. To simplify, let us label the objective probability of a verdict in the plaintiff's favor

$$v = W(1 - Q_1) + (1 - W)Q_2. \tag{17.5}$$

If one of the parties has private information on compliance, his estimate of W is equal to 1 in the case of non-compliance, or 0 in the case of compliance. Thus, to take one example, if the defendant is informed and innocent, $P_d = P'_d = Q_2$.

The fourth component is a *heteroscedasticity assumption* regarding the error variances of the predictions.[6] From the perspective of a litigant, the outcome of a dispute is most uncertain when the rational component of the litigants' prediction is equal to 0.5. This is the case in which the outcome of the dispute is viewed by the litigant as a coin toss; the litigant may have a great deal of information on the case, but the sum total of his information leads him to believe that a finding of guilt (or liability) is just as likely as a finding of innocence (non-liability). Consistent with Priest and Klein (1984), we therefore assume that the variance of the prediction error term is a function of the rational component of the litigant's prediction, and that the variance reaches a maximum when the rational component is 0.5 and with minima at 0 and 1 (see Figure 17.1 below).

3.2. Frequency of Litigation

The probability of litigation is

$$f = prob((P_p - P_d) > \gamma) \tag{17.6}$$

which, given (17.2) and (17.3), is

$$f = prob(\varepsilon_p - \varepsilon_d > \gamma - \Delta), \tag{17.7}$$

where $\Delta = P'_p - P'_d$. We assume that the error difference $\varepsilon_p - \varepsilon_d$ is generated by a truncated normal distribution with mean zero and standard deviation σ, where $\varepsilon_p - \varepsilon_d \in [-1 - \Delta, 1 - \Delta]$. The variance of the error difference can be decomposed as $\sigma^2 = \sigma_p^2 + \sigma_d^2 - 2\rho$.

Based on the foregoing, the frequency of litigation is given by

---

[6] Wittman (1985) emphasizes the importance of the heteroscedasticity assumption in the Priest-Klein analysis.

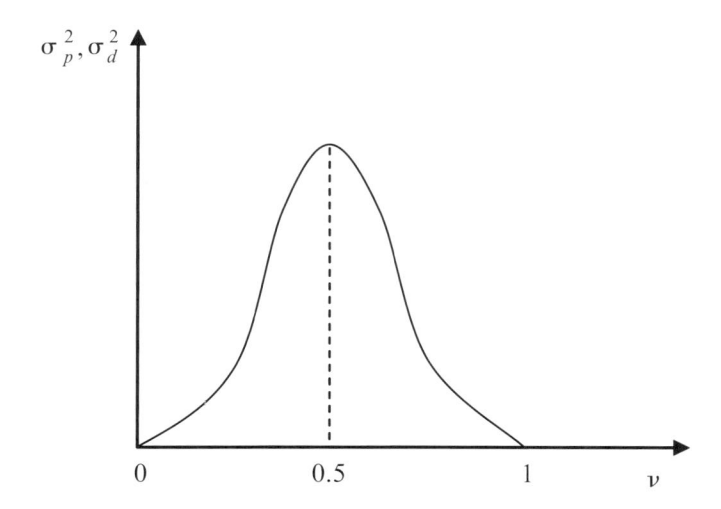

Figure 17.1 Prediction error variance

$$f = 1 - G, \qquad (17.8)$$

where G, which is the probability of settlement, is

$$G(\gamma - \Delta; -1 - \Delta, 1 - \Delta) = \frac{\Phi\left(\frac{\gamma - \Delta}{\sigma}\right) - \Phi\left(\frac{-1 - \Delta}{\sigma}\right)}{\Phi\left(\frac{1 - \Delta}{\sigma}\right) - \Phi\left(\frac{-1 - \Delta}{\sigma}\right)}. \qquad (17.9)$$

The heteroscedasticity assumption implies that as the degree of uncertainty concerning the judgment increases (as reflected in the variance terms in the denominator), the probability of litigation rises (Priest and Klein, 1984).[7]

The frequency of litigation function combines features from several models of the litigation process. Note that as the cost of litigation rises relative to the judgment – i.e., as γ increases – the probability of litigation falls, a prediction of the Landes-Posner-Gould framework. The Priest-Klein model is also incorporated by the assumption of heteroscedastic prediction-error variances. Over-optimism appears as a factor that gener-

---

[7] This result is in Hylton (2006), but is based on a non-truncated normal, which is technically inappropriate. The same result holds for the truncated case, but the proof is complicated; we have explored it in a separate paper (in progress).

ates litigation (Shavell, 1982). Over-optimism is incorporated in the model by assuming a negative correlation between prediction errors, which reduces σ (because $\sigma^2 = \sigma_p^2 + \sigma_d^2 - 2\sigma$). When the correlation between the parties' prediction errors is negative, plaintiffs overestimate the size of the judgment, while defendants underestimate the size of the judgment.

3.2.1. Priest-Klein case   Under the Priest-Klein analysis, litigation is driven by uncertainty and the plaintiff win rate equals 50 percent. The reason is that only disputes that are as uncertain as coin tosses make it all the way to judgment.

The frequency of litigation function f can generate the analysis of Priest and Klein when the rational predictions of the plaintiff and the defendant are the same ($P'_p = P'_d$, or $\Delta = 0$). In this case, the key factor leading to litigation is uncertainty, as reflected in the error variance in the denominator of (17.9). The Priest-Klein model assumes that uncertainty regarding trial-outcome predictions increases as the defendant's conduct comes closer to the legal standard, which implies that the rational component of the trial-outcome prediction is 50 percent ($P'_p = P'_d = 0.5$).

A precise description of the Priest-Klein theorem within the context of this model can be achieved by examining the plaintiff's win rate. The average plaintiff win rate takes into account the frequency of litigation, which is a function of the probability of litigation conditional on v (the f function) and the distribution of v. If the distribution of v is uniform, this can be expressed as:

$$\bar{\pi} = \int_0^1 v f(v) \, dv. \tag{17.10}$$

Given the assumptions on the error variances (see Figure 17.1), f is symmetric around $v = 0.5$. Under these assumptions $\bar{\pi} = 0.5$.[8]

3.2.2. Asymmetric information case   There are two asymmetric information cases to consider: where the defendant has the informational advantage and where the plaintiff has the informational advantage.

When the defendant has the informational advantage, the frequency of litigation will depend on the defendant's type. If the plaintiff is uninformed

---

[8] For a sketch of this special case, see Hylton (2006), but the argument is incomplete and the more general problem of ascertaining the conditions under which the Priest-Klein result holds is not examined in that paper. We examine the Priest-Klein model in a more general setting in a separate paper in progress.

and the defendant is innocent, $P'_p = W(1 - Q_1) + (1 - W)Q_2$, $P'_d = Q_2$. Thus, $\Delta_I = W(1 - Q_1 - Q_2)$. Let f_I be the probability of litigation evaluated at Δ_I. If the defendant is guilty, $P'_p = W(1 - Q_1) + (1 - W)Q_2$, $P'_d = 1 - Q_1$, and $\Delta_G = -(1 - W)(1 - Q_1 - Q_2)$. Let f_G be the probability of litigation evaluated Δ_G. In the nontruncated normal case examined in Hylton (2006), it is immediately clear that the frequency of litigation is larger for cases involving innocent defendants, i.e., $f_I > f_G$. In the truncated case, the same result holds in most cases.[9] This is because guilty defendants settle their cases at a higher rate than the innocent.

The average win rate, when the defendant has the informational advantage, is

$$\bar{\pi}_2 = \int_0^1 [Wf_G(1 - Q_1) + (1 - W)f_I Q_2] dv. \tag{17.11}$$

Because the frequency of litigation is greater for innocent defendants, the average win rate expression implies that instead of a tendency toward 50 percent, the average win rate when the defendant has the informational advantage will tend toward some level less than 50 percent, i.e., $\bar{\pi}_2 < \bar{\pi}$.

Now suppose the plaintiff has the informational advantage. There are two cases to consider: when the plaintiff deserves to win (*meritorious* plaintiff), and when the plaintiff deserves to lose (*non-meritorious* plaintiff). In the non-meritorious case, the plaintiff brings a claim that deserves to be called frivolous. The plaintiff brings it because he knows that with probability Q_2 he will be awarded damages by the court.

In the meritorious plaintiff case, the probability of litigation f_I where $\Delta_I = (1 - W)(1 - Q_1 - Q_2)$. In the non-meritorious case, the probability of litigation is f_G, where $\Delta_G = -W(1 - Q_1 - Q_2)$. The pairing between the uninformed defendant and the informed and meritorious (innocent) plaintiff is more likely to litigate than that of the frivolous (guilty) plaintiff. The reason is that the guilty plaintiff tends to settle his claim. This leads to high win rates, exceeding 50 percent.

The foregoing analysis can be summarized in the form of a simple proposition offered in Hylton (1993):

Divergent Expectations/Asymmetric Information Selection Hypothesis: If neither the plaintiff nor the defendant has the informational advantage in litigation, the plaintiff win rate will tend toward 50 percent. If the

---

[9] The proofs have been omitted from this paper, and are presented in a separate paper.

defendant (plaintiff) has the informational advantage, the plaintiff win rate will be less than (greater than) 50 percent.

This proposition provides a general selection theory based on the parties' possession of information relevant to the probability of a verdict for the plaintiff. The Priest-Klein hypothesis is a special case that holds in the absence of a substantial informational disparity.

4. Strategic Behavior Models of Litigation: Some Practical Considerations

As we noted at the outset, the signaling and screening approaches in the literature have generated different implications in the models analyzing the selection effect. The screening model generates no clear implication with respect to the level of the plaintiff win rate (Shavell, 1996). The signaling model, however, generates results more in line with the view that informational asymmetry leads to predictable deviations from the 50 percent plaintiff win rate prediction. Neither approach clearly yields the Priest-Klein model's 50 percent prediction – though the prediction is consistent with the signaling model. The model presented in the previous section has the desirable feature of generating the Priest-Klein prediction and also including the asymmetric information models as special cases.

The success of the foregoing model in delivering the Priest-Klein prediction raises the question whether the screening approach is preferable to the signaling model in the analysis of selection effects. There are good reasons to prefer either the signaling model or a different version of the screening model than that used in the analysis of litigation outcomes.

First, if one considers the nature of litigation as a transaction, it seems intuitive that the signaling model should be preferred to the screening model.[10] The screening model is especially appropriate in the case of an uninformed actor that must set a contract term for many informed actors on the other side of the contact: e.g., an insurer setting terms for the uninsured (Rothschild and Stiglitz, 1976), a bank setting the interest rate on a loan (Stiglitz and Weiss, 1981), an employer setting the wage, or an airline setting the price of a plane ticket. In these settings, the uninformed actor can be said to have acted first, and is more or less forced by the circumstances to choose the contract term without being able to observe signals that would allow him to sort the contracting parties by type. The screening

---

[10] In a general assessment of signaling and screening models, Stiglitz and Weiss (1994) conclude that history and knowledge of the particular setting should inform decisions on the type of asymmetric information model.

model provides a useful description of the informed actor's incentives, and the general characteristics of the market equilibrium.

In the litigation context, there is no plausible sense in which the plaintiff or the defendant acts first, or is forced by the circumstances to choose a contract term (settlement offer) before observing any signals identifying the type of the other party. When the plaintiff makes a settlement demand, he is not setting a price for some faceless mass of counterparties; settlement involves a one-on-one bargaining relationship. The plaintiff can and typically does observe some signals from the defendant that would lead him to update his beliefs about the defendant's guilt. While the screening model is well suited to the scenarios in which it was originally applied, its appropriateness in the case of litigation is questionable.

One argument in favor of the screening model is that it leads to simple outcomes. The signaling models, in contrast, generate complicated results with more than one equilibrium outcome.[11] However, the simplicity advantage of the screening model has to be balanced against the cost of using such a model in the litigation setting. The screening model delivers general statements that offer a broad-brush view of the outcome (e.g., litigation will occur), but it does not offer specific testable predictions that are useful in the analysis of selection effects in litigation.

5. Empirical Evidence

In this section, we examine the empirical evidence on trial selection theory. Before examining the evidence, a few preliminary points are in order.

First, although trial selection theories are distinguishable from models of settlement, there is a close connection between the two. The divergent expectations (Priest-Klein) and asymmetric information selection theories are, as the model in the previous section shows, derivable from settlement models.

Indeed, one could generate a selection theory based on any particular variable that plays a role in the settlement decision. In settlement models, such as the LPG framework $[(P_p - P_d) > \gamma]$, the settlement decision is influenced by several major factors: the parties' predictions of the outcome of trial, the expected judgment, and the litigation costs borne by the parties. Each of these factors imparts some influence on the decision to go to trial. It follows that each of these factors also imparts some influence on the rate at which plaintiffs win at the trial level. The litigious-plaintiff hypothesis of Eisenberg and Farber employs variation in the parties' costs of litigation to generate a theory of trial selection (see also Langlais, Chopard, and

---

[11] Stiglitz and Weiss (1994).

Cortade, 2010). One could also use the variation in the plaintiff's award to generate a theory of selection (Miceli, 2008).

What distinguishes the Priest-Klein and asymmetric information theories is that they focus on the parties' trial outcome expectations and generate testable predictions on key trial outcome parameters. The best example is the Priest-Klein model, which generates a prediction that plaintiffs will win 50 percent of trials (unless stakes are asymmetric). Theories of selection based on variation in litigation costs or in the expected judgment are unlikely to generate equivalently strong testable predictions on the key trial outcome parameters.[12]

The other preliminary point worth noting is that the divergent expectations and asymmetric information models apply across a broad spectrum of hypotheses concerning factors that might influence trial outcomes. Suppose, for example, that one hypothesizes that trial judges are biased in favor of plaintiffs.[13] Under the Priest-Klein model, that should not lead to a prediction of a higher win rate for plaintiffs, as long as the bias is public information. If the bias is public information, both plaintiffs and defendant will take it into account in settlement discussions, and the 50 percent win rate prediction will still be observed. Other than asymmetric stakes, only unexpected shocks – say, an unannounced change in the decision standard – will cause the plaintiff win rate to deviate from its 50 percent tendency.

Similarly, informational asymmetry could be present in many different forms relevant to litigation. The common assumption is that the defendant knows more about the facts of his own compliance with the legal standard than does the plaintiff (P'ng, 1983; Bebchuk, 1984). But either party could have an informational advantage with respect to some variable that influences the trial outcome. Consider possible judicial biases. If the plaintiff has private information with respect to the bias of a particular judge, that information will influence the plaintiff's settlement conduct and impart an upward influence on plaintiff win rates (Hylton, 2006).

Asymmetric information theories could operate on a wide array of variables influencing the trial outcome and could be consistent with a wide array of trial outcome parameters (win rate, trial rate, etc). The defendant could have an informational advantage with respect to the facts of the case, while the plaintiff could have an informational advantage with

---

[12] For example, the litigious-plaintiff hypothesis of Eisenberg and Farber (1997) generates the prediction that on average individual plaintiffs will win less than corporate plaintiffs, but this offers no prediction on the win rate level.

[13] See, e.g., Eisenberg and Heise (2009), at 125.

respect to judicial biases. If the informational advantages are roughly the same on both sides, the conditions could be equivalent to the equal information assumption of Priest-Klein. If the advantages are not the same, then an analyst would have to assess whether the effect of one type of informational advantage dominates. An empirical test would have to start by specifying the variable with respect to which information is asymmetric, and a prediction of the selective effect that variable will have as a result of informational asymmetry.

5.1. Win Rate Observations

There are now several studies that present win rate patterns across several case categories (property, torts, malpractice, etc). These studies allow researchers to examine win rate evidence directly to check for consistency with a particular selection theory. Deviations from 50 percent can be explained under the Priest-Klein theory by asymmetric stakes. Alternatively, deviations from 50 percent can be explained by the asymmetric information model.

5.1.1. Across case categories Hylton (1993) argues that win rates tended in general to conform with the Priest-Klein prediction but that substantial deviations were observed in pockets in which one party was likely to have a significant informational advantage. The most obvious pockets are medical malpractice and product liability litigation, where defendants are likely to have a significant advantage with respect to information on their own compliance with the legal standard. Win rates for medical malpractice and products liability are consistently less than 50 percent (Eisenberg, 1990). Products liability is governed largely by the "risk-utility" standard, which is a type of negligence test that focuses on the incremental risk and incremental utility presented by the defendant's design in comparison with a safer alternative. The standard gives the defendant an informational advantage over the plaintiff. Similarly, the negligence standard for medical malpractice, which is based on the doctor's compliance with medical custom, gives the doctor an informational advantage over the plaintiff.

Win rates for contract actions tend to be greater than those for tort actions (Eisenberg, 1990, p. 357). This is consistent with the asymmetric information theory. Tort actions often involve defendants with private information on their own compliance with the legal standard. Contract actions, in comparison, generally look at the conduct of both parties in relation to objective rules governing offer and acceptance. Since defendant-side informational advantage is more common in the tort setting, lower plaintiff win rates are predicted under the informational asymmetry model. The asymmetric stakes theory, on the other hand, could explain this pattern only if plaintiffs generally have greater stakes in contract than in tort actions.

5.1.2. Within case categories Even within the products liability category, win rate patterns appear to be consistent with the asymmetric information theory. When the plaintiffs bring products liability claims based on contract – e.g., a claim that the product failed to perform as warranted – plaintiff win rates tend to be greater than 50 percent.[14] Products liability claims based on tort law tend have win rates less than 50 percent (Eisenberg, 1990). The asymmetric information model suggests that the key difference between product-liability contract and product-liability tort actions is that the defendant does not have an informational advantage under the legal standard used in the contract actions (Hylton, 2006).[15] In contrast to the asymmetric information theory, the stakes theory fails to explain the pattern of win rates observed within the products liability category. If defendants have greater stakes in these cases, as the stakes theory posits, they should tend to win more often than plaintiffs both in product-liability tort actions and in product-liability contract actions. However, one observes the opposite in the case of product-liability contract actions.

5.2. Other Observations of Trial Outcome Parameters and More Sophisticated Tests

Several recent studies have examined other trial outcome parameters or conducted more sophisticated tests of selection theories.

Waldfogel (1998) presents an empirical model that attempts to test the degree to which the divergent expectations and asymmetric information theories are consistent with data on trial outcomes. The study concludes

---

[14] Eisenberg (1990) reports 0.57 in the case of contract-based actions, 0.25 for tort-based actions.

[15] Those standards come in essentially two varieties: express and implied warranty rules. Express warranties are simply the terms of the contract, and there is no reason to believe that either party has an informational advantage in reading the contract. However, contract law doctrines generally favor the consumer in these cases. Since state courts are rather idiosyncratic in this regard, it is quite possible that lawyers on the plaintiff's side, who are more likely than the product seller's lawyers to be familiar with the law and the behavior of juries in their jurisdiction, generally have the best prediction of the effective legal standard. In the case of implied warranties, the court's determination of a contract breach will often depend on the type of use to which the consumer put the product. In these cases, the plaintiff-consumer is again likely to have an informational advantage.

that the evidence is consistent with the divergent expectations theory but not with the asymmetric information theory.

The core empirical test in the Waldfogel article involves an examination of the correlation between trial rates and the plaintiff win rate. He argues, based on the Bebchuk model, that the asymmetric information theory implies a positive relationship between the trial rate and the plaintiff win rate, and a positive relationship between the plaintiff win rate and the size of the award. He finds evidence of a negative relationship in both cases and concludes that the asymmetric information model is rejected.

The usefulness of the empirical strategy of Waldfogel depends on the extent to which the screening model (Bebchuk model) serves as a complete account of the asymmetric information theory. However, the screening model, we have argued, does not serve as a complete account of the asymmetric information theory. Indeed, given the strong incentives for and low cost of signaling in the litigation context, the screening provides a rather incomplete account of the asymmetric information theory. Hence, Waldfogel's approach should be regarded as inconclusive because it rejects an incomplete version of the asymmetric information theory.

Eisenberg and Heise (2009) present evidence that defendants appear to win at the appellate level more frequently than do plaintiffs. The "defendant advantage" result appears at first glance to be inconsistent with trial selection theories. The evidence of a defendant advantage appears to hold for several categories of litigation. The defendant advantage result appears to be inexplicable on the basis of the Priest-Klein model. Moreover, the nearly uniform result appears to be inconsistent with the informational asymmetry theory, since that theory would imply variation according to case category.

On closer inspection, the defendant advantage result does not appear to be inconsistent with trial selection theories. Trial and appellate courts have different areas of competence; with trial courts resolving factual issues and appellate courts resolving issues of law. Given these differences, it is not difficult to see how a settlement process that produces Priest-Klein results at the trial level might still generate the appearance of a defendant advantage at the appellate level.

Other things equal, plaintiffs will tend to push forward at the trial level with cases that they perceive as strong on factual grounds (e.g., sympathetic plaintiff), even if they are weak on legal grounds. Such a strategy would be successful for plaintiffs in the vast majority of cases in which it is employed, because relatively few defendants will have an incentive to appeal a trial court decision. Of the cases that are generated from this particular process, defendants will gain an advantage at the appellate level precisely because the appellate court will focus on the law rather than the particular facts of the case.

In some respects, this theory is supported by the data presented in the Eisenberg and Heise article. The defendant advantage result is particularly strong for torts cases, which generally comply with the Priest-Klein hypothesis at the trial level. Thus, at the trial level, the Priest-Klein hypothesis is confirmed, while at the appellate level, the "defendant advantage" hypothesis is confirmed. In case categories where informational asymmetry is present, such as medical malpractice and products liability, Eisenberg and Heise find no evidence of a defendant advantage. This suggests that appeals from medical malpractice and products liability cases tend to be based on law, with respect to which neither party has an informational advantage. Trial court decisions in these areas reflect the superior information of defendants. Appellate decisions fail to reflect or to be suggestive of any informational advantage for either side.

Moreover, the defendant advantage result reported by Eisenberg and Heise is particularly strong for jury trials, which suggests that plaintiffs are assuming that sympathetic facts will give them the strongest chances in front of juries.[16] The defendant advantage hypothesis receives weak confirmation at best in the case of bench trials.[17]

Kessler, Meites, and Miller (1996) use a multimodal empirical examination of the selection hypothesis. Specifically, they estimate a regression model that includes variables that they argue should explain deviations from the 50 percent win rate prediction. Their results are consistent with both the divergent expectations and asymmetric information hypotheses.

The difficult part of such a study is the creation of variables that effectively distinguish the effects of various selection influences. Among the selection influences included in the regression model of Kessler, Meites, and Miller are informational asymmetry, stakes asymmetry, and biased legal standards. These three influences are difficult to distinguish. For example, Kessler, Meites, and Miller describe medical malpractice as an area in which stakes are asymmetric.[18] However, medical malpractice is clearly a category in which informational asymmetry favors defendants. It is unclear, in their framework, which coding approach would be correct for the medical malpractice category.[19] Given that three of

---

[16] Eisenberg and Heise (2009), at 142.
[17] Id.
[18] Kessler, Meites, and Miller (1996), at 242.
[19] Hylton (1993) confronts the same problem, but argues that the data are more consistent overall with the asymmetric information hypothesis than with the differential stakes hypothesis.

the variables in their model (information asymmetry, stakes asymmetry, and biased standard) are at least partially measuring informational asymmetry, their results can be read as providing empirical confirmation for the combined divergent expectations/information asymmetry proposition presented in the conclusion of the theory discussion in this chapter.[20]

Siegelman and Waldfogel (1999) present an alternative multimodal regression approach to selection theory. They focus on three determinants of litigation identified in the Priest-Klein model: the decision standard, the variance in the parties' predictions of the decision standard, and the asymmetry of stakes. They also estimate a second model that includes a proxy for the asymmetry in variance predictions (asymmetric uncertainty). They find that the four parameter model performs better in explaining the win rate and the trial rate than does the three parameter model.

The Siegelman and Waldfogel results are broadly consistent with those of Kessler, Meites, and Miller. Their inclusion of an asymmetric uncertainty measure should be viewed as an attempt to include a proxy for informational asymmetry. In addition, some of the observations that they code for asymmetric stakes could probably be coded more accurately as informational asymmetry. The results should be interpreted as confirming the divergent expectation/asymmetric information theory.

6. Conclusion

If this review has appeared at times to argue in favor of a simple and bold statement of the selection hypothesis, that is by design. Priest and Klein offered a spare model with a bold and falsifiable proposition: plaintiff win rates should tend toward 50 percent unless the litigating parties have asymmetric stakes. Some of the more recent contributions, however, have stated the Priest-Klein theory (or divergent expectations selection theory) in a weaker form, weighted down with qualifications, perhaps in order to avoid rejecting it. Selection theory is better advanced, in our view, through the bold statement approach of the Priest-Klein article.

The asymmetric information selection theory holds that win rates will tend toward 50 percent unless one of the parties has the informational advantage, in which case the win rate will be higher for the side with the advantage. We have presented a simple model that communicates the

---

[20] The same problem is present in Eisenberg and Farber (1997). The litigious-plaintiff hypothesis is confirmed by finding that plaintiff win rates are lower when the plaintiff is an individual. But cases in which the plaintiff is an individual will overlap considerably with cases in which the defendant has an informational advantage.

asymmetric information theory, and shows its connection to the divergent expectations model.

These two theories do not exhaust the realm of potential trial selection theories. As we noted earlier, a selection theory can be based on expectations, the amount at stake, or the costs of litigation. The distinguishing feature of the divergent expectations and asymmetric information theories is that they deliver clear predictions on important trial outcome parameters, and for the path through which common law rules evolve (Priest, 1980; Priest and Klein, 1984; Hylton, 2006).

As the selection literature has expanded, empirical tests have been employed to distinguish the importance of divergent expectations and asymmetric information as determinants of trial outcomes statistics. Although the results of the empirical tests appear to confirm both theories to some extent, the empirical work so far has to be considered preliminary. The main difficulties are: (1) attempting to construct an empirical framework that embodies a richer model of information-based selection, and (2) coding variables that distinguish information from other influences (e.g., stakes asymmetry).

References

Bebchuk, Lucian A. (1984), "Litigation and Settlement under Imperfect Information", *Rand Journal of Economics*, 15(3), 404–15.
Daniels, Stephen and Joanne Martin (1995), *Civil Juries and the Politics of Reform*, Evanston, IL: Northwestern University Press.
Daughety, Andrew F. and Jennifer F. Reinganum (1993), "Endogenous Sequencing in Models of Settlement and Litigation", *Journal of Law, Economics, and Organization*, 9, 314–48.
Eisenberg, Theodore (1990), "Testing the Selection Effect: A New Theoretical Framework with Empirical Tests", *Journal of Legal Studies*, 19 (2), 337–58.
Eisenberg, Theodore and Henry S. Farber (1997), "The Litigious Plaintiff Hypothesis: Case Selection and Resolution", *Rand Journal of Economics*, 28, S92–S112.
Eisenberg, Theodore and Michael Heise (2009), "Plaintiphobia in State Courts? An Empirical Study of State Court Trials on Appeal", *Journal of Legal Studies*, 38, 121–55.
Gould, John P. (1973), "The Economics of Legal Conflicts", *Journal of Legal Studies*, 2, 279–300.
Hay, Bruce L. (1995), "Effort, Information, Settlement, Trial", *Journal of Legal Studies*, 24, 29–62.
Hylton, Keith N. (1993), "Asymmetric Information and the Selection of Disputes for Litigation", *Journal of Legal Studies*, 22, 187–210.
Hylton, Keith N. (2002), "An Asymmetric Information Model of Litigation", *International Review of Law and Economics*, 22, 153–75.
Hylton, Keith N. (2006), "Information, Litigation, and Common Law Evolution", *American Law and Economics Review*, 8, 33–61.
Kessler, Daniel, Thomas Meites, and Geoffrey Miller (1996), "Explaining Deviations from the Fifty-percent Rule: A Multimodal Approach to the Selection of Cases for Litigation", *Journal of Legal Studies*, 25, 233–59.
Landes, William M. (1971), "An Economic Analysis of the Courts", *Journal of Law and Economics*, 14, 61–107.
Langlais, Eric, Bertrand Chopard, and Thomas Cortade (2010), "Trial and Settlement

Negotiations between Asymmetrically Skilled Parties", *International Review of Law and Economics*, 30, 18–27.
Miceli, Thomas J. (2008), "Legal Change and the Social Value of Lawsuits", University of Connecticut Economics Department Working Paper 2008-34, available at http://www.econ.uconn.edu/working/2008-34.pdf.
P'ng, Ivan P.L. (1983), "Strategic Behavior in Suit, Settlement and Trial", *Bell Journal of Economics*, 14, 539–50.
P'ng, Ivan P.L. (1987), "Litigation, Liability, and Incentives for Care", *Journal of Public Economics*, 34, 61–85.
Posner, Richard A. (1973), "An Economic Approach to Legal Procedure and Judicial Administration", *Journal of Legal Studies*, 2, 399–458.
Priest, George (1977), "The Common Law Process and the Selection of Efficient Rules", *Journal of Legal Studies*, 6, 65–82.
Priest, George and Benjamin Klein (1984), "The Selection of Disputes for Litigation", *Journal of Legal Studies*, 13, 1–55.
Rothschild, Michael and Joseph E. Stiglitz (1976), "Equilibrium in Competitive Insurance Markets: An Essay on the Economics of Imperfect Information", *Quarterly Journal of Economics*, 90, 629–49.
Shavell, Steven (1982), "Suit, Settlement and Trial: A Theoretical Analysis under Alternative Methods for the Allocation of Legal Costs", *Journal of Legal Studies*, 11, 55–82.
Shavell, Steven (1996), "Any Frequency of Plaintiff Victory at Trial is Possible", *Journal of Legal Studies*, 25, 493–501.
Siegelman, Peter and Joel Waldfogel (1999), "Toward a Taxonomy of Disputes: New Evidence through the Prism of the Priest/Klein Model", *Journal of Legal Studies*, 28, 101–30.
Spier, Kathryn E. (1992), "The Dynamics of Pretrial Negotiation", *Review of Economic Studies*, 59, 93–108.
Stiglitz, Joseph E. and Andrew Weiss (1981), "Credit Rationing in Markets with Imperfect Information", *American Economic Review*, 71, 393–410.
Stiglitz, Joseph E. and Andrew Weiss (1994), "Sorting Out the Differences between Screening and Signaling Models", in M.O.L. Bacharach, M.A.H. Dempster and J.L. Enos (eds.), *Mathematical Models in Economics*, Oxford: Oxford University Press.
Waldfogel, Joel (1998), "Reconciling Asymmetric Information and Divergent-Expectations Theories of Litigation", *Journal of Law and Economics*, 41, 451–76.
Wittman, Donald (1985), "Is the Selection of Cases for Trial Biased?" *Journal of Legal Studies*, 14, 185–214.

Index

Abrams, D. 127, 131
absent class members *see* class action
Acemoglu, D. 317
adversarial versus inquisitorial justice 1–18
   adverse selection and opt-out, and intra-class conflict 75–7
   and attorney-client confidentiality 58
   centralized versus decentralized evidence production 7–11
   comparison using model of litigation between two parties 5–7, 14
   competing experts and decision making 15
   cost and variance, tradeoff between 10–11
   definitions and comparisons 5–11
   differences between 1–3
   evidence, theoretical models 232–3
   experimental tests of sophistication 14–15
   future research 16
   incentive alignment problem 14
   and institutional organization 3
   model assumptions 3–4
   naïve decision makers and evidence production 11–12, 15, 16
   principal-agent problem 11, 13, 16
   sophisticated decision makers and tradeoff between cost of evidence and accuracy 12–14, 15, 16
   theoretical literature 11–14
Albonetti, C. 132
Alchian, A. 101
Alexander, J. 71
Allais, M. 221
Allen, R. 55–6, 221, 222
Allen, W. 91
Anderson, D. 291, 295–6
Anderson, G. 100
Anderson, J. 132–3
Anderson, R. 29
anti-pooling rationale
   and self-incrimination 367–70, 371, 372, 373–8
   see also pooling strategy
Antonovics, K. 122
Anwar, S. 122
appeal and supreme courts 19–51
   case space and distinguishing practice 23–4
   case-by-case adjudication 32–4
   civil law legal systems, precedent in 25–6
   common law precedential practices 21
   common law precedential practices and horizontal *stare decisis* 21–4
   constitutional system, models of adjudication embedded in 42–5
   convergence to compromise rule 24
   and criminal procedure 139–40
   empirical studies of *stare decisis* 24–5, 31
   fact space and adjudication 29
   information-based explanation of horizontal *stare decisis* 23
   issue-by-issue adjudication 32–4
   judges' reputation concerns and horizontal *stare decisis* 23, 24
   judicial accuracy and Condorcet Jury Theorem 28, 29, 32
   and judicial preferences and separability 29
   judicial review effects on administrative agencies 42–3, 45
   median justice rule 27, 28, 29, 30
   overruling precedent 24
   political model of doctrine 36–7
   political model for horizontal *stare decisis* 22–3
   and political theory model of legislation 20, 26–7, 41
   precedential practices 21–6, 36–7

sentencing decisions and separation of powers game 44
separation of powers models 42–5
separation of powers models, empirical studies 45
see also judicial organization and administration; US Court of Appeals; US Supreme Court
appeal and supreme courts, collegiality 26–34
  adjudication and doctrinal paradox 32–4
  adjudication models 28
  of appellate courts, reasons for 27–8
  and competing opinions 29–30
  and consistency and coherence 31–2, 33
  and one-dimensional spatial preferences in policy 26–7
  and panel effects 30–31
  policy choice on collegial courts 28–30
  and sincere versus sophisticated voting 34
  voting protocols in collegial courts 32–4
appeal and supreme courts, hierarchical organization 34–42
  and discretionary review 41–2
  and doctrinal structure 35–8, 39
  and doctrinal structure, and CART estimation technique 38
  and lower court compliance with higher courts 35–41
  and political agency models 38–9
  reasons for 34–5
  and team models of error correction 39–41
  and team models of error correction, and cases selected for review 40–41
  and team models of error correction, and defendant's type 40
Aranson, P. 310–11
Arnold, M. 2
Arrow, K. 120
Arther, R. 150
Ashenfelter, O. 315
asymmetric information
  imperfect information comparisons, and settlement negotiation 435–8
  informational advantage for defendant 495–6, 499–500, 502
  informational advantage for plaintiff 496–7, 499–500, 502–3
  litigation investment and nonparty preclusion rule 363
  and negative-expected-value suits 342–3
  one-sided, settlement process models 423–35
  and protection of contracting parties 103, 104
  and settlement negotiation 393–8, 400, 402, 407, 414, 417, 419–35, 443
  settlement negotiation and consistent versus inconsistent priors 398–401, 419, 439, 440
  settlement and strategic behavior 489–91, 495–7, 499–502, 504
  structured bargaining with, and fee shifting 284–6
  versus other models of settlement bargaining 439–41
  see also evidence; imperfect information; information; private information
Atkins, R. 124, 126
attorney-client confidentiality 52–66
  accuracy and primary activity incentives 59–62
  and adversarial versus inquisitorial justice 58
  capacity to conceal information produced by an attorney, effect of 61–2
  and competition between interested parties 57–8, 63–4
  confidentiality of information shared or generated during litigation over completed acts 55–7
  confidentiality of information shared prior to contemplated act 54–5, 56–7
  confidentiality and strategic revelation of information to courts 57–9

equilibrium decision on use of legal services 59, 60
future research 60–61, 64–5
legal advice and strategic revelation 53–9
and litigation costs 62–4
and litigation costs, and distortion created in markets for legal goods and services 63–4
litigation costs, and dynamic quality of law 64–5
and litigation costs, and propensity for and timing of settlement 64
social welfare effects of legal information production and exchange 59–65
social welfare value of confidentiality protection 53–9
unfavorable information, risk of discovering and effects on incentives 61
work-product doctrine 52
attorneys
experience and career paths, and criminal procedure 131
settlement negotiation 441–3
auctioning counsel, class action 80
Aumann, R. 394
Austen-Smith, D. 332–3
Axelrod, R. 93
axiomatic approach to solutions, settlement negotiation 392, 403–4, 407–13, 454–5, 463
Ayres, I. 92, 98, 99, 127

Babcock, L. 401, 465
Bafumi, J. 314
bail, and pretrial release 126–7
Bailey, M. 314
Baird, D. 386, 403, 404, 417
Baker, S. 459
Baker, T. 301–2
Baldus, D. 134
Banerjee, A. 102
bankruptcy scenario model and concession limits 411–13
Banks, J. 332–3
Bar-Gill, O. 401

bargaining
charge bargaining and criminal procedure 128, 129–30
and cost allocation rules, fee shifting 295–6
range and bargaining efficiency model 407
under threat of trial, fee shifting 294–5
Baxter, W. 90, 91
Baye, M. 281
Baysinger, B. 101
Beale, J. 85
Bebchuk, Lucian A. 161, 284, 285, 292, 341–9, 393, 419, 420, 423, 426, 451, 452–3, 455, 460, 478, 489, 490, 491, 499, 502
Beccaria, C. 148
Beckenstein, A. 150
Becker, G. *ix*, 117, 118, 120, 145, 148, 161–5, 167–70, 173, 205
Beckerman, J. 79
Beckner, C. 288
Bell, A. 98
Bell, G. 2
Benoit, J.-P. 34
Benson, B. 101
Bentham, J. 148, 369
Bergara, M. 45
Berkowitz, D. 318
Bernardo, A. 206, 253–5
Bernheim, B. 403
Bernstein, D. 2
Bernstein, L. 275
Bernstein, R. 69, 71
Bierschbach, R. 371, 375
Bikhchandani, S. 102
Binmore, K. 386, 394, 399–400, 403, 454
Bjerk, D. 128, 129, 459
Block, M. 5, 14–15
Blume, L. 22
Bohn, J. 70
Bone, Robert G. 67–84, 188–202, 349–65
Bonnefon, J.-F. 33
Borchers, P. 95–6
Borenstein, S. 75
Boudreau, C. 15
Bowles, R. 332

Boylan, R. 130–31
Brace, P. 314–15
Braeutigam, R. 206, 275, 277
Brazil, W. 2, 150, 188
Brenner, S. 25
Breyer, S. 132
Briggs, H. 445
Brilmayer, L. 85, 86, 89, 90, 91, 94
British Rule *see* English Rule
Brosi, K. 128
Brown, J. 472
Bruce, C. 88
Buckley, F. 98
Bull, J. 233, 252, 256
Bundy, S. 54–5, 56, 57, 61
Bushway, S. 129–30, 132, 134, 135
Butler, H. 98, 101

Cabranes, J. 132
Calfee, J. 476
Cameron, C. 22, 27, 29, 30, 36, 38, 40–41, 42, 313, 314
Campbell, J. 2
card game model, settlement negotiation 389–90, 394–5, 396–7, 408, 420, 421–3, 425
Carney, W. 98, 99, 106
Cary, W. 98, 105
Cassell, P. 125, 126, 369–70
Cavers, D. 85
Cecil, J. 1, 2
Chang, H. 285, 292, 455
Chang, K. 314
Chapman, B. 33
Che, Y.-K. 57, 59, 60, 62, 63, 72, 76, 287, 288, 358–9, 444–5, 447–8, 456–7, 476
Chen, K. 286, 442
Chen, Z. 346
Chien, H.-K. 457
Choi, A. 167, 288, 457
Choi, S. 70, 79, 327
choice of laws *see* conflict of laws and choice of laws
Chopard, B. 285, 498–9
Chu, C. 457
Chung, T.-Y. 291, 419
civil law system
 and common law, differences between, in judicial
 organization and administration 317–19
 lawsuits by jail and prison inmates 140
 precedent in 25–6
 and right to silence 377–8
 see also common law system
claim preclusion *see* preclusion law
Clark, T. 27, 313, 314
Clarke, S. 126
class action 67–84
 agency costs 72–5, 77, 78
 and asymmetry of litigation costs 69
 attorney fees 71, 74–5
 auctioning counsel 80
 benefits of 68–72
 Class Action Fairness Act (CAFA) 74–5, 79–80
 coupon settlements 75
 and economies of scale 68–9, 70
 fee award rules, adjusting 80
 frivolous and weak suits 77, 80–81
 intra-class conflict, and adverse selection and opt-out 75–7
 judicial review, bolstering 79–80
 large claim 68–70, 73, 74, 76
 mass tort settlement actions 78, 80
 monitoring of class counsel, improving 78–9
 monitoring, lack of 73
 nonmonetary settlements 74–5
 opportunistic behavior, control of 74–5
 and prediction of outcomes 402–3, 446–8
 Private Securities Litigation Reform Act (PSLRA) 73, 78–9, 80
 public and private enforcement coordination 71–2
 reform proposals 78–81
 reversionary fund settlement 75
 securities fraud 78–9, 80
 settlement, special case of 78
 small claim 70–73, 74, 76–7
 small claim costs 71
 social costs of sweetheart settlements 74
 subclassing 77

sweetheart settlements 73–5, 78, 79, 80
treatment costs 72–7
client confidentiality *see* attorney-client confidentiality
Coase, R. 105
Coffee, J. 68, 70, 72, 73, 74, 77, 78
Cohen, Laurence 223
Cohen, Linda 36–7, 43, 45
Cohen, M. 312–13
collegiality *see* appeal and supreme courts, collegiality
commerce law and cost-exportation theory 106–7
common law system
    and civil law, differences between, in judicial organization and administration 317–19
    and enforcement of contractual choice of law 103–4
    precedential practices and horizontal *stare decisis* 21–4
    see also civil law system
compensation scheme for plaintiffs' lawyers 442–3
competition
    between interested parties, and attorney-client confidentiality 57–8, 63–4
    jurisdictional *see* jurisdictional competition
complete-information model, settlement negotiation 446, 457
Condorcet jury theorem 28, 29, 32, 332–3
    see also juries
confessions
    economics of 378–84
    false, and admissibility rules 381
    reasons for 378–81
    see also self-incrimination, privilege against
confidentiality *see* attorney-client confidentiality
conflict of laws and choice of laws 85–115
    adhesion contracts 103
    Allstate Insurance Co v. Hague 107
    'balance of state interests' approach 90, 91

choice-of-law approach in practice 94–6
and choice-of-law monitoring and precedents 93
commerce law and cost-exportation theory 106–7
common law and enforcement of contractual choice of law 103–4
comparative regulatory advantages and forum law 88–9
conflict of laws problem 87–96
constitutional law 106–8
contract validity issues 91–2
Cooley v. Board of Wardens 106
corporate internal affairs rule 105–6
CTS Corp. v. Dynamics Corp. of America 107
Edgar v. Mite Corp 107
escape devices 86
federal law 108
First Restatement of Conflicts 85–6, 89, 91, 92, 93, 94, 95, 96
foreign law, reasons for and against choosing 87–90
forum law, costs and benefits of 87–9
Home Insurance v. Dick 89
inefficiency and forum shopping 88
information asymmetry and protection of contracting parties 103, 104
interest analysis 89–91, 100
interstate compacts 93–4
jurisdictional competition and contractual choice of law 101–2, 105, 106
jurisdictional competition and evolutionary theories 101–2
jurisdictional competition and herd behavior 101–2
Leflar's 'better law' 89, 90, 94, 95, 96
legislators' weak incentives to innovate 99
mandatory rules, evasion of 102
'most significant relationship' test 89, 90
recovery-favoring modern approach 94–6
rule versus standard-based approaches 89–92

rule-based approaches, coordination problems with 92–4
Second Restatement of Conflicts 90, 95, 103–4
state competition incentives for corporate law 98–9
state competition incentives for lawyers 99–100, 106
state competition incentives for non-corporate law 100
statutory law and enforcement of contractual choice of law 104–5
Supreme Council of the Royal Arcanum v. Green 107–8
territorial approach, criticism of 85–6
conflict of laws and choice of laws, contractual choice of law 96–108
benefits of enforcing 97–102
and clarification of applicable law 97
costs of 102–3
and elimination of inconsistency 97
enforcement 103–8
and jurisdictional competition 97–101
constitutional system
conflict of laws and choice of laws 106–8
courts and judicial organization and administration 330
and criminal procedure 123
models of adjudication embedded in 42–5
contingent fees
and retainer arrangements 346–7
settlement negotiation 442, 457
contracts scholarship, questioning emphasis on verifiability in 251–3
contractual choice of law *see* conflict of laws and choice of laws, contractual choice of law
Cooter, R. 2, 64, 191, 192, 193, 195, 197–8, 201, 240, 284, 291, 311, 320, 324, 386, 463, 481
Corchón, L. 206
Cornell, B. 280, 345
corporate internal affairs rule 105–6
Cosgel, M. 23, 24, 481
cost-exportation theory and commerce law 106–7

Coughlan, P. 333
coupled awards 457–8
coupon settlements, and class action 75
Coursey, D. 294–5
courts
congestion 330–31
functions of 316–20
organization of 321–7
see also judicial organization and administration
Cover, A. 313, 314
Cover, R. 106
Cox, J. 73, 79
Crain, W. 100
Craswell, R. 476
Crémer, J. 256
criminal procedure 116–44
appeals 139–40
Apprendi v. New Jersey 138
and attorney experience and career paths 131
bail amounts and probability of re-arrest 127
bail and pretrial release 126–7
Bivens v. Six Unknown Named Agents 123
charge bargaining 128, 129–30
civil lawsuits by jail and prison inmates 140
and constitutional law 123
criminal punishment statistics 116
death penalty and plea bargaining 129
death penalty reversal rates 140
defendant characteristics and prosecutor preferences 130
demographic characteristics and sentencing 134–5
discretionary sentencing 131–2
economic studies and criminology, differences between 117–18
exclusionary rule 122–6
exclusionary rule and defendant's statement 124–5
exclusionary rule, effect on crime rates 124
federal sentencing grid 132
indeterminate sentencing, abandonment of 134
inmate litigation 140

judicial characteristics and sentencing 136
judicial discretion, regulation of 131–9
jury trial rights and mandatory sentencing 138
mandatory sentencing 128–9, 132, 133, 137–9
Mapp v. Ohio 124
Miranda case, and confession rates 125–6
Miranda case, effects of 124–6
Miranda case, effects on police behavior 125
parole boards 134
plea bargaining and length of sentence 128
plea bargaining and pretrial release 126–7
police discretion and regulation of investigations 118–26
policing levels and crime rates 118–19
political affiliation of judge, and sentencing 136–7
post-conviction litigation 139–40
prosecutor behavior 127–31
and prosecutors' career patterns 130–31
punishment imposition 131–40
recidivism and sentencing 134, 136
and right to silence 373–4
sentencing guidelines and prosecutors' discretion 128–30, 131–2
sentencing and inter-judge disparity 132–3, 139
three-strikes laws 129
truth-in-sentencing laws 134
United States v. Booker 138–9
criminal procedure, racial disparities 116
in bail 127
and discretionary sentencing 131–2
and post-guidelines sentencing 134–6
racial profiling 118–22
racial profiling of black motorists 119–22
Croson, D. 346

Cross, F. 31
Currie, B. 85, 89–90, 356

Dam, K. 71, 72
Dana, D. 77
Daniels, R. 98
Daniels, S. 487
Daughety, Andrew F. 11, 23, 57, 58, 61, 231–2, 386–471, 489
Davies, G. 116
Davies, T. 124
deadline effects, and settlement negotiation 460–61, 462
death penalty
 and plea bargaining 129
 reversal rates 140
defendants
 advantage theory, and trial selection theory 502–3
 asymmetric information and informational advantage for 495–6, 499–500, 502
 characteristics, and prosecutor preferences 130
 innocent, an indirect benefit of right to silence 377
 insolvent defendant model, settlement negotiation 446
 strategic search models and possibility of pro-plaintiff or pro-defendant bias 231–2
 see also plaintiffs; prosecutor
Deffains, B. 461
Demsetz, H. 2
Deneckere, R. 248, 416
detection avoidance and enforcement theory 145–87
 complementarities, accounting for, across orders of detection avoidance 179–80
 conventional approach to enforcement 148–9
 conventional enforcement model with detection avoidance added 150–54
 and court's inherent powers 146–7
 detection avoidance, theoretical possibility of preventing increases in 176–8

deterrence mechanics, effects on 150–54, 156
evidence of reasonableness of destruction 147
and firms' document retention policies 147
incorporation of detection avoidance and effect on enforcement model 148–54
Malik's qualification, and counter qualifications 155, 161–7, 168–9
misconduct penalties 146–7
policies directed at detection avoidance 152–4
regulation overview 145–7
regulation scope 147
responsive increases in detection avoidance, effects of 156
responsive increases in detection avoidance, effects when violation is a continuous variable 157–61
social cost-benefit accounting, effect of responsive increases in detection avoidance 161–7
social cost-benefit analysis in conventional approach 149, 151–2, 154
technological approach 147, 180–85
technological approach, implementing 183–5
technological approach, mechanics of 180–82
and US Federal Rule of Civil Procedure 146, 147
see also evidence, theoretical models
detection avoidance and enforcement theory, recursivity of detection avoidance 170–80
nature of, and substitution effect 171–3
practical assessment of state involvement 178–9
practical import of 170–71
detection avoidance and enforcement theory, sanctioning
detection avoidance, and assuming no recursivity 167–70
for detection avoidance, importance of 167–8

for detection avoidance, potentially decisive impact of adding 168–70
first-order 152, 153, 155–6, 169, 170, 172, 173–7, 179–80
hierarchies 173–9
hierarchies, uniform 174–5
hierarchies, variable 175–9
for misconduct 146–7, 149, 151, 152–3
public detection costs and comparison to 183
second-order 152–3, 170, 172, 179–80
of underlying activity 155–67
Dewatripont, M. 3, 5, 14, 15
Dharmapala, D. 121
Dicey, A. 87
Dinkin, S. 73, 79
discovery process 188–202
abusive discovery 197, 198–9, 200
concealment of information, and benefit of trial surprise 190
cost shifting 201
excessive discovery 197–8, 201
filing incentives, benefits for 196
limits 200
mandatory disclosure 199–200
primary activity incentive, benefits for 196–7
Prisoner's Dilemma and discovery abuse 198–9, 200
rational processing of information 190
reforms 199–201
settlement benefits 191–5
settlement quality 193–5
settlement rate 192–3
social benefits of 189–97
social costs of 197–9
trial outcomes, benefits for 195
truthfulness verification 190
voluntary disclosure 189–91, 192–3, 463
voluntary disclosure of favorable information 189–90
voluntary disclosure of unfavorable information 190–91
discretionary sentencing, criminal procedure 131–2

diversity jurisdiction 330
Dixit, A. 6
Djankov, S. 318
doctrinal structure
  and adjudication paradox 32–4
  and appeal and supreme courts, hierarchical organization 35–8, 39
  and CART estimation technique 38
  and self-incrimination, privilege against 370–76
documentary evidence
  firms' document retention policies 147
  and self-incrimination, privilege against 373
Dodd, P. 98
Dominitz, J. 121
Donohue, J. 119, 122, 126, 274, 297, 369
Dorf, M. 35
Doriat, M. 461
double jeopardy rule, and self-incrimination 382
Durand, A. 75

Easterbrook, F. 2, 26, 31–2, 98, 101, 116, 188, 198
efficiency
  levels, and fee shifting 274–5, 279–80
  loss, and settlement negotiation 395, 404, 407, 415, 416, 419–20, 426, 433, 438
Ehrenzweig, A. 85
Eichenberger, R. 98
Eisenberg, T. 71, 73, 79, 80, 297, 315, 488–90, 498–9, 500, 501, 502, 503, 504
Elder, H. 312
electoral pressures, judicial organization and administration 326–7
Elhauge, E. 54–5, 56, 57, 61
Ellsberg, D. 221
Ely, J. 85
Emons, W. 13, 240
enforcement theory *see* detection avoidance and enforcement theory

English rule
  fee shifting 271, 273, 274, 276–89, 292, 295–7, 298–301
  settlement negotiation 455, 461
  social versus private incentive to sue 482
Epstein, L. 313
Eskridge, W. 43, 45
Europe
  'most significant relationship' test 90
  see also France; UK
Evans, D. 77, 81
evidence
  evidentiary misconduct *see* detection avoidance and enforcement theory
  generation following plea bargaining 459
  see also asymmetric information; imperfect information; information
evidence, theoretical models 203–70
  adversarial versus inquisitorial justice 232–3
  assume-the-worst rule 225–6, 229–30, 232
  binary cost interpretation of omission models 231, 242–3
  character evidence and conduct 251
  contracts scholarship, questioning emphasis on verifiability in 251–3
  damages accuracy assessment, effect on incentives 251
  endogenous cost signaling 248–56
  exogenous cost signaling 244–8
  exogenous cost signaling, applied to legal evidence 245
  exogenous cost signaling, and comparison to emission models 246–8
  false evidence, costs of 243
  feasible presentation 230, 233
  feasible presentation, lingering problems in 240–42
  Herring v. New York 227
  infinite or zero cost 230–31, 246
  infinite or zero cost, illusory solution of adopting 242–3

jury's role, historical evolution of 265–6
and law and economics of litigation 204–7
link to primary activities 233
Lipman and Seppi on partial provability 234–8, 243
multiple informed parties with conflicting interests 226–7, 233
omission models 223–43
partial provability in a multi-party context 233–8
partial provability in a multi-party context, partial solution of 243
and plaintiff victory, probability of 205–7
predictive evidence 251
presumptions and litigation-primary activity feedback 253–5
private information, correlated 256–66
private information, correlated, implementing caution without endogenous cost signaling 259–62
proof burdens' allocations and strategic complementarities in evidentiary choice 255–6
single party model 224–6, 233–4
and spoliation 225–6
strategic search models and possibility of pro-plaintiff or pro-defendant bias 231–2
subset reporting 227, 228–9
subset reporting, no-lying assumption 239–41
third-party information, efficacy of 257–9
trace evidence as byproduct of conduct 251
trial error minimization and deterrence maximization, link between 250–51
truth revelation versus primary activity incentive setting 249–50
truth-consistent presentation 227–30, 241
truth-consistent presentation, no-lying assumption 239–40

see also detection avoidance and enforcement theory
evidence, theoretical models, pure probabilistic deduction 207–23
accounting for interests of parties 222–3
conjunction problem 221–2
gatecrasher paradox 222, 223, 226
paradoxes and criticisms 221–3
evidence, theoretical models, pure probabilistic deduction, Bayes' rule 208–11, 254
across-person hindsight bias and its rational twin 217–21
basic rate neglect 213–14
iterated application of 211–12
likelihood ratio 211
loss function 212–13
trial selection bias and past crimes evidence 215–17
exclusionary rule 122–6
and defendant's statement 124–5
effect on crime rates 124

Fagan, J. 116
Fairly, W. 207
false statements, and self-incrimination, privilege against 371–2
Fang, H. 122
Farber, H. 393, 488, 490, 498–9, 504
Farmer, A. 12, 58, 61, 62, 193, 279–80, 281, 346, 455, 463–4
Farnsworth, W. 314
Farrell, J. 224
Farrell, M. 2
Fawcett, J. 86
Feddersen, T. 332, 333
federal judges, nomination of 313–14, 316
fee shifting 271–307
agency problems in lawyer-client relationship 278
Alyeska Pipeline Service Co. v. Wilderness Society 273
American rule as default rule 274
asymmetric information, structured bargaining with 284–6
bargaining and cost allocation rules, laboratory experiment 295–6

Index   517

bargaining under threat of trial, laboratory experiment 294–5
conditioned on offers made in settlement 289–92
Contract with America (Republican Party) proposal 271, 290
court-awarded fees 273, 274
and damage multipliers 287–8
and decisions to file and contest lawsuits 278–81
econometric evidence of actual disputes 297–302
and efficiency levels 274–5, 279–80
empirical evidence on effects of 294–302
English rule 271, 273, 274, 276–89, 292, 295–7, 298–301
externalities in litigation decision making 272
and Federal Rules of Civil Procedure 273–4, 289–91, 292, 293, 295–6
indemnification rules 271, 272, 273–4, 276–81, 282–3, 286–7, 291–2, 293–4
and Internal Revenue Code 292
laboratory experiments 294–6
liability disputes and damages 290–91
and litigation settlement 281–6, 288–9
Marek v. Chesny 289
and margin of victory 292–4
marginal-cost effect 276–7, 278
medical malpractice cases experiments 298–302
multi-phase models 280–81, 285–6
Nash equilibrium of litigation expenditure 275, 277–8
offer based, and settlement negotiation 455–6
offer-of-judgment procedure 273–4, 290–92, 296
one-way policies 273, 274
and optimal incentives 287
practical extent of 273–5
pretrial settlements and effect of switching between English and American rules, laboratory experiment 296

primary behavior, simulation of effects on 297
relative optimism models 282–5, 291–2
settlement behavior, econometric model of 298
and settlement negotiation 442
settlement timing and effect of English rule experiment 300–302
simulation of quantitative effects 296–7
and substantive behavior 286–9
and trial outcomes 285
trial and pretrial expenditures, effect on 275–8
Feeney, F. 126
Feld, L. 324
Fenn, P. 461, 462
Ferejohn, J. 36, 42–3
Fernandez, P. 24
Fernandez, R. 415
finite-horizon model
    settlement negotiation 393, 434, 460, 461
    see also infinite-horizon model
Finkelstein, M. 207
Fischel, D. 63, 98, 107
Fischhoff, B. 217
Fischman, J. 31, 137
Fisher, T. 382
Fluet, C. 13
Fon, V. 26
foreign law, reasons for and against choosing 87–90
Forst, B. 128
forum law, costs and benefits of 87–9
Fournier, G. 298, 461
Fowles, R. 126, 369–70
France
    adjudication specialization 327–8
    jurisprudence constante 25
    legal structures, evolution of 319
    settlement and deadline effect 461
    see also Europe
Frankel, L. 198
Frankel, M. 131
Franzoni, L. 148, 162, 459, 460
Frey, B. 98

Friedman, D. 76, 434, 435, 440
Friedman, G. 74
Friedman, J. 93
frivolous (weak) lawsuits 77, 80–81, 452
Froeb, Luke M. 1–18, 57, 58, 61, 62, 231–2
future research
 adversarial versus inquisitorial justice 16
 attorney-client confidentiality 60–61, 64–5
 inmate litigation 140
 negative-expected-value suits 347
 preclusion law 365

Gabel, H. 150
Garoupa, N. 148, 162
Garrett, B. 382
Garth, B. 70, 188, 197
Geanakoplos, J. 394
Geistfeld, M. 286, 472, 482
Gelman, A. 140
Gely, R. 36, 42, 43, 45
Gennaioli, N. 23–4, 481
Gerken, L. 98, 101
Gertner, R. 440, 464–5
Gilles, M. 74
Gilson, R. 198
Ginsburg, T. 324
Glaeser, E. 130, 318–19
Glazer, J. 415
Goldman, J. 330
Gong, J. 285–6
Good, I. 28
Gordon, S. 44
Gorelick, J. 146
Gould, J. ix, 205, 275, 278, 282, 284, 291, 341, 488, 491, 494, 498
Gravelle, H. 288
Green, E. 93
Greenberg, J. 403
Greenberg, P. 312
Griffin, L. 168
Grogger, J. 118, 119–20
Grossman, G. 128, 458, 459
Grossman, S. 57–8, 224
Gruhl, J. 37
Grundfest, J. 346
Guarnaschelli, S. 333

Guarnieri, C. 326
Guthrie, C. 190, 213
Guzman, A. 97, 346

Hadfield, Gillian K. 52–66
Hagan, J. 134
Haire, S. 38
Haley, James 312
Haley, John 324
Hammond, T. 27
Hansen, R. 80
Hanssen, F. 323, 327
Harcourt, B. 121
Harel, A. 80
Harsanyi, J. 4, 400
Hart, O. 251
Harvey, A. 313
Hause, J. 297
Hay, B. 64, 69, 72, 73, 80, 81, 93, 190, 191, 195, 196, 197–8, 351–2, 356, 358, 359–61, 386, 489
Hay, P. 90, 92
Hayek, F. 2, 101, 106
Heiner, R. 22
Heise, M. 139–40, 316, 499, 502, 503
Helland, E. 74, 127, 326
Helmke, G. 325
Hensler, D. 68, 74, 80–81
Hermalin, B. 256, 257
Hersch, P. 277, 297
heteroscedasticity assumption, trial selection theory 493, 494
Hettinger, V. 31
hierarchical organization *see* appeal and supreme courts, hierarchical organization
Higgins, R. 311–12
Hofer, P. 132, 133
Holmstrom, B. 171
Huang, P. 346
Huber, G. 44
Hughes, J. 277, 298–300
Hyde, C. 277, 278
Hylton, Keith N. 288, 297, 303, 443, 476, 487–506

Iaryczower, M. 325
ideology views, and judicial organization and administration 314–16, 323–4

imperfect information
  asymmetric information
    comparisons, and settlement
      negotiation 435–8
  model, settlement negotiation
    410–11
  see also asymmetric information;
    evidence; information; private
    information
incentive compatibility condition,
  settlement negotiation 430–31
indemnification rules, and fee shifting
  271, 272, 273–4, 276–81, 282–3,
  286–7, 291–2, 293–4
infinite-horizon model
  settlement negotiation 414–15, 417,
    454, 461
  see also finite-horizon model
information
  acquiring from experts, and
    settlement negotiation 464
  acquiring from other player, and
    settlement negotiation
    462–4
  capacity to conceal information
    produced by an attorney, effect
    of 61–2
  confidentiality of information shared
    prior to contemplated act 54–5,
    56–7
  confidentiality and strategic
    revelation of information to
    courts 57–9
  role in settlement negotiation
    393–401
  unfavorable, risk of discovering and
    effects on incentives 61
  see also asymmetric information;
    evidence; imperfect information;
    private information
inmate litigation 140
Innes, R. 162–3, 167
innocent defendants, indirect benefit of
  right to silence 377
inquisitorial justice see adversarial
  versus inquisitorial justice
insolvent defendant model 446
interrogation, coercive, and self-
  incrimination, privilege against
  381–2

interstate compacts 93–4
Issacharoff, S. 199, 200

Japan, judicial independence 322,
  323–4, 326
Jehl, S. 222
Jensen, M. 328
Johnson, S. 315
judges
  characteristics and sentencing 136
  discretion, regulation of 131–9
  judicial accuracy and Condorcet
    Jury Theorem 28, 29, 32
  judicial preferences and separability
    29
  judicial review, bolstering, and class
    action 79–80
  judicial review effects on
    administrative agencies 42–3, 45
  political affiliation of, and sentencing
    136–7
  promotion of efficiency, and
    incentive to sue 481
  reputation concerns and horizontal
    stare decisis 23, 24
  sentencing and inter-judge disparity
    132–3, 139
  and settlement negotiation 443–4
judicial organization and
  administration 308–40
  adjudication organization 327–31
  appointment and tenure of judges
    325–7
  case and controversy requirement
    328
  civil and common law systems,
    differences between 317–19
  constitutional courts 330
  court congestion 330–31
  court organization 321–7
  courts, functions of 316–20
  diversity jurisdiction 330
  electoral pressures 326–7
  fact-finding process 331–5
  federal judges, nomination of
    313–14, 316
  ideology views 314–16, 323–4
  independence of judiciary 321–5
  independence of judiciary, and
    political pressure 324–5, 326

independence of judiciary, and size of jurisdiction 322–3
judicial decisions and case arguments 313
judicial motivation and preferences 309–16
judicial preferences over policies 310, 311–12
judicial reputation among peers 310, 311
judicial self-interest 310, 311–12
jurisdiction 328–30
legal functions of courts 317
legal system development and mechanisms 318–19
monitoring mechanisms 312
non-ideological judicial preferences 309–13
non-pecuniary benefits 312
performance of appointed versus elected judges 327
policy preferences 313–16
policy preferences, measurement of 313–15
promotion prospects 311–12, 323–4
public versus private adjudication 320
sentencing pattern and promotion 312–13
sequential versus unitary trials 331
social cost of court congestion 330–31
social cost of jury system 332
social functions of courts 317–19
specialization 327–8
specialized courts versus courts of general jurisdiction 328–30
utility maximizing and judicial power 311
voting on cases and policy preferences 314
see also appeal and supreme courts
juries
 Condorcet Jury Theorem 28, 29, 32, 332–3
 jurors' strategic behavior 332–3
 jury trial rights and mandatory sentencing 138
 role, historical evolution of 265–6
 selection 332, 334
 and settlement negotiation 443–4
 size and voting rules 332–5
 social cost of jury system 332
 system 319, 331–5
 voting rule 334–5
jurisdictional competition
 and contractual choice of law 101–2, 105, 106
 and evolutionary theories 101–2
 and herd behavior 101–2

Kahan, D. 161
Kahan, M. 442, 457
Kahneman, D. 213
Kakalik, J. 188
Kalai, E. 413
Kalven, J. 71, 333
Kamin, K. 217
Kaplow, L. 10, 55, 56, 57, 161, 251, 287, 328, 482
Karlan, P. 41–2
Kastellec, J. 38
Katz, Avery Wiener 198–9, 206, 271–307, 313, 342, 451–2, 478
Katz, M. 128, 256, 257, 458, 459
Kaye, D. 222, 223, 226
Kennan, J. 419
Kerber, W. 98, 101
Kessler, D. 128, 129, 461–2, 490, 503, 504
Keyes, M. 92, 97, 102
Kim, J.-Y. 417–18, 433, 434, 444, 460
Kitch, E. 106, 107
Kleck, G. 134
Klein, B. 95, 97, 99, 439, 440, 487–91, 493–5, 497, 499–500, 502–5
Klein, D. 316
Klement, Alon 72, 73, 79, 80, 288–9, 341–9, 452, 455
Klerman, D. 319, 325
Klevorick, A. 333–4
Klick, J. 74, 100
Knight, B. 122
Knowles, J. 120, 121–2
Kobayashi, Bruce H. 1–18, 57, 58, 61, 62, 79, 94, 97–101, 103, 105, 231–2, 293, 459
Koesel, M. 146
Kornhauser, Lewis A. 19–51, 77, 308–40, 354, 446

Korobkin, R. 190
Kort, F. 38
Kozyris, J. 86
Kramer, L. 91
Kreps, D. 170, 223, 386
Kritzer, H. 37
Kuziemko, I. 129, 134

La Porta, R. 317
LaCasse, C. 133
Landa, D. 32
Landeo, C. 443, 457, 465
Landes, W. *ix*, 88, 100, 126, 127–8, 131, 275, 278, 282, 285, 291, 311, 320, 322, 328, 331, 341, 345, 454, 458, 472, 488, 491, 494, 498
Landsman, S. 227
Langbein, J. 1
Langlais, E. 163–4, 285, 498–9
Lauderdale, B. 314
Lax, D. 402
Lax, J. 29, 30, 32, 42
Lee, I. 319
Leflar, R. 89, 90, 94, 95, 96
Leftwich, R. 98
Leibman, V. 140
Leiken, L. 125
Lempert, R. 207, 208–9, 215, 223
Leo, R. 125
Leonard, D. 33
LePoidevin, N. 2
Leshem, Shmuel 52–66, 377
Leubsdorf, J. 274
Levine, R. 317
Levitt, S. 118, 119, 122
Levmore, S. 107, 222
Liang, M.-Y. 416
Lim, Y. 25
Lin, Haizhen 487–506
Lindquist, S. 25, 316
Lipman, B. 2, 11, 234–8, 243
litigation
 litigious-plaintiff hypothesis, and trial selection theory 490, 498–9
 post-conviction 139–40
 settlement, and fee shifting 281–6, 288–9
litigation costs
 and attorney-client confidentiality 62–4
 and distortion created in markets for legal goods and services 63–4
 and dynamic quality of law 64–5
Loewenstein, G. 199, 200
Long, C. 131
LoPucki, L. 88
loser pays all *see* English rule
Lowenstein, G. 190

McAfee, R. 11, 285–6
McChesney, F. 2, 7
McConnell, M. 86
McCormick, R. 100
McCubbins, M. 15
Macey, J. 71, 72, 73, 74, 80, 99, 106, 108, 354
MacIntosh, J. 99
McLean, R. 256
McNollgast 36, 37, 39, 42
Mahoney, P. 317, 319, 325
Main, B. 296
Malik, A. 155, 161–7, 168–9
mandatory disclosure, impact of, settlement negotiation 463–4
mandatory sentencing, criminal procedure 128–9, 132, 133, 137–9
Marcus, N. 446
Marks, B. 42
Marks, K. 330
Martin, A. 313, 314, 332
Martin, J. 487
Martin, L. 273
Mas-Colell, A. 386–7, 402, 422
Maskin, E. 323
Mause, P. 282
medical malpractice cases
 and fee shifting 298–302
 trial selection theory 500, 503, 503–4
Menell, P. 472, 481, 482, 485
Mershon, C. 313
Mezzetti, C. 459
Mialon, H. 377
Miceli, Thomas J. 23, 24, 346, 459, 460, 472–86, 499
Miles, Thomas J. 116–44
Milgrom, P. 2, 5, 11, 13, 57–8, 171, 189, 224–7, 231, 232, 234, 239, 463
Miller, A. 67

Miller, G. 71–5, 77, 79, 80, 99, 290, 291, 386, 440, 442, 464–5, 490, 503, 504
Miller, M. 130
Mirrlees, J. 244
Mnookin, R. 198, 284, 291, 346
Moore, J. 251
Morawetz, N. 77
Moss. S. 200
'most significant relationship' test 89, 90
most-favored-nation clauses, and settlement negotiation 448–9
Mullenix, L. 188
Mustard, D. 134–5
Myers, G. 293
Myers, S. 126–7
Myerson, R. 291

Nagin, D. 118
Nalebuff, B. 449–50, 457, 460
Nardulli, P. 124
Nash Bargaining Solution, and settlement negotiation 404, 410, 411–13, 415, 419, 436, 438, 454–5, 463
Neeman, Z. 80, 288–9, 455
negative-expected-value suits 341–9
    and asymmetric information 342–3
    contingent fees and retainer arrangements 346–7
    definition 341
    and divisibility of litigation cost 343–4
    future research 347
    meritorious suits 347
    and new information at intermediate points 345–6
    normative implications 347–8
    puzzle of 341–7
    repeat playing and reputation 346
    and settlement negotiation 451–4
    upfront costs by defendant 345
    see also positive-expected-value suits
Nikitin, M. 443, 457
Nisbett, R. 213
Noam, E. 330–31
North, P. 86
Note 69, 77, 356, 358, 360–61

nuisance suits 451
Nussim, J. 155, 157–61, 167, 179, 182

Oaks, D. 123
offer-of-judgment procedure, and fee shifting 273–4, 290–92, 296
O'Hara O'Connor, Erin 23, 85–115
Okada, A. 403
Okuno-Fujiwara, M. 234
Olson, M. 100
opportunistic behavior, control of, and class action 74–5
Ordover, J. 7

Palumbo, G. 14
Parchomovsky, G. 98
Parisi, F. 1, 5, 12, 26
Park, A. 296
Parker, J. 5, 15, 101, 293
parole boards 134
Payne, A. 133
Pecorino, P. 12, 58, 61, 62, 193, 279–80, 281, 346, 455, 463–4
Pepe, S. 150
perfect-information model, settlement negotiation 407–10, 414–18, 429–30, 454–5
Persico, N. 121, 122
Pesendorfer, W. 332, 333
Pettit, B. 116
Pfaff, J. 138–9
Pfennigstorf, W. 292
Piehl, A. 128, 129–30, 132, 134, 135, 140
Pinello, D. 316
plaintiffs
    asymmetric information and informational advantage for 496–7, 499–500, 502–3
    compensation scheme for plaintiffs' lawyers 442–3
    litigious-plaintiff hypothesis 490, 498–9
    strategic search models and possibility of pro-plaintiff or pro-defendant bias 231–2
    victory, probability of 205–7
    see also defendants; prosecutor
plea bargaining
    and length of sentence 128

and pretrial release 126–7
settlement negotiation 458–60
Plott, C. 277
P'ng, I. 287, 341, 393, 451, 476, 489, 490, 491, 499
Polemarchakis, H. 394
police
   discretion and regulation of investigations 118–26
   policing levels and crime rates 118–19
Polinsky, A. 75, 148, 161, 162, 285–8, 293, 367, 442, 456–7, 476
political affiliation of judge, and sentencing 136–7
political pressure, and independence of judiciary 324–5, 326
political theory models of legislation 20, 22–3, 26–7, 36–9, 41
Ponzetto, G. 24
pooling strategy
   settlement negotiation 422–3, 425–6, 429
   see also anti-pooling rationale
Porter, R. 93
positive-expected-value suits
   and settlement negotiation 451–2
   see also negative-expected-value suits
Posner, R. *ix*, 27, 34, 63, 88, 100, 101, 107, 205–7, 253, 275, 291, 310–12, 320, 322, 327–9, 341, 363–4, 380, 384, 455, 472, 481, 488, 491, 494, 498
Post, D. 33
post-conviction litigation 139–40
precedential practices 21–6, 36–7
   stare decisis see stare decisis
preclusion law 349–65
   asymmetric litigation investment and nonparty preclusion rule 363
   Blonder-Tongue Laboratories, Inc. v. University of Illinois Foundation 356
   claim preclusion 350–51
   claim preclusion by agreement 351–2
   claim preclusion scope 352–3
   complete preclusion system 362–3
   costs associated with nonmutual issue preclusion 356–8
   costs associated with nonparty issue preclusion 362
   error cost reduction and claim preclusion 352
   future research 365
   issue preclusion 350, 351, 354–65
   legal right test and claim preclusion 353
   mutuality doctrine and issue preclusion 355
   nonmutual issue preclusion 355–61, 362
   nonparty preclusion 361–5
   Parklane Hosiery v. Shore 356, 357
   settlement effects and issue preclusion 358–61
   settlement effects and nonparty preclusion rule 364–5
   stare decisis and issue preclusion, difference between 354–5, 359
   Taylor v. Sturgell 361
   transaction cost reduction and claim preclusion 352
   transaction test and claim preclusion 353
   trial effects and nonmutuality doctrine 356–8
   trial effects and nonparty preclusion 361–4
prediction of outcome, and settlement negotiation 401–4
predictive evidence 251
Prescott, J. 138
pretrial settlements and effect of switching between English and American rules 296
Prichard, J. 303
Priest, G. 77, 95, 97, 99, 290, 291, 439, 440, 481, 487–91, 493–5, 497, 499–500, 502–5
prison inmate litigation 140
Prisoner's Dilemma game, and settlement negotiation 404
private incentive to sue *see* social versus private incentive to sue
private information
   correlated 256–66
   correlated, implementing caution without endogenous cost signaling 259–62

and differences in player assessment 419–35, 447, 448–9, 461, 462–4
procedures for monitoring effects of 464–5
see also asymmetric information; evidence; imperfect information; information
products liability cases, and trial selection theory 500–501, 503
prosecutor
  behavior, and criminal procedure 127–31
  career patterns, and criminal procedure 130–31
  disclosure requirements from, and self-incrimination, privilege against 377
  discretion and sentencing guidelines 128–30, 131–2
  preferences, and defendant characteristics 130
  see also defendants; plaintiffs
pure probabilistic deduction *see* evidence, theoretical models, pure probabilistic deduction

Quinn, K. 313, 314

Rachlinski, J. 213, 217
racial disparities *see* criminal procedure, racial disparities
Rader, K. 30
Ramseyer, J. 322–4
random proposer game 414, 420, 435, 440, 453
Rasmusen, E. 22–3, 323–4, 354, 385
recidivism and sentencing 134, 136
recursivity of detection avoidance *see* detection avoidance and enforcement theory, recursivity of detection avoidance
Reese, W. 86
Reid, J. 150
Reinganum, Jennifer F. 11, 23, 57, 58, 61, 128, 231–2, 284, 341, 386–471, 489
Reny, P. 11
retainer arrangements and contingent fees 346–7
Revesz, R. 30, 41–2, 315–16, 329, 446

Rhodes, W. 128
Ribstein, Larry E. 79, 85–115
Richards, M. 37
Richman, D. 168
Rickman, N. 442, 461, 462
Ridgeway, G. 119–20
right to silence *see* self-incrimination, privilege against, right to silence
Riker, W. 106
risk aversion, settlement negotiation 390, 454–5, 458
Roberts, J. 2, 5, 11, 13, 57, 58, 189, 224, 225, 226, 227, 231, 232, 234, 239, 394–5, 463
Roe, M. 319
Rogers, J. 32, 33, 35
Rolfs, C. 127
Romano, R. 98, 101
Rose-Ackerman, S. 99, 106, 286, 472, 482
Rosen-Zvi, I. 382
Rosenberg, D. 69, 72, 73, 80, 81, 279, 345, 364, 451, 452
Rosenberg, M. 86, 92
Rosenfeld, M. 71
Ross, S. 121
Roth, A. 401
Rothschild, M. 333–4, 497
Rowe, T. 80–81, 295–6, 298
Rubenstein, W. 71
Rubin, P. 124, 126, 311–12, 481
Rubinfeld, D. 2, 22, 64, 75, 191–3, 195, 197–8, 201, 206, 245–6, 285–7, 293, 386, 442, 444, 458, 463, 481
Rubinstein, A. 392, 414–15, 417, 434, 440–41, 454
Ryu, K. 444

Sager, L. 28, 31, 32, 33
Salop, S. 33
Saltzburg, S. 215
Sanchirico, Chris William 3, 13, 145–87, 198–9, 203–307, 457
sanctioning *see* detection avoidance and enforcement theory, sanctioning
Sappington, D. 206, 245–6, 444, 458
Satterthwaite, M. 291
Savage, L. 221
Schanzenbach, M. 98, 136, 137

Scharfstein, D. 102
Schazenbach, M. 137
Schlanger, M. 140
Schmalbeck, R. 293
Schrag, J. 250–51
Schulhofer, S. 125–6
Schwab, S. 297
Schwartz, A. 103, 251
Schwartz, E. 29, 36, 37, 334–5
Schwartz, J. 389
Schwartz, W. 334–5, 343, 344, 393, 453–4, 460
Schwarzer, W. 2
Schweizer, U. 434
Scoles, E. 90, 92
Scotchmer, S. 250–51
Scott, K. 101
Scott, R. 139
screening model
  with continuum of types 426–8
  and settlement negotiation 420, 421, 423–8, 434, 435, 438, 439, 450, 455, 457, 458, 463–4
  trial selection theory 489, 490, 491, 497–8, 502
Sebenius, J. 402
securities fraud, class action 78–9, 80
Segal, J. 24–5, 36, 38, 41, 42, 45, 310, 313, 314
Seidmann, D. 11, 367, 369, 370, 372, 373, 376
self-incrimination, privilege against 366–85
  admissibility rules and false confessions 381
  anti-pooling rationale 367–70, 371, 372, 373–8
  collective entity rule 375–6
  confessions, reasons for 378–81
  and disclosure requirements from prosecution 377
  doctrinal fit 370–76
  and documentary evidence 373
  double jeopardy rule 382
  economics of confessions 378–84
  emergency exception to the right to silence 374–5
  and false statements 371–2
  Gilbert v. California 373
  Harris v. New York 383
  innocent defendants, indirect benefit of right to silence 377
  and interrogation, coercive 381–2
  Johnson v. United States 369
  and law-enforcers personal interests 379–81
  Lego v. Twomey 381
  Mincey v. Arizona 383
  and *Miranda* rights 366, 369, 370, 383–4
  monitoring law-enforcers 383–4
  New York v. Quarles 375
  non-verbal responses 372–3
  and punishment for remaining silent 378
  true and false confessions, separation of 381–2
  Twining v. New Jersey 369
  United States v. Hubbell 373
  United States v. Mezzanatto 384–5
  United States v. Patane 383
  voluntariness, meaning of 378–81, 382
  waiver of 384–5
  Withrow v. Williams 366
  see also confessions
self-incrimination, privilege against, right to silence
  as anti-pooling device 367–70
  as applying to every phase of the criminal process 371–2
  and asymmetrical information 367–70, 380, 382
  as belonging to persons, not corporations 375–6
  as confined to criminal trials 373–4
  as confined to same-sovereign prosecutions 374
  and false positives and negatives 367
  and intermediate cases 368
  as legal regime 368
  and privilege against adverse inferences to some civil cases 377–8
  problem of removing from trial 371–2
  as restricted to testimonial evidence 372–3
  and social welfare 376–7
  utility of 367–76

sentencing
   guidelines and prosecutors'
      discretion 128–30, 131–2
   and inter-judge disparity 132–3, 139
   pattern and judicial promotion
      312–13
   and recidivism 134, 136
   and separation of powers game 44
separation of powers models 42–5
Seppi, D. 2, 11, 234–8, 243
sequential rationality, settlement
      negotiation 392, 415, 416–17, 421,
      433–4, 444–5, 447–8, 464
sequential versus unitary trials 331
Setear, J. 198
settlement
   asymmetric information and
      settlement and strategic
      behavior 489–91, 495–7,
      499–502, 504
   econometric model of, and fee
      shifting 298
   effects and issue preclusion 358–61
   effects and nonparty preclusion rule
      364–5
   settlement-trial decision, and
      incentive to sue 477–9
   special case of, and class action 78
   timing, and effect of English rule
      experiment 300–302
   and trial selection theory 488–9
settlement negotiation 386–471
   actions and strategies 388–90,
      449–54
   admissible settlement model 405–7
   asymmetric information, one-sided,
      settlement process models
      423–32
   asymmetric information, one-sided,
      settlement process models,
      robustness of 433–5
   asymmetric information versus other
      models of settlement bargaining
      439–41
   and asymmetrical information
      393–8, 400, 402, 407, 414, 417,
      419–35, 443
   asymmetrical information and
      consistent versus inconsistent
      priors 398–401, 419, 439, 440

   attorneys 441–3
   axiomatic approach to solutions 392,
      403–4, 407–13, 454–5, 463
   bankruptcy scenario model and
      concession limits 411–13
   bargaining range and bargaining
      efficiency model 407
   card game model 389–90, 394–5,
      396–7, 408, 420, 421–3, 425
   class action suits and prediction of
      outcomes 402–3, 446–8
   common value attribute 416
   compensation scheme for plaintiffs'
      lawyers 442–3
   complete-information model 446,
      457
   confidentiality agreements 448
   contingent-fee contract 442, 457
   counterclaims 454
   coupled awards 457–8
   credibility of proceeding to trial
      should negotiations fail 449–50
   damage awards 456–8
   deadline effects 460–61, 462
   decoupled liability 456–7
   delay, reasons for 461–2
   discovery and voluntary disclosure,
      impact of 463
   divergent expectations approach 401,
      439–40
   and efficiency loss 395, 404, 407, 415,
      416, 419–20, 426, 433, 438
   English system 455, 461
   evidence generation following plea
      bargaining 459
   and fee shifting 442
   and fee shifting, offer based 455–6
   filing and pursuing claim 451–4
   finite-horizon model 393, 434, 460,
      461
   frivolous lawsuits 452
   imperfect and asymmetric
      information comparisons
      435–8
   imperfect-information model 410–11
   imperfect-information model in
      noncooperative case 414, 415,
      417, 418, 426
   incentive compatibility condition
      430–31

infinite-horizon model 414–15, 417, 454, 461
information, acquiring from experts 464
information, acquiring from other player 462–4
information role 393–401
information role, and modeling uncertainty 395–8
insolvent defendant model 446
interdependent value attribute 416
judges and juries 443–4
mandatory disclosure, impact of 463–4
models 404–41
most-favored-nation clauses 448–9
multiple litigants 444–9
and Nash Bargaining Solution 404, 410, 411–13, 415, 419, 436, 438, 454–5, 463
and negative-expected-value (NEV) suits 451–4
nuisance suits 451
outcomes and payoffs 390–91, 454–60
overview 386–8
perfect-information model 407–10, 454–5
perfect-information model in noncooperative case 414–18, 429–30
players 441–9
plea bargaining 458–60
pooling strategy 422–3, 425–6, 429
and positive-expected-value (PEV) suits 451–2
prediction of outcome 401–4
prediction of outcome, and cooperative solutions 403–4
prediction of outcome, and Nash equilibrium in noncooperative games 401–4
primary participants 388
and Prisoner's Dilemma game 404
private information and differences in player assessment 419–35, 447, 448–9, 461, 462–4
private information, procedures for monitoring effects of 464–5

proposal/response periods, number of 414
random proposer game 414, 420, 435, 440, 453
revealing equilibrium 423, 429, 431
risk aversion 390, 454–5, 458
screening model 420, 421, 423–8, 434, 435, 438, 439, 450, 455, 457, 458, 463–4
screening model, with continuum of types 426–8
sequential rationality 392, 415, 416–17, 421, 433–4, 444–5, 447–8, 464
signaling model 420, 421–3, 428–32, 438, 439, 463–4
signaling model, with continuum of types 431–2, 443–4
and simultaneous proposals 388, 391, 392, 395, 433–4, 435, 440, 446, 464
split-award statutes 442, 457
strategic approach to solutions 392–3, 399, 403, 404, 414–35, 454–5
subgame perfect equilibrium 417
time factors 391–3, 415–16, 417–18, 460–62
ultimatum game 414, 415, 417, 419, 420, 424–38, 441–5, 449–50, 452, 455, 456, 458, 460–61
variations on basic models 441–65
Severinov, S. 57, 59, 60, 62, 63, 248
Shapiro, M. 106
Shavell, S. 39, 54–8, 60–64, 148, 161, 162, 189–92, 198, 205, 224, 251, 275, 278–9, 282, 287, 320, 328, 345, 347, 367, 393, 401, 439, 451, 452, 455, 462, 472, 476, 477, 481, 482, 488–90, 495, 497
Shepherd, G. 199
Shepherd, J. 134, 326
Sherman, L. 118
Shin, H. 4, 5, 13, 15, 57, 58, 232
Shipan, C. 36, 42–3, 44
Shleifer, A. 23–4, 319, 481
Shughart, W. 98, 101
Siegelman, P. 504

signaling model
  with continuum of types 431–2, 443–4
  settlement negotiation 420, 421–3, 428–32, 438, 439, 463–4
  trial selection theory 489, 490, 491, 497–8, 502
silence, right to *see* self-incrimination, privilege against; self-incrimination, privilege against, right to silence
Silver, C. 73, 77, 79
simultaneous proposals, and settlement negotiation 388, 391, 392, 395, 433–4, 435, 440, 446, 464
Singer, L. 75
Sisk, G. 316
Sitkoff, R. 98
Skaperdas, S. 206
Smith, J. 45
Smorodinsky, M. 413
Snyder, E. 155, 298–300
Sobel, J. 2, 5, 12, 193, 224, 434, 463
social cost
  of court congestion 330–31
  detection avoidance, effect of responsive increases in 161–7
  of jury system 332
  social cost-benefit analysis in conventional approach 149, 151–2, 154
  sweetheart settlements 74
social functions of courts 317–19
social versus private incentive to sue 472–86
  alternative cost rules 482
  bilateral care accidents 482–3
  corrective policies 475–6
  deterministic damages 481–2
  English rule 482
  and judges' promotion of efficiency 481
  model 473–6
  model under negligence rule 476–7
  model when settlement is possible 477–80
  numerical example 475
  settlement-trial decision 477–9
  social costs when settlement is possible 479–80
  trials, lawmaking function of 480–81
social welfare
  effects of legal information production and exchange 59–65
  and right to silence 376–7
  value of confidentiality protection 53–9
Solimine, M. 86, 89, 94, 95
Songer, D. 25, 36, 37–8, 41, 42, 316
sorting model *see* screening model
Spaeth, H. 24–5, 310
specialization
  judicial organization and administration 327–8
  specialized courts versus courts of general jurisdiction 328–30
Spence, A. 244–5
Spier, K. 291, 386, 393, 414, 416, 433, 444, 446, 447–9, 456, 457–8, 460, 461, 489
Spiller, P. 34, 36, 37, 42, 43, 44, 45
Spiotto, J. 123, 124
Spitzer, M. 34, 36–7, 43, 45
split-award statutes 442, 457
Spurr, S. 356, 357–8, 359
Ståhl, I. 389, 392
Stanley, L. 294–5
stare decisis
  empirical studies of 24–5, 31
  horizontal, and common law precedential practices 21–4
  information-based explanation of horizontal 23
  and issue preclusion, difference between 354–5, 359
  judges' reputation concerns and horizontal 23, 24
  political model for horizontal 22–3
state competition incentives
  for corporate law 98–9
  for lawyers 99–100, 106
  for non-corporate law 100
state involvement
  'balance of state interests' approach 90, 91
  and recursivity of detection avoidance 178–9

Stearns, M. 31–2, 33, 328
Stein, Alex 80, 222, 366–85
Stein, J. 102
Steir, M. 25
Stephenson, M. 45, 323
Sterk, S. 88, 93, 94
Stigler, G. 161
Stiglitz, J. 497, 498
Stith, K. 132, 382
Stone, R. 23
strategic approach to solutions, and settlement negotiation 392–3, 399, 403, 404, 414–35, 454–5
strategic behavior models of litigation 497–8
Stuntz, W. 117, 168
Subrin, S. 188
subset reporting
  evidence, theoretical models 227, 228–9
  no-lying assumption, evidence, theoretical models 239–41
suing incentives *see* social versus private incentive to sue
Sullivan, J. 72
Sunstein, C. 31
sweetheart settlements 73–5, 78, 79, 80
Symeonides, S. 86

Tabarrok, A. 127, 326
Tabbach, A. 155, 157–61, 162, 164–8, 179, 182
Tahk, A. 29
team models of error correction, and appeal and supreme courts, hierarchical organization 39–41
Thibault, J. 1
Thiel, S. 87, 96
third-party information
  efficacy of 257–9
  see also evidence
Thomas, G. 125
Thomas, R. 73, 79, 80
three-strikes laws 129
Tiebout, C. 98
Tiller, E. 31, 37, 44, 136, 137
time factors, settlement negotiation 391–3, 415–16, 417–18, 460–62
Tirole, J. 3, 5, 14, 15, 323

Todd, P. 121, 122
Tollison, R. 98, 100, 101
Toma, E. 43–4
Tonry, M. 128
trial
  effects and nonmutuality doctrine 356–8
  effects and nonparty preclusion 361–4
  lawmaking function of 480–81
  outcomes, and fee shifting 285
  and pretrial expenditures, effect on fee shifting 275–8
trial selection theory 487–506
  asymmetric information and informational advantage for defendant 495–6, 499–500, 502
  asymmetric information and informational advantage for plaintiff 496–7, 499–500, 502–3
  asymmetric information and settlement and strategic behavior 489–91, 495–7, 499–502, 504
  defendant advantage theory 502–3
  divergent expectations 488, 499, 501–2, 504
  empirical evidence 498–504
  heteroscedasticity assumption 493, 494
  importance of 487–8
  literature review 488–91
  litigious-plaintiff hypothesis 490, 498–9
  medical malpractice cases 500, 503, 503–4
  model 491–7
  model and frequency of litigation 493–5
  products liability cases 500–501, 503
  selection hypothesis or effect 489–90
  settlement decision 488–9
  signaling and screening approaches 489, 490, 491, 497–8, 502
  strategic behavior models of litigation 497–8
  and win rates 500–501
Triantis, G. 251
Tribe, L. 221

Trubek, D. 297
truth revelation versus primary activity incentive setting 249–50
truth-consistent presentation
 evidence, theoretical models 227–30, 241
 no-lying assumption, evidence, theoretical models 239–40
truth-in-sentencing laws 134
Tuckman, B. 442, 457
Tullock, G. 1, 5–7, 12, 14, 28
Tversky, A. 213

UK
 English rule *see* English rule
 judicial review 321
 jury system 332
 legal structures, evolution of 319
 'payment into court' settlement 289
 Vita Food Products Inc. v. Unus Shipping Co. 104
 see also Europe
ultimatum game, settlement negotiation 414, 415, 417, 419, 420, 424–38, 441–5, 449–50, 452, 455, 456, 458, 460–61
US
 Class Action Fairness Act (CAFA) 74–5, 79–80
 Contract with America (Republican Party) proposal 271, 290
 Equal Protection Clause of the 14th Amendment 119, 120
 Federal Rules of Civil Procedure (FRCP) 2, 67, 76, 146, 147, 188, 199, 200, 273–4, 289–93, 295–6, 456
 First Restatement of Conflicts 85–6, 89, 91–6
 Internal Revenue Code 292
 Prison Litigation Reform Act (PLRA) 140
 Private Securities Litigation Reform Act (PSLRA) 73, 78–9, 80
 Second Restatement of Conflicts 90, 95, 103–4
US Court of Appeals
 Chavez v. Illinois State Police (racial disparity) 119
 see also appeal and supreme courts

US Supreme Court
 Allstate Insurance Co v. Hague 107
 Alyeska Pipeline Service Co. v. Wilderness Society 273
 Apprendi v. New Jersey 138
 Bivens v. Six Unknown Named Agents 123
 Blonder-Tongue Laboratories, Inc. v. University of Illinois Foundation 356
 Chevron USA Inc. v Natural Resources Defense Council Inc 43
 collegiality 28
 and conflict of laws and choice of laws 89, 106, 107–8
 Cooley v. Board of Wardens 106
 and criminal procedure 123, 124, 138–9
 CTS Corp. v. Dynamics Corp. of America 107
 discretionary review 41–2, 43–4, 45
 Edgar v. Mite Corp 107
 exclusionary rule 123, 124–5
 fee shifting 273, 289
 Gilbert v. California 373
 Harris v. New York 383
 Herring v. New York 227
 Home Insurance v Dick 89
 INS v Chadha 43
 Johnson v. United States 369
 and judicial ideology 316
 Lego v. Twomey 381
 Mapp v. Ohio 124
 Marek v. Chesny 289
 Mincey v. Arizona 383
 Miranda v. Arizona 124–6, 366, 369, 370, 383–4
 New York v. Quarles 375
 Parklane Hosiery v. Shore 356, 357
 precedent adherence 24–5
 and preclusion law 356, 357, 361
 and right to silence 366, 369, 373, 375, 381, 383–5
 and self-incrimination, privilege against 366, 369, 370, 373, 375, 381, 383–5
 and Sentencing Guidelines 137–8
 Supreme Council of the Royal Arcanum v. Green 107–8

Taylor v. Sturgell 361
Twining v. New Jersey 369
United States v. Booker 138–9
United States v. Hubbell 373
United States v. Mezzanatto 384–5
United States v. Patane 383
Warren Court, precedent adherence 25
Withrow v. Williams 366
see also appeal and supreme courts

Vanberg, V. 98, 101
Vidmar, N. 295
Vihanto, M. 101
Vincent, D. 416
Voigt, S. 324
voting protocols in collegial courts 32–4

Wald, M. 125
Waldfogel, J. 127, 133, 439, 490, 501–2, 504
Wang, G. 417–18, 433, 434, 460
Wang, J.-S. 286, 442
Ware, S. 87
Watanabe, Y. 297, 300–301, 302
Watson, J. 233
Watts, A. 441–2, 464
weak (frivolous) suits 77, 80–81, 452
Weimar, D. 128
Weiss, A. 79, 497, 498
Weitzman, P. 7

welfare *see* social welfare
Wen, Q. 389
Western, B. 116
Whincop, M. 92, 97, 102
White, M. 99, 393
Whitman, D. 24
Wickelgren, A. 61, 343, 344, 378, 393, 453–4, 460
Wilde, L. 103, 284, 341, 419, 420, 423, 431, 455
Willging, T. 2, 67, 68, 70, 188, 189, 197
Williams, P. 277
Williamson, O. 105
Wilson, R. 419
win rates, and trial selection theory 500–501
Winter, E. 11
Winter, R. 98
Wittman, D. 434, 435, 440, 489, 493
Woglom, G. 277
Wright, R. 71
Wright, R. 130

Yang, B. 445
Yeazell, S. 67
Yi, J. 358–9, 417–18, 433, 434, 444–5, 460
Yildiz, M. 440–41
Yoon, A. 131, 301–2

Zeisal, H. 333
Zuehlke, T. 298, 461
Zywicki, T. 7